D1387503

*The Nuttall Dictionary
of English Synonyms
and Antonyms*

The Nuttall Dictionary of English Synonyms and Antonyms

12,000 WORDS SHOWING 100,000 PARALLEL
EXPRESSIONS WITH OPPOSITE EXAMPLES

Edited by G. Elgie Christ

FREDERICK WARNE
London · New York

NEW EDITION
Revised, enlarged and reset

1943

Twenty-first Reprint 1976
Twenty-second Reprint 1977
Twenty-third Reprint 1978
Twenty-fourth Reprint 1979
Twenty-fifth Reprint 1980
Twenty-sixth Reprint 1982

ISBN 0 7232 0164 1—Cased
ISBN 0 7232 2292 4—Limp

Printed in Great Britain by Butler & Tanner Ltd
Frome and London
D 6193·380

PREFACE

In compiling this Dictionary it has been the editor's intention to appeal to those who want to find, with the least possible delay, an alternative word to that used first in a sentence, thus avoiding tautology in writing or speaking.

Included in the synonyms are certain archaic words, mainly such as occur in biblical or legal phraseology, and these have been printed in italics.

It is necessary to explain the use of the dagger sign (†). Its object is to refer the reader to the previous entry, where the same word, or a word easily derivable from it, will be found. By continuing the previous entry from this point he will obtain further synonyms for the original word. Thus ' abandoned,' see † at ' discarded,' and refer to the previous group of words, where the word ' discard ' will be found, and is followed by ' quit,' etc. Another example will be seen in the synonym of ' barrier,' where a † is placed against the word ' obstruction,' which refers the reader to the synonyms of the preceding word. The required words can then easily be obtained, and space is thereby saved by avoiding much unnecessary repetition. It has, therefore, enabled the editor greatly to extend the number of references in a way that would otherwise have been impossible in the space at his command.

An outstanding feature of this work, apart from its easy reference, is the introduction of the antonyms, where they exist, in conjunction with the word for which synonyms are provided. The antonym is printed in heavy *italic* type at the end of the line. Although only one antonym is given for a word that has several synonyms, the reader may obtain further suitable words by turning up the antonym given and finding the synonym for it. Thus, as an antonym for ' adroit,' only the word ' clumsy ' is given, but, by looking under ' clumsy,' a further selection can be obtained.

In certain instances there will be found more than one group of synonyms for a word ; each of these groups represents a different meaning.

Abbreviations of the " Parts of Speech " are printed in italics, as follows :—

a.	..	representing	adjective.
adv.	..	,,	adverb.
conj.	..	,,	conjunction.
interj.	..	,,	interjection.
n.	..	,,	noun.
prep.	..	,,	preposition.
v.a.	..	,,	verb active (or transitive).
v.n.	..	,,	verb neuter (or intransitive).
v.a. & n.	..	,,	verb active and neuter.

THE NUTTALL DICTIONARY

OF

ENGLISH SYNONYMS AND ANTONYMS

A

ABACK

Aback, Backwards, aft, rearward, back, behind. ***Onward***

Abaft, Aft, astern, behind, back. ***Afore***

Abandon, *v.,* Desert, leave, forsake, discard, quit, surrender, cede, evacuate, vacate, yield, relinquish, renounce, abjure, resign, drop, forego, withdraw, abdicate. ***Hold***
n., Dash, heartiness, impulsiveness, frankness, verve. ***Timidity***

Abandoned, Deserted, left, forsaken, discarded.† ***Held***
Depraved, demoralized, wicked, vicious, dissolute, profligate, corrupt, licentious, sinful, bad, shameless, lost, obdurate, hardened, impenitent. ***Virtuous***

Abase, Degrade, lower, disgrace, humiliate, reduce, sink, depress, drop, dishonour, detrude, debase. ***Exalt***

Abasement, Degradation, lowering, disgrace,† abjectness, shame, ignominy, baseness, degeneration, depravation. ***Exaltation***

Abash, Confound, confuse, awe, disconcert, daunt, shame, discompose, embarrass, humble, snub.

Abashment, Confusion, shame, embarrassment, humiliation, mortification.

Abate, *v.a.,* Lessen, reduce, deduct, diminish, moderate, soothe, assuage, soften, allay, calm, appease, pacify. ***Increase***
v.n., Decrease, diminish, lessen, subside, sink, decline, wane, slacken.

Abatement, Decrease, diminution, lessening,† reduction.
Discount, rebate, allowance, reduction.

Abbreviate, Condense, shorten, abridge, compress, epitomize, reduce, curtail. ***Amplify***

Abbreviation, Condensation, abridgment, compression, epitome, reduction, curtailment. ***Amplification***

Abdicate, Resign, retire, abandon, relinquish, vacate, surrender, cede, renounce. ***Usurp***

ABJECT

Abdomen, Belly, paunch.

Abdominal, Ventral, visceral, hemal.

Abduce, Separate, part, retract. ***Adjoin***

Abduct, Appropriate, remove, kidnap, carry off. ***Restore***

Abduction, Seizure, kidnapping, appropriation, rape. ***Restoration***

Aberrant, Erratic, devious, deviating, wandering, disconnected, irregular, abnormal, eccentric, singular, peculiar, unusual, idiotic, inconsistent. ***Regular***

Aberration, Deviation, divergence, irregularity.† ***Regularity***

Abet, Aid, assist, support, encourage, countenance, help, succour, sustain, favour, advocate, sanction, incite. ***Oppose***

Abettor, Accomplice, helper, aider, assistant, advocate, adviser, promoter, instigator, coadjutor, confederate. ***Opponent***

Abeyance, Suspension, intermission, dormancy, reservation, expectation. ***Revival***

Abhor, Hate, loathe, abominate, detest, nauseate. ***Love***

Abhorrence, Hatred, loathing,† horror, disgust, antipathy, aversion. ***Sympathy***

Abide, *v.a.,* Tolerate, bear, suffer, sustain, endure.
Await, attend.
v.n., Tarry, rest, lodge, wait, sojourn. ***Depart***
Dwell, settle, reside, live.
Endure, last, remain, persist, sustain, tolerate, continue. ***Perish***

Abiding, *n.,* Dwelling, abode.
a., Lasting, permanent, enduring, changeless, durable, continuing. ***Changing***

Ability, Power, force, might, vigour, efficiency, aptitude, cleverness, capacity, skill, competency, capability, talent. ***Incapacity***

Abject, Base, degraded, vile, mean, low, servile, menial, cringing, worthless, despicable, outcast, miserable, ignoble,

I

dirty, sordid, low-minded, scurvy, pitiable. **_Honourable_**

Abjectness, Baseness, abjection, vileness, meanness.†

Abjure, Recant, forego, recall, withdraw, disclaim, renounce, disown, abandon, repudiate, forswear, reject, disavow, discard. **_Acknowledge_**

Able, Powerful, mighty, strong, masterly, talented, skilful, clever, expert, accomplished, adroit, competent, efficient, qualified, proficient, capable, practical. **_Incapable_**

Ablocate, Lease, rent, let, hire out.

Ablution, Washing, purification, cleansing, bathing. **_Pollution_**

Abnegate, Deny, abjure, reject, renounce. **_Profess_**

Abnegation, Denial, surrender, abjuration. **_Profession_**

Abnormal, Irregular, unusual, exceptional, monstrous, extraordinary, aberrant, singular, peculiar, strange, devious, divergent, eccentric, erratic. **_Ordinary_**

Abnormity, Abnormality, irregularity,† idiosyncrasy. **_Regularity_**

Aboard, On board, afloat, within, inside. **_Ashore_**

Abode, Dwelling, habitation, lodging, home, house, seat, place, quarters.

Abolish, Destroy, eradicate, suppress, annihilate, overthrow, extirpate, abrogate, obliterate.
Annul, repeal, revoke, rescind, suppress, cancel, expunge. **_Support_**

Abolition, Destruction, eradication, suppression.†

Abominable, Odious, hateful, detestable, horrible, execrable, horrid, damnable, accursed, offensive, obnoxious, foul, vile, disgusting, repulsive, shocking. **_Lovable_**

Abominate, Abhor, detest, hate, loathe. **_Love_**

Abomination, Abhorrence, detestation.†
Pollution, defilement, taint, contamination, corruption, impurity.
Infliction, plague, torment, curse, annoyance, nuisance. **_Blessing_**

Aboriginal, Primitive, primeval, primary, native, original, first, indigenous. **_Exotic_**

Aborigines, Natives, indigenes. **_Aliens_**

Abortion, Miscarriage, failure, disappointment, mishap, frustration, blundering. **_Achievement_**

Abortive, Miscarrying, failing,† untimely, immature, incomplete, stunted, vain, imperfect, fruitless, ineffective, futile, unavailing. **_Successful_**

Abound, Flow, teem, overflow, increase, swarm, multiply, flourish. **_Lack_**

About, _prep._, Near, round, around, surrounding, encircling, through, over.
Touching, respecting, concerning, anent.
adv., Roughly, approximately, almost, nearly. **_Precisely_**
Ready, prepared.

Above, _prep._, Over, beyond, exceeding.
adv., Overhead, aloft, before, previously. **_Below_**

Above-board, Frank, candid, open, sincere, honest, fair, ingenuous, artless. **_Cunning_**

Abrasion, Attrition, rubbing, scraping, wearing, disintegration.

Abreast, Beside, alongside, aligned, against.

Abridge, Abbreviate, epitomize, condense, compress, shorten, contract, curtail, cut down, lessen, reduce, diminish. **_Amplify_**
Deprive of, divest of.

Abridgment, Abbreviation, epitome, condensation,† summary, compendium, abstract, digest, synopsis, outline. **_Amplification_**
Deprivation, dispossession, limitation.

Abroad, Apart, far, away, dispersed, adrift. **_Near_**
Extensively, publicly, widely.

Abrogate, Repeal, revoke, annul, cancel, abolish, quash, overrule, invalidate, expunge. **_Enact_**

Abrogation, Abolition, repeal, revocation, annulment.† **_Enactment_**

Abrupt, Sudden, unexpected, precipitate, hasty.
Steep, precipitous, craggy, broken, rough, jagged.
Blunt, curt, rough, short, unceremonious, brusque, rugged. **_Courteous_**

Abscess, Sore, boil, gathering, ulcer, fester.

Abscond, Decamp, elope, withdraw, flee, fly, escape, bolt, retreat, disappear, hide. **_Emerge_**

Absence, Lack, want, deficiency, default, defect.
Distraction, inattention, preoccupation.
Non-attendance, non-appearance. **_Presence_**

Absent, _a._, Away, left, gone abroad. **_Present_**
Distracted, inattentive, preoccupied. **_Attentive_**
_v.a._, Stay away, keep aloof. **_Come_**

Absolute, Complete, perfect, entire, unconditional, unlimited, unrestricted, unqualified, unadulterated, unmixed, pure. **_Conditional_**
Despotic, autocratic, arbitrary, supreme,

dictatorial, tyrannical, tyrannous, irresponsible. **Dependent**
Actual, real, veritable, certain. **Dubious**
Absolutely, Completely, perfectly, definitely, entirely.† **Partly**
Actually, really,† indeed, unquestionably, infallibly, positively, indubitably. **Probably**
Absolution, Remission, forgiveness, pardon, acquittal, discharge, release, deliverance, liberation. **Condemnation**
Absolve, Forgive, pardon, acquit,† loose, clear, free, exonerate. **Condemn**
Absonant, Discordant, dissonant, unmusical, inharmonious, repugnant. **Agreeable**
Absorb, Imbibe, swallow, drown, engulf, consume, engross, appropriate, assimilate, exhaust, monopolize. **Exude**
Absorbent, Imbibing, assimilating.
Absorbing, Engrossing,† interesting. **Dull**
Abstain, Forbear, refrain, refuse, desist, withhold, demur, avoid. **Indulge**
Abstemious, Abstinent, temperate, moderate, sober, sparing, frugal. **Greedy**
Abstract, v.a., Separate, part, remove, isolate, disjoin, disunite, dissociate, disengage, detach. **Unite**
Steal, take, seize, appropriate, purloin, pilfer. **Return**
Abbreviate, shorten, curtail, lessen, abridge, epitomize. **Amplify**
a., Separate, isolated, unrelated. **United**
Vague, abstruse, recondite, occult. **Concrete**
n., Abbreviation, abridgment, epitome, summary, synopsis, digest, outline. **Amplification**
Abstracted, a., Separated, preoccupied, inattentive, absent-minded. **Attentive**
Abstraction, Separation, isolation, disconnection, disjunction. **Union**
Stealing, taking, seizure, appropriation, purloining, pilfering, abduction. **Restoration**
Inattention, reverie, musing, preoccupation, absence, absorption. **Attention**
Abstruse, Hidden, obscure, vague, recondite, occult, abstract, remote, dark, indefinite, mystic, curious, subtle, refined. **Clear**
Absurd, Irrational, unreasonable, preposterous, monstrous, foolish, stupid, silly, ridiculous, asinine, nonsensical, senseless. **Rational**
Abundance, Plenty, plenteousness, luxuriance, profusion, fertility, ampleness, richness, largeness, wealth, store, affluence, flow, flood, overflow, exuberance. **Scarcity**

Abundant, Plentiful, luxuriant, profuse,† lavish, replete, full, bountiful, liberal. **Scarce**
Abuse, v.a., Misuse, misemploy, misapply, pervert, pollute, profane, desecrate, dishonour. **Honour**
Injure, harm, maltreat, hurt, ill-treat, ill-use, ravish, outrage. **Tend**
Reproach, slander, disparage, revile, defame, traduce, calumniate, satirize, upbraid, vituperate. **Extol**
n., Misuse, misemployment, misapplication.†
Outrage, maltreatment, ill-treatment. **Protection**
Reproach, slander, disparagement.† **Panegyric**
Abusive, a., Insulting, reviling, ribald, offensive. **Complimentary**
Abut, Extend, project, meet, terminate. **Recede**
Abyss, Gulf, gorge, abysm, chasm, bottomless pit.
Academic, Scholastic, literary, collegiate. Unreal, artificial, unimportant. **Illiterate**
Academy, School, college, university, institute, seminary.
Accede, Agree, consent, comply, assent, acquiesce, accept. **Dissent**
Succeed, inherit, ascend.
Accelerate, Hasten, hurry, quicken, urge, speed, precipitate, expedite, despatch. **Retard**
Accent, v.a., Accentuate, emphasize, stress.
n., Tone, modulation, intonation, cadence, emphasis, beat, stress, rhythm.
Accents, n.pl. Language, words, utterances, tones, expressions.
Accept, Take, receive. **Refuse**
Agree to, accede to, assent to, admit, avow, embrace, acknowledge. **Repudiate**
Acceptable, Welcome, pleasant, pleasing, agreeable, gratifying. **Unwelcome**
Acceptance, Receipt, accepting, reception, acknowledgment. **Refusal**
Approval, satisfaction, agreement.
Access, Admission, admittance, approach, entrance, entry, audience, interview. **Exit**
Addition, increment, gain, enlargement, increase, aggrandizement. **Decrease**
Attack, fit, paroxysm, onset, recurrence.
Accessible, Affable, easy, approachable, friendly. **Unfriendly**
Accession, Addition, augmentation, extension, enlargement, increase. **Decrease**
Attainment, arrival.
Accessory, n., Accomplice, abettor, confederate, coadjutor, associate, assistant, aider. **Opponent**

Accessory, Detail, supplement, subsidiary, attendant, element, minor part. *Essential*

a., Assisting, abetting, aiding, helping. *Opposing*

Subsidiary, supplementary, subordinate, additional, minor. *Chief*

Accident, Mishap, misadventure, chance, fortuity, casualty, calamity, contingency, mischance. *Purpose*

Accidental, Casual, fortuitous, unintended, undesigned, contingent, unforeseen, unexpected. *Designed*

Acclamation, Applause, cheers, shouting, enthusiasm, plaudit, homage. *Denunciation*

Acclimatize, Acclimate, inure, habituate, season.

Acclivity, Ascent, hill, height, incline, rising ground, slope. *Declivity*

Accommodate, Oblige, furnish, serve, supply, give, spare. *Disoblige*

Adapt, adjust, fit, suit, settle, compose, harmonize, reconcile. *Aggravate*

Accommodating, Conciliatory, obliging, considerate, unselfish, polite, yielding, kind. *Selfish*

Accommodation, Supply, provision, service, convenience, advantage, privilege. Adaptment, adjustment, conformity, fitness.

Accompaniment, Attendant, adjunct, appendage, appurtenance, attachment.

Accompany, Escort, chaperon, convoy, attend, wait on, consort, follow, go with. *Desert*

Accomplice, Accessory, abettor, confederate, aider, helper, assistant, coadjutor, associate, co-operator, second. *Opponent*

Accomplish, Complete, finish, achieve, execute, effect, perfect, perform, fulfil, consummate. *Fail*

Accomplished, Talented, skilled, expert, instructed, educated, experienced, finished, consummate, qualified, proficient, able, cultured, refined, elegant, polished. *Unskilled*

Accord, *v.a.,* Grant, concede, vouchsafe, allow, resign, yield, deign, give. *Deny*

v.n., Agree, harmonize, consent, tally, be in unison. *Differ*

n., Concord, harmony, unanimity. *Discord*

Accordance, Accord, concord, agreement, harmony, conformity, unison, unanimity. *Difference*

Accordant, Agreeing, agreeable, suitable, harmonious. *Discordant*

Accordingly, Agreeably, suitably, harmoniously, *Discordantly*

Accordingly, Consequently, therefore, and so, so, then.

Accost, Confront, approach, salute, greet, address, stop, hail. *Avoid*

Account, *v.a.,* Judge, esteem, deem, regard, think, estimate, consider, reckon. *Underrate*

v.n., Explain, elucidate, expound.

n., Tale, narrative, narration, description, history, chronicle, report, recital, statement, explanation, exposition, elucidation.

Record, score, inventory, bill, reckoning, calculation, count, tally.

Consideration, reason, motive, ground.

Importance, consequence, repute, worth, benefit, profit, advantage.

Accountable, Responsible, answerable, liable, amenable. *Irresponsible*

Accoutre, Dress, furnish, equip, array.

Accoutrements, Dress, equipments, trappings, gear, array.

Accredit, Believe, credit, trust. *Suspect*

Authorize, entrust, delegate, commission, depute. *Dismiss*

Accretion, Growth, accumulation, adhesion, increase. *Dispersion*

Accrue, Come, result, issue, proceed, inure, accumulate. *Diminish*

Accumulate, *v.a.,* Collect, store, heap, amass, pile, lay up, garner, hoard. *Dissipate*

v.n., Increase, grow, accrue. *Diminish*

Accumulation, Store, hoard, accretion, mass, heap, collection, pile, aggregation, assembly. *Dissipation*

Accuracy, Correctness, exactness, exactitude, accurateness, precision, niceness, nicety, truth. *Error*

Accurate, Correct, exact, precise, nice, truthful, rigorous, unerring. *Careless*

Accursed, Doomed, damned, unholy, diabolical. *Blessed*

Accusation, Charge, indictment, impeachment, arraignment. *Defence*

Accuse, Charge, indict,† tax, taunt, summon, cite, inculpate, inform against, censure. *Defend*

Accuser, Plaintiff, complainant, informer, prosecutor. *Defendant*

Accustom, Habituate, use, inure, familiarize, train, drill, addict. *Alienate*

Ace, Atom, particle, unit, item, iota, jot, tittle, whit, bit, scrap, trifle, mite.

Acephalous, Headless, disorganized, disorderly, anarchical, confused. *Orderly*

Acerbity, Harshness, sourness, bitterness, tartness, acidity, roughness, acridity, acrimony, asperity, sternness, sullenness, churlishness. *Sweetness*

Ache, *v.n.,* Hurt, be in pain, grieve, sorrow, suffer.

n., Pain, agony, anguish, pang. *Soothe*

Achieve, Accomplish, complete, finish, perfect, perform, execute, do, consummate, effect, carry out, conclude, attain, obtain, win, acquire. *Fail*

Achievement, Accomplishment, completion, perfection,† exploit, feat, work, deed. *Failure*

Achromatic, Untinged, colourless, uncoloured, transparent, hueless. *Tinged*

Acid, Sour, sharp, tart, bitter, rough, stinging. *Sweet*

Acidulous, Sourish, slightly acid, subacid, vinegarial.

Acknowledge, Recognize, remember, admit, own, confess, grant, allow, avow, profess, accept, endorse. *Deny*

Acknowledgment, Recognition, remembrance, admission.† *Disclaimer*

Acme, Top, summit, apex, zenith, vertex, pinnacle, peak, pitch, culmination, climax, crisis. *Base*

Acolyte, Acolythe, acolyth, attendant, follower, assistant, retainer.

Acquaint, Inform, tell, teach, advertise, apprize, notify, make known, advise, familiarize. *Hoodwink*

Acquaintance, Friend.

Familiarity, experience, knowledge. *Ignorance*

Acquiesce, Assent, agree, concur, accede, consent. *Dissent*

Rest, yield, submit, comply, repose, bow. *Object*

Acquiescence, Assent, agreement.† *Dissension*

Yielding, submission.† *Demurring*

Acquire, Gain, attain, earn, win, achieve, obtain, procure, purchase, get, secure. *Lose*

Learn, master.

Acquirement, Gaining, attainment, earning, acquisition, procuration, purchase. *Loss*

Learning, mastery.

Acquisition, Acquirement, gaining.†

Acquit, Release, set free, liberate, clear, absolve, discharge, pardon, forgive, exonerate, exculpate. *Charge*

Acquittal, Release, liberation, clearance.†

Acrid, Sharp, biting, sour, harsh, pungent, bitter, acrimonious. *Sweet*

Acrimonious, Acrid, severe, harsh, virulent, bitter, sarcastic, malignant, petulant, testy, peevish, snappish, snarling, hard, spiteful, ill-tempered, ill-natured, censorious, crabbed, cross, sour, tart, mordacious, mordant. *Amicable*

Acrimony, Acridity, severity, harshness.† *Mildness*

Acroamatic, Secret, private, profound, obscure, abstruse, deep, esoteric, difficult. *Open*

Across, Crosswise, transversely, athwart, over against. *Along*

Act, *v.a.,* Do, perform, carry out, execute.

v.n., Work, function, operate, behave.

Play, pretend, simulate, represent, personate, mimic, counterfeit.

n., Action, deed, feat, achievement, exploit, performance.

Law, bill, statute, ordinance, decree, enactment, edict.

Action, Act, deed, feat,† operation, movement, agency, exercise. *Rest*

Gesture, gesticulation, movement.

Battle, engagement, encounter, skirmish, combat, contest, conflict.

Performing, enacting, representation, plot, fable, subject.

Suit, case, prosecution.

Active, Operative, efficient, effective, potent, powerful, influential, living, vigorous, busy, employed, diligent, assiduous, industrious, sedulous, laborious. *Indolent*

Agile, alert, nimble, quick, smart, prompt, ready, animated, enterprising, energetic. *Slow*

Activity, Operation, efficiency.†

Agility, alertness.† *Lassitude*

Actual, Real, true, veritable, certain, demonstrable, positive, absolute, genuine, determinate, substantial, present, existing. *Virtual*

Actually, Really, truly, verily,† indeed. *Virtually*

Actuary, Registrar, clerk, manager, agent, superintendent, overseer, supervisor.

Actuate, Urge, instigate, induce, incline, move, impel, dispose, persuade, prompt, drive, incite, encourage. *Deter*

Acumen, Keenness, perception, quickness, acuteness, astuteness, sharpness, sagacity, penetration, discernment, shrewdness, perspicacity, ingenuity, talent. *Stupidity*

Acute, Keen, quick, astute, sharp, sagacious, penetrating, discerning, shrewd, perspicacious, ingenious, talented. *Obtuse*

Intense, distressing, violent, severe, poignant, pungent, sore.

Acuteness, Keenness, quickness,† acumen, perception.

Intensity, violence.†

Adage, Saying, proverb, saw, precept, tag, aphorism, dictum, maxim.

Adamantine, Indestructible, hard, unyielding. *Soft*

Adapt, Adjust, accommodate, suit, fit, prepare, attune, harmonize, match, conform, co-ordinate. *Misfit*

Adaptation, Adjustment, accommodation, suitability,† adaptability, aptness, appropriateness.

Add, Join, adjoin, subjoin, annex, adduce, affix, append, tag, connect, sum up, aggregate, reckon up. *Subtract*

Addendum, Addition, adjunct, appendage, appendix, appurtenance, annexation, acquisition. *Detraction*

Addict, Devote, give up, apply, dedicate, accustom, habituate.

Addicted, Devoted, given,† inclined, prone, disposed. *Free*

Addition, Adding, adjoining, subjoining, annexing, appending.

Increase, augmentation, extension, aggrandizement. *Decrease*

Addendum, adjunct, appendage, appendix, appurtenance, annexation, acquisition. *Subtraction*

Additional, Supplementary, supplemental, extra, more, further, superadded.

Address, *v.a.,* Accost, greet, approach, speak to, direct, invoke, appeal to, entreat. *Ignore*

n., Appeal, invocation, suit, request, imploration, entreaty, discourse, speech, oration, sermon, harangue.

Direction, superscription.

Ability, dexterity, skill, cleverness, art, ingenuity, tact, adroitness, readiness, expertness. *Clumsiness*

Adduce, Allege, give, assign, advance, present, cite, name, mention, quote. *Retract*

Adept, *a.,* Proficient, skilled, practised, versed, good, experienced, expert, adroit, handy, clever. *Clumsy*

n., Master, expert, artist. *Novice*

Adequacy, Adequateness, enough, completeness, sufficiency, fitness. *Insufficiency*

Adequate, Enough, complete, sufficient, equal, full. *Inadequate*

Adhere, Stick, cohere, cling, cleave, hold, unite, belong, pertain. *Sever*

Adherence, Tenacity, fixedness, fidelity, adhesion, constancy, devotion, attachment. *Severance*

Adherent, *a.,* Adhering, sticking, cohering, adhesive, constant, devoted.

n., Disciple, follower, supporter, partisan, henchman, satellite, ally, admirer, backer. *Opponent*

Adhesion, Adherence, tenacity, fixedness,

fidelity, constancy, devotion, attachment.

Adhesive, Sticky, gummy, glutinous, viscous, tenacious, sticking, clinging, viscid.

Adieu, *interj.,* Good-bye, farewell. *Hullo*

n., Valediction, farewell, parting. *Greeting*

Adjacent, Adjoining, near, close, neighbouring, bordering, contiguous. *Remote*

Adjoin, Approximate, abut, touch, unite, attach, annex. *Separate*

Adjourn, Postpone, put off, procrastinate, defer, delay, protract, suspend, prorogue, interrupt. *Complete*

Adjournment, Postponement, putting off, procrastination.† *Conclusion*

Adjudge, Award, assign, settle, determine, allot, decide, adjudicate, arbitrate. *Reserve*

Adjudicate, *v.a.,* Adjudge, award, settle.†

v.n., Judge, determine, arbitrate, decide.

Adjudication, Judgment, decision, sentence, award.

Adjunct, Appendage, appendix, addition, additament, addendum, attachment, appurtenance, dependency, accessory, auxiliary, amplification. *Detraction*

Adjure, Urge, entreat, implore, supplicate, beg, pray, beseech, command, enjoin, invoke, conjure. *Deprecate*

Adjust, Arrange, trim, rectify, dispose, regulate, set, harmonize, collocate, adapt, fit, suit, accommodate. *Dislocate*

Reconcile, make up, pacify, compose, settle.

Adjustment, Arrangement, disposal, regulation.†

Reconciliation, pacification.†

Adjutant, Subordinate, helper, assistant.

Admeasurement, Size, measurement, measure, dimensions. *Misfit*

Division, partition, adjustment.

Administer, Award, distribute, dole, give, dispense, afford, furnish, supply, contribute, control, conduct, execute, manage, direct, superintend. *Mismanage*

Administration, Distribution, dispensation, direction, execution.

Government, executive, cabinet.

Admirable, Excellent, fine, superb, wonderful, praiseworthy. *Despicable*

Admiration, Esteem, liking, love, wonder, approval, respect. *Contempt*

Admire, Esteem, like, love, prize, appreciate, approve, extol, adore, revere, respect. *Despise*

Admissible, Permissible, allowable, lawful, proper, just, fair, right, reasonable, justifiable, possible, probable, warrantable. **Preposterous**

Admission, Acknowledgment, concession, allowance, avowal, acceptance. **Denial**

Admittance, introduction, access, entrance. **Exclusion**

Admit, Acknowledge, concede, allow, avow, accept, confess, grant, own. **Deny** Receive, let in. **Exclude**

Admittance, Admission, introduction, access, entrance, pass, reception, welcome. **Exclusion**

Admixture, Mixture, mingling, seasoning, sprinkling, spice, dash, infusion, smack, tinge, suggestion, hint.

Admonish, Warn, advise, censure, rebuke, remind, caution, reprove, enjoin, counsel, instruct, teach, inform. **Encourage**

Admonition, Admonishment, warning, reminder, advice,† monition. **Applause**

Ado, Fuss, bustle, flurry, stir, hubbub, excitement, tumult, turmoil, commotion, trouble, difficulty. **Tranquillity**

Adolescence, Youth, minority, teens, nonage, juvenility. **Maturity**

Adolescent, Youthful, juvenile, young, growing.

Adopt, Appropriate, assume, father, affiliate. **Abandon** Accept, approve, choose, endorse, avow. **Reject**

Adorable, Divine, admirable, estimable, worthy, venerable. **Abominable**

Adoration, Devotion, worship, homage, veneration, admiration, reverence. **Blasphemy**

Adore, Worship, honour, venerate, admire, idolize, reverence. **Despise**

Adorn, Decorate, embellish, beautify, deck, garnish, enrich, gild, grace. **Mar**

Adrift, Afloat, agog, abroach, distracted, abroad, parted, loose, disordered. **Secure**

Adroit, Expert, dexterous, able, apt, clever, handy, skilful, adept, masterly. **Clumsy**

Adscititious, Superfluous, supplementary, adventitious, redundant, alien, smuggled, artificial, spurious, additional, accessory. **Essential**

Adulation, Flattery, compliment, sycophancy, fawning, blandishment, cajolery, cringing, courtship. **Obloquy**

Adult, *n.*, Man, woman, grown-up. **Child** *a.*, Mature, ripe, full. **Immature**

Adulterate, Debase, deteriorate, corrupt, contaminate, vitiate, alloy. **Ameliorate**

Adulterated, Debased, deteriorated,† spurious, impure, concocted. **Pure**

Adultery, Infidelity, unchasteness, dissoluteness, advoutry. **Purity**

Adumbrate, Shadow, foreshadow, indicate, hint, suggest, presage, symbolize, typify, represent, denote. Darken, obscure, dim, bedim, becloud, hide, conceal. **Reveal**

Advance, *v.a.*, Push, send, propel. **Retard** Elevate, raise, promote, augment, increase, improve, further, strengthen, benefit, aggrandize, enhance, dignify, exalt, forward. **Lower** Lend, loan. **Foreclose** Allege, adduce, propound. **Disprove** *v.n.*, Progress, rise, proceed, prosper, improve, thrive, grow. **Retrogress** *n.*, Push, progress, march. **Retreat** Advancement, elevation, rise, promotion.† **Degrade** Offer, proposal, address, proposition, tender. **Retract**

Advantage, *v.a.*, Help, benefit, serve, profit. **Hinder** *n.*, Help, benefit, assistance, blessing, boon, avail, gain, profit, expediency, emolument, superiority. **Hindrance**

Advantageous, Helpful, beneficial.† **Prejudicial**

Advent, Coming, arrival, approach, visitation, appearing, accession. **Departure**

Adventitious, Adscititious, extrinsic, superfluous, redundant, casual, accidental, incidental, extraneous, fortuitous. **Essential**

Adventure, *v.a.*, Venture, risk, hazard, imperil. *v.n.*, Venture, dare. *n.*, Venture, hazard, risk, experiment, trial, crisis, incident, occurrence, romance, transaction, speculation.

Adventurous, Venturesome, bold, daring, brave, enterprising, gallant, fearless, courageous, rash, reckless, foolhardy, hazardous. **Timid**

Adversary, Opponent, enemy, foe, rival, antagonist, opposer. **Ally**

Adverse, Unfavourable, contrary, opposing, opposed, conflicting, hostile, inimical, antagonistic, harmful, disastrous, unfortunate, unlucky, hard. **Favourable**

Adversity, Ill-luck, misfortune, calamity, misery, disaster, failure, ruin, affliction, trouble, woe, distress, suffering, sorrow, desolation. **Prosperity**

Advertence ⎰ Attention, regard, heed, observance, notice, consideration. **Carelessness** **Advertency** ⎱

Advertise, Announce, proclaim, publish, notify, inform, declare, promulgate, broadcast. **Conceal**

Advertisement, Announcement, proclamation.†

Advice, Counsel, admonition, persuasion, warning, caution, instruction, suggestion, recommendation.
Information, tidings, word, intelligence, notification.

Advisability, Advisableness, propriety, expediency, prudence, judiciousness, desirability.

Advisable, Proper, expedient,† advantageous, fit.

Advise, *v.a.*, Counsel, admonish, suggest, recommend, persuade, urge, prompt. *Deter*
Inform, apprize, notify, acquaint, tell.
v.n., Consult, deliberate, confer.

Advocacy, Support, defence, vindication, countenance. *Opposition*

Advocate, *v.a.*, Support, defend, vindicate, countenance, uphold, maintain, justify, plead for. *Oppose*
n., Supporter, defender, vindicator,† friend, intercessor. *Opponent*
Lawyer, counsel, barrister, attorney, solicitor.

Aegis, Shield, buckler, protection, defence, safeguard.

Aerial, Ethereal, airy, gaseous, vaporous, light, empyreal, empyrean, high, lofty. Atmospheric.

Aeriform, Airy, gaseous, vaporous, ethereal.

Aerolite, Meteorite.

Aeronaut, Balloonist, pilot, airman, aviator.

Aeronautics, Ballooning, aviation, aerostation, aerostatics.

Aeroplane, Flying-machine, 'plane.

Aesthetic, Beautiful, gratifying, tasteful, becoming, fit, appropriate. *Ugly*

Afar, Far off, away, aloof, abroad, remote. *Near*

Affability, Courtesy, courteousness, condescension, graciousness, complaisance, accessibility, ease, easiness, amiability, amenity, suavity, urbanity, politeness, civility, sociability. *Haughtiness*

Affable, Courteous, condescending, gracious,† free, frank, open, cordial, familiar, obliging, benign, mild. *Haughty*

Affair, Matter, business, concern, function, duty, subject, question, circumstance, transaction.
Incident, event, occurrence, performance.
Battle, engagement, skirmish, conflict, brush, encounter.

Affairs, Administration, business, finances, property, estate.

Affect, Assume, adopt, feign, sham, simulate. *Feel*
Influence, change, alter, transform.
Concern, interest.
Touch, overcome, pierce, melt, move, subdue, impress.
Desire, like, crave. *Dislike*

Affectation, Hypocrisy, pretence, artifice, foppery. *Naturalness*

Affected, Hypocritical, pretending,† canting, unnatural, insincere, vain, conceited. *Natural*
Altered, influenced, transformed.

Affection, Love, feeling, kindness, partiality, fondness, liking, tenderness, regard, devotion, passion, inclination.
Indifference

Affiance, Betrothal, engagement, plighting.

Affidavit, Evidence, statement, testimony, declaration, deposition.

Affiliate, Adopt, annex, incorporate, graft, join, unite. *Sever*

Affiliation, Adoption, annexation, incorporation.† *Separation*

Affinity, Relationship, kith, kin, propinquity, connection, similarity, harmony, sympathy, attraction, interconnection, interdependence, correlation, analogy, correspondence, likeness, resemblance.
Antipathy

Affirm, Assert, maintain, declare, aver, asseverate, vouch, state, say, allege, testify, profess, ratify, endorse. *Deny*

Affirmation, Assertion, declaration, averment.† *Denial*

Affirmative, Assertory, assertical, declaratory, ratifying, indorsing, positive.
Negative

Affix, *v.a.*, Attach, fasten, connect, annex, join, subjoin, add, append. *Detach*
n., Suffix, postfix. *Prefix*

Afflatus, Inspiration, ecstasy.

Afflict, Trouble, distress, grieve, try, torment, pain, agonize, hurt, wound, harass, plague, persecute, smite, grind, exercise. *Console*

Afflicting, Troublous, distressing, grievous,† harrowing, sorrowful, piteous, calamitous, afflictive, sad, dire, wretched, hard, deplorable, sore. *Relieving*

Affliction, Trouble, distress, grief, trial, torment, calamity, adversity, misfortune, sorrow, woe, tribulation, pain, depression, scourge, agony. *Blessing*

Affluence, Opulence, wealth, riches, abundance, plenty, exuberance. *Poverty*

Affluent, *a.*, Opulent, wealthy, rich, moneyed. *Poor*
n., Tributary, branch, feeder.

Afford, Produce, yield, supply, give, furnish, grant, lend, impart, confer, bestow, spare, endure, support. **Deny**

Affranchise, Enfranchise, liberate, free.
Subjugate

Affray, Brawl, broil, mêlée, tumult, disturbance, fray, struggle, conflict, contest, quarrel, strife, outbreak, fracas, scuffle, tussle, rumpus. **Order**

Affright, v.a., Terrify, frighten, alarm, dismay, daunt, scare, appal, startle, astonish, shock, intimidate, dishearten.
Reassure
n., Terror, fright, alarm, dismay, panic.

Affront, v.a., Abuse, outrage, insult, offend, vex, annoy, provoke, chafe, irritate, displease, fret, nettle, anger.
Pacify
n., Abuse, outrage, insult, offence.†
Defence

Affusion, Sprinkling, bedewing.

Afire, Ablaze, ignited, burning, alight.
Extinguished

Afloat, Adrift, abroad. loose, abroach, at sea. **Ashore**

Afoot, Forthcoming, agoing, preparing, started, inaugurated, instituted, established, launched, on foot, walking.

Afore, Before, beyond, afront, ahead, sooner. **Behind**

Aforesaid, Afore-mentioned, above-mentioned, stated, fore-named, above-named. **Subjoined**

Aforethought, a., Premeditated, deliberate, prepense, considerate, considered, calm, sober, collected. **Hasty**
n., Premeditation, deliberation.†

Afraid, Timid, alarmed, fearful, apprehensive, anxious, terrified, frightened.
Bold

Afresh, Newly, anew, again.
Continuously

Aft, Abaft, back, behind, rearward, astern. **Forward**

After, prep., Behind, following, succeeding. **Before**
adv., Afterwards, afterward, later, subsequently.
a., Succeeding, later, subsequent, following. **Preceding**

After-thought, After wit, reflection, esprit d'escalier.

Afterwards, Subsequently, after, later, thereafter.

Again, Anew, afresh, frequently, often, repeatedly, further, moreover, furthermore, besides.

Against, Opposite, facing, over, abutting, resisting, opposing, counter, across, despite, athwart. **For**

Agape, Gazing, curious, wondering, inquisitive, amazed, astare, astonished, dazed, yawning, stupefied, thunderstruck, dumbfounded. **Incurious**

Age, Period, stage, epoch, time, century, generation.
Antiquity, senility, seniority, old age, maturity. **Youth**

Aged, Old, elderly, ancient, antiquated.
Young

Agency, Instrumentality, mediation, charge, direction, means, action, operation, superintendence, influence, supervision, management.

Agent, Executor, actor, performer, factor, doer, representative, procurator, middleman, deputy, substitute. **Opponent**

Agglomerate, Gather, lump, mass, accumulate, conglomerate, heap, confuse, entangle, amalgamate. **Scatter**

Agglomeration, Gathering, lump, mass,† aggregation. **Division**

Agglutinate, Conglutinate, unite, weld, stick, glue, cement, gum, attach, paste, splice, solder, consolidate. **Detach**

Agglutination, Conglutination, union, welding,† cohesion. **Disintegration**

Aggrandize, Promote, advance, exalt, dignify, elevate, ennoble, honour. **Debase**

Aggrandizement, Promotion, advancement.† **Debasement**

Aggravate, Increase, heighten, worsen, magnify, exaggerate, enhance. **Mitigate**
Exasperate, annoy, provoke, irritate, enrage, tease. **Soothe**

Aggravation, Increase, heightening.†
Mitigation
Exasperation.†

Aggregate, v.a., Collect, heap, pile, amass, gather, accumulate, agglomerate.
Scatter
a., Total, sum collected.
n., Total, totality, sum, whole, mass, collection, result, lump, amount. **Unit**

Aggregation, Aggregating, collecting, heaping.†
Accumulation, mass, heap, collection, pile. **Distribution**

Aggress, Invade, attack, encroach.
Retreat

Aggression, Attack, invasion, encroachment, assault, onslaught, provocation.
Resistance

Aggressive, Attacking, invading, encroaching. **Peaceful**

Aggressor, Attacker, invader, encroacher, assaulter.

Aggrieve, Trouble, annoy, hurt, pain, wound, vex, aggravate, molest, injure, wrong, maltreat, abuse, oppress. **Soothe**

Aghast, Agape, terrified, horrified, dismayed, frightened, appalled, astonished, startled, dumbfounded, bewildered, astounded, astare. *Calm*

Agile, Nimble, active, quick, lively, brisk, smart, fleet, alert, spry, sprightly, ready, lithe, supple, prompt. *Clumsy*

Agility, Nimbleness, activity, quickness.† *Clumsiness*

Agitable, Movable, excitable. *Immobile* Debatable, investigable, discussable.

Agitate, Trouble, excite, disturb, move, rouse, ruffle, toss, perturb, stir, confuse, flurry, fluster, disconcert. *Calm* Discuss, examine, debate, investigate, moot, ventilate, meditate, consider, propound, resolve, deliberate, devise. *Settle*

Agitation, Agitating, trouble, excitement, disturbance.† Discussion, examination, debate.†

Agitator, Firebrand, extremist, incendiary, demagogue.

Agnostic, Sceptic, doubter, unbeliever, positivist, rationalist.

Ago, Past, gone, gone by, since. *Future*

Agog, Agitated, excited, eager, impatient. *Cool*

Agonize, *v.a.*, Torture, torment, pain, distress. *Ease* *v.n.*, Suffer, writhe, struggle.

Agony, Torment, torture, pain, anguish, pangs, distress. *Ease*

Agree, Accord, harmonize, coincide, correspond, tally, suit, match, fit, comport, consort, conform, cohere. *Differ* Assent, acquiesce, accede, comply, consent. *Dissent* Promise, bargain, stipulate, undertake, engage. *Refuse*

Agreeable, Accordant, harmonious, coincident,† pleasant, pleasing, gratifying, welcome, sweet, charming, acceptable, good, delicious, delectable. *Obnoxious*

Agreeably, Pleasantly, pleasingly, gratifyingly.†

Agreement, Bond, contract, undertaking, compact, treaty, obligation. *Difference*

Agriculture, Farming, cultivation, tillage, husbandry.

Aground, Stranded, ashore, beached, stopped. *Afloat*

Ague, Fever, chill, cold, shivering, rigor.

Ahead, Onwards, forward, afore, afront. *Behind*

Aid, *v.a.*, Help, assist, succour, relieve, support, encourage, abet, serve, second, back, co-operate with, prosper, befriend. *Oppose*

Aid, *n.*, Help, assistance, succour, relief,† alms, subsidy, bounty. *Opposition* Aider, helper, assistant, backer, second, aide-de-camp. *Opponent*

Aider, Helper, assistant, backer, second, associate, ally, abetter, coadjutor, follower, retainer, subordinate, accessory, acolyte. *Opponent*

Ail, *v.a.*, Pain, trouble, afflict, distress. *v.n.*, Suffer, peak, pine, be in pain.

Ailing, Sickly, sick, ill, indisposed, unwell, weakly, poorly, diseased. *Healthy*

Ailment, Ail, illness, disease, complaint, sickness, malady, weakness, infirmity, disorder, distemper. *Health*

Aim, *v.a.*, Direct, point, level. Intend, prepare, mean, design. *Shun* *n.*, Direction, tendency, course, bearing. Intention, purpose, design, scheme, idea, reason, end, mark, target.

Aimless, Purposeless, objectless, useless, random, chance, haphazard. *Purposeful*

Air, *v.a.*, Expose, display, ventilate. *n.*, Atmosphere, gas, breeze. Manner, look, aspect, bearing, port, behaviour, deportment, carriage, conduct, mien, cast, appearance, demeanour. Song, melody, tune, poem.

Airiness, Lightness, openness, buoyancy, grace, gracefulness, flexibility. *Heaviness* Vivacity, liveliness, gaiety, hilarity, levity, sprightliness. *Sullenness*

Airing, Stroll, promenade, ride, drive, walk, ventilation.

Airs, Affectation, affectedness, pretention, mannerism. *Naturalness*

Airy, Aerial, ethereal, unsubstantial, light, sublimated, buoyant, graceful. *Heavy* Gay, jolly, jovial, merry, sprightly, vivacious, lively, hilarious, light-hearted, blithe. *Sullen* Garish, gaudy, showy, empty, windy. *Dull*

Aisle, Passage, path, walk.

Akin, Related, kindred, allied, agnate, cognate, consanguineous, similar, congenial, like, corresponding, connected, homogeneous, sympathetic. *Alien*

Alack, Alas, welladay, lackaday, alackaday.

Alacrity, Quickness, promptness, readiness, promptitude, eagerness, alertness, agility, activity, compliance, willingness, cheerfulness, sprightliness. *Reluctance*

Alarm, *v.a.*, Terrify, frighten, affright, intimidate, scare, startle, appal, daunt. *Compose* *n.*, Fear, terror, intimidation, fright,

apprehension, dismay, consternation.
Quiet
War-cry, tocsin, alarum, warning, reveille.

Alarming, Fearful, terrible, intimidating, ominous, threatening, frightful.
Encouraging

Alas, Alack, welladay, lackaday, alackaday.

Albeit, Although, notwithstanding.

Alchemy, Chemistry, magic, astrology.

Alcohol, Spirits, wine, intoxicant.

Alcoholic, Ardent, spirituous.

Alcove, Arbour, recess, retreat.

Alert, Active, vigilant, watchful, ready, prepared, wakeful, wary, circumspect, heedful, prompt, brisk, agile, smart, on guard. *Sleepy*

Alertness, Activity, vigilance, watchfulness.† *Inactivity*

Alias, Otherwise.

Alibi, Elsewhere.

Alien, *a.*, Foreign, strange, estranged, unallied, differing, remote, separated, unconnected, irrelevant, inappropriate, exotic. *Akin*
n., Foreigner, stranger. *Native*

Alienate, Convey, assign, consign, abalienate, transfer, demise, devolve.
Entail
Estrange, disaffect, wean, withdraw.
Conciliate

Alienation, Conveyance, assignment, consignment.†
Estrangement, disaffection.†
Breach, rupture, division, variance.
Insanity, aberration, derangement, hallucination, imbecility, lunacy, madness, delusion, craziness, delirium, mania.
Sanity

Alight, Descend, perch, drop, rest, stop, land, settle, dismount. *Ascend*

Alike, *a.*, Similar, like, resembling, allied, analogous. *Unlike*
adv., Equally, akin, together, both.

Aliment, Food, sustenance, sustentation, nourishment, nutriment, subsistence, victuals, viands, meat, provision, 'fare, diet, rations, forage.

Alive, Living, live, breathing, quick, active, operative. *Dead*
Alert, quick, smart, prompt, cheerful, sprightly, animated, lively, brisk, joyous, susceptible, sensitive. *Dull*

All, *a.*, Whole, entire, complete, total.
Some
adv., Altogether, wholly, completely, entirely, totally, quite. *Partly*
n., Total, totality, aggregate, everything, whole. *Nothing*

Allay, Soothe, alleviate, repress, mitigate,

assuage, appease, pacify, compose, soften, quiet, still, calm, smooth, lull, hush, tranquillize, restrain, silence, check, subdue, solace, modify, moderate, abate, lessen, mollify, relieve, ease. *Aggravate*

Allegation, Assertion, statement, declaration, averment, affirmation, excuse, plea. *Denial*

Allege, Assert, state, declare,† maintain, say, adduce, assign, cite, quote, advance, produce. *Contradict*

Allegiance, Loyalty, fealty, obedience, homage, subjection, fidelity, obligation, duty. *Treason*

Allegorical, Metaphorical, figurative, typical. *Literal*

Allegory, Parable, fable, story, tale, myth, metaphor, illustration, *Fact*

Alleviate, Allay, assuage, lighten, mitigate, palliate, soothe, soften, moderate, mollify, quell, abate, lessen, diminish, relieve, ease, quiet, still. *Aggravate*

Alleviation, Allaying, assuagement.†
Aggravation

Alley, Passage, walk, aisle, lane, by-way, slum.

Alliance, Compact, treaty, union, co-operation, coalition, confederation, confederacy, league, combination, federation, affiliation. *Disunion*
Relation, relationship, affinity, inter-marriage.

Allied, In compact, united, confederated, co-operating.†
Related, akin, alike, analogous, cognate, similar.

Allocate, Allot, assign, divide, distribute, deal, grant. *Appropriate*

Allodial, Independent, freehold, free.
Feudal

Allonge, Lunge, thrust, stab, longe, pass, tilt.

Allot, Allocate, apportion, divide, distribute, measure, deal, dispense, portion, mete, fix, specify, administer, assign, grant. *Withhold*

Allotment, Allocation, apportionment, division,† quota, contingent, parcel, piece, dole.

Allow, Admit, acknowledge, concede, own, confess, grant, yield. *Deny*
Permit, justify, sanction, approve, let, authorize, tolerate, suffer, endure, bear.
Resist
Allot, apportion, assign, remit, abate, deduct. *Withhold*

Allowable, Permissible, justifiable, proper, lawful, warrantable, admissible.
Unlawful

Allowance, Permission, leave, permit,

authorization, approval, sufferance, sanction, license, limit, ration, grant. **Prohibition**

Alloy, *v.a.*, Debase, admix, deteriorate, adulterate, impair, diminish, decrease, depreciate. **Purify**
n., Base metal, admixture, deterioration, adulteration,† combination, amalgam, alloyage, compound.

Allude, Refer, point, indicate, suggest, hint, insinuate, imply.

Allure, Tempt, entice, bait, lure, seduce, attract, decoy, troll, ensnare, coax, cajole, lead, persuade, engage, inveigle. **Scare**

Allurement, Temptation, enticement, lure.† **Determent**

Allusion, Reference, suggestion, hint, insinuation, implication, intimation, innuendo.

Allusive, Suggestive, hinting, insinuating, innuent, emblematic, figurative, symbolical, typical.

Alluvium, Silt, sediment, deposit.

Ally, *v.a.*, Combine, unite, join, league, marry. **Separate**
n., Confederate, coadjutor, aider, helper, assistant, friend, colleague, co-operator, partner, accomplice, abettor, accessory. **Opponent**

Almanac, Calendar, register, ephemeris.

Almighty, All-powerful, all-sufficient, omnipotent. **Impotent**

Almoner, Distributor, allocator, dispenser.

Almost, Well-nigh, nearly, towards, about.

Alms, Gift, gratuity, bounty, charity, dole.

Aloft, Above, overhead, on high, skyward, heavenward. **Below**

Alone, Lone, lonely, sole, solitary, single, isolated, unaccompanied, forsaken, deserted, unhelped. **Together**

Along, *adv.*, Lengthwise, longitudinally, beside.
Together, simultaneously.
Onward, forward.
prep., Alongst, by, through.

Aloof, Apart, away, far off, superior, distant. **Near**

Aloud, Loudly, clamorously, vociferously, audibly, distinctly. **Silently**

Alpine, High, mountainous, elevated.

Already, Before, previously. **Later**

Also, Too, likewise, besides, withal, moreover, furthermore, in addition.

Altar, Shrine, sanctuary, Holy of Holies.

Alter, Change, vary, substitute, modify, turn, exchange, convert, shift, transform, transmute. **Conserve**

Alterable, Changeable, variable,† mutable, movable, revocable. **Permanent**

Alteration, Change, variation, modification, transformation, permutation, diversification.

Altercation, Contention, strife, dispute, difference, controversy, quarrel, wrangle, dissension. **Agreement**

Alternate, *v.n.*, Reciprocate.
a., Reciprocal, in turn.

Alternative, Choice, option, resource. **Necessity**

Although, Though, albeit, notwithstanding, granted, supposing.

Altiloquence, Inflateness, bombast.

Altitude, Height, loftiness, elevation. **Depth**

Altogether, Wholly, completely, entirely, totally, quite, fully, utterly, perfectly, thoroughly. **Partially**
Collectively, conjointly, combined, simultaneously, in the aggregate, en masse. **Separately**

Altruistic, Unselfish, philanthropic, devoted. **Selfish**

Alumnus, Graduate, pupil, disciple.

Alveary, Beehive.

Alveolate, Honeycombed, cellular.

Always, Ever, evermore, continually, eternally, everlastingly, unceasingly, perpetually, aye. **Never**

Amain, Furiously, violently, forcibly, headlong, suddenly. **Gently**

Amalgam, Compound, composite, mixture, combination, alloy.

Amalgamate, Unite, fuse, blend, mix, incorporate, mingle, compound, combine, commingle, consolidate. **Separate**

Amalgamation, Union, fusion, blending,† intermarriage. **Disunion**

Amanuensis, Secretary, copyist, writer, transcriber, scribe.

Amaranthine, Unfading, lasting, fadeless, imperishable, undying, deathless, immortal, perennial. **Fading**

Amass, Collect, accumulate, heap, pile, gather, aggregate. **Scatter**

Amateurish, Unskilled, dilettantish, untrained, inexpert, novice. **Professional**

Amatory, Amorous, lovesome, erotic, passionate, tender.

Amaze, Astonish, astound, bewilder, daze, dumbfound, stagger, nonplus, perplex, confuse, confound.

Amazement, Astonishment, bewilderment,† wonder, marvel, surprise, stupefaction. **Composure**

Amazing, Astonishing, astounding, bewildering,† striking, prodigious, extraordinary, stupendous. **Ordinary**

Ambages, Windings, turnings, verbosity, accumulation, wordiness, subterfuges, deviations, evasions, circumlocution. *Brevity*

Ambagious, Winding, turning, verbose.† *Brief*

Ambassador, Envoy, plenipotentiary, minister, legate, deputy.

Ambient, Encompassing, enfolding, surrounding, encircling.

Ambiguity, Vagueness, obscurity, doubtfulness, dubiousness. *Lucidity*

Ambiguous, Vague, obscure, doubtful, dubious, uncertain, equivocal, indistinct, indeterminate, indefinite, enigmatical. *Lucid*

Ambition, Desire, yearning, aspiration.

Ambitious, Aspiring, eager, intent, emulous.

Amble, Dawdle, walk, saunter, stroll. *Hurry*

Ambrosial, Fragrant, delicious, balmy, odorous, sweet, luscious, dainty. *Obnoxious*

Ambush, Ambuscade, hiding place, cover, lurking place.

Ameliorate, Amend, improve, promote, raise, better, advance, elevate. *Mar*

Amelioration, Amendment, improvement, promotion.†

Amenability, Liability, accountability, responsibility, answerableness, amenableness. *Obstinacy*

Amenable, Liable, accountable,† impressible, pliant, subject, docile, ductile. *Obstinate*

Amend, Ameliorate, mend, improve, reform, correct, rectify, better, repair. *Deteriorate*

Amendment, Improvement, alteration, change, reform, correction.

Amends, Recompense, compensation, indemnity, reparation, satisfaction, atonement, apology, redress. *Injury*

Amenity, Pleasantness, agreeableness, geniality, graciousness, mildness, blandness, softness, affability, gentleness, courtesy, amiability, politeness. *Austerity*

Amerce, Fine, condemn, bind, mulct. *Remit*

Amiability, Kindness, kindliness, amiableness, benignity, amenity, attractiveness, loveliness, affability, obligingness, winsomeness, friendliness, benevolence. *Churlishness*

Amiable, Kind, benign, benignant, attractive,† engaging, charming, good, charitable. *Churlish*

Amicable, Friendly, cordial, neighbourly, kind, amiable, harmonious, peaceable. *Hostile*

Amicableness, Friendliness, kindness, cordiality.†

Amidst, Between, among, amongst, betwixt, mid.

Amiss, *a.,* Wrong, inaccurate, incorrect, false, untrue, improper, erroneous. *Right* *adv.,* Wrong, wrongly, inaccurately.†

Amity, Amicableness, friendliness, cordiality, amiableness, harmony, peacefulness, peaceableness. *Hostility*

Ammunition, Munition, munitions, stores, shells.

Amnesty, Pardon, forgiveness, acquittal, remission, absolution. *Punishment*

Amongst, Amid, amidst, between, mid.

Amorous, Enamoured, fond, loving, ardent, longing, tender, passionate, impassioned, amatory, erotic.

Amorphous, Shapeless, irregular, formless, unformed, incomplete, inchoate, vague, structureless, chaotic, confused. *Ordered*

Amount, *v.n.,* Reach, rise, come to, attain, aggregate. *n.,* Total, sum, aggregate, whole, quantity. *Deficit*

Ample, Large, bountiful, liberal, sufficient, plentiful, abundant, great, wide, capacious, extensive, spacious, broad, rich, lavish, exuberant, unrestricted. *Scanty*

Amplification, Expansion, enlargement, dilation, greatening, extension, broadening, development, diffuseness, prolixity. *Abbreviation*

Amplify, Expand, enlarge,† augment, magnify. *Abbreviate*

Amplitude, Largeness, size, bulk, volume, capaciousness, width, breadth, extent, dimensions, mass, bigness, greatness, range, sweep, compass.

Amputate, Remove, cut off, sever, separate, prune, clip, curtail, lop.

Amuse, Entertain, cheer, divert, gladden, solace, please, charm, enliven, recreate. *Bore*

Amusement, Entertainment, diversion,† pastime, game, sport, fun, frolic.

Amusing, Entertaining, diverting, droll, ludicrous, comic, ridiculous, funny. *Boring*

Anacreontic, Amatory, amorous, jovial, erotic, convivial.

Anæmic, Bloodless, thin-blooded.

Analeptic, Restorative, invigorating, strenghtening, comforting. *Depressing*

Analogous, Similar, alike, like, resembling, corresponding. *Different*

Analogy, Similarity, likeness.†

Analysis, Decomposition, resolution, segregation, dissection, separation, partition. *Synthesis*

Anarchist, Demagogue, Jacobin, agitator.

Anarchy, Lawlessness, disorder, confusion, misrule, violence, tumult, riot, chaos. *Order*

Anathema, Curse, excommunication, ban, denunciation, malediction, imprecation. *Blessing*

Anatomize, Dissect, vivisect, analyse, examine, sift, probe, scrutinize.

Anatomy, Structure, skeleton, dissection, analysis.†

Ancestor, Forebear, forefather, progenitor, father, predecessor. *Descendant*

Ancestral, Patrimonial, hereditary, inherited.

Ancestry, Race, house, family, line, lineage, progeniture, generation, descent, stock, pedigree, genealogy.

Anchor, n., Security, stay, defence, hold. v.a., Fasten, secure, fix. *Loose*

Anchorage, Harbour, port, road, roadstead.

Anchorite, Recluse, hermit, anchoret, solitary.

Ancient, Old, olden, primeval, aged, primitive, pristine, antiquated, antique, archaic, obsolete. *Modern*

Ancillary, Helping, auxiliary, accessory, helpful, contributory, instrumental, subsidiary, subordinate, subservient. *Preventative*

Anecdote, Story, incident, tale, memoir, narrative, occurrence.

Anew, Again, newly, afresh, once more, repeatedly.

Anfractuous, Devious, winding, crooked, tortuous, sinuous, intricate, meandering, ambagious, angular. *Straight*

Angel, Seraph, cherub, spirit. *Devil*

Angelical, Seraphic, cherubic, heavenly, celestial, ethereal, adorable, rapturous, entrancing, ravishing, divine, pure. *Diabolical*

Anger, v.a., Displease, infuriate, annoy, aggravate, exasperate, irritate, offend, rouse, provoke, enrage, vex. *Appease* n., Displeasure, fury, annoyance,† wrath, resentment, choler, indignation, ire, rage, passion, temper, animosity. *Mildness*

Angle, v.n., Fish, bob, scheme. n., Corner, bend, crotch, elbow, knee, divergence, hook.

Angry, Displeased, infuriated, annoyed, wrathful, exasperated, irritated, provoked, irate, furious, "riled," "mad,"
hot, passionate, piqued, chafed, moody, indignant. *Calm*

Anguish, v.a., Agonize, torture, distress, hurt, pain. *Ease* n., Agony, torture, torment, distress, woe, suffering, pain. *Ecstacy*

Anile, Old, senile, decrepit, aged, imbecile, doting.

Animadversion, Censure, blame, disapproval, rebuke, condemnation, reproof, aspersion, reprobation, criticism, comment. *Praise*

Animal, n., Creature, being, beast, brute. a., Carnal, physical, beastly, brutal, brutish, sensual, natural, fleshly. *Human*

Animate, v.a., Waken, enliven, stimulate, stir, encourage, quicken, vivify, invigorate, fortify, revive, rouse, whet, excite, urge, provoke, goad, embolden. *Depress*

Animated, Brisk, lively, vigorous, sprightly, buoyant, spirited, elated, gay, blithe, jocund, vivacious, stirred, excited. *Dull*

Animosity, Hatred, hate, antipathy, aversion, animus, grudge, antagonism, malice, bitterness, rancour, malignity, hostility, virulence, spleen, enmity. *Love*

Animus, Animosity, malice, hatred.† Intention, aim, purpose, disposition, temper, spirit.

Annals, History, chronicles, records, archives, registers, rolls, memorials.

Annex, Add, append, adjoin, attach, tag, subjoin, super-add, connect, join, unite. *Separate*

Annexation, Addition, adding, appending.† *Separation*

Annihilate, Abolish, destroy, extinguish, exterminate, raze, nullify, annul, obliterate, blast, kill, quench, efface. *Preserve*

Annihilation, Abolition, destruction, extinction.† *Preservation*

Annotate, Comment, explain, elucidate, illustrate.

Annotation, Comment, note, explanation, elucidation, illustration, commentary, remark, observation, criticism.

Announce, Declare, proclaim, publish, herald, notify, report, intimate, propound, promulgate, blazon, advertise, reveal. *Conceal*

Announcement, Declaration, proclamation, publication,† ratification, manifestation. *Suppression*

Annoy, Vex, anger, tease, enrage, irritate, affront, molest, disturb, trouble, harass, pain, worry, hector, badger, pester, bother. **Soothe**

Annoyance, Vexation, anger, irritation.† Bore, nuisance, infliction.

Annual, Yearly.

Annually, Yearly, per annum.

Annul, Annihilate, obliterate, extinguish, nullify, cancel, abrogate, repeal, revoke, quash, abolish, recall, countermand, invalidate. **Confirm**

Annular, Circular, round, ring-shaped.

Annulment, Annulling, annihilation, obliteration, extinction.†

Anodyne, Narcotic, sedative, opiate, palliative, lenitive, drug, mitigative, assuasive. **Stimulant**

Anoint, Rub, smear, consecrate, anele.

Anomalous, Abnormal, anomalistic, irregular, unusual, unnatural, monstrous, erratic, eccentric, singular, peculiar, exceptional. **Normal**

Anomaly, Abnormity, abnormality, irregularity, monstrosity.†

Anon, Soon, shortly, immediately, ere, quickly, forthwith, directly, presently.

Anonymous, Nameless, unacknowledged, unidentified, unsigned. **Authentic**

Answer, v.a., Reply to, respond to, satisfy, fulfil, refute. **Question**
v.n., Reply, respond, rejoin.
Suit, serve, do, pass.
n., Reply, response, retort, rejoinder, plea, refutation, defence, confutation.

Answerable, Liable, responsible, accountable, amenable, suited, correlative, proportionate.

Antagonism, Opposition, hostility, enmity, feud, disharmony, dissonance, conflict, discord, discordancy, discordance, contradiction, abashing, repugnance, contrariety. **Amity**

Antagonist, Opponent, enemy, foe, adversary, rival, competitor.

Antagonistic, Opposing, hostile, disharmonious, dissonant, inimical. **Friendly**

Antecedence, Priority, precedence, anteriority, introduction. **Posteriority**

Antecedent, a., Prior, preceding, anterior, previous, precursory. **Posterior**
n., Precursor, forerunner. **Postcursor**

Antedate, Anticipate, forestall, foretaste.

Anterior, Preceding, foregoing, previous, prior, introductory. **Posterior**

Ante-room, Ante-chamber, hall, lobby, vestibule.

Anthem, Hymn.

Anthology, Collection, excerpts, selections, extracts.

Anthropoid, Manlike, anthropomorphic.

Anthropophagi, Maneaters, cannibals.

Antic, a., Fantastic, odd, fanciful, merry, ludicrous, grotesque, ridiculous, wild.
n., Trick, prank, lark, gambol, caper.
Freak, mountebank, fool, buffoon, clown, jester, harlequin.

Anticipate, v.a., Forestall, foretaste, prevent, antedate.
Expect, foresee, forecast, meet, intercept, prepare for, reckon upon.

Anticipation, Forestalling, foretaste.†
Expectation, foresight, forecast.†

Antidote, Remedy, cure, restorative, counteractive, specific, corrective. **Poison**

Antipathy, Hatred, loathing, dislike, repugnance, disgust, abhorrence, detestation, aversion. **Sympathy**

Antiquarian, Archaeologist, archaeologian, antiquary.

Antiquated, Archaic, antique, quaint, old-fashioned, obsolete, ancient, bygone. **Modern**

Antique, Old, archaic, quaint.†

Antithesis, Opposition, contrast. **Comparison**

Anxiety, Trouble, care, carefulness, misgiving, concern, solicitude, apprehension, uneasiness, disquiet, disquietude, foreboding, fear, pain, worry, perplexity. **Ease**

Anxious, Troubled, careful, concerned, solicitous.† **Careless**

Apace, Quickly, rapidly, eagerly, fast, speedily, swiftly, hastily, expeditiously. **Slowly**

Apart, Aside, separately, aloof, away, asunder. **Together**

Apartment, Room, hall, chamber, lodging.

Apathetic, Cold, unfeeling, indifferent, insensible, passionless, impassible, impassive, unconcerned, callous, dead, senseless, sluggish, stoical, unimpressible, soulless, phlegmatic, dull, obtuse, torpid, tame. **Eager**

Apathy, Coldness, unfeelingness, indifference, insensibility.† **Eagerness**

Ape, v.a., Mimic, imitate, copy, counterfeit.
n., Simian, troglodyte, monkey.
Imitator.
Guy, imitation, image, likeness, type.

Aperture, Hole, gap, opening, perforation, cleft, rift, passage, eye, loop-hole, orifice, chasm. **Enclosure**

Apex, Acme, top, zenith, summit, pinnacle, height. **Base**

Aphorism, Dictum, adage, apothegm, saying, maxim, proverb, saw, precept.

Apiary, Bee-hive, bee-house, bee-stand, bee-shed.

Apiece, Severally, separately, individually, distributively, each. *Collectively*

Apish, Imitative, mimicking, foppish, affected, trifling.

Aplomb, Collectedness, poise, assurance, self-confidence, self-possession, self-balance. *Excitement*

Apocalypse, Revelation, disclosure, manifestation, unveiling. *Eclipse*

Apocryphal, Uncanonical, unauthentic, legendary, dubious, false, fictitious, spurious. *Authentic*

Apodeictic } Unquestionable, certain, de-
Apodictic } monstrative. *Doubtful*

Apologetic, Excusatory, exculpatory, defensive, vindicative.

Apologist, Supporter, defender, advocate, vindicator. *Adversary*

Apologize, Excuse, plead, explain.

Apologue, Allegory, fable, parable, fiction. *Precept*

Apology, Defence, justification, vindication, excuse, plea, explanation, reparation. *Accusation*

Apostasy, Desertion, dereliction, defection, fall, backsliding. *Steadfastness*

Apostate, n., Deserter, backslider, turncoat, pervert, renegade. *Loyalist* a., Treacherous, traitorous, disloyal, perfidious, false, backsliding, recreant, unfaithful, untrue. *Loyal*

Apostle, Messenger, missionary, preacher.

Apothecary, Chemist, druggist, pharmacist.

Apothegm, Adage, saying, proverb, maxim, precept.

Appeal, Alarm, affright, terrify, scare, dismay, daunt, frighten, shock, horrify, petrify, astound. *Reassure*

Apparatus, Utensils, tools, means, appliances, instruments, mechanism, contrivances.

Apparel, v.a., Clothe, dress, attire, equip, array, accoutre, robe, habit. *Strip* n., Clothes, clothing, dress, attire, equipment, raiment, accoutrement, robes, habit, habiliments, costume, garments, vesture, vestments.

Apparent, Obvious, discernible, perceptible, visible, manifest, plain, open, clear, conspicuous, patent, evident, indubitable, ostensible, external. *Hidden*

Apparently, Obviously, discernibly, perceptibly.† *Dimly*

Apparition, Ghost, spirit, spectre, phantom, vision, spook, illusion. *Reality*

Appeal, v.n., Address, entreat, implore, urge, invoke, petition, accost, solicit, request, resort. *Disclaim* n., Address, entreaty, imploration.†

Appear, Emerge, open, dawn, break, arrive, be present. *Disappear* Seem, look, present, show.

Appearance, Emergence, coming, manifestation, advent, arrival. *Disappearance* Semblance, seeming, look, show, pretence, colour, aspect, manner, mien, air, bearing, demeanour.

Appeasable, Reconcilable, placable, forgiving. *Unrelenting*

Appease, Pacify, assuage, mitigate, moderate, calm, lessen, still, abate, soothe, quiet, alleviate, mollify, tranquillize, allay, compose, lull, ease, placate, satisfy, reconcile, propitiate. *Aggravate*

Appellation, Name, designation, title, denomination, term, cognomen.

Append, Attach, affix, add, hang, fasten, join, subjoin, supplement, tag, tack, annex. *Separate*

Appendage, Appendix, attachment, adjunct, supplement, annexation, addition.

Appendant, Attached, annexed, supplementary, hanging, pendent, attendant.

Appendix, Appendage, attachment, adjunct, supplement, codicil, addendum, annexation, addition.

Appertain, Belong, pertain, adhere, touch, refer, concern.

Appetite, Desire, passion, want, craving, longing, liking, relish, hunger, proneness, disposition. *Apathy*

Applaud, Praise, cheer, clap, laud, approve, encourage, commend, compliment, extol. *Denounce*

Applause, Praise, plaudit, laudation, acclamation, acclaim, approbation, eulogy, approval. *Denunciation*

Appliance, Contrivance, tool, instrument, mechanism, apparatus, utensil, means, agency.
Application, use, exercise, practice.

Applicable, Appropriate, available, useful, suitable, convenient, adjustable, apt, fitting, pertinent, relevant, proper, apposite, ancillary, conducive. *Useless*

Applicant, Candidate, suitor, petitioner.

Application, Request, petition, appeal, suit, solicitation.
Perseverance, assiduity, industry, persistency, study, attention, use, exercise, practice.

Apply, v.a., Use, appropriate, employ, exercise, execute. *Disuse* Devote, dedicate, addict, direct, engage, refer. *Divert* v.n., Suit, make application.

Appoint, Nominate, name, prescribe, determine, fix, establish, constitute, create, install. *Recall*

Command, direct, require, ordain, decree, enjoin, order, bid. *Cancel*

Allot, assign, distribute, supply, furnish, equip.

Appointment, Office, station, position, place.

Appointing, nomination.†

Tryst, arrangement, agreement, assignation.

Command, direction, requirement, ordination.†

Allotment, assignment, equipment.†

Apportion, Allot, assign, divide, allocate, administer, distribute, partition, measure, share, dispense, deal. *Retain*

Apportionment, Allotment, assignment, division.†

Apposite, Pertinent, apt, fit, fitting, suitable, befitting, relevant, appropriate. *Irrelevant*

Appraise, Value, estimate, survey, price, prize, rate. *Undervalue*

Appraisement, Appraisal, valuation,† judgment. *Condemnation*

Appreciate, *v.a.*, Esteem, value, acknowledge, respect. *Deprecate*

v.n., Rise in value.

Appreciation, Esteem, valuation.†

Rise in value. *Depreciation*

Apprehend, Seize, capture, arrest. *Release*

Fear, forebode.

Conceive, view, regard, imagine, understand, perceive, realize, appreciate, opine, suppose, think, fancy, presume, conjecture.

Apprehension, Seizure, capture, arrest.

Fear, foreboding.

Conception, view.† *Misapprehension*

Apprize, Acquaint, inform, notify, advertise, advise, tell, warn, admonish. *Mislead*

Approach, *v.n.*, Come, draw near, approximate. *Depart*

v.a., Come near, advance, broach.

n., Advent, advance, coming, nearing, approximation.

Access, admittance, admission, entrance, adit, path, avenue. *Exit*

Approbation, Praise, approval, laudation, commendation, satisfaction, encouragement, assent, consent, support, sanction. *Censure*

Appropriate, *v.a.*, Adopt, convert, apply, use, employ. *Ignore*

Assign, allot, apportion, devote.

a., Fitting, fit, proper, timely, adapted, apt, befitting, apposite, pertinent, felicitous, germane, seemly, becoming. *Irrelevant*

Appropriateness, Fitness, propriety, timeliness.†

Appropriation, Adoption, seizure, capture, use, employment, application, assignment, allotment, apportionment, devotion. *Release*

Approval, Approbation, praise, commendation, satisfaction, appreciation, encouragement, assent, consent, support, sanction. *Censure*

Approve, Praise, commend, recommend, value, prize, appreciate, like, encourage, assent, consent, support, sanction, uphold. *Reprove*

Approximate, *v.n.*, Approach, come near, resemble.

a., Proximate, approaching, near, rough. *Differ*

Approximately, Nearly, about, near, approaching, close.

Appulse, Impact, shock, collision, meeting, jar.

Appurtenance, Appendage, adjunct, belonging, connection, attachment, concomitant, supplement, annexation, addition.

Appurtenant, Pertaining, appertaining, belonging, connected, attached, concomitant, supplementary.

A Priori, Theoretically.

Apropos, Opportune, timely, suitable, seasonable, fit, apt.

Apt, Apposite, fit, fitting, appropriate, pertinent, opportune, suitable, timely, germane, befitting, felicitous. *Irrelevant*

Disposed, liable, prone, addicted, inclined.

Quick, clever, dexterous, expert, prompt, sharp, able, adroit, ready. *Slow*

Aptitude, Disposition, inclination, talent, leaning, bent, bias, turn, genius, gift, knack, aptness, ability, cleverness, quickness, readiness. *Stupidity*

Aptness, Appositeness, fitness, appropriateness.†

Aptitude, disposition, inclination.†

Aqueous, Wet, moist, watery, damp, humid.

Aquiline, Bent, hooked, curved, curving. *Straight*

Arab, Arabian, Saracen, Moor.

Arable, Cultivable, tillable.

Arbiter, Judge, arbitrator, referee, umpire, controller, governor, ruler, sovereign, lord, master.

Arbitrament, Adjudication, decision, determination, decree, award, settlement judgment, verdict.

Arbitrary, Despotic, tyrannical, dictatorial, autocratic, harsh, imperious, overbearing, wilful, selfish, capricious. *Just*

Arbitrate, *v.a.*, Judge, determine, decide. *v.n.*, Mediate, interpose, intervene, adjust, settle.

Arbitration, Judgment, determination, decision, adjudication, mediation, intervention, intercession, arbitrament.

Arbitrator, Arbiter, judge, referee, umpire.

Arboreal, Treelike, dendriform.

Arbour, Bower, recess, retreat.

Arcade, Colonnade, piazza, peristyle, loggia.

Arcadian, Pastoral, rustic, elysian, amaranthine.

Arch, *n.*, Curve, bend, bending, curving. *a.*, Principal, chief, main, first class. *Minor*
Playful, merry, roguish, sly, sportive, waggish, mirthful, cunning, knowing, shrewd.

Archaeologist, Archaeologian, antiquary, antiquarian.

Archaic, Ancient, obsolete, old, antiquated, bygone, old-fashioned. *Modern*

Arched, Vaulted, concave, bowed.

Archetype, Type, model, pattern, prototype, protoplast, original, paragon, example.

Arching, Vaulted, curving, bending.

Architect, Designer, author, maker, contriver.

Architecture, Fabric, structure, frame, framework, workmanship.

Archives, Records, annals, rolls, registers, documents.

Arctic, Northern, boreal. *Antarctic*

Ardent, Warm, hot, passionate, burning, fiery, fervent, eager, excited, impassioned, intense, keen, zealous, earnest, fervid, vehement. *Cool*

Ardour, Warmth, heat, passion, fire. *Apathy*

Arduous, Difficult, hard, onerous, laborious, toilsome, tiresome, steep, lofty, precipitous, uphill. *Easy*

Area, District, region, territory, realm, sphere, surface.
Yard, enclosure.

Arena, Amphitheatre, theatre, ring, field, stage.

Argent, *a.*, Silvery, radiant, bright, shining, brilliant, resplendent.
n., Silveriness, radiance, brightness.†

Argosy, Ship, galleon, carack.

Argue, *v.n.*, Dispute, debate, reason, plead, discuss. *Acquiesce*
v.a., Denote, indicate, show, imply, prove, betoken.

Argument, Dispute, debate, discussion, disputation, controversy, question, subject, theme, topic, matter.
Proof, ground, reason, reasoning, evidence.
Abstract, epitome, summary, outline, condensation. *Amplification*

Arid, Dry, parched, barren, sterile, infecund, pointless, dull. *Fertile*

Aridity, Aridness, dryness, parchedness.† *Humidity*

Arise, Rise, get up, ascend, mount, soar, appear, emerge. *Sink*
Begin, originate, spring, proceed, issue, result, flow. *End*
Rise, rebel, revolt.

Arising, Commencing, beginning, inchoative, incipient, originating.† *Ending*

Aristocracy, Peerage, nobility, noblesse, gentry, upper classes. *People*

Aristocratic, Noble, titled, patrician, princely, gentle. *Low*
Proud, overbearing, haughty, arrogant, disdainful. *Humble*

Arm, *v.a.*, Equip, cover, prepare, furnish, array, protect, fortify, guard, strengthen. *Disarm*
n., Limb, bough, brand.
Inlet, estuary, creek, cove.
Power, strength, might, weapon.

Armada, Fleet, flotilla, squadron.

Armament, Munitions, arms, weapons.

Armistice, Truce.

Armorial, Heraldic.

Armoury, Arsenal, magazine.

Arms, Weapons, munitions, armour, array, mail, shield, crest, scutcheon.
War.

Army, Force, troops, host, multitude, throng, array.

Aroma, Fragrance, odour, redolence, perfume, scent.

Aromatic, Scented, fragrant, spicy, odoriferous, redolent.

Around, About, round, encircling, encompassing, environing, surrounding. *Amid*

Arouse, Excite, stir, incite, instigate, provoke, animate, stimulate, warm, awaken, rouse, disturb, alarm, kindle, inspirit. *Pacify*

Arraign, Summon, accuse, indict, persecute, impeach, charge, denounce, tax. *Condone*

Arraignment, Summons, accusation, indictment.†

Arrange, Group, classify, dispose, assort, array, class, marshal, place, distribute, order, adjust, locate. *Disperse*

Arrange, Plan, contrive, devise, organize, prepare, agree. **Disagree**

Arrangement, Grouping, classification, disposition.†
Plan, contrivance, preparation, scheme, economy, regulation, management.

Arrant, Vile, atrocious, notorious, infamous, monstrous, rank, utter, veritable, emphatic, unqualified. **Mitigated**

Array, *v.a.,* Arrange, dispose, rank, range, marshal, place. **Derange**
Dress, equip, accoutre, attire, habit, vest, enrobe, robe, wrap, clothe, invest, deck, bedeck, adorn. **Strip**
n., Arrangement, disposition, order, marshalling, display, show, exhibition, army, soldiery, troops.
Apparel, dress, clothes, attire, garments.

Arrears, Arrearage, deficiency. **Sufficiency**

Arrest, *v.a.,* Seize, apprehend, capture, take, detain, stop, hinder, interrupt, check, obstruct, restrain, hold, fix, engage, rivet, occupy, engross. **Release**
n., Seizure, apprehension, capture, detention.†

Arrival, Coming, advent. **Departure**
Comer, new-comer.

Arrive, Come, reach, attain, land. **Depart**

Arrogance, Pride, haughtiness, disdain, effrontery, contemptuousness, insolence, discourtesy, hauteur, loftiness, lordliness, contumely, assumption, superciliousness, assurance, self-assertion, self-conceit. **Modesty**

Arrogant, Proud, haughty, disdainful.† **Modest**

Arrogate, Usurp, assume, demand, vindicate, assert. **Waive**

Arrow, Shaft, dart, bolt, reed.

Arsenal, Armoury, magazine, depository.

Art, Skill, aptitude, dexterity, aptness, cleverness, ingenuity, knack, adroitness. **Clumsiness**
Address, readiness.
Artfulness, shrewdness, deceit, guile, astuteness, artifice, craft, duplicity. **Simplicity**
Craft, trade, calling, vocation, business, employment.

Artful, Cunning, shrewd, sharp, designing, knowing, deceitful, astute, crafty, subtle, insidious, wily, sly. **Simple**

Article, Essay, paper, piece.
Commodity, thing, substance, part, item, portion, brand, division.

Articulate, *v.a.,* Pronounce, enunciate, speak.
Join, connect, fasten, unite. **Sever**

Articulate, *a.,* Distinct, clear, audible, intelligible, connected, articulated.

Artifice, Cunning, deceit, trickery, guile, deception, subtlety, wile, trick, art, contrivance, invention, fraud, subterfuge, manoeuvre, stratagem, machination, cheat, imposture, circumvention, duplicity. **Simplicity**

Artificer, Maker, craftsman, worker, workman, artisan, artist, mechanic, contriver, plotter, machinator.

Artificial, Unreal, unnatural, assumed, feigned, sham, spurious, fictitious, counterfeit, fake. **Real**

Artillery, Cannon, gunnery, guns, ordnance, enginery.

Artisan, Workman, worker, craftsman, operative, hand, mechanic, labourer.

Artist, Painter, sketcher, limner, carver, sculptor, modeller, master, adept.

Artistic, Tasteful, beautiful. **Ugly**
Masterly, skilful.

Artless, Simple, unaffected, plain, frank, honest, open, fair, straightforward, truthful, ingenuous, sincere, true. **Artful**
Ignorant, rude, untaught, unlearned.

As, Because, since.
Similarly, like, while.

Ascend, *v.a.,* Climb, scale, mount. **Descend**
v.n., Rise, arise, mount, soar, climb, aspire.

Ascendancy ⎫ Superiority, control, power,
Ascendency ⎬ authority, mastery, influence, supremacy, sway, government, command, rule, dominion, advantage, domination, sovereignty. **Servitude**

Ascendant, *n.,* Superiority, supremacy, predominance, ascendancy.
a., Rising, superior, prevailing, ruling, predominant, surpassing.

Ascension, Rising, rise, ascent, ascending, mounting. **Descent**

Ascent, Ascension, rising, rise, ascending, mounting, climbing, scaling. **Descent**
Acclivity, elevation, height, eminence.

Ascertain, Discover, perceive, verify, certify, determine, settle, define, fix, establish, prove, confirm. **Surmise**

Ascetic, *a.,* Stern, severe, puritanical, abstemious, rigid, austere. **Lax**
n., Hermit, recluse, anchorite, eremite.

Ascribable, Attributable, traceable, assignable, referable, chargeable, imputable.

Ascribe, Attribute, assign, refer.† **Deny**

Ashamed, Confused, abashed. **Proud**

Ashen, Ashy, pale, hueless, gray, colourless, pallid, blanched, wan. **Coloured**

Ashore, On shore, on land, aground, stranded. **Afloat**

Ashy, Ashen, pale, hueless, gray, colourless, pallid, blanched, wan.

Aside, Away, apart, aloof, separately, laterally.

Asinine, Stupid, foolish, senseless, mad, idiotic, doltish, absurd. **Clever**

Ask, Question, inquire, interrogate. **Answer**
Request, entreat, desire, invite, beg, pray, supplicate, implore, crave, petition, sue, solicit, seek, beseech.

Askance -ant, Awry, aslant, askew, asquint, obliquely, sloping, aslope, sideways. **Straight**

Askew, Askance, awry, aslant.†

Aslant, Askance, slanting, awry, obliquely.†

Asleep, Sleeping, slumbering, dormant, dead. **Awake**

Aslope, Sloping, aslant, slanting, obliquely, askew, askance.

Aspect, Look, bearing, mien, appearance, phase, presentation, air, feature, expression. **Obverse**
Outlook, position, situation, view, prospect.

Asperity, Harshness, acrimony, sullenness, moroseness, bitterness, tartness, pungency, poignancy, sourness, sharpness, sternness, severity, virulence, crabbedness, acerbity, churlishness, roughness, ruggedness. **Mildness**

Asperse, Slander, calumniate, censure, defame, abuse, disparage, depreciate, assail, vilify, traduce, slur, impugn, malign, vituperate, defile, befoul, besmirch, bespatter, blemish, blacken, attack, backbite, revile. **Eulogize**

Aspersion, Slander, calumny, censure.†

Aspirant, Aspirer, seeker, suitor, candidate, competitor.

Aspirate, Aspirated, toneless, surd, atonic, unintonated.

Aspiration, Longing, desire, hope, ambition, aim, effort, endeavour, eagerness, yearning, craving. **Apathy**

Aspire, Long, desire, hope, aim, yearn, crave, mount, soar, rise, ascend. **Reject**

Asquint, Askance, askant, awry, askew, obliquely. **Straight**

Ass, Fool, idiot, dunce, donkey, dolt, blockhead, simpleton. **Sage**

Assail, Attack, assault, invade, oppugn. **Defend**
Asperse, slander, calumniate, censure, defame, abuse, disparage, vilify, traduce, slur, impugn, malign, vituperate, defile, befoul, besmirch, bespatter, blemish, blacken, attack, backbite, deride. **Vindicate**

Assailable, Vulnerable, sensitive, censurable.

Assailant, Attacker, assaulter, aggressor, assailer, invader. **Helper**

Assassin, Murderer, assassinator, slayer, cut-throat.

Assassinate, Kill, slay, murder, despatch.

Assassination, Murder.

Assault, v.a., Attack, assail, charge, storm, invade. **Defend**
n., Attack, onslaught, charge, thrust, invasion, onset, aggression. **Defence**

Assay, v.a., Test, try, analyse, examine, prove.
n., Test, trial, examination, analysis.

Assemblage, Assembly, concourse, gathering, meeting, congregating, congregation, throng, company, crowd. **Dispersal**
Collection, combination, union, conjunction, association, group, aggregate, body, bunch, mass, clump, cluster.

Assemble, Collect, muster, congregate, gather, levy, call, convene, convoke, summon. **Disperse**

Assembly, Assemblage, concourse, gathering.†
Collection, combination, union.†
Ball, dance.

Assent, v.a., Acquiesce, agree, yield, concur, accord, consent, subscribe, approve. **Dissent**
n., Acquiescence, agreement, concurrence, consent, alliance, approval, approbation, accord. **Dissension**

Assert, Maintain, declare, affirm, pronounce, aver, allege, say, state, express, asseverate, depose, avow, avouch, predicate. **Deny**

Assertion, Declaration, affirmation, averment.† **Denial**

Assertive, Positive, decided, confident, peremptory.

Assess, Tax, assign, impose, appraise, value, estimate, compute, rate.

Assessment, Valuation, tax, charge, impost, rate, levy.

Assets, Estate, property, possessions. **Liabilities**

Asseverate, Affirm, assert, maintain, declare, pronounce, allege, say, state, express, depose, avow, avouch, predicate. **Deny**

Asseveration, Affirmation, assertion, declaration.† **Denial**

Assiduity, Industry, assiduousness, diligence, sedulousness, application, carefulness, care, devotion, devotedness, patience, preservance, persistence, pains, activity, labour, attention, exertion, effort. **Indolence**

Assiduous, Industrious, diligent, sedulous.† **Indolent**

Assign, Allot, apportion, appoint, appropriate, cast, fix, specify, determine.

Adduce, advance, offer, show, give, present, allege. **Refuse**

Assignment, Allotment, apportionment.†

Adducing, offering, showing.†

Assimilate, Digest, absorb, incorporate, liken, compare, match. **Reject**

Assist, Aid, help, support, succour, befriend, sustain, second, patronize, further, promote, relieve, abet, back. **Hinder**

Assistance, Aid, help, support.† **Hindrance**

Assistant, Helper, aider, second, ally, auxiliary, abettor, accessory, collaborator, coadjutor. **Opponent**

Associate, v.a., Combine, unite, join, conjoin, connect, like, affiliate. **Sever**

v.n., Consort, fraternize.

n., Companion, ally, friend, colleague, co-partner, helpmate, confederate, mate, consort, partner, coadjutor. **Foe**

Association, Society, union, company, alliance, body, corporation, fraternity, combination, amalgamation, connection, conjunction, consortment, companionship, friendship, community, partnership, band, firm, guild, house, lodge, club, coterie. **Separation**

Assort, v.a., Group, sort, arrange, array, class, classify, rank, distribute.

v.n., Suit, agree, consort.

Assorted, Mixed, various, varied, miscellaneous.

Assortment, Variety, kinds, class, group, set, lot, batch, parcel, stock, collection, arrangement, distribution, allotment.

Assuage, Mitigate, soothe, soften, console, moderate, pacify, appease, mollify, compose, allay, abate, quell, still, tranquillize, quiet, ease, lessen, lull, alleviate. **Aggravate**

Assuagement, Mitigation, pacification, appeasement.†

Assuasive, Mitigating, soothing, softening.†

Assume, Pretend, feign, sham, affect, counterfeit, simulate.

Take, undertake, usurp, arrogate. **Surrender**

Suppose, presuppose, presume, imply. **Prove**

Assuming, Presuming, presumptuous, arrogant, forward, bold, overbearing, proud, conceited, audacious, haughty, shameless. **Modest**

Assumption, Presumption, arrogance, forwardness.†

Assuming, taking, undertaking, usurpation.

Supposition, conjecture, guess, postulate, theory, hypothesis, presumption. **Proof**

Assurance, Certainty, security, conviction, surety, assuredness, persuasion. **Doubt**

Pledge, promise, engagement, averment, asseveration, protestation, declaration.

Arrogance, boldness, effrontery, impertinence, impudence, conceit. **Modesty**

Courage, confidence, intrepidity, firmness. **Timidity**

Assure, Pledge, promise, engage, aver,† guarantee, warrant.

Embolden, encourage, reassure, hearten, enhearten. **Deter**

Assured, Indubitable, certain, sure, unquestionable, secure. **Doubtful**

Assuredly, Indubitably, certainly.†

Astern, Behind, back, abaft, aft, rearward, backward. **Afore**

Asthenia -eny, Debility, weakness, feebleness, exhaustion, prostration. **Strength**

Astir, Active, alert, roused, awake, stirring, excited. **Apathetic**

Astonish, Startle, surprise, confound, alarm, terrify, scare, amaze, astound, stagger, stupefy, daze, stun, petrify, overwhelm. **Assure**

Astonishing, Surprising, striking, wonderful, admirable.

Astonishment, Surprise, confusion, alarm.†

Astound, Astonish, startle, surprise, confound, alarm, amaze, stagger, stupefy, daze, stun, petrify, overwhelm.

Astral, Starry, stellar.

Astray, Erring, wandering, wrong, loose, abroad, absent, missing, straying. **Safe**

Astringent, Costive, binding, contracting, styptic. **Laxative**

Astute, Cute, cunning, shrewd, crafty, knowing, sharp, acute, keen, penetrating, ingenious, intelligent, discerning, deep, quick. **Simple**

Astuteness, Cuteness, cunning, shrewdness.†

Asunder, Apart, separate, divided, discordant, divergent, disunited. **United**

Asylum, Sanctuary, retreat, refuge, shelter, home.

Atheistic, Godless. **Godly**

Athirst, Thirsty, dry, eager.

Athletic, Strong, muscular, lusty, sturdy, stalwart, powerful, strapping, stout, robust, brawny, sinewy. *Weak*

Athwart, *prep.*, Over, across. *Along*
adv., Across, crosswise, sidewise, awry, askew, aslant, obliquely. *Straight*
Wrong, wrongfully, unsuitably, unreasonably.

Atom, Molecule, monad, particle, corpuscle, jot, iota, tittle, ace, bit, mite, scrap, whit.

Atomical, Small, tiny, minute, infinitesimal.

Atone, Expiate, satisfy. *Offend*

Atonement, Expiation, propitiation, satisfaction, reparation, amends. *Offence*
Reconciliation, agreement, pacification, concord. *Estrangement*

Atonic, Asthenic, aspirate, surd, unaccented.

Atrabilious, Dejected, depressed, melancholy, hypochondriac, dispirited, gloomy, sad, desponding, downcast. *Buoyant*

Atrocious, Monstrous, nefarious, enormous, shameful, heinous, cruel, flagitious, infamous, horrible, infernal, diabolical, outrageous, vile. *Noble*

Atrocity, Atrociousness, monstrosity, enormity,† ferocity, depravity, wickedness, savagery. *Nobility*

Atrophy, Decline, emaciation, wasting, consumption.

Attach, Join, fasten, affix, tie, fix, annex, connect, adhere, apply, bind, cement, append, tack, subjoin, hitch. *Loose*
Win, attract, engage, charm, endear, enamour, captivate. *Alienate*
Take, seize, distrain, bind, distress. *Release*

Attached, Fond, loving, enamoured, attracted.

Attachment, Joining, fastening,† adjunct, appendage, addendum, addition, appurtenance.
Affection, love, liking, regard, fondness, friendship, devotion, adherence. *Hatred*
Seizure, distraint.

Attack, *v.a.*, Assault, charge, invade, assail, storm, violate, oppugn, impugn, contravene. *Defend*
n., Assault, charge, invasion,† descent, aggression, onslaught, onset, encounter. *Defence*

Attacker, Assaulter, charger, invader.† *Defender*

Attain, Acquire, get, reach, secure, procure, win, gain, obtain, achieve, effect, grasp, accomplish, master. *Lose*

Attainable, Acquirable, reachable,† possible, feasible, practicable. *Impossible*

Attainment, Acquisition, getting, reaching.†
Acquirement, learning, wisdom, erudition, accomplishment, enlightenment, information, qualification, grace.

Attaint, Taint, stain, pollute, corrupt, disgrace. *Purify*

Attemper, Assuage, alleviate, allay, moderate, subdue, temper, soothe, soften, mollify, pacify, appease. *Aggravate*
Adapt, adjust, harmonize, suit, fit, proportion, attune, blend.

Attempt, *v.a.*, Try, essay, undertake, endeavour.
Assail, assault, attack, charge, invade, storm, force, violate, oppugn, impugn. *Defend*
v.n., Try, strive, aim, endeavour, seek.
n., Trial, aim, effort, endeavour, essay, undertaking, experiment, enterprise.

Attend, *v.a.*, Accompany, serve, escort, watch, guard, protect, follow, await, abide. *Desert*
v.n., Tend, wait, serve.
Listen, hearken, hear, heed, notice, observe. *Wander*

Attendance, Service, ministration, attendants, train, retinue.
Presence. *Absence*

Attendant, Follower, companion, associate, satellite, escort, squire, retainer, servant, servitor, flunkey, lackey, dependant, footman, valet, waiter.
Attender, frequenter.
Consequence, accompaniment, concomitant.

Attention, Regard, respect, courtesy, civility, deference, politeness.
Addresses, court, suit, devotion.
Care, heed, regard, alertness, notice, observation, consideration, advertence, study, application.

Attentive, Careful, heedful, alert, considerate, mindful, diligent, sedulous. *Careless*

Attenuate, Rarefy, thin, reduce, lessen, diminish. *Increase*

Attenuation, Rarefying, thinning.†
Thinness, slenderness, elongation, emaciation. *Fatness*

Attest, Adjure, invoke, endorse, witness, confirm, ratify, support, corroborate, certify. *Deny*
Prove, display, confess, manifest, show, exhibit.

Attestation, Confirmation, testimony, proof, evidence, authentication, seal, voucher, witness. *Denial*

Attic, *a.*, Classic, classical, correct, refined, pure, chaste, elegant, polished, delicate. *Rude*

Attic, *n.,* Loft, garret. ***Basement***

Attire, *v.a.,* Dress, apparel, robe, array, clothe, rig, accoutre, equip, furnish. ***Strip***

n., Dress, apparel, robes,† costume, vesture, vestments, outfit.

Attitude, Pose, posture, position.

Aspect, state, standing, situation, phase, condition, posture, predicament.

Bearing, relation.

Attorney, Agent, deputy, substitute, proxy, factor.

Attract, Draw, allure, pull, entice, drag, win, captivate, engage, fascinate, endear, charm. ***Repulse***

Attraction, Draw, allurement, pull.† ***Repulsion***

Attractive, Drawing, alluring, pulling,† sweet, lovely, magnetic, pleasing. ***Repulsive***

Attributable, Ascribable, traceable, chargeable, connecting, applicable, assignable, imputable, referable.

Attribute, *v.a.,* Ascribe, trace, charge.† *n.,* Quality, characteristic, sign, indication, mark, note, peculiarity, property.

Attrition, Abrasion, wearing, friction, rubbing.

Sorrow, repentance, penitence, remorse.

Attune, Tune, harmonize, accord, moderate, attemper, adjust, adapt. ***Disturb***

Audacious, Courageous, fearless, bold, daring, dauntless, venturesome, valiant. ***Afraid***

Forward, brazen, arrogant, impertinent, assuming, presumptuous, impudent, insolent, shameless. ***Modest***

Audacity, Courage, fearlessness, boldness.† ***Fear***

Forwardness, arrogance, impertinence,† effrontery, assurance. ***Modesty***

Audience, Assembly, assemblage, congregation.

Reception, hearing, interview.

Audit, Examine.

Audition, Hearing, test.

Auditor, Examiner, hearer.

Augment, *v.a.,* Increase, enlarge, magnify, swell, amplify, enrich, enhance, improve. ***Decrease***

v.n., Increase, grow, swell.

Augmentation, Increase, enlargement.†

Augur, *v.a.,* Foreshadow, portend, forebode, presage, foreshow, foretell, predict, prophesy.

n., Prophet, soothsayer, seer, foreteller.

Augury, Prophecy, soothsaying, prediction, presage, omen, portent, sign.

August, Venerable, kingly, regal, princely, imposing, exalted, pompous, awful, majestic, solemn, stately, grand, dignified, noble. ***Vulgar***

Aura, Aroma, odour, effluvium, effluence, smell.

Aureate, Golden, gold-coloured, yellow, gilded.

Aureola, Aureole, glory, halo, irradiance.

Aurora, Morn, dawn, daybreak, morning, sunrise. ***Evening***

Auspice, Omen, augury, portent, sign, presage.

Auspices, Patronage, favour, influence, protection, support.

Auspicious, Bright, happy, favourable, promising, satisfactory, seasonable, opportune, propitious, fortunate, lucky, successful, hopeful, encouraging. ***Hopeless***

Austere, Rough, rigid, severe, ascetic, hard, stern, uncompromising, unrelenting, harsh, strict. ***Loose***

Austerity, Roughness, ridigity, severity.† ***Looseness***

Authentic, Genuine, veritable, pure, real, true, reliable, accurate, trustworthy, accepted, certain, legitimate. ***Spurious***

Authenticate, Verify, attest, seal, prove, confirm, substantiate, identify, establish, ratify. ***Disprove***

Author, Writer, composer, originator, producer, parent, creator, constructor, maker, contriver, fabricator, perpetrator, inventor, cause, agent. ***Annihilator***

Authoritative, Official, authentic, conclusive, sure, decisive, certain, potent, powerful, imperative. ***Vague***

Imperious, dictatorial, arrogant, firm, commanding, dogmatic, arbitrary, peremptory. ***Affable***

Authority, Power, rule, sway, government, dominion, sovereignty, ascendancy, influence, control, direction, right. ***Weakness***

Ground, justification, authenticity, genuineness.

Permission, liberty, sanction, precept, warrant, leave.

Authorize, Sanction, empower, support, order, commission, licence, warrant, legalize, permit, allow. ***Forbid***

Autochthonous, Native, primitive, original, indigenous, first, primeval.

Autocracy, Dictatorship, despotism, absolutism. ***Constitutionalism***

Autocrat, Dictator, despot, absolute monarch.

Autocratic, Dictatorial, despotic, absolute, arrogant, tyrannous, tyrannical, overbearing, oppressive, independent, arbitrary. ***Constitutional***

Automatic, Mechanical, reflex, self-acting.

Autonomy, Independence, self-government, freedom. *Dependence*

Auxiliary, *a.*, Accessory, ancillary, aiding, abetting, helping, assisting, helpful, subsidiary. *Obstructive*
n., Accessory, aider, abettor,† ally, confederate, co-operator, second, coadjutor. *Opponent*

Avail, *v.a.*, Benefit, profit, advantage, help. *Hinder*
v.n., Answer, tell, profit, suffice, hold, stand, endure. *Fail*
n., Benefit, profit, advantage, use, service.

Available, Useful, serviceable, beneficial, advantageous, procurable, handy, applicable, attainable, suitable. *Useless*

Avarice, Greed, cupidity, rapacity, covetousness, sordidness, acquisitiveness, miserliness. *Liberality*

Avaricious, Greedy, covetous.† *Liberal*

Avast, Stop, stay, hold, enough.

Avaunt, Away, begone, hence.

Avenge, Revenge, vindicate, retaliate, right, visit. *Pardon*

Avenue, Approach, adit, entrance, access, passage, entry, alley, route, way, pass, path, road, street.

Aver, Affirm, assert, asseverate, declare, depose, avouch, pronounce, avow, allege, predicate, say, state. *Deny*

Average, *v.a.*, Equate, proportion.
n., Mean, medium. *Extreme*
a., Mean, medium, medial, middling, ordinary, tolerable, passable, moderate.

Averment, Affirmation, assertion, asseveration, declaration, deposition, avowal, predication, statement, allegation, word. *Denial*

Averse, Unwilling, indisposed, hostile, disinclined, adverse, reluctant, loath, opposed. *Ready*

Aversion, Dislike, hatred, loathing, repugnance, disgust, abhorrence, antipathy, horror, detestation, distaste, disrelish, reluctance, disinclination. *Love*

Avert, Divert, prevent, preclude, forefend, avoid. *Encourage*

Avid, Greedy, eager.

Avidity, Greediness, eagerness, voracity, rapacity, ravenousness, longing. *Apathy*

Avocation, Vocation, occupation, calling, trade, pursuit, business, employment, profession, lot. *Idleness*

Avoid, Shun, abandon, desert, quit, forsake, fly, elude, eschew. *Seek*

Avouch, Aver, asseverate, protest, maintain, say, avow, state, declare, affirm, profess, propound, assert, depose, avow. *Deny*

Avow, Acknowledge, own, admit, confess, avouch, aver.† *Contradict*

Avowal, Acknowledgment, admission, confession.† *Denial*

Await, Abide, expect, attend, wait, stay, remain, tarry. *Depart*

Awake, Alert, attentive, vigilant, watchful, ready, alive. *Asleep*

Awaken, *v.a.*, Awake, wake, rouse, arouse, excite, stimulate, spur, kindle, incite, provoke. *Lull*
v.n., Wake, be roused.

Award, *v.a.*, Give, grant, distribute, assign, apportion, allot, bestow, divide, adjudge, decree. *Withdraw*
n., Gift, grant, distribution.†

Aware, Conscious, sensible, informed, cognisant, guarded, apprized, mindful, observant, certified, assured, familiar, convinced. *Ignorant*

Away, *a.*, Absent, far, abroad, afar, loose, separate, detached, gone, off, distant. *Near*
interj., Avaunt, hence, begone.

Awe, *v.a.*, Affright, intimidate, frighten, terrorize, daunt, cow, subdue, terrify, alarm, scare, dismay, appal, startle. *Reassure*
n., Fear, dread, reverence, veneration, terror, alarm, dismay. *Confidence*

Awful, Fearful, dreadful.†

Awhile, Briefly, sometime, shortly, soon.

Awkward, Ungainly, clownish, unskilful, clumsy, maladroit, bungling, inapt, lumbering, rough, ungraceful, coarse. *Dexterous*

Awning, Canopy, baldequin, tilt.

Awry, *a.*, Oblique, askant, athwart, aslant, wry, bent, slanting, crooked, distorted, askew, asquint. *Straight*
adv., Obliquely, askance.†

Axiom, Truism, postulate.

Axiomatic, Absolute, positive, certain, necessary, a priori.

Aye, Always, evermore, forever, continually, unending.

Azure, Blue, sky-coloured, cerulean.

B

Babble, *v.a.,* Tell, utter, state, blab.
v.n., Chatter, prattle, jabber, prate, chat, gossip, tell.
n., Chatter, prattle,† nonsense, drivel. *Wisdom*

Babbler, Gossip, chatterbox, prattler.†

Babbling, Gossiping, prattling.†

Babe, Baby, infant, suckling, nursling.

Babel, Hubbub, tumult, disorder, jargon, discord, din, confusion, clamour. *Quiet*

Baby, Infant, babe, nursling, suckling.

Babyhood, Infancy, babehood.

Babyish, Childish, infantile.

Bacchanal, Bacchanalian, revelling, riotous, noisy, gay. *Sober*

Bacchante, Hag, vixen, fury, shrew.

Back, *v.a.,* Aid, assist, abet, second, help, support, countenance, favour. *Hinder*
v.n., Retreat, retire, withdraw. *Advance*
n., Rear end, posterior. *Front*
a., Remote, hindmost. *Foremost*
adv., Backward, rearward, abaft. *Onward*

Backbite, Abuse, malign, slander, defame, vilify, asperse, libel, blacken, traduce, revile, calumniate, detract. *Praise*

Backbiter, Abuser, maligner, slanderer.† *Upholder*

Backbiting, Abuse, malignity, slander, defamation, aspersion, libel, calumny, detraction. *Praise*

Backed, Supported, seconded, financed, patronized, countenanced.

Backbone, Spine, nerve, courage, pluck, resolution, firmness, stability, steadfastness, hardihood, manhood, decision. *Weakness*

Backhanded, Unfair, unfavourable, indirect.

Backslider, Apostate, abjurer, renegade, recreant, deserter. *Adherent*

Backward, *a.,* Dull, stupid, sluggish, stolid, slow, behind, tardy, late, retrogressive. *Forward*
Averse, antipathetical, reluctant, unwilling, disinclined, loath. *Prompt*
adv., Backwards, abaft, aback, behind, rearwards, regressively. *Forward*

Bad, Wicked, abandoned, depraved, immoral, dishonest, unprincipled, corrupt, rascally, villainous. *Virtuous*
Evil, pernicious, baneful, hurtful, injurious, unwholesome, detrimental, noxious, deleterious. *Good*
Unlucky, unfortunate, unhappy, sad, unwelcome, serious, hard, heavy, distressing, depressing, discouraging. *Splendid*
Poor, wretched, vile, mean, defective, shabby.

Badge, Sign, mark, emblem, token, stamp, brand.

Badger, Harass, torment, tease, try, worry, plague, persecute, hector, vex, annoy, bait, harry, trouble. *Pacify*

Badinage, Banter, raillery.

Baffle, Foil, balk, check, mar, upset, frustrate, thwart, defeat, confound, bewilder, perplex. *Abet*

Bag, Sack, wallet, pouch.

Bagatelle, Small, unconsequential, trifle, unimportant.

Baggage, Belongings, luggage.

Bail, Surety, security.

Bailiff, Manager, overseer, steward, factor, supervisor.

Bairn, Babe, baby, child, infant.

Bait, *v.a.,* Badger, harry, harass, worry, torment, trouble, try, vex, annoy, tease, plague, persecute, bother, hector. *Pacify*
n., Allurement, lure, decoy, snare, enticement, morsel, inducement, temptation. *Warning*

Bake, Harden, parch, dry up.

Balance, *v.a.,* Poise, weigh, estimate, compare, counterpoise, counteract, compensate, counterbalance, neutralize.
Adjust, equalize, square. *Upset*
n., Equipoise, comparison, weighing, counterpoise, surplus, residue, remainder, overplus, excess.
Self-control, self-possession, equilibrium.

Bald, Hairless, bare, verdureless, uncovered, literal, undisguised, plain, unadorned, inelegant, dull, prosaic, tame, naked. *Ornamented*

Balderdash, Bombast, verbiage, prating, palaver, jargon, flummery, gasconade, chatter, nonsense, drivel. *Wisdom*

Bale, Bundle, package, parcel, case.
Hurt, ruin, injury, harm, mischief, calamity, misery.

Baleful, Baneful, hurtful, ruinous,† pernicious, noxious. *Good*

Balk, Baffle, thwart, prevent, frustrate, defeat, confound, undo, foil, disappoint, hinder. *Abet*

Ball, Dance, assembly, party, reception.
Globe, sphere.
Shot, projectile, bullet.

Ballast, Packing, weight, filling.

Balance, judgment, sense, prudence, discretion, equipoise, steadiness, stability.

Ballot, Voting-ticket, vote, ticket.

Balm, Ointment, unguent, cure, soothing, mitigant, assuager, healing. *Aggravation*

Balmy, Soothing, mitigatory, assuaging, sedative, fragrant, sweet.

Bamboozle, Cheat, deceive, mislead, trick, hoax, defraud, mystify.

Ban, *v.a.*, Prohibit, bar, interdict, outlaw, forbid, curse, execrate.

n., Prohibition, interdiction,† proclamation, edict, decree.

Band, Company, party, troop, troupe, gang, body, coterie.

Tie, bandage, ligature, ligament, girth, girdle, belt, binding, chain, fetter, cord, bond.

Bandage, Band, binding, ligament, ligature, belt.†

Bandit, Brigand, outlaw, robber, footpad.

Bandy, *v.a.*, Toss, exchange, interchange, dispute, agitate. *Drop*
a., Bent, crooked. *Straight*

Bane, Bale, hurt, ruin, injury, harm, mischief, calamity, misery.

Poison, venom.

Baneful, Baleful, hurtful, ruinous.†

Poisonous, venemous.

Bang, *v.a.*, Knock, beat, strike, thump, pound, pommel, slam.

v.n., Rattle, resound, echo, clatter, ring.

n., Clang, whack, knock, blow.

Banish, Abandon, expel, expatriate, forswear, disclaim, repudiate, exclude, eject, extrude, relegate, exile, dismiss. *Harbour*

Banishment, Abandonment, expulsion, expatriation.†

Bank, Shore, border, margin, brink, brim.

Mound, knoll, heap, pile, shoal, bar.

Bankrupt, Insolvent.

Banner, Standard, flag, colours, ensign.

Banquet, Feast, dinner, treat, regalement, cheer, entertainment, carouse.

Banter, *v.a.*, Rally, chaff, twit, deride, joke, mock, badinage, bandy, ridicule, jeer.

n., Raillery, irony, chaff, derision.†

Bantling, Baby, babe, infant, child, bairn, nursling, suckling.

Bar, *v.a.*, Ban, hinder, exclude, prohibit, restrain, stop, prevent, obstruct, impede. *Admit*

n., Ban, barrier, hindrance, exclusion,† obstacle. *Help*

Rod, rail, pole, ingot.

Tribunal, bench.

Barb, Point, wattles, beard.

Barbarian, Savage, ruffian, brute.

Barbarity, Cruelty, brutality, ferocity, inhumanity.† *Humanity*

Barbarous, Uncivilized, ignorant, savage, rough, coarse, uncouth, rude, harsh, rugged, vulgar, brutal, ruthless, cruel, ferocious, inhuman. *Humane*

Bare, Naked, nude, unclothed, undressed, uncovered, exposed, unprotected, destitute. *Clothed*

Bald, simple, plain, unadorned, unvarnished. *Ornamented*

Barefaced, Impudent, brazen, shameless, audacious, glaring, conspicuous, undisguised, palpable, notorious. *Concealed*

Barely, Scarcely, hardly, merely, simply, just.

Poorly, meanly, slenderly, meagrely. *Richly*

Bargain, *v.n.*, Agree, contract, stipulate, haggle, reckon.

n., Agreement, contract, compact, stipulation, transaction, purchase, negotiation, speculation, proceeds, result.

Bark, Yelp, bay, clamour.

Barm, Ferment, yeast, leaven.

Barren, Unfertile, sterile, unproductive, infecund, unfruitful, ineffectual, bare. *Fertile*

Barricade, *v.a.*, Obstruct, block, stop, fortify.

n., Obstruction, barrier, obstacle, bar, hindrance, impediment.

Barrier, Barricade, obstruction,† embargo.

Barrister, Advocate, counsel, lawyer.

Barrow, Wheelbarrow, truck, handbarrow, handcart.

Mound, hillock, tumulus.

Hog.

Barter, Exchange, bargain, trade, dealing, traffic.

Base, *v.a.*, Establish, found, rest.

n., Basis, foundation, bottom, foot, ground. *Top*

a., Vile, mean, despicable, low, venal, pitiful, sorry, worthless, servile, menial, sordid, contemptible, abject, disgraceful, shameful, dishonourable. *Honourable*

False, debased, spurious, corrupt, cheap, counterfeit.

Vulgar, lowly, humble, plebeian. *Aristocratic*

Baseness, Vileness, meanness.†

Bashful, Shy, timid, modest, timorous, coy, diffident. *Bold*

Bashfulness, Shyness, timidity, modesty.

Basis, Base, foundation, bottom, ground, foot.

Bask, Revel, bathe, luxuriate, lounge, repose, dally, lie, prosper, rejoice.

Bass, Low, deep, grave. *Treble*

Bastard, Illegitimate, base-born, natural, spurious, fake. *Legitimate*

Baste, Beat, buffet, thrash, cudgel, cane, pound.

Bat, Stick, club, cudgel.

Batch, Collection, quantity, crowd, lot, amount.

Bate, Abate, decrease, reduce, lessen, abridge, diminish, curtail, rebate, remit. *Increase*

Bath, Ablution, washing, bathing.

Bathe, Wash, immerse, purify, lave. *Pollute*

Bathos, Anticlimax, bombast. *Pathos*

Bating, Except, excepting, bar, barring.

Baton, Staff, wand, truncheon, rod.

Batter, *v.a.*, Beat, baste, smite, shatter, bruise, break, strike, smash, destroy, wear, mar, abrade, indent, deface.
n., Paste.
Batsman, striker.

Battle, *v.n.*, Struggle, contend, fight, contest, strive, war. *Agree*
n., Combat, engagement, fight, contest, war, affair, action, brush. *Peace*

Bauble, Trifle, toy, trinket, gewgaw.

Bavin, Twig, bough, faggot.

Bawd, Procurer, procuress, strumpet.

Bawdry, Whoredom, fornification, lechery, impurity, indecency.

Bawdy, Filthy, indecent, lewd, obscene, impure, smutty. *Chaste*

Bawl, Yell, clamour, howl, shout, roar, cry, vociferate. *Whisper*

Bay, *v.a., & n.*, Bark, yelp.
n., Bight, inlet, recess, opening, compartment.
Thwart, check, desperation.

Bays, Garland, wreath, chaplet, crown.
Renown, praise, glory, applause, fame, honours.

Bazaar, Mart, market, market-place, exchange.

Be, Exist, subsist.

Beach, Shore, strand, sands, margin, rim.

Beacon, *v.a.*, Signal, guide, light, enlighten.
n., Signal, mark, sign.

Bead, Drop, globule, pellet, bubble.
Moulding, astragal.

Beadle, Constable, servitor, crier.

Beak, Stem, bow, prow, bill, mandible.,

Beaker, Cup, goblet, bowl.

Beam, *v.n.*, Beacon, shine, glitter, gleam, glisten.

Beam, *n.*, Glimmer, ray, streak, gleam, glitter.

Beaming, Gleaming, shining, bright, beautiful, radiant, transparent, translucid. *Dull*

Bear, *v.a.*, Carry, transport, lift, convey, waft, hold, uphold, support, sustain. *Drop*
Suffer, endure, abide, tolerate, brook, undergo, allow, admit, permit, submit to. *Resist*
Produce, generate, yield, hold, possess, keep, maintain, harbour, cherish, entertain.
v.n., Suffer, submit, endure.
Concern, affect, relate.
n., Growler, grumbler, snarler.

Bearable, Endurable, tolerable, supportable. *Intolerable*

Beard, *v.a.*, Defy, oppose.
n., Whiskers.
Barb, guard.

Bearing, Behaviour, appearance, manner, style, aspect, deportment, conduct, mien. *Misbehaviour*
Direction, course, aim, aspect.
Socket, receptacle, bed.

Bearish, Coarse, rough, rude, ungentlemanly, boorish, coarse, savage. *Polite*

Beast, Brute, animal, savage, sensualist, ruffian.

Beastly, Brutish, brutal, sensual, vile, abominable, inhuman, loathsome, filthy, bestial, repulsive, coarse. *Humane*

Beat, *v.a.*, Strike, hit, pound, thrash, batter, cudgel, knock, thwack, whack, bang, thump, belabour, maul, pommel, pound, hammer, bruise, smite. *Caress*
Subdue, vanquish, overcome, defeat, baffle, conquer, worst. *Foul*
v.n., Throb, pulsate.
n., Throb, pulsation, beating.
Course, round.
Blow, stroke, striking.

Beaten, Defeated, baffled, subdued.†

Beatific, Ecstatic, enchanting, enrapturing, ravishing, rapturous, transporting.

Beatitude, Beatification, bliss, blessedness, blissfulness, felicity.

Beau, Dandy, fop, coxcomb.
Gallant, admirer, lover, suitor.

Beautiful, Handsome, beauteous, fine, elegant, fair, graceful, comely, lovely, seemly, attractive. *Ugly*

Beautify, Adorn, gild, bedeck, array, ornament, embellish, deck, garnish. *Mar*

Beauty, Elegance, grace, fairness, comeliness, loveliness, seemliness, attractiveness, embellishment, adornment. *Ugliness*

Becalm, Quiet, still, pacify, soothe, appease, calm, tranquillize. **Aggravate**

Because, As, since, for, owing to.

Becharm, Charm, enchant, captivate, fascinate. **Repulse**

Beck, *v.a., & n.,* Beckon, nod.

n., Nod, sign, signal, symbol, token.

Beckon, Call, wave, signal, invite.

Becloud, Cloud, darken, dim, bedim, obscure, hide. **Lighten**

Become, *v.a.,* Suit, befit, grace, beseem, behove, adorn. **Disgrace**

v.n., Grow, get, change to, come to be.

Becoming, Comely, suitable, befitting,† decorous, neat, pretty. **Ugly**

Bed, Couch, berth.

Layer, strata, accumulation.

Bedaub, Besmear, smear, daub, soil, bespatter, befoul, mar, disfigure, deface, spoil, stain. **Beautify**

Bedeck, Array, adorn, decorate, beautify, embellish, gild, deck, ornament, emblazon, garnish, grace. **Strip**

Bedew, Damp, dampen, moisten, wet, sprinkle.

Bedim, Dim, darken, bedarken, obscure, cloud, becloud , hide. **Lighten**

Bedizen, Bedeck, adorn, array, gild, deck.

Bedizened, Gaudy, tawdry, flashy, dressy.

Beetle, *v.n.,* Protrude, jut, project.

n., Mallet, maul.

Befall, *v.a.,* Overtake, bechance, betide.

v.n., Happen, occur, chance, supervene, betide.

Befit, Fit, suit, become.

Befitting, Fitting, suitable, becoming, proper, appropriate, right, seemly, meet. **Unsuitable**

Befog, Puzzle, confuse, muddle, perplex, bewilder, embarrass.

Befool, Fool, dupe, cheat, deceive, hoodwink, bamboozle, elude, mystify, mislead, ensnare, infatuate, delude, beguile, trick, hoax.

Before, *prep.,* Preceding, ahead of, in front of, prior to, previous to. **After**

adv., Ahead, formerly, already, previously, hitherto, above.

Befoul, Bedaub, soil, mar, spoil, besmear, smear, pollute, bemire, besmirch, dirty. **Cleanse**

Befriend, Assist, help, encourage, patronize, favour, support, sustain, defend, advocate, protect, aid, benefit. **Oppose**

Beg, Crave, ask, beseech, supplicate, implore, petition, appeal, request, entreat. **Demand**

Beget, Produce, generate, engender, procreate, get, breed.

Beggar, *v.a.,* Ruin, impoverish, exhaust, surpass, exceed. **Assist**

n., Mendicant, suitor, applicant, pauper.

Beggarly, Destitute, poor, indigent, needy, abject, low, low-minded, mean, sorry, wretched, despicable, pitiful, base, paltry, shabby, vile, miserable, slavish. **Noble**

Begin, *v.a.,* Commence, institute, originate, inaugurate, initiate, start. **End**

v.n., Arise, originate, commence. **Finish**

Beginner, Novice, learner, pupil, tyro. **Expert**

Originator, inaugurator, author, starter, creator.

Beginning, Commencement, start, origin, source, emergence, opening, initiation, inception. **End**

Begird, Gird, engird, surround, encircle, environ, enclose, encompass.

Begone, Away, avaunt, depart.

Begrime, Defile, foul, befoul, bedaub, soil, spoil, mar, pollute, besmirch, besmear, bemire. **Cleanse**

Begrudge, Envy, grudge.

Beguile, Befool, fool, delude, cheat, deceive, bamboozle, trick, hoax, hoodwink.

Entertain, cheer, divert, amuse, solace.

Behalf, Side, interest, advantage, benefit, aid.

Behave, Act, bear, comport, deport.

Behaviour, Conduct, deportment, comportment, bearing, demeanour, mien, carriage, air, port, action. **Misconduct**

Behead, Decapitate, decollate.

Behest, Injunction, command, instruction, mandate, order, precept, bidding, charge.

Behind, *prep.,* Abaft, after, following. **Before**

adv., Back, backward, abaft, aft, astern, rearward. **Forward**

Behold, *v.a.,* See, observe, look at, contemplate, scan, survey, eye, regard, view, consider, discern. **Miss**

interj., Look, mark, observe, see.

Beholden, Obliged, bound, indebted, obligated, grateful, thankful. **Ungrateful**

Behove, Become, befit, fit, suit, beseem.

Being, Existence, subsistence, reality, actuality, essence.

Belabour, Beat, strike, thump, thwack, cudgel, hit, pound, thrash, batter, knock, whack, bang, pommel, bruise, smite.

Belate, Delay, retard, hinder. **Accelerate**

Belated, Delayed, retarded, hindered.

Belaud, Overpraise, overlaud.

Belay, Fasten, hold.

Beleaguer, Besiege, beset, blockade, obstruct, encompass, encumber. *Relieve*

Belie, Contradict, controvert, falsify, misrepresent.

Belief, Faith, believing, trust, credence, avowal, confidence, assurance, persuasion, conviction, creed, doctrine, dogma. *Distrust*

Believe, *v.a.*, Credit, trust, assent to, confide in, rely upon. *Doubt*
v.n., Opine, think, hold, suppose, fancy, imagine, conceive.

Belike, Perhaps, maybe, probably, perchance.

Bellicose, Quarrelsome, pugnacious, irascible, belligerent, contention. *Genial*

Belligerent, Hostile, warlike, rival, contending, fighting, antagonistic, conflicting, bellicose, pugnacious. *Peaceful*

Bellow, Roar, bawl, clamour, yell, howl, cry. *Whisper*

Belly, Abdomen, paunch.

Belonging, *n.*, Property, possession, estate, appurtenance, appendage. Attribute, quality, endowment.
a., Related, connected, appertaining, cognate, accompanying, obligatory, congenial. *Independent*

Beloved, Dear, darling.

Below, Under, underneath, beneath. *Above*

Belt, Band, girdle, girth, zone.

Bemire, Bedaub, besmirch, begrime, befoul, foul, soil, pollute, dirty, bedraggle. *Cleanse*

Bemoan, Lament, bewail, moan, mourn, deplore. *Rejoice*

Bemused, Bewildered, confused, stupefied, muddled. *Collected*

Bench, Seat, form. Court, tribunal.

Bend, *v.a.*, Curve, bow, incurvate, crook, flex, deflect, draw. *Straighten*
Subdue, mould, influence, dispose, bias, incline, direct, turn.
v.n., Lean, deflect, incline, turn, deviate, diverge, swerve, crook.
Yield, stoop, bow, submit, kneel.
Stoop, condescend, deign.
n., Curve, curvity, curvature, angle, turn, turning.

Beneath, Under, underneath, below, inferior, subordinate. *Above*

Benediction, Blessing, benison, beatitude, benefit, grace. *Curse*
Thanks, thanksgiving, gratitude.

Benefaction, Present, gift, donation, alms, grant, endowment, bequest.

Benefactor, Patron, supporter, friend, donor. *Rival*

Benefice, Living.

Beneficence, Generosity, liberality, benevolence, charity, bounty. *Meanness*

Beneficent, Generous, liberal,† munificent, benign, benevolent, bountiful, benignant, favourable. *Hard*

Beneficial, Helpful, useful, salutary, wholesome, favourable, improving, profitable, serviceable, advantageous. *Useless*

Benefit, *n.*, Boon, advantage, favour, profit, blessing, gain, utility, service. *Loss*
v.a., Help, serve, befriend, profit, avail, enrich, advantage, gain. *Damage*

Benevolence, Kindness, charity, beneficence, liberality, benignity, philanthropy, humanity, tenderness, goodwill. *Hardness*

Benevolent, Kind, charitable, beneficent.† *Hard*

Benighted, Belated, retarded. Ignorant, darkened, unenlightened.

Benign, Benevolent, gracious, humane, kind, kindly, obliging, friendly, amiable, gentle, sweet, good. *Malevolent*

Benignant, Benign, benevolent, gracious.† *Harsh*

Benignity, Benevolence, graciousness, kindness.† *Harshness*

Benison, Benediction, blessing, beatitude, benefit, grace. *Curse*

Bent, *a.*, Crooked, curved, hooked, deflected. *Straight*
n., Bias, inclination, tendency, disposition, leaning, turn, aptitude, predilection, predisposition, partiality, liking, fondness.

Benumb, Stupefy, deaden, paralyse, blunt. *Quicken*

Bepraise, Belaud, overpraise, puff.

Bequeath, Leave, demise, will, transmit, give, grant, bestow, impart. *Alienate*

Bequest, Legacy, inheritance.

Berate, Reprove, rate, reprimand, chide, scold.

Bereave, Deprive, despoil, rob, divest, spoil, dispossess, strip.

Bereft, Stripped, deprived, destitute, spoiled. *Consoled*

Berth, Bed, cabin.
Post, place, position, appointment, situation.

Beseech, Adjure, implore, beg, entreat, ask, pray, supplicate, petition, conjure, importune, crave, solicit. *Demand*

Beseem, Behove, befit, suit, become.

Beset, Beleaguer, surround, encompass, encircle, environ, besiege, hem in. *Relieve*

Beset, Entangle, embarrass, perplex.

Beshrew, Curse, execrate. *Bless*

Beside, Near, close to, alongside.
Out of, aside from.

Besides, *prep.*, Except, save, distinct from.
adv., Moreover, further, furthermore, too, also.

Besiege, Beleaguer, surround, encompass, encircle, beset, invest. *Relieve*

Besmear, Bedaub, daub, besmirch, foul, smear, bespatter, dirty, soil, defile, befoul, pollute, contaminate, begrime. *Cleanse*

Besot, Intoxicate, soak, delude, stupefy, stultify, infatuate, befool. *Sober*

Bespatter, Besmear, bedaub, daub, foul, besmirch, smear, dirty, soil, defile, befoul, pollute, contaminate, begrime. *Cleanse*

Bespeak, Order, engage, book.
Solicit, accost, address, declare, betoken, proclaim.

Besprinkle, Bedew, sprinkle, bestrew, wet.

Best, Choice, pick, flower, élite.

Bestial, Brutish, brutal, brute, brute-like, beastly, vile, low, inhuman, mean, depraved, degraded, sensual.

Bestir, Labour, strive, work, toil, be alert, hasten, rouse, awaken. *Slack*

Bestow, Confer, give, grant, accord, impart, present, award. *Keep*

Bestrew, Strew, sprinkle, besprinkle, spread, bespread, scatter, bescatter.

Bet, Wager, stake, gamble, pledge.

Betide, Befall, happen, chance, bechance.

Betimes, Early, soon, seasonably, in time. *Late*

Betoken, Denote, betray, imply, indicate, show, argue, represent, teach, proclaim, foretell, foreshow, foreshadow, presage, augur, portend. *Hide*

Betray, Seduce, ruin, undo, corrupt, lure, mislead, ensnare, inveigle, beguile, delude, entrap. *Befriend*
Violate, divulge, reveal, expose, tell, show. *Conceal*

Betroth, Plight, engage, pledge, affiance.

Betrothal, Plighting, engagement.†

Better, *n.*, Superiority, advantage, victory. *Inferiority*
a., Superior.
v.a., Amend, emend, reform, improve, correct, rectify, meliorate, ameliorate, advance, promote. *Spoil*
v.n., Grow better, reform, improve, advance, mend. *Deteriorate*

Bettering, Betterment, improvement, melioration, amelioration, amendment. *Deterioration*

Between, Betwixt, amidst, amid.

Betwixt, Between, amidst, amid.

Bevel, Slope, inclination, chamfer, slant.

Beverage, Drink, potion.

Bevy, Group, throng, company, party, flock, swarm, flight.

Bewail, Bemoan, moan, lament, grieve, deplore, mourn, sorrow. *Rejoice*

Beware, Mind, take care, heed, avoid, remember, consider. *Ignore*

Bewilder, Muddle, bemuddle, confound, perplex, astonish, confuse, embarrass, befog, daze, puzzle, stagger, mystify. *Enlighten*

Bewilderment, Muddle, confusion, perplexity.†

Bewitch, Fascinate, enchant, captivate, charm, enamour, allure, enravish, enrapture, transport, entrance.

Beyond, Over, farther, past, more, above. *Near*

Bias, *n.*, Bent, inclination, proneness, propensity, disposition, predisposition, predilection, leaning, tendency, prejudice, proclivity.
v.a., Bend, incline, influence, prejudice.

Bibacious, Drunken, tippling, fuddling. *Sober*

Bibulous, Absorbent, porous, spongy, imbibing, soaking, drinking.

Bicker, Quarrel, dispute, squabble, wrangle. *Agree*
Vibrate, tremble, quiver.

Bickering, Quarrelling, disputing.† *Agreement*

Bid, *v.a.*, Charge, order, enjoin, command, direct, summon. *Restrain*
Request, ask, invite, call, solicit, wish.
Offer, propose, proffer, tender.
n., Bidding, offer, proposal, tender.

Bidding, Charge, order, injunction, behest, precept.
Offer, bid, proposal, tender.

Bide, *v.a.*, Abide, await, tarry.
Endure, abide, tolerate, bear, suffer.
v.n., Abide, wait, stay, remain, dwell. *Quit*

Big, Large, great, huge, massive, bulky, full, inflated, swollen. *Small*
Arrogant, proud, important, haughty, pompous, blustering, boastful, conceited. *Humble*
Pregnant, fecund, teeming.

Bight, Coil, bend, loop.
Bay, cove, inlet.

Bigot, Fanatic, zealot, dogmatist.

Bigoted, Obstinate, prejudiced, intolerant, dogmatic. *Tolerant*

Bigotry, Obstinacy, prejudice,† zealotry, fanaticism. *Tolerance*

Bijou, Gem, jewel, trinket, beauty, ornament.
Small, compact.

Bile, Anger, rage, fury, choler, indignation, resentment.

Bilk, Thwart, deceive, frustrate, balk, elude, disappoint.

Bill, *v.n.,* Fondle, kiss, toy, caress.
n., Account, charge, check, reckoning, fee, score.
Poster, notice, advertisement, placard.
Beak, nib, mandible.

Billet, *v.a.,* Allot, apportion, distribute, quarter, assign.
n., Quarters, rooms, lodgings.
Note, letter.
Stick, faggot, splinter.

Billow, *v.n.,* Roll, heave, surge, swell.
n., Wave, surge, breaker.

Billowy, Rolling, heaving, surging, swelling, undulating.

Bin, Receptacle, box, tub.

Binary, Double, dual, twofold.

Bind, *v.a.,* Tie, secure, fasten, lace, twine, wrap, bandage. *Loose*
Restrict, confine, crab, restrain. *Liberate*
Oblige, indenture, apprentice.
v.n., Hold, be obligatory.

Binding, Bandage, band, fillet, covering, cover.
Obligatory, holding, contracting.

Biography, Life, history, memoir.

Birch, Whip, rod, lash.

Bird, Fowl.

Birth, Nativity, origin, beginning, source, start. *Death*
Ancestry, line, lineage, descent, extraction, family, race, blood, nobility.

Bisect, Halve, cut in two. *Dissect*

Bishop, Prelate, patriarch.

Bishopric, Diocese, see, episcopate.

Bit, Morsel, crumb, scrap, mouthful, piece, fragment. *Whole*
Ace, atom, mite, whit, jot, tittle, iota, grain, particle.
Bridle, mouthpiece, borer, tool.
Coin, piece.

Bite, Chew, gnaw, champ, tear, rend, nip, pierce.
Burn, sting, tingle, smart.
Nip, blast, blight.
Clutch, grip, grasp, catch, grapple.

Biting, Burning, stinging, hot, pungent, sharp, piquant.
Caustic, cutting, severe, sarcastic. *Genial*
Piercing, cold, freezing, blasting, blighting, nipping. *Warm*

Bitter, Acrid, acid, harsh, sour, sharp, tart, acetose. *Sweet*

Bitter, Acrimonious, severe, harsh, stern. *Genial*
Fierce, intense, savage, cruel, virulent. *Mild*
Sad, affective, sore, painful, distressing, grievous, poignant. *Cheery*

Bitterness, Acridity, acridness, acidity.† *Sweetness*
Acrimony, severity,† spleen, gall, asperity, acerbity, spite, malice, hatred, rancour. *Love*
Fierceness, intensity, cruelty, virulence. *Mildness*
Pain, distress, grief, poignancy, sorrow, affliction.

Bizarre, Strange, singular, weird, odd, fantastic, whimsical. *Usual*

Blab, Prate, tell, prattle, tattle.

Black, Dark, inky, swarthy, dusky, murky, ebon, pitchy, dingy. *White*
Sombre, doleful, mournful, dismal, dark, gloomy, calamitous, disastrous, sullen, depressing, forbidding. *Bright*
Atrocious, wicked, monstrous, nefarious, infamous, heinous, horrible. *Good*

Blackamoor, Black, negro, Moor.

Blacken, Darken, soil, stain, bedaub, bespatter, befoul, defame, decry, calumniate, dishonour, abuse, sully, deface, defile, malign, traduce, besmirch, slander, asperse, vilify. *Vindicate*

Blackguard, Scoundrel, rascal, villain, rapscallion, scamp, rogue. *Gentleman*

Blackguardism, Scoundrelism, rascality, villainy, worthlessness, ribaldry, scurrility, indecency, obscenity. *Decency*

Blackmail, Hush-money, tribute, extortion.

Blain, Blister, sore, pustule, blotch.

Blamable, Blameworthy, censurable, culpable, reprehensible, faulty. *Blameless*

Blame, *v.a.,* Censure, disapprove, reproach, condemn, reprehend, chide, rebuke, vituperate. *Praise*
n., Censure, disapproval, reproach, reproof. *Approval*

Blameless, Inculpable, irreproachable, faultless, pure, innocent, guiltless, unspotted, unsullied, spotless, undefiled, stainless, unblemished, irreprehensible, irresponsible. *Blameworthy*

Blameworthy, Blamable, censurable, culpable, faulty, reprehensible. *Blameless*

Blanch, Bleach, whiten, fade. *Darken*

Bland, Mild, gentle, affable, soft, suave, amiable, benign, soothing. *Rough*

Blandiloquence, Adulation, flattery, humbug, blarney, speciousness. *Bluntness*

Blandishment, Flattery, compliment, cajolery, coaxing, wheedling, caressing, toying, fawning. **Bluntness**

Blank, *a.*, Empty, void, bleak, bare. **Full**
Amazed, astonished, dumbfounded, confounded, confused, disconcerted, nonplussed. **Calm**
Pure, simple, utter, unmixed, unmitigated, unqualified, entire, complete, perfect. **Mitigated**
n., Void, vacancy, bareness.

Blare, *v.a.*, Proclaim, trumpet, blazon.
v.n., Blow, sound, peal.
n., Peal, clang, blast, clangour.

Blarney, Flattery, cajolery, compliment, fawning, blandishment, blandiloquence, adulation. **Bluntness**

Blasé, Satiated, surfeited, cloyed, exhausted. **Fresh**

Blaspheme, Speak impiously, revile, defame, swear. **Adore**

Blasphemous, Profane, impious, sacrilegious. **Reverent**

Blasphemy, Profanity, impiousness, impiety, swearing, sacrilege. **Reverence**

Blast, *v.a.*, Destroy, kill, ruin, blight, wither, shrivel, annihilate, burst, split.
n., Blight, pestilence.
Explosion, discharge, burst, outbreak.
Peal, clang, clangour, blare.
Gust, squall, blow, breeze, storm. **Calm**

Blatant, Clamorous, noisy, bellowing, braying, vociferous, loud, obstreperous. **Quiet**

Blattering, Swaggering, noisy, blustering. **Unassuming**

Blaze, *v.a.*, Proclaim, publish, blazon, broadcast.
v.n., Flame, burn.
n., Flame, burning, glow.

Blazon, *v.a.*, Proclaim, blaze, publish, broadcast, trumpet, blare, herald. **Suppress**
Exhibit, display. **Hide**
Emblazon, emblaze, adorn.
n., Proclamation, publication.†
Exhibition, show, display.

Blazonry, Emblazonry, heraldry.

Bleach, Blanch, whiten, etiolate. **Darken**

Bleak, Cold, bare, exposed, open, unprotected, unsheltered, piercing, desolate, drear, chilly, raw, nipping, cheerless. **Sheltered**

Blear, Dim, make watery.

Bleary, Watery, rheumy.

Bleb, Blob, blister, tumour, vesicle.

Bleed, *v.a.*, Let blood.
v.n., Lose blood, lose sap, die, exude, secrete, drop.

Blemish, *v.a.*, Sully, taint, soil, stain, impair, disgrace, reproach. **Honour**
n., Flaw, speck, spot, defect, fault, imperfection.
Ruin, spoil, mar.

Blench, Shrink, evade, avoid, flinch, shy, shudder, yield, weaken, shirk, recoil, start. **Face**

Blend, Mix, mingle, harmonize, coalesce, intermingle, commingle, combine, unite, amalgamate. **Separate**

Bless, Praise, exalt, magnify, laud, glorify, extol, thank, adore. **Curse**
Gladden, delight, beatify, enrich. **Sadden**

Blessed, Sacred, holy, hallowed.
Blissful, happy, beatified. **Sad**

Blessing, Glory, praise, honour, laud, thanksgiving, gratitude. **Curse**
Boon, advantage, benefit, gain, profit. **Loss**
Benison, donation, benediction. **Curse**

Blight, *v.a.*, Kill, blast, destroy, wither, shrivel, crush, annihilate.
n., Withering, blast, pestilence.

Blind, *a.*, Sightless, eyeless, unseeing. **Seeing**
Ignorant, unaware, uninformed, unenlightened, benighted, undiscerning. **Enlightened**
Injudicious, careless, rash, heedless, indiscriminate, thoughtless, inconsiderate. **Careful**
Closed, shut, issueless. **Open**
v.a., Blindfold, hoodwink.
n., Curtain, cover, screen, shade.
Pretext, feint, ruse, disguise, stratagem, concealment.

Blindfold, Blind, hoodwink.

Blink, *v.n.*, Wink, flicker, twinkle, glitter, gleam, flutter.
v.a., Ignore, overlook, evade, avoid, disregard, connive. **Notice**
n., Glimpse, wink, glance, sight, view.
Glimmer, gleam, twinkle.

Bliss, Blessedness, blissfulness, happiness, joy, ecstasy, felicity, beatification, rapture. **Misery**

Blissful, Blessed, happy, joyful.† **Miserable**

Blister, Blob, bleb, blain, vesicle, pustule.

Blithe, Merry, gay, bright, joyful, joyous, cheerful, happy, elastic, lively, animated, sprightly, jocund, vivacious, mirthful, elated. **Dejected**

Bloat, Swell, inflate, dilate, distend. **Deflate**

Bloated, Swollen, inflated.†

Blob, Bubble, blister, blain, bleb, vesicle.

Block, *v.a.*, Stop, obstruct, arrest, blockade. ***Clear***
n., Stoppage, obstruction, jam, pack. ***Passage***
Dunce, fool, blockhead, simpleton. Mass, mould.

Blockade, *v.a.*, Block, close, beset, beleaguer, besiege. ***Relieve***
n., Closure, siege.

Blockhead, Dunce, block, fool, simpleton, dolt, booby, dullard, ignoramus. ***Sage***

Blockish, Stupid, foolish, simple, doltish, dull. heavy, stolid, unintelligent, ignorant. ***Wise***

Blonde, Light, fair, flaxen. ***Brunette***

Blood, Progeny, children, offspring, descendants, posterity, lineage, line, family, house, kin, kindred, relations.
Feeling, temper, passion, disposition, spirit.

Bloodshed, Murder, slaughter, butchery, massacre, carnage.

Bloodthirsty, Bloody, cruel, barbarian, ferocious, ruthless, savage, inhuman, murderous.

Bloody, Sanguinary, gory, ensanguined. Bloodthirsty, cruel, barbarian.†

Bloom, *v.n.*, Blossom, bud, flower, blow. ***Decay***
n., Blossom, bud, flower, efflorescence, flowering.
Beauty, freshness, delicacy, vigour, prime. ***Decadence***

Blossom, *v.n.*, Bloom, bud, flower, blow. ***Decay***
n., Bloom, bud, flower.

Blot, *v.a.*, Erase, expunge, obliterate, cancel, efface. ***Perpetuate***
Soil, sully, deface, disfigure, mar, tarnish, obscure, spoil, spot, blur, stain, disgrace, dishonour. ***Cleanse***
n., Erasure, obliteration.
Blemish, stain, spot, blur, disgrace, dishonour.

Blotch, Blain, bleb, blemish, spot, pimple, pustule, patch, splotch.

Blow, *v.a.*, Impel, drive, force.
Sound, wind.
Spread, diffuse.
v.n., Puff, pant.
Bloom, flower, blossom, bud.
Sound, breathe.
n., Knock, stroke, bang, thwack, whack, rap, wound.
Calamity, disaster, affliction, misfortune, disappointment.
Gale, gust, blast, puff.

Blown, Breathless, puffed, exhausted, fatigued, swollen, inflated.

Blubber, Weep, whine, cry, whimper.

Bludgeon, Cudgel, club.

Blue, Azure, sky-coloured, sapphire, sapphirine.
Pallid, ghastly, livid.
Dejected, depressed, sad, melancholy, dismal, gloomy, downhearted, dispirited, glum, downcast. ***Blithe***

Blues, Dejection, depression, dumps, melancholy, despondency.

Bluff, *a.*, Blunt, hearty, frank, open, good-natured. ***Polished***
n., Deceit, stratagem, concealment, disguise, feint.
v.a., & *n.*, Deceive, pretend, conceal, disguise, feint.

Blunder, *v.n.*, Err, bungle, miss, mistake, wander. ***Correct***
n., Error, mistake, misunderstanding, oversight. ***Foresight***

Blunt, *a.*, Dull, obtuse, stolid, pointless. ***Sharp***
Bluff, plain, unceremonious, uncourtly, abrupt. ***Polished***
Rude, brusque, rough, harsh, ungracious. ***Polite***
v.a., Dull, deaden, benumb, stupefy, paralyse, quiet, soften, abate, allay, alleviate, mitigate.

Blur, *v.a.*, Dim, bedim, obscure.
Blot, stain, spot, tarnish, soil, sully, blemish.
n., Confusion. ***Clarity***
Blot, spot, tarnish, blotch, disgrace, defect, dishonour, aspersion.

Blush, *v.n.*, Colour, redden, flush. ***Blanch***
n., Reddening.
Guiltiness, confusion, shame. ***Innocence***

Bluster, *v.n.*, Boast, swagger, vaunt, roar, swell, bully, domineer, storm, fume, brag.
n., Noise, tumult, boisterousness, turbulence, boasting, swaggering.†

Blustering, Windy, gusty, stormy, tempestuous, noisy, tumultuous, turbulent. ***Quiet***

Board, *v.a.*, Enter.
Feed, provide.
n., Plank.
Table, food, provision, meals, fare, victuals.
Committee, council, conclave.

Boast, *v.n.*, Vaunt, brag, swagger, swell, bluster, vapour, crow.
n., Vaunt, brag.†

Boaster, Braggart, blusterer, bully, vaunter.

Boastful, Vaunting, boasting, bragging.†

Boat, Craft, ship, vessel, bark, skiff.

Bob, *v.a.*, Jerk, knock, tap, strike, rap.
n., Pendant, wig, shilling.

Bode, *v.n.*, Presage, forebode.

v.a., Portend, shadow, foreshadow, foreshow, betoken, augur, predict, foretell.

Bodice, Stays, corset, waist.

Bodily, Wholly, entirely, completely, altogether. ***Partly***

Body, Substance, mass, whole, bulk, substantiality. ***Part***

Person, being, creature, mortal, individual.

Corpse, carcass, trunk.

Company, band, collection, corporation, coterie, party, association.

Bog, Swamp, marsh, quagmire, fen, morass, slough.

Bogey, Hobgoblin, spirit, ghost.

Boggle, Halt, hesitate, falter, dubitate, waver, vacillate, demur, shrink.

Bogus, False, counterfeit, sham, fraudulent, spurious. ***Genuine***

Boil, *v.n.*, Seethe, foam, bubble, froth, rage, fume. ***Cool***

n., Tumour, ulcer, fester, gathering, pustule.

Boisterous, Loud, noisy, stormy, roaring, turbulent, obstreperous, clamorous, vociferous, furious, tumultuous, violent, vehement. ***Quiet***

Bold, Valiant, daring, brave, fearless, dauntless, heroic, gallant, courageous, manly, spirited, doughty, audacious, undaunted. ***Timid***

Confident, assured, forward, pushing, rude, insolent, assuming. ***Modest***

Prominent, striking, conspicuous. ***Faint***

Boldness, Valour, daring, bravery.†
Timidity

Confidence, assurance.† ***Modesty***

Prominence, conspicuousness.

Bolster, *v.a.*, Support, hold up, maintain, defend, sustain, aid, help, patch, buoy, prop. ***Relax***

n., Cushion.

Bolt, *v.n.*, Abscond, run away, quit, retire, fly, flee. ***Stay***

v.a., Swallow, gulp.

Fasten, secure.

n., Dart, shaft, missile, arrow.

Sieve.

Fastening.

Bomb, Shell, bombard, pelt.

Bombast, Pomposity, fustian, gasconade, bluster, rant, magniloquence.
Moderation

Bonbon, Sweet, sweetmeat, confection.

Bond, *n.*, Binding, contract, compact, obligation.

Link, connection, tie, attachment, attraction, union.

Band, cord, fastening, ligament, ligature.

Bond, *a.*, Captive, enslaved, slave. ***Free***

Bondage, Slavery, captivity, servitude, imprisonment, confinement, fetters, chains. ***Freedom***

Bondsman, Slave, captive, serf.
Freeman

Bonny, Fair, pretty, handsome, beautiful, fine. ***Ugly***

Buxom, plump, healthy, round, chubby.

Joyous, blithe, cheerful, gay, merry, jolly, jocose. ***Dull***

Bonus, Award, gift, reward, subsidy, honorarium, premium.

Booby, Dunce, fool, simpleton, blockhead, idiot. ***Sage***

Trap.

Book, Work, volume, part, pamphlet, manual, compendium, brochure, monograph, tract, treatise.

Bookish, Studious, learned, erudite, pedantic. ***Ignorant***

Boom, *v.n.*, Roar, hum, resound.

v.a., Boost, push.

n., Roar, booming, humming, droning.

Boon, *n.*, Blessing, benefit, advantage, present, benefaction. ***Drawback***

a., Benign, benignant, generous, kind, bountiful, liberal. ***Unkind***

Merry, jovial, jolly, jocose. ***Sad***

Boor, Rustic, lout, clown, bumpkin, lubber, clodhopper.

Boorish, Rustic, loutish, clownish, rude, clumsy, rough, ungainly, coarse, lubberly.
Refined

Boost, Recommend, eulogize, strengthen, push.

Boot, *n.*, Gain, advantage, profit, benefit.
Loss

v.a., Advantage, profit, benefit, avail.

Bootless, Unavailing, useless, profitless, abortive, futile, vain, fruitless, worthless, ineffectual. ***Useful***

Booty, Spoil, plunder, loot, prey, pillage.

Boozy, Drunk, fuddled, tipsy, inebriated, intoxicated.

Border, Boundary, bound, margin, marge, limit, edge, edging, enclosure, confine, frontier, skirt, brim, rim, hem. ***Centre***

Bore, *v.a.*, Tire, weary, fatigue, vex, annoy, worry. ***Please***

Drill, pierce, perforate.

n., Proser, talker.

Hole, calibre.

Boreal, Arctic, northern, northerly.
Antarctic

Boredom, Weariness, dulness, tedium.

Borough, Corporation, town, township.

Borrow, Take, appropriate, imitate, adopt. ***Lend***

Feign, assume, simulate, dissemble.

Bosh, Nonsense, foolishness, balderdash.

Bosk, Grove, thicket, bushes.

Bosky, Bushy, leafy, shady, woody, sylvan.

Bosom, Heart, breast, affection, mind, soul, will.
Depth, hollow, deep, centre, bed, valley.

Boss, *n.,* Knob, stud, protuberance.
Foreman, ganger, master, overseer, superintendent, employer.
v.a., Stud, bestud, emboss.

Botch, *n.,* Blotch, blain, sore, blister, pustule.
Failure, bungling, miscarriage. **Success**
v.a., Mend, patch.

Both, Twain, the two. **Neither**

Bother, *v.a.,* Trouble, annoy, harass, vex, tease, perplex, worry, disturb, plague, molest, pester, flurry, *pother.* **Calm**
n., Trouble, annoyance, vexation.†

Bottom, Base, foot, basis, groundwork, floor, foundation. **Top**
Seat, buttocks, fundament.
Stamina, stay, strength.
Lees, dregs, sediment, grounds.
Ship, vessel.

Bottomless, Abysmal, unfathomable.

Boudoir, Apartment, room, chamber, cabinet.

Bough, Limb, branch, shoot. **Trunk**

Bounce, *v.n.,* Spring, leap, bolt, rebound, recoil.
n., Bound, spring, leap, jump.
Knock, blow, thump.
Boast, lie, vaunt, brag.

Bound, *v.a.,* Border, limit, confine, terminate.
v.n., Spring, leap, jump, rebound.
n., Border, limit, confine, boundary, bourn, termination.
Spring, leap, jump, bounce.

Boundary, Border, limit, confine, bourn, termination, bound, march.

Bounden, Binding, obligatory.

Boundless, Unbounded, infinite, unlimited, illimitable, unconfined, undefined. **Finite**

Bounteous, Bountiful, liberal, benevolent, generous, munificent, princely. **Stingy**

Bountiful, Generous, liberal, beneficent, munificent, bounteous. **Niggardly**

Bounty, Present, gift, reward, bonus, donation.

Bouquet, Bunch, nosegay, posy, cluster.

Bourgeoisie, Middle classes, townspeople, tradesmen, shopkeepers. **Proletariat**

Bourn, Boundary, border, limit, bound, confine, march, termination.
Brook, stream, burn, torrent, rivulet.

Bourse, Exchange.

Bout, Turn, conflict, contest.

Bow, *v.a.,* Bend, incline, inflect, curve, droop, drop.
Subdue, depress, crush, sink, weigh down.
v.n., Bend, incline, buckle.
n., Prow, beak, stem.

Bowels, Interior, inside, entrails, intestines.
Pity, compassion, sympathy, mercy, feeling, tenderness. **Hardness**

Bower, Recess, arbour, alcove, summerhouse.

Bowl, Beaker, goblet, receptacle.

Box, *v.a.,* Encase.
Cuff, buffet, strike.
v.n., Spar, fight.
n., Case, chest, receptacle.
Cuff, buffet, stroke, blow.

Boy, Lad, youth, stripling, youngster.

Boycott, Shun, ostracize, blackball.

Boyish, Youthful, puerile, childish, young.

Brace, *v.a.,* Tighten, strengthen, fortify, prop, support, tie, bind, strap, lash. **Loose**
n., Support, prop.
Pair, couple.

Bracing, Invigorating, strengthening, stimulating. **Relaxing**

Bracket, Shelf, stay, support, corbel, console, brace.

Brackish, Saltish.

Brag, *v.n.,* Boast, vaunt, swagger, bully, bluster, gasconade, flourish. **Whine**
n., Boast, vaunt, swaggering.†

Braggart, *n.,* Boaster, swaggerer, bully, blusterer, bravo.
a., Boastful, vaunting, bragging, blustering.

Braid, Interlace, interweave, interwine, plait. **Unwind**

Brains, Mind, sense, understanding, intellect, reason.

Brainless, Irrational, silly, unreasonable, absonant, nonsensical, thoughtless, witless. **Clever**

Brake, Jungle, brushwood, thicket, fern.

Branch, *n.,* Limb, bough, shoot, arm, offshoot. **Stem**
Tributary, affluent.
Subsection, subdivision, section, department.
v.n., Ramify, diverge.

Brand, *v.a.,* Mark, stigmatize, denounce.
n., Stigma, disgrace, mark, infamy, blot. **Honour**
Kind, grade, quality, make.
Bolt, thunderbolt.

Brandish, Flourish, shake, agitate, wave, wield.

Brangle, Wrangle, quarrel, squabble, bicker, dispute, argue. *Agree*

Brass, Assurance, front, boldness, forwardness, effrontery, face, audacity, impudence. *Modesty*

Brat, Urchin, child, infant.

Bravado, Brag, boasting, boast, bluster, vaunting.

Brave, *a.*, Valiant, heroic, dauntless, undaunted, courageous, daring, fearless, manly, doughty, bold, gallant, intrepid, plucky. *Timid*
v.a., Dare, defy, challenge.

Bravery, Valour, heroism, dauntlessness.†

Bravo, *n.*, Bandit, murderer, assassin, assassinator.
interj., Well done.

Brawl, *v.n.*, Wrangle, quarrel, squabble, dispute, bicker, roar. *Agree*
n., Wrangle, quarrel, squabble, dispute, bickering, altercation, tumult, row, broil. *Harmony*

Brawny, Powerful, muscular, strong, athletic, stalwart, herculean, sinewy, robust, stout, sturdy, lusty, strapping. *Weak*

Bray, *v.a.*, Bruise, pound, beat, pulverize, grind, crush.
v.n., Clamour, vociferate.
n., Blare, roar, crash.

Brazen, Bold, impudent, brassy, forward, pert, saucy. *Modest*

Breach, Rupture, fracture, break, gap, crack, flaw, opening, rift, rent, chasm.
Violation, infringement, infraction.
Quarrel, row, rupture, difference, dissension, disagreement, alienation. *Reconciliation*

Bread, Food, fare, provisions, victuals, aliment, sustenance, nourishment, nutriment, diet.

Breadth, Width.
Largeness, generosity, liberality, openness, tolerance, freedom. *Narrowness*

Break, *v.a.*, Fracture, rend, sever, tear, destroy, smash, shatter, shiver. *Mend*
Violate, transgress, infringe, disobey. *Obey*
Assuage, lessen, mitigate, abate. *Increase*
Weaken, enfeeble, tame, impair, enervate. *Strengthen*
Dismiss, discard, discharge.
Stop, interrupt.
v.n., Burst, explode.
Open, appear, dawn.
Decline.
n., Fracture, rupture, rent, breach, gap, rift, opening, chasm.

Break, Pause, interruption.
Dawn, dawning, sunrise.

Breakdown, Collapse, fall, downfall, failure, ruin.

Breakwater, Pier, jetty, mole.

Breast, *n.*, Bosom, chest, udder.
Conscience, heart, affections.
v.a., Face, withstand, oppose, resist, stem. *Yield*

Breath, Breathing, respiration, animation, life, existence.
Odour, aroma, exhalation.
Pause, instant, moment, rest, respite.

Breathe, *v.n.*, Respire, exist, live.
Rest, pause.
v.a., Emit, exhale, respire. *Inhale*
Show, express, whisper, indicate.

Breathing, *n.*, Respiration.
a., Alive, living, live. *Dead*

Breathless, Lifeless, dead, defunct, blown, puffed, winded.

Breeches, Trousers, pantaloons, knickerbockers.

Breed, *v.a.*, Bear, produce, conceive, bring forth, engender, beget, generate, originate.
Train, instruct, teach, educate, discipline, school, rear, raise, nourish, foster, nurture.
n., Race, progeny, stock, line, lineage, pedigree, family, extraction.

Breeding, Procreation, bearing, begetting.
Training, instruction, teaching,† deportment, manners.

Breeze, Wind, zephyr, gust.

Breviary, Digest, epitome, condensation, abbreviation, abridgment, outline, synopsis, summary, abstract. *Amplification*

Brevity, Briefness, shortness, closeness, conciseness, terseness. *Prolixity*

Brew, *v.a.*, Plot, contrive, hatch, foment, devise, project, concoct.
v.n., Make beer.

Bribe, *v.a.*, Suborn, reward.
n., Reward.

Bridal, Nuptial, conjugal, matrimonial, connubial.

Bridge, Span, traverse, surmount, overcome.

Bridle, *v.a.*, Curb, restrain, check, control, govern, master. *Liberate*
n., Curb, restraint, check.

Brief, *a.*, Concise, short, curt, laconic, terse, pithy. *Lengthy*
Transitory, transient, fleeting. *Long*
n., Summary, epitome, condensation, abstract, abridgment, compendium, compression, synopsis. *Amplification*

Briefly, Concisely, in short.

Brigand, Footpad, highwayman, robber, bandit, outlaw.

Bright, Luminous, shining, brilliant, flashing, gleaming, glowing, beaming, burnished, glossy, sunny, vivid, dazzling, sparkling, resplendent, glittering, radiant, scintillating. *Dull*
Intelligent, keen, acute, clever, ingenious, smart, discerning, witty. *Stupid*
Happy, merry, cheerful, gay, cheering, inspiring, smiling, pleasant, animated, vivacious, genial, auspicious, favourable. *Sad*
Famous, illustrious, glorious, great.
Lucid, lucent, clear, transparent. *Muddy*

Brighten, *v.a.*, Polish, furbish, illuminate, illumine.
Enliven, make cheerful, inspire, encourage, exhilarate, hearten. *Dishearten*
v.n., Grow bright, improve, clear. *Darken*

Brilliancy, Brightness, splendour, lustre, brilliance, radiance, sheen, glitter, glow. *Dulness*
Distinction, glory, fame, renown, eminence, illustriousness.

Brilliant, Bright, splendid, lustrous.† *Dull*
Distinguished, glorious, famous.†

Brim, Border, edge, rim, brink, margin, marge, skirt, verge, shore. *Centre*

Brindled, Striped, tabby, particoloured.

Brine, Salt water, sea, ocean, pickle.

Bring, Bear, fetch, conduct, convey, convoy, lead, accompany, attend. *Remove*
Obtain, draw, produce, gain, procure.

Brink, Border, verge, margin, marge, edge, brow, brim, bank, shore. *Middle*

Brisk, Quick, agile, active, nimble, alert, smart, spry, sprightly, lively. *Slow*

Bristle, Roughen, ruffle, corrugate. *Smooth*

Bristling, Full, crowded, stocked, swarming.

Brittle, Fragile, frail, brash, crumbling.

Broach, Approach, break, hint, suggest, open.
Pierce, tap, open. *Seal*
Publish, announce, proclaim, utter.

Broad, Large, wide, vast, ample, spacious, capacious, extensive. *Narrow*
Liberal, large, open, hospitable, tolerant.
Vulgar, indecent, gross, coarse.

Broaden, Widen, enlarge, amplify.

Broadcast, *v.a.*, Transmit, utter, publish, spread.
a., Scattered, dispersed.

Broadside, Poster, bill, placard.

Broil, Brawl, affray, quarrel, feud, strife, contention.

Broken, Destroyed, shivered, rent, shattered, fractured, ruptured, torn, separated, severed. *Mended*
Feeble, enfeebled, shaken, exhausted, spent, weakened, impaired, imperfect, defective. *Sound*
Defective, hesitating, imperfect, stammering, halting.
Steep, craggy, precipitous, rough, abrupt. *Smooth*

Broker, Agent, middleman, factor.

Brooch, Pin, clasp.

Brood, *v.n.*, Lie, sit, incubate, meditate.
n., Breed, offspring, family, progeny, issue.

Brook, *n.*, Stream, rivulet, rill, beck, run.
v.a., Stand, bear, abide, endure, suffer, allow, tolerate.

Brother, Kinsman, mate, pal, friend, comrade, companion.

Brotherhood, Brotherliness, fraternity, friendliness.

Brotherly, Fraternal, friendly, affectionate, kind. *Unkind*

Brow, Forehead.
Brink, border, edge, rim.

Browbeat, Overbear, intimidate, bully.

Browse, Nibble, crop, feed.

Bruise, *n.*, Contusion.
v.a., Batter, crush, break, contuse, pound, pulverize, indent.

Bruit, Report, rumour, hearsay.
v.a., Noise, report, blazon.

Brunt, Shock, impulse, aggression.

Brush, Skirmish, engagement, fight, conflict, affair, action, contest, scrap, encounter.
Wipe, cleanse, sweep, dust, scrub.
Brushwood, thicket, shrubs, bushes.

Brusque, Rude, gruff, abrupt, short, bluff, blunt, rough, unceremonious. *Polite*

Brutal, Cruel, inhuman, ferocious, savage, barbarous, ruthless. *Humane*
Harsh, gruff, rude, abrupt, short, bluff, blunt, brusque, unceremonious. *Polite*
Coarse, sensual, carnal, beastly, bestial, gross. *Refined*

Brutality, Cruelty, ferocity.†
Harshness, gruffness.†
Coarseness, sensuality.†

Brute, *n.*, Beast, quadruped, animal, ruffian, barbarian, monster.
a., Dumb, speechless, bestial, savage, rough, rude, uncivilized.

Bubble, Blob, bleb, blain, blister, vesicle.

Buccaneer, Pirate, freebooter, sea-rover.

Buckish, Gay, dashing, foppish.

Buckle, *n.*, Brooch, clasp, pin.

v.n., Bend, bow, double up.

Buckler, Aegis, shield, safeguard, protection, defence.

Bud, *n.*, Shoot, germ, flower.

v.n., Sprout, shoot, flower, vegetate. *Decay*

Budge, Move, stir, go, flinch.

Budget, Parcel, package, batch, store, collection.

Buffer, Bumper, guard, cushion, fender.

Buffet, *v.a.*, Strike, box, smite, blow, beat. Knock, slap, resist.

n., Stroke, box, knock, cuff, slap, rap. Bar, counter, sideboard.

Buffoon, Mountebank, jester, fool, antic, droll, wag, harlequin, clown. *Sage*

Buffoonery, Jesting, foolery, tomfoolery. *Wisdom*

Bugbear, Ogre, spectre, hobgoblin, bogey.

Build, Erect, construct, raise, make, fabricate. *Raze*

Building, Erection, construction, fabric, edifice, pile, structure.

Bulb, Knob, bulge, protuberance. Tuber, corm.

Bulbous, Round, roundish, protuberant.

Bulge, *v.n.*, Protrude, swell.

n., Protuberance, swelling, bilge.

Bulk, Size, largeness, bulkiness, magnitude, volume, massiveness, mass, dimensions.

Mass, most, majority. *Minority*

Bulky, Large, massive, huge, great, vast, big, enormous. *Small*

Bulletin, Statement, news, report.

Bully, *n.*, Browbeater, blusterer, hector, swaggerer, villain.

v.a., Browbeat, intimidate, overbear.

Bulwark, Rampart, redoubt, safeguard, protection, fortification, security.

Bump, *n.*, Blow, knock, shock, jar, thump, jolt.

Swelling, lump, protuberance.

Gift, faculty, endowment, talent, power.

v.a., Hit, strike, thump, knock.

Bumper, Buffer, guard, fender.

Large, generous, full, crowded, brimming.

Bumpkin, Clown, rustic, boor, hind, clod, lubber.

Bumptious, Conceited, vain. *Modest*

Bunch, Cluster, tuft, collection, assortment, set, batch, parcel, lot, group.

Lump, knob, protuberance, bump.

Bundle, Parcel, budget, package.

Bungle, Miss, fail, botch. *Succeed*

Bungler, Fumbler, botcher, novice, mismanager. *Expert*

Bunker, Bench, hollow, stowage bin, crib, hazard.

Bunkum, Nonsense, claptrap.

Buoy, Float, support, sustain, cheer, elevate. *Swamp*

Buoyancy, Gaiety, lightness, vivacity, levity, sprightliness, cheerfulness. *Despondency*

Buoyant, Gay, light, vivacious.† *Despondent*

Burden, *n.*, Burthen, load, weight, impediment, incubus, grievance, trouble, sorrow, affliction, encumbrance. *Ease*

Drift, chorus, refrain.

Cargo, lading, freight, capacity, tonnage.

v.a., Load, surcharge, afflict, overload, oppress.

Bureau, Department, office, dresser, drawer.

Burgher, Citizen, townsman, bourgeois. *Villager*

Burial, Burying, inhumation, interment, entombment. *Exhumation*

Burke, Suffocate, smother, suppress.

Burlesque, Caricature, travesty, parody, satire, irony, humour, wit.

Burly, Portly, bulky, stout, lusty. *Frail*

Burn, *v.a.*, Parch, char, scorch, shrivel, bronze, brown, toast, tan.

v.n., Flame, glow, blaze, flash, smoulder, tingle. *Extinguish*

Burning, Flaming, glowing, fiery, hot, scorching, ardent, fervent, vehement, earnest, intense, feverish. *Cool*

Burnish, Polish, brighten, furbish, glaze. *Dull*

Burrow, Tunnel, mine, excavate.

Bursar, Treasurer, cashier.

Burst, *v.n.*, Split, crack, explode, break.

v.a., Rend, break, split.

n., Explosion, bursting, disruption, blast, blasting.

Bursting, Burst, explosion.†

Bury, Inter, inhume, cover, obliterate, conceal, hide, entomb, inearth. *Exhume*

Burying, Burial, interment, inhumation.† *Exhumation*

Business, Vocation, occupation, calling, trade, employment, avocation, pursuit, profession, craft. *Leisure*

Commerce, traffic, trade, dealing.

Concern, affair, duty, function.

Bustle, *v.n.*, Stir, fuss.

n., Stir, fuss, hurry, commotion, flurry, tumult, *pother*. *Calm*

Busy, Occupied, employed, engaged. *Free*

Assiduous, diligent, sedulous, active, industrious, working. *Lazy*

Bustling, stirring, fussing, meddling, officious.

Busybody, Bustler, meddler, inter-meddler, prig.

But, Yet, however, nevertheless, still.
Unless, save, saving, except, excepting, moreover, furthermore, only.

Butcher, *v.a.*, Slay, slaughter, kill, murder, massacre.
n., Slaughterer, slayer, killer, murderer, assassin.

Butchery, Slaughter, murder, massacre, carnage.

Butt, Object, mark, target.

Buttonhole, Persuade, catch, detain, bore, importune.

Buttress, Support, stay, prop, brace, shore.

Buxom, Plump, healthy, vigorous, gay, hearty, comely, fresh, lively, jocund, jolly, bonny, blithe, cheerful.   *Slim*

Buy, Purchase, bribe, corrupt, pervert, cheapen.   *Sell*

Buzz, Hum, whisper, murmur.

By, Through, with.
At, on.
Per.
Along, over, through.
From.
Near.
Past.

Bygone, Past, gone by.

Bypath, By-way, sidepath.   *Highway*

Bystander, Onlooker, spectator, watcher, observer.

Byword, Saw, adage, dictum, tag, precept, proverb, saying, aphorism, maxim.
Reproach, taunt.

C

Cabal, *n.,* Junto, faction, combination, clique, gang, coalition, coterie, set, league, confederacy.

Conspiracy, plot, intrigue.

v.n., Conspire, plot, intrigue. *Legislate*

Cabalistic, Mystic, occult, secret, mysterious, fanciful, symbolical. *Patent*

Cabaret, Inn, tavern, public-house, place of entertainment.

Cabin, Shed, hut, hovel, cottage.

Cabinet, Case, collection.

Boudoir, chamber, closet.

Government, ministry, administration.

Cabriolet, Cab, hansom, brougham.

Cachinnation, Laughter, chuckle, titter, cackle, grin, snigger, giggle.

Cackle, *v.n.,* Titter, laugh, chuckle, snigger, giggle.

Babble, prate, prattle, palaver, chatter.

n., Prate, prattle, twaddle.

Cacophonous, Discordant, jarring, harsh, cacophonic, caocphonical, cacophonious, grating. *Harmonious*

Cacophony, Discord, jarring, jar.

Concord

Cadaver, Body, corpse, ashes, remains.

Cadaverous, Deathlike, ghastly, pale, pallid, wan, ashy. *Chubby*

Cadence, Intonation, tone, sound, accent.

Caducity, Decline, decrepitude, senility, infirmity, decadence, dotage. *Youth*

Caducous, Declining, decrepit, senile.†

Cafe, Restaurant, tea-shop, coffee-house.

Cage, Imprison, cabin, crib, confine, incarcerate. *Liberate*

Caitiff, Miscreant, rascal, villain, ruffian, rogue, churl, wretch, vagabond, traitor, scoundrel, knave, coward, sneak.

Gentleman

Cajole, Coax, tempt, wheedle, flatter, lure, delude, deceive, dupe, inveigle, fawn, impose, mislead, persuade, beguile, blandish, entrap. *Warn*

Cajolery, Coaxing, temptation, wheedling, flattery.†

Cake, Solidify, harden, bake.

Cover.

Calamitous, Disastrous, unfortunate, adverse, catastrophic, afflictive, unlucky, unhappy, untoward, sad, severe, hapless, dreadful, deplorable, baleful, distressing, ill-fated, ill-starred. *Fortunate*

Calamity, Disaster, misfortune, adversity, catastrophe, affliction, evil, trouble, mischance, dispensation, blight,

visitation, reverse, set-back, blow, trial.

Blessing

Calcine, Burn, powder.

Calculate, Compute, reckon, number, count, value, consider, weigh, estimate, rate, assess, appraise, cast.

Suit, fit, adjust, adapt.

Calculated, Suited, fitted, adapted, conducive, congenial.

Calculating, Cautious, wary, careful, guarded, sagacious, circumspect, farsighted. *Rash*

Crafty, scheming, selfish, hard, cool.

Reckless

Calculation, Computation, reckoning, numbering, counting, valuation, estimation, weighing, assessment.

Foresight, forethought, prudence, care, caution, cautiousness, discretion, deliberation, circumspection, wariness.

Rashness

Anticipation, prospect, expectation, contemplation.

Calculous, Stony, gritty, sandy, arinaceous.

Ca(u)ldron, Boiler, copper, kettle, pot.

Caledonian, *a.,* Scottish, Scotch.

n., Scot, Scotsman, Scotchman.

Calefacient, *a.,* Heating, warming.

Cooling

Vesicatory, rubefacient.

n., Vesicant, vesicatory, rubefacient.

Calefaction, Warming, warmth, heating, heat. *Cooling*

Calefy, Warm, heat. *Cool*

Calembourg, Pun, quibble, witticism.

Calendar, *n.,* Almanac, catalogue, list, schedule, register.

v.a., Catalogue, list, register, enroll, enter.

Calendered, Rolled, smooth, glossy.

Calibre, Gauge, diameter, bore.

Capacity, ability, force, power, strength, gifts, faculty, parts, talent, scope, endowment.

Calid, Hot, burning, glowing, fiery, ardent, fervent.

Caliginous, Dim, cloudy, dark, obscure, dusky, indistinct, gloomy. *Bright*

Call, *v.a.,* Name, entitle, dub, style, christen, term, designate, denominate, phrase.

Summon, invite, bid, assemble, convoke, muster, convene. *Dismiss*

Ordain, elect, appoint, designate.

v.n., Cry, cry out, exclaim.

n., Cry, outcry, voice.

Call, Summons, appeal, invitation, election, choice, appointment.
Claim, demand, requisition.

Calling, Profession, vocation, avocation, trade, business, occupation, employment, pursuit, craft.

Callous, Unfeeling, hard, obdurate, indurated, hardened, indifferent, insensible, torpid, obtuse, dull, apathetic, unimpressible. *Feeling*

Callow, Naked, unfledged.
Soft, simple, silly, green, inexperienced.

Calm, *a.*, Serene, tranquil, undisturbed, unruffled, placid, peaceful, still, smooth, quiet, mild, composed, cool, sedate, collected, self-possessed. *Disturbed*
v.a., Pacify, placate, tranquillize, still, quiet, assuage, allay, smooth, compose, hush, appease, becalm, soften, lull, alleviate, moderate, mollify. *Agitate*
n., Lull, peace, serenity, tranquillity, quiet, repose, calmness, stillness, placidity, equanimity. *Storm*

Calmness, Calm, lull, peace, peacefulness.† *Storm*
Composure, self-possession, sedateness, coolness, mildness, serenity, repose, equanimity, quiet, tranquillity, placidity. *Agitation*

Calumniate, Asperse, slander, vilify, malign, libel, abuse, blacken, defame, blemish, traduce, revile, detract, backbite. *Eulogize*

Calumniator, Slanderer, vilifier, maligner.†

Calumnious, Slanderous, libellous, abusive, defamatory, insulting, contumelious, vituperative, scurrilous, opprobrious.

Calumny, Aspersion, slander, libel, abuse, defamation, insult, vituperation, scandal, detraction, backbiting, obloquy. *Eulogy*

Camarilla, Cabal, clique, gang, junto, ring.

Camber, *n.*, Arch, arching, curve, rounding, convexity.
v.a., Arch, curve, bend.

Cambrian, *a.*, Welsh, Cymric.
n., Welshman, Cymro.

Camerated, Arched, bowed, vaulted.

Camp, *v.n.*, Encamp, pitch a tent.
n., Encampment.

Campaign, Operation, crusade, drive.

Campanile, Belfry, bell-tower.

Canaille, People, populace, proletariat, mob, multitude, herd, rabble, scum, riff-raff. *Aristocracy*

Canal, Channel, waterway, duct, pipe, tube.

Canard, Rumour, fabrication, hoax. *Truth*

Cancel, Obliterate, erase, abolish, discharge, countervail, expunge, efface, blot, abrogate, quash, repeal, revoke, rescind, nullify, annul. *Confirm*

Cancellated, Cross-barred, reticulated.

Candelabrum, Chandelier.

Candid, Frank, honest, open, fair, straightforward, plain, sincere, naive, above-board, witless, guileless, unreserved. *Cunning*

Candidate, Aspirant, solicitant, applicant, petitioner, claimant, competitor.

Candle, Light, taper.

Candour, Frankness, honesty, openness, fairness, straightforwardness, plainness, sincerity, artlessness, guilelessness, simplicity, truthfulness. *Cunning*

Canker, *n.*, Infection, bane, bale, blight, rot, corrosion, erosion, corruption.
v.a., Infect, blight, rot, corrode, erode, corrupt, poison, envenom, embitter. *Purify*

Canon, Law, rule, formula, standard.

Canonical, Authorized, authentic, received. *Doubtful*

Canopy, Awning, baldaquin, tilt, dias, firmament.

Canorous, Tuneful, musical, melodious.

Cant, Hypocrisy, sham piety.
Tilt, slant, turn, bevel.

Cantankerous, Obdurate, headstrong, self-willed, perverse, crabbed, obstinate, stubborn, unyielding, stiff, intractable.

Canter, Gallop.

Canticle, Song, psalm.

Canting, Hypocritical, insincere, affected, hollow, sanctimonious.

Canvas, Tarpaulin, sail, painting, tent.

Canvass, *v.a.*, Debate, dispute, discuss, agitate.
Examine, sift, investigate, scrutinize, consider, study.
Solicit.
n., Debate, dispute, discussion.
Examination, sifting, investigation, scrutiny, study.

Canyon, Ravine, gulch, gorge.

Cap, *n.*, Headgear, cover, covering, bonnet.
Top, peak, summit, pitch, crown, height, acme, head. *Bottom*
v.a., Cover, surmount, complete, finish, crown.
Overtop, surpass, exceed, transcend.

Capability, Ability, capableness, capacity, skill, power, brains, competency, calibre, force, faculty. *Inability*

Capable, Able, skilful, efficient, clever,

competent, gifted, accomplished, qualified, fitted, suited, ingenious, intelligent. *Incompetent*

Capacious, Spacious, voluminous, wide, roomy, ample, large, broad, comprehensive, extensive, accommodative, vast. *Narrow*

Capaciousness, Spaciousness, width, roominess,† breadth, freedom. *Narrowness*

Capacitate, Qualify, make able, enable. *Incapacitate*

Capacity, Volume, magnitude, dimensions, size, amplitude.
Calibre, power, faculty, ability, force, strength, gifts, parts, talent, scope, endowment, aptitude, aptness, brains, wit, discernment, skill, efficiency, competency, readiness, cleverness. *Inaptitude*
Position, office, function, sphere, duty, appointment, charge, service, province.

Cape, Promontory, headland.

Caper, *v.n.,* Hop, skip, jump, dance, gambol, romp, leap, frisk, bound, spring.
n., Hop, skip, jump.†

Capillary, Delicate, slender, fine, filiform, minute.

Capital, *a.,* Principal, chief, cardinal, first, main, leading. *Minor*
Fatal.
First-rate, first-class, prime, splendid, good, excellent. *Poor*
n., Metropolis.
Stock, principal.

Capitalist, Investor, speculator.

Capitulate, Yield, surrender, submit. *Resist*

Capitulation, Yielding, surrender, submission. *Resistance*

Caprice, Whim, whimsy, fancy, oddity, humour, vagary, crotchet, freak.

Capricious, Whimsical, fanciful, odd, humorsome, variable, changeable, wayward, fantastical, fickle, uncertain, queer, crotchety, freakish, inconstant. *Firm*

Capsize, Upset, overturn.

Capsule, Shell, covering, case, sheath, wrapper, envelope.
Pod, seed-vessel.

Captain, Officer, commander, leader, chief, chieftain, warrior, soldier.

Caption, Arrest, apprehension.
Title, heading, certificate.

Captious, Carping, cavilling, hypercritical, censorious. *Appreciative*
Acrimonious, crabbed, snarling, contentious, testy, touchy, cantankerous, waspish, cross, splenetic. *Sweet*
Insidious, ensnaring, luring.

Captivate, Fascinate, charm, enamour, win, gain, catch, take, enchant, bewitch. *Repulse*

Captivating, Fascinating, charming, winning.† *Repulsive*

Captive, Prisoner.

Captivity, Imprisonment, incarceration, confinement, durance, duress, bondage, servitude, enthralment, thraldom, slavery, subjection. *Freedom*

Capture, *v.a.,* Arrest, take, seize, apprehend, catch, imprison. *Release*
n., Arrest, seizure, apprehension, catching, catch, imprisonment.

Carack, Galleon, argosy, ship.

Caravansary | Caravansera | Khan, inn, tavern, public-house.

Carcass, Corpse, corse, body.

Cardinal, Capital, principal, chief, main, vital, essential, central, important, first. *Minor*

Care, *n.,* Concern, anxiety, solicitude, trouble, worry, perplexity. *Indifference*
Attention, watchfulness, pains, regard, carefulness, heed, caution, vigilance, circumspection, prudence, economy, thrift, wariness, foresight, direction, management, preservation. *Neglect*
Charge, burden.
v.n., Worry, be anxious, be troubled.
Like, feel interested.

Career, *n.,* Progress, course, race, walk, conduct, procedure, life, history.
v.n., Rush, course, sweep.

Careful, Attentive, watchful, painstaking, heedful, cautious, vigilant, circumspect, prudent, economical, thrifty, wary, provident, thoughtful. *Careless*
Anxious, troubled, weary, concerned, solicitous, worried, perplexed. *Easy*

Careless, Inattentive, negligent, remiss, neglectful, heedless, incautious, rash, imprudent, unmindful, thriftless, forgetful, improvident, thoughtless, unconcerned, regardless, listless. *Careful*
Untroubled, easy, unperplexed, undisturbed. *Anxious*

Carelessness, Inattention, neglect, heedlessness.†

Caress, *n.,* Endearment, fondling, wheedling, coaxing, blandishment, striking, kiss, embrace. *Persecution*
v.a., Fondle, wheedle, coax, blandish, stroke, kiss, embrace, hug, pet. *Tease*

Cargo, Load, lading, burden, freight, consignment, *burthen.*

Caricature, Burlesque, parody, travesty, mimicry.

Carious, Putrid, decayed, corrupt, rotten, mortified, ulcerated. *Fresh*

Cark, Worry, annoy, vex, fret, harass, grieve, perplex. *Appease*

Carking, Worrying, annoying, vexing, grievous, distressing. *Appeasing*

Carle, Boor, lout, clown, rustic, bumpkin, churl.

Carlock, Fish-glue, ichthyocol, ichthyocolla, isinglass.

Carnage, Butchery, slaughter, massacre, havoc, bloodshed.

Carnal, Sensual, lecherous, voluptuous, licentious, self-indulgent, lustful, fleshly, base, lascivious, lubricous. *Temperate* Earthly, worldly, secular, temporal, natural, unspiritual, unregenerate. *Spiritual*

Carnality, Sensuality, lust, self-indulgence, grossness, lechery, lubricity. *Temperance*

Carnival, Masquerade, revel, festivity, carousal.

Carol, *n.*, Song, chorus, ditty, lay.
v.n., Sing, warble, hymn, hum, chant, chirp.

Carousal, Carnival, festivity, festival, feast, banquet, entertainment, revel, revelry, revelling, masquerade, debauchery, carouse, bacchanals, orgies.

Carouse, *n.*, Carousal, carnival, festivity.†
v.n., Revel, feast, tipple, debauch.

Carouser, Bacchanalian, bacchanal, reveller, tippler.

Carp, Cavil, censure, object, hypercriticise. *Appreciate*

Carper, Caviller, censurer, critic.

Carping, *a.*, Captious, censorious, hypercritical, cavilling. *Appreciative*
n., Censure, blame, hypercriticism, cavil. *Appreciation*

Carriage, Conveyance, vehicle, cab, transportation.
Deportment, bearing, behaviour, mien, demeanour, air, conduct. *Miscarriage*

Carry, Transport, convey, transfer.
Uphold, support, sustain.
Impel, urge. *Deter*
Effect, accomplish, secure, gain, attain, compass. *Fail*

Cart, Wagon, vehicle, van, conveyance.

Carve, Cut, chisel, engrave, grave, sculpture, form, hack, shape, mould, fashion, hew, divide, slice.

Carving, Sculpture.

Cascade, Cataract, fall, waterfall.

Case, *n.*, Box, chest, carton.
Capsule, covering, sheath.
Condition, predicament, plight, state, situation.
Circumstance, event, instance, example.
Action, suit, lawsuit, cause, trial, process.

Case, *v.n.*, Encase, enclose, cover, wrap, protect, envelop, box, pack.

Casehardened, Obdurate, brazen, hardened, reprobate.

Casement, Window, lattice.

Cash, Money, coin, specie, currency, payment.

Cashier, *n.*, Cash-keeper.
v.a., Discharge, dismiss, discard, break.

Casino, Saloon, dancing-hall, gaming-house, clubhouse.

Casque, Helmet, helm, cask, morion.

Cast, *v.a.*, Throw, fling, pitch, sling, hurl, toss, send, drive, thrust, force, impel. *Keep*
Calculate, reckon, compute.
Found, form.
Shed, divest, drop. *Retain*
n., Throw, fling, toss, drive, thrust.
Mould, form, style, mien, manner, air, character, tone, look.
Shade, touch, tint, tinge.

Castaway, Outcast, vagabond, reprobate, wreck.

Caste, Class, order, lineage, blood, race, rank, dignity, respect.

Castigate, Whip, cane, chastise, beat, lash, flog, thrash, punish, chasten, discipline, correct, upbraid, censure, flagellate. *Caress*

Castigation, Whipping, caning, chastisement.†

Castle, Citadel, keep, fortress, stronghold.

Castrate, *Glib*, geld, emasculate, weaken, subdue, mortify.

Castration, *Glibbing*, gelding, emasculation, orchotomy.

Casual, Occasional, accidental, fortuitous, incidental, contingent. *Regular*

Casualty, Accident, contingency, fortuity, chance, mischance, mishap, reverse, disaster, trial, catastrophe, ill, misfortune, calamity, stroke, blow, visitation, affliction, misadventure. *Blessing*

Casuistry, Sophistry, quibble, refinement, fallacy. *Reason*

Catachrestic-al, Strained, far-fetched, forced, recondite.

Cataclysm, Flood, deluge, overflow, inundation.

Catacomb, Vault, crypt, tomb, cellar.

Catalogue, Record, list, inventory, invoice, roll, schedule, register.

Cataract, Cascade, fall, waterfall.

Catastrophe, Calamity, disaster, misfortune, visitation, blow, stroke, misadventure, mishap, mischance, reverse, trial, trouble, affliction, evil, misery, distress, casualty, adversity, ill. *Blessing*

Catastrophe, Conclusion, termination, end, upshot, finale, denouement, consummation, issue. *Beginning*

Catastrophic, Disastrous, calamitous, distressing, changing.

Catch, *v.a.*, Seize, grasp, snatch, grip, clutch, take. *Miss*
Capture, entrap, ensnare, entangle, arrest, apprehend. *Lose*
Captivate, charm, fascinate, enchant, win, bewitch. *Repulse*
Overtake.
Surprise.
n., Seizure, taking, capture, arrest, apprehension.
Snatch, chorus, refrain.
Hook, hasp, clasp.
Quantity, take.

Catching, *a.*, Infectious, contagious, pestilential.
Captivating, winning, charming, enchanting, fascinating, bewitching, attractive, taking. *Repulsive*

Catchword, Shibboleth.
Cue, clue.

Catechise, Interrogate, question, examine.

Catechism, Interrogation, compendium, socratics, creed, examination.

Catechumen, Pupil, novice, learner, scholar, tyro, neophyte, proselyte, convert. *Master*

Categorical, Plain, positive, distinct, affirmative, absolute, emphatic, downright, unreserved, unconditional, unqualified, direct, explicit, express. *Hazy*

Category, Class, sort, order, rank, division, kind, state.

Catenation, Conjunction, link, joint, union, connection.

Cater, Provide, purvey.

Cathartic, Cleansing, purgative, evacuant, abstergent.

Catholic, General, universal, world-wide, wide, liberal, tolerant, unexclusive. *Narrow*

Causal, Causative.

Causality, Causativity, causativeness, causation, potentiality, effectuality, operativeness.

Causation, Production, creation.

Cause, *n.*, Source, origin, agent, creator, producer.
Reason, ground, motive, purpose, inducement, incitement, incentive, object, aim, end.
Undertaking, attempt, enterprise.
Action, case, trial, suit.
v.a., Create, originate, produce, effect.

Caustic, Burning, mordant, pungent,

catheretic, corrosive, corroding, acrid, virulent, biting, bitter, severe, sarcastic, trenchant, sharp, cutting, stinging, scathing. *Mild*

Cauterize, Burn, sear.

Caution, *n.*, Carefulness, wariness, discretion, heed, heedfulness, care, vigilance, watchfulness, providence, prudence. *Rashness*
Admonition, advice, warning, counsel, injunction.
v.a., Admonish, warn, forewarn, advise.

Cautious, Careful, wary, discreet.† *Careless*

Cavalcade, Procession, caravan, equipage, cortege, retinue.

Cavalier, *n.*, Chevalier, knight, equestrian, royalist. *Roundhead*
a., Arrogant, haughty, disdainful, curt, proud, scornful, supercilious, insolent. *Meek*

Cave, Cavern, grotto, den, grot.

Cavern, Cave, grotto, den, grot.

Cavernous, Hollow.

Cavil, *v.n.*, Carp, censure, object, hypercriticise. *Appreciate*
n., Carping, censure, objection, hypercriticism. *Appreciation*

Caviller, Carper, censurer, critic.

Cavilling, Carping, captious, censorious, hypercritical. *Appreciative*

Cavity, Hollow, void, vacuum, pocket.

Cease, *v.n., & a.*, Stop, desist, end, terminate, finish, discontinue, stay. *Start*
v.n., Fail, be extinct.

Ceaseless, Unceasing, continuous, continual, perpetual, endless, interminable, incessant, eternal, uninterrupted. *Fitful*

Cede, Yield, resign, surrender, abandon, forego, grant, relinquish. *Annex*

Celebrate, Honour, commemorate, commend, solemnize, observe, keep, glorify, laud, praise, extol, magnify, applaud. *Ignore*

Celebrated, Famous, distinguished, eminent, noted, illustrious, famed, notable, renowned, exalted. *Obscure*

Celebration, Honour, commemoration, solemnization, observance, glorification, laudation, praise, extolment.

Celebrity, Notability, star, lion. *Nonentity*
Fame, distinction, eminence, note, renown, honour, glory, repute, reputation, credit. *Ignominy*

Celerity, Velocity, quickness, speed, rapidity, swiftness, fleetness, despatch, haste. *Slowness*

Celestial, Heavenly, divine, immortal,

supernatural, angelic, ethereal, radiant, empyrean, empyreal. *Earthly*

Celibate, Single, unmarried. *Married*

Cellular, Alveolated, honey-combed.

Cement, *v.a.*, Unite, stick, join, connect, attach, bind, consolidate. *Loose*
v.n., Cohere, unite, cleave. *Part*
n., Mortar, bond, adhesive.

Cemetery, Graveyard, churchyard, necropolis, burial-ground.

Cenotaph, Monument, memorial, tomb.

Censor, Critic, censurer, inspector, caviller, carper.

Censorious, Captious, cavilling, hypercritical, severe. *Appreciative*

Censurable, Blamable, blameworthy, faulty, reprehensible, culpable.
Blameless

Censure, *v.a.*, Blame, reprehend, rebuke, reprove, remonstrate, reproach, reprimand, condemn, chide. *Praise*
n., Blame, reprehension,† animadversion, stricture, disapprobation, disapproval.

Central, Convenient, accessible, mediate.
Remote

Centralize, Localize, concentrate, nationalize, collect. *Delocalize*

Centralization, Localization, concentration.† *Delocalization*

Centre, Middle, midst. *Outskirts*

Century, Hundred, centenary.

Cereals, Grain, corn.

Cerement, Cerecloth, graveclothes.

Ceremonial, *a.*, Formal, official, functional, ministerial, imposing, pompous, scenic, sumptuous. *Quiet*
n., Formalities, rites, ritual, ceremony,† etiquette.

Ceremonious, Formal, courtly, lofty, stately, starched, precise, stiff, punctilious. *Blunt*

Ceremony, Formality, form, rite, ceremonial, observance, solemnity, show, parade, stateliness, pomp.

Certain, Plain, positive, unquestionable, unquestioned, indubitable, indisputable, undisputed, undoubted, absolute, manifest, undeniable, incontestable, incontrovertible. *Doubtful*
Sure, confident, assured, positive, convinced.
Infallible, unfailing.
Real, actual, existing.
Determinate, true, fixed, established, regular, constant, stated, definite, settled.

Certainly, Plainly, positively, unquestionably.
Willingly, surely.

Certainty, Surety, unquestionableness, indubitableness. *Uncertainty*

Certainty, Certitude, confidence, assurance assuredness, conviction.
Truth, fact. *Fiction*

Certificate, Credential, testimonial, voucher.

Certify, Witness, attest, testify, avouch, avow, aver, acknowledge, declare, prove, demonstrate, show, inform. *Disprove*

Cerulean, Blue, azure, sky blue.

Cess, Tax, assessment, rate.

Cessation, Stop, halt, stoppage, intermission, respite, pause, ceasing, discontinuance, rest, abeyance, suspension, quiescence, remission. *Continuance*

Cession, Surrender, renunciation, yielding, abandonment, grant, relinquishment.
Annexation

Cestus, Belt, girdle, band, cincture.
Glove, gauntlet.

Chafe, *v.a.*, Rub, irritate, vex, anger, incense, nettle, annoy, exasperate, provoke, tease, enrage, offend, fret, fidget, worry, harass, gall, grieve, chagrin.
Soothe
v.n., Fume, fret, rage, grieve.

Chaff, *n.*, Husks, refuse, hulls, trash. *Gist*
v.a., Mock, scoff, ridicule, jeer, deride.

Chaffer, Haggle, bargain, negotiate.

Chagrin, *n.*, Irritation, vexation, anger, annoyance, exasperation, displeasure, mortification, disquiet. *Pleasure*
v.a., Irritate, vex,† chafe, provoke.
Soothe

Chain, *v.a.*, Fasten, fetter, restrain, confine, shackle, enslave. *Loose*
n., Fetter, shackle, bond, manacle.
Series, succession.

Chair, Seat.
Professorship.

Chaldaic, Chaldee, Aramaean, Aramaic.

Chalice, Goblet, cup, bowl.

Challenge, *v.a.*, Dare, defy, brave.
Question, summon, investigate, interrogate. *Pass*
n., Defiance.
Question, summons, investigation, interrogation.

Chamber, Room, apartment, closet, hall.
Hollow, cavity.

Chambers, Rooms, apartments, lodgings, quarters.

Chamfer, *v.a.*, Groove, flute, channel.
n., Furrow, fluting, channel.

Champ, Chew, gnaw, bite, crunch.

Champion, *n.*, Hero, combatant, challenger, warrior, defender, vindicator, protector, victor. *Renegade*
v.a., Uphold, defend, vindicate, protect.
Oppose

Chance, *v.n.*, Occur, happen, betide, befall. *v.a.*, Risk.

n., Hap, fortuity, fortune, casualty, accident, luck. ***Design***
Opening, opportunity, occasion.
Risk, hazard, chance, gamble, jeopardy, peril.
Uncertainty, possibility, contingency. ***Certainty***

Change, *v.a.*, Alter, vary, modify, transmute, remove, replace, transform, convert, shift. ***Conserve***
Exchange, substitute, commute, barter. ***Retain***

v.n., Alter, veer, vary, modify, shift, turn, alternate, fluctuate. ***Endure***

n., Alteration, modification, variation, turning, revolution, mutation, transition, transformation, transmutation. ***Conservation***
Variety, alternation, innovation, novelty, vicissitude.

Changeable, Wavering, variable, mutable, capricious, vacillating, irregular, inconstant, unsteady, fickle, unsettled, fluctuating, irresolute, uncertain, unstable, unsteadfast, fitful, giddy, mercurial, volatile. ***Steadfast***

Changeless, Steadfast, constant, unchanging, regular, settled, immutable, consistent, resolute, reliable, abiding, permanent, fixed, unvarying, invariable, unalterable. ***Changeable***

Channel, *n.*, Canal, passage, duct, conduit, strait, chamfer, gutter, fluting furrow, way, avenue.
v.a., Chamfer, flute, groove.

Chant, *v.n.*, Sing, intone, carol, warble.
n., Song, intonation, carol.

Chaos, Disorder, confusion, anarchy. ***Order***

Chaotic, Disordered, confused, confounded, intermingled. ***Ordered***

Chap, *v.a.*, *& v.n.*, Open, crack, split, cleave.
n., Opening, crack, split, cleft.
Boy, fellow, youth.

Chapfallen, Crestfallen, despondent, dejected, depressed, downcast, sad, discouraged, dispirited, disheartened, downhearted. ***Happy***

Chaplet, Wreath, garland, bouquet, coronal.

Chaps, Mouth, jaws.

Char, *v.a.*, Scorch, burn, carbonize.
n., Charwoman, cleaner.

Character, Symbol, letter, figure, type, emblem, sign.
Nature, disposition, temperament, quality, turn, cast, constitution, bent.

Character, Reputation, repute. ***Disrepute***
Person, individual.

Characteristic, *a.*, Distinctive, specific, special, peculiar. ***General***
n., Distinction, peculiarity, singularity, speciality, individuality. ***Generality***

Characterize, Mark, describe, distinguish, designate, specialize, individualize. ***Hint***

Charge, *v.a.*, Command, direct, enjoin, admonish, require, order, bid. ***Beg***
Entrust, commit, load, lade, burden, freight.
Accuse, impeach, impute, arraign, indict, inculpate, tax, criminate. ***Clear***
Attack, assail, assault. ***Retreat***
n., Command, direction,† mandate, instruction, exhortation.
Trust, commission, load, lading,† cargo, custody, care, ward, duty, office.
Accusation, imputation, indictment, crimination.
Attack, assault, onslaught, onset.
Price, cost, outlay, expenditure.

Chargeable, Traceable, imputable, attributable, referable.

Charger, Plate, dish.
Horse, mount, warhorse.

Charily, Warily, carefully, cautiously, circumspectly, heedfully, sparingly, reluctantly, slowly. ***Eagerly***

Charitable, Kind, benign, benevolent, beneficent, benignant, generous, liberal, philanthropic, bountiful. ***Selfish***
Lenient, forgiving, considerate, compassionate, mild, placable. ***Harsh***

Charity, Love, kindness, benignity, benevolence,† humanity, goodness, goodwill. ***Selfishness***

Charlatan, Quack, mountebank, cheat, empiric, impostor, pretender.

Charm, *v.a.*, Enchant, fascinate, captivate, bewitch, win, allure, please, catch, mesmerize, delight, entrance, enravish, transport, enamour, enrapture. ***Repulse***
n., Enchantment, fascination, witchery,† spell, magic, sorcery. ***Repulsion***
Trinket, amulet, talisman.

Charming, Enchanting, fascinating, captivating.† ***Repulsive***

Charter, *n.*, Prerogative, right, privilege.
v.a., Incorporate.
Hire.

Chary, Wary, careful, cautious, prudent, circumspect, heedful, sparing, reluctant, slow, shy. ***Rash***

Chase, *v.a.*, Hunt, pursue, follow, prosecute, track. ***Abandon***
n., Hunt, hunting, pursuit, race.

Chasm, Cavity, hollow, opening, rift, cleft, gap, fissure, aperture, hiatus.

Chaste, Pure, modest, simple, undefiled, uncontaminated, continent, incorrupt, virtuous. *Corrupt*

Chasten, Correct, discipline, chastise, improve, punish, castigate, humble. *Pamper*

Chastening, Correction, discipline.†

Chastise, Correct, discipline, punish, castigate, flog, whip, lash, beat, chasten, humble, restrain, repress. *Caress*

Chastisement, Correction, discipline.†

Chastity, Virtue, purity, modesty, simplicity, continence, decency, cleanness. *Corruption*

Chat, v.n., Babble, gossip, prattle, chatter, prate, confabulate.
n., Babbling, gossip, prattle, conversation, talk.

Chattels, Goods, belongings, property, effects, furniture, movables. *Freehold*

Chatter, v.n., Prattle, prate, chat, gossip, babble, tattle, palaver, jabber.
n., Prattle, prate, chat,† balderdash.

Chatterer, Prattler, prater, tattler, babbler, gossip.†

Cheap, Inexpensive, common, uncostly. *Dear*
Mean, paltry, vile, poor, worthless, indifferent, inferior. *Noble*

Cheapen, Depreciate, belittle, reduce. *Appreciate*

Cheat, v.a., Beguile, hoodwink, deceive, dupe, defraud, hoax, befool, fool, trick, gull, bamboozle, delude, cajole, swindle, ensnare, jockey, *cozen, chouse.* *Guide*
v.n., Prevaricate, dissemble, inveigle, juggle, deceive, shuffle, *cozen.*
n., Deception, hoax, fraud, wile, trick, imposture, snare, swindle, artifice, lie, fiction, illusion, delusion, stratagem, pitfall, *chouse.*
Deceiver, fraud, impostor, trickster, swindler, liar, cheater, shuffler, rogue, dissembler, sharper, knave, charlatan, pretender, mountebank, *chouser.*

Check, v.a., Curb, restrain, hinder, stop, stay, obstruct, repress, control, bridle, impede. *Accelerate*
Chide, rebuke, reprove, reprimand, censure, blame. *Encourage*
n., Curb, restraint, hindrance,† bar, barrier.
Chiding, rebuke, reproof.† *Encouragement*
Register, counter, mark, tally, sign, symbol.

Checkmate, Corner, frustrate, beat, defeat, vanquish, conquer.

Cheek, Impertinence, insolence.

Cheer, v.a., Applaud, praise, clap. *Decry*
Encourage, gladden, enliven, animate, exhilarate, inspirit, console, comfort, solace. *Depress*
n., Cheerfulness, gladness, gladsomeness, happiness, gleefulness, liveliness, joy, mirth, gaiety, solace, merriment, contentedness, joyfulness, buoyancy, mirthfulness, blithesomeness, hope. *Dejection*
Comfort, entertainment, hospitality, plenty, food, provision, repast, conviviality.
Acclamation, applause.

Cheerful, Glad, gladsome, happy, gleeful, lively, joyful, mirthful, gay, merry, content, contented, buoyant, blithesome, hopeful, bright, animated, sprightly, jolly, cheery, jocund. *Dull*

Cheerfulness, Cheer, gladness, gladsomeness, happiness.† *Dejection*

Cheerless, Lifeless, dull, gloomy, dispiriting, depressing, joyless, sullen, unhappy, dreary, dark, desolate, forlorn, sombre, melancholy, doleful, mournful, dismal, spiritless, despondent, rueful, discouraged, disconsolate, depressed, dejected. *Cheerful*

Cheery, Gay, cheerful, blithe, merry, sprightly, lively, hearty, joyous, buoyant, cheering, enlivening, animating. *Disheartening*

Chequer, Variegate, diversify.

Chemise, Slip, smock, shift, wall.

Cherish, Foster, promote, nurse, nurture, nourish, support, sustain, entertain, value, encourage, harbour, treasure. *Abandon*

Cherub, Angel, power, child.

Cherup, Chirrup, chirp.

Chest, Coffer, coffin, box, trunk, case. Breast, thorax, trunk.

Chevalier, Cavalier, knight, horseman, equestrian.

Chew, Munch, masticate, bite, champ, gnaw.

Chicanery, Chicane, artifice, quibble, trickery, sophistry, duplicity, shift, prevarication, underhandedness, subterfuge, deception, intrigue, stratagems, wiles. *Candour*

Chide, Rebuke, scold, rate, trounce, check, objurgate, censure, blame, reprove, reprimand, upbraid, admonish. *Applaud*

Chief, n., Leader, captain, commander, chieftain, head, ruler, principal. *Minion*
a., Principal, cardinal, capital, main, supreme, leading, first, paramount, grand, prime, especial, essential, vital. *Minor*

Chiefly, Principally, mainly, especially, mostly.†

Chieftain, Leader, captain, commander, head, ruler, principal, chief.

Chiffonier, Cabinet, cupboard, sideboard.

Child, Babe, baby, infant, nursling, suckling, progeny, issue, offspring. *Man*

Childbirth, Travail, labour, delivery, parturition.

Childhood, Babyhood, infancy, nonage, minority. *Manhood*

Childish, Infantile, infantine, puerile, tender, young, silly, weak, imbecile, foolish, trivial, paltry, trifling. *Manly*

Chill, *a.*, Chilly, cold, bleak, frigid. *Warm*

v.a., Freeze, dampen, depress, dishearten, discourage. *Encourage*

Chilled, Frozen, cold, shivering, refrigerated. *Heated*

Chime, *v.n.*, Accord, harmonize.

n., Consonance, harmony. *Discord*

Chimera, Dream, hallucination, fantasy, illusion, delusion, phantom, fancy, crotchet. *Reality*

Chimerical, Illusory, fanciful, fantastic, imaginary, visionary, wild, shadowy, Utopian. *Real*

Chine, Spine, backbone.

Ravine, cleft.

Chink, *n.*, Crevice, cleft, opening, crack, cranny, rift, gap, fissure.

v.a., & n., Jingle, ring, clink.

Chip, *n.*, Scrap, fragment, flake, portion, piece.

v.a., Cut, hew.

Chirography, Handwriting, penmanship, hand, fist.

Chiromancy, Palmistry.

Chirrup, Chirp, cherup.

Chisel, Carve, cut, sculpture, engrave.

Chit, Memo, memorandum, note, voucher, slip, recommendation.

Shoot, sprout, baby, child.

Chivalrous, Courageous, gallant, knightly, generous, heroic, valiant, brave, adventurous, bold, warlike, spirited, highminded. *Recreant*

Chivalry, Courage, gallantry, knighthood, valour, bravery, boldness.

Chock, Wedge, choke, block, stop.

Choice, *a.*, Exquisite, select, dainty, precious, cherished, valuable, rare, unusual, uncommon, excellent, superior. *Cheap*

n., Option, election, selection, adoption, preference, alternative. *Refusal*

Choke, Throttle, burke, suffocate, gag, stifle, strangle, smother, overcome, overpower, suppress.

Choler, Bile.

Anger, ire, wrath, spleen, fury, resentment, rage, indignation, animosity. *Mildness*

Choleric, Testy, hasty, hot, passionate, fiery, irritable, impetuous, irascible, angry, petulant, touchy, waspish. *Cool*

Choose, Select, elect, adopt, prefer, cull, pick. *Reject*

Chop, *v.a.*, Cut, mince.

v.n., Change, veer, vary, alter, shift. *Endure*

Chord, Harmony, consonance.

String.

Chorus, Concord, concert, harmony, unity. *Discord*

Chouse, *v.a.*, Cozen, cheat, hoodwink, beguile, deceive, dupe, defraud, hoax, befool, fool, trick, gull, bamboozle, delude, cajole, swindle, ensnare, jockey, outwit, mislead, circumvent, entrap, gammon, inveigle. *Guide*

n., Trick, deception, fraud, imposition, blind, wile, imposture, snare, swindle, artifice, lie, fiction, hoax, illusion, delusion, stratagem, pitfall.

Tool, gull, dupe, simpleton.

Christen, Baptize, name, entitle, dub, designate, term, style, call.

Chronic, Inveterate, virulent.

Chronicle, *n.*, Journal, history, register, diary, record, annals, narrative, narration, account, recital.

v.a., Register, relate, tell, record, narrate.

Chronometer, Watch, timepiece, clock.

Chubby, Plump, buxom. *Lean*

Chuck, *v.a.*, Throw, cast, hurl, push, thrust, toss.

n., Throw, thrust, toss, push.

Chuckle, *v.n.*, Cackle, grin, crow, titter, giggle, laugh, exult, triumph.

n., Chuckling, laughter, laugh, giggle, titter.

Chump, Log, chunk.

Chunk, Chump, piece, log, cut.

Church, Temple, chapel, kirk, meetinghouse, denomination.

Churchyard, Cemetery, graveyard, necropolis, burial-ground.

Churl, Boor, lout, clown, rustic, peasant, bumpkin, clodhopper, countryman. *Gentleman*

Niggard, miser, scrimp.

Churlish, Rude, impolite, harsh, snarling, snappish, waspish, rough, uncivil, surly, brutish, brusque, sullen, morose, crabbed. *Polite*

Illiberal, unsociable, miserly, niggardly, inhospitable, unneighbourly, mean, close, stingy. *Generous*

Churlishness, Rudeness, impoliteness, harshness,† tartness, acrimony, asperity, acerbity. *Politeness*
Illiberality, unsociability, miserliness.† *Generosity*

Churn, Upset, agitate, jostle, foam.

Cicatrice⎱ Scar, seam.
Cicatrix⎰

Cicerone, Guide, conductor.

Cicisbeo, Admirer, suitor, beau, gallant, lover.

Ci-devant, Former, late, quondam.

Cimmerian, Dark, black. *Light*

Cincture, Cestus, belt, girdle, band.

Cinders, Embers, ashes, dross, slag.

Cinereous, Ashy, ashen, cineritious.

Cipher, Nothing, zero, nought, dot.
Nonentity, nobody.
Character, symbol, monogram, device.

Circean, Magical, magic, enchanting.

Circle, Circumference, round, hoop, loop, ring, periphery, orb, sphere, globe.
Coterie, fraternity, clique, society, company, set. *Exclusion*
Region, neighbourhood, circuit, province, sphere, field, compass, tract, enclosure, bounds, range.

Circuit, Region, neighbourhood, province,† circle, space, boundary.
Revolution, tour, course, journey, perambulation, round.

Circuitous, Roundabout, devious, indirect, tortuous, winding, turning. *Direct*

Circular, Round, annular, spherical, globular, discoid. *Square*

Circulate, *v.a.*, Diffuse, publish, propagate, spread, disseminate, promulgate. *Hush*
v.n., Travel, spread, move. *Stagnate*

Circulation, Diffusion, propagation, spread, spreading, publication, dissemination, promulgation.

Circumambient, Surrounding, circling, encircling, encompassing, ambient, circumjacent.

Circumference, Periphery, circuit, enclosure, girth, outline, boundary. *Diameter*

Circumjacent, Surrounding, circling, encircling, enclosing, enfolding, bordering, encompassing, ambient, circumambient.

Circumlocution, Verbosity, periphrasis, periphrase, inconciseness, ambiguousness, ambiguity. *Terseness*

Circumlocutory, Verbose, periphrastic,† diffuse, indirect, involved, ambiguous, roundabout. *Terse*

Circumscribe, Surround, encircle, enclose, bound, confine, limit, restrict, fence, define, designate, delineate. *Distend*

Circumspect, Cautious, careful, vigilant, wary, watchful, scrupulous, heedful, observant, prudent, discreet, judicious, thoughtful, considerate, attentive. *Rash*

Circumspection, Caution, care, carefulness.† *Rashness*

Circumstance, Incident, event, fact, occurrence, happening, detail, feature, point, topic, condition, particular.

Circumstances, Position, condition, situation, environment, surroundings.

Circumstantial, Inferential, indirect, presumptive, constructive, minute, specific, detailed, elaborate, particular. *Positive*

Circumvent, Check, checkmate, thwart, outwit, ensnare, entrap, deceive, cheat, defraud, beguile, mislead, dupe, trick, overreach, delude, bamboozle, gull, hoodwink, inveigle, *chouse, cozen*. *Guide*

Circumvention, Deception, deceit, cheating, fraud, imposture, wiles, chicanery, trickery. *Honesty*

Cirrus, Tendril, filament.

Cistern, Tank, reservoir.

Citadel, Fortress, keep, castle, stronghold, bulwark.

Citation, Quotation, quoting, excerpt, extract, mention, enumeration.
Summons, call. *Rejection*

Cite, Quote, extract, mention, enumerate, adduce.
Summon, call. *Reject*

Citizen, Townsman, burgher, burgess, resident, dweller, inhabitant, subject. *Alien*

Civic, Municipal, political, corporate, civil. *Rural*

Civil, Civic, municipal, political, domestic.
Courteous, civilized, complaisant, polite, urbane, suave, affable, refined, respectful, obliging, accommodating, gracious, easy. *Churlish*

Civility, Courtesy, politeness, urbanity.†

Civilization, Refinement, cultivation, humanization, culture. *Barbarism*

Civilize, Refine, cultivate, humanize, educate, improve, enlighten, polish.

Clack, *v.n.*, Clink, click.
Prattle, prate, chatter, clatter, gossip, babble, gabble, jabber.
n., Clink, click.
Prattle, prate,† palaver.

Claim, *v.a.*, Demand, require, ask, insist, challenge, usurp, appropriate, assume, arrogate. *Waive*
n., Demand, requisition, call, assertion, right, privilege, pretension, title.

Claimant, Appellant, litigant, assertor.

Clamber, Climb, scramble.

Clammy, Damp, glutinous, slimy, sticky, wet, viscous, dauby, adhesive, smeary, viscid, gummy. *Dry*

Clamour, *v.n.*, Shout, vociferate, cry.

n., Shout, shouting, vociferation, outcry, uproar, fuss, noise, hubbub, blare, excitement. *Quiet*

Clamorous, Vociferous, uproarious, noisy, blatant, obstreperous, boisterous.

Clan, Family, tribe, race, coterie, group, set, clique, gang, fraternity, band, company, brotherhood.

Clandestine, Furtive, surreptitious, sly, secret, hidden, clancular, concealed, stealthy, private; underhand. *Open*

Clang, *v.n.*, Clash, clank.

n., Clank, clash, clashing, clangour.

Clangour, Clang, clank, clash, clashing.

Clank, *v.n.*, Clash, clang.

n., Clangour, clash, clang, clashing, clatter, rattle.

Clap, *v.a.*, Applaud, cheer.

Slam, thrust, force, slap, pat.

n., Slam, slap, knock, blow, peal, burst, explosion.

Clarification, Purification, straining, clearing. *Pollution*

Clarify, Purify, strain, clear, defecate, precipitate, infiltrate. *Pollute*

Clash, *n.*, Collision, clashing, clank, clang, clangour, crash, rattle, clatter.

Interference, jar, jarring, contradiction, disagreement, clashing, opposition. *Harmony*

v.n., Collide, clash, clank.†

Interfere, disagree, jar, differ, contend. *Agree*

Clashing, Collision, clash, clanking.†

Interference, jar, jarring, contradiction, disagreement, opposition, clash, hostility. *Harmony*

Clasp, *v.a.*, Connect, fasten, unite, bracket. *Detach*

Grasp, embrace, fold, hug, grip, grapple, clutch, concatenate. *Relax*

n., Hasp, catch, hook, buckle.

Embrace, clutch, grip, hug.

Class, *v.a.*, Rank, range, arrange, order, group, dispose, distribute, classify. *Derange*

n., Collection, set, group, division, category, head.

Order, rank, degree, grade, kind, sort.

Classic-al, First-rate, masterly, standard, model, pure, elegant, refined, polished, chaste. *Uncouth*

Greek, Grecian, Latin, Roman, Augustan.

Classification, Arrangement, grouping, distribution, division, assortment. *Isolation*

Classify, Arrange, group, distribute, divide, assort, class, tabulate, collocate, rank, range, dispose. *Muddle*

Clatter, *n.*, Clattering, rattling, rattle, clutter, clangour, clang, clash, clashing.

v.n., Clash, rattle, clang, clank, crash.

Clause, Provision, proviso, article, stipulation, condition.

Portion, part, passage, section, paragraph.

Clavate-d, Claviform, club-shaped.

Clavis, Guide, clue, key, explanation.

Claw, Tear, scratch, lacerate.

Clean, *v.a.*, Cleanse, clear, purify, clarify. *Pollute*

a., Spotless, unspotted, unsullied, unsoiled, neat, immaculate. *Dirty*

Pure, purified, unmixed, unadulterated. *Impure*

Complete, perfect, entire, whole, unblemished, faultless. *Imperfect*

Delicate, graceful, neat, adroit, shapely, light, dexterous. *Untidy*

adv., Completely, perfectly, entirely, wholly, fully, altogether, thoroughly.

Cleanse, Clean, clear, purify, clarify. *Pollute*

Cleansing, *n.*, Purification, purifying. *Pollution*

a., Purifying, redemptive, regenerating, regenerative, cathartic, purgative, abstergent. *Contaminating*

Clear, *v.a.*, Liberate, free, disenthral, loose, emancipate. *Enslave*

Absolve, vindicate, acquit, discharge, exonerate, justify. *Charge*

Purify, cleanse, refine, clarify. *Pollute*

Disencumber, disentangle, disengage, extricate, disembarrass, loosen. *Encumber*

Clean, scour, sweep.

a., Transparent, serene, cloudless, unclouded, crystalline, bright, pellucid, light, sunny, luminous, undimmed, unobscured. *Thick*

Plain, obvious, visible, apparent, lucid, perspicuous, intelligible, distinct, evident, patent, unquestionable, indubitable, manifest, indisputable, palpable, unmistakable, conspicuous, unequivocal, undeniable. *Dubious*

Open, free, unobstructed, unencumbered, unhindered, unimpeded, unhampered. *Encumbered*

Prompt, quick, sharp, acute, discerning, perspicacious. *Slow*

Musical, euphonious, silvery, mellifluous, liquid, sonorous. *Discordant*

Clear, Guiltless, innocent, pure, spotless, unspotted, unblemished, unsullied, clean, undefiled, sinless, irreproachable, stainless, immaculate.   *Contaminated*
v.a., Balance, settle.

Clearance, Acquittal, discharge, exoneration, release.

Cleave, *v.n.,* Adhere, cling, stick, cohere, hold.   *Leave*
v.a., & n., Separate, divide, sever, part, sunder, crack, split, open, rend.   *Unite*

Cleft, Rift, fissure, hole, gap, opening, crevice, chasm, fracture, chink, interstice, break, crack, cranny, breach.

Clemency, Mercy, lenience, lenity, compassion, tenderness, mildness, gentleness, kindness, forgivingness.   *Harshness*

Clement, Merciful, lenient, compassionate.†   *Harsh*

Clergyman, Parson, minister, priest, pastor, divine, ecclesiastic, churchman.   *Layman*

Clerk, Secretary, scribe, registrar, recorder.

Clever, Able, talented, ready, adroit, quick, sharp, dexterous, ingenious, apt, expert, skilful, smart, capable, handy, gifted.   *Stupid*

Cleverness, Ability, talent, readiness.†   *Stupidity*

Click, *v.n.,* Clack, clink, tick, beat, vibrate.
n., Clack, clink, tick, beat.

Client, Dependant, retainer, henchman.   *Master*

Clientele, Clientage, clientelage.

Cliff, Crag, headland, precipice.

Climate, Weather, clime, temperature, region, country.

Climax, Culmination, consummation, height, acme, top, zenith, head.

Climb, Ascend, mount, clamber, scramble, scale, surmount, creep, swarm.   *Drop*

Clime, Climate, region, country, place.

Clinch, *v.a.,* Secure, fasten, grip, grapple, clash, grasp, clutch.   *Relax*
n., Grip, grasp, clutch, catch.

Clinched, Riveted, fastened, gripped.

Cling, Cleave, hold, stick, attach, adhere, clasp, embrace, hug, hang.   *Surrender*

Clink, Ring, chime, jingle, chink, tinkle, rhyme.

Clip, Trim, cut, prune, pare, shear, curtail, abridge, contract,   *Elongate*
Rap, knock, whack, thump, blow.

Clique, Clan, gang, set, coterie, fraternity, brotherhood, party, cabal, junto.

Cloak, *v.a.,* Hide, conceal, disguise, mask, cover, veil, screen.   *Expose*

Cloak, *n.,* Cover, screen, mask, veil, pretext, blind.
Mantle, coat.

Clock, Chronometer, timepiece, timekeeper.
Embroidery, broidery.

Clod, Sod, turf, earth, lump, ground.

Clodhopper, Churl, bumpkin, rustic, boor, clown, dolt, dunce, hind, peasant, yokel, countryman.   *Townsman*

Clodpoll, Dunce, fool, simpleton, blockhead, clodpate.

Clog, *v.a.,* Obstruct, hinder, choke, encumber, trammel, impede, restrain, burden, load, embarrass, hamper, cumber, shackle, fetter.   *Free*
n., Obstruction, hindrance, encumbrance.†
Shoe, sabot.

Cloister, Colonnade, arcade, piazza.
Monastery, priory, abbey, convent, nunnery.

Cloistral, Monastic, solitary, recluse, secluded, sequestered.   *Sociable*

Close, *v.a.,* Shut, stop, obstruct, clog, choke, seal.   *Open*
Finish, end, terminate, cease, conclude, complete.   *Begin*
v.n., Finish, end, terminate, cease.
Agree, coalesce, unite, grapple.   *Part*
a., Hidden, private, secret, reticent, reserved, secretive, taciturn, closed, incommunicative, tight, confined, secluded, retired, withdrawn.   *Open*
Mean, near, stingy, niggardly, miserly, illiberal, ungenerous, parsimonious, churlish.   *Generous*
Near, adjacent, adjoining, neighbouring.   *Distant*
Assiduous, intent, ardent, intense, fixed, earnest, hard.
Nice, exact, accurate, strict, faithful, true, precise.   *Vague*
Stagnant, motionless, oppressive, uncomfortable, stuffy, stifling, confined, dense, thick, solid, compressed, firm.   *Fresh*
Dear, near, intimate, devoted, attached.   *Distant*
n., End, conclusion, termination, cessation.   *Beginning*
Precinct, enclosure, grounds, yard, court.

Closet, Room, chamber, cabinet.

Clot, *n.,* Concretion, crassament, coagulation.
v.n., Concrete, coagulate, curdle, thicken, curd.

Clothe, Attire, robe, dress, array, apparel, drape, cover, invest, swathe, enwrap.   *Strip*

Clothes, Attire, robes, dress, array, apparel, vestments, vesture, raiment, garments, clothing, costume, habiliments, habits, garb.

Cloud, v.a., Dim, bedim, darken, overcast, begloom, becloud, obscure, overspread, shadow. **Clear**
n., Haze, vapour, mist, fog.
Darkness, eclipse, gloom, obscurity, blur.
Mass, horde, army, throng, host, assemblage, multitude.

Cloudy, Dim, dark, overcast, gloomy, obscure, murky, muddy, lurid, lowering, lustreless, confused. **Clear**

Clown, Lout, boor, bumpkin, peasant, rustic, yokel, clodhopper, countryman, churl, hind. **Gentleman**
Fool, dunce, harlequin, buffoon, jester, dolt.

Clownish, Loutish, boorish, rustic, churlish, rude, rough, coarse, ungainly, clumsy, awkward. **Apt**

Cloy, Surfeit, sate, satiate, glut, pall.

Club, v.n., Co-operate, unite, combine, join, amalgamate.
Beat, cudgel, bludgeon.
n., Society, coterie, association, set, company, brotherhood, fraternity, league.
Cudgel, bat, truncheon, bludgeon, hickory.

Clue, Guide, hint, indication, key, solution.

Clump, Bunch, collection, group, cluster, muster, assemblage, gathering.

Clumsy, Bungling, awkward, maladroit, inexpert, unskilful, unapt, blundering, unhandy, unwieldy, lumbering, ponderous, heavy. **Dexterous**

Cluster, Clump, bunch, collection, group, muster, assemblage, gathering.

Clutch, n., Clasp, clinch, grasp, seizure, grip, gripe.
v.a., Clasp, clinch, grasp, seize, grip, gripe, snatch, catch, grapple. **Release**

Clutches, Power, hands, paws, claws, talons.

Clutter, Clatter, clattering, racket, bustle.
Litter, mess, disorder, disarray, confusion.

Coadjutor, Helper, aider, abettor, accessory, assistant, colleague, co-partner, co-operator, collaborator, ally, partner, auxiliary, accomplice, confederate, associate. **Opponent**

Coagulate, Clot, concrete, thicken, curdle. **Dissipate**
Mix, blend, fuse, condense, amalgamate.

Coalesce, Combine, fraternize, unite, blend, harmonize, mix, amalgamate.
Part

Coalition, Combination, fraternity, union, amalgamation, alliance, league, federation, confederation, confederacy, compact. **Disruption**

Coarse, Impure, rough, crude, unpurified.
Refined
Rude, vulgar, common, churlish, rough, lewd, brutish, gross, indecent, vile, broad, inelegant, impolite, indelicate, unpolished. **Polished**

Coast, Seaside, shore, strand, beach.

Coat, v.a., Cover, lay, spread.
n., Cover, covering, coating, layer, garment.

Coating, Layer, covering.

Coax, Cajole, flatter, wheedle, fawn, allure, seduce, overcome, persuade.
Coerce

Cobble, Mend, tinker, patch, botch, clout.

Cobweb, Web, snare, entanglement, toils, meshes.
Trappings, traditions, custom.

Cock, Male bird, chanticleer, rooster.
Hen
Tap, valve, faucet, spout.
Rick, shock, pile.
Yawl, boat.

Cockatrice, Basilisk.

Cockle, Wrinkle, corrugate, pucker.

Cockney, Londoner.

Coddle, Humour, indulge, pamper, pander, pet, nurse, fondle, caress.
Harden

Code, Laws, digest.

Codger, Miser, scrimp, niggard, skinflint.

Codicil, Supplement, postscript.

Codify, Systematize, digest, summarize, condense, reduce. **Rescind**

Coerce, Force, constrain, impel, compel, inhibit, drive, restrain, repress, curb, check. **Coax**

Coercion, Force, constraint, compulsion.†

Coercive, Forcing, constraining, compelling, compulsory.†

Coetaneous, Coeval, synchronous, simultaneous, contemporary, coexistent.

Coeval, Coetaneous, coexistent, synchronous, simultaneous, contemporary.

Coexistent, Coeval, coetaneous, synchronous.†

Coffer, Chest, trunk, case, box, casket, cask.

Coffin, Sarcophagus, casket, chest, cist.

Cogency, Conclusiveness, force.
Weakness

Cogent, Conclusive, powerful, potent.
Weak
Urgent, irresistible, persuasive, forcible, convincing, effective.

Cogitate, Think, ruminate, reflect, muse,

meditate, ponder, speculate, contemplate, brood, deliberate, consider, weigh.

Cogitation, Thought, rumination, reflection.†

Cognate, Related, connected, allied, akin, kin, kindred, like, similar, alike, analogous, affiliated. *Apart*

Cognition, Cognizance, k n o w l e d g e, notice, knowing, observation, experience, recognition. *Ignorance*

Cognizance, Cognition, knowledge, notice.†

Cognizant, Aware, informed.

Cognize, Know, recognize, notice, observe.

Cognomen, Surname, title, name, denomination, nickname, sobriquet.

Cohere, Cleave, adhere, stick, join, unite, coalesce. *Part*

Coherence, Cohesion, adhesion, adherence, union, coalition, connection, unity, harmony, agreement, congruity, consistency. *Disunity*

Coherent, Adherent, united, connected, congruous, consistent, logical, compact. *Loose*

Cohesion, Coherence, adhesion, adherence, union, coalition, connection.† *Disintegration*

Cohort, Battalion, legion, squadron, line, band, company.

Cohibit, Inhibit, prevent, restrain, hinder. *Help*

Coil, Spiral, convolution, curl, loop, wind. Entanglements, perplexities, bustle, care, turmoil, clamour, tumult, uproar, confusion. *Tranquillity*

Coin, *v.a.*, Fabricate, devise, make, invent, counterfeit, create, mould, form, stamp.

n., Money, cash, specie.

Corner, quoin, wedge, plug, key, prop.

Coincide, Correspond, harmonize, tally, square, agree, concur. *Clash*

Coincidence, Correspondence, harmony, agreement, concurrence. *Difference* Chance, fortuity, accident. *Design*

Coincident, Corresponding, agreeing, concurring, tallying, squaring. *Differing* Conterminous, overlaying, identical.

Cold, Cool, cooled, frigid, gelid, arctic, icy, frosty, polar, boreal, chilly, biting, cutting, wintry, raw, bleak, nipping. *Hot* Unfeeling, spiritless, apathetic, dead, dull, passionless, stoical, indifferent, unsympathetic, sluggish, torpid, unconcerned, distant, phlegmatic, unresponsive, unimpressible, unsusceptible, lukewarm. *Fiery*

Collapse, *v.n.,* Subside, fall, faint, break down. *Recover*

n., Subsidence, fall, falling, breakdown, downfall, failure, faint, coma, exhaustion, sinking, prostration. *Recovery*

Collar, Ruff, gorget, belt, band, ring, fillet.

Collate, Compose, collect, gather, adduce. *Disperse*

Collateral, Parallel, indirect, related, subordinate.

Collation, Comparison, collection, adduction.

Colleague, Helper, partner, friend, companion, co-partner, aider, co-operator, auxiliary, coadjutor, assistant, associate, abettor, collaborator, ally. *Opponent*

Collect, Gather, collate, muster, assemble, amass, heap, accumulate, glean, aggregate, pile. *Scatter*

Collection, Gathering, collation, muster,† crowd, cluster, group, hoard, store. *Distribution* Offertory, alms, contribution.

College, School, seminary, academy, university. Community, association, body, guild, society, corporation.

Collide, Crash, encounter, interfere, oppose, clash.

Colligate, Bind, fasten, combine, unite.

Colliquate, Melt, dissolve, drain.

Collision, Crash, encounter, interference, opposition, conflict, clash, concussion.

Collocate, Locate, arrange, place, allocate, order, tabulate, dispose, classify. *Dislocate*

Collocation, Location, arrangement, placing.† *Dislocation*

Colloquial, Conversational. *Grammatical*

Colloquy, Discourse, talk, conversation, dialogue.

Colluctation, Competition, wrestling, contention, strife. *Agreement*

Collude, Connive, conspire.

Collusion, Connivance, conspiracy, confederacy, accompliceship. *Defeat*

Collusive, Dishonest, fraudulent, deceptive, deceitful. *Honest*

Colour, *n.,* Tinge, tint, hue, dye, shade, paint, complexion. Disguise, guise, appearance, semblance, pretence, pretext, plea, excuse, varnish. *Genuineness*

v.a., Tinge, tint, paint, stain, dye. Disguise, varnish, garble, pervert, distort.

v.n., Blush, flush, redden. *Blanch*

Colourless, Achromatic, hueless, livid,

uncoloured, untinged, untinted, blanched, pale, pallid. **Vivid**
Monotonous, dull, blank, characterless, expressionless.

Colours, Banner, ensign, standard, flag.

Colossal, Enormous, immense, huge, vast, gigantic, prodigious, tremendous, monstrous, herculean. **Insignificant**

Colt, Foal, filly, youth, junior.

Coltish, Spirited, frisky, sportive, gay, rampant, frolicsome, playful. **Lethargic**

Column, Pillar, cylinder, file, row, line.

Coma, Stupor, lethargy, torpor. **Liveliness**
Cluster, tuft, bunch, clump.

Comatose, Sleepy, lethargic, stupefied, drowsy, heavy. **Wakeful**

Comb, v.a., Disentangle, dress.
v.n., Curl.

Combat, v.a., Withstand, oppose, battle, fight, resist. **Submit**
v.n., War, contend, struggle, fight, contest. **Agree**
n., War, conflict, struggle, fight, strife, contention, battle, contest, action, brush, engagement, affair, fray, skirmish, encounter. **Peace**

Combatant, Fighter, contestant, champion. **Neutral**

Combination, Association, union, connection, combine, conjunction, consortment, co-operation, confederacy, league, cabal, coalition, alliance, conspiracy, amalgamation, compound, mixture, synthesis. **Disruption**

Combine, n., Combination, association, union.†
v.a., Compound, amalgamate, unite, mix, incorporate, blend. **Separate**
v.n., Amalgamate, coalesce, unite, mix, mingle, blend.

Combustible, Inflammable, consumable.

Combustion, Consuming, burning.

Come, Reach, attain, approach, arrive, advance. **Depart**
Issue, originate, proceed, ensue, result, arise, flow, follow.
Befall, betide, occur, happen.

Comedian, Player, performer, actor.

Comeliness, Seemliness, grace, gracefulness, elegance, symmetry, beauty, propriety, suitableness, fitness. **Unseemliness**

Comely, Seemly, graceful, elegant,† becoming, shapely, decorous, decent, handsome, pretty. **Unseemly**

Comfort, v.a., Console, relieve, gladden, cheer, enliven, inspirit, solace, revive, animate, encourage, strengthen, invigorate, refresh. **Trouble**

Comfort, n., Consolation, relief, solace, encouragement, succour, help, aid, assistance, support.
Satisfaction, peace, enjoyment, ease.

Comfortable, Gratifying, grateful, pleasant, pleasing, pleasurable, acceptable, agreeable, welcome. **Aggravating**
Snug, satisfied, happy, cosy. **Troubled**

Comforter, Consoler, solacer.†
Scarf, muffler, coverlet, quilt, muff.
Dummy, coral.

Comfortless, Desolate, forlorn, cheerless, wretched, miserable, drear, dreary, bleak, disconsolate. **Cheerful**

Comic-al, Funny, amusing, laughable, ludicrous, absurd, droll, humorous, farcical, diverting. **Sad**

Coming, a., Future, nearing, imminent, approaching, ensuing. **Past**
n., Arrival, advent, approach. **Departure**

Comity, Urbanity, affability, blandness, pleasantness, politeness, suavity, amenity, civility, courtesy. **Roughness**

Command, v.a., Govern, rule, order, enjoin, bid, direct, charge, require, instruct.
Demand, compel, claim, exact, challenge. **Entreat**
n., Direction, order, charge, injunction, instruction, bidding, behest, commandment, requisition, requirement, hest, mandate.
Government, authority, control, sway, power, dominion, supremacy.

Commandeer, Seize, take, annex. **Surrender**

Commander, Captain, chief, chieftain, leader, head, ruler.
Beetle, mallet, instrument.

Commandment, Command, direction, order, charge, instruction, injunction, bidding, behest, precept, requisition, requirement, hest, mandate.

Commemorate, Solemnize, perpetuate, celebrate, keep. **Ignore**

Commemoration, Solemnization, perpetuation.†

Commemorative, Memorial.

Commence, v.n., Begin, start, originate, open. **End**
v.a., Begin, start, inaugurate, initiate, open, originate, institute. **Terminate**

Commencement, Beginning, start, opening, outset, origin, inauguration, institution. **Termination**

Commend, Laud, praise, extol, applaud, eulogize, encourage, approve, recommend. **Censure**
Intrust, commit, give, yield.

Commendable, Laudable, praiseworthy. *Blamable*

Commendation, Approval, approbation, praise, eulogy, panegyric, encomium.

Commensurate, Commeasurable, co-extensive, equal, conterminous. *Unequal* Proportioned, proportionate, adequate, sufficient, appropriate, due, corresponding. *Undue*

Comment, *v.n.,* Remark, note, annotate, observe, illustrate, propound, interpret, explain, criticise, dilate.

n., Remark, note, annotation,† commentary, exposition.

Commentary, Comment, remark, note, annotation, observation, interpretation, explanation, criticism.

Commentator, Commenter, expounder, critic, annotator, explainer, interpreter, elucidator.

Commentitious, Fictitious, invented, fabricated, supposititious.

Commerce, Trade, business, merchandise, exchange, barter, traffic, dealing.
Communication, communion, intercourse, converse.

Commercial, Trading, mercantile, business.

Commination, Denunciation, threat, menace, threatening.

Commingle, Mingle, intermingle, mix, commix, intermix, blend, amalgamate, join, unite, combine. *Separate*

Comminute, Grind, pulverize, break, powder, levigate, triturate, bruise.

Comminution, Grinding, pulverization.†

Commiserate, Pity, condole, compassionate, sympathize.
Condemn, despise. *Envy*

Commiseration, Pity, condolence, compassion, sympathy.

Commission, *v.a.,* Authorize, empower, depute, delegate.
Order, bespeak.
n., Errand, duty, task, care, office, job, employment, charge, trust, warrant.
Perpetration.
Delegation, committee.
Allowance, rebate, compensation, fee.

Commissioner, Delegate, deputy, agent.

Commissure, Juncture, conjunction, joint, seam, closure.

Commit, Do, perform, perpetrate, enact, execute.
Intrust, deposit, consign, resign, commend, confide.
Compromise, endanger, implicate, pledge, engage.
Imprison.

Commitment, Intrusting, depositing, delivery, consignment.
Implication, pledge, engagement.
Imprisonment, committal.

Committal, Intrusting, depositing, delivery, consignment.
Implication, pledge, engagement.
Imprisonment, commitment.
Performance, perpetration.

Commix, Mingle, commingle, intermingle, mix, unite, blend, coalesce, amalgamate, compound, combine. *Separate*

Commixture, Mingling, commingling, intermingling.†

Commodious, Spacious, ample, easy, convenient, roomy, comfortable, fit, suitable, proper, advantageous, useful. *Narrow*

Commodities, Goods, wares, produce, merchandise.

Common, Universal, general, public. *Private*
Ordinary, familiar, frequent, everyday, customary, habitual, usual, stale, trite, hackneyed, commonplace. *Rare*
Vulgar, low, inferior, undistinguished, rude, lewd. *Refined*

Commonplace, Stale, trite, common, hackneyed, threadbare, obvious. *Deep*

Commons, Food, fare, provisions.

Commonwealth, Republic, nation, state, people.

Commotion, Turmoil, tumult, agitation, excitement, disturbance, perturbation, bustle, violence, disorder, turbulence, *pother*. *Calm*

Commune, Communicate, converse, speak, talk, correspond.

Communicant, Participator, sharer, partaker.

Communicate, *v.n.,* Commune, converse, speak, talk, correspond.
Lead.
v.a., Confer, bestow, impart, give, grant, vouchsafe.
Declare, announce, reveal, divulge, disclose.
Touch, join, adjoin.

Communicative, Open, unreserved, sociable, affable, chatty, free. *Reserved*

Communion, Converse. intercourse, fellowship, participation.
Sacrament, Eucharist.

Community, Society, association, state, brotherhood, college, people, public, body.
Sameness, similarity, likeness.

Commute, Change, alter, replace.
Exchange, barter.

Compact, *a.,* Close, dense, solid, firm, snug, compressed. ***Ductile***
Short, terse, concise, brief, pithy, laconic, succinct. ***Extended***
n., Contract, agreement, bargain, treaty, pact, arrangement, convention, covenant.
v.a., Condense, compress, consolidate, join, bind, unite. ***Diffuse***

Companion, Partner, comrade, fellow, associate, consort, mate, compeer, sharer, participant, participator, partaker. ***Foe***

Companionship, Fellowship, association, company, friendship, society. ***Loneliness***

Company, Companionship, association, friendship, fellowship, society.
Assembly, assemblage, collection, group, association, body, set, congregation, meeting, troop, gathering, gang, circle, concourse, corporation, firm, house, partnership.
Guests, visitors, party.

Comparable, Like, similar, approximate, resembling. ***Incomparable***

Comparative, Relative. ***Absolute***

Compare, *n.,* Comparison, similitude.
v.a., Collate, liken, assimilate. ***Contrast***

Comparison, Compare, collation, similitude, illustration. ***Contrast***

Compartment, Partition, division, allotment, space, part, section.

Compass, *n.,* Circumference, range, scope, bound, boundary, limit, reach, stretch, circuit, extent.
Area, enclosure.
v.a., Encompass, surround, enclose, encircle, circumscribe, environ, embrace, engird, beset, besiege, beleaguer, block, blockade, invest.
Consummate, attain, achieve, effect, realize, procure, accomplish, obtain, perform. ***Fail***

Compassable, Attainable, procurable, obtainable.

Compasses, Dividers.

Compassion, Commiseration, pardon, mercy, tenderness, sympathy, clemency, pity, kindness, kindliness. ***Harshness***

Compassionate, *a.,* Pitying, merciful, tender.† ***Harsh***
v.a., Commiserate, pity, sympathize.

Compatible, Congruous, consistent, consonant, reconcilable, accordant.
Antagonistic

Compatriot, Countryman, fellow-countryman. ***Alien***

Compeer, Peer, equal, mate, companion, fellow, comrade, associate. ***Superior***

Compel, Force, coerce, drive, restrain, make, oblige, necessitate, bow, bend, subdue, subject. ***Coax***

Compend, Synopsis, abridgment, abbreviation, curtailment, condensation, compression, summary, compendium, abstract, syllabus, digest, epitome.
Amplification

Compendious, Abridged, abbreviated, curtailed,† short, brief, concise, comprehensive, compact, succinct. ***Diffuse***

Compendium, Synopsis, abridgment, abbreviation, curtailment, condensation, compression, summary, abstract, syllabus, digest, epitome. ***Amplification***

Compensate, *v.n.,* Atone, amend.
v.a., Recompense, reward, reimburse, requite, indemnify, satisfy, remunerate, counterbalance. ***Injure***

Compensation, Recompense, reward,† atonement, reparation, amends. ***Injury***

Compete, Contest, contend, struggle, strive, emulate, rival. ***Combine***

Competence, Capableness, ability, power, capacity, fitness, suitableness, qualification. ***Weakness***
Sufficiency, enough, wealth, adequacy, adequateness. ***Poverty***

Competent, Capable, able, powerful,† endowed. ***Weak***
Sufficient, wealthy.† ***Poor***

Competition, Contention, contest, emulation, rivalry. ***Combination***

Competitive, Competing, contending, rival.

Competitor, Rival, opponent, adversary, antagonist, candidate, aspirant, emulator. ***Partner***

Compilation, Compiling, selecting, selection, combining, combination, composition.

Compile, Select, combine, arrange, compose, prepare.

Complacence, Pleasure, satisfaction, content, contentment, gratification.
Complaisance, affability, politeness, civility, courtesy, manners.
Churlishness

Complacent, Pleased, satisfied.†
Complaisant, affable, polite.† ***Churlish***

Complain, Lament, repine, grumble, murmur, bewail, groan. ***Rejoice***

Complainant, Accuser, petitioner, plaintiff. ***Defendant***

Complaint, Lamentation, repining, grumbling.†
Disease, illness, malady, sickness, disorder, indisposition, distemper. ***Health***

Complaisance, Complacence, affability, politeness, civility, courtesy, manners, urbanity, graciousness, suavity, compliance, obligingness. ***Churlishness***

Complaisant, Complacent, affable, polite.† *Churlish*

Complement, Quota, crew, tale, total, totality, completeness, fulfilment.

Complete, *a.*, Completed, finished, ended, perfect, fulfilled, concluded, consummated, consummate, entire, whole, total, undivided, unimpaired. *Unfinished*
v.a., Finish, end, perfect, fulfil, conclude, consummate, effect, execute, terminate, perform, achieve, attain, realize.

Completion, Finishing, ending, perfection, fulfilment.

Complex, Manifold, mingled, mixed, composite, compounded, confused, involved, intricate, complicated. *Simple*

Complexion, Colour, hue, look, appearance, aspect.

Complexity, Complication, entanglement, intricacy. *Simplicity*

Compliance, Yielding, submission, docility, obedience, acquiescence, concession, consent, assent, concurrence, agreement. *Refusal*

Compliant, Yielding, submissive,† docile. *Obstinate*

Complicate, Entangle, involve, confuse. *Simplify*

Complicated, Complex, manifold, involved, confused, intricate, entangled, mixed, mingled, composite, compounded. *Simple*

Complication, Complexity, tangle, entanglement, confusion, intricacy, mixture, complexus.

Complicity, Sharing, partnership, participation.

Compliment, *v.a.*, Praise, flatter, laud, commend, congratulate, extol. *Insult*
n., Praise, flattery,† encomium.

Complimentary, Flattering, laudatory, commendatory, encomiastic. *Insulting*

Comply, Yield, submit, obey, acquiesce, concede, consent, assent, agree, conform, perform, do, execute, meet, complete, observe, fulfil, satisfy, discharge. *Refuse*

Component, *a.*, Constituent, constituting, composing.
n., Element, ingredient, rudiment, part, integral, content, constituent, particle.

Comport, Agree, tally, harmonize, accord, square, correspond, match, suit, coincide. *Differ*
Behave, demean, conduct, carry, act.

Compose, Form, make, contrive, frame, invent, write, indite, build, create, constitute, compound.
Pacify, soothe, calm, appease, tranquillize, assuage, still, quiet. *Aggravate*

Compose, Adjust, arrange, dispose, organize, settle, regulate. *Disorganize*

Composed, Calm, appeased, tranquil, still, quiet, cool, sedate, collected, unmoved, imperturbable, placid, undisturbed, unruffled. *Excited*

Composite, Complex, mixed, compounded.

Composition, Making, formation, framing, invention, constitution, writing. Compound, mixture.

Compost, Manure, dung, ordure, fertilizer.

Composure, Calmness, quiet, tranquillity, placidity, sedateness, equanimity, coolness. *Riot*

Compotation, Revelling, revelry, revel, debauch, bacchanal, carouse, carousal, carousing, conviviality, jollification.

Compound, *v.a.*, Mix, intermingle, intermix, blend, combine, unite, mingle, amalgamate, fuse. *Separate*
n., Mixture, admixture, combination, medley, miscellany, composition.
v.n., Compromise, agree, arrange.
a., Complex, compounded, composite, complicate, intricate.

Comprehend, Understand, apprehend, grasp, see, perceive, conceive, discern.
Include, comprise, embrace, enclose, contain, involve. *Exclude*

Comprehension, Understanding, apprehension,† conception, intellect, intelligence, reason, mind. *Misunderstanding*
Inclusion, scope, sphere, range, compass, sweep, field, limits.

Comprehensive, Wide, full, sweeping, extensive, large, capacious, broad, exhaustive, deep. *Narrow*

Compress, Condense, press, contract, compact, pinch, squeeze, close, shut, summarize, shorten, epitomize, abridge. *Expand*

Compression, Condensation, pressure, contraction.† *Expansion*

Comprise, Include, enclose, comprehend, embody, embrace, contain. *Exclude*

Compromise, *v.n.*, Agree, compound, concede. *Differ*
v.a., Commit, engage, pledge, implicate. Imperil, jeopardize, endanger.
Compound, compose, settle, adjust.
n., Settlement, agreement, adjustment, concession.

Compulsion, Force, constraint, coercion. *Inducement*

Compulsory, Obligatory, binding, enforced, unavoidable, imperative, necessary. *Voluntary*

Compunction, Misgiving, remorse, regret, repentance, sorrow, qualm, contrition, reluctance, penitence.
Satisfaction

Compunctious, Remorseful, sorrowful, sorry, contrite, repentant, penitent.

Computation, Reckoning, estimate, account, valuation, calculation.

Compute, Reckon, estimate, count, value, calculate, number, rate, measure.
Guess

Comrade, Associate, mate, compeer, fellow, companion, confederate, ally, chum, pal. *Enemy*

Con, Study, learn, read, consider, pore over.

Concamerated, Arched, vaulted, concave.

Concatenate, Join, connect, unite, link, string. *Sever*

Concatenation, Connection, linking, stringing, continuity, chain, sequence, succession, series.

Concave, Hollow, hollowed, scooped, excavated, concamerated, depressed.
Convex

Conceal, Disguise, hide, cover, secrete, screen, dissemble, suppress, cloak.
Reveal

Concealment, Disguise, hiding, cover,† privacy, shelter, retreat, ambush.
Revelation

Concede, Yield, grant, allow, admit, surrender, deliver, compromise, resign.
Deny

Conceit, Vanity, egotism, conceitedness, opinionatedness. *Modesty*
Notion, idea, thought, fancy, belief, image, imagination, impression, estimate, estimation, opinion, judgment, quip, whim, illusion, vagary. *Substance*

Conceited, Vain, egotistical, opinionated, opinionative. *Modest*

Conceivable, Possible, thinkable, imaginable, picturable, rational, probable.
Inconceivable

Conceive, Imagine, think, picture, comprehend, fathom, apprehend, suppose, fancy, understand.
Plan, purpose, contrive, devise, design.
Misconceive
Bear, be pregnant.

Concentrate, Centralize, converge, draw, muster, assemble, congregate, convene, conglomerate, localize, condense.
Disperse

Concentration, Centralization, convergence, mustering,† application.
Dispersal

Concept, Conception, idea, notion, impression, thought, conceit, fancy.

Conception, Concept, idea, notion.†
Imagination, apprehension, comprehension, supposition. *Misapprehension*

Concern, *v.a.*, Interest, touch, affect, regard.
Disturb, trouble, disquiet.
n., Affair, business, matter, transaction.
Firm, business, establishment, house.
Anxiety, regard, interest, regret, sorrow, sympathy, care, solicitude. *Indifference*
Consequence, weight, interest, importance, moment.

Concerning, About, touching, regarding, anent, of, respecting. *Disregarding*

Concert, *n.*, Agreement, co-operation, union, unison, combination, association, concord, harmony. *Opposition*
Entertainment.
v.a., Plan, plot, contrive, devise, design, concoct, manage. *Oppose*

Concession, Yielding, grant, allowance, boon, admission, surrender, resignation.
Denial

Conciliate, Win, gain, enlist, pacify, propitiate, reconcile, appease. *Estrange*

Conciliation, Pacification, peace, propitiation, reconciliation, reconcilement.
Estrangement

Conciliatory, Reconciling, pacific, pacifying, pacificatory, persuasive, winning.
Irritating

Concise, Compact, terse, pointed, short, summary, pithy, brief, compressed, condensed, laconic, sententious, compendious, succinct, neat. *Diffuse*

Conclave, Council, assembly, meeting, synod, cabinet.

Conclude, *v.a.*, Close, end, terminate, finish, complete. *Begin*
Infer, judge, deduce, determine, decide, settle, arrange, bar, hinder, restrain, argue, gather.
v.n., Resolve, decide, determine, end, close, terminate, syllogize, settle.

Conclusion, Close, end, termination, finish, completion, upshot, result, event, issue. *Beginning*
Inference, deduction, decision.†

Conclusive, Final, ultimate, positive, indisputable, definite, decisive, clinching, irrefutable, unanswerable, convincing.
Inconclusive

Concoct, Contrive, plot, plan, devise, brew, hatch, prepare, compound, make, mix, invent, design, frame, project. *Mar*

Concomitant, Attendant, concurrent, accompanying, attending, synchronous.
Independent

Concord, Harmony, concert, accord, agreement, accordance, amity, unanimity, peace, unity, union, friendship. *Discord*

Concordance, Concord, harmony, accord.†

Index, vocabulary, glossary, catalogue.

Concordat, Covenant, agreement, compact, bargain, treaty, stipulation, convention.

Concourse, Assembly, assemblage, meeting, crowd, mob, throng, multitude, gathering, collection, cluster.

Concrete, *n.*, Cement, mixture, admixture.

a., Solid, solidified, consolidated, firm. Particularized, individualized, real. *Abstract*

Concubine, Mistress, paramour.

Concupiscence, Passion, lasciviousness, lust, desire, craving, lechery, pruriency. *Temperance*

Concur, Agree, harmonize, coincide, combine, co-operate, help. *Part*

Concurrence, Agreement, harmony, union, alliance, combination, co-operation. *Disagreement*

Concurrent, Agreeing, harmonizing. Concomitant, attendant, synchronous, associated.

Concuss, Compel, force, oblige, coerce, constrain.

Concussion, Collision, crash, clash, shock, shaking, agitation.

Condemn, Doom, sentence, convict. *Acquit*

Censure, blame, disapprove, reprove, upbraid, proscribe, reprobate. *Praise*

Condemnation, Dooming, doom, sentence, conviction, penalty, judgment. *Acquittal*

Censure, blame, disapproval. *Praise*

Condemnatory, Disapproving, reproachful, censuring, damnatory, blaming, deprecatory. *Praiseworthy*

Condensation, Contraction, compression, reduction, abridgment, curtailment, abbreviation, concentration, diminution, epitome, summary. *Amplification*

Condense, Contract, compress, reduce,† compact, consolidate, shorten. *Amplify*

Condescend, Descend, stoop, deign vouchsafe, grant.

Condescension, Stooping, affability, favour, grace, graciousness. *Haughtiness*

Condign, Deserved, adequate, merited, suitable. *Unmerited*

Condiment, Sauce, seasoning, relish, appetizer, flavour.

Condition, Stipulation, arrangement, term, proviso, provision, consideration, qualification.

State, case, plight, situation, circumstances.

Estate, rank.

Conditional, Relative, provisional, hypothetical.

Condole, Console, sympathize, commiserate.

Condolence, Sympathy, commiseration.

Condonation, Pardon, indulgence, amnesty, forgiveness. *Punishment*

Condone, Pardon, indulge, overlook, forgive. *Punish*

Conduce, Lead, tend, aid, subserve, contribute, promote, help, advance, forward. *Defeat*

Conducive, Conducing, leading, tending.† *Preventative*

Conduct, *n.*, Behaviour, bearing, manners, mien, demeanour, deportment, carriage, actions. *Misconduct*

Leadership, management, guidance, control, administration, direction.

Guard, escort, convoy.

v.a., Lead, manage, guide, administer, direct, bring, escort, convoy, superintend, operate, govern, command, control, carry, transmit, propagate. *Mislead*

Conductor, Guide, leader, manager, director.

Propagator, transmitter.

Conduit, Canal, passage, pipe, duct, tube, alveus, channel.

Confabulate, Chatter, prate, gossip, chat, prattle.

Confectionery, Sweetmeats, confections, comfits.

Confederacy, League, confederation, federation, coalition, union, alliance. *Secession*

Confederate, *a.*, Allied, leagued, federated, confederated, united. *Opposed*

n., Ally, associate, abettor, aider, helper, accomplice, accessory, second, coadjutor. *Opponent*

v.a., & n., Combine, ally, unite, league. *Separate*

Confederation, Confederacy, league, federation, coalition, union, alliance.

Confer, *v.a.*, Bestow, grant, give, vouchsafe, present. *Withhold*

v.n., Converse, talk, parley, consult, deliberate, collate, discourse.

Conference, Conversation, parley, consultation, meeting.

Confess, Own, acknowledge, aver, avow, admit, grant, recognize, concede. *Deny*

Confess, Attest, prove, show, manifest, exhibit, shrive. *Disprove*

Confession, Acknowledgment, averment, avowal, admission, recognition. *Denial*

Confide, Trust, hope, rely, depend, believe. *Mistrust*

Confidence, Trust, faith, belief, assurance, reliance, dependence. *Doubt*
Courage, boldness, firmness, assurance, intrepidity. *Timidity*
Intimacy, secrecy.

Confident, Trustful, hopeful, assured, sure, positive, certain. *Doubtful*
Courageous, bold, firm, assured, intrepid. *Afraid*

Confidential, Private, intimate, secret. *Public*
Trustworthy, reliable.

Configuration, Figure, form, shape, outline, formation.

Confine, *n.,* Frontier, march, limit, border, edge, boundary.
v.a., Bound, limit, circumscribe, restrict, restrain, immune, imprison, incarcerate. *Extend*

Confinement, Restraint, imprisonment, incarceration, durance, duress, captivity. *Liberation*
Childbirth, delivery, parturition.

Confirm, Ratify, assure, fix, establish, strengthen. *Annul*
Corroborate, substantiate, verify, avouch, endorse, countersign. *Refute*

Confirmation, Ratification, establishment, proof, verification, substantiation.†

Confiscate, Seize, distrain, sequester, dispossesses. *Restore*

Conflagration, Fire, flare, ignition, combustion, burning.

Conflict, *v.n.,* Interfere, clash, disagree.
n., Interference, clash, disagreement, struggle, contest, battle, encounter, combat, fight, opposition, discord. *Agreement*

Confluence, Concourse, conflux, meeting, union, convergence, assembly, assemblage, congregation, collection, crowd, throng, multitude, host.

Confluent, Meeting, converging, mingling, commingling, blending.

Conflux, Confluence, concourse, meeting, union, convergence, assembly, assemblage, congregation, collection, crowd, throng, multitude, host.

Conform, Comply, agree, assent, consent. *Dissent*
Comport, tally, suit, harmonize, unite, adapt.

Conformity, Compliance, agreement, assent, consent, obedience, submission, yielding. *Dissension*
Congruity, harmony, likeness, resemblance, similitude, correspondence.

Confound, Confuse, mystify, astound, perplex, astonish, bewilder, flurry, amaze, stupefy, stun, dumbfound, dumbfounder, surprise, startle, disturb. *Compose*
Abash, mortify, embarrass, trouble, shame, disconcert, discompose. *Rally*
Ruin, upset, overthrow, demolish, destroy, annihilate, overwhelm.

Confounded, Miserable, shameful, horrid, odious, detestable, cursed, abominable, excessive, hateful, damnable.
Confused, mystified, astounded.† *Orderly*

Confront, Oppose, resist, face, threaten, menace, challenge, intimidate.

Confuse, Confound, mingle, intermingle, blend, mix, disorder.
Derange. *Arrange*
Mystify, astound, perplex, bewilder, flurry, disturb. *Clarify*
Abash, mortify, embarrass, trouble, shame, disconcert, discompose. *Rally*

Confusion, Confusedness, chaos, anarchy, disorder, disarray, derangement, disarrangement, jumble, stir, ferment, agitation, perplexity, astonishment, distraction, bewilderment, embarrassment, turmoil, commotion, tumult, mess. *Order*
Abashment, mortification, embarrassment, shame, disconcertion.
Ruin, overthrow, demolition, destruction, annihilation, defeat. *Rally*

Confute, Refute, disprove, overthrow, overcome. *Prove*

Congeal, Freeze, benumb, congealate. *Thaw*

Congenial, Natural, suitable, concordant, consonant, suited, proper, adapted, fit, favourable, agreeable, genial. *Abhorrent*
Similar, sympathetic, kindred, alike. *Antagonistic*

Congenital, Inherent, innate, coeval, coetaneous, incarnate, ingrained, inborn, natural, connate. *Extraneous*

Congestion, Accumulation, cluster, crowd, agglomeration, conglomeration, aggregate, aggregation, congeries. *Clearance*

Conglomeration, Congestion, accumulation, cluster.†

Congratulate, Compliment, felicitate.

Congregate, Convene, gather, muster, meet, collect, assemble, throng. *Disperse*

Congregation, Gathering, muster, meeting, collection, assembly, throng.

Congress, Assembly, meeting, council, conference, convention, Parliament, legislature.

Congruity, Agreement, conformity, fitness, suitableness, suitability, consistency, harmony.   ***Discord***

Congruous, Agreeing, fit, suitable, consistent, consonant, harmonious, coherent, accordant, compatible, seemly, appropriate.   ***Discordant***

Conjecture, *v.a.*, Guess, divine, suppose, fancy, suspect.   ***Deduce***
n., Guess, divination, supposition, surmise, hypothesis.   ***Deduction***

Conjoin, Join, connect, string, link, combine, fasten, unite, associate.   ***Sever***

Conjoint, Joined, connected, strung.†

Conjointly, Together, jointly.†

Conjugal, Connubial, matrimonial, married, nuptial, bridal, hymeneal.

Conjunction, Connection, link.
Combination, union, association, embodiment.

Conjuncture, Juncture, emergency, contingency, exigency, crisis, point, occasion·

Conjuration, Adjuration, conjuring, spell, enchantment, sorcery, magic.

Conjure, *v.a.*, Adjure, beseech, implore, pray, importune, crave, beg, entreat, supplicate.   ***Command***
Charm, fascinate, bewitch, enchant, captivate, win.   ***Repel***
v.n., Juggle.

Conjuror, Magician, wizard, juggler, sorcerer, charmer, necromancer.

Connate, Inherent, congenital, coeval, coetaneous, innate, inborn, incarnate, ingrained, natural.   ***Extraneous***

Connect, Join, conjoin, string, link, combine, communicate, concatenate, unite, associate, couple.   ***Sever***

Connected, Joined, strung.
     Disconnected
Communicating.
Akin, allied, related.

Connection ⎱ Junction, union, association,
Connexion ⎰ alliance.
Communication, commerce, intercourse.
Kindred, relative, relation, kinsman.

Connivance, Forbearance, consent, blindness, blinking, abettal, approval, participation.   ***Opposition***

Connive, Overlook, permit, pass, wink, blink.   ***Oppose***

Connoisseur, Critic, expert, judge, virtuoso.

Connotation, Implication, meaning, intention, force, comprehension.

Connubial, Conjugal, matrimonial, married, nuptial, bridal, hymeneal.   ***Celibate***

Conquer, Defeat, vanquish, overcome, beat, overpower, overthrow, subdue, master, subjugate, rout, reduce, crush, discomfort, humble, humiliate, checkmate, surmount.   ***Surrender***

Conqueror, Victor, winner, vanquisher, subduer, subjugator.   ***Victim***

Conquest, Victory, triumph, subjugation, overthrow, defeat, rout, reduction, mastery, discomfiture, humiliation. ***Failure***

Consanguinity, Kindred, relationship, blood, lineage.

Conscience, Sense, principle, integrity, intuition.

Conscientious, Honest, principled, just, fair, good, upright, scrupulous, straight, straightforward, strict, exact, uncorrupt, incorruptible, honourable, faithful, careful.   ***Reprobate***

Conscious, Aware, awake, sensible, cognizant, apprized.   ***Ignorant***
Thinking, intelligent, intellectual, knowing, rational, reflecting, sensible, sentient, percipient.   ***Irrational***

Consecrate, Dedicate, sanctify, hallow, devote, enshrine, ordain.   ***Desecrate***

Consecutive, Continuous, successive, coherent, arranged, orderly.   ***Chaotic***

Consensus, Agreement, unison, concord, unanimity, consent.   ***Dissension***

Consent, *v.n.*, Concur, agree, assent, acquiesce, submit, comply, yield, accede.   ***Refuse***
n., Concurrence, agreement, assent.†
     Refusal
Accord, concord, consensus, harmony, agreement, coherence, unison.
     Dissension

Consequence, Issue, result, conclusion, effect, end, event.   ***Cause***
Weight, importance, moment, influence, standing, concern.

Consequent, Consequential, resulting, following.
Arrogant, pompous, proud, important, conceited.   ***Modest***

Conservation, Preservation, maintenance, perpetuation, protection, keeping.
     Abolition

Conservative, Moderate, preservative, Tory.   ***Liberal***

Conserve, Preserve, maintain, perpetuate, protect, keep, save.   ***Abolish***

Consider, *v.a.*, Care for, remember, regard, respect, consult.   ***Ignore***
v.a., & n., Reflect, ponder, meditate, study.
Contemplate, think, mark, weigh, judge, opine, deem, infer, cogitate, muse, examine, ruminate, heed, mind.

Considerable, Large, important, respectable. *Trifling*

Considerate, Thoughtful, kind, charitable, heedful, serious, sober, staid, mindful, careful, judicious, prudent, discreet. *Careless*

Consideration, Notice, contemplation, heed, attention, deliberation, meditation, regard.

Consequence, significance, import, importance, weight, moment. *Insignificance*

Motive, reason, ground, inducement, score, account, remuneration.

Consign, Send, deliver, ship, transmit, commit, entrust, intrust.

Consignee, Agent, factor, receiver.

Consignment, Delegation, custody, commission.

Sending, delivery, shipping, transmission.

Load, shipment.

Consignor, Sender, transmitter, shipper.

Consistent, Congruous, compatible, reconcilable, accordant, agreeing, conformable, corresponding, harmonious, logical. *Contradictory*

Consist, Constitute, compose, form, make, lie.

Consolation, Comfort, solace, encouragement, cheerfulness, relief. *Oppression*

Console, Solace, relieve, encourage, comfort, soothe, cheer, assuage. *Irritate*

Consolidate, Solidify, condense, compact, compress, conglutinate, weld, solder, harden, cement, unite, fuse. *Disintegrate*

Consonance⎫ Congruity, consistency, concord, accord, agreement,
Consonancy⎭ unison, harmony. *Discord*

Consonant, Congruous, consistent, accordant, according, harmonious, compatible, *Discordant*

Consort, *n.*, Companion, associate, fellow, comrade, compeer, partner. *Foe*
v.n., Associate, fraternize, herd.

Conspectus, Outline, synopsis, summary, compend, compendium, epitome, abstract, syllabus, digest. *Amplification*

Conspicuous, Manifest, obvious, visible, plain, eminent, pre-eminent, clear, outstanding, noticeable, discernible, perceptible, marked, noted, prominent, distinguished, celebrated, remarkable, apparent. *Microscopic*

Conspiracy, Intrigue, plot, cabal, combination, treason, treachery, machination.

Conspire, Intrigue, plot, combine, co-operate, machinate.

Constancy, Regularity, uniformity, permanence, stability, steadfastness, steadiness, unchangeableness, firmness, determination, inflexibility, decision, loyalty, faithfulness, fidelity, devotion. *Fickleness*

Constant, Regular, uniform, permanent.† *Fickle*
Incessant, unbroken, perpetual, continuous, sustained, uninterrupted. *Intermittent*

Constellation, Collection, group, cluster, assemblage, galaxy.

Consternation, Terror, horror, dismay, alarm, amazement, fright, astonishment. *Expectancy*

Constituent, *a.*, Component, constituting, composing, forming.
n., Component, ingredient, particle, element.
Voter, elector.

Constitute, Compose, make, form, establish, appoint, enact, fix, depute, empower, set up. *Dissolve*

Constitution, Organization, formation.
Temperament, temper, spirit, character, humour, quality, peculiarity.

Constitutional, Lawful, legitimate, legal. *Unlawful*
Inherent, inherited, innate, inborn, inbred, organic, natural, congenital, connate. *Extraneous*

Constrain, Coerce, force, make, compel, drive, oblige, impel, urge. *Coax*
Restrain, curb, confine. *Free*

Constraint, Coercion, force, compulsion.†
Restraint, confinement, imprisonment, durance, duress, incarceration, captivity. *Freedom*

Constrict, Squeeze, tighten, compress, contract, cramp. *Expand*

Construct, Make, build, frame, form, create, erect, raise, fabricate, organize, arrange, invent, compose, institute, originate. *Destroy*

Construction, Making, building, framing.† *Destruction*

Construe, Render, translate, do, interpret, explain, expound, resolve, parse, analyse.

Consult, *v.a.*, Ask, question, interrogate, convass.
v.n., Deliberate, confer.

Consultation, Conference, counsel, deliberation, council, parley, interview, colloquy.

Consume, *v.a.*, Devour, dissipate, spend, waste, use, assimilate, lavish, exhaust, destroy, squander, expend. *Save*
v.n., Perish, decay, vanish. *Remain*

Consummate, *v.a.*, Finish, perfect, complete, end, accomplish, achieve, effect, compass, execute, conclude. *Drop* *a.*, Finished, perfect, complete, excellent, superb, supreme, masterly. *Mediocre*

Consummation, Perfection, finishing, completion, close, termination, achievement, realization. *Frustration*

Consumption, Waste, dissipation, expenditure, use, extinction, destruction, decline, emaciation.

Contact, Touch, union, contiguity, junction, apposition, juxtaposition. *Isolation*

Contagion, Infection, contamination, corruption, pestilence.

Contagious, Infectious, catching, pestilential, poisonous, deadly.

Contain, Hold, include, embrace, comprise, comprehend, embody, enclose, restrain. *Exclude*

Contaminate, Corrupt, infect, sully, defile, taint, poison, pollute, tarnish, stain, soil. *Cleanse*

Contamination, Corruption, infection, defilement.†

Contemn, Scorn, spurn, despise, disdain, deride, slight, disregard, scout. *Respect*

Contemplate, Behold, observe, study, ponder, meditate, survey, resolve, reflect, consider. *Ignore* Intend, purpose, design, project. *Abandon*

Contemplation, Reflection, study, meditation, thought, pondering, deliberation, cogitation, speculation. Prospect, expectation, view.

Contemplative, Reflective, studious, thoughtful, meditative, musing. *Thoughtless*

Contemporary, Contemporaneous, coetaneous, coeval, coexistent.

Contempt, Scorn, disdain, derision, mockery. *Respect*

Contemptible, Despicable, paltry, vile, base, mean, low, abject, disreputable. *Honourable*

Contemptuous, Disdainful, haughty, scornful, insolent, supercilious. *Meek*

Contend, Compete, struggle, strive, cope, contest, combat, grapple, vie. *Surrender* Claim, maintain, assert, argue, hold, affirm. *Disclaim*

Content, *v.a.*, Satisfy, appease, mollify. *a.*, Contented, satisfied, willing. *Dissatisfied* *n.*, Contentment, satisfaction, ease. *Dissatisfaction*

Contented, Content, satisfied, willing. *Dissatisfied*

Contention, Strife, discord, struggle, dissension, dispute, wrangle, altercation, rupture, quarrel, squabble, bickering, controversy. *Agreement* Claim, assertion, argument, point.

Contentious, Captious, quarrelsome, perverse, petulant, cavilling, pugnacious, wayward. *Obliging*

Contentment, Content, satisfaction, ease. *Dissatisfaction*

Contents} Capacity, dimensions, volume, **Content }** filling, area, length, quantity. Topics, matters, subjects.

Conterminous, Adjacent, adjoining, abutting, commensurate, contiguous, meeting, touching.

Contest, *n.*, Contention, strife, discord, fight, struggle, combat, battle, conflict, dissension, dispute, wrangle, altercation, rupture, quarrel, squabble, bickering, controversy. *v.a. & n.*, Contend, strive, fight.†

Context, Treatment, composition, texture, matter.

Contexture, Structure, constitution, composition, framework.

Contiguity, Expanse, continuity, proximity, nearness, contact, meeting, juxtaposition.

Contiguous, Meeting, touching, conterminous, adjacent, adjoining, commensurate, abutting.

Continence, Restraint, chastity, moderation, temperance, self-control, abstinence, sobriety. *Licentiousness*

Continent, *a.*, Chaste, moderate, restrained, temperate, sober. *Licentious* *n.*, Mainland.

Contingency, Casualty, accident, incident, event, occurrence, chance, uncertainty.

Contingent, *a.*, Accidental, fortuitous, incidental, casual, uncertain, conditional, dependent. *n.*, Force, quota, contribution, division, proportion, share.

Continual, Incessant, constant, perpetual, eternal, endless, unceasing, everlasting, continuous, uninterrupted, persistent, unremitting, permanent, enduring. *Fitful*

Continually, Incessantly, constantly.† *Fitfully*

Continuance, Continuation, extension, perpetuation, persistence, perseverance, endurance, constancy, succession, sequence, prolongation. *Cessation*

Continuation, Continuance, extension.† *Interruption*

Continue, Persist, last, endure, remain, abide, tarry, stay, persevere, prolong, extend, perpetuate. *Cease*

Continuity, Connection, cohesion, contiguity, continuance.

Continuous, Unbroken, continued, connected, uninterrupted. *Broken*

Contort, Distort, deform, twist, writhe. *Straighten*

Contortion, Distortion, deformity, twist, convulsion.

Contour, Profile, outline, sketch.

Contraband, Illicit, illegal, unlawful, prohibited, banned. *Lawful*

Contract, *v.a.*, Reduce, shorten, condense, abridge, diminish, lessen, narrow, curtail, epitomize, retrench, abbreviate. *Expand*
v.n., Shrink, shrivel.
Stipulate, bargain, agree, covenant. *Cancel*
n., Agreement, bargain, covenant, bond, compact, stipulation, pact, treaty.

Contraction, Lessening, abbreviation, abridgment, diminution, reduction, shortening, shrinkage, shrivelling. *Expansion*
Summary, abstract, compend, compendium, epitome. *Amplification*

Contradict, Deny, contravene, dissent, oppose, negative, gainsay, refute, confute, disprove. *Confirm*

Contradiction, Contrariety, denial, opposition, gainsaying, antagonism, repugnance. *Harmony*
Inconsistency, incongruity.

Contradictory, Contrary, antagonistic, repugnant, inconsistent, opposite. *Affirmative*

Contrariety, Contradiction, opposition, antagonism, repugnance, clashing, contrast. *Harmony*

Contrary, Contradictory, opposing, opposite, antagonistic, adverse, counter, counteracting, conflicting, repugnant. *Favourable*

Contrast, *v.a. & v.n.*, Differ, show difference.
n., Difference, contrariety, opposition. *Similarity*

Contravene, Contradict, oppose, cross, annul, nullify, abrogate, defeat, traverse, obstruct, impede, counteract, hinder, thwart. *Help*

Contravention, Contradiction, opposition, obstruction.†

Contretemps, Accident, mistake, mischance, mishap.

Contribute, *v.a.*, Supply, furnish, give, bestow, assist, aid, grant, afford, subscribe. *Retain*
v.n., Conduce, add, minister, tend.

Contribution, Subscription, grant, offering, donation, gift. *Retention*

Contributory, Helpful, conducive, instrumental, accessory.

Contrite, Penitent, repentant, humble.

Contrition, Penitence, repentance, sorrow, remorse, compunction, regret. *Satisfaction*

Contrivance, Device, invention, machine, plan, scheme, artifice, plot, design.

Contrive, Devise, invent, plan, scheme, plot, project, design, concoct, brew, hatch, frame, consider. *Copy*
Manage, succeed. *Fail*

Control, *v.a.*, Manage, guide, direct, govern, sway, rule, regulate, command, superintend. *Free*
n., Management, direction, government,† mastery, dominion.

Controversial, Disputable, problematic, doubtful, uncertain, debatable. *Certain*

Controversy, Dispute, disputation, debate, altercation, argument, wrangle, bickering. *Agreement*

Controvert, Dispute, debate, argue, wrangle, bicker, contest, contend. *Agree*

Contumacy, Rebelliousness, stubbornness, intractableness, intractability, obstinacy, obduracy, perverseness, insolence, disobedience. *Docility*

Contumacious, Rebellious, stubborn.†

Contumelious, Insolent, insulting, rude, abusive, arrogant, calumnious, overbearing, disdainful, scornful, supercilious. *Respectful*

Contumely, Insolence, rudeness, abuse,† obloquy, opprobrium, reproach. *Respect*

Contuse, Bruise, squeeze, crush, knock. *Caress*

Contusion, Bruise, knock, blow.

Convalescence, Recovery, recuperation.

Convalescent, Recovering, improving, recuperating.

Convene, Congregate, meet, muster, assemble, gather, summon. *Disband*

Convenience, Fitness, suitableness, propriety.
Accommodation, ease, satisfaction, comfort. *Discomfort*

Convenient, Fit, suitable, proper, adopted, suited, appropriate. *Unsuitable*
Advantageous, useful, serviceable, comfortable, beneficial, helpful, favourable, handy. *Inconvenient*

Convention, Convocation, meeting, assembly, congress. *Recess*
Arrangement, agreement, compact, understanding, contract, stipulation.

Conventional, Usual, habitual, ordinary,

customary, standard, orthodox, regular, approved, common. **Unusual**

Converge, Tend, approach, incline. **Diverge**

Conversable, Communicative, affable, open, sociable.

Conversant, Familiar, learned, skilled, acquainted, versed, experienced, proficient. **Ignorant**

Conversation, Talk, chat, parley, converse, dialogue, conference.

Converse, v.n., Talk, chat, commune, confabulate, confer.

n., Conversation, talk, chat, parley, dialogue, conference.

Opposite, reverse.

Conversely, Reversely, reciprocally, contrary, contradictory, opposite. **Identical**

Conversion, Transformation, change, alteration, reversal, reformation, regeneration.

Convert, Transform, change, alter, interchange, transpose, turn.

Apply, appropriate.

Convex, Protuberant, gibbous, rounding. **Concave**

Convey, Carry, take, transfer, transport, remove, bear, bring, conduct, convoy, escort.

Conveyance, Conveying, carrying, transfer, convoyance, transference.†

Carriage, cab, vehicle.

Convict, v.a., Condemn, sentence, convince. **Acquit**

n., Felon, prisoner, criminal, culprit, malefactor.

Conviction, Sentence, condemnation. **Acquittal**

Persuasion, belief, principle, convincing. **Doubt**

Convince, Persuade, satisfy, prove. **Unsettle**

Convivial, Social, jovial, festive, gay, festal, jolly. **Mournful**

Convocation, Meeting, assembly, convention, congress, council.

Convoke, Convene, muster, parade, collect, gather, assemble, summon. **Disperse**

Convolution, Coil, fold, curl, twist, spiral, roll, bight.

Convoy, Escort, guard, attendant, attendance.

Convulse, Disturb, agitate, shake, perturb. **Compose**

Convulsion, Disturbance, agitation, commotion, tumult.

Spasm, cramp.

Cool, a., Cold, frigid. **Warm**

Composed, calm, collected, dispassionate,

unimpassioned, placid, quiet, unexcited, unruffled, undisturbed, unconcerned, lukewarm, indifferent. **Ardent**

Impudent, assured, shameless.

v.a., Refrigerate. **Warm**

Damp, dampen, quench, temper, attemper, assuage, allay, moderate, quiet, abate, calm. **Excite**

Coop, Confine, imprison, cage, incage. **Liberate**

Co-operate, Help, aid, assist, abet, conspire, combine. **Oppose**

Co-operator, Helper, aider, assistant, abettor, coadjutor, ally, auxiliary. **Opponent**

Co-ordinate, Equal, co-equal, equivalent, tantamount, coincident.

Co-partner, Partner, associate, colleague, confederate, companion, aider, abettor, accomplice, coadjutor, partaker, helper, assistant, ally, auxiliary, sharer. **Opponent**

Co-partnership, Partnership, association, fraternity. **Enmity**

Business, house, firm, company, concern, establishment.

Cope, Compete, contend, struggle, deal, vie, combat, encounter, engage. **Submit**

Copious, Plentiful, plenteous, abundant, rich, profuse, ample, exuberant, full, overflowing. **Scanty**

Copiousness, Plenty, abundance, richness.†

Copse, Coppice, grove, thicket.

Copulative, Uniting, connecting, coition, coupling.

Copy, v.a., Transcribe, portray, imitate, duplicate, reproduce, trace. **Originate**

n., Transcription, portrait, imitation, duplicate, facsimile, pattern, model.

Copyist, Copier, transcriber, imitator.

Coquet, Philander, flirt.

Coquetry, Philandering, flirtation.

Cord, Line, string, rope, braid.

Cordate, Heartshaped.

Cordial, Friendly, warm, affectionate, kind, hearty, sincere, heartfelt, earnest, ardent. **Distant**

Cordiality, Friendliness, warmth, affection.† **Coldness**

Core, Centre, heart, kernel.

Cormorant, Glutton, rapacious.

Corner, Bend, angle, crotch, knee, elbow, joint.

Retreat, recess, nook, cranny, cavity, hole, niche.

Confound, confuse, puzzle, perplex.

Corollary, Inference, deduction, conclusion, consequence.

Rider addendum.

Coronal, Garland, chaplet, wreath, crown, laurels.

Corporal, Bodily, fleshly, physical, corporeal.   *Spiritual*

Corporation, Company, association, council, mayoralty.

Corporeal, Corporal, material, fleshly, physical.   *Spiritual*

Corps, Body, company, band, troop, regiment, squadron, contingent.

Corpse, Body, carcass, corse, dust, remains, ashes.

Corpulence, Fatness, rotundity, stoutness, plumpness, obesity, fleshiness.   *Thinness*

Corpulent, Fat, rotund, stout,† portly.   *Thin*

Corpuscle, Particle, atom, monad, molecule, mite, jot, iota, ace, scintilla, grain, scrap.

Correct, *a.*, Accurate, true, faultless, right, exact, precise, proper.   *Wrong*
v.a., Amend, improve, redress, reform, rectify, reclaim, mend.   *Spoil*
Punish, chasten, discipline.   *Indulge*

Correction, Amendment, improvement.† Punishment, chastening, discipline.   *Indulgence*

Corrective, Reformatory, improving, correcting, alternative, modifying, amending.
Regulative, restorative.

Correctness, Accuracy, truth, faultlessness, exactness, precision, propriety, niceness.   *Faultiness*

Correlative, Corresponding, reciprocal, mutual, complementary, complemental.   *Independent*

Correlation, Correspondence, mutuality, interdependence, interrelation, apposition.   *Independence*

Correption, Reproof, chiding, blame, reproach.

Correspond, Accord, correlate, suit, agree, answer, match, tally, square, harmonize, fit, comport.   *Differ*
Communicate, write.

Correspondence, Correlation, interrelation, interdependence, agreement, fitness, match, harmony, concurrence, coincidence.   *Difference*
Communications, letters, despatches.

Corridor, Passage, gallery.

Corrigible, Docile, tractable, amenable.   *Stubborn*

Corroborate, Support, confirm, ratify, strengthen, establish, substantiate, sustain, fortify.   *Invalidate*

Corroboration, Confirmation, ratification.†   *Invalidation*

Corrode, Gnaw, wear, rust, canker, erode, eat, consume, crumble, waste.   *Repair*

Corrosion, Gnawing, wearing, erosion.†

Corrosive, Corroding, gnawing, wearing, erosive, wasting, consuming, crumbling.

Corrugate, Wrinkle, pucker, contract, rumple, crumple, ruffle, furrow, groove, crease.   *Smooth*

Corrupt, *a.*, Corrupted, putrid, contaminated, polluted, tainted, soiled, unsound, infected, defiled, debased.   *Pure*
Depraved, abandoned, wicked, vicious, immoral, profligate, dissolute, loose, reprobate, dishonest.   *Virtuous*
v.a., Putrefy, contaminate, pollute, taint, soil, infect, defile, debase, spoil, vitiate, deteriorate, impair.   *Purify*
Deprave, vitiate, demoralize, pervert, entice, bribe, sophisticate, deflower.   *Correct*

Corruption, Putrefaction, putrescence, contamination.†   *Purity*
Depravity, depravation, demoralization.†   *Amelioration*

Corsair, Buccaneer, pirate, rover.

Corse, Corpse, ashes, body, remains.

Corset, Stays, bodice.

Coruscate, Sparkle, flash, blaze, shine, glitter, scintillate, flame, glisten, gleam, twinkle.

Coruscation, Sparkle, flash, blaze.†

Corypheus, Chief, leader, director, guide.

Cosmopolitan, Universal, general.   *Local*

Cosmos, Universe, order.

Cosset, Caress, pet, fondle.

Cost, *v.n.*, Require, absorb, consume.   *Produce*
n., Price, charge, outlay, expenditure, payment, disbursement.
Loss, damage, detriment, suffering, pain.

Costly, Dear, expensive, sumptuous, valuable, rich, gorgeous, luxurious, splendid, rare, fine.   *Cheap*

Costume, Uniform, robes, livery, dress.

Cosy, Comfortable, easy, snug.   *Uncomfortable*

Coterie, Brotherhood, fraternity, set, gang, association, clique, club, band, company, circle, society.

Cottage, Lodge, hut, cot.

Couch, *v.n.*, Lie, recline, stoop, bend, crouch, squat.
v.a., Utter, express.
Cover, hide, conceal.
n., Bed, sofa, seat.

Couchant, Lying squatting.   *Rampant*

Council, Assembly, congress, diet, parliament, synod, ministry, cabinet, chamber, conclave.

Counsel, *n.*, Advice, caution, admonition, warning, instruction, deliberation, forethought, consultation, suggestion, opinion.
Advocate, barrister, lawyer.
v.a., Advise, caution, admonish.†

Count, *v.a.*, Number, enumerate, compute, reckon, estimate, sum up, calculate, cast.
Esteem, judge, hold, consider, regard, deem. *Misjudge*
n., Enumeration, computation.†

Countenance, *n.*, Look, aspect, mien, expression.
v.a., Help, aid, encourage, patronize, support. *Oppose*

Counter, Contrary, contrariwise, adverse, opposed, against. *Aid*

Counteract, Neutralize, oppose, foil, counterfoil, counterinfluence, baffle, hinder, frustrate, resist, contravene, check, defeat, thwart, traverse. *Abet*

Counteraction, Neutralization, opposition.†

Counterbalance, Balance, counterpoise, compensate, countervail.

Counterfeit, *v.a.*, Forge, feign, sham, simulate, impersonate, copy, imitate.
a., Forged, fraudulent, feigned, sham, spurious, simulated, false, mock, copied, imitated. *Genuine*
n., Forgery, copy, trick, artifice, fabrication. *Reality*

Countermand, Revoke, annul, repeal, rescind, abrogate, recall. *Order*

Counterpart, Correlate, correlative, match, copy, fellow, supplement, complement, twin, brother. *Contrast*

Counterpoise, Counterbalance, balance, compensate, countervail, equalize.

Countersign, Watchword, password.

Countervail, Counterpoise, counterbalance, balance, compensate, equalize.

Countless, Innumerable, unnumbered, myriad, incalculable. *Few*

Country, *n.*, Region, nation, band, people, fatherland, state.
a., Rural, rustic, landed, territorial. *Urban*
Rough, rude, uncouth, unpolished, unrefined, countrified, uncultivated. *Polished*

Countryman, Compatriot, yeoman.
Boor, churl, clown, lout, peasant, hind, rustic, yokel.

Couple, *v.a.*, Connect, unite, join, pair, conjoin, bracket, splice, brace. *Separate*
v.n., Pair, unite.
n., Pair, brace, twain.

Courage, Valour, boldness, audacity, bravery, intrepidity, fearlessness, gallantry, pluck, fortitude, heroism, daring, spirit, manhood, resolution, hardihood, mettle. *Timidity*

Courageous, Valiant, valorous, bold, audacious,† dauntless. *Timid*

Courier, Runner, messenger, express.

Course, *v.a.*, Hunt, pursue, chase.
n., Order, continuity, sequence, succession, regularity. *Disorder*
Route, track, path, round, beat, way, road, direction.
Progress, process.
Conduct, proceeding, behaviour, deportment.

Court, *n.*, Courtyard, quadrangle.
Tribunal.
Homage, solicitation, attention, respects, addresses, civilities.
v.a., Woo, solicit, invite, flatter, coddle. *Avoid*

Courteous, Gracious, polite, courtly, elegant, respectful, polished, ceremonious, affable, civil, obliging, complaisant, urbane, debonair. *Churlish*

Courtesan⎫ Harlot, prostitute, wanton,
Courtezan⎭ strumpet, whore.

Courtesy, Graciousness, politeness, courtliness.† *Churlishness*

Courtly, Courteous, gracious, polite, elegant, respectful, polished, ceremonious, affable, civil, obliging, complaisant, urbane, debonair. *Churlish*

Courtship, Wooing.

Courtyard, Area, quadrangle, court.

Cove, Bay, bight, inlet.

Covenant, Bargain, stipulation, agreement, compact, arrangement, pact, contract, convention, treaty.

Cover, *v.a.*, Cloak, veil, conceal, shroud, screen, mask, secrete, hide, disguise, overspread, overlay. *Expose*
Defend, shield, protect, guard, shelter.
Include, embrace, embody, contain, comprise.
Clothe, envelop, wrap, invest, dress. *Strip*
n., Cloak, veil, shroud, screen, mask, disguise, covering.
Defence, shield, protection, guard, shelter.
Envelope, wrap, wrapper.

Covert, *n.*, Underwood, thicket, shade, shrubbery.
Shelter, harbour, sanctuary, asylum, refuge, retreat.
a., Clandestine, secret, concealed, hidden, stealthy, underhand, disguised, sly, insidious. *Open*

Covet, Desire, long for, hanker after. *Despise*

Covetous, Desirous, avaricious, greedy, eager, acquisitive, grasping, rapacious. *Unselfish*

Covetousness, Desire, avarice, greed,† cupidity.

Covey, Brood, flock, bevy, party, set, company.

Covinous, Deceitful, dishonest, collusive, fraudulent. *Honest*

Cow, Frighten, awe, overawe, subdue, intimidate, browbeat, oppress, abash, break, discourage, daunt, dishearten. *Encourage*

Coward, Dastard, craven, poltroon, renegade, recreant. *Hero*

Cowardice, Poltroonery, cowardliness, timidity, fear, pusillanimity. *Bravery*

Cowardly, Timid, fearful, pusillanimous, craven, dastardly, timorous, base, recreant. *Brave*

Cower, Cringe, fawn, crouch, stoop, shrink. *Confront*

Coxcomb, Dandy, fop, prig, puppy, beau, pedant.

Coy, Bashful, modest, demure, retiring, shy, reserved, timid, shrinking, diffident. *Forward*

Cozen, *Chouse*, cheat, dupe, trick, gull, beguile, circumvent, defraud, swindle, victimize, over-reach, deceive.

Crabbed, Morose, captious, surly, sour, bitter, tart, acrid, acrimonious, splenetic, harsh, sullen, rough, testy, censorious, touchy, churlish, caustic, cantankerous, peevish, petulant, waspish, snarling, snappish, crusty. *Genial*

Crabbedness, Moroseness, surliness, sourness,† asperity, acerbity. *Geniality*

Crack, *n.*, Fissure, hole, gap, break, opening, cleft, rift, breach, rent, chink, cranny. Burst, explosion, report, snap, clap, pop. *v., a., & n.,* Split, open, burst, break, chop, cleave. *Mend*

Craft, *n.*, Power, skill, talent, ability, dexterity, aptness, aptitude, cleverness, expertness. *Clumsiness*
Art, trade, vocation, avocation, calling, occupation, employment, business.
Vessel, ship, barque, boat.
Artfulness, artifice, deceit, guile, cunning, intrigue, strategem, dodge, underhandedness, duplicity, chicanery, trickery, wiliness, shrewdness, deceitfulness, deception, subtlety. *Artlessness*

Craftsman, Artisan, mechanic, artificer, workman, operative.

Crafty, Artful, deceitful, cunning.† *Artless*

Craggy, Rough, uneven, broken, scraggy, jagged. *Smooth*

Cram, *v.a.*, Stuff, fill, glut, press, crowd, squeeze, pack, choke, ram, compress.
Coach, grind.
v.n., Overeat, stuff, gorge, gluttonize.
Study, read.

Cramp, *v.a.*, Hinder, obstruct, restrain, impede, confine, check. *Loose*
Convulse.
n., Convulsion, spasm.

Cranium, Skull.

Crank, *v.n.*, Twist, bend, crankle, crinkle, turn, wind.
n., Twist, bend, winding, turn, quirk, involution.
a., Unsteady, loose, shaky, cranky, unstable, disjointed. *Firm*
v.n. Crankle, twist, bend, crinkle, turn, wind.

Cranny, Crack, rift, opening, fissure, cleft, gap, hole, crevice, chink, breach, break, interstice.

Crapulent, Drunk, inebriated, intoxicated, tipsy, fuddled. *Sober*

Crash, *v.a.*, Smash, shatter, break, shiver, splinter, dash.
v.n., Fall, collapse, tumble.
n., Clash, clang, jar, resonance, noise, sound.

Crass, Thick, unrefined, raw, coarse, gross, unabated, unmitigated.

Crate, Hamper, case.

Cravat, Necktie, neckerchief, neckcloth.

Crave, Desire, yearn, hanker after, long for.
Beseech, entreat, implore, beg, cry, supplicate, petition, solicit. *Demand*

Craven, Coward, recreant, poltroon, dastard, milksop.

Craving, Longing, yearning, hungering, desiring.

Crawl, Creep, glide, steal.
Abase.

Craze, Madden, derange, dement, disarrange, impair, weaken, confuse.
Novelty, fashion.

Crazy, Mad, deranged, demented, insane, idiotic, lunatic, aberrant, daft, delirious, distracted. *Sane*

Create, Cause, produce, make, form, fashion, originate, occasion, constitute, appoint, invent. *Destroy*

Creation, Production, making, forming. *Destruction*
Universe, cosmos.

Creator, Maker, former, originator, inventor. *Imitator*
God, First Cause.

Creature, Animal, being, man, person, brute.
Wretch, miscreant.

Credence, Faith, trust, belief, confidence, credit, reliance, acceptance. *Distrust*

Credential, Certificate, letter, warrant, testimonial, diploma, testament, seal, missive, voucher.

Credible, Believable, reliable, trustworthy, probably, likely, thinkable. *Unlikely*

Credit, *n.*, Credence, faith, trust, belief, confidence, reliance, acceptance. *Distrust*

Honour, merit, praise. *Blame*
Trust, loan.
Repute, reputation, regard, esteem, character.
v.a., Believe, rely on, trust, accept, confide in. *Disbelieve*
Trust, loan.

Creditable, Praiseworthy, honourable, meritorious, estimable, reputable. *Blameworthy*

Creditor, Lender, mortgagee, claimant. *Debtor*

Credulous, Confiding, trusting, believing, simple. *Cautious*

Creed, Belief, dogma, doctrine, tenet, confession, profession.

Creek, Canal, rivulet, inlet, cove, bay, bight.

Creep, Crawl, glide, steal, fawn, cringe, grovel, trail.

Crenate, Indented, notched, scalloped. *Smooth*

Crepitate, Crackle, snap.

Crest, Top, apex, summit, head, crown, ridge. *Foot*
Bearings, arms, device.

Crestfallen, Depressed, dejected, downhearted, disheartened, desponding, discouraged, abashed, humiliated, dispirited, despondent, melancholy, chapfallen, sad, downcast. *Elated*

Crevasse, Gap, hole, opening, cleft, rift, crevice, rent, breach, break, chasm.

Crew, Company, set, gang, mob, crowd, party, band, throng, herd, horde, swarm.

Crib, *v.a.*, Confine, imprison, cage, incage, enclose, coop, restrict, hedge, limit. *Liberate*
Purloin, steal, pilfer, cheat.
n., Bed, cot, rack, manger, box.
Situation, job, theft.

Crick, Cramp, spasm, convulsion.

Crime, Wrong, sin, offence, fault, felony, misdemeanour, transgression, misdeed, enormity, iniquity, delinquency. *Duty*

Criminal, *a.*, Illegal, wicked, wrong, felonious, iniquitous, guilty, culpable. *Lawful*

Criminal, *n.*, Felon, malefactor, culprit, delinquent, offender, transgressor, convict, trespasser.

Criminate, Implicate, charge, accuse, impeach, arraign. *Acquit*

Crimp, Plait, curl, crisp, ridge.

Cringe, Stoop, bend, crouch, bow, fawn, grub, truckle, sneak.

Cringing, Stooping, bending,† servile.

Crinkle, Crankle, bend, wind, turn, wrinkle, curl, corrugate.

Cripple, Lame, impair, weaken, disable, maim, mutilate. *Strengthen*

Crisis, Emergency, conjuncture, juncture, exigency, pass, height, turn, strait.

Crisp, Brittle, crimp, friable.

Criterion, Touchstone, proof, standard, test, rule, canon, measure.

Critic, Judge, reviewer, censor, arbiter, savant, connoisseur, carper, caviller, censurer.

Critical, Fastidious, captious, cavilling, carping, censorious. *Appreciative*
Accurate, nice, exact. *Loose*
Crucial, important, decisive, determining, psychological.

Criticise, Judge, review, examine, analyse, scan, discuss, anatomize, censor.

Criticism, Judgment, review, examination.†

Croak, Complain, grumble, murmur, groan, mumble. *Rejoice*

Crockery, Earthenware, pots, dishes.

Crone, Witch, hag, beldame, harridan.

Crony, Ally, mate, associate, chum, friend, companion. *Enemy*

Crook, Bend, curve, turn, wind, incurvate, inflect, bow.

Crooked, Bent, curved, incurved, bowed, twisted, winding, disfigured, disformed, askew, awry, wry, distorted. *Straight*
Dishonest, underhanded, unfair, crafty, deceitful, dishonourable, unscrupulous, intriguing, insidious. *Honest*

Crop, *n.*, Harvest, yield.
v.a., Mow, reap, clip, lop, pluck, cut, gather, pick.
Reduce, share, shorten, curtail.

Cross, *n.*, Gibbet.
Affliction, misfortune, trouble, trial, worry, persecution, vexation.
v.a., Traverse, pass over.
Interbreed, intermix, hybridize.
Hinder, obstruct, thwart, prevent. *Help*
a., Petulant, peevish, irritable, fretful, pettish, crusty, fractious, ill-tempered, ill-humoured, snappish, snarling, testy, sullen, waspish, morose, sour, surly, cynical, splenetic, touchy, churlish, sulky, ill-natured, captious. *Amiable*

Cross-grained, Obdurate, stubborn, wayward, perverse, cantankerous, peevish, refractory, intractable, headstrong. *Obliging*

Crotch, Angle, corner, fork.

Crotchet, Fancy, whim, whimsy, quirk, vagary, freak, caprice.

Crotchety, Fanciful, fantastic, whimsical, freakish, capricious, fitful, odd, humoursome, queer.

Crouch, Stoop, bend, cower, cringe, truckle, fawn, bow.

Croup, Buttocks, rump, crupper.

Crow, Boast, brag, vaunt, exult, cackle, rejoice, triumph, swagger, gasconade, bluster. *Croak*

Crowd, *n.,* Host, multitude, throng, horde, herd, rabble, mob, concourse, pack, swarm. *Elite*
v.n., Swarm, flock, press, congregate, herd, huddle.
v.a., Press, compress, cram.

Crown, *n.,* Diadem, coronet, coronal, laurel, garland, chaplet, wreath.
Sovereignty, royalty.
Top, summit, crest, apex, brow, head. *Foot*
v.a., Adorn, dignify, honour, reward, recompense.
Complete, consummate, perfect, conclude, finish, cap, seal.

Crucial, Critical, piercing, severe, snarp, searching, probing, trying, discriminating, decisive. *Superficial*

Cruciform, Cruciate, cross-shaped.

Crucify, Sacrifice, torture.
Overcome, subdue, mortify.

Crude, Raw, rough, unrefined, coarse, unshaped, harsh, unfinished, unprepared, unconsidered, immature. *Finished*

Crudeness, Rawness, roughness, coarseness, crudity, awkwardness, immaturity.

Cruel, Savage, barbarous, malignant, harsh, unmerciful, pitiless, relentless, ferocious, severe, bitter, unrelenting, inhuman, ruthless, unfeeling, brutal, merciless, dire. *Humane*

Cruelty, Savagery, barbarity, malignance.† *Humanity*

Cruet, Cruse, vial, caster.

Cruise, *n.,* Voyage, trip, sail.
v.n., Rove, journey, sail, voyage.

Crumble, *v.n.,* Perish, disintegrate. *Endure*
v.a., Pulverize, disintegrate, crush.

Crumple, Rumple, wrinkle, crinkle, corrugate, ruffle. *Smooth*

Cruse, Vial, cruet, caster.

Crush, Crumble, triturate, squeeze, pulverize, powder, disintegrate, bruise, contuse, compress, demolish. *Consolidate*
Overpower, subdue, overcome, conquer, suppress, overwhelm.

Crust, Coating, incrustation.

Crusty, Peevish, touchy, cross, petulant, irritable, fretful, pettish, fractious, illtempered, ill-humoured, snappish, snarling, testy, cynical, splenetic, sullen, waspish, morose, sour, surly, churlish, ill-natured, captious. *Amiable*

Cry, *n.,* Lament, lamentation, plaint, weeping, crying. *Rejoicing*
Outcry, yell, scream, howl, shriek, screech, roar, exclamation, slogan.
v.n., Sob, weep, lament. *Rejoice*
Exclaim, yell, scream, howl, shriek, roar, vociferate, clamour, bawl.
v.a., Proclaim, blazon, publish, noise.

Crying, *n.,* Weeping, lament, lamentation, cry. *Smiling*
a., Weeping, lamenting.
Enormous, great, heinous, notorious, nefarious, flagrant.

Crypt, Tomb, vault, catacomb.

Cryptic, Secret, latent, occult, mysterious.

Cuddle, Nestle, snuggle, hug, fondle, embrace.

Cudgel, *v.a.,* Pound, beat, buffet, batter, bruise, baste, drub, cane, thrash.
n., Bludgeon, club, stick.

Cue, Sign, hint, wink, suggestion, signal, nod, intimation.

Cuff, *v.a.,* Beat, buffet, strike, punch, slap, box, smack, pommel.
n., Stroke, punch, slap, box, smack, blow.

Cuisine, Cookery, cooking, kitchen, culinary.

Culinary, Cooking, kitchen, cuisine.

Cull, Pick, choose, elect, select, collect, gather, bunch, pluck.

Culmination, Zenith, apex, top, acme, consummation, completion, meridian, success. *Defeat*

Culpable, Blameworthy, blamable, guilty, wrong, censurable, faulty, sinful, reprehensible. *Innocent*

Culprit, Delinquent, offender, criminal, malefactor, felon. *Hero*

Cult, Worship, homage, ritual, system.

Cultivate, Till, work.
Promote, improve, foster, nourish, cherish, develop, train, refine, discipline, elevate, meliorate, civilize. *Neglect*
Investigate, study, pursue, search.

Cultivation, Tillage, husbandry, agriculture.
Promotion, improvement, fostering.†
Study, investigation, pursuit.

Culture, Cultivation, civilization, refinement, improvement, elevation.
Barbarity

Cumber, Encumber, oppress, load, clog, impede, obstruct, hamper, incommode.
Liberate
Harass, distract, plague, annoy, worry, torment, trouble, embarrass, perplex.
Relieve

Cumbersome, Encumbering, oppressive.† *Light*

Cumulative, Increasing, gaining, collective. *Reducing*

Cunning, *a.,* Artful, crafty, crooked, diplomatic, underhanded, deceitful, sly, shrewd, wily, sharp, clever, tricky, astute, designing. *Artless*
Ingenious, skilful, dexterous. *Clumsy*
n., Art, craft, crookedness.† *Artlessness*
Ingenuity, skill, dexterity. *Clumsiness*

Cup, Chalice, bowl, beaker, goblet.

Cupidity, Avarice, desire, acquisitiveness, greed, covetousness, hankering, longing, lust.

Curative, Healing, restorative, remedial, sanatory, medicinal. *Poisonous*

Curator, Guardian, keeper, custodian, varden.

Curb, *v.a.,* Restrain, hold, repress, moderate, check, control, bridle. *Incite*
n., Restraint, repression, check, control, bridle.

Curb-stone, edge-stone.

Curd, Curdle, coagulate, congeal, thicken, chill, stiffen.

Cure, *n.,* Healing, remedy, restoration, restorative, antidote, specific, corrective, reparative, help, alleviation.
Aggravation
v.a., Heal, remedy, restore.† *Aggravate*

Curiosity, Interest, inquisitiveness.
Indifference
Phenomenon, rarity, sight, wonder, spectacle, marvel, oddity, freak. *Trite*

Curious, Prying, inquisitive, scrutinizing, peering, peeping, interested. *Indifferent*
Phenomenal, rare, wonderful, odd, unusual, uncommon, queer, strange, unique, singular, freakish, extraordinary.
Common

Curl, Twist, wind, turn, bend, writhe, crisp, wave, coil.

Curmudgeon, Miser, skinflint, niggard, screw, churl.

Currency, Money.
Circulation, publicity, acceptance.

Current, *a.,* General, common, popular, rife.
Present, existing. *Obsolete*
n., Tide, stream, course, progression.

Curse, *v.a.,* Execrate, anathematize, maledict, imprecate, denounce, destroy, blight, blast, plague, torment. *Bless*
n., Execration, anathema, malediction.†
Blessing

Cursory, Superficial, careless, hasty, brief, passing, transient, slight, desultory, rapid. *Thorough*

Curt, Terse, short, laconic, blunt, concise, brief, rude, tart.

Curtail, Diminish, abbreviate, shorten, contract, lessen, decrease, abridge, lop, cut. *Amplify*

Curtailment, Diminution, abbreviation.†
Amplification

Curvature, Curve, incurvation, bend, bending, curvity, flexure.

Curve, *n.,* Curvature, incurvation, bend.†
v., a. & n., Wind, bend, turn, twist, inflect. *Straighten*

Curvet, Leap, bound, caper, frisk, frolic, vault.

Cushion, Pad, bolster, pillow, hassock.

Cusp, Horn, point, angle.

Cuspidate, Pointed, sharp, acute.

Custodian, Guardian, curator, keeper, warden.

Custody, Care, protection, keeping, watch, ward, observation.
Confinement, imprisonment, duress, prison, durance.

Custom, Habit, manner, convention, fashion, practice, use, usage, rule.
Tax, impost, toll, tribute, duty.

Customary, Habitual, conventional, usual, fashionable.† *Unusual*

Customer, Client, buyer, purchaser, patron. *Seller*

Cut, *v.a.,* Sever, slice, divide, sunder, wound, chop. *Splice*
Carve, chisel, sculpture.

Cut, Avoid, slight.
n., Incision, gash, wound, piece, slice.
Channel, passage way, path.

Cutting, Sharp, sardonic, cruel, bitter, malignant, stinging, piercing, sarcastic, trenchant, severe, satirical. *Soothing*

Cycle, Period, circle, age, era.

Cyclopean, Gigantic, vast, massive, colossal, enormous, immense. *Small*

Cynical, Petulant, peevish, touchy, cross, irritable, fretful, pettish, fractious, illtempered, ill-humoured, sneering, snappish, snarling, testy, splenetic, sullen, waspish, morose, sour, surly, churlish, sulky, ill-natured, captious, censorious, sophisticated. *Amiable*

Cynosure, Centre, point, attraction.

D

Dab, *v.a.*, Strike, lunge, pat, slap.
n., Stroke, pat, blow.
Mass, pat, lump, piece.
Adept, expert, dabster.

Dabble, *v.n.*, Meddle, trifle, mix.
v.a., Sprinkle, moisten, spatter, wet, soak, dip.

Dabster, Adept, expert, dab.

Daedalian, Daedal, intricate, involved, mazy.   *Simple*

Daft, Silly, stupid, foolish, idiotic, lunatic, insane, soft, fond, absurd.   *Sensible*

Dagger, Dirk, stiletto, poniard, bayonet.

Daggle, Dirty, befoul, besmire, draggle, soil, foul, defile, sully.   *Cleanse*

Dainty, Choice, rare, tasty, delicate, exquisite, fine, neat, refined, elegant, delicious, nice, palatable, savoury, luscious, luxuriant, tender, beautiful.   *Coarse*
Squeamish, fastidious, epicurean, scrupulous, particular.

Dale, Dell, valley, vale, dingle, glen, ravine.   *Hill*

Dalliance, Trifling, caressing, endearments, fondling.

Dally, Trifle, caress, fondle, toy, play, sport, wanton.
Dawdle, delay.   *Hurry*

Damage, *v.a.*, Hurt, harm, injure, impair, mar, spoil.   *Repair*
n., Hurt, harm, injury, impairment, detriment, loss, mischief.   *Reparation*

Damages, Compensation, reparations, indemnity, satisfaction, forfeiture, fine.

Dame, Madam, matron, mistress, lady.

Damn, Doom, condemn, ruin, kill.   *Bless*

Damnable, Abominable, execrable, hateful, detestable, odious, horrible, horrid, atrocious, outrageous, accursed.
                                                                                       Splendid

Damp, *v.a.*, Dampen, moisten.   *Dry*
Discourage, depress, cool, discountenance, blunt, moderate, repress, allay, restrain, chill, abate, deaden, deject.
                                                                                       Encourage
n., Moisture, dampness, fog, vapour.
a., Moist, wet, dank, humid, clammy.

Dampen, Damp, moisten.
Discourage, depress.†

Damper, Obstacle, hindrance, check, impediment, depression, discouragement.

Damsel, Girl, maid, maiden, lass, miss, lassie.

Dance, Frisk, caper, hop, bob.

Dandle, Caress, pet, fondle, amuse.

Dandy, Fop, beau, coxcomb, swell.

Danger, Peril, risk, venture, jeopardy, hazard.   *Safety*

Dangerous, Perilous, risky, hazardous, unsafe.   *Safe*

Dangle, Swing, suspend, oscillate, pendulate.

Dank, Damp, moist, wet, humid, clammy.
                                                                                       Dry

Dapper, Smart, spruce, neat, natty, nice, pretty.   *Slovenly*
Smart, spry, alert, ready, active, brisk, quick, nimble, agile.   *Slow*

Dapple, Spotted, variegated, brindle, streak, chequer.

Dare, *v.a.*, Defy, brave, challenge.
v.n., Hazard, venture, presume.   *Cower*

Daring, *a.*, Adventurous, dashing, bold, heroic, valiant, valorous, gallant, undaunted, dauntless, intrepid, brave, doughty, courageous, fearless.   *Timid*
n., Boldness, heroism, valiance.†
                                                                                       Timidity

Dark, *a.*, Black, dusky, shadowy, opaque, swarthy, lurid, ebon, Cimmerian, sable, dim, rayless, unilluminated, sunless, murky, pitchy, cloudy, overcast.   *Light*
Unenlightened, ignorant, rude, benighted, untaught, blind.   *Enlightened*
Obscure, enigmatical, abstruse, recondite, mystic, mysterious, occult, unintelligible, incomprehensible.   *Plain*
Cheerless, dismal, gloomy, sombre, joyless, mournful, sorrowful, discouraging, disheartening.   *Festive*
Atrocious, horrible, wicked, vile, damnable, infamous, infernal, nefarious, foul.
                                                                                       Good
n., Darkness, obscurity, dimness.   *Light*
Ignorance, blindness.
Secrecy, concealment, privacy.

Darken, Dim, obscure, shade, cloud.
                                                                                       Lighten
Blind, benight, stupefy, stultify.
                                                                                       Enlighten
Obscure, perplex.
Blot, stain, defile, sully, soil, dull, dim.
Damp, chill, depress, discourage.
                                                                                       Encourage

Darkness, Dark, obscurity, dimness.
                                                                                       Light
Ignorance, blindness.
Secrecy, concealment, privacy, gloom, despondency, cheerlessness.

Darling, *n.*, Dear, pet, favourite, sweetheart, love, idol.

Darling, *a.*, Dear, beloved, precious, sweet, favourite.

Dart, *v.n.*, Fly, rush, spring, dash, run.
v.a., Hurl, project, propel, throw, fling, launch.

Dash, *v.n.*, Dart, fly, rush, spring, run.
v.a., Hurl, strike, cast, throw.
n., Rush, onset.
Blow, stroke.
Tinge, touch, spice, sprinkling, infusion, tincture, smack.
Show, flourish, vigour, spirit.

Dashing, Showy, adventurous, spirited, brave, impetuous, rushing, sweeping, precipitate, gay, brilliant. **Timid**

Dastard, *n.*, Coward, recreant, poltroon, craven.
a., Cowardly, recreant, base, dastardly, craven, pusillanimous. **Brave**

Dastardly, Dastard, cowardly, recreant.†

Data, Facts, grounds, basis, premises, postulates, axioms.

Date, Age, time, period, era, epoch.

Daub, *v.a.*, Bedaub, begrime, defile, sully, soil, stain, smear, besmear, deface, cover, plaster. **Cleanse**
n., Smirch, smear.

Dauby, Smeary, sticky, viscous, viscid, glutinous, clammy, adhesive.

Daunt, Intimidate, dismay, terrify, confront, scare, check, stop, thwart, deter, cow, discourage, appal, tame, subdue. **Encourage**

Dauntless, Undaunted, courageous, valiant, valorous, brave, gallant, indomitable, intrepid, fearless, unconquerable, bold, undismayed, heroic, doughty, daring. **Timid**

Dawdle, Lag, dally, idle, trifle, fiddle. **Hurry**

Dawdler, Laggard, drone, idler, lounger, trifler, sluggard.

Dawn, *n.*, Daybreak, dawning, dayspring, sunrise, opening. **Sunset**
v.n., Gleam, begin, break, open, rise, appear. **Set**

Day, Daylight, daytime, sunlight, sunshine. **Night**
Generation, epoch, age, era, time, lifetime.

Daybreak, Dawn, dawning, dayspring. **Darkness**

Dayspring, Dawn, dawning, daybreak.

Daze, Bewilder, confuse, dazzle, stun, blind, stupefy, amaze, perplex, glare, flare.

Dazzle, *v.a.*, Daze, bewilder, confuse.† **Dim**
n., Brightness, splendour, brilliance.

Dead, Lifeless, defunct, deceased, gone, departed, inanimate, breathless. **Alive**
Spiritless, cheerless, dull, inert, indifferent, cold, unfeeling, frigid, callous, lukewarm, torpid, obtuse. **Stirring**
n., Midst, depth, darkest, coldest, gloomiest.

Deaden, Damp, dampen, blunt, subdue, weaken, impair, restrain, abate, paralyse, benumb. **Quicken**

Deadlock, Standstill, stoppage, uncompromising.

Deadly, Mortal, malignant, fatal, murderous, venomous, destructive, pernicious, noxious, baleful, deleterious, rancorous, sanguinary, implacable. **Vital**

Deaf, Heedless, regardless, inattentive, insensible, inaudible.

Deafen, Confuse, stun.

Deal, *v.a.*, Divide, distribute, dispense, bestow, give, allot, share, apportion, mete, dole.
Treat, reward, punish.
v.n., Trade, traffic, bargain.
Act, behave.
n., Extent, quantity, amount, degree.
Transaction, business, bargain.

Dealer, Merchant, trader, vendor, monger, trafficker, tradesman, shopkeeper.

Dealing, Commerce, business, traffic, trade, conduct, action, behaviour.

Dear, Darling, precious, beloved. **Vile**
Costly, expensive. **Cheap**

Dearth, Lack, want, scarcity, deficiency, need, shortness, insufficiency, shortage, famine. **Abundance**

Death, Departure, decease, dissolution, dying, demise, exit, expiration, mortality. **Birth**

Deathless, Immortal, imperishable, undying, everlasting, unfading. **Mortal**

Debacle, Stampede, rush, rout, cataclysm, break-up.

Debar, Stop, hinder, exclude, prohibit, deny, thwart, restrain, prevent, obstruct, withhold. **Allow**

Debase, Degrade, lower, deteriorate, abase, reduce, depress, injure, impair, vitiate, alloy, taint, corrupt, foul, befoul, soil, sully, contaminate, defile, deprave, dishonour, shame, mortify, humiliate, humble. **Raise**

Debasement, Degradation, lowering, deterioration.†

Debatable, Disputable, contestable, doubtful, moot, dubious. **Certain**

Debate, *v.*, *a.* & *n.*, Dispute, contest, argue, discuss, contend, question. **Admit**
n., Disputation, dispute, contest,† controversy, altercation.

Debauch, *v.a.,* Deprave, corrupt, pollute, seduce, vitiate, deflour. *Purify*

n., Debauchery, gluttony, orgy, riot, revel, revelry, carousal, bacchanal, excess, lust, indulgence, intemperance, dissoluteness, licentiousness, dissipation. *Temperance*

Debauchery, Debauch, gluttony, orgy.†

Debilitate, Enfeeble, weaken, enervate, prostrate, relax, exhaust. *Strengthen*

Debility, Feebleness, weakness, enervation, prostration, exhaustion, lassitude, languor, frailty, infirmity. *Strength*

Debit, Liability, obligation.† *Credit*

Debonair, Affable, civil, graceful, easy, gracious, polite, courteous, urbane, kind, obliging, refined, complaisant, elegant, lithe. *Brusque*

Buoyant, bright, cheery, sprightly, vivacious, elegant, graceful. *Dull*

Debris, Remains, rubbish, ruins, pieces, fragments.

Debt, Liability, obligation, debit, due, default, arrears. *Asset*

Decadence, Decay, decline, declension, sinking, wasting, degeneracy, deterioration, caducity, waning, fall. *Rise*

Decamp, Abscond, bolt, fly, flee, escape.

Decapitate, Behead, execute, guillotine, decollate.

Decay, *n.,* Decadence, decline, declension, sinking, wasting, degeneracy, deterioration, caducity, waning, fall. *Growth*

v.n., Decline, sink, waste,† perish, decrease, ebb, rot, wither. *Flourish*

Decayed, Rotten, unsound, corrupt, decomposed, putrified. *Sound*

Decease, Death, departure, dissolution, dying, demise, exit, expiration, mortality. *Birth*

Deceased, Dead, lifeless, defunct, departed, gone, inanimate, breathless, late. *Alive*

Deceit, Fraud, cheating, guile, deception, underhandedness, chicanery, duplicity, artifice, trickery, imposition, imposture, deceitfulness, *cozenage.* *Honesty*

Deceitful, Fraudulent, guiletul, false, misleading, deceptive, dissembling, counterfeit, illusory, illusive, delusive, insincere, hollow, tricky, double, designing. *Honest*

Deceive, Cheat, trick, beguile, fool, mislead, delude, dupe, gull, hoodwink, circumvent, over-reach, *cozen, chouse.* *Guide*

Deceiver, Cheat, impostor, sharper, humbug, charlatan.

Decency, Propriety, purity, modesty, decorum, delicacy. *Impropriety*

Decent, Proper, pure,† seemly, becoming, befitting, fit, suitable, comely. *Improper*

Deception, Deceit, imposture, fraud, cheating, guile, underhandedness, chicanery, duplicity, artifice, trickery, trick, ruse, stratagem, wile, imposition, deceitfulness, *cozenage.* *Honesty*

Deceptive, Deceitful, false, misleading, deceiving, counterfeit, illusory, illusive, delusive, insincere, hollow, double, false, subtle. *Honest*

Decide, *v.a.,* Conclude, settle, terminate, determine, end. *Waive*

v.n., Determine, resolve. *Waver*

Decided, Unwavering, determined, resolved, resolute, positive, unhesitating, firm. *Vacillating*

Certain, unquestionable, indisputable, clear, absolute, positive, unequivocal, unmistakable. *Dubious*

Decipher, Explain, reveal, expound, read, unravel, interpret, unfold, spell, solve. *Mystify*

Decision, Determination, resolution, firmness, conclusion. *Uncertainty*

Judgment, settlement, verdict.

Decisive, Conclusive, final, ultimate, determinative. *Uncertain*

Deck, Cover, adorn, bedeck, clothe, robe, array, don, apparel, dress, beautify, decorate, ornament, embellish. *Strip*

Declaim, Recite, harangue, debate, speak, apostrophize, rant.

Declamation, Declaiming, recitation, harangue, speech, elocution, oratory, effusion, ranting.

Declamatory, Fustian, grandiloquent, rhetorical, loud, bombastic, noisy, turgid, pompous, incoherent, discursive, loose, swelling. *Quiet*

Declaration, Avowal, assertion, asseveration, statement, affirmation, averment, protestation, profession, proclamation, publication, announcement. *Denial*

Declare, Avouch, assert, asseverace,† say, aver, maintain. *Deny*

Declension, Decay, decadence, degeneracy, deterioration, decline, fall, diminution. *Rise*

Refusal, rejection.

Declination, Inclination, bending, deviation, departure, declivity, slope, descent, divergence. *Acclivity*

Decline, *v.n.,* Decay, degenerate, deteriorate, fall, diminish, sink, waste, wane, droop, pine, languish, lessen, decrease. *Increase*

v.a., Refuse, reject, avoid, inflect, vary.

n., Decay, decadence, degeneracy.†

Declivity, Descent, slope, fall, incline. *Ascent*

Decollate, Behead, decapitate, execute, guillotine.

Decompose, *v.n.,* Decay, dissolve, putrefy.

v.a., Analyse, disintegrate, segregate, resolve, dissolve, decompound. *Compose*

Decomposition, Decay, dissolution, putrescence, rotting, disintegration, corruption, crumbling.

Analysis, disintegration, resolution. *Synthesis*

Decompound, Decompose, disintegrate, segregate, resolve, dissolve. *Compose*

Decorate, Embellish, ornament, adorn, deck, bedeck, garnish, beautify, enrich, gild. *Mar*

Decoration, Embellishment, ornament, adornment.† *Defacement*

Decorous, Decent, befitting, fitting, becoming, proper, suitable, comely, seemly. *Unseemly*

Decorum, Decency, propriety, dignity, order, seemliness. *Unseemliness*

Decoy, *v.a.,* Lure, allure, ensnare, entice, entrap, seduce, inveigle, mislead, tempt. *Guide*

n., Lure, allurement.

Decrease, *v.a.,* Lessen, curtail, reduce, diminish, lower, retrench. *Increase*

v.n., Lessen, diminish, decline, contract, wane, ebb, fall, subside, abate, dwindle.

n., Lessening, diminution, decline, declension,† reduction, curtailment, decrement.

Decree, *v.a.,* Enact, order, command, enjoin, appoint, ordain, decide, determine.

n., Enactment, order,† law, edict, mandate, regulation, statute, fiat, rule, verdict, ukase.

Decrement, Decrease, lessening, diminution, decline, declension, contraction, wane, ebb, ebbing, fall, abatement, reduction, curtailment. *Increment*

Decrepit, Aged, weak, infirm, tottering, effete, superannuated, crippled. *Youthful*

Decrepitate, Snap, crackle, crepitate.

Decrial, Disparagement, condemnation, depreciation. *Appreciation*

Decry, Disparage, condemn, depreciate, traduce, discredit, underrate, undervalue, belittle, vituperate, defame, denounce,† vilify. *Appreciate*

Dedicate, Consecrate, devote, sanctify, hallow, apportion, assign, apply. *Desecrate*

Dedication, Consecration, devotion. *Desecration*

Address, inscription.

Deduce, Gather, infer, draw, conclude, derive. *Hazard*

Deduct, Withdraw, subtract, remove, bate. *Add*

Deduction, Withdrawal, subtraction, removal, abatement, discount, reduction, allowance, defalcation. *Addition*

Conclusion, inference, corollary.

Deed, Action, act, performance, feat, achievement, perpetration, exploit, fact, reality, truth, atrocity, doings. *Omission*

Document, indenture, charter, transaction.

Deem, *v.n.,* Believe, think, opine, hold, fancy, suppose, consider.

v.a., Believe, think, hold, suppose, consider, count, account, estimate, judge, regard, imagine. *Misjudge*

Deep, *a.,* Subterraneous, submerged. *Shallow*

Profound, mysterious, dark, unfathomable, difficult, hard, knotty, intricate. *Obvious*

Recondite, learned, astute, shrewd, penetrating, discerning, intelligent, sagacious. *Superficial*

Wrapt, engrossed, absorbed, silent, still, hushed.

n., Water, ocean, main, sea.

Depth, bottom, abyss, midst, stillness, silence.

Deface, Disfigure, mar, injure, spoil, deform, soil, sully, tarnish. *Decorate*

Defacement, Disfigurement, injury. *Decoration*

De facto, Real, actual, practical.

Defalcate, Reduce, curtail, cut, lop, abate, retrench, deduct. *Add*

Defalcation, Reduction, abatement, deduction, diminution, discount. *Addition*

Deficit, arrears, deficiency, shortage, default. *Balance*

Defamation, Aspersion, calumny, abuse, scandal, slander, detraction, obloquy, vilification, backbiting, libel. *Praise*

Defamatory, Calumnious, abusive, scandalous, libellous, slanderous. *Praising*

Defame, Asperse, abuse, libel, slander, calumniate, blacken, vilify, blemish, traduce, revile. *Eulogize*

Default, Failure, omission, want, lapse, neglect, absence, lack, destitution, defect, delinquency, deficiency, defalcation. *Satisfaction*

Defaulter, Delinquent, offender, embezzler. *Liquidator*

Defeat, *v.a.*, Vanquish, overcome, conquer, beat, rout, discomfit, frustrate, checkmate, worse, thwart, balk, foil, repulse. ***Baffle***
n., Overthrow, rout, discomfiture, repulse, frustration, downfall. ***Victory***

Defecate, Clear, purify, cleanse, clarify, purge, depurate, refine. ***Pollute***

Defecation, Purification, cleansing.†
Pollution

Defect, Shortcoming, imperfection, blemish, fault, omission, lack, want, deficiency, default, flaw, failing. ***Faultless***

Defective, Imperfect, blemished, faulty, lacking, wanting, deficient, insufficient, short, inadequate, marred, incomplete.
Perfect

Defence, Protection, guard, resistance, shelter, maintenance, shield, buckler, bulwark. ***Attack***
Plea, vindication, excuse, apology, justification. ***Accusation***

Defenceless, Unprotected, unguarded, unarmed, unshielded, exposed, unsheltered, helpless, weak. ***Protected***

Defend, Protect, guard, resist, shield, shelter, ward, cover, harbour. ***Attack***

Defender, Champion, advocate, protector, upholder, pleader, vindicator. ***Assailant***

Defendant, Accused, prisoner. ***Plaintiff***

Defer, Delay, waive, procrastinate, postpone, adjourn. ***Hasten***

Deference, Respect, obedience, reverence, consideration, allegiance, homage, veneration, esteem, regard, honour. ***Defiance***

Deferential, Respectful, obedient, reverent.† ***Defiant***

Defiance, Disobedience, opposition, contumacy, disregard, contempt. ***Deference***
Challenge, daring.

Defiant, Recalcitrant, contumacious, resistant. ***Deferential***
Daring, bold, brave, courageous, intrepid, fearless, heroic. ***Timid***

Deficiency, Lack, shortage, shortness, scarcity, want, defectiveness, deficit, insufficiency, scarceness, dearth, meagreness, imperfection, incompleteness, weakness. ***Sufficiency***

Deficient, Lacking, short, scarce,† blemished, defective, faulty, inadequate, marred. ***Perfect***

Deficit, Lack, shortage, deficiency, defectiveness, insufficiency. ***Balance***

Defile, Contaminate, pollute, taint, soil, sully, stain, debase, dirty, tarnish, begrime, corrupt, poison, vitiate, seduce, deflour, debauch. ***Purify***

Definable, Specific, determinable.
Indeterminable

Define, Specify, determine, designate, limit, describe, circumscribe, bound, elucidate, explain. ***Confuse***

Definite, Specified, determinate, defined, clear, certain, ascertained, exact, precise.
Vague

Definition, Defining, meaning, explanation, limitation.

Definitive, Final, decisive, conclusive, positive, explicit, unconditional.
Uncertain

Deflect, *v.a.*, Divert, turn, bend.
Straighten
v.n., Deviate, turn, wind, bend, swerve, twist, diverge. ***Continue***

Deflection, Deviation, turning, twist, bending, bend, divergence. ***Straightness***

Deflower, Corrupt, defile, debauch, rape, seduce, sophisticate, ravish.

Deform, Disfigure, mar, spoil, deface, distort, injure. ***Adorn***

Deformity, Ugliness, hideousness, disfigurement, defacement, distortion, abnormity, irregularity, monstrosity, inelegance, malformation. ***Beauty***

Defraud, Cheat, deceive, trick, gull, dope, bamboozle, circumvent, beguile, overreach, hoodwink, delude, *cozen, chouse.*

Defray, Meet, pay, discharge, liquidate, settle, bear. ***Repudiate***

Deft, Clever, expert, dexterous, neat, apt, handy, skilful, practised, adroit, ready.
Clumsy

Defunct, Dead, gone, deceased, departed, obsolete. ***Living***

Defy, Flout, spurn, disregard, brave, ignore, scorn, despise, slight, dare, challenge. ***Defer***

Degeneracy, Decline, declension, deterioration, corruption, retrogression, caducity, degeneration, degradation, debasement, depravity, decrease.
Amelioration
Poverty, poorness, meanness, inferiority, lowness.

Degenerate, *v.n.*, Decline, deteriorate, retrograde, decrease, decay. ***Improve***
a., Depraved, degenerated, fallen, corrupt, debased, decayed, impaired, poor, mean, inferior, low. ***Superior***

Degeneration, Degeneracy, decline, declension, deterioration, retrogression, caducity, degradation, debasement, depravation, decrease. ***Amelioration***
Poverty, poorness, meanness, inferiority, lowness.

Degradation, Degeneration, degeneracy, decline.†
Disgrace, dishonour, humiliation.
Honour

Degrade, Lower, debase, deteriorate, injure, impair, disgrace, humble, humiliate, disparage, decry, depreciate, sink, vitiate, alloy, pervert. *Ameliorate*

Degree, Grade, rank, class, order, standing, station.
Division, mark, space, step, interval, stage.

Dehort, Discourage, dissuade, depress.

Deify, Elevate, exalt, idolize, apotheosize. *Debase*

Deign, Condescend, vouchsafe, stoop, descend.

Deject, Dispirit, depress, dishearten, discourage, sadden. *Inspirit*

Dejected, Dispirited, depressed,† downhearted, gloomy, chapfallen, crestfallen, pessimistic, downcast, despondent, desponding, melancholy, doleful. *Cheerful*

Dejection, Depression, sadness, gloominess, gloom, despondency, melancholy. *Cheer*

Dejecture, Excrement, excretion, soil.

Delay, *v.a.,* Obstruct, hinder, impede, block, stop, detain, retard. *Hasten*
Defer, procrastinate, postpone.
v.n., Dawdle, linger, tarry, stop, dally, procrastinate.
n., Obstruction, hindrance, impediment, stoppage, detention, retardation. *Hastening*
Deferring, procrastination, postponement.
Dawdling, lingering, tarrying, dalliance.

Dele, Delete, erase, efface, obliterate. *Insert*

Delectable, Pleasant, delightful, enjoyable, pleasing, gratifying, agreeable. *Unpleasant*

Delectation, Pleasure, delight, enjoyment, joy, gladness, rapture, ecstasy.

Delegate, *n.,* Commissioner, deputy, representative.
v.a., Depute, appoint, commission. *Recall*
Commit, instruct.

Delete, Dele, erase, efface, obliterate. *Insert*

Deleterious, Noxious, injurious, destructive, poisonous, pernicious, deadly, harmful, hurtful, noisome, unwholesome, bad. *Beneficial*

Deliberate, *v.n.,* Consider, consult, think, cogitate, ruminate, meditate, ponder, muse, reflect, debate.
a., Purposed, designed, intentional, grave. Studied, slow, unhurried, leisurely. *Hurried*
Cautious, considerate, careful, thoughtful, heedful, wary, circumspect, resolute. *Rash*

Deliberation, Discussion, consultation, consideration, cogitation, rumination, meditation, reflection, thought.

Delicacy, Dainty, luxury, morsel, relish, savoury.
Weakness, frailty, tenderness, slenderness, slightness. *Robustness*
Purity, refinement, softness, tact, feeling, sensibility, scruple, scrupulousness, discrimination, fastidiousness. *Roughness*
Finesse, elegance, daintiness, savouriness, deliciousness, pleasantness, agreeableness, softness, smoothness, lightness.

Delicate, Weak, frail, fragile, tender, slender, slight. *Robust*
Dainty, luxurious, savoury, delicious, pleasant, agreeable, palatable. *Loathsome*
Pure, refined, soft, tactful, careful, scrupulous, discriminating, fastidious. *Rough*

Delicious, Delicate, luxurious, delightful, dainty, choice, luscious, palatable, nice, savoury, exquisite, charming, pleasant. *Loathsome*

Delight, *v.a.,* Charm, ravish, enchant, please, rejoice, enrapture, transport, gratify. *Disappoint*
n., Charm, ravishment, delectation, gladness, joy, ecstasy, satisfaction. *Disappointment*

Delightful, Charming, ravishing, enchanting, pleasing, pleasant, enrapturing, transporting, gratifying, rapturous. *Disappointing*

Delineate, Describe, depict, picture, portray, draw, figure, design, paint, sketch, limn. *Caricature*

Delineation, Description, picture, portrayal, drawing, design, sketch, outline, draught.

Delinquency, Crime, offence, fault, misdeed, misdemeanour. *Innocence*

Delinquent, Criminal, offender, misdoer, culprit, malefactor, miscreant. *Innocent*

Deliquescent, Liquefying, melting, disappearing, vanishing.

Delirious, Raving, wandering, demented, frenzied, crazy, frantic, mad, insane, deranged. *Sane*

Delitescent, Concealed, latent, hidden. *Open*

Deliver, Transfer, intrust, consign, commit, hand, cede, yield, grant, resign, relinquish, surrender. *Appropriate*
Release, rescue, liberate, free, discharge, emancipate, save, redeem, extricate. *Capture*
Declare, pronounce, promulgate, speak, utter.

Deliverance, Release, rescue, liberation.†

Delivery, Conveyance, transmission, transference, surrender, handing, giving, distribution. *Appropriation*
Speech, pronunciation, elocution, enunciation, utterance.

Dell, Dale, glen, valley, vale, ravine, dingle. *Hill*

Delude, Deceive, mislead, dupe, gull, beguile, cheat, circumvent, overreach, trick, *cozen, chouse.* *Guide*

Deluge, *n.,* Flood, cataclysm, inundation, rush, overflow. *Drought*
v.a., Inundate, flood, overflow, overwhelm, submerge, drown.

Delusion, Illusion, hallucination, error, deception, phantasm, mockery, mirage, fallacy. *Reality*
Trick, artifice, ruse, snare, deceit, imposture, imposition, wile, fraud, dodge.

Delusive, Illusive, illusory, deceptive, deceiving, fallacious, deceitful, misleading. *True*

Delve, Dig, excavate, scoop, penetrate, search, investigate.

Demand, *v.n.,* Ask, question, inquire, query. *Answer*
v.a., Claim, require, ask, insist, exact, challenge, necessitate. *Obviate*
n., Question, inquiry, query, interrogation.
Claim, requirement, requisition, exactment.

Demarcation, Distinction, division, definition, inclosure, plan, separation, boundary, bound, confine, limit.

Demean, Lower, degrade, disgrace, debase. *Exalt*

Demeanour, Behaviour, deportment, manner, mien, air, conduct, carriage, bearing.

Demented, Insane, idiotic, deranged, daft, crazy, man, lunatic, infatuated, foolish. *Sane*

Dementia, Idiocy, lunacy, insanity.

Demerit, Fault, delinquency, misdeed, crime, offence. *Virtue*

Demesne, Estate, lands, domain, property, possessions.

Demise, *n.,* Decease,† dissolution, death. *Birth*
Convergence, transference.
v.a., Bequeath, leave, will, convey, devise, transfer.

Demiurgic, Creative, formative.

Democratic, Popular, representative. *Autocratic*

Demolish, Raze, destroy, level, overthrow, ruin, break, dismantle. *Build*

Demolition, Destruction, overthrow, ruin.

Demon, Fiend, spirit, devil, goblin, evil one. *Angel*

Demoniacal, Fiendish, devilish, diabolical, infernal. *Angelic*

Demonstrate, Show, prove, establish, exhibit, illustrate. *Disprove*

Demonstration, Show, proof,† display, manifestation, exhibition. *Concealment*

Demonstrative, Open, expressive, unreserved, natural, free. *Close*
Certain, conclusive, sure, absolute, apodictic. *Dubious*

Demoralize, Deprave, deflower, corrupt, debauch, contaminate, vitiate. *Improve*
Dishearten, depress, weaken, dispirit. *Encourage*

Demulcent, Soothing, lenitive, softening, mild, sedative, allaying, emollient. *Irritating*

Demur, Dubitate, halt, hesitate, waver, stop, pause, scruple, object. *Consent*

Demure, Modest, grave, prudish, staid, discreet, sober, sedate. *Wanton*

Den, Cave, cavern.
Haunt, resoɹt, retreat, snuggery.

Dendriform, Branching, arborescent, arboriform, treeshaped.

Denial, Contradiction, refutation, negation, controverting. *Confirmation*
Disavowal, renunciation, disowning, disclaimer, abjuration, abnegation. *Acknowledgment*
Refusal, rejection. *Compliance*

Denizen, Citizen, resident, subject, inhabitant, dweller. *Alien*

Denominate, Designate, name, call, christen, specify, denote, entitle, style, term.

Denomination, Designation, name, title, style, appellation. *Misnomer*
Sect, kind, class, school, sort, set.
Value.

Denote, Mean, signify, mark, designate, imply, indicate, betoken, typify.

Dénouement, Catastrophe, issue, conclusion, *finale,* termination.

Denounce, Upbraid, menace, threaten, censure, decry, reprobate, defame, vituperate, stigmatize, brand. *Eulogize*

Dense, Condensed, compact, compressed, close, heavy, solid, thick. *Rarefied*
Stupid, dull, foolish, slow, thick, stolid. *Clever*

Density, Compactness, closeness, thickness.

Dent, *v.a.,* Indent, notch.
n., Indentation, notch, niche, dint, cavity.

Dentated } Dented, notched, jagged,
Denticulated } serrate, serrated, toothed.

Denude, Strip, bare, divest, spoil. *Clothe*

Denudate, Strip, divest, bare, denude, divest, disarm, dispossess.

Denunciation, Menace, threat, censure, vituperation, defamation, branding, arraignment. *Eulogy*

Deny, Contradict, negative, controvert, refute, gainsay. *Confirm* Disavow, renounce, dispute, disclaim, disown, abjure, abnegate. *Acknowledge* Reject, refuse, withhold. *Comply*

Depart, Go, leave, start, disappear, vanish, decamp, withdraw, retire. *Arrive* Die, decease.

Department, Province, branch, division, section, part, portion. Office, function, station, bureau, store.

Departure, Exit, removal, retirement, disappearance, withdrawal. *Arrival* Deviation, variation, abandonment, forsaking. Death, decease, exit, demise.

Depauperate, Impoverish.

Depend, Rely, hang, rest, hinge, turn.

Dependant, Minion, retainer, henchman, vassal, satellite. *Freeman* Concomitant, corollary, consequence.

Dependence, Reliance, trust, prop, stay, support, buttress, staff. *Independence* Subordination, subjection. Interdependence, connection, concatenation. *Separation*

Dependent, Conditioned, hanging, pendent, relying, resting. *Independent*

Depict, Delineate, portray, sketch, paint, draw, pencil, outline, colour, limn. *Caricature*

Deplete, Empty, exhaust, strain, drain, reduce, evacuate. *Fill*

Depletion, Emptying, exhausting, exhaustion.†

Deplorable, Lamentable, wretched, sad, grievous, calamitous, pitiable, mournful, melancholy, miserable, disastrous. *Felicitous*

Deplore, Lament, mourn, grieve, bemoan, bewail, sorrow. *Rejoice*

Deploy, Open, extend, expand, desplay, unfold.

Deport, Banish, expel.

Deportment, Behaviour, carriage, demeanour, manner, conduct, air, mien, bearing, breeding.

Depose, *v.a.,* Dethrone, cashier, oust, displace, degrade. *Enthrone* *v.n.,* Declare, testify, avouch.

Deposit, *v.a.,* Lay, drop, place, precipitate. Store, hoard, put, save, lodge, intrust, commit.

Deposit, *n.,* Sediment, precipitate. Security, stake, pawn, pledge.

Depositary, Trustee, guardian, fiduciary.

Deposition, Affidavit, declaration, evidence, testimony. Dethroning, removal, dismissal, displacement. *Enthronement*

Depository, Depôt, magazine, warehouse, storehouse, deposit.

Depôt, Depository, magazine.†

Depravation, Deterioration, degeneracy, degeneration, impairment, injury, vitiation, debasement, abasement, corruption, depravity, demoralization, wickedness. *Improvement*

Deprave, Corrupt, demoralize, deteriorate, debase, vitiate, contaminate, pollute, degrade. *Improve*

Depraved, Corrupted, corrupt, demoralized, immoral, wicked, vicious, bad, lost, abandoned, profligate, licentious, dissolute, reprobate, hardened, shameless, graceless. *Virtuous*

Depravity, Corruption, demoralization, immorality, degeneracy, depravation. *Virtue*

Deprecate, Intercede, expostulate, disavow, disclaim. *Entreat*

Depreciate, *v.a.,* Disparage, underrate, underestimate, undervalue, degrade, traduce, belittle, malign, decry, censure. *Appreciate* *v.n.,* Decline, fall.

Depreciation, Disparagement, traducing, belittling, maligning, censure, derogation, detraction. *Appreciation* Decline, fall.

Depredation, Havoc, spoliation, plunder, pillage, pilfering, robbery, rapine, theft, trespass, encroachment, invasion, inroad. *Compensation*

Depredator, Robber, thief, plunderer, spoiler, trespasser, invader, brigand.

Depress, Dishearten, discourage, dispirit, damp, dampen, weaken, deject, sadden, chill. *Encourage* Humble, lower, debase, abase, degrade, disgrace, abash, humiliate, detrude, reduce, bow, sink, drop. *Elevate*

Depression, Discouragement, dejection, sadness, gloom, gloominess, melancholy, despondency, dolefulness, dolour. *Gaiety* Humiliation, lowering, debasement, degradation, abashment, detrusion, reduction. *Elevation* Cavity, hollow, dent, dip, valley, vale, hollowness, concavity, indentation, pit, excavation, dimple. Stagnation, inactivity, dulness. *Activity*

Deprivation, Privation, bereavement, robbery, dispossession, spoliation, loss. *Endowment*

Deprive, Strip, rob, divest, bereave, dispossess, despoil. *Endow*

Depth, Deepness, profundity, profoundness, perspicacity, astuteness, sagacity, penetration, wisdom, shrewdness, discernment. *Superficiality*
Measure, extent.
Middle, midst.
Abyss, chasm.

Depurate, Clarify, purify, cleanse.

Deputation, Commission, delegation, delegates, deputies, legation, embassy.

Depute, Appoint, commission, charge, delegate, intrust, authorize, credit. *Dismiss*

Deputy, Delegate, agent, representative, envoy, commissioner, legate, nuncio, substitute, proxy, lieutenant.

Deracinate, Uproot, extirpate, exterminate, eradicate.

Derange, Disorder, disarrange, disturb, confuse, displace, disconcert, upset, ruffle, discompose, madden, unbalance. *Arrange*

Derangement, Disorder, disarrangement, disturbance,† lunacy, mania, insanity, hallucination, delirium. *Order*

Derelict, Relinquished, abandoned, forsaken, deserted, left, quitted, stranded.

Dereliction, Relinquishment, abandonment, desertion, renunciation, neglect, faithlessness, delinquency, negligence, failure, shortcoming. *Observance*

Deride, Mock, laugh, ridicule, scoff, jeer, scout, scorn, taunt, lampoon, satirize. *Respect*

Derision, Mockery, laughter, ridicule, scorn, contumely, disrespect, contempt, irony. *Respect*

Derisive, Mocking, laughing, ridiculing.† *Respectful*

Derivation, Source, origin, origination, foundation, beginning, rise, descent, extraction, genealogy, growth, spring, root, cause. *Conclusion*

Derive, Deduce, follow, trace, track.
Draw, obtain, receive, get.

Derogate, Disparage, detract, diminish, lessen, depreciate,† decry.† *Appreciate*

Derogation, Disparagement, detraction.† *Appreciation*

Derogatory, Disparaging, detracting, depreciative, dishonouring. *Appreciative*

Descant, *v.n.,* Dilate, discourse, talk, enlarge, expatiate, discuss, dissert, dwell, amplify. *Abridge*
n., Melody, tune, variation.

Descend, Dismount, alight, drop, sink, fall. *Rise*
Originate.

Descendants, Offspring, children, progeny, posterity, issue. *Ancestors*

Descent, Fall, drop, descending. *Ascent*
Slope, decline, declivity. *Rise*
Origin, origination, extraction, derivation, genealogy.
Attack, raid, invasion, assault, onset, incursion, foray.

Describe, Delineate, portray, show, tell, explain, draw, illustrate, picture, trace, depict, relate, narrate, recount, define, specify, characterize. *Mystify*

Description, Delineation, portrayal, explanation,† account, report, recital.
Class, order, kind, sort, shape, form, species.

Descry, Detect, see, perceive, discover, recognize, discern, espy, behold, glimpse, distinguish, mark, observe. *Miss*

Desecrate, Abuse, pollute, profane, secularize, misuse. *Sanctify*

Desecration, Abuse, pollution.† *Sanctification*

Desert, *v.a.,* Abandon, leave, quit, forsake, renounce, relinquish, resign. *Hold*
v.n., Abscond, fly, run.
a., Forsaken, desolate, wild, barren, uninhabited, sterile, waste, untilled, solitary. *Fertile*
n., Wild, wilderness, waste, solitude.
Deserving, worth, merit, due.

Deserted, Abandoned, forsaken, left, relinquished, forlorn, derelict, lonely.

Deserter, Renegade, turncoat, quitter, runaway, recreant, delinquent.

Desertion, Abandonment, dereliction, relinquishment, renunciation.

Deserve, Earn, justify, merit, win. *Forfeit*

Deserving, Worthy, meritorious, needful, suitable, adequate. *Unworthy*

Desiccate, Dry, exsiccate. *Moisten*

Desiderate, Want, desire, need, require, miss, lack. *Forget*

Desideratum, Requisite, want, need, complement, essential. *Drawback*

Design, *v.a.,* Plan, plot, scheme, propose, purpose, mean, intend, devise, contrive, concoct, project, brew, prepare, contemplate. *Chance*
Delineate, draw, sketch, paint, describe, trace, limn.
n., Plan, plot, scheme,† aim.
Delineation, drawing, sketch, painting, outline, draught, plan.

Designate, Name, style, call, christen, entitle, denominate, term,

Characterize, particularize, distinguish, mark, denote, specify, show, define, indicate, describe.

Appoint, allot, allocate, assign.

Designation, Name, style, title, denomination, appellation, epithet.

Characterization, particularization, distinction, specification, indication, description.

Class, sort, order, kind, species, description.

Designing, Artful, crafty, wily, crooked, tricky, trickish, deceitful, dishonest, cunning, astute, foxy, scheming, sly, treacherous, insidious, intriguing, arch, diplomatic, subtle. *Artless*

Desinence, Conclusion, end, finality, termination, cessation, discontinuance, period. *Inception*

Desirable, Valuable, expedient, acceptable, profitable, good, eligible, enviable, beneficial. *Detestable*

Desire, *v.a.,* Want, wish for, covet, crave, long for, fancy, yearn for, lust after, hanker after, solicit, request, ask. *Detest*

n., Want, wish, craving,† proclivity, impulse, inclination, will, appetite, passion, longing, eagerness, lust. *Aversion*

Desirous, Longing, yearning, eager. *Apathetic*

Desist, Stop, cease, stay, discontinue, end, forbear, pause. *Persist*

Desolate, *a.,* Lone, lonely, lonesome, solitary, uninhabited, companionless, desert, forsaken, deserted. *Frequented*

Forlorn, dreary, wild, barren, waste, ruined, desolated, devastated, ravaged, destroyed, bare, bleak, miserable, cheerless, wretched, comfortless, bereaved. *Cheerful*

v.a., Ravage, destroy, devastate, ruin, waste, spoil, sack, despoil, depopulate, plunder, pillage. *Cultivate*

Desolation, Ravage, destruction, devastation.†

Gloom, misery, desolateness, loneliness, solitude, dreariness, bleakness, bareness, barrenness, wildness, wretchedness, unhappiness, gloominess, bereavement, sadness. *Joy*

Despair, *v.n.,* Faint, despond. *Hope*

n., Despondency,† hopelessness, desperation.

Despatch, *v.a.,* Hasten, hurry, accelerate, expedite, quicken, speed, forward, send, finish, end, terminate, conclude. *Impede*

Murder, kill, slay, slaughter, assassinate.

n., Haste, acceleration, expedition, quickness, speed, rapidity, celerity, diligence. *Sloth*

Despatch, Message, communication, report, missive.

Despatching, sending. *Receive*

Desperado, Ruffian, marauder, thug, gangster, apache, villain.

Desperate, Desponding, hopeless, despairing, irredeemable, inextricable, irretrievable, abandoned, wretched, forlorn. *Hopeful*

Daring, heroic, wild, audacious, rash, reckless, frantic, precipitate, extreme, determined. *Cautious*

Desperation, Despondency, hopelessness, despair. *Hope*

Recklessness, rashness, fury, rage. *Coolness*

Despicable, Contemptible, low, vile, mean, base, paltry, abject, pitiful, unworthy, worthless. *Praiseworthy*

Despise, Disdain, contemn, spurn, scorn, slight, scout, ignore, disregard. *Admire*

Despite, *n.,* Spite, malice, malevolence, malignity. *Charity*

prep., Notwithstanding, opposing, resisting.

Despoil, Pillage, plunder, spoil, rob, strip, divest, deprive, denude, bereave, devastate, desolate, ravage, spoliate, rifle. *Endow*

Despond, Despair, faint.† *Hope*

Despondency, Despair, desperation, melancholy, hopelessness, depression, gloom, sadness, discouragement, dejection. *Hopefulness*

Despondent, Despairing, desperate, melancholy,† disheartened, dispirited, downcast, downhearted. *Hopeful*

Despot, Tyrant, autocrat, dictator, oppressor. *Subject*

Despotic, Tyrannical, tyrannous, autocratic, dictatorial, oppressive, imperious, absolute, arbitrary, irresponsible. *Limited*

Despotism, Tyranny, autocracy, dictatorship.†

Destination, Haven, goal, harbour, objective, end, terminus. *Beginning*

Lot, doom, fate, destiny, fortune.

Destine, Ordain, design, purpose, intend, devote, decree, appoint, allot, consecrate. *Divert*

Destiny, Lot, destination, fate, star, fortune, doom.

Destitute, Poor, necessitous, needy, indigent, distressed, penniless. *Rich*

Wanting, lacking, devoid, without.

Destitution, Poverty, need, indigence, distress, penury, want, privation. *Wealth*

Destroy, Demolish, subvert, annihilate,

raze, ruin, overthrow, overturn, quench, extinguish, devastate, desolate, waste, devour, ravage, eradicate, extirpate, slay, kill. ***Create***

Destruction, Demolition, subversion, annihilation.† ***Creation***

Destructive, Pernicious, noxious, baneful, harmful, hurtful, baleful, injurious, detrimental, fatal, deadly, deleterious, ruinous, mischievous. ***Beneficial***

Desuetude, Obsolescence, obsoleteness, discontinuance, disuse, non-observance. ***Observance***

Desultory, Cursory, discursive, casual, spasmodic, irregular, fitful, unmethodical, loose, rambling, wandering, vague, aberrant, capricious, roving, erratic, inexact, unsystematic. ***Methodical***

Detach, Separate, part, sever, dissever, divide, split, disconnect, disunite, disjoin, disengage. ***Attach***
Detail, appoint, despatch.

Detail, *v.a.*, Recount, relate, enumerate, particularize, describe, delineate, portray, rehearse, narrate.
Detach, appoint, despatch.
n., Part, point, component, particular, item.

Detain, Delay, stay, stop, hinder, check, restrain, restrict, hold, retain, keep, confine. ***Loose***

Detect, Descry, discover, find, unmask, expose, reveal, ascertain. ***Hide***

Detection, Discovery, exposure.

Deter, Hinder, discourage, restrain, withhold, prevent, dissuade, stop, scare, terrify, disincline, warn. ***Encourage***

Detergent, Cleansing, purging, mundatory, detersive, abstergent, detersion.

Deteriorate, *v.n.*, Decline, degenerate. ***Improve***
v.a., Vitiate, impair, debase, depreciate, degrade.

Deterioration, Decline, declension, degeneration, degeneracy, vitiation, impairment, debasement, depreciation, degradation, depravation, caducity. ***Improvement***

Determinable, Fixable, definable. ***Uncertain***

Determinate, Fixed, definite, positive, certain, absolute, settled, limited, established, explicit, express. ***Vague***

Determination, Decision, firmness, resolution, constancy, certainty, fixity, resoluteness, persistence. ***Weakness***
Conclusion, decision, resolve, result, purpose, judgment.

Determine, *v.a.*, Conclude, decide, resolve, judge, settle, fix, end, adjust.

Determine, Certify, verify, ascertain. Lead, induce, influence, incline.
v.n., Decide, conclude, resolve. ***Waive***

Detersion, Detergent, abstergent, cleansing, purifying.

Detest, Abominate, abhor, loathe, hate, execrate. ***Love***

Detestable, Abominable, abhorrent, abhorred, loathsome, hateful, execrable, cursed, accursed, damnable, odious, vile, horrid, horrible, repulsive, nauseating, sickening, disgusting, offensive. ***Adorable***

Detestation, Abomination, abhorrence, loathing.† ***Love***

Dethrone, Depose. ***Crown***

Detonate, Explode, detonize, blast.

Detour, Deviation, roundabout, indirect, circuitous.

Detract, Disparage, depreciate, asperse, slander, decry, derogate, traduce, belittle, vilify, defame, abuse, calumniate, lessen, lower, diminish, deteriorate. ***Appreciate***

Detraction, Disparagement, depreciation, slur, aspersion.† ***Appreciation***

Detriment, Injury, damage, loss, hurt, harm, evil, mischief, prejudice. ***Benefit***

Detrimental, Injurious, hurtful, harmful, evil, mischievous, pernicious, bad, baneful, baleful, deleterious, prejudicial. ***Beneficial***

Detrude, Lower, dash, drop, depress, sink, thrust. ***Raise***

Detruncate, Cripple, maim, lame, mutilate, mangle, amputate, dismember.

Detrusion, Lowering, dashing, dropping.†

Devastate, Despoil, ravage, waste, rob, plunder, pillage, spoil, spoliate, strip, sack, desolate. ***Endow***

Devastation, Despoiling, ravage, wasting.†

Develop } *v.n.*, Grow, open, unfold, expand, evolve. ***Restrict***
Develope }
v.a., Evolve, expand, enlarge, amplify, unfold, disclose, disentangle, unravel, exhibit, show.

Development, Growth, evolution, opening, increase, progress, advance. ***Retrogression***
Amplification, expansion, disentanglement, exhibition, disclosure, unravelling, unfolding.

Deviate, Veer, diverge, wander, digress, depart, stray, err, deflect, turn, tack, wheel, swerve. ***Continue***
Vary, differ, diverge, change.

Deviation, Divergence, wandering, digression, departure.† ***Continuity***
Variation, variance, difference, divergence, change.

Device, Scheme, invention, contrivance, artifice, plan, ruse, idea, stratagem, wile, design, expedient, manœuvre, fraud, shift, resort.

Design, emblem, symbol, type, bearing, motto, legend, inscription.

Devil, Demon, evil spirit, goblin, Satan, Lucifer. *Angel*

Devilish, Diabolical, demonic, demoniac, demon, satanic, fiendish, infernal, wicked, atrocious, shocking, cruel, evil, malicious. *Angelic*

Devious, Erratic, divergent, wandering, deviating, crooked, strange, obscure, tortuous, roundabout, ambiguous, distorted, mazy, labyrinthine, circuitous, meandering, trackless, untracked, pathless. *Straight*

Devise, Scheme, invent, contrive, plan, project, design, manœuvre, manage, compass, concoct.

Devoid, Void, empty, wanting, lacking, vacant, blank, destitute, unendowed. *Replete*

Devolve, Place, impose, transfer, depute, commission. *Pass*

Devote, Resign, give, dedicate, yield, consecrate, appropriate, destine. *Keep*

Devoted, Ardent, fond, attached, affectionate, loving, dedicated, zealous, earnest, assiduous. *Faithless*

Devotee, Zealot, enthusiast, fanatic, bigot. *Votary*

Devotion, Religion, devoutness, piety, devotedness, holiness, saintliness, adoration, worship. *Profanity*

Consecration, dedication.

Zeal, ardour, eagerness, enthusiasm, earnestness, devotedness.

Love, attachment, affection.

Devotional, Religious, pious, devout, saintly, godly.

Devour, Consume, eat, gorge, gobble, bolt, swallow, absorb. *Vomit*

Devout, Devotional, religious, pious, devoted, holy, saintly, solemn, grave, sincere. *Profane*

Dexterity, Cleverness, skill, skilfulness, readiness, expertness, quickness, handiness, adroitness, aptitude, aptness, tact, ability, knack, facility, art. *Clumsiness*

Dexterous, Clever, skilled, skilful.† *Clumsy*

Diabolical, Devilish, demonic, demoniac, demon, satanic, fiendish, infernal, wicked, atrocious, shocking, cruel, evil, malicious. *Angelic*

Diadem, Crown, coronal, coronet, wreath, tiara, chaplet.

Diagnosis / **Diagnostic** Indication, distinction, clue, feature, character, sign, symptom.

Diagram, Sketch, figure, graph, drawing, delineation.

Dialect, Tongue, speech, language, parlance.

Idiom, provincialism, accent.

Dialectic, Logical, argumentative, critical, rhetorical. *Colloquial*

Dialogue, Conversation, conference, confabulation, colloquy, discourse.

Diametrically, Direct, opposition, antagonistically.

Diaphaneity, Clarity, transparency, translucency, pellucidness. *Muddiness*

Diaphanous, Clear, transparent, translucent, pellucid. *Muddy*

Diary, Chronicle, record, register, account, journal.

Diatribe, Abuse, invective, tirade, philippic, reviling. *Eulogy*

Dissertation, effusion, disquisition, disputation.

Dicacity, Flippancy, pertness, sauciness, 'cheek'.

Dictate, *v.a.*, Command, direct, order, enjoin, ordain, decree, bid, pronounce, require.

Speak, utter.

n., Command, direction,† rule, precept, maxim.

Dictator, Despot, ruler, autocrat, tyrant, oppressor.

Dictatorial, Despotic, autocratic, tyrannous, absolute, imperious, arbitrary, domineering, overbearing. *Affable*

Diction, Speech, expression, style, language, phraseology, grammar, rhetoric.

Dictionary, Lexicon, vocabulary, glossary, encyclopaedia, cyclopaedia, nomenclature.

Dictum, Saying, saw, tag, maxim, precept, assertion, affirmation.

Didactic, Moral, instructive, preceptive, directive. *Misleading*

Diddle, Trifle, dawdle.

Die, *v.n.*, Depart, decease, cease, expire. *Live*

Decline, wane, languish, fall, fade, perish, wither, decay, sink, faint, disappear, vanish. *Grow*

n., Stamp, cube, tablet.

Diet, Food, fare, sustenance, nourishment, nutriment, repast, meal, provisions, victuals, aliment, commons, rations, viands.

Parliament, congress, council, assembly, convocation, chamber.

Differ, Diverge, vary, deviate. *Correspond*

Disagree, argue, contend, wrangle, dispute, bicker. *Agree*

Difference, Divergence, diversity, deviation, contrast, disparity, dissimilarity, unlikeness, contrariety, dissimilitude. *Similarity*

Disagreement, argument, contention, wrangle, dispute, bickering, strife, contest, discord, dissonance, dissension, variance, debate, altercation, controversy, misunderstanding, jarring, alienation, schism, rupture, breach. *Agreement*

Different, Divergent, diverse, deviating.† *Alike*

Differentiate, Distinguish, particularize, individualize, discriminate, disseminate. *Generalize*

Difficult, Hard, up-hill, herculean, arduous. *Easy*

Intricate, obscure, involved, deep, perplexing, enigmatical. *Simple*

Unamenable, reserved, austere, rigid, unmanageable, intractable, unaccommodating, unyielding. *Tractable*

Difficulty, Hardness, arduousness. *Ease*

Trouble, impediment, obstacle, hindrance, barrier, bar, obstruction.

Exigency, dilemma, embarrassment, emergency, perplexity.

Diffidence, Modesty, shyness, bashfulness, timidity, doubt, distrust, hesitation, sheepishness, reluctance. *Assurance*

Diffident, Modest, shy, bashful.†

Diffuse, *v.a.,* Scatter, spread, disperse, disseminate, propagate, circulate, publish, distribute, lavish. *Gather*

a., Copious, prolix, rambling, discursive, loose, vague, wordy, verbose. *Terse*

Diffusion, Scattering, spread, dispersion,† extension.

Diffusive, Expansive, spreading, permeating. *Contracting*

Dig, *v.a.,* Delve, excavate, scoop, grub, channel, quarry.

n., Punch, thrust, poke.

Digest, *v.a.,* Systematize, codify, classify, arrange, array, order, sort, methodize, dispose, tabulate, prepare. *Disarrange*

Assimilate, master, study, ponder, contemplate, consider, reflect, meditate, revolve.

n., System, code.

Abridgment, epitome, summary, abstract, compendium, compend, synopsis, syllabus, conspectus, abbreviation. *Amplification*

Digit, Finger, toe.

Symbol.

Dignified, Noble, honourable, stately, majestic, august, decorous, imposing, grand, great, grave. *Lowly*

Dignify, Ennoble, honour, elevate, exalt, raise, advance, promote, aggrandize, adorn, grace. *Degrade*

Dignity, Nobility, nobleness, honour, stateliness, majesty, grandeur, greatness, importance, elevation, exaltation, advancement, rank, station, standing, preferment, height, eminence, glory, respectability, reputableness, decorum, gravity, worth. *Lowliness*

Dignitary, magistrate, ruler.

Digress, Deviate, diverge, wander, err, turn, swerve, depart. *Continue*

Digression, Deviation, divergence.†

Dilacerate, Lacerate, tear, rend.

Dilapidate, Disintegrate, ruin, destroy, waste, demolish, dismantle. *Renovate*

Dilapidated, Disintegrated, ruined.† *Renovated*

Dilapidation, Disintegration, downfall, ruin,† decay, crumbling. *Renovation*

Dilatation, Amplification, expansion, expanding, swelling, enlargement, dilation. *Contraction*

Dilate, *v.a.,* Amplify, expand, swell, enlarge, extend, widen, distend, stretch. *Contract*

v.n., Expand, widen, stretch, extend.

Descant, yarn, expatiate.

Dilation, Dilatation, amplification, expansion, expanding.† *Contraction*

Dilatory, Slow, tardy, tedious, procrastinating, dawdling, behindhand, lagging, laggard, lingering, sluggish, dallying, backward, loitering. *Prompt*

Dilemma, Difficulty, plight, case, problem, fix, quandary, predicament, strait.

Dilettante, Critic, amateur, pretender.

Diligence, Industry, assiduity, assiduousness, attention, heed, care, application, sedulousness, perseverance, activity. *Sloth*

Diligent, Industrious, assiduous, attentive,† busy. *Slothful*

Dilly-dally, Loiter, lag, dally, dawdle, idle, linger, delay, saunter.

Dilute, Water, reduce, attenuate, thin, weaken. *Strengthen*

Dim, *a.,* Obscure, dark, cloudy, clouded, dusky, blurred, dull, dulled, tarnished, darkened, dingy, faint, confused, hazy, shadowy, indistinct, indefinite, vague, mysterious. *Bright*

v.a., Obscure, darken, cloud, becloud, blur, dull, tarnish, confuse. *Brighten*

Dimension, Measurement, measure, extent, size, extension, capacity, volume, mass, magnitude, bulk.

Dimidiate, Bisect, halve.

Diminish, *v.a.*, Lessen, decrease, reduce, contract, retrench, curtail, cut, abate. *Increase*

v.n., Lessen, decrease, contract, abate, subside.

Diminution, Lessening, decrease, reduction.†

Diminutive, Small, little, minute, tiny, pygmy, dwarfish, puny. *Large*

Din, Noise, clamour, uproar, clangour, clash, clashing, crash, crashing, clatter, rattle, racket, resonance, hubbub, reverberation. *Quiet*

Dingle, Dell, dale, glen, valley, vale.

Dingy, Dull, dulled, dim, dark, dusky, obscure, brown, sombre, faded, colourless, soiled, sullied, smirched, dirty. *Bright*

Dint, Blow, stroke, dent, indentation, notch, nick.

Power, force.

Diocese, See, bishopric, episcopate, jurisdiction, charge.

Dip, *v.a.*, Douse, immerse, duck, souse, plunge.

v.n., Plunge, dive, pitch.

Incline.

n., Slope, depression, declivity. *Acclivity*

Diplomacy, Tact, negotiation, outwitting, circumvention.

Diplomat, Diplomatist, negotiator, ambassador, envoy, plenipotentiary.

Diplomatic, Prudent, wise, careful, tactful, knowing, sagacious, judicious, artful. *Bungling*

Dire, Dreadful, terrible, horrible, horrid, direful, fearful, shocking, dismal, gloomy, destructive, calamitous, portentous, terrific, tremendous, awful, disastrous.

Direct, *a.*, Straight. *Crooked*
Express, plain, unambiguous, categorical, unequivocal. *Ambiguous*
Sincere, open, frank, outspoken, ingenuous, artless. *Crafty*

v.a., Order, enjoin, command, bid, require, prescribe, instruct, govern, rule, regulate, conduct, manage, dispose.

Guide, lead, point, show, conduct. *Mislead*

Aim, point, make.

Superscribe, address.

Direction, Order, injunction, instruction, command.†

Guidance, lead.

Aim, tendency.

Superscription, address.

Directly, Soon, presently, immediately, promptly, quickly, speedily, instantly, forthwith, anon, straightway. *Previously*

Director, Instructor, ruler, controller, adviser, manager, master, superintendent, leader, monitor, mentor, conductor, guide.

Direful, Dire, dreadful, terrible, horrible, horrid, fearful, shocking, dismal, gloomy, destructive, calamitous, disastrous, portentous, terrific, tremendous, awful.

Dirge, Requiem, elegy, lament, threnody, coronach.

Dirt, Filth, foulness, sordidness, uncleanness, soil, muck, grime, mud, puddle. *Cleanness*

Dirty, Filthy, foul, sordid, unclean, soiled, mucky, grimy, muddy, begrimed, sullied, nasty, squalid. *Clean*
Clouded, dark, dull, cloudy, sullied, sloppy, muddy, rainy, squally.
Mean, vile, abject, base, paltry, low, despicable, contemptible, pitiful, grovelling. *Honourable*

Disability, Disqualification, impotency, impotence, inability, unfitness, incapacity, incompetence, incapability. *Fitness*

Disable, Disqualify, unfit, incapacitate. *Fit*
Enfeeble, weaken, cripple, paralyse. *Strengthen*

Disabuse, Correct, undeceive, enlighten. *Deceive*

Disadvantage, Inconvenience, unfavourableness, detriment, loss, drawback, damage, injury, harm, hurt. *Benefit*

Disadvantageous, Inconvenient, unfavourable,† deleterious, baneful. *Beneficial*

Disaffect, Estrange, alienate. *Win*

Disaffected, Disloyal, unfaithful, untrue, undutiful, estranged, alienated, dissatisfied. *Faithful*

Disaffection, Estrangement, alienation, disagreement, breach, disloyalty, dissatisfaction.

Disagree, Differ, vary, diverge, deviate. *Correspond*
Dissent, argue, dispute, wrangle, differ, bicker, debate, quarrel, contend. *Assent*

Disagreeable, Offensive, unpleasant, unpleasing, displeasing, nasty, obnoxious, unwelcome, distasteful. *Pleasant*

Disagreement, Difference, dissension, argument, dispute, wrangle, bickering, debate, strife, contention, contest, quarrel, discord, variance, misunderstanding, clashing, jarring. *Harmony*
Difference, divergence, dissimilarity,

diversity, deviation, discrepancy, dissimilitude *Similarity*

Disallow, Forbid, prohibit, refuse, reject, deny, disclaim, disapprove, discountenance, disavow, disown. *Sanction*

Disannul, Annul, repeal, nullify, abolish, rescind, cancel, void, quash, abrogate, invalidate, extinguish, obliterate. *Confirm*

Disappear, Vanish, fade, dissolve, melt, recede, cease. *Appear*

Disappoint, Frustrate, baffle, confound, thwart, defeat, foil, check, balk, disconcert, delude, deceive, betray, vex, mortify. *Satisfy*

Disappointment, Frustration, baffling, confounding.† *Satisfaction*

Disapprobation, Disapproval, condemnation, blame, censure, dislike, displeasure. *Approval*

Disapproval, Disapprobation, condemnation.† *Approbation*

Disapprove, Condemn, blame, censure, dislike. *Condone*

Disarm, Disable, incapacitate, weaken, strip, divest.

Disarrange, Derange, disorder, disturb upset, unsettle, confuse. *Order*

Disarray, Disarrangement, disorder, derangement, disturbance, confusion, muddle. *Arrange*

Disaster, Calamity, misfortune, mischance, mishap, accident, catastrophe, reverse, casualty, stroke, blow, affliction, adversity, visitation. *Blessing*

Disastrous, Calamitous, catastrophic, unfortunate, unlucky, adverse, afflicting, hapless, untoward, ill-fated, ruinous, unprosperous, destructive. *Auspicious*

Disavow, Disallow, deny, reject, disclaim, disown. *Acknowledge*

Disband, Disperse, separate, break up, scatter, disembody. *Gather*

Disbelief, Unbelief, doubt, rejection, distrust. *Faith*

Disbelieve, Doubt, reject, distrust, discredit. *Credit*

Disburden, Ease, unburden, unload, disencumber, relieve, free, *disburthen.* *Encumber*

Disburse, Spend, expend.

Discard, Cast, abandon, reject, discharge, repudiate, dismiss, cashier.

Discern, Descry, see, perceive, recognize, ascertain, observe, espy, behold, discover. *Ignore*

Distinguish, separate, discriminate, differentiate, choose, judge.

Discernible, Visible, conspicuous, manifest, palpable.† *Obscure*

Discernment, Descrying, perception, recognition.†

Discrimination, sagacity, judgment, perspicacity, shrewdness, insight, cleverness, observation, perception, far-sightedness, clear-sightedness, sharpness, ingenuity, astuteness, brightness, intelligence, wit. *Dulness*

Discharge, *v.a.*, Expel, eject, cashier, discard, dismiss, emit, excrete. *Absorb*

Free, liberate, acquit, absolve, exonerate, release, loose, clear, relieve. *Detain*

Disburden, unload, unburden, disencumber, empty. *Load*

Perform, fulfil, execute, observe, do. *Neglect*

n., Expulsion, ejection, dismissal, emission, flow, vent, evacuation, excretion. *Absorption*

Liberation, acquittal, absolution, exoneration, release, clearance, quittance. *Detention*

Disburdening, unloading, disencumbering, emptying. *Loading*

Performance, fulfilment, doing, execution, observation. *Neglect*

Disciple, Follower, votary, adherent, supporter, believer, student, scholar, learner, pupil. *Master*

Discipline, *v.a.*, Train, educate, instruct, teach, drill, exercise, train, breed.

Govern, regulate, control, school, correct, punish, chastise, coerce. *Indulge*

n., Training, education, instruction.† Government, regulation, control,† subjection. *Disorder*

Disclaim, Disown, deny, disavow, reject, renounce. *Confess*

Disclaimer, Repudiation, denial, disavowal, abjuration, disowning, rejection, renunciation, relinquishment. *Confession*

Disclose, Reveal, expose, uncover, discover, show, divulge, betray, tell, utter, communicate, unveil, unfold. *Hide*

Disclosure, Revelation, exposure, discovery.†

Discolour, Stain, disfigure, tarnish, daub, taint, tinge. *Embellish*

Discomfit, Defeat, rout, balk, frustrate, disconcert, upset, overthrow, overpower, overwhelm, overcome, beat, subdue, conquer, vanquish, check, checkmate, confound. *Rally*

Discomfiture, Defeat, rout, balking.† *Encouragement*

Discomfort, Disquiet, unpleasantness, annoyance, trouble, vexation, uneasiness, disagreeableness. *Ease*

Discommode, Annoy, disturb, disquiet, molest, trouble, inconvenience.

Discompose, Disconcert, perplex, worry, harass, bewilder, abash, embarrass, agitate, vex, plague, annoy, irritate, provoke, disquiet, ruffle, displease, fret, trouble, chafe, nettle, excite. *Quiet* Derange, disorder, disarrange, upset, unsettle, confuse, jumble, embroil, disturb. *Arrange*

Discomposure, Disconcertion, perturbation, perplexity, worry,† uneasiness. *Easiness* Derangement, disorder, disarrangement.† *Arrangement*

Disconcert, Discompose, perplex, worry, bewilder, abash, embarrass, agitate, perturb, unbalance, confuse, disturb. *Compose* Discomfit, defeat, rout, balk, frustrate, upset, overthrow, overpower, overwhelm, beat, overcome, subdue, conquer, vanquish, check, checkmate, confound, baffle, thwart, contravene. *Rally*

Disconnect, Detach, sever, disunite, disjoin, separate, disengage, dissever, divide, part. *Join*

Disconnection, Detachment, severance, disunion, disjunction, separation, isolation, disassociation. *Union*

Disconsolate, Forlorn, unhappy, sad, desolate, melancholy, comfortless, cheerless, woeful, sorrowful, inconsolable. *Joyous*

Discontent, Discontentment, dissatisfaction, restlessness, uneasiness. *Satisfaction*

Discontinue, Stop, cease, intermit, interrupt, suspend, end, terminate. *Continue*

Discontinuous, Broken, interrupted, intermittent, discrete. *Unbroken*

Discord, Discordance, dissonance, harshness, dissension, jarring, strife, contention, disagreement, difference, wrangling, rupture, variance. *Harmony*

Discordant, Dissonant, harsh, jarring,† contrary, incongruous, contradictory, repugnant, unharmonious. *Harmonious*

Discount, Rebate, allowance, abatement, deduction, reduction. *Premium*

Discountenance, Disapprove, discourage, check, frown, disfavour. *Encourage*

Discourage, Damp, dampen, depress, deject, dishearten, dispirit. *Rally* Discountenance, disfavour, disapprove, deter, dissuade. *Countenance*

Discourse, *v.n.,* Talk, converse, speak, expatiate, confer, confabulate, parley. *n.,* Talk, conversation, speech,† disquisition, sermon, dissertation, homily.

Discourteous, Rude, brusque, abrupt, ill-mannered, unmannerly, uncivil, impolite, disrespectful, uncourtly, ungentlemanly, ill-bred, short, curt. *Polite*

Discourtesy, Rudeness, brusqueness.† *Civility*

Discover, Detect, ascertain, find, find out, See, discern, glimpse, behold, descry, espy. *Miss* Disclose, reveal, show, exhibit, uncover, expose, bare, divulge, betray, unfold, manifest. *Conceal*

Discovery, Detection, ascertainment, finding, finding-out. Disclosure, revelation, showing.† *Concealment*

Discredit, *v.a.,* Disbelieve, doubt, question, distrust. *Believe* Dishonour, disgrace. *Honour* *n.,* Disbelief, doubt, question, distrust. *Belief* Dishonour, disgrace, shame, ignominy, disrepute, reproach, odium, obloquy, opprobrium. *Honour*

Discreditable, Dishonourable, disgraceful, shameful, ignominious. *Honourable*

Discreet, Wise, sagacious, cautious, prudent, wary, circumspect, judicious, heedful, considerate, thoughtful, careful. *Rash*

Discrepancy, Disagreement, disharmony, difference, dissonance, incongruity, inconsistency, contrariety, discord, discordance, divergence, variance. *Correspondence*

Discrepant, Disagreeing, inharmonious, differing,† conflicting, clashing, jarring. *Corresponding*

Discrete, Separate, distinct, disjunct, discontinuous.

Discretion, Wisdom, sagacity, prudence, caution, wariness, circumspection, care, judiciousness, heedfulness, consideration, thought, carefulness, judgment. *Rashness*

Discretional, Optional, voluntary. *Compulsory*

Discriminate, Distinguish, differentiate, discern, judge. *Indiscriminate*

Discrimination, Distinction, differentiation. Penetration, discernment, judgment, wisdom, shrewdness, sagacity, acuteness, insight. *Shortsightedness*

Discursive, Rambling, desultory,† wandering, roving.

Discus, Quoit, disc, disk.

Discuss, Consider, debate, argue, deliberate, sift, reason.

Discussion, Consideration, deliberation, debate, debating, argument, reasoning.

Disdain, *v.a.*. Scorn, spurn, despise, contemn, scout, ignore.　　**Respect**
n., Scorn, contempt, sneer, annoyance, superciliousness, haughtiness, contumely.

Disdainful, Scornful, contemptuous, sneeringly, arrogant.†　　**Respectful**

Disease, Sickness, illness, complaint, malady, distemper, ailment, ail, disorder, infirmity, indisposition.　　**Health**

Diseased, Decayed, unsound, sickly.†

Disembark, Land, debark.　　**Embark**

Disembarrass, Clear, rid, free, ease, disencumber, disengage, extricate, disentangle.　　**Puzzle**

Disembodied, Spiritual, incorporeal, bodiless, unbodied, immaterial.
　　Material

Disembogue, Discharge, empty.

Disembowel, Eviscerate, wound, gut.

Disenable, Disable, disqualify, incapacitate, unfit, hinder, prevent.　　**Qualify**

Disencumber, Disburden, disengage, unburden, free, relieve, ease, release.
　　Burden

Disengage, Disburden, unburden, disencumber, free, relieve, ease, release, loose, disembarrass, disembroil, disentangle, unloose.　　**Entangle**
Separate, disjoin, disunite, detach, sever, dissever, dissociate, divide.　　**Join**

Disengaged, Free, unoccupied, unengaged.　　**Busy**

Disennoble, Disgrace, degrade.

Disentangle, Extricate, free, loose, liberate, detach, disconnect, sever, unravel, unwind, unfold, untwist.

Disenthral, Liberate, free, release, discharge, emancipate, enfranchise.
　　Enslave

Disestablish, Overthrow, annul, discontinue, abolish, abrogate.

Disesteem, Disfavour, disregard, disapprove, disrespect, dislike, disgrace.
　　Favour

Disfavour, Disesteem, disregard, disapprove.†

Disfigure, Deface, deform, spoil, mar, blemish, stain, injure.　　**Adorn**

Disfigurement, Defacement, deformity, blemish, injury.　　**Adornment**

Disgorge, Surrender, yield, give, resign, relinquish, discharge, eject, emit, vomit, spew, vent.

Disgrace, *v.a.*, Dishonour, discredit, disfavour, degrade, humiliate, humble, taint, stain, sully, tarnish, shame, debase, disparage.　　**Honour**
n., Dishonour, disesteem, degradation,

disfavour, disrepute, discredit, reproach, odium, obloquy, ignominy, shame, opprobrium, infamy, scandal, disparagement.

Disgraceful, Dishonourable, disreputable, discreditable, degrading, infamous, scandalous, shameful, ignominious, opprobrious.　　**Honourable**

Disguise, *v.a.*, Mask, conceal, cloak, cover, hide, muffle, dissemble, veil, shroud.　　**Expose**
n., Mask, concealment, cloak, cover, pretext, blind, pretence.

Disgust, *v.a.*, Sicken, offend, displease, nauseate, repulse, repel.　　**Please**
n., Sickness, nausea, repulsion, aversion, loathing, hatred, abhorrence, distaste, disrelish, antipathy, repugnance, abomination, dislike, detestation.　　**Relish**

Disgusting, Sickening, nauseating, repulsive.†

Dish, *n.*, Plate, saucer, bowl, vessel.
Viand, food.
v.a., Thwart, disappoint, frustrate, upset, balk.

Dishearten, Discourage, damp, dampen, deject, depress, dispirit.　　**Encourage**

Dishevelled, Disordered, disorderly, untidy, disarranged, muddled, loose. **Tidy**

Dishonest,. Fraudulent, tricky, trickish, false, faithless, deceitful, unfair, perfidious, crooked, unscrupulous, treacherous, knavish.　　**Fair**

Dishonesty, Fraud, fraudulence, fraudulency, trickery,† improbity, chicanery, guile.　　**Integrity**

Dishonour, *n.*, Reproach, disgrace, discredit, disesteem, disrepute, degradation, odium, obloquy, ignominy, shame, opprobrium, infamy, scandal.　　**Respect**
v.a., Reproach, disgrace, discredit, degrade, shame, debase.

Dishonourable, Disgraceful, disreputable, shameful, scandalous, infamous.
　　Honest

Disinclined, Indisposed, unwilling, reluctant, averse.　　**Willing**

Disinfect, Purify, cleanse, fumigate.
　　Contaminate

Disingenuous, Dishonest, unfair, artful, sinister, insincere, hollow, crafty.
　　Artless

Disintegrate, Crumble, analyse, break up.

Disinter, Exhume, disentomb, exhumate, unbury.　　**Inhume**

Disinterested, Impartial, open, fair, just, unbiassed.　　**Biassed**
Generous, open, liberal, magnanimous, unselfish.　　**Selfish**

Disjoin, Detach, sever, dissever, disunite, disjoint, separate, part, divide, dissociate, sunder, disconnect. *Unite*

Disjoint, Disjoin, detach, sever,† disarrange, derange, luxate, dislocate.

Disjointed, Desultory, incoherent, loose, broken, disconnected. *Connected*

Disjunction, Parting, isolation, separation, disjoining, disconnection, disunion, severance. *Unity*

Dislike, *v.a.*, Hate, disapprove, disrelish, detest, loathe, abominate, abhor. *Love*
n., Hatred, disapproval, disrelish, aversion, distaste, disinclination, repugnance, disgust, antipathy, displeasure.

Dislocate, Disjoint, displace, luxate, disconnect, disturb, derange, disarrange. *Arrange*

Dislocation, Disjointing, displacement, luxation.† *Arrangement*

Dislodge, Remove, eject, oust, expel. *Place*

Disloyal, Perfidious, false, faithless, recreant, treacherous, unfaithful, untrue, disaffected, undutiful. *True*

Disloyalty, Perfidy, falseness, faithlessness, treachery, unfaithfulness, disaffection, undutifulness. *Allegiance*

Dismal, Dreary, gloomy, cheerless, sad, mournful, melancholy, hopeless, dark, dull, doleful, dolorous, sombre, black, funereal, lugubrious, tragic, ominous, foreboding. *Joyous*

Dismantle, Strip, disrobe, despoil, denude, divest. *Equip*

Dismay, *n.*, Terror, fear, fright, affright, horror, alarm, consternation. *Assurance*
v.a., Terrorize, terrify, frighten, affright, horrify, alarm, appal, scare, daunt, dishearten, intimidate. *Rally*

Dismember, Detruncate, disintegrate, disjoint, mutilate, divide, dilacerate, sever, separate, disincorporate, dislimb. *Engraft*

Dismiss, *v.a.*, Discharge, cashier, banish, discard, abandon, remove. *Retain*
v.n., Disband, part, separate, break up.

Dismissal, Discharge, removal, liberation, release. *Retention*

Dismount, *v.n.*, Descend, alight. *Ascend*
v.a., Unhorse, dismantle, displace.

Disobedience, Disobeying, contumacy, indiscipline, unruliness, frowardness, undutifulness, *Compliance*

Disobedient, Disobeying, undisciplined, unruly, froward, undutiful, obstinate, refractory, unsubmissive. *Dutiful*

Disobey, Disregard, ignore, violate, transgress, infringe, break. *Submit*

Disoblige, Offend, displease, annoy. *Accommodate*

Disobliging, Unkind, unfriendly, unaccommodating, perverse, rude, discourteous. *Kind*

Disorder, *v.a.*, Disarrange, derange, confuse, disturb, upset, unsettle, disorganize, dislocate, discompose. *Arrange*
n., Disarrangement, derangement,† disarray, irregularity, jumble, medley, riot, tumult, tumultuousness, turmoil. *Arrangement*
Disease, complaint, sickness, ail, ailment, malady, distemper, indisposition. *Health*

Disorderly, Lawless, unruly, riotous, turbulent, unmanageable, confused, untidy, chaotic, irregular. *Orderly*

Disorganize, Disarrange, derange, disorder, confuse, disturb, upset, unsettle, dislocate, discompose, destroy. *Order*

Disown, Deny, repudiate, disclaim, renounce, reject, disavow, ignore. *Acknowledge*

Disparage, Depreciate, underestimate, undervalue, despise, belittle, decry, underrate, asperse, derogate, reproach, vilify, defame, traduce. *Extol*

Disparagement, Depreciation, underestimation, undervaluation,† detraction, derogation. *Appreciation*

Disparity, Difference, gap, inequality, disproportion, dissimilitude, unlikeness. *Equality*

Dispart, Separate, cleave, split, open, disunite, sever, rend, burst. *Unite*

Dispassionate, Calm, collected, composed, cool, unruffled, unexcited, inexcitable, unimpassioned, undisturbed, imperturbable, serene, quiet, sober, staid, impassive, temperate, urbane. *Spirited*
Disinterested, unbiassed, neutral, fair, impartial, candid. *Biassed*

Dispatch, Send, expedite, accelerate, hasten, execute, conclude. *Retain*

Dispel, Disperse, dismiss, scatter, banish, dissipate. *Collect*

Dispensable, Needless, unnecessary, redundant, superfluous. *Essential*
Apportionable, allotable, distributable, divisible.

Dispensation, Administration, stewardship, rule.
Distribution, distributing, dispersion-dispersing, allotment, assignment, apportionment, apportioning. *Retention*
Economy, scheme, plan, system, arrangement, order, dealing.
License, exemption, immunity, privilege.

Dispense, Administer, rule, execute, apply.

Dispense, Distribute, allot, assign, apportion.

Dispenser, Distributer, divider, mixer, compounder.

Disperse, Dispel, scatter, dissipate, separate, dissolve, disseminate, spread, diffuse. *Collect*

Dispirit, Discourage, depress, deject, damp, dampen, dishearten. *Encourage*

Dispirited, Discouraged, depressed,† down-hearted, downcast, crestfallen, chapfallen, despondent. *Blithe*

Displace, Dislocate, dislodge, move, remove, oust, dismiss, discharge, cashier, eradicate, transplant. *Fix*

Display, *v.a.,* Parade, exhibit, show, flaunt, vaunt, expose, unfold, evince, spread, extend, open, expand. *Hide*
n., Parade, exhibition, show.†

Displease, Offend, provoke, annoy, vex, irritate, fret, anger, chafe, nettle, pique, aggravate, affront, disgust, dissatisfy, disoblige. *Placate*

Displeasure, Offence, provocation, annoyance.†

Disport, *v.n.,* Sport, gambol, play, frolic, frisk, caper, wanton. *Work*
v.a., Entertain, divert, cheer, relax, amuse, solace, beguile.

Dispose, Arrange, group, rank, range, place, set, array, marshal, order, settle, regulate, adjust. *Derange*
Predispose, bias, move, induce, lead, incline.
Sell, convey, transfer.

Disposition, Character, humour, nature, temper, inclination, turn, propensity, predisposition, proneness, proclivity, tendency.

Dispossess, Strip, divest, deprive, derobe.
Eject, evict, oust, dislodge. *House*

Dispraise, Censure, blame, discredit, shame, reproach, dishonour, disgrace.

Disprofit, Damage, loss, detriment.

Disproof, Confutation, refutation, rebuttal. *Confirmation*

Disproportion, Disparity, inequality, inadequacy, insufficiency. *Equality*

Disproportionate, Unequal, inadequate, insufficient, unsuitable, incommensurate, unsymmetrical. *Commensurate*

Disprove, Confute, refute, rebut.
Confirm

Disputable, Questionable, debatable, controversial, open, doubtful, moot.
Certain

Disputant, Debater, arguer, contender, disputer, wrangler, controversialist.†
Advocate

Dispute, *n.,* Disputation, debate, wrangle, controversy, argument, discussion, contest, altercation, disagreement, squabble, bickering. *Agreement*
v.n., Debate, argue, wrangle, disagree, squabble, quarrel, bicker, brawl. *Agree*
v.a., Debate, argue, discuss, contradict, deny, controvert, impugn. *Uphold*

Disqualify, Incapacitate, disable, unfit, injure. *Qualify*
Preclude, disenable, prohibit.

Disquiet, *v.a.,* Trouble, annoy, worry, disturb, harass, plague, pester, molest, bother, *pother.* *Appease*
n., Disquietude, uneasiness, anxiety, trouble, worry, disturbance, unrest, inquietude, agitation, commotion. *Peace*

Disquisition, Dissertation, treatise, discussion, thesis, essay, discourse. *Diatribe*

Disregard, *v.a.,* Ignore, slight, disobey, contemn, overlook. *Heed*
n., Ignoring, slight, disobedience.

Disrelish, Loathe, dislike, detest, abhor, distaste, aversion, repugnance, antipathy. *Like*

Disreputable, Discreditable, opprobrious, shameful, derogatory, infamous, scandalous, disgraceful, dishonourable, shabby, low, vulgar, base, mean. *Respectable*

Disrepute, Discredit, shame, derogation.†
Respect

Disrespect, Disregard, rudeness, discourtesy, impoliteness, incivility, neglect, slight, irreverence, disesteem. *Regard*

Disrespectful, Rude, discourteous, impolite.† *Polite*

Disrobe, Strip, divest, undress, unclothe, undrape, uncover, bare, expose, denude.
Drape

Disruption, Rupture, disintegration, burst, breach, rent. *Union*

Dissatisfaction, Discontent, disquiet, disquietude, uneasiness, anxiety, trouble, agitation, inquietude, unrest, disturbance, disapproval, disapprobation, displeasure, dislike. *Contentment*

Dissatisfied, Discontented, anxious,† uneasy. *Content*

Dissect, Anatomize, examine, study, investigate, analyse, scrutinize, explore, sift. *Unite*

Dissemble, Hide, cloak, conceal, cover, disguise, repress, smother. *Reveal*

Disseminate, Disperse, diffuse, spread, circulate, distribute, publish, proclaim, propagate, promulgate, preach. *Stifle*

Dissemination, Dispersion, diffusion.†

Dissension, Disagreement, discord, strife, contention, clashing, quarrel, difference, variance. *Agreement*

Dissent, Disagree, differ refuse. *Agree*

Dissenter, Nonconformist, dissident, sectary. *Churchman*

Dissentient, Disagreeing, differing, dissenting, objecting. *Agreeing*

Dissertation, Discourse, treatise, disquisition, essay, thesis.

Disservice, Disfavour, harm, hurt, injury, mischief, disadvantage. *Favour*

Dissever, Sever, disjoin, disjoint, disconnect, disunite, dissociate, part, separate, divide, sunder, rend, split, cleave. *Unite*

Dissident, Dissenter, nonconformist, sectary.

Dissilience, Antipathy, avoidance, aversion, repugnance, repulsion. *Affection*

Dissimilar, Unlike, divergent, various, different, diverse, heterogeneous. *Alike*

Dissimilarity, Unlikeness, divergence,† disparity, dissimilitude. *Likeness*

Dissimilitude, Dissimilarity, unlikeness, divergence, difference, diversity, heterogeneity, disparity. *Similarity*

Dissimulation, Dissembling, concealment, duplicity, hypocrisy, deceit, disguise, pretence. *Honesty*

Dissipate, Spend, consume, waste, squander, lavish, fritter away. *Hoard*

Scatter, disperse, spread, dispel, disseminate. *Collect*

Dissipation, Expenditure, waste, squandering, lavishing, excess, prodigality, debauchery, dissoluteness, profligacy. *Frugality*

Scattering, dispersion, spreading, distribution, dissemination, vanishing. *Collection*

Dissociate, Sever, dissever, disunite, disconnect, disjoin, disjoint, detach, divide, part, sunder. *Join*

Dissociation, Severance, severing, disseverance, dissevering.†

Dissolute, Loose, lewd, debauched, dissipated, wanton, depraved, profligate, abandoned, licentious, rakish, corrupt, reprobate, graceless, shameless. *Strict*

Dissolution, Decomposition, putrefaction, corruption.

Termination, end, extinction, death, overthrow, destruction, ruin. *Union*

Solution, melting, liquefaction.

Dissolve, *v.a.,* and *n.,* Melt, liquefy. *Solidify*

v.a., Sever, dissever, separate, part, divide, disunite, disconnect, dislocate, disorganize, loose. *Unite*

Terminate, end, extinguish, overthrow, destroy, ruin.

v.n., Disappear, vanish, depart, fade, perish, crumble. *Endure*

Dissonance, Disagreement, discord, discordance, jarring, clash, harshness, incongruity, inconsistency, discrepancy. *Harmony*

Dissonant, Disagreeing, discordant,† grating. *Harmonious*

Dissuade, Deter, disincline, indispose, discourage, depress, dehort. *Urge*

Distance, Space, interval, interspace.

Remoteness, removal, separation, absence. *Nearness*

Reserve, frigidity, aloofness, coldness, coolness, stiffness. *Cordiality*

Distant, Far, remote, removed, absent. *Near*

Reserved, frigid,† uncordial, aloof. *Cordial*

Faint, obscure, indirect, indistinct, slight. *Clear*

Distaste, Disgust, disrelish, dislike, antipathy, aversion, repugnance, displeasure, dissatisfaction. *Relish*

Distasteful, Disgusting, repugnant, unpleasing, repulsive, nauseating, nauseous, loathsome, offensive, hateful, disagreeable, unpleasant, unsavoury, unpalatable. *Pleasant*

Distemper, Disorder, disease, malady, ailment, ail, complaint, illness, sickness, indisposition. *Health*

Distend, Dilate, enlarge, extend, stretch, expand, swell, bloat, inflate, gape. *Compress*

Distension, Dilatation, dilation, enlargement.† *Compression*

Distil, Drop, drip, emanate, percolate.

Distinct, Detached, separate, independent, different, unconnected. *One*

Clear, defined, definite, unmistakable, plain, obvious, visible, palpable, conspicuous, unconfused. *Dim*

Distinction, Repute, reputation, fame, note, name, renown, eminence, dignity, superiority, account, mark, significance, celebrity, respectability, credit. *Insignificance*

Difference, separation. *Similarity*

Distinctive, Distinguishing, discriminating, outstanding, notable, characteristic. *Hazy*

Distinguish, Characterize, differentiate, mark, separate, divide. *Confuse*

Discern, descry, see, observe, perceive. *Overlook*

Distinguished, Marked, conspicuous, extraordinary. *Ordinary*

Famous, notable, renowned, eminent, celebrated, noted, illustrious. *Unknown*

Distort, Deform, twist, turn, misrepresent, pervert, falsify, wrest. *Straighten*

Distortion, Deformity, twist,† wryness.

Distract, Confuse, perplex, bewilder, harass, confound, embarrass, disconcert, disturb, mystify, divert, discompose, craze, derange, convulse. ***Compose***

Distracted, Insane, wild, mad, frantic, deranged, discomposed, crazed, furious, convulsive, raving, delirious. ***Sane***

Distraction, Insanity, wildness,† mania, lunacy, aberration, incoherence. ***Sanity*** Confusion, perplexity, bewilderment, embarrassment, disconcertion, disturbance, diversion, mystification, discomposure, abstraction. ***Composure***

Distrain, Attach, distress, seize, rend, tear. ***Release***

Distress, *v.a.*, Harass, embarrass, trouble, vex, grieve, torment, torture, pain, afflict, worry. ***Soothe*** *n.*, Trouble, grief, torment, torture, pain, affliction, worry, adversity, misfortune, calamity, disaster, trial, sorrow, agony, anguish, straits, poverty, destitution, privation. ***Joy***

Distribute, Divide, allot, apportion, assign, dispense, share, parcel, deal, mete. ***Collect***

Distribution, Division, allotment, apportionment.† ***Collection***

District, Region, territory, tract, quarter, part, province.

Distrust, *v.a.*, Doubt, mistrust, disbelieve, question, suspect. ***Believe*** *n.*, Doubt, mistrust, disbelief, suspicion, misgiving. ***Belief***

Distrustful, Doubting, suspicious, dubious. ***Trustful***

Disturb, Disarrange, derange, upset, unsettle, confuse, disorder. ***Arrange*** Molest, worry, harass, plague, annoy, vex, irritate, ruffle, trouble, incommode, disquiet, discompose, agitate, rouse, stir, shake. ***Placate***

Disturbance, Tumult, uproar, excitement, riot, turmoil, disorder, commotion. ***Quiet*** Discomposure, annoyance, agitation, derangement.

Disunite, Disconnect, disjoin, disjoint, dissociate, detach, sever, dissever, divide, part, separate, sunder. ***Join***

Disuse, Desuetude, abandonment, disusage, neglect, discontinuance.

Ditch, Drain, moat, channel, trench.

Diurnal, *a.*, Daily, daytime, quotidian. *n.*, Daybook, journal.

Divagate, Wander, roam, stray, ramble, digress, deviate. ***Halt***

Divaricate, Fork, diverge, separate, part, deviate, divide. ***Converge***

Divarication, Forking, divergence.† ***Convergence***

Dive, Plunge, sound, fathom, explore, penetrate.

Diverge, Divide, separate, fork, divaricate, part, deviate, radiate. ***Converge***

Divergence, Dividing, separation.† ***Convergence*** Disagreement, difference. ***Agreement***

Divergent, Dividing, separating, parting, divaricating, deviating, radiating. ***Convergent*** Disagreeing, differing, different, dissimilar, diverse. ***Similar***

Divers, Manifold, different, many, various, sundry, numerous, several. ***Few***

Diverse, Different, divergent, differing, disagreeing, changed, varied, chequered, variegated, dissimilar, unlike, variant. ***Similar***

Diversify, Vary, change, alter, variegate, modify.† ***Stereotype***

Diversion, Amusement, recreation, pastime, entertainment, sport, relaxation. ***Work***

Diversity, Difference, divergence, unlikeness, variation, dissimilarity, dissimilitude, variety. ***Similarity***

Divert, Distract, amuse, entertain, relax, recreate, refresh, exhilarate. Change, alter, deflect, alienate. ***Continue***

Divest, Strip, disrobe, deprive, undress, denude, bare, unclothe, dispossess. ***Clothe***

Divide, Sever, dissever, sunder, part, separate, disunite, disconnect, cleave. ***Join*** Alienate, estrange. ***Unite*** Allot, assign, distribute, apportion, share, parcel, mete, dispense. ***Collect***

Dividend, Share, division, profit.

Divination, Magic, witchcraft, sorcery, prophecy, presage, prediction, foretelling, soothsaying, divining, augury.

Divine, *a.*, Godlike, angelic, spiritual, heavenly, sacred, holy, celestial, seraphic, superhuman. ***Diabolical*** Exalted, lofty, noble, high, supreme, rapturous, transcendent. ***Low*** *v.a.*, & *n.*, Predict, prophesy, foretell, augur, presage, prognosticate, surmise, guess, fancy, suspect.

Diviner, Magician, seer, conjurer. Conjecturer, guesser, predictor.

Divinity, God, Godhead, Deity, theology.

Division, Demarcation, compartment, partition, section, head, category, class. Portion, allotment, distribution, apportionment, dispensation, sharing. ***Collection***

Division, Separation, severance. *Union*
Disagreement, divergence, discord, disunion, variance, breach, rupture, feud, estrangement, alienation. *Harmony*

Divorce, Separate, part, sever, dissever, alienate. *Join*

Divulge, Disclose,. show, exhibit, manifest, reveal, communicate, tell, spread, blaze, publish, impart, discover, uncover. *Hide*

Dizzy, Giddy, careless, rash, thoughtless, heedless.

Do, *v.a.*, Perform, execute, accomplish, achieve, complete, perfect, effect, conclude, end, finish, terminate, transact, practise, work, make, produce. *Neglect*
Cheat, hoax, swindle.
Cook, prepare.
Translate, render.
v.n., Act, work, perform, behave, fare, function, answer, suffice.

Docile, Tractable, amenable, compliant, teachable, tame, pliant, yielding. *Obstinate*

Docility, Tractableness, compliance, tameness, pliancy. *Obstinacy*

Dock, Clip, reduce, curtail, lessen, diminish, shorten. *Increase*

Doctrinaire, Thinker, theorist, ideologist.

Doctrine, Dogma, creed, principle, teaching, tenet, precept, article, maxim, opinion, belief.

Document, Writing, paper, title, writ, certificate.

Dodge, *v.n.*, Evade, duck, quibble, shuffle.
n., Artifice, trick, evasion.

Doer, Performer, actor, operator, agent, executor.

Doff, Remove, cast, divest. *Don*

Dog, *v.a.*, Follow, trace, track, haunt, pursue. *Elude*
n., Cur, pup, whelp, canine.

Dogged, Stubborn, obstinate, stolid, headstrong, inflexible, indomitable, wilful, pertinacious, intractable, resolute, unyielding. *Weak*
Sullen, churlish, surly, sour, morose, snappish, growling, snarling. *Genial*

Dogma, Doctrine, creed, belief, principle, teaching, article, maxim, tenet, precept, opinion.

Dogmatic, Arbitrary, arrogant, overbearing, peremptory, dictatorial, magisterial, positive. *Reasonable*
Categorical, certain, authoritative.

Dogmatize, Assert, dictate. *Reason*

Doings, Deeds, actions, movements, works, performance, acts, transactions.

Dole, *v.a.*, Distribute, apportion, allot, assign, dispense, divide, share, deal, parcel, mete. *Withhold*
n., Apportionment, allotment.†
Benefit, gift, gratuity, grant, donation, bounty, alms. *Wage*
Sorrow, dolour, grief, distress, woe, affliction. *Joy*

Doleful, Sorrowful, dolorous, dolesome, gloomy, unhappy, dismal, cheerless, piteous, rueful, sad, woeful, melancholy, dark, lugubrious. *Joyful*

Dolorous, Doleful,† sorrowful, dolesome. *Happy*

Dolt, Dunce, fool, simpleton, idiot, ignoramus, booby, blockhead, dullard, ass. *Genius*

Doltish, Foolish, simple,† stolid, blockish. *Clever*

Domain, Dominion, power, majesty, sway.
Dominion, kingdom, realm, land, empire, territory, province, region, district, estate, demesne. *Wilderness*

Domestic, *a.*, Civil, intensive, internal. *Foreign*
Homely, home, family, household, private. *Public*
Tame, domesticated. *Wild*
n., Servant, maid, help, menial, drudge.

Domesticate, Tame, adopt, cultivate, naturalize, settle, colonize, localize.

Domicile, House, dwelling, abode, home, residence, quarters, habitation.

Dominant, Predominant, predominating, ascendant, prevailing, prevalent, ruling. *Subsidiary*

Dominate, Predominate, ascend, prevail, rule, control, sway, reign, command, surmount, override. *Liberate*

Domineer, Overbear, swagger, bully, tyrannize, hector, lord. *Bow*

Dominion, Domain, majesty, sway, command, rule, sovereignty, ascendancy, mastery, government, supremacy, authority. *Submission*
Domain, territory, land, province, realm, kingdom, empire, region, country.

Don, Wear, assume, invest. *Doff*

Donation, Grant, gift, present, subscription, offering, boon, contribution, gratuity, dole, charity, alms, benefaction, bounty, largess. *Wage*

Done, Performed, executed, accomplished, achieved, completed, perfected, effected, concluded, ended, finished, terminated, transacted. *Neglected*
Translated, rendered.

Donkey, Mule, ass.
Dunce, dolt, idiot, fool, simpleton, ignoramus, dullard. *Genius*

Donor, Donator, giver, bestower.
Recipient

Doom, *v.a.,* Judge, sentence, condemn, appoint, destine, decree.

n., Judgment, sentence,† fate, lot.

Door, Entrance, passage, avenue, way, portal, exit.

Dormant, Sleeping, slumbering, quiescent, latent, inert, undeveloped, inactive, unexerted. *Active*

Dormitory, Bedroom, chamber.

Dose, Draught, portion, drench, quantity.

Dot, Period, point, stop, speck.
Dowry.

Dotage, Senility, imbecility, dementedness. *Vigour*

Dote, Love. *Hate*

Double, *a.,* Twofold, coupled, twice, paired, duplex, dual. *Single*
Deceitful, dishonest, insincere, hollow, perfidious, false. *Open*

v.a., Duplicate, fold, plait, repeat.

n., Faults, turn, artifice, duplicate.
Doubling, plait, fold.
Trick, ruse, wile, manoeuvre, strategem.
Counterpart, twin.

adv., Twice, twofold.

Double-faced, Deceitful, dishonest, insincere, hollow, perfidious, false, hypocritical. *Frank*

Doublet, Jacket, jerkin.

Doubt, *v.a.,* Suspect, question, query, mistrust, distrust. *Trust*

v.n., Waver, vacillate, hesitate, demur, dubitate. *Resolve*

n., Suspicion, distrust, mistrust. *Trust*
Wavering, vacillation, irresolution, hesitation, dubitation, suspense, uncertainty, misgiving, indecision. *Resolution*

Doubtful, Wavering, vacillating, irresolute.† *Resolute*
Obscure, dubious, uncertain, questionable, debatable, problematical, undecided, ambiguous. *Certain*

Doubtless, Precisely, certainly, clearly, indisputably.

Doughty, Redoubtable, valiant, valorous, brave, courageous, heroic, bold, intrepid, gallant, fearless, dauntless, undaunted.
Timid

Douse, Souse, dip, submerge, plunge, duck, immerse.

Dowdy, Shabby, slovenly, awkward, scrubby, dingy, slatternly. *Smart*

Dowel, Peg, pin, pinion, tenon, socket.

Dower, Dowry, gift, endowment, bequest.

Down, *n.,* Feathers, fluff, fur.
Bank, pasture, hill.

a., Downcast, depressed, dejected, low-spirited. *Cheerful*

Down, Alee, lee-side.
Prostrate, low, below, beneath, adown.
Up

Downcast, Discouraged, down-hearted, dispirited, depressed, dejected, despondent, disheartened, sad, crestfallen, chapfallen. *Elated*

Downfall, Fall, ruin, destruction. *Rise*

Down-hearted, Downcast, discouraged, dispirited, depressed, dejected, despondent, disheartened, sad, crestfallen, chapfallen. *Elated*

Downright, Absolute, positive, plain, unequivocal, simple, explicit, clear, categorical, sheer. *Evasive*
Honest, frank, open, sincere, straightforward, blunt. *Insincere*

Dowry, Dower, gift, endowment, bequest, dot.

Doze, *v.n.,* Sleep, slumber, drowse. *Wake*

n., Sleep, slumber, nap, drowse.

Drab, Prostitute, courtezan, strumpet, whore, harlot, trull.

Draff, Dregs, refuse, lees, waste, stuff, scum, sediment, leavings.

Draft, *v.a.,* Delineate, outline, sketch, select, prepare.
Conscript, impress, commandeer.

n., Delineation, outline,† conscription.
Bill, check, outline, delineation, rough.

Drag, Tug, draw, pull, heave, haul. *Push*

Draggle, Trail, drabble, befoul, besmirch, besmear, daggle. *Raise*

Dragoon, Force, compel, make, drive, harass, harry, persecute, coerce. *Coax*

Drain, *v.a.,* Empty, exhaust, evacuate, strain, dry, draw, drip. *Fill*

n., Ditch, sewer, channel, passage, trench, gutter.

Drape, Cover, clothe, robe, array, deck, adorn, dress, invest. *Denude*

Drastic, Extreme, violent, active, forcible, robust, efficacious, powerful, strong.
Mild

Draught, Dose, drench, quantity, potion, cup, drink.
Pulling, drawing, hauling.
Breeze.
Sketch, draft, outline.†

Draw, *v.a.,* Drag, pull, heave, haul, tug, tow. *Push*
Attract, allure, entice, induce, influence, persuade, engage, lead, move. *Repulse*
Prepare, draft, write, compose, formulate.
Delineate, trace, describe, sketch, depict, limn.
Extract, extort.
Inhale, suck, drain, siphon.
Protract, extend, lengthen, stretch.
Curtail

Draw, *v.n.,* Sketch, depict.
Proceed, move, go, come.
Inflame, vesicate, blister.
Draft.

Drawback, Detriment, disadvantage, defect, deficiency, imperfection, fault. *Advantage*

Drawing, Dragging, pulling, heaving, hauling, tugging. *Pushing*
Sketch, delineation, portrait, picture, plan, outline, etching.

Drawl, Drone, lag, drag. *Gabble*

Dread, *n.,* Fear, terror, apprehension, horror, alarm, intimidation, awe. *Confidence*
a., Fearful, terrible,† awesome.
v.a., Fear.

Dreadful, Fearful, terrible, horrible, alarming, intimidating, dire, direful, horrid, frightful, tremendous, terrific, awful. *Hopeful*

Dream, *n.,* Vision, illusion, delusion, reverie, hallucination, vagary, fancy, conceit, trance. *Reality*
v.n., Fancy, imagine.

Dreamer, Visionary, idealist, enthusiast.

Dreary, Cheerless, dark, gloomy, dispiriting, depressing, dull, uninteresting, tiresome, monotonous, lonesome, drear, comfortless, chilling, dismal, lonely, solitary. *Inspiring*

Dregs, Lees, grounds, draff, waste, sediment, leavings, stuff, scrum, dross, refuse. *Pickings*

Drench, Soak, wet, saturate, steep, imbrue, duck, immerse, drown, inundate. *Dry*

Dress, *v.a.,* Clothe, robe, cover, array, rig, accoutre, invest, equip, deck, bedeck, attire, adorn, drape, decorate, embellish. *Strip*
Arrange, adjust, prepare, fit, dispose. *Derange*
n., Clothes, robes, investments, attire, garments, garb, raiment, clothing, habit, habiliment, apparel, guise, costume, vesture, suit, gown, clothing.

Dressing, Manure, compost, fertilizer.
Forcemeat, stuffing, garnishing, preparation.

Dribble, Trickle, drip, drop, ooze.

Driblet, Portion, part, fragment, scrap, bit, morsel.

Drift, *v.n.,* Wander, drive, edge, bear, float. *Steer*
n., Aim, object, purpose, intent, intention, design, mark, tendency, meaning, scope, direction, bearing, course.
Current, sweep, rush.
Pile, heap, accumulation, mass.

Drill, *v.a.,* Teach, instruct, exercise, train.
Pierce, bore, perforate.
n., Furrow, trench, channel.
Tool, borer.
Training, discipline, exercise.

Drink, *v.a.,* Imbibe, swallow, quaff, absorb, draught. *Exude*
v.n., Indulge, tipple, tope, carouse, revel.
n., Potion, beverage, cup, draught.

Drip, Drop, dribble, trickle, percolate, ooze.

Drive, *v.a.,* Urge, press, compel, coerce, dragoon, force, oblige, persecute, prosecute, harass. *Coax*
Propel, send, impel, hurl.
n., Airing, ride.
Road, course.

Drivel, *v.n.,* Dote, slobber, babble.
n., Drivelling, slobbering, babble, fatuity, twaddle, nonsense, rubbish, prate, stuff, balderdash. *Sense*

Driveller, Dotard, babbler, idiot, simpleton, fool, gabbler, imbecile.

Droll, *a.,* Funny, amusing, comic, comical, ludicrous, laughable, farcical, fantastic, whimsical, facetious, queer, odd, diverting. *Sad*
n., Buffoon, jester, fool, mountebank, harlequin, clown.

Drollery, Fun, comicality, facetiousness, waggery, waggishness, buffoonery, pleasantry.

Drone, *n.,* Idler, lounger, sluggard. *Worker*
v.n., Drawl, drag, lag, lounge, dawdle, idle. *Gabble*

Drool, Drivel, dribble, slaver, slobber.

Droop, Sink, drop, fade, wither, wilt, weaken, faint, sink, languish, pine, decline, flag, sag, bend, fail. *Flourish*

Drop, *v.a.,* Sink, lower, depress, droop.† *Raise*
Desert, abandon, relinquish, resign, forswear, quit, leave, omit, discontinue, cease. *Continue*
Distil.
v.n., Fall, drip, distil.
n., Globule, bead, spot.
Pendant, ear-ring.

Dross, Scum, waste, dregs, refuse, recrement, scoria, lees.

Drought, Aridity, dryness, parching. *Deluge*

Drove, Flock, herd, crowd, collection, congregation.

Drover, Driver, herdsman, dealer.

Drown, Suffocate, submerge, immerse, sink.
Swamp, overcome, inundate, deluge, overwhelm, overpower, overflow, flood.

Drowse, Doze, sleep, slumber, nap. *Wake*

Drowsy, Dozy, sleepy, lethargic, somnolent, heavy, drooping, stupid, comatose, soporific. *Alert*

Drub, Flog, beat, thrash, pound, thump, cane, cudgel, maul, pommel.

Drudge, *v.n.*, Toil, slave, labour, work, plod.

n., Toiler, slave, labourer, worker, plodder, menial, scullion.

Drudgery, Toil, slavery, labour, work.

Drug, Remedy, physic, medicine.

Drunkard, Tippler, toper, sot, inebriate, carouser, reveller, dipsomaniac.

Drunk, Inebriated, intoxicated, drunken, drenched, saturated, soaked, fuddled, tipsy, muddled. *Sober*

Dry, *v.a.*, Parch, drain, exsiccate, desiccate. *Moisten*

a., Parched, arid, dried, thirsty. *Wet* Barren, dull, jejune, tedious, boring, uninteresting, dreary, tiresome, fatiguing, wearisome, tame, vapid, meagre, plain. *Lively*

Sarcastic, ironic, sly, keen, severe, sharp, cutting.

Dub, Name, christen, call, style, designate, denominate, entitle, term, grace, dignify, honour.

Dubious, Doubtful, uncertain, hesitant, wavering, vacillating, undecided, unsettled, fluctuating. *Determined*

Doubtful, uncertain, ambiguous, questionable, equivocal. *Certain*

Duck, *v.a.*, Submerge, immerse, douse, dip, sink, plunge.

v.n., Plunge, dive, dip.

Duct, Conduit, passage, channel, canal, tube, pipe.

Ductile, Docile, yielding, compliant, facile, tractable, pliant, malleable, flexible, extensible, tractile. *Obdurate*

Dudgeon, Indignation, anger, spleen, resentment, ire, wrath, malice. *Satisfaction*

Duds, Clothes, garments, effects, things, traps.

Due, *a.*, Owing, owed, fit, befitting, proper, becoming, appropriate, just, fair, suitable, obligatory, necessary. *Deficient*

n., Right, debt.

Duel, Combat, fight, affair of honour.

Dug, Nipple, teat, pap, udder.

Dulcet, Sweet, pleasing, charming, pleasant, agreeable, soft, melodious, soothing, harmonious, euphonious, delightful, luscious, honeyed, delicious. *Horrid*

Dull, *v.a.*, Blunt, alleviate, modify, assuage, lessen, allay, mitigate, moderate, soften, abate. *Aggravate*

Benumb, deaden, paralyse, stupefy, deject, depress, dispirit, dishearten, discourage. *Rally*

Dim, stain, sully, tarnish, soil. *Brighten*

a., Blunt, dulled, obtuse. *Sharp*

Sad, gloomy, dark, cheerless, dismal. *Joyous*

Foolish, stupid, unintelligent, doltish, stolid. *Clever*

Opaque, dim, cloudy, obscure. *Clear*

Insensible, callous, passionless, unimpassioned, dead, inert, heavy, apathetic, lifeless, torpid, inanimate, inactive, sluggish, slow. *Lively*

Tiresome, boring, dry, uninteresting, barren, jejune, fatiguing, tame, vapid, meagre, plain, dreary. *Lively*

Dullard, Dunce, fool, simpleton, blockhead, dolt, ignoramus, booby. *Genius*

Duly, Rightly, properly, fitly, regularly. *Unduly*

Dumb, Silent, mute, speechless, voiceless, inarticulate. *Articulate*

Dumbfound-er, Astonish, astound, confuse, amaze, bewilder, nonplus.

Dummy, Mute, dumb.

Sham, puppet.

Dump, *v.a.*, Unload, tilt, deposit.

n., Counter, quoit, ball, heap.

Dun, Urge, importune, press.

Dunce, Fool, dullard, simpleton, blockhead, dolt, ignoramus, booby, clodpoll, clodpate. *Genius*

Dung, Manure, compost, soil.

Dungeon, Cell, prison, keep, gaol.

Dupe, *v.a.*, Cheat, guile, beguile, befool, deceive, overreach, circumvent, gull, outwit, delude, trick, *cozen, chouse. Guide*

n., Gull, cully, simpleton, victim.

Duplicate, *v.a.*, Double, repeat, copy.

a., Double, twofold.

n., Copy, counterpart, transcription. *Original*

Duplicity, Guile, trickery, deceit, fraud, falseness, artfulness, craftiness, chicanery, dissimulation, deception, dishonesty, circumvention, artifice, hypocrisy, perfidy. *Honesty*

Durable, Stable, lasting, permanent, constant, abiding, continuing, persistent. *Transient*

Durance, Duress, confinement, imprisonment, captivity, constraint, restraint, incarceration. *Liberty*

Duration, Continuance, term, period, time.

Duress, Durance, confinement, restraint,

imprisonment, captivity, constraint, incarceration. **Freedom**

During, Throughout, pending. **Excepting**

Dusk, Twilight, nightfall, eve, eventide.

Dusky, Dark, dim, cloudy, clouded, obscure, opaque, shadowy, overcast, shady, murky. **Light**
Swarthy, dark, tawny.

Dutiful, Obedient, respectful, duteous, submissive, deferential, reverential. **Rebellious**

Duty, Obligation, function, business, part, responsibility, trust, commission, service. **Licence**
Tax, impost, excise, toll, custom, tariff

Dwarf, *v.a.*, Stunt, lower, depress.
n., Pygmy, imp, midget. **Giant**

Dwarfish, Stunted, small, undersized, pygmy, pygmean, little, tiny, dwarfed, diminutive, lilliputian. **Gigantic**

Dwell, Live, reside, inhabit, stay, tarry, sojourn, abide, linger, stop. **Wander**

Dwelling, Residence, habitation, abode, house, home, quarters, lodgings, domicile.

Dwindle, Diminish, lessen, decrease, shrink, melt, decline, waste, pine, decay. **Increase**

Dye, Colour, hue, shade, cast, stain, tinge, tint.

Dying, *a.*, Expiring, mortal, perishable, moribund. **Living**
n., Death, expiration, departure, demise, decease, dissolution, end, exit. **Life**

Dynasty, House, succession, line.
Government, domain, dominion, empire, sway, rule, sovereignty.

Dyspepsia, Indigestion.

E

Eager, Ardent, earnest, longing, anxious, keen, yearning, desirous, impatient, impetuous, fervent, zealous, hot, fervid, enthusiastic, animated, vehement.   *Indifferent*

Eagerness, Ardour, earnestness, longing,† avidity.   *Indifference*

Ear, Heed, hearing, regard, attention.   *Neglect*

Early, *a.,* Seasonable, timely, premature, forward, prime.   *Late*
adv., Betimes, beforehand, soon, shortly, ere, anon, seasonably, forward.

Earn, Win, gain, get, deserve, procure, merit, obtain, acquire, achieve.   *Forfeit*

Earnest, *n.,* Seriousness, steadiness, fixity, sincerity, determination, truth, reality.   *Flippancy*
Pledge, promise, security.
a., Serious, steady, intent, fixed, sincere, determined, truthful, true.   *Flippant*
Ardent, keen, anxious, desirous, vehement, fervent, zealous, eager, fervid, enthusiastic, animated, hot.   *Indifferent*

Earnings, Wages, income, profits, takings, proceeds, salary, stipend, emolument, pay, remuneration, reward.   *Spending*

Earth, Land, soil, turf, sod, clay, loam, dirt, ground.
Globe, world, planet, mankind.

Earthly, Terrestrial, mundane.
Low, carnal, worldly, sensual, base, sordid, gross, unspiritual.   *Spiritual*

Ease, *v.a.,* Assuage, alleviate, allay, abate, mitigate, soothe, relieve, pacify, still, quiet, calm, moderate, disencumber, disburden, release, lighten.   *Aggravate*
n., Comfort, tranquillity, quiet, quietude, quietness, repose, rest, contentment, content, peace, satisfaction, refreshment, enjoyment, relief.   *Disquiet*
Easiness, readiness, facility.   *Difficulty*

Easy, Tranquil, quiet, restful, content, contented, satisfied, relieved, untroubled, undisturbed, comfortable.   *Disturbed*
Facile, light.   *Difficult*
Pliant, complaisant, compliant, complying, yielding, tractable, submissive.   *Unmanageable*
Natural, simple, unaffected, unconstrained, affable, graceful, moderate, gentle, smooth.   *Unnatural*

Eat, Swallow, chew, masticate, feed, devour, consume.
Erode, corrode.

Eatable, Edible, esculent.   *Poisonous*

Eating, Erosive, corroding, corrosive, caustic.

Eavesdropper, Listener, hearkener.

Ebb, *v.n.,* Recede, retire, sink, subside, decline, wane, decay, decrease.   *Flow*
n., Regress, regression, decline, wane, waning, decay, decrease, diminution, abatement, caducity, deterioration, degeneracy, degeneration, decrement, subsidence, retrogression, refluence, reflux, retrocession, return.

Ebony, Black, dark, ebon, inky.

Ebriety, Inebriation, inebriety, intoxication, drunkenness.   *Sobriety*

Ebullience⎫ Ebullition, boiling, fermenta-
Ebulliency⎭ tion, effervescence, burst, overflow, outburst, eruption.

Ebullient, Boiling, effervescent, bursting, eruptive, throbbing, stormy.   *Quiet*

Ebullition, Ebullience, ebulliency, boiling, fermentation, effervescence, burst, overflow, outburst, eruption, paroxysm.   *Composure*

Eccentric, Irregular, peculiar, singular, aberrant, odd, erratic, abnormal, uncommon, strange, anomalous, whimsical, wayward, unnatural.   *Normal*

Eccentricity, Irregularity, peculiarity, singularity.†

Ecclesiastic, Parson, clergyman, minister, priest, pastor, divine, churchman.   *Layman*

Echo, *n.,* Resonance, repetition, reverberation, answer, imitation.
v.a., Resound, repeat.†
v.n., Resound, reverberate.

Éclat, Splendour, show, pomp, brilliancy, lustre, effect, striking, glory, pageantry.

Eclectic, Selective, selecting, choosing, picking, broad.   *Petty*

Eclipse, *v.a.,* Extinguish, obscure, blot, hide, dim, darken, shroud, veil, surpass, overshadow.   *Brighten*
n., Extinction, obscuration,† eclipsing, occultation, obliteration.

Economic-al, Thrifty, careful, saving, frugal, provident, sparing.   *Extravagant*

Economize, Save, utilize, husband, retrench.   *Squander*

Economy, Thrift, thriftiness, care, frugality, husbandry, providence, retrenchment.   *Extravagance*
Administration, dispensation, rule, order, system, plan, arrangement, management, regulation.   *Disorder*

Ecstasy, Trance, transport, delight, rapture, ravishment, fervour, inspiration.
Indifference

Ecstatic, Entrancing, transporting,† beatific.
Local

Ecumenical, Universal, general, catholic.
Local

Eddy, Whirlpool, current, swirl, ripple, vortex.

Edge, *n.,* Brink, border, rim, brim, verge, margin.

Sharpness, keenness, sting, zest, intensity, animation.
Dulness

v.n., Fringe, border, rim, frill, move. Sharpen.

Edging, Border, fringe, rim, frill.

Edible, Eatable, esculent, wholesome.
Poisonous

Edict, Decree, order, ordinance, proclamation, mandate, command, law, ukase.

Edification, Improvement, upbuilding, uplifting, elevation, invigoration, strengthening.
Corruption

Edifice, Building, structure, erection, fabric.
Ruin

Edify, Improve, upbuild, uplift, elevate, invigorate, strengthen, instruct, enlighten.
Corrupt

Edit, Correct, revise, preface, annotate, emend, conduct, arrange, manage, supervise, superintend.

Edition, Impression, print, issue, number.

Editor, Corrector, reviser, reader, annotator, supervisor, superintendent.

Educate, Instruct, train, teach, initiate, school, ground, discipline, develop, cultivate, nurture, rear.

Educated, Cultured, literate, initiated, lettered, trained, instructed, taught, schooled, developed.
Ignorant

Educe, Elicit, produce, draw, derive, extract.
Insert

Efface, Erase, obliterate, annihilate, expunge, blot, cancel, remove, dele, delete.
Imprint

Effect, *v.a.,* Consummate, complete, achieve, do, perform, execute, accomplish, effectuate, realize, compass, carry. Cause, create, produce.
Frustrate

n., Event, result, issue, consequence.
Cause

Meaning, intent, import, drift, purport. Efficiency, power, reality, fact, truth, being, validity, weight, force.

Effective, Efficient, operative, powerful, potent, cogent, able, competent, talented, telling, effectual, sufficient, adequate, efficacious, energetic, forcible, active.
Useless

Effects, Goods, chattels, furniture, movables, property.

Effectual, Efficient, operative, powerful.†

Effectuate, Effect,† consummate, carry, achieve, accomplish, complete, execute, secure, perform, do.
Hinder

Effeminate, Weak, feminine, unmanly, womanish, timid, timorous, soft.
Manly

Effervesce, Bubble, boil, ferment, foam, froth, explode.
Subside

Lively, hilarious, gay.

Effervescence, Bubbling, boiling,† ebullition.

Effete, Spent, exhausted, worn, wasted, decayed, decrepit.
Vigorous

Barren, unproductive, fruitless, abortive, unfruitful, unprolific, sterile, stale.
Fertile

Efficacious, Effective, efficient, effectual, operative, powerful, potent, active, vigorous, competent, energetic, productive, useful.
Useless

Efficacy, Effectiveness, efficiency, power, potency, activity, vigour, competence, energy, productivity, use, force.
Uselessness

Efficiency, Efficacy, effectiveness.†

Efficient, Skilful, skilled, able, ready, energetic, competent, fitted, active, capable, potent, powerful, effective, effectual, efficacious, operative.
Unskilled

Effigy, Image, statue, portrait, picture, representation, figure, likeness.

Effloresce, Flower, blow, bloom, bud, blossom, luxuriate.
Decay

Efflorescence, Flowering, bloom, budding.†

Effluence, Efflux, effusion, flow, emanation, discharge, emission, abundance, overflow.
Retention

Effluvium, Vapour, exhalation, emanation, stench, stink, smell.

Efflux, Effluence, effusion, flow, emanation, discharge, emission, overflow.
Influx

Effort, Attempt, essay, trial, endeavour, exertion, struggle, striving, straining, strain, stretch.
Inactivity

Effrontery, Audacity, impudence, face, boldness, sauciness, barefacedness, brass, presumption, assurance, shamelessness, hardihood.
Bashfulness

Effulgence, Splendour, brilliance, lustre, refulgence, radiance, brightness, luminosity, blaze, glow.
Darkness

Effulgent, Splendid, brillaint, lustrous,† flaming, beaming, shining, burning.
Dark

Effuse, *v.n.,* Emanate, issue.
Absorb

v.a., Pour, spill, shed.

Effuse, *a.*, Profuse, abundant, effluent, copious, diffused, lavish, generous. *Scanty*

Effusion, Emission, effluence, discharge, pouring, efflux, outpouring, gush, spilling, waste, shedding. *Absorption*
Utterance, oration, address, speech.

Effusive, Diffused, lavish, generous, effuse, profuse, expansive, abundant, effluent, copious. *Scanty*

Egg, Urge, press, push, encourage, incite, impel, stimulate, provoke, harass. *Deter*

Egoism, Egotism, selfishness, self-conceit, self-opinionatedness, self-esteem, self-importance, vanity. *Humility*

Egotism, Egoism, selfishness.†

Egotistic, Conceited, self-opinionated, opinionated, self-important, vain.
Humble

Egregious, Monstrous, remarkable, outrageous, extraordinary, peculiar, enormous, huge, tremendous, great, prodigious. *Ordinary*

Egress, Exit, outlet, emergence, departure. *Entrance*

Ejaculate, Cry, utter, exclaim, blurt.

Ejaculation, Cry, utterance, exclamation, interjection.

Eject, Expel, evict, dismiss, cashier, discharge, oust, evacuate, vomit, emit, void, banish, reject, throw out. *Retain*

Ejection, Expulsion, eviction, dismissal.†

Eke, *v.a.*, Stretch, lengthen, enlarge, help, raise.
adv., Likewise, also.

Elaborate, *a.*, Studied, laboured, ornate.
Simple
v.a., Refine, prepare, improve, mature, ripen, develop, concoct, forge.

Elapse, Lapse, intervene, pass, slip. *Hold*

Elastic, Rebounding, springy, recoiling, resilient, flexible, extensile, ductile.
Rigid

Elasticity, Springiness, resilience, flexibility, ductility. *Rigidity*

Elate, Excite, cheer, exhilarate, animate, rouse, elevate, flush, inflate, inspirit.
Depress

Elated, Excited, cheered,† joyed, proud.
Depressed

Elbow, *n.*, Flexure, bend, curve, turn, angle, corner.
v.n., Jostle, push, crowd, shoulder, force, nudge.

Elder, *n.*, Senior, presbyter.
a., Older, senior, earlier, eldest, aged, venerable. *Younger*

Elect, *v.a.*, Choose, select, pick, prefer, appoint, cull. *Reject*
a. & n., Elite, elected, chosen, selected, picked. *Rejected*

Election, Choice, selection, preference, acceptance. *Rejection*

Elector, Voter, constituent, selector, chooser.

Electric, Exciting, thrilling, flashing, stirring.

Electrify, Thrill, stir, amaze, astound, astonish, rouse, excite. *Compose*

Elegance, Beauty, grace, refinement, propriety, symmetry, gentility, polish, politeness, taste, gracefulness.
Coarseness

Elegant, Beautiful, graceful, refined,† fine, handsome, chaste, classical, neat, courtly, fashionable, cultivated, accomplished. *Coarse*

Elegiac, Dirgelike, plaintive, mournful, sad, sorrowful. *Gay*

Elegy, Dirge, lament, threnody, plaint.

Element, Component, constituent, part, particle, material, ingredient, rudiment, factor, principle.

Elementary, Rudimentary, rudimental, simple, basic, fundamental, primordial, primary, uncompounded. *Advanced*

Elephantine, Gigantic, immense, huge, large, big, gargantuan, tremendous, enormous, colossal, mammoth, brobdingnagian. *Minute*

Elevate, Lift, raise, hoist, erect. *Lower*
Dignify, promote, ennoble, exalt, aggrandize, improve. *Degrade*
Elate, cheer, exhilarate, inspirit, animate, flush, excite, rouse. *Depress*

Elevated, Lofty, high, dignified, raised, grandiose. *Lowered*

Elevation, Lifting, raising, elevating.
Lowering
Dignity, promotion, exaltation, ennobling.†
Height, hill, altitude. *Depth*

Elf, Sprite, spirit, brownie, fairy, fay, gnome, urchin, puck, dwarf, imp, pixy.

Elicit, Educe, extract, draw, evoke, worm.
Instil

Eligible, Qualified, able, fit, preferable, worthy. *Ineligible*

Eliminate, Eradicate, erase, remove, expel, exclude, dislodge, oust, banish, eject, reject. *Include*

Elimination, Eradication, erasure, removal.† *Inclusion*

Elite, Select, chosen, flower, cream, best.

Ellipsis, omission, hiatus, gap.

Elliptical, Oval, oblong.
Incomplete, defective. *Perfect*

Elocution, Delivery, speech, eloquence, declamation, oratory.

Elongate, Extend, stretch, lengthen.
Curtail

Elope, Abscond, disappear, leave.

Eloquence, Declamation, oratory, elocution, delivery, force, power.

Eloquent, Powerful, fluent, flowing, impassioned, ardent, vigorous, impressive, persuasive.   *Halting*

Else, *a.*, Other, beside, different.
adv. and conj., Otherwise, differently. Besides.

Elucidate, Explain, expound, clear, unfold, illustrate.   *Obscure*

Elucidation, Explaining, explanation, clearing, unfolding, illustrating, illustration, elucidating, commentary, comment, exposition, annotation.

Elude, Evade, avoid, escape, shun.
    Encounter
Baffle, fence, parry, frustrate, mock, foil, thwart, balk, disconcert.   *Persist*

Elusive, Elusory, evasive, illusory, deceptive, delusive, slippery, intangible, fraudulent, fugitive, unsubstantial, unstable, undetainable, fallacious.   *Stable*

Elusory, Elusive, evasive, illusory.†

Eluxation, Dislocation, disjointing.

Elysian, Blissful, heavenly, celestial, enchanting, delightful, happy, charming, glorious, ravishing.   *Abominable*

Emaciate, Waste, decline, pine.

Emaciated, Wasted, lean, thin, skinny, gaunt, lank, attenuated, meagre.   *Fat*

Emaciation, Leanness, attenuation, thinness.†   *Fatness*

Emanate, Proceed, originate, rise, arise, flow, spring, issue, emerge.   *Culminate*

Emanation, Origin, rising, flowing, springing, issuing, issuance, emerging, emergence, issue, efflux, effluence.
    Culmination

Emancipate, Liberate, free, enfranchise, release, rescue, unshackle, unfetter, loose, unchain, disenthrall, manumit.   *Enslave*

Emancipation, Liberation, freeing, enfranchisement, manumission.†

Emasculate, Weaken, unman, enervate, effeminize, effeminate, debilitate.
    Strengthen
Castrate, geld.

Emasculation, Weakening, weakness.†

Embalm, Scent, perfume, preserve, conserve, cherish, keep, enshrine, store, treasure, consecrate.   *Abandon*

Embargo, Restraint, restriction, prohibition, ban, veto, bar, stoppage, hindrance.
    Permit

Embark, Start, enter, launch, begin, engage, undertake.   *Arrive*

Embarrass, Abash, confound, confuse, perplex, disconcert, dumbfound, nonplus.   *Extricate*

Embarrass, Harass, annoy, vex, plague, worry, encumber, trouble, distress, clog, hamper.   *Assist*

Embarrassment, Abashment, confusion, perplexity,† difficulty.   *Ease*
Plague, annoyance, vexation, worry, trouble, distress.   *Assistance*

Embellish, Deck, bedeck, adorn, ornament, decorate, beautify.   *Disfigure*

Embellishment, Decking, bedecking, adorning, ornamentation, adornment.†
    Disfigurement

Embers, Cinders, ashes.

Embezzle, Steal, appropriate, misappropriate, falsify, confuse, purloin, pilfer, peculate.

Embezzlement, Stealing, appropriation.†

Embitter, Exasperate, aggravate, anger, exacerbate, madden, enrage.   *Soothe*

Emblazon, Emblaze, blaze, adorn, decorate, ornament, deck, bedeck, embellish.

Emblem, Badge, token, device, symbol, representation, type, mark, sign, figure.

Embodiment, Embodying, incorporation, expression, incarnation, conjunction, union, association.

Embody, Incorporate, express, incarnate, integrate, compact, combine, codify, systematize, methodize, aggregate.
    Dismember
Embrace, include, contain, comprise, comprehend.   *Exclude*

Embogue, Empty, fall, discharge.   *Rise*

Embolden, Reassure, rally, encourage, inspirit, animate, hearten, cheer, incite, urge, impel, stimulate, instigate.
    Discourage

Embolismic-al, Interpolated, inserted, intercalated, intercalary, embolic.

Embosom, Enfold, conceal, wrap, envelop, hide, surround, bury, encircle, encompass, nurse, foster, cherish. *Expose*

Embowed, Bowed, bent, arched, arcuate, arcuated, curved.   *Straight*

Embowel, Bury, conceal, hide, embed. Disembowel, eviscerate, gut.

Embrace, Clasp, hug, seize, welcome, enfold, accept.   *Release*
Include, comprehend, comprise, contain, cover, encompass, embody, encircle, enclose.   *Exclude*

Embroider, Emboss, embellish, emblazon, decorate, enrich.   *Patch*

Embroil, Disturb, distract, perplex, trouble, discompose, disorder, confuse.
    Compose
Implicate, involve, commingle, entangle.
    Extricate

Embryo, Rudiment, beginning, embryon,

germ, bud, nucleus, imperfect, undeveloped. **Maturity**

Emend, Correct, amend, rectify, improve, reform, better. **Err**

Emendation, Correction, rectification, improvement, amendment, reformation. **Error**

Emerge, Appear, rise, emanate, issue, escape. **Disappear**

Emergence, Emerging, appearing, emanation.† **Disappearance**

Emergency, Urgency, crisis, exigency, juncture, conjuncture, strait, difficulty, necessity, extremity, pinch. **Deliverance**

Emigrate, Migrate, remove, depart. **Settle**

Emigration, Migration, removal, exodus.

Eminence, Distinction, celebrity, prominence, renown, fame, note, notoriety, mark, exaltation, reputation, repute, loftiness, conspicuousness. **Obscurity** Height, hill, elevation, projection.

Eminent, Distinguished, celebrated, prominent,† illustrious. **Unknown**

Emissary, Scout, agent, messenger, spy.

Emission, Emitting, ejection, issue, issuing, issuance, emanation.

Emit, Eject, issue, discharge, breathe, exhale, vent, emanate. **Inhale**

Emollient, Soothing, softening, laxative, relaxing. **Stimulating**

Emolument, Advantage, gain, benefit, profit, profits, remuneration, pay, wages, salary, stipend, income, living, lucre, compensation, reward. **Loss**

Emotion, Feeling, passion, excitement, agitation. **Indifference**

Emphasis, Weight, significance, impressiveness, force, stress, accent.

Emphatic, Positive, certain, decided, distinct, absolute, definite, earnest, unequivocal, strong, energetic, forcible, significant, expressive. **Uncertain**

Empire, Dominion, rule, sway, sovereignty, command, control, supremacy, government.

Empiric, *a.,* Experimental, hypothetical, provisional, tentative. **Definite** Quackish, charlatanic.

n., Quack, charlatan, cheat, fraud, pretender, impostor, mountebank.

Employ, Use, occupy, engross, engage, exercise. **Discard**

Employee, Agent, hand, workman, man, artisan, servant. **Master**

Employment, Occupation, situation, work, engagement, craft, avocation, vocation, trade, profession, calling, business, pursuit, service.

Emporium, Store, shop, market, mart.

Empower, Commission, authorize, warrant, allow, permit, encourage, enable, qualify. **Disqualify**

Empty, *v.a.,* Disembogue, pour, discharge, drain, exhaust, deplete, evacuate. **Fill**

a., Vacant, void, devoid, unoccupied, destitute, unfilled, unfurnished, deserted, waste, desolate, uninhabited, unfrequented, clear. **Full** Hollow, unsatisfying, unsatisfactory, insincere, unsubstantial. **Sincere** Idle, silly, weak, senseless, vacuous, frivolous. **Serious**

Empyreal, Aerial, ethereal, sublime, sublimated, empyrean, airy.

Emulate, Vie, compete, rival, copy.

Emulation, Competition, rivalry, strife, jealousy, envy.

Emulous, Competing, rivalling.† **Content**

Enable, Empower, capacitate, qualify, permit, allow. **Prevent**

Enact, Order, decree, ordain, establish, authorize, command. **Abrogate** Act, represent, play, personate.

Enactment, Act, decree, law, edict, ordinance.

Enamour, Fascinate, charm, win, captivate, enchant, bewitch, enslave, endear. **Repel**

Encamp, Camp, pitch, settle. **Move**

Encampment, Camp, bivouac.

Enchain, Enslave, bind, hold, fetter, manacle, fix, shackle, rivet. **Loose**

Enchant, Captivate, charm, win, enamour, gain, bewitch, fascinate, enslave, rapture, enrapture, ravish, enravish, delight, please, transport. **Repel**

Enchanting, Captivating, charming, winning.† **Repulsive**

Enchantment, Witchery, witchcraft, sorcery, magic, wizardry, charm, spell, charming, incantation, conjuration, fascination, transport, bliss, delight, pleasure, ravishment, rapture. **Repulsion**

Encircle, Encompass, surround, enclose, circumscribe, hem, environ, embrace, gird, engird, belt.

Enclose, Encircle, encompass, surround.† **Exclude** Cover, envelop, wrap.

Enclosure, Precinct, ring, yard, close, compound, palisade, paddock, circle, compass. **Space**

Encomiastic, Eulogistic, complimentary, commendatory, panegyrical, laudatory. **Vituperative**

Encomium, Eulogy, compliment,† praise.
Vituperation

Encompass, Encircle, enclose, surround, hem, circumscribe, environ, gird, engird, belt, compass.

Encounter, *v.a.*, Meet, face, confront.
Avoid
Attack, withstand.

n., Collision, meeting, clash, rencounter. Brush, affair, battle, fight, attack, skirmish, combat, engagement, conflict, assault, onset, contest, dispute, action.

Encourage, Hearten, enhearten, rally, rouse, cheer, inspirit, animate, refresh, reassure, assure, stimulate, embolden, incite, comfort.
Depress
Aid, abet, help, promote, further, countenance, support, advance, foster, prompt, favour, patronize, allow, permit.
Discountenance

Encroach, Advance, intrude, invade, creep, trespass, trench, infringe. *Recede*

Encrust, Plaster, coat, face, line.

Encumber, Hinder, impede, obstruct, load, oppress, overload, clog, burden.
Free

Encumbrance, Hindrance, impediment,† drag, deadweight, incubus.

End, *v.*, *a.* & *n.*, Conclude, finish, close, terminate, cease.
Begin
v.a., Kill, destroy.

n., Conclusion, finish, close, termination, cessation, finis, finale, expiration, completion.
Limit, extremity, bound, boundary.
Beginning
Aim, object, purpose, intent, intention, drift, bearing, design.
Scrap, fragment, rump, remnant.
Upshot, consequence, issue, result, event, sequel.

Endanger, Imperil, peril, expose, risk, jeopardize, hazard, compromise, commit.
Shield

Endear, Attach, conciliate, bind, gain, win, captivate, charm.
Alienate

Endearment, Attachment, love, fondness, tenderness.
Hatred
Caress, caressing, fondling, blandishment.

Endeavour, *v.n.*, Attempt, try, aim, strive, labour, essay.

n., Attempt, trial, aim, essay, struggle, effort, exertion.

Endemic, Local, indigenous, present.

Endless, Unending, boundless, interminable, eternal, infinite, perpetual, incessant, unceasing, continual, continuous, unlimited, illimitable, limitless, ceaseless, uninterrupted, immeasurable, immortal, everlasting, imperishable, deathless.
Brief

Endorse, Superscribe.
Ratify, confirm, second, support, warrant, sanction, approve.

Endow, Endue, enrich, bequeath, furnish, supply, qualify, adorn, invest, grant, present.
Divest

Endowment, Bequest, grant, gift, provision, bounty, present, largess, boon, benefit, revenue, property. *Spoliation*
Talent, qualification, attainment, capacity, quality, ability, aptness, aptitude, genius, power, faculty, parts. *Incapacity*

Endue, Endow, enrich, clothe, supply, furnish, invest.
Denude

Endurance, Fortitude, courage, patience, resignation.

Endure, *v.n.*, Abide, remain, continue, last, persist.
Perish
v.a., Abide, tolerate, bear, allow, sustain, support, brook, experience, undergo, stand.

Enemy, Adversary, opponent, foe, rival, antagonist.
Ally

Energetic, Vigorous, powerful, active, potent, strong, lively, forcible, efficacious, effective.
Lethargic

Energize, Animate, excite, force.

Energy, Vigour, power, activity,† intensity, might, zeal, spirit, spiritedness, life, animation.
Lethargy

Enervate, Unnerve, debilitate, weaken, relax, enfeeble, unhinge, unstring, effeminize, effeminate, paralyse, break, emasculate.
Strengthen

Enfeeble, Enervate, unnerve, debilitate.†

Enfold, Envelop, enclose, wrap, embrace, comprise.

Enforce, Force, compel, oblige, constrain, coerce, require, exact, exert. *Waive*

Enfranchise, Emancipate, liberate, free, manumit, release.
Enslave

Engage, *v.n.*, Contend, contest, struggle, fight, combat, battle.
Withdraw
Agree, bargain, promise, undertake, stipulate.
Decline
v.a., Encounter, meet, attack.
Busy, employ, occupy, engross. *Dismiss*
Pledge, bind, promise, vouch, undertake, commit, plight, betroth, affiance.
Attract, hold, attack, win, gain, allure, arrest.
Repulse

Engagement, Battle, contest, combat, encounter, brush, skirmish, affair, conflict, fight, action.
Withdrawal
Occupation, employment, situation, work, business.
Agreement, appointment, assignment, contract, compact, pact, stipulation,

covenant, pledge, obligation, assurance, plighting, affiancing, betrothing, betrothal.

Engaging, Charming, delightful, attractive, captivating, enchanting, winning, pleasing, agreeable, interesting. *Repulsive*

Engender, Produce, breed, beget, generate, procreate, cause, occasion, propagate, create. *Stifle*

Engine, Machine, implement, agent, instrument, weapon, device, method.

Engird, Gird, surround, encompass, encircle, environ.

Engorge, Gorge, gulp, engulf, swallow, bolt, devour. *Digest*

Engrained, Indelible, ineffaceable.

Engrave, Grave, print, imprint, cut, carve, sculpture, chisel. *Erase*

Engraving, Graving, print, imprinting.†

Engross, Monopolize, absorb, occupy, engage, forestall.

Engulf, Absorb, overwhelm, engorge, swallow, devour.

Enhance, Increase, swell, raise, heighten, advance, augment. *Depreciate*

Enhearten, Hearten, encourage, rally, rouse, inspirit, assure, reassure, embolden, console, comfort, cheer, fortify, animate, stimulate, incite. *Depress*

Enigma, Puzzle, conundrum, riddle, mystery.

Enigmatical, Puzzling, hidden, obscure, mysterious, mystic, mystical, occult, dark, perplexing, unintelligible, recondite, incomprehensible, ambiguous. *Plain*

Enjoin, Command, bid, direct, prescribe, order, require, urge, admonish, impress, advise. *Absolve*

Enjoy, Like, relish, love, appreciate. *Detest*
Possess. *Lose*

Enjoyment, Delight, pleasure, happiness, gratification.

Enkindle, Kindle, ignite, inflame, excite, instigate, incite, stimulate, provoke, rouse. *Damp*

Enlarge, *v.a.*, Expand, extend, amplify, increase, magnify, augment, stretch. *Diminish*
v.n., Expand, extend, increase, grow, swell.
Descant, dilate, expatiate.

Enlargement, Expansion, extension, amplification, increase, augmentation, dilatation, expatiation. *Contraction*

Enlighten, Illumine, illume, illuminate, irradiate. *Darken*
Edify, instruct, teach, inform. *Mystify*

Enlightened, Intelligent, instructed, informed, taught, wise, educated, refined. *Ignorant*

Enlist, *v.a.*, Engage, enroll, register, record, secure.
v.n., List, enroll, engage, embark.

Enliven, Wake, rouse, animate, excite, inspirit, invigorate, quicken. *Deaden*

Enmesh, Entangle, net, trap, ensnare. *Release*

Enmity, Discord, strife, war, bitterness, rancour, hate, animosity, animus, hatred, malevolence, malice, aversion, hostility, malignity, opposition. *Friendship*

Ennoble, Elevate, aggrandize, exalt, raise, dignify, glorify, enlarge, promote. *Degrade*

Ennui, Boredom, langour, listlessness, weariness, tedium, tiresomeness, lassitude. *Energy*

Enormity, Atrocity, atrociousness, depravity, wickedness, heinousness, flagitiousness, flagrancy, outrageousness, nefariousness.

Enormous, Huge, gigantic, large, vast, tremendous, immense, colossal, elephantine, gargantuan, prodigious. *Small*
Monstrous, atrocious, wicked, heinous, depraved, flagitious, flagrant, outrageous, nefarious.

Enough, Sufficient, adequate, ample, plenty, abundant. *Insufficient*

Enquire, Investigate, ask, inquire, question.

Enrage, Incense, infuriate, anger, aggravate, exasperate, exacerbate, annoy, provoke, madden, chafe, incite, inflame, rouse. *Pacify*

Enrapture⎫ Delight, transport, enchant,
Enravish ⎬ beautify, entrance, captivate, charm, win, ravish. *Repel*

Enrich, Endow, endue, supply, store. *Impoverish*
Fertilize.
Bedeck, deck, ornament, embellish, adorn, decorate, emblazon. *Disfigure*

Enrobe, Robe, dress, invest, clothe, cover, drape, attire, array, apparel. *Strip*

Enrol, Register, list, enlist.
Record, chronicle.

Ensconce, Hide, screen, shield, cover, protect, shelter, harbour. *Expose*

Ensemble, Together, all, group, effect, impression.

Enshrine, Embalm, preserve, treasure, cherish, consecrate. *Desecrate*

Ensign, Banner, standard, flag, colours, badge.

Enslave, Enthral, subjugate, bind, dominate, captivate, overpower, master. *Emancipate*

Ensnare, Entrap, enmesh, net, seduce, inveigle, trap, allure, entangle. *Loose*

Ensue, Result, proceed, issue, rise, arise, follow, succeed, come, accrue. *Precede*

Ensure, Insure, assure, secure, fix, determine, seal. *Imperil*

Entail, Leave, bequeath. *Alienate*
Involve, necessitate, induce.

Entangle, Entrap, ensnare, involve, catch, confuse, mat, ravel, implicate, tangle, knot, perplex, embarrass, encumber, puzzle, bewilder. *Extricate*

Entanglement, Confusion, perplexity, intricacy, bewilderment, complication, involution.

Enter, Invade, penetrate, pierce, perforate, trespass. *Leave*
Register, note, record, inscribe, chronicle, insert.
Embark, enlist, begin, start, commence.

Enterprise, Undertaking, attempt, essay, effort, emprise, endeavour, venture, adventure.
Energy, adventurousness, activity, daring, boldness. *Timidity*

Enterprising, Venturesome, venturous, active, daring, bold, ready, eager, prompt, dashing, audacious, alert, efficient, smart, spirited, adventurous, stirring, energetic, strenuous, zealous. *Timid*

Entertain, Amuse, divert, please, recreate *Bore*
Receive, lodge, harbour, cherish, hold, foster.
Consider, conceive. *Banish*

Entertainment, Amusement, recreation, diversion, pastime, sport, treat, festival, feast, banquet.

Enthral, Enslave, bind, overcome, master, subjugate, subdue, captivate, capture, hold. *Free*

Enthralment, Enslavement, bondage, captivity, thraldom, servitude, serfdom, slavery, vassalage. *Freedom*

Enthrone, Crown, install, elevate, exalt. *Depose*

Enthusiasm, Zeal, ardour, devotion, passion, vehemence, earnestness, frenzy, excitement, fanaticism. *Apathy*

Enthusiast, Zealot, devotee, fanatic, bigot.

Enthusiastic, Zealous, ardent, devoted, passionate, vehement, earnest, excited, fanatical, bigoted, fervent, fervid, impassioned, burning. *Apathetic*

Entice, Seduce, allure, attract, lure, tempt, inveigle, cajole, wheedle, coax, decoy. *Deter*

Enticement, Seduction, allurement,† bait. *Deterrent*

Entire, Complete, perfect, whole, unbroken, pure, mere, sheer, undiminished, undivided, unimpaired, full, unalloyed, unmitigated, thorough. *Partial*

Entirely, Completely, perfectly.† *Partially*

Entirety, Entireness, completeness, wholeness.†

Entitle, Qualify, fit, enable, empower, allow. *Disqualify*
Name, style, call, term, designate, denominate, christen, dub.

Entity, Existence, being, essence. *Chimera*

Entomb, Bury, inter, inhume, sepulchre. *Exhume*

Entrails, Inside, inwards, intestines, bowels, guts, offal.

Entrammel, Entangle, entrap, impede, involve, perplex, hinder, obstruct, hamper, ensnare, embarrass. *Extricate*

Entrance, *v.a.,* Enrapture, charm, enchant, captivate, ravish, enravish, delight, transport, please. *Repel*
n., Access, ingress, approach.
Avenue, way, passage, adit, portal, entry, mouth, inlet, gate, door, doorway, lobby, vestibule. *Exit*
Beginning, debut, initiation, introduction, commencement, admission, entrée. *Departure*

Entrap, Entrammel, entangle, impede, hinder, obstruct, hamper, ensnare, catch, involve, embarrass, perplex. *Extricate*
Seduce, tempt, entice, allure, lure, decoy, inveigle.

Entreat, Beg, implore, supplicate, crave, adjure, ask, cry, pray, beseech, importune, petition, enjoin. *Insist*

Entrée, Admittance, admission, access.

Entry, Entrance, ingress, access, arrival.
Avenue, way, passage, entrance, adit, portal, mouth, inlet, gate, door, doorway, lobby, vestibule. *Exit*
Note, record, memorandum, minute.

Entwine, Weave, twine, lace, interlace, twist. *Dissever*

Enumerate, Number, count, reckon, cite, compute, tell, numerate, recount, specify, detail, mention. *Confound*

Enumeration, Numbering, counting, recounting.†

Enunciate, Propound, promulgate, utter, publish, pronounce, proclaim, declare, say, assert, articulate, express, speak, relate, state, announce. *Stammer*

Enunciation, Promulgation, utterance publication.†

Enunciatory, Enunciative, declarative, declaratory, expressive.

Envelop, Wrap, fold, enfold, enwrap, encase, cover, hide, surround, encompass, encircle. *Expose*

Envelope, Wrapper, case, cover, covering, wrapping, veil, vesture, wrap, skin.

Envenom, Poison, embitter, anger, exasperate, rouse, annoy, enrage, aggravate, incense, madden, provoke, inflame, irritate. *Soothe*

Enviable, Desirable, happy, pleasant. *Unpleasant*

Envious, Jealous, grudging. *Content*

Environ, Encircle, surround, encompass, gird, besiege, beset, engird, begird, envelop, enclose, hem.

Environment, Surroundings, influences, atmosphere.

Environs, District, vicinity, neighbourhood.

Envoy, Minister, plenipotentiary, ambassador, legate, messenger.

Envy, *v.a.*, Begrudge, grudge, covet, desire.

n., malice, malignity, rivalry, ill-will, jealousy, suspicion.

Ephemeral, Short, transient, transitory, passing, fleeting, evanescent, brief, fugacious, fugitive, flitting, momentary, short-lived. *Permanent*

Epic, Heroic, narrative.

Epicure, Voluptuary, gourmand, glutton, sensualist, gourmet.

Epigrammatic, Laconic, terse, short, concise, pointed, graphic, pungent, sharp, piquant, poignant. *Diffuse*

Episode, Incident, happening, event, digression, occurrence.

Epistle, Letter, communication, missive note.

Epitaph, Inscription.

Epithet, Adjective, appellation, designation, name, title, description.

Epitome, Summary, synopsis, digest, abstract, breviary, compend, compendium, abridgment, conspectus, abbreviation, contraction. *Amplification*

Epitomize, Summarize, abstract, abridge, abbreviate, contract, curtail, cut, shorten, diminish, lessen, reduce, condense. *Amplify*

Epoch, Age, era, time, period, date, cycle.

Equable, Equal, serene, even, calm, uniform, regular, smooth, steady. *Variable*

Equal, *a.*, Commensurate, proportionate, adequate, sufficient, fit, competent, co-ordinate. *Disproportionate*

Equal, Equivalent, alike, like, tantamount. *Disparate*

Equable, serene, even, uniform, smooth, regular, steady. *Variable*

n., Peer, compeer, fellow.

v.a., Equalize, even, proportionate. Rival.

Equality, Evenness, uniformity, sameness. *Disparity*

Equanimity, Tranquillity, serenity, calmness, collectedness, composure, peace, self-possession. *Impatience*

Equestrian, Rider, horseman, cavalier, knight. *Pedestrian*

Equilibrium, Balance, equipoise.

Equip, Supply, furnish, rig, fit, provide, arm, accoutre, array, prepare, dress, invest. *Dismantle*

Equipage, Equipment, furniture, accoutrements, baggage, impedimenta, effects.

Train, retinue, suite, attendants, attendance, procession, following.

Equipment, Equipage, furniture, accoutrements, baggage, impedimenta, effects, outfit, apparatus.

Equipoise, Balance, equilibrium.

Equitable, Just, fair, right, proper, reasonable, upright, impartial, indifferent, disinterested. *Unjust*

Equity, Justice, fairness,† rectitude.

Equivalence, Parity, equality. *Disparity*

Equivalent, Commensurate, equal, equipollent, tantamount, interchangeable, synonymous. *Unequal*

Equivocal, Doubtful, questionable, uncertain, debatable, dubious, indeterminate, ambiguous. *Clear*

Equivocate, Prevaricate, fence, quibble, cavil, shift, evade, dodge, shuffle.

Equivocation, Prevarication, quibbling.†

Era, Epoch, age, date, period, time, cycle.

Eradicate, Annihilate, destroy, uproot, exterminate, extirpate, abolish. *Implant*

Eradication, Annihilation, destruction,† excision.

Erase, Expunge, blot, efface, obliterate, cancel, delete. *Engrave*

Erasure, Expunging, blotting, effacement.†

Erect, *v.a.*, Construct, build, raise, establish, plant, form, institute, found. *Demolish*

a., Upright, firm, stiff, tall. *Stooping*

Erection, Constructing, building, raising, erecting. *Demolition*

Building, edifice, structure, fabric.

Eremite, Recluse, hermit, solitary, anchorite, anchoret.

Ergo, Consequently, therefore, hence.

Eristic-al, Polemic, polemical, controversial, controversive, disputable, disputative, debatable. **Certain**
Disputatious, cavilling, captious.
Embarrassing, perplexing, entangling,
ensnaring, entrapping, catching.

Erode, Corrode, consume, canker, wear,
eat, destroy.

Erosive, Corrosive, corroding, consuming,
caustic, virulent, acrid, eating.

Err, Offend, sin, stumble, blunder, mis-
take, misjudge, fail, fall, trip, trespass.
Rectify
Wander, deviate, rove, roam, ramble.

Errand, Commission, mission, charge,
delegation.

Errant, Rambling, wandering, roving.

Errata, Misprints, errors, mistakes, cor-
rections.

Erratic, Aberrant, changeful, changeable,
capricious, unreliable, unequal, irregular,
eccentric, desultory, rambling, vagrant,
wandering. **Steady**

Erratum, Misprint, error, mistake, correction, corrigendum.

Erroneous, Wrong, false, untrue, inaccurate, inexact, mistaken, heretical.
True

Error, Inaccuracy, inexactitude, mistake,
heresy, blunder, misapprehension, oversight, untruth, fallacy. **Truth**
Offence, fault, crime, sin, delinquency,
iniquity, transgression, trespass, misdeed, misdoing.

Erubescent, Rubicund, red, reddish,
blushing. **Pale**

Erudite, Learned, scholarly, polished,
instructed, literate. **Illiterate**

Erudition, Learning, knowledge, lore,
scholarship.

Eruption, Outbreak, outburst, explosion.
Rash.

Escapade, Adventure, prank, vagary,
frolic, indiscretion.

Escape, v.a., Avoid, shun, elude, evade.
Meet
v.n., Fly, abscond, decamp, flee, retreat,
slip.
n., Release, leakage, flight, passage,
passing, running.

Eschew, Shun, avoid, miss, elude. **Court**

Escort, v.a., Protect, guard, attend,
accompany, conduct.
n., Guard, attendance, company, convoy,
safeguard.

Esculent, Edible, eatable.

Escutcheon, Scutcheon, shield, arms,
ensign, blazon.

Esoteric, Special, private, secret, inmost,
inner. **External**

Especial, Special, marked, distinguishing, distinguished, particular, unusual,
peculiar. **Ordinary**

Espial, Discovery, notice, observation,
spying.

Espousal, Marriage, plighting, betrothing, espousing, affiancing.
Support, adoption, maintenance, defence.

Espouse, Marry, plight, betroth, affiance.
Support, adopt, maintain, defend, embrace, champion, uphold. **Attack**

Espy, v.a., Descry, perceive, see, discern,
discover, observe, notice. **Miss**
v.n., Spy, observe, watch, look.

Essay, v.a., & n., Try, attempt, endeavour.
n., Trial, attempt, endeavour, aim, effort,
struggle.
Discourse, paper, dissertation, article,
composition, disquisition.

Essence, Quintessence, being, substance.
Nature, entity, life, existence.

Essential, Necessary, vital, indispensable,
important, innate, inherent.
Superfluous

Establish, Plant, place, fix, secure, settle,
form, found, originate, organize, institute, constitute, enact, decree, ordain.
Demolish
Prove, demonstrate, verify, substantiate,
ratify, confirm. **Refute**

Establishment, Establishing, planting,
placing.† **Demolition**
Proof, demonstration.† **Refutation**
Household, menage.
Firm, concern, house, business, organiza-
tion.
Income, allowance, salary, stipend, sub-
sistence.

Estate, Condition, state, class, position,
order, rank, standing.
Property, lands, effects, possessions.

Esteem, v.a., Regard, consider, deem,
count, reckon, think, estimate, believe,
judge, imagine, fancy, account, hold.
Disregard
Value, appreciate, respect, like, prize,
love, affect, admire, revere, honour.
Deprecate
n., Respect, appreciation, regard, honour,
reverence, love, admiration.

Estimable, Honourable, admirable,
worthy, delectable, amiable, excellent,
splendid, good, deserving, meritorious.
Bad
Computable, calculable, appreciable.

Estimate, v.a., Count, judge, reckon,
calculate, rate, value, appraise, prize.
Miscalculate
n., Judgment, reckoning, calculation,

computation, estimation, rating, valuation, appraisement.

Estimation, Estimate, judgment, reckoning.†

Estop, Stop, bar, impede, preclude.

Estrange, Alienate, disaffect, withdraw, withhold, divert. *Conciliate*

Estuary, Creek, firth, inlet.

Etch, Engrave, corrode, draw, sketch.

Etching, Drawing, sketch, picture.

Eternal, Everlasting, perpetual, incessant, unceasing, ceaseless, unbroken, continuous, endless, unending, unchanging, unchangeable, imperishable, immutable, infinite, interminable, continual, uninterrupted, perennial, persistent, undying, deathless, immortal. *Transient*

Ethereal, Aerial, airy, celestial, heavenly, empyreal, empyrean, sublime, delicate, light, fairy, fugitive, volatile. *Material*

Ethical, Moral.

Ethnic-al, Pagan, heathen, gentile.

Etiolate, Bleach, whiten, blanch.

Etiquette, Breeding, manners, decorum, form, fashion, usage, formality, conventionality. *Rudeness*

Eucharist, Sacrament, communion, mass.

Eulogistic, Laudatory, encomiastic, commendatory, panegyrical, flattering. *Depreciatory*

Eulogize, Laud, commend, praise, applaud, extol, magnify, worship, panegyrize. *Censure*

Eulogy, Laudation, commendation,† encomium, eulogium.

Euphonic } Musical, silvery, clear, mel-
Euphonious } lifluous, harmonious, melodious, mellow. *Harsh*

Euphony, Smoothness, ease, felicity, melody, harmony.

Euphuism, Affectation, purism, pedantry, fastidiousness. *Simplicity*

Evacuant, Purgative, cathartic, emetic, abstergent, clearing, cleansing.

Evacuate, Leave, quit, vacate, abandon, desert, relinquish, forsake. *Occupy*
Empty, clear, void, eject, expel, discharge, purge, excrete.

Evacuation, Leaving, quitting,† retreat, withdrawal.

Evade, *v.a.,* Elude, escape, shun, miss, avoid, dodge, decline, baffle, foil. *Encounter*
v.n., Quibble, prevaricate, equivocate, fence, hedge, shuffle.

Evanesce, Disappear, vanish, fade, pass. *Appear*

Evanescent, Vanishing, transitory, transient, passing, brief, ephemeral, fleeting, flying, fugitive, flitting. *Permanent*

Evaporate, *v.n.,* Evanesce, disappear, vanish, dissolve.
v.a., Vaporize. *Consolidate*
Exhale.

Evaporation, Evanescence, disappearance.†
Vaporization.
Exhalation.

vasion, Prevarication, equivocation, quibble, shuffle, shuffling, subterfuge, shift, sophistry, tergiversation. *Answer*

Evasive, Prevaricating, equivocating,† elusive, elusory. *Helpful*

Even, *a.,* Level, regular, smooth, flat, plane, uniform, constant, equal, equable, steady. *Variable*
Fair, just, equitable, direct, impartial, straightforward. *Unjust*
adv., Just, exactly, precisely, verily, actually.

Evening, Even, eventide, eve, dusk, twilight, nightfall. *Morning*

Event, Incident, affair, occurrence, circumstance, fact, adventure, happening. *Cause*
Issue, result, conclusion, termination, end, consequence, sequel. *Origin*

Eventful, Memorable, notable, important, remarkable, critical, momentous, stirring, signal. *Ordinary*

Eventual, Final, ultimate, consequential, last, conditional, possible.

Eventuate, Result, accrue, occur, happen, issue, close, terminate, end. *Begin*

Ever, Always, continually, perpetually, eternally, evermore, aye, forever. *Never*
Sometimes, occasionally.

Everlasting, Eternal, endless, unending, perpetual, incessant, unceasing, ceaseless, continuous, unchangeable, immutable, imperishable, interminable, uninterrupted, undying, deathless, immortal. *Passing*

Evermore, Always, ever, eternally, continually, perpetually, aye, forever.

Every, All, each. *None*

Everyday, Usual, common, customary, habitual, routine, accustomed, commonplace, general. *Unusual*

Evict, Dispossess, expel, eject. *Lodge*

Evidence, *v.a.,* Evince, manifest, show.
n., Proof, manifestation, indication, testimony, witness.

Evident, Apparent, plain, clear, obvious, patent, manifest, indisputable, incontrovertible, unmistakable, palpable. *Doubtful*

Evil, *n.,* Wrong, sin, badness, wickedness, crime, depravity, corruption, baseness, malignity, harm. *Good*

Evil, Mischief, injury, wrong, harm, ill, curse, blast.

Disaster, sorrow, affliction, ill, calamity, suffering, visitation, reverse, pain, misery, woe.

a., Wrong, sinful, bad, ill, wicked, vicious, corrupt, base, malicious, malign, malevolent, perverse, vile, nefarious. *Good*

Harmful, hurtful, pernicious, deleterious, bad, injurious, baneful, baleful, noxious, mischievous. *Beneficial*

Disastrous, adverse, ill, woeful, calamitous, unfortunate, unpropitious, unhappy, inauspicious. *Fortunate*

Evince, Evidence, show, display, manifest, exhibit, indicate, establish, prove.
Conceal

Eviscerate, Embowel, disembowel, gut, draw. *Stuff*

Evoke, Extract, summon, educe, provoke, call, rouse, excite, arouse, elicit. *Stifle*

Evolution, Development, evolvement, evolving, growth, expansion.
Retardation

Evolve, Exhibit, develop, educe, open, unfold, expand, unroll. *Mask*

Exacerbate, Exasperate, irritate, provoke, aggravate, infuriate, rouse, excite, inflame, enrage, embitter. *Pacify*

Exacerbation, Exasperation, irritation.†
Pacification

Exact, *v.a.,* Extort, demand, claim, elicit, mulct, ask, requisition, take, compel, impose.

a., Precise, accurate, correct, faithful, literal, true, faultless. *Untrue*

Critical, nice, fine, strict, rigid, severe, scrupulous, exacting, rigorous. *Vague*

Careful, particular, precise, prim, regular, methodical, orderly. *Loose*

Exacting, Critical, exactive, rigid, difficult.

Exaction, Extortion, tribute.

Exactitude ⎱ Correctness, precision, accuracy, faultlessness, faithfulness, care, carefulness, scrupulousness. *Looseness*
Exactness ⎰

Exactly, Precisely, accurately, correct, true, literally, definitely. *Otherwise*

Exaggerate, Stretch, magnify, overstate, overdraw, overestimate, overcolour, strain, romance. *Disparage*

Exaggeration, Stretching, overstatement.†

Exalt, Elevate, ennoble, raise, aggrandize, dignify, honour. *Degrade*

Praise, extol, magnify, glorify, bless.

Exaltation, Elevation, nobility, grandeur, dignity, loftiness.

Examination, Inquiry, scrutiny, observation, inspection, investigation, search, interrogation, test, research, perusal, survey, exploitation, trial, review.

Examine, Inquire, scrutinize,† study.
Discard

Example, Model, copy, pattern, prototype, ensample, representative, standard. Illustration, instance, sample, specimen, exemplification, exemplar, precedent, warning.

Exasperate, Anger, aggravate, vex, annoy, exacerbate, inflame, provoke, chafe, irritate, enrage, rouse, incense, nettle. *Appease*

Exasperation, Anger, aggravation, vexation.†

Excavate, Dig, delve, trench, hollow, burrow, scoop, disinter. *Bury*

Excavation, Digging, delving.†

Trench, hollow, cutting, cut, cavity.

Exceed, Surpass, pass, overstep, cap, transcend, outstrip, outdo, excel.

Exceedingly, Greatly, very, tremendously, enormously, hugely, extremely, highly, vastly. *Slightly*

Excel, *v.a.,* Outvie, outdo, surpass, beat, outrival, outstrip, exceed.

v.n., Shine, succeed.

Excellent, Worthy, good, pre-eminent, eminent, superior, first-rate, sterling, prime, transcendent, admirable, estimable, choice. *Inferior*

Except, *v.a.,* Omit, exclude, negative, reject, bar, ban, veto. *Include*

prep., Save, excepting, omitting, excluding, bar, barring. *Including*

Exception, Omission, exclusion.

Objection, affront, offence.

Anomaly, abnormality. *Rule*

Exceptional, Anomalous, abnormal, unusual, rare, irregular, peculiar, uncommon, unnatural, aberrant. *Normal*

Excerpt, *v.a.,* Extract, cut, cite, quote, select, take.

n., Extract, cutting,† citation.

Excess, Surplus, overplus, remainder, balance, superabundance, abundance, superfluity, surfeit, glut. *Deficiency*

Excess, Extravagance, overdoing, immoderation. *Moderation*

Debauchery, intemperance, immoderation, dissipation, dissoluteness.
Temperance

Excessive, Superfluous, enormous, undue, overmuch, superabundant, exuberant, disproportionate, outrageous, inordinate, extravagant. *Deficient*

Intemperate, immoderate, extreme, violent, vehement. *Moderate*

Exchange, *v.a.*, Change, barter, commute, interchange, substitute, trade, swap, shuffle.

n., Barter, trade, traffic, dealing, change, substitution, commutation.

Bourse, market, fair, bazaar.

Excise, Duty, impost, tax, revenue.

Excitable, Irritable, passionate, sensitive, irascible. *Imperturbable*

Excite, Rouse, arouse, wake, inflame, animate, incite, kindle, stimulate, awaken, provoke, evoke, raise, elicit. *Allay*
Agitate, discompose, irritate, disturb, provoke. *Pacify*

Excitement, Agitation, discomposure, irritation, sensation, commotion, perturbation, passion. *Calmness*
Incitement, motive, stimulus.

Exclaim, Cry, roar, vociferate, call, shout, ejaculate.

Exclamation, Cry, roar,† clamour, outcry.

Exclude, Except, omit, reject, bar, debar, preclude, interdict, veto. *Admit*
Prohibit, ban, hinder, stop, restrain, withhold. *Encourage*
Expel, extrude, eject, eliminate.

Exclusion, Exception, omission.†
Admission
Prohibition, ban, interdict, veto.
Expulsion, extrusion, ejection.

Exclusive, Excluding, barring, debarring, omitting. *Inclusive*
Snobbish, fastidious, choice, aristocratic, select, cliquish, selfish, narrow.
Only, sole, special.

Excogitate, Contrive, create, imagine, invent, coin, fabricate, frame.

Excommunicate, Anathematize, exclude, expel, eject, bar, banish, dismiss, proscribe, exscind, denounce. *Admit*

Excoriate, Skin, abrade, flay, gall, strip, score, scar, scarify.

Excrement, Excretion, dung, dropping, stool, excreta.

Excrete, Discharge, eject, eliminate, separate.

Excruciate, Torture, agonize, rack, torment, pain, wring, writhe. *Soothe*

Excruciating, Torturing, agonizing.†
Soothing

Exculpate, Exonerate, vindicate, clear, absolve, acquit, discharge, free, release.
Charge

Excursion, Trip, outing, journey, tour, ramble, expedition, jaunt.
Episode, digression.

Excursive, Discursive, rambling, devious, erratic, wandering, roaming, roving.
Direct

Excuse, *v.a.*, Acquit, pardon, clear, absolve, exonerate, exculpate, forgive, vindicate, condone, remit, overlook, justify, champion. *Condemn*
Exempt, free, release.

n., Plea, justification, apology, defence.
Pretext, subterfuge, disguise, guise, makeshift, pretence, evasion, colour.

Execrable, Abominable, hateful, detestable, odious, horrid, horrible, abhorrent, cursed, accursed, damnable, vile, disgusting, obnoxious, revolting, nauseating, nauseous, loathsome, repulsive, offensive, sickening, bad, wretched.
Desirable

Execrate, Abominate, hate, detest, abhor, curse, damn. *Like*

Execute, Consummate, finish, perfect, complete, perform, achieve, do, effect, effectuate, accomplish, administer, enforce.

Execution, Performance, achievement, operation, accomplishment, consummation, effect.

Executive, Government, administration.
Legislature

Exegetic, Explanatory, explicatory, explicative, expository.

Exemplary, Model, excellent, worthy, honourable, estimable, admirable, praiseworthy, good, fine, splendid, laudable, commendable, correct. *Vile*

Exemplify, Illustrate, show, represent, exhibit, manifest. *Falsify*

Exempt, *v.a.*, Excuse, relieve, free, privilege, release, except. *Compel*
a., Exempted, excused, free, privileged, released, excepted, liberated, immune.
Liable

Exemption, Freedom, privilege, exception, release, immunity, license.
Liability

Exercise, *v.a.*, Use, employ, exert, apply.
Disuse
Drill, discipline, cultivate, train, develop.
Rest
Produce, effect, exert, wield, pursue, practise.
Trouble, afflict, try, test, annoy, burden, worry.

n., Use, employment, exertion, application, operation, performance. *Disuse*
Drill, drilling, discipline, culture, training, development, schooling, task, lesson.
Labour, toil, effort, exertion, work. *Rest*

Exert, Exercise, use, employ, apply.
Disuse
Wield, exercise, produce, effect.

Exertion, Exercise, use,† exerting.
Labour, toil, effort, attempt, trial,

Exertion, endeavour, stretch, struggle, strain. *Rest*

Exhalation, Mist, damp, effluvium, fog, vapour, steam, fume, reek.

Evaporation, emission. *Absorption*

Exhale, Evaporate, emit, breathe, reek, emanate. *Absorb*

Exhaust, *v.a.*, Drain, empty, draw, expend, squander, impoverish, destroy, dissipate, void, use, consume, spend, waste. *Replenish*

Tire, weary, weaken, prostrate, debilitate, cripple, disable. *Strengthen*

n., Valve, opening, vent, escape.

Exhibit, Display, show, manifest, evince, demonstrate, disclose, indicate, express, evidence. *Mask*

Exhibition, Display, show, manifestation, demonstration, spectacle, sight, pageant, representation.

Scholarship, grant, allowance, pension.

Exhilarate, Stimulate, elate, cheer, gladden, inspirit, inspire, animate, enliven. *Depress*

Exhilaration, Stimulating, elating, cheering.†

Glee, animation, elation, cheer, gaiety, gladness, cheerfulness, hilarity, joyousness. *Depression*

Exhort, Enjoin, persuade, urge, counsel, advise, encourage, incite, stimulate. *Deprecate*

Exhortation, Enjoinder, counsel, advice, encouragement. *Deprecation*

Exhume, Disentomb, disinter, unbury, unearth, disinhume. *Bury*

Exigency, Crisis, emergency, pass, strait, juncture, point, conjuncture, pinch, quandary. *Provision*

Urgency, pressure, necessity, demand, want, need, requirement.

Exigent, Critical, urgent, pressing, importunate.

Exiguity, Smallness, exiguousness, exility, slenderness, attenuation, fineness, diminutiveness. *Fatness*

Exiguous, Small, slender,† slim, tiny, minute. *Large*

Exile, *v.a.*, Expel, expatriate, banish, relegate, proscribe, ostracize. *Welcome*

n., Expulsion, expatriation,† banishment.

Exility, Smallness, exiguity, exiguousness, slenderness, attenuation, diminutiveness, fineness, thinness, subtlety. *Fatness*

Exist, Live, breathe, be, subsist, remain, endure, last, continue, abide. *Die*

Existence, Life, breath, being, animation, subsistence, entity, essence, continuance, duration. *Death*

Exit, Egress, passage, outlet. *Entrance*

Withdrawal, departure, end, demise.

Exodus, Emigration, withdrawal, removal, departure. *Arrival*

Exonerate, Absolve, pardon, clear, exculpate, acquit, excuse, justify, vindicate, discharge, free, release. *Charge*

Exorable, Merciful, yielding, gracious, kind, lenient, pitiful. *Hard*

Exorbitant, Excessive, extravagant, inordinate, enormous, unreasonable, outrageous. *Moderate*

Exorcism, Spell, charm, incantation.

Exordium, Preamble, preface, prelude, introduction, foreword, opening, proem, prologue. *Epilogue*

Exoteric, External, open, public, outer, superficial. *Esoteric*

Exotic, Extraneous, foreign, acquired. *Native*

Expand, Open, stretch, evolve, unfold, spread, dilate, swell, extend, distend. Amplify, enlarge, diffuse, increase. *Contract*

Expanse, Stretch, breadth, space, expansion, extent, void, vast. *Confine*

Expansion, Opening, stretching, evolution, unfolding, spreading, dilatation, swelling, extension, distension, amplification, enlargement, dilation, diffusion, increase. *Contraction*

Expanse, stretch, breadth, space, extent. *Enclosure*

Expansive, Vast, wide, comprehensive, diffusive. *Narrow*

Expanding, stretching, dilating, swelling.

Expatiate, Dilate, enlarge, descant. *Epitomize*

Expatriate, Exile, expel, banish, proscribe, ostracize. *Reinstate*

Expatriation, Exile, expulsion,† banishment.

Expect, Anticipate, forecast, await, forebode, hope, contemplate.

Expectant, Waiting, hopeful.

Expectation, Anticipation, assurance, presumption, reliance, confidence, contemplation, hope, trust.

Expedience⎱ Utility, advantage, interest, **Expediency**⎰ gain, profit.

Advisability, advantageousness, desirability, wisdom, suitableness, fitness, usefulness, propriety, judiciousness, profitableness. *Detriment*

Expedient, *a.*, Advisable, advantageous.† *Unwise*

n., Means, way, contrivance, resort, shift, resource, method.

Expedite, Accelerate, hasten, precipitate, speed, hurry, advance, despatch, quicken, forward. *Delay*

Expedition, Celerity, haste,† alacrity, promptness, alertness. *Tardiness*
Undertaking, enterprise, excursion, march, voyage.

Expeditious, Swift, quick, prompt, speedy, fast, rapid, alert, nimble. *Slow*

Expel, Eject, remove, banish, exscind, exclude, exile, expatriate, proscribe, ostracize, discharge. *Welcome*
Evacuate, void, eject, dislodge, discharge.

Expend, Spend, disburse, dissipate, exhaust, consume, waste, scatter, use, employ, exert. *Save*

Expenditure, Spending, disbursement, outlaying, outlay, outgo, outgoing. *Income*
Expense, cost, charge, outlay, payment. *Receipt*

Expense, Cost, charge, outlay, expenditure, price, payment. *Receipt*

Expensive, Dear, costly, extravagant, rich, valuable, lavish, wasteful. *Cheap*

Experience, *v.a.,* Feel, undergo, try, suffer, endure, encounter, meet. *Miss*
n., Feeling, trial, observation, practice.

Experienced, Skilled, versed, practised, able, instructed, expert, wise, trained, accomplished, qualified, conversant. *Unqualified*

Experiment, Trial, test, observation, examination, essay, experience, ordeal.

Experimental, Empiric, empirical, tentative, essaying, trying, testing. *Perfect*

Expert, *n.,* Specialist, connoisseur.
a., Dexterous, apt, adroit, smart, clever, skilful, able, prompt, quick. *Clumsy*

Expiation, Reparation, atonement, satisfaction.

Expiration, End, death, decease, exit, close, departure, demise, conclusion, termination, cessation. *Beginning*

Expire, End, die,† stop. *Begin*

Explain, Expound, interpret, illustrate, unfold, elucidate, teach, solve, justify, warrant. *Obscure*

Explanation, Exposition, interpretation, illustration,† elucidation, explication, reason. *Mystery*
Account, solution, key, secret, justification, warrant, deduction, description, recital, detail.

Explanatory, Expository, illustrative, elucidative, justifying, justificatory, warranting, accounting. *Mystifying*

Expletive, *a.,* Unnecessary, superfluous, redundant. *Essential*
n., Oath.

Explication, Explanation, exposition, interpretation, illustration, elucidation, justification.

Explicit, Plain, categorical, clear, express, detailed, unambiguous, definite, positive, absolute, determinate. *Implied*

Explode, Burst, displode, detonate, discharge.
Scorn, discard, repudiate, scout.

Exploit, *v.a.,* Use, utilize, victimize.
n., Achievement, deed, feat, act, accomplishment.

Exploration, Search, research, scrutiny, examination, inquisition, inquiry, investigation.

Explore, Search, scrutinize, examine, investigate, prospect, plumb, fathom, pry, inquire.

Explosion, Crack, blast, burst, bursting, pop, detonation, displosion, discharge.

Exponent, Advocate, propounder, interpreter, representative, indication, example, symbol, specimen, illustration.

Export, Ship, produce, send, carry. *Import*

Expose, Exhibit, uncover, unmask, reveal, disclose, bare. *Cover*
Denounce, detect. *Condone*
Endanger, risk, jeopardize, venture.

Exposé, Exhibit, manifests, revelation, denouncement, publication, exposure.

Exposition, Display, show, exhibition.
Disclosing, exposure. *Concealment*
Explanation, explication, elucidation, interpretation.

Expostulate, Object, remonstrate, reason, protest. *Abet*

Expostulation, Objection, remonstrance, protest.

Exposure, Exposition, divulgement, disclosure, revelation.

Expound, Explain, elucidate, interpret, develop, unfold, rehearse.

Express, *v.a.,* State, declare, assert, say, utter.
Exhibit, evince, show, manifest, denote, signify, represent, indicate, intimate.
a., Rapid, speedy, quick, fast, swift. *Slow*
Special, particular. *General*
Positive, definite, clear, specific, plain, unambigious, unmistakable, explicit, categorical, determinate. *Vague*

Expression, Look, countenance.
Utterance, statement, declaration, assertion, communication.
Phrase, word, term, saying.
Tone, feeling, effect, exhibition, modulation, execution.

Expressive, Strong, forcible, forceful,

violent, emphatic, energetic, vivid, eloquent, lively, demonstrative.
Indicative, significant.
Sympathetic, appropriate, modulated.

Expulsion, Banishment, extrusion, exclusion, ejection, discharge, expatriation, exile. ***Welcome***

Expunge, Obliterate, erase, efface, delete, cancel, abrogate, annul. ***Insert***

Expurgate, Cleanse, clean, clarify, purify, purge, wash. ***Stain***
Bowdlerize, emasculate.

Expurgation, Cleansing, cleaning.†

Exquisite, Rare, choice, fine, nice, excellent, capital, splendid, refined, delicate, valuable, precious, choice, select, consummate, perfect, complete, matchless. ***Common***

Exsiccate, Desiccate, dry. ***Moisten***

Extant, Existent, existing, visible, present, undestroyed, current, surviving. ***Defunct***

Extemporaneous, Extempore, extemporary, unpremeditated, improvised, impromptu, unprepared, spontaneous. ***Prepared***

Extemporary, Extempore, extemporaneous, unpremeditated, improvised.†

Extempore, *a.*, Extemporary, extemporaneous.†
adv., Suddenly.

Extend, *v.a.*, Stretch, reach, spread, range, lie, expand. ***Limit***
v.a., Lengthen, protract, stretch, expand, dilate, elongate, increase, widen, enlarge, continue, prolong, augment, diffuse. ***Contract***
Offer, give, impart, yield.

Extension, Lengthening, stretching, expansion.†

Extensive, Broad, large, wide, spacious, capacious, comprehensive. ***Narrow***

Extent, Degree, quantity, amount, content. ***Restriction***
Volume, size, length, stretch, bulk, reach, magnitude, measure, proportions, breadth, width, height, depth, latitude, scope, range, area, field.

Extenuate, Mitigate, qualify, palliate, lessen, reduce, diminish. ***Aggravate***

Exterior, *n.*, Outside, surface, face. ***Inside***
a., Outside, outer, outward, external, superficial, exotic. ***Interior***

Exterminate, Annihilate, destroy, extirpate, eliminate, eradicate, abolish, uproot. ***Establish***

Extermination, Annihilation, destruction,† extinction. ***Establishment***

External, Exterior, outside, superficial, outer, entrinsic, foreign, exotic. ***Inside***
Visible, apparent, outward.

Extinct, Dead, defunct, extinguished, obsolete, finished, ended, terminated, closed, done. ***Living***

Extinction, Destruction, annihilation, cessation, suffocation, stifling, extirpation, abolition, extinguishment, abolishment, excision, extermination, eradication. ***Survival***

Extinguish, Destroy, annihilate, suffocate,† quench, kill, suppress. ***Promote***
Obscure, eclipse.

Extirpate, Exterminate, destroy, annihilate, abolish, eradicate, uproot. ***Establish***

Extirpation, Extermination, destruction.† ***Establishment***

Extol, Laud, praise, eulogize, exalt, magnify, applaud, panegyrize, glorify, commend. ***Decry***

Extort, Exact, extract, wring, wrest, force, wrench, elicit, squeeze. ***Coax***

Extortionate, Exorbitant, exacting, hard, heavy, severe, oppressive, excessive, harsh. ***Moderate***

Extra, Supplementary, supplemental, additional, accessory, spare.
Special, extraordinary, extreme, unusual. ***Ordinary***

Extract, *v.a.*, Educe, draw, extort. ***Insert***
Distil, draw, squeeze, derive.
Quote, select, cite, determine, find.
n., Excerpt, quotation, selection, citation.
Decoction, juice, essence, distillation, infusion.

Extraction, Parentage, lineage, descent, birth, origin.
Essence, distillation, derivation.

Extradition, Surrender, delivery.

Extraneous, Extrinsic, alien, foreign, external, adscititious, superfluous. ***Intrinsic***

Extraordinary, Singular, unusual, rare, strange, signal, remarkable, uncommon, egregious, peculiar, unwonted. ***Usual***

Extravagance, Wildness, folly, absurdity, monstrosity, excess, irregularity. ***Regularity***
Profusion, prodigality, waste, recklessness, wastefulness. ***Economy***
Preposterousness, enormity, excess, unreasonableness. ***Moderation***

Extravagant, Wild, foolish, absurd.† ***Regular***
Profuse, prodigal,† lavish, spendthrift. ***Economical***
Preposterous, unreasonable, enormous, excessive, inordinate. ***Moderate***

Extreme, *a.*, Greatest, last, final, terminal, farthest, ultimate, utmost, uttermost, outermost.   *Initial*
Immoderate, extravagant, unreasonable, excessive.   *Moderate*
n., Extremity, verge, end, termination, edge, apex, acme, climax, crest, top.
               Beginning

Extremity, Extreme, verge, end.†
               Commencement

Extricate, Disentangle, release, free, disengage, disembarrass, clear, relieve, deliver, liberate.   *Involve*

Extrinsic, Extraneous, exotic, outside, foreign, alien, superficial, external, outward.   *Internal*

Extrude, Banish, expel, discharge, eject.
               Introduce

Extrusion, Banishment, expulsion.†
               Introduction

Exuberance, Abundance, plenty, copiousness, plenitude, redundance, profusion, excess, luxuriance, superabundance, lavishness.   *Scarcity*

Exuberant, Abundant, plentiful, rich, copious,† prolific.   *Scarce*

Exudation, Sweating, excretion, discharge, oozing, percolation, dripping, infiltrating, secretion.   *Absorption*

Exude, *v.a.*, Excrete, discharge, secrete.
               Absorb
v.n., Ooze, sweat, drip, percolate, infiltrate.

Exult, Crow, triumph, rejoice, gloat, taunt, vaunt, jubilate.   *Mourn*

Exultant, Exulting, triumphant, rejoicing, jubilant, joyous, elated.
               Depressed

Eye, Observe, watch, notice, view, regard, look.
Perforation, aperture, eyelet.
Bud, shoot.

Eyrie, Retreat, nest.

F

Fable, Story, tale, allegory, myth, parable, apologue, legend.
Untruth, lie, fiction, falsehood, fabrication, invention. *Fact*

Fabric, Building, edifice, structure, pile, erection.
Web, texture. *Ruin*

Fabricate, Build, make, form, construct, manufacture. *Demolish*
Forge, invent, feign, falsify, coin.

Fabrication, Building, construction, manufacture. *Demolition*
Forgery, invention, fable, fiction, falsehood, mendacity, figment. *Fact*

Fabulous, Monstrous, incredible, fictitious, legendary, unreal, mythical, marvellous, fabricated, invented. *Real*

Face, *v.a.*, Front, confront, oppose, defy, dare, meet. *Avoid*
Cover, coat, veneer, incrust, polish, dress, level, smooth.
n., Countenance, look, appearance, visage, expression, aspect, semblance.
Surface, front, cover, facet, breast, escarpment.
Boldness, effrontery, audacity, assurance, shamelessness, brass, impudence, confidence. *Timidity*

Facetious, Merry, gay, jolly, jocose, jocular, witty, amusing, entertaining, sportive, lively, humorous, buoyant, sprightly, pleasant, waggish, funny, droll, comical. *Dull*

Facile, Easy, dexterous, able, ready, skilful. *Clumsy*
Pliant, compliant, pliable, easy, tractable, affable, mild, complaisant, docile, indulgent, weak, manageable, ductile, yielding. *Obstinate*

Facilitate, Expedite, forward, advance.

Facility, Ease, easiness, dexterity, ability, readiness. *Clumsiness*
Pliancy, pliability, ease.† *Obstinacy*
Aid, advantage, help, convenience, resource, means, applicancy.

Facsimile, Copy, duplicate, reproduction. *Original*

Fact, Truth, actuality, reality, certainty. *Fiction*
Event, happening, occurrence, incident, circumstance, act, performance, deed. *Romance*

Faction, Cabal, conspiracy, confederation, league, party, junta, combination, clique.
Turbulence, disorder, tumult, anarchy, discord, sedition, dissension, strife, recalcitration, rebellion. *Order*

Factious, Turbulent, disorderly, tumultuous.† *Orderly*

Factitious, False, artificial, unnatural.

Factor, Middleman, agent, substitute.
Broker, steward, bailiff.
Element, part, divisor.

Faculty, Dexterity, skill, skilfulness, ability, power, capacity, talent, expertness, competency, capability, endowment, gift, adroitness, address, aptness, aptitude, cleverness, knack, facility. *Clumsiness*
Body, department, profession.
Right, license, privilege, power, authority, prerogative.

Fade, Disappear, vanish, recede, evanesce, dwindle, decrease, fail, fall, decline, droop, sink, decay, languish, wither, bleach, etiolate. pale, change, blanch. *Endure*
Dissolve, disperse.

Fag, Fatigue, weary, tire, toil, droop, sink, flag, drudge. *Refresh*
Drudge, menial, slave.

Fagged, Fatigued, weary, wearied, tired, jaded, exhausted.

Fail, *v.n.*, Fall, miss, miscarry. *Succeed*
Neglect, forget, omit.
Decay, wane, sink, decline, fade, cease, break, collapse. *Wax*
v.a., Disappoint.

Failing, Failure, miscarriage, abortion. *Success*
Decay, decline.
Fault, weakness, defect, imperfection, infirmity, shortcoming, deficiency, slip, frailty, sin, error. *Virtue*

Failure, Failing, miscarriage, abortion, breakdown, collapse, fiasco. *Success*
Decay, decline, declension, omission, neglect, deficiency, loss.
Insolvency, bankruptcy, ruin.

Fain, Willingly, gladly, cheerfully, readily, joyfully, eagerly. *Reluctantly*

Faint, *v.n.*, Swoon, droop, languish, sink, fade, fail.
a., Drooping, languid, weak, ill, fatigued.
Weak, small, slight, little, imperceptible, inconsiderate, dull, indistinct, dim, pale. *Strong*

Faint-hearted, Timid, cowardly, fearful, timorous. *Brave*

Fair, Just, right, honourable, equitable,

proper, reasonable, frank, honest, upright. **Unjust**

Blond, white, light, clear, unstained, unsullied, untarnished, unblemished, unspotted, spotless, unclouded. **Dark**

Favourable, promising, hopeful.

Open, plain, distinct, clear, unencumbered.

Moderate, middling, satisfactory, passable, tolerant.

Handsome, beautiful, pretty, comely, pleasing. **Ugly**

Pleasant, uncloudy, sunny, clear, cloudless, bright. **Stormy**

Fairy, Sprite, elf, elfin, pixie, fay, brownie.

Charming, lovely, dainty, fascinating.

Faith, Creed, doctrine, dogma, tenet, religion, persuasion, conviction.

Belief, credit, credence, confidence, assurance, hope, reliance, dependence. **Doubt**

Faithfulness, fidelity, loyalty, truth, truthfulness, steadfastness, constancy. **Perfidy**

Faithful, Loyal, truthful, true, steadfast, constant, devoted, leal, trusty, trustworthy, reliable. **Perfidious**

Exact, close, accurate, nice, strict. **Loose**

Faithless, Disloyal, unfaithful, untrustworthy, unreliable, perfidious, false, treacherous, unbelieving. **Loyal**

Fall, v.n., Sink, drop, descend. **Rise**

Err, lapse, sin, trespass, offend, trip, transgress, stumble.

Decrease, decline, subside, ebb, abate.

Perish, die.

Happen, pass, come, befall, chance, occur, become, get.

n., Sinking, drop, dropping, descent, falling, tumble. **Rise**

Degradation, failure, lapse, sin, slip, apostasy, decline, declension.

Decrease, decline, diminution, ebb, subsidence, sinking, depreciation.

Death, destruction, overthrow, ruin, downfall, collapse, surrender.

Waterfall, cascade, rapids, cataract.

Declivity, inclination, incline, slope.

Autumn.

Fallacious, False, untrue, fictitious, misleading, illusory, illusive, sophistical, worthless, delusive, erroneous, incorrect, wrong, disappointing, deceptive, deceiving. **True**

Fallacy, Falsehood, untruth, fiction,† blunder, chimera, misconception. **Truth**

Fallible, Weak, uncertain, imperfect, unsafe, erring, frail, ignorant. **Unerring**

Fallow, Idle, dormant, quiescent, inactive, inert, untilled, unsowed, uncultivated, neglected. **Fertile**

False, Fallacious, untrue, fictitious, misleading, illusory, illusive, sophistical, worthless, delusive, disappointing, deceptive, deceiving, erroneous, incorrect, wrong. **True**

Perfidious, faithless, disloyal, treacherous, dishonourable, dishonest. **Faithful**

Spurious, counterfeit, forged, feigned. **Genuine**

Unveracious, untrue, untruthful, mendacious, unreliable, untrustworthy, lying. **Veracious**

Falsehood, Lie, untruth, falsity, fiction, fabrication, mendacity. **Truth**

Falsify, Misrepresent, misinterpret, belie, mistake, " doctor," adulterate, fake, alter, counterfeit.

Falsity, Falsehood, lie, untruth, fiction, fabrication, mendacity. **Truth**

Falter, Hesitate, waver, stumble, stammer, stutter, tremble, fail, totter, halt, vacillate, demur. **Flow**

Fame, Renown, honour, repute, reputation, credit, name, glory, celebrity. **Oblivion**

Familiar, Common, well-known, household. **New**

Intimate, close, friendly, cordial, near, amicable, fraternal, easy, affable, open, free, unconstrained, unceremonious, informal, sociable, social, friendly. **Distant**

Conversant. **Ignorant**

Familiarity, Intimacy, closeness, friendliness.†

Familiarize, Habituate, inure, accustom, use, train.

Family, Household, house, tribe, race, lineage, clan, kindred.

Subdivision, group, genera, kind, class.

Famine, Dearth, scarcity, starvation. **Plenty**

Famish, Starve, exhaust, hunger. **Feed**

Famous, Renowned, honoured, honourable, reputable, celebrated, eminent, illustrious, great, famed, noted, remarkable, distinguished. **Unknown**

Fan, Agitate, excite, rouse, inflame, stimulate, increase, thresh, move, blow, winnow. **Allay**

Cool, refresh.

Fanatic, Zealot, visionary, enthusiast, bigot. **Cynic**

Fanatical, Zealous, bigoted, enthusiastic, visionary, rabid, wild, frenzied, mad. **Cool**

Fanciful, Capricious, grotesque, unreal,

imaginary, chimerical, wild, fantastic, whimsical, fitful. ***Real***

Fancy, *v.a.*, Imagine, conceive, think, like.
v.n., Imagine, believe, suppose, think, conjecture, apprehend.
n., Image, conception, conceit, thought, idea, notion, apprehension, impression.
Liking, inclination, fondness, predilection. ***Aversion***
Whim, caprice, fantasy, vagary, freak, humour, crotchet.
a., Ornamental, elegant, fine, nice, extravagant, fanciful, imaginative, fancied.

Fang, Tooth, tusk, nail, claw, talon.

Fantastic-al, Fanciful, capricious, odd, grotesque, imaginary, unreal, chimerical, wild, whimsical, queer, fitful. ***Realistic***

Fantasy, Fancy, image, conceit, thought, idea, notion.
Whim, caprice, vagary, freak, humour, crotchet.

Far, Distant, remote, removed, long, protracted. ***Near***
Alienated, hostile, estranged.

Farce, Comedy, burlesque, parody, travesty, caricature. ***Tragedy***
Force, forcemeat, stuffing.

Farcical, Absurd, comic, ridiculous, funny, amusing, ludricous, droll. ***Tragic***

Fardel, Pack, burden, load, bundle.

Fare, *v.n.*, Do, manage, subsist, feed, live.
n., Food, victuals, provisions, rations, commons, board.
Charge, price.
Passenger.
Fortune, luck, condition, experience, outcome.

Farewell, Valediction, adieu, good-bye, leave, departure, parting.

Farm, Till, cultivate.

Farrago, Jumble, mixture, medley, pot-pourri.

Farther, *adv.*, Further, beyond, past.
Nearer
Moreover, furthermore, besides.
a., Further, remoter, ulterior, distant.
Additional.

Fascinate, Charm, captivate, enchant, bewitch, enamour, entrance, enrapture, stupefy, delight. ***Repel***

Fascinating, Charming, captivating,† attractive, alluring. ***Repulsive***

Fash, Tease, plague, vex, harass, torment, trouble, worry, care.

Fashion, *v.a.*, Make, form, mould, shape.
n., Form, mould, shape, figure, stamp, cast, guise, appearance, style, cut, make, model, pattern.
Method, manner, sort, way, wise.
Gentility, gentry, quality.

Fashion, Convention, conventionality, practice, custom, style.

Fashionable, Conventional, usual, customary, modish, prevailing, current, smart. ***Eccentric***

Fast, *a.*, Rapid, swift, quick, fleet, speedy, accelerated. ***Slow***
Firm, steadfast, unmovable, immovable, constant, fixed, close, fastened, secure.
Loose
Dissolute, dissipated, extravagant, wild, reckless, gay, thriftless. ***Temperate***
adv., Firmly, immovably, tightly.
Quickly, swiftly, rapidly, recklessly, wildly, extravagantly.

Fasten, Bind, secure, unite, join, attach, tie, connect, chain, bolt, strap, tether, belay, bend. ***Detach***

Fastidious, Dainty, squeamish, particular, critical, censorious. ***Careless***

Fat, Plump, corpulent, portly, large, obese, fleshly, oleaginous. ***Thin***
Rich, profitable, lucrative, fertile, fruitful, productive.

Fatal, Deadly, destructive, lethal, mortal, pernicious, baleful, baneful, ruinous, calamitous. ***Beneficial***

Fatality, Destiny, calamity, disaster, mortality.

Fate, Destiny, lot, doom, fatality, destination. ***Choice***

Fated, Destined, doomed, predestined, preordained, decreed.

Fateful, Ominous, momentous, portentous.

Father, *v.a.*, Adopt, nurture, cherish, succour.
Engender, beget.
n., Progenitor, ancestor, forefather.
Mother
Inventor, creator, author.

Fatherly, Paternal, kind, tender, protecting, benign.

Fathom, Measure, sound, penetrate, pierce, gauge, probe, reach, comprehend, understand. ***Skim***

Fathomless, Bottomless, deep, abysmal, profound. ***Shallow***

Fatigue, *v.a.*, Weary, tire, jade, exhaust, fag, harass. ***Refresh***
n., Weariness, tiredness,† lassitude.
Freshness

Fatuity, Folly, absurdity, foolishness, idiocy, imbecility, stupidity, infatuation, madness. ***Sense***

Fatuous, Foolish, absurd, idiotic, imbecile, infatuated, mad, witless, senseless, stupid. ***Sensible***

Fault, Flaw, blemish, failing, weakness, defect, frailty, imperfection. ***Perfection***

Fault, Sin, offence, error, lapse, omission, crime, failing, misdeed, mistake, delinquency, trespass, slip, misdemeanour, transgression, wrong. ***Virtue***

Faultless, Perfect, whole, complete, flawless, accurate. ***Defective***
Innocent, sinless, stainless, guiltless, blameless, unsullied, spotless, unspotted. ***Sinful***

Faulty, Defective, imperfect, bad, incomplete. ***Perfect***

Favillous, Ashen, ashy, cinereous.

Favour, *v.a.,* Approve, encourage, countenance, patronize, befriend, help, support, aid, oblige, facilitate, assist. ***Discourage***
Spare, indulge, humour, ease, palliate, extenuate.
n., Countenance, approval, friendliness, kindness, popularity, patronage, support, championship. ***Disapproval***
Permission, leave, pardon, goodwill.
Gift, present, token.
Rosette, decoration, colours.
Letter, communication, epistle.
Advantage, indulgence, protection, cover, prejudice, bias, partiality.

Favourable, Auspicious, advantageous, beneficial. ***Adverse***
Kind, willing, friendly, partial, fond. ***Impartial***

Favourite, Beloved, precious, dear, darling, chosen.

Fawn, Cringe, crouch, kneel, stoop, bow, bend, flatter. ***Dare***

Fawning, Cringing, flattery, sycophancy, servility. ***Independence***

Fay, Fit, join.
Elf, fairy.

Fealty, Loyalty, allegiance, fidelity, homage, honour, faithfulness, devotion. ***Treason***

Fear, *v.a.,* Apprehend, dread.
Reverence, venerate, revere.
n., Apprehension, dread, terror, awe, trepidation, fright, affright, alarm, dismay, consternation, horror, panic, timidity. ***Boldness***
Anxiety, apprehension, concern, solicitude, worry. ***Assurance***
Reverence, veneration, awe.

Fearful, Apprehensive, trepid, frightened, alarmed, dismayed, timid, afraid, shrinking, timorous. ***Bold***
Dreadful, terrible, awful, horrible, dire, frightful, shocking. ***Reassuring***

Fearless, Undaunted, dauntless, bold, brave, heroic, gallant, intrepid, courageous, valiant, valorous. ***Timid***

Feasible, Practicable, manageable, possible, contrivable. ***Impossible***

Feast, *n.,* Banquet, entertainment, carousal, treat, holiday, festival.
v.a., Delight, gladden, rejoice, gratify.

Feat, Achievement, exploit, act, deed, performance, accomplishment, trick.

Feature, Characteristic, part, portion, mark, element, component, item, outline, fashion, make, aspect, lineament.

Feculence, Dregs, lees, sediment, muddiness, turbidity. ***Clarity***

Fecund, Fruitful, productive, fertile, prolific, impregnated, rich. ***Barren***

Federal, United, confederate, federate, treaty, alliance.

Federation, Confederation, union, league, alliance, coalition, federacy, confederacy, combination.

Fee, Remuneration, pay, reward, compensation, charge, toll, bill, account, reckoning.

Feeble, Weak, faint, infirm, frail, languid, drooping, enervated, debilitated. ***Strong***

Feed, *v.n.,* Eat, subsist. ***Starve***
v.a., Provide, nourish, cherish, supply, sustain.
n., Fodder, food, provender, feeder.

Feel, Touch, handle, perceive.
Try, test, sound, prove.
Experience, suffer, enjoy, sense.

Feeling, *n.,* Sense, sensation, touch, contact, perception.
Sensibility, passion, emotion, sensitiveness, sentiment, susceptibility, tenderness. ***Callousness***
a., Sensitive, passionate, tender, moving, touching, sympathetic, affecting. ***Callous***

Feign, Counterfeit, sham, pretend, forge, affect, invent, devise, fabricate, imagine, simulate, assume.

Feint, Pretence, pretext, sham, blind, artifice, trick, expedient, stratagem, dodge.

Felicitate, Congratulate, compliment.

Felicitous, Happy, apt, timely, fortunate, proper, appropriate, successful, opportune, pertinent, seasonable, auspicious, fit, lucky. ***Unfortunate***

Felicity, Happiness, aptness, timeliness.†
Bliss, blissfulness, happiness, blessedness. ***Sadness***

Fell, *v.a.,* Hew, cut, prostrate, level, subvert, demolish. ***Plant***
a., Barbarous, savage, cruel, inhuman, ferocious, direful, bloody, sanguinary, unrelenting, relentless, ruthless, merciless, malicious, unmerciful, malignant. ***Humane***

Fellow, Companion, compeer, peer, mate, equal, associate, comrade, partner. *Stranger*

Fellowship, Companionship, equality, brotherhood, intimacy, friendship, intercourse, familiarity, society, communion, sociability, company. *Enmity*

Felon, Criminal, convict, culprit, malefactor, offender, outlaw.

Felonious, Criminal, wicked, bad, base, nefarious, infamous, heinous, perfidious, villainous. *Proper*

Felony, Crime, offence, sin, trespass, misdemeanour.

Female, Fertile, pistillate, breeding, bearing. *Male*

Feminine, Womanly, soft, effeminate, tender, unmanly, delicate, weak. *Manly*

Fen, Bog, marsh, swamp, moor, morass, quagmire.

Fence, *v.a.*, Enclose, protect, fortify, defend, circumscribe, guard, parry. *Expose*

v.n., Hedge, shuffle, evade, prevaricate, equivocate.

n., Hedge, wall, barrier, rampart, shield, defence, protection, guard. Receiver.

Ferine, Savage, wild, untamed, fierce, ferocious,† rapacious, brutal. *Tame*

Ferment, *v.a.*, Excite, rouse, heat, agitate. *Calm*

v.n., Seethe, chafe, effervesce.

n., Excitement, heat, agitation, tumult, commotion, fever. *Peace* Yeast, leaven.

Ferocious, Savage, wild, cruel, barbarous, fell, relentless, unrelenting, ruthless, unmerciful, merciless, harsh, inhuman, sanguinary, bloody, fierce, ferine, rapacious, pitiless, unpitying, brutal. *Humane*

Fertile, Fecund, fruitful, productive, teeming, rich, prolific, luxuriant, pregnant. *Barren*

Fervent, Fervid, hot, eager, ardent, keen, glowing, seething, melting, zealous, earnest, warm, animated. *Apathetic*

Fervid, Fervent, hot, eager.†

Fervour, Fervency, heat, eagerness, zeal, ardour, keenness, earnestness, warmth, animation, intensity. *Apathy*

Festal, Festive, jovial, convivial, gay, merry, jolly, joyous. *Mournful*

Fester, *v.n.*, Rankle, ulcerate, corrupt, suppurate, putrefy, rot.

n., Ranking, sore, gathering, boil, ulcer, pustule, abscess.

Festival, Feast, gala, holiday, fête, treat, banquet, carnival, celebration, anniversary.

Festive, Festal, jovial, convivial, gay, merry, jolly, joyous. *Mournful*

Festivity, Conviviality, joviality, gaiety, merriment, joyfulness, joyousness, feast, festival. *Mourning*

Festoon, Decorate, loop, wreath, garland.

Fetch, *v.a.*, Bring, convey, carry.

n., Dodge, trick, ruse, stratagem, artifice, wile.

Fête, Festival, gala, holiday, carnival, feast, anniversary, treat.

Fetid, Foul, stinking, corrupt, offensive, noxious, rank, mephitic, noisome. *Fresh*

Fetish, Charm, talisman, superstition.

Fetter, *v.a.*, Chain, shackle, manacle, tie, bind, trammel, encumber, clog. *Loose*

n., Chain, shackle, bond, manacle.

Feud, Quarrel, row, strife, bickering, contention, rupture, enmity, discord, dissension, jarring, clashing, broil, hostility, vendetta. *Concord*

Fever, Ferment, agitation, excitement, flush, heat, passion. *Composure*

Few, Rare, scanty, scant, lacking, little, scarce. *Many*

Fiasco, Failure, farce, fizzle. *Success*

Fiat, Order, ordinance, law, decree, proclamation, command, word.

Fibre, Thread, pile, staple, filament, strand.

Sinews, toughness, strength. *Debility*

Fickle, Fitful, weak, variable, changeable, vacillating, wavering, irresolute, unstable, volatile, unsteady, unreliable, inconstant, capricious, mercurial, unsettled, veering, shifting. *Steadfast*

Fiction, Story, tale, romance, fabrication, invention, imagination, fancy, fantasy, fable. *Fact*

Fictitious, Invented, untrue, imaginary, fabricated, fanciful, feigned, unreal, false, artificial, mythical, spurious. *True*

Fiddle, Trifle, idle, dawdle, dally.

Fiddling, Trifling, idle, trivial, small, foolish, nonsensical. *Important*

Fidelity, Loyalty, faithfulness, devotion, fealty, allegiance, truth, devotedness, attachment. *Perfidy*

Closeness, exactness, accuracy, faithfulness, precision. *Looseness*

Fidget, Worry, fret, chafe, twitch.

Fidgety, Impatient, uneasy, fretful, restless. *Restful*

Fiducial, Precise, accurate, exact, true. *Loose*

Confident, fiduciary, trustful, unwavering, undoubting, steadfast, firm. *Doubtful*

Fiduciary, Fiducial, confident, trustful.† Reliable, trusty, trustworthy. *Untrustworthy*

Field, Ground, meadow, glebe.

Region, province, realm, sphere, domain, department.

Range, scope, extent, sphere, surface, room.

Fiend, Demon, devil, monster, wretch. *Angel*

Fiendish, Demoniac, devilish, malignant, cruel, malevolent, diabolical, infernal, malicious. *Angelic*

Fierce, Savage, ferocious, furious, cruel, barbarous, fell, violent, raging, ruthless, wild, bloody, ferine, sanguinary, rapacious. *Tame*

Fiery, Fervent, hot, ardent, eager, flaming, burning, heated, lurid, glowing, fervid, vehement, passionate, fierce. *Cold*

Fight, *v.n.*, Battle, combat, contend, strive, contest, struggle, war, wrestle.

v.a., Battle against, combat, contend against.†

n., Battle, combat, contention, contest, struggle, war, conflict, fray, affair, brush, engagement, action, affray, onset, encounter, riot, broil, brawl. *Peace*

Fighting, Battle, combat, contention.†

Figment, Fiction, fable, story, fabrication, invention, falsehood. *Fact*

Figurative, Metaphorical, emblematic, representative, illustrative, typical. *Literal*

Rhetorical, poetical, flowery, purple, ornate, florid. *Plain*

Figure, *v.a.*, Calculate, reckon, compute.

Picture, conceive, imagine.

Represent, signify, depict, symbolize.

v.n., Appear, perform, act.

n., Outline, shape, form, configuration, appearance, pattern, image, design, likeness, representation, effigy.

Number, digit, cipher.

Drawing, diagram.

Emblem, symbol, type.

Evolution.

Filament, Thread, fibre, pile, staple, strand.

Filch, Crib, steal, pilfer, purloin, thieve.

File, Rasp, smooth, perfect, finish, polish, refine. *Roughen*

Bundle, roll, list.

Fill, Replenish, satisfy, supply, furnish, stock, sate, glut, content, satiate. *Empty*

Hold, occupy, fulfil, perform, do, discharge, execute. *Withhold*

Film, Thread, pellicle, skin, veil, scum, cloud.

Filter, *v.a.*, Strain, distil, refine, clarify, filtrate. *Thicken*

v.n., Exude, ooze, transude, percolate, leak.

n., Strainer, clearer.

Filth, Dirt, pollution, corruption, defilement, grossness, uncleanness, foulness, impurity, nastiness. *Cleanliness*

Filthy, Dirty, polluted, corrupt.† *Clean*

Fimbriate, Fringed, filamentous, tasselled. *Hemmed*

Final, Ultimate, last, latest, conclusive, decisive, terminal, eventual. *First*

Finale, End, conclusion, termination, climax, finis. *Beginning*

Finality, Conclusiveness, completeness, definiteness.

Finally, Lastly, ultimately, eventually. *Firstly*

Financial, Fiscal, monetary, pecuniary.

Find, *v.a.*, Discover, notice, perceive, remark, observe, detect, catch. *Lose*

Provide, furnish, contribute, supply.

v.n., Decide, declare, determine, rule.

n., Discovery. *Loss*

Fine, *v.a.*, Mulct, amerce.

n., Mulct, amercement, forfeiture, forfeit. *Reward*

a., Splendid, beautiful, choice, handsome, elegant, excellent, superior, admirable, honourable. *Mean*

Small, thin, little, minute, delicate, slender, tenuous, attenuated. *Thick*

Refined, exquisite, pure, clear, unadulterated. *Coarse*

Keen, exact, sharp. *Blunt*

Finery, Decorations, ornaments, trimmings, trinkets, trappings, show, display. *Simplicity*

Finesse, Wiles, stratagems, cunning, strategy, artifice, craft, subtlety.

Finical, Particular, squeamish, fastidious, faddy, dainty. *Careless*

Finish, *v.a.*, Complete, perfect, end, terminate, fulfil, achieve, close, execute, accomplish, consummate, conclude, do, perform. *Begin*

n., Completion, perfection, end.† *Beginning*

Polish, elaboration.

Finished, Complete, completed, perfect, consummate, elegant. *Incomplete*

Experienced, qualified, practised, proficient, accomplished, able. *Unqualified*

Finite, Limited, conditioned, bounded, restricted. *Unbounded*

Fire, *v.a.*, Discharge, eject, expel, hurl.

Kindle, inflame, rouse, animate, excite, invigorate, inspire, inspirit, ignite. *Damp*

Fire, *n.*, Burning, combustion, conflagration, blaze.

Fervour, ardour, heat, vigour, animation, excitement, passion, fervency, force, violence, intensity, enthusiasm, spirit. *Coldness*

Light, radiance, splendour, lustre, vivacity, inspiration, imagination.

Fireside, Hearth, home.

Firm, *n.*, Company, business, concern, house, establishment, partnership.

a., Steady, steadfast, immovable, secure, rooted, grounded, established, fixed, stable, fast, constant, staunch, durable, sure. *Wavering*

Solid, hard, compact, dense, compressed. *Soft*

Firmament, Sky, heavens, welkin. *Earth*

First, Earliest, foremost. *Last*

Chief, foremost, greatest, leading, principal, highest, capital. *Least*

Rudimentary, primitive, primary, elementary, primeval, original. *Advanced*

Fissure, Rent, rift, breach, break, gap, opening, cleft, cranny, crevice, fracture, hole, chasm, interstice, crack.

Fit, *v.a.*, Adapt, adjust, suit.

Provide, accommodate, furnish, supply, equip, qualify, prepare.

n., Paroxysm, spasm, whim, humour.

a., Proper, decent, fitting, befitting, suitable, becoming, right, appropriate, apt, seemly, fitted, meet. *Improper*

Fitful, Irregular, desultory, variable, inconstant, unreliable, spasmodic, fickle, capricious, fanciful, unstable, impulsive. *Regular*

Fitness, Propriety, decency, suitability, appropriateness, aptness, seemliness, pertinence. *Impropriety*

Fix, *v.a.*, Establish, fasten, plant, settle, place, root, secure, set, rivet. *Move*

Fasten, tie, join, connect, bind, attach, hitch. *Sever*

Settle, determine, limit, define, decide, appoint.

n., Dilemma, predicament, quandary, plight.

Fixed, Steady, steadfast, firm, constant, immovable, unchanging, established, fast, secure, rooted, grounded, settled. *Movable*

Flabbergast, Dumbfound, astound, surprise, astonish, amaze, stagger, nonplus.

Flabby, Tabid, flaccid, soft, limp, drooping, lax, yielding. *Firm*

Flaccid, Flabby, tabid.†

Flag, *v.n.*, Droop, languish, pine, tire, faint, weary, decline, sink, drop, succumb, fall, fail. *Persevere*

Flag, *n.*, Standard, banner, colours, ensign, pennant, streamer.

Flagellate, Scourge, flog, whip, chastise, castigate, thrash, beat.

Flagitious, Disgraceful, monstrous, atrocious, shameful, wicked, outrageous, wanton, profligate, notorious, heinous, enormous, vile, flagrant, crying, scandalous, nefarious, corrupt, shocking, infamous, villainous. *Honourable*

Flagrant, Flagitious, disgraceful, monstrous.†

Flame, *v.n.*, Burn, blaze, glow.

n., Fire, blaze.

Ardour, eagerness, enthusiasm, keenness, fervency, fervour, fire, warmth, heat, intensity. *Coolness*

Flank, *v.a.*, Touch, border, lie.

n., Side.

Flap, *v.*, *a. & n.*, Vibrate, flutter, wave, swing, shake, beat.

n., Flapping, swinging, vibration.

Flare, Dazzle, blaze, flicker, glare, flutter, waver.

Flaring, Glaring, flaming, flashy, conspicuous, showy, gaudy, bright. *Subdued*

Flash, Glare, gleam, spark, glint, sparkle, glisten.

Twinkling, moment, second, instant.

Flashy, Showy, gaudy, tawdry, ostentatious. *Quiet*

Flat, *n.*, Lowland, plain, strand, shoal, sandbank, shallow, bar.

Apartment, rooms, floor, story.

a., Plain, level, even, smooth, unbroken, low, prostrate, horizontal. *Undulating*

Vapid, uninteresting, tasteless, lifeless, dull, insipid, tame, stale, pointless, prosaic, spiritless, tedious, wearisome, boring. *Sensational*

Positive, downright, clear, direct, absolute, peremptory.

Flatter, Compliment, praise, blandish, coax, cajole, court, eulogize, adulate. *Insult*

Flatterer, Fawner, wheedler, sycophant, toady.

Flattery, Compliment, praise, fawning, adulation, sycophancy, blandishment, blarney, cajolery, obsequiousness, eulogy. *Frankness*

Flatulent, Windy, gassy, empty, vain.

Flaunt, Boast, display, vaunt, flourish, parade. *Hide*

Flaunting, Showy, boastful, flashy, ostentatious, gaudy, garish. *Quiet*

Flavour, Savour, smack, taste, relish, seasoning, admixture, essence, aroma, zest. *Insipidity*

Flaw, Defect, fault, blemish, spot, imperfection. ***Perfect***
Breach, break, fissure, hole, gap, cleft, rift, crack, crevice, cranny, rent, fracture.

Flawless, Perfect, whole, complete, unblemished, intact. ***Defective***

Flay, Skin, excoriate, strip, criticise.

Fleck, *v.a.*, Streak, speckle, spot, variegate.
n., Streak, spot, freckle.

Flee, Abscond, fly, run, escape, retreat. ***Stand***

Fleece, Shear, clip, strip, despoil, spoliate, plunder, rob. ***Invest***

Fleet, *a.*, Rapid, fast, quick, swift, nimble. ***Slow***
n., Armada, squadron, flotilla, navy.

Fleeting, Ephemeral, transitory, transient, evanescent, passing, brief, temporary. ***Eternal***

Fleetness, Rapidity, speed, quickness, celerity, swiftness, nimbleness, velocity. ***Slowness***

Flesh, Body, carnality, meat. ***Spirit***
Kindred, race, family, stock, man, mankind.

Fleshly, Carnal, mortal, earthly, lustful, lecherous, lascivious, sensual. ***Spiritual***
Fat, obese, corpulent, plump, rotund, stout, adipose. ***Thin***

Flexible, Ductile, pliable, pliant, elastic, lithe, supple, tractable, complaisant, compliant, yielding, lissom. ***Rigid***

Flexuous, Tortuous, winding, curving, bending, serpentine. sinuate, sinuous, turning. ***Straight***

Flexure, Winding, curve, curvature, bending, bend, turn, turning, incurvation, fold.

Flicker, Flare, flutter, waver, fluctuate, quiver, glimmer, scintillate, falter. ***Beam***

Flight, Soaring, mounting, flying, volitation.
Flying, fleeing, retreat, departure, escape, rout, stampede, exodus. ***Return***
Stairs, steps.
Shower, volley.
Group, unit.

Flighty, Frivolous, wild, giddy, fickle, volatile, capricious, mercurial. ***Steady***

Flimsy, Frail, thin, slight, weak, light, trivial, feeble, puerile. ***Strong***

Flinch, Wince, shrink, cower, blench, recoil, withdraw, swerve, retreat, quail. ***Endure***

Fling, *v.a.*, Hurl, toss, throw, shy, pitch, cast, dart.
n., Toss, throw, shy. ***Grasp***

Flippancy, Pertness, impertinence, sauce, glibness. ***Gravity***

Flippant, Pert, impertinent, saucy, glib, malapert, bold, irreverent. ***Grave***

Flirt, *v.n.*, Philander, coquet.
n., Philanderer, coquette.
v.a., Pitch, toss, throw, fling, hurl, shy, chuck, twirl, whirl, whisk, flutter.

Flit, Fly, dart, dash, flutter, flicker, hover, hasten.

Flitting, Fleeting, passing, ephemeral, transitory, transient, brief, short, evanescent, fugitive. ***Lengthy***

Float, *v.n.*, Waft, swim, sail, soar, ride, glide, hang, drift. ***Sink***
n., Buoy, raft.
v.a., Support, launch, start.

Flock, *v.n.*, Congregate, collect, herd, crowd, swarm, run, gather. ***Disperse***
n., Congregation, collection, company, herd.

Flog, Scourge, castigate, chastise, whip, beat, lash, flagellate, thrash.

Flood, *v.a.*, Inundate, overflow, deluge, overwhelm, submerge, swamp. ***Drain***
n., Inundation, overflow, deluge, freshet, outburst, spate, downpour, excess, tide, abundance. ***Drought***

Floor, *v.a.*, Nonplus, beat, conquer, overthrow, baffle.
n., Deck, stage, bottom, pavement, story. ***Ceiling***

Flora, Vegetation, plants.

Florid, Flowery, figurative, rhetorical, ornate, purple, meretricious. ***Plain***

Flounce, Fling, jerk, spring, wince, toss.

Flounder, Wallow, flounce, sink, tumble, struggle, toss.

Flourish, *v.n.*, Prosper, succeed, grow, thrive, speed, triumph. ***Fail***
v.a., Brandish, wave, swing, flaunt, shake.
n., Show, parade, ostentation, display, dash, fustian, bombast, fanfare, blast, tantivy.

Flout, Mock, gibe, jeer, sneer, deride, scoff, insult. ***Respect***

Flow, *v.n.*, Proceed, issue, come, emanate, arise, rise, spring.
Run, pour, stream, abound, glide, wave, undulate, float. ***Stop***
n., Copiousness, abundance, stream. ***Paucity***
Stream, flood, current, flux, gush, discharge, rush. ***Trickle***

Flower, *v.n.*, Bloom, blow, blossom, develop. ***Wither***
n., Bloom, blossom.
Prime, best, finest, essence, elite.

Flowery, Ornate, florid, figurative, embellished. ***Plain***

Flowing, Fluent, easy, copious, smooth, exuberant. ***Laboured***

Fluctuate, Vacillate, oscillate, waver, vary, undulate, change, veer. *Stay*

Fluctuation, Vacillation, oscillation,† inconstancy, unsteadiness. *Fixity*

Fluency, Exuberance, ease, copiousness, smoothness.

Fluent, Exuberant, easy,† ready, flowing, voluble, gliding, liquid, fluid. *Laboured*

Fluid, *n.*, Liquid, gas, vapour. *Solid*
a., Liquid, gaseous, running, fluent.

Flume, Race, channel, chute, ravine, gorge.

Flummery, Emptiness, trash, chaff, froth, trifling, nonsense, adulation, blandishment, flattery. *Reason*

Flunkey, Footman, lacquey, servant. Toady, snob.

Flurry, *v.a.*, Agitate, bustle, excite, confuse, perturb, disturb, fluster, disconcert, hurry, ruffle. *Compose*
n., Agitation, bustle, excitement.† *Composure*

Flush, *v.a.*, Colour, redden. *Blanch*
Encourage, animate, excite, elate, erect, elevate.
Drench, flood, cleanse, wash.
v.n., Colour, redden, blush, glow.
n., Colour, redness, blush, glow, excitement.
a., Exuberant, easy, free, lavish, abundant, generous, prodigal. *Mean*
Even, level, flat, plane.

Fluster, *v.a.*, Flurry, agitate, bustle, excite, confuse, perturb, disturb, disconcert, hurry, ruffle. *Compose*
n., Flurry, agitation, bustle.† *Composure*

Fluted, Corrugate, corrugated, grooved, channelled.

Flutter, *v.n.*, Flap, palpitate, tremble, vibrate, flicker, quiver, fluctuate, waver, oscillate. *Repose*
Flit, hover.
n., Tremor, confusion, flurry, fluster, stir, disturbance, agitation, perturbation, hurry. *Composure*

Flux, Progression, flow, flowing, transition, change, mutation, transmutation. *Stagnation*
Fusion, melting.

Fly, *v.n.*, Mount, soar, hover.
Flee, run, abscond, retreat, escape, decamp. *Remain*
Burst, explode, break.
Flap, flutter, float, sail, soar, play.
Pass, slip, glide.
n., Flap, lap, gallery, scenery.
Coach, cab, vehicle.

Foam, *v.n.*, Spume, froth.
n., Spume, froth, spray.

Fodder, Food, provisions, provender, rations, forage.

Foe, Opponent, enemy, adversary, foeman, antagonist. *Friend*

Fog, Mist, haze, vapour.

Foggy, Misty, hazy, obscure, muddled, dim, indistinct, blurred, muddy, confused. *Clear*

Foible, Defect, failing, infirmity, fault, weakness, imperfection, blemish. *Virtue*

Foil, *v.a.*, Baffle, frustrate, thwart, balk, defeat, circumvent. *Assist*
n., Set-off, setting, contrast, background.
Flake, film, lamina.

Foist, Impose, palm, thrust, pass, falsify, interpolate. *Expose*

Fold, *v.a.*, Double, lap.
Inwrap, wrap, envelop, enfold, furl. *Unfurl*
n., Folding, plait.
Pen, enclosure, cot.
Flock.

Folk, People, kindred, nation, persons, individuals.

Follow, *v.a.*, & *n.*, Succeed. *Lead*
v.a., Chase, pursue, hunt.
Practise, pursue, seek, cultivate. *Elude*
Copy, imitate.
Accompany, attend. *Quit*
Obey, observe, heed. *Disobey*
v.n., Succeed, ensue, proceed, result, arise, spring, come, issue.

Follower, Adherent, disciple, partisan, retainer, associate, supporter, attendant, dependant, companion. *Leader*
Copier, imitator.

Folly, Madness, silliness, foolishness, nonsense, stupidity, fatuity, absurdity, imbecility, indiscretion. *Wisdom*

Foment, Excite, encourage, stimulate, promote, propagate, fan, abet, brew. *Quench*

Fomentation, Excitement, encouragement, stimulation.†

Fond, Affectionate, loving, attached. *Averse*
Foolish, absurd, silly, weak, empty, doting, senseless. *Sensible*

Fondle, Coddle, pet, caress, dandle, spoil, indulge. *Tease*

Fondness, Affection, love, attachment, liking, partiality, predilection. *Aversion*
Folly, absurdity, silliness, weakness, emptiness. *Sense*

Font, Fount, source, spring.

Food, Victuals, nutriment, nourishment, aliment, provisions, commons, rations, fare, sustenance, viands, board, cheer, subsistence.
Fodder, feed, provender, forage.

Fool, *v.a.*, Deceive, dupe, gull, cheat, hoax, beguile, delude, hoodwink, trick, *cozen, chouse.*   *Guide*

v.n., Jest, play, trifle.

n., Idiot, blockhead, dunce, simpleton, dolt, ninny, clown, jester, buffoon, harlequin, antic.   *Sage*

Foolery, Folly, foolishness, nonsense, absurdity, buffoonery, silliness.   *Sense*

Foolhardy, Reckless, risky, rash, bold, venturous, venturesome, daring, desperate, precipitate, dangerous.   *Cautious*

Foolish, Silly, weak, absurd, ridiculous, idiotic, unreasonable, indiscreet, unwise, senseless, irrational, injudicious, puerile, idle, contemptible, mad.   *Sensible*

Foolishness, Silliness, weakness,† folly.   *Sense*

Foot, *v.a.*, Pay, discharge, meet, settle, stand.

n., Bottom, base.   *Head*

Paw, hoof.

Footfall, Step, tread, footstep.

Footing, Standing, status, condition, state, rank, grade.

Basis, establishment, settlement, foothold, purchase, groundwork, foundation.

Footman, Lacquey, flunkey, runner, servant.

Footprint, Footmark, trace, track.

Footstep, Footfall, step, tread.

Footmark, trace, track.

Fop, Dandy, coxcomb, swell, beau.

Foppery, Foppishness, dandyism, coxcombry, vanity.

Foppish, Dressy, finical, dandyish, coxcombical.   *Slovenly*

For, *conj.*, Since, because, as.

prep., During, concerning.

Owing to.

Towards, toward.   *Against*

Forage, *n.*, Fodder, provender, food.

v.n., Seek, search, ravage, pillage, plunder.

Foray, inroad, raid, sally, invasion.   *Flight*

Forbear, *v.n.*, Stay, hold, refrain, abstain, pause, cease, stop, desist, withhold.

Tolerate, endure.   *Retaliate*

v.a., Avoid, decline, shun, omit, withhold, abstain.

Forbearance, Forbearing, abstinence, moderation, tolerance, toleration, lenity, patience.   *Impatience*

Forbid, Prohibit, ban, inhibit, interdict, proscribe, veto, taboo.   *Allow*

Forbidding, Menacing, threatening, unpleasant, offensive, repulsive, repellent, odious, abhorrent, disagreeable.   *Attractive*

Force, *v.a.*, Compel, impel, make, coerce, urge, drive, constrain, press.   *Coax*

n., Compulsion, coercion, constraint, violence, enforcement.   *Coaxing*

Power, might, strength, vigour, cogency, efficacy, potency, puissance, energy, emphasis, stress.   *Weakness*

Army, legion, host, troop, squadron.

Forced, Unnatural, strained, artificial.   *Natural*

Enforced, compelled, compulsory, necessary, constrained.   *Voluntary*

Forcible, Powerful, mighty, strong, vigorous, cogent, impressive, weighty, irresistible, efficacious, potent, puissant.   *Weak*

Violent, impetuous, compulsory, coercive.

Ford, Current, stream, brook, flood.

Fore, Front, first, prior, preceding, antecedent, anterior, previous, foregoing, foremost, head, leading.   *Back*

Forebear, Ancestor, progenitor, forefather.   *Offspring*

Forebode, Portend, betoken, augur, promise, foreshow, foreshadow, predict, foretell, presage.

Foreboding, Token, augury, prediction, premonition, presentiment, omen.

Forecast, Anticipate, foresee, prophesy, predict, estimate, calculate, plan, contrive, scheme, devise, project.

Foreclose, Prevent, stop, hinder, bar, preclude, deprive.

Forefather, Father, ancestor, progenitor.   *Descendant*

Forefend, Prevent, avert, hinder.

Forego, Yield, resign, surrender, relinquish, abandon, drop, renounce.   *Claim*

Foregoing, Previous, preceding, antecedent, prior, fore, former, anterior.   *Following*

Foregone, Past, previous, former, bygone, predetermined.

Foreign, Alien, strange, exotic, extraneous, exterior, extrinsic, external, remote, distant.   *Native*

Foreknowledge, Prescience, foresight.

Foreland, Cape, headland, promontory.

Foreman, Superintendent, overseer, officer, ganger.

Foremost, Chief, first, leading, front.   *Least*

Forensic, Argumentative, debative, disputative, judicial.

Forerunner, Precursor, predecessor, harbinger, herald, preclude, omen, sign, premonition.   *Follower*

Foresee, Anticipate, expect, forecast, predict, prophesy, foretell.   *Recall*

Foreshadow, Foreshow, foretell, augur, forebode, presage, prophesy, predict.

Foreshow, Foreshadow, foretell.†

Foresight, Forethought, prudence, care, anticipation, precaution, providence.   *Blindness*

Forest, Woods, woodland, wood, grove, boscage.

Forestall, Anticipate, thwart, frustrate, prevent, hinder, preclude, engross, antedate, monopolize.

Foretell, Foreshadow, foreshow, predict, presage, augur, prophesy, prognosticate, portend, forecast, bode, forebode. *Detail*

Forethought, Foresight, prudence, care, anticipation, precaution, providence.

Forever, Ever, evermore, always, eternally, aye, everlastingly, perpetually.

Forewarn, Warn, caution, admonish, advise.

Forfeit, *v.a.*, Lose, renounce, forego, alienate.   *Earn*

n., Loss, penalty, fine, amercement, mulct, forfeiture.   *Reward*

Forge, *v.a.*, Make, fabricate, beat, frame, devise, invent.

Falsify, counterfeit, feign, coin.

v.n., Progress, advance.   *Recede*

n., Smithy, furnace, ironworks, foundry.

Forged, Counterfeit, spurious, imitation, sham, faked, false, coined.   *Genuine*

Forgery, Falsification, counterfeit, counterfeiting.†

Forget, Overlook, neglect, slight.   *Remember*

Forgetful, Negligent, oblivious, heedless, mindless, unmindful, careless, inattentive, neglectful.   *Mindful*

Forgive, Pardon, acquit, absolve, exonerate, remit, discharge, excuse.   *Punish*

Forgiveness, Pardon, acquittal, absolution.†   *Punishment*

Forgotten, Neglected, slighted, lost, unremembered.   *Remembered*

Fork, *v.n.*, Divide, branch, separate, part, divaricate.   *Join*

n., Division, branch, branching, divarication.

Forlorn, Desolate, destitute, miserable, deserted, forsaken, abandoned, lost, solitary, wretched, helpless, disconsolate, comfortless, friendless, luckless, hapless, pitiable.   *Cheered*

Form, *v.a.*, Fashion, create, make, mould, fabricate, conceive, model, build, devise, contrive, invent, frame, shape, produce, construct.   *Deform*

Compose, constitute, arrange, dispose, combine.   *Disorganize*

Form, *n.*, Mould, shape, figure, configuration, cut, fashion.

Bench, seat, class, rank.

Pattern, model, mould, fashion.

Method, mode, ritual, practice, formula, system, manner, order, ceremony, formality, rite, etiquette, arrangement.

Formal, Precise, exact, stiff, punctilious, ceremonious, pompous, dignified, correct, stately.   *Easy*

Regular, methodical, set, fixed, constitutional, essential.   *Irregular*

Formality, Ceremony, ritual, order, custom, etiquette, form.   *Simplicity*

Formation, Making, creation, construction, production.   *Deformity*

Composition, constitution.

Order, array, arrangement, classification, combination.   *Distortion*

Former, Antecedent, anterior, previous, prior, preceding, earlier, bygone, past, foregoing.   *Latter*

Formerly, Previously, anciently, heretofore, aforetime, hitherto.   *Latterly*

Formidable, Alarming, terrifying, dreadful, fearful, awful, horrible, frightful, tremendous, redoubtable, terrible, terrific, dangerous, difficult.   *Contemptible*

Formless, Chaotic, distorted, shapeless.

Formula, Prescription, recipe, rule, model.

Forsake, Abandon, leave, quit, desert, renounce, relinquish, yield, abjure, drop, forswear.   *Hold*

Forsooth, Surely, truly, certainly, indeed, really.

Forswear, Abjure, forsake, yield, relinquish, deny, resign, retract, renounce, abandon, quit, recant, drop.   *Reiterate*

Fort } Fortification, fastness, citadel,
Fortress } bulwark, defence, stronghold, castle.

Forth, Abroad, out, away.

Forward, onward, ahead.

Forthwith, Directly, instantly, forthright, immediately, instanter. *Presently*

Fortification, Fort, fortress, fastness, citadel, bulwark, defence, stronghold.

Fortify, Strengthen, confirm, garrison, reinforce, brace, stiffen, encourage.   *Dismantle*

Fortitude, Courage, endurance, strength, hardihood, bravery, patience, firmness, resolution, resignation, calmness.   *Timidity*

Fortuitous, Contingent, chance, accidental, casual, undesigned.   *Designed*

Fortunate, Lucky, happy, felicitous, propitious, advantageous, prosperous, successful, favourable, auspicious.   *Unlucky*

Fortune, Accident, chance, luck, destiny, future, fate, lot, doom.
Wealth, opulence, estate, substance, possessions, property, felicity, affluence, riches. *Poverty*
Result, issue, success, event.

Forward, *a.*, Advancing, progressive, onward, advanced, early, premature. *Late*
Bold, brazen, assuming, presuming, presumptuous, impertinent, immodest, confident. *Modest*
Earnest, ready, eager, willing, prompt.
Head, anterior, front, fore. *Back*
adv., Ahead, onward. *Backward*
v.a., Further, promote, foster, advance, encourage, aid, support, quicken, hasten, expedite, speed, accelerate, hurry, despatch. *Hinder*
Ship, transmit, post, send, despatch.

Fosse, Depression, canal, moat, ditch, graff.

Foster, Cherish, support, promote, advance, favour, forward, stimulate, sustain, feed, nourish, rear, nurse, mother, cultivate.

Foul, Dirty, filthy, unclean, impure, defiled, polluted, sullied, tainted, stained, nasty, loathsome, disgusting, offensive. *Pure*
Coarse, low, scurrilous, vulgar, abusive, ribald. *Clean*
Unfair, dishonourable, illegal, shameful, scurvy, base. *Fair*
Cloudy, rainy, murky, muddy, stormy, lowering, rough, wet, thick, turbid. *Fine*
Collide, tangle, entangle, collision.

Found, Establish, start, originate, institute, plant, root, ground, base, fix, set, place, erect, raise, contract, build, mould. *Subvert*

Foundation, Basis, footing, groundwork, bottom, base. *Superstructure*
Establishment, institution, endowment.

Founder, *v.n.*, Sink, fall, fail, miscarry, trip, collapse, stumble. *Float*
n., Originator, author, institutor, planter, establisher, organizer, builder, caster, moulder.

Fountain, Spring, well, fount, jet.
Source, cause, origin.

Foxy, Wily, artful, cunning, sly, crafty, scheming, subtle. *Artless*

Fracas, Quarrel, uproar, tumult, brawl, row, disturbance.

Fraction, Part, particle, piece, fragment, portion, section, bit. *Whole*

Fractious, Snappish, snarling, cross, petulant, peevish, irritable, captious, waspish, splenetic, testy, touchy, fretful. *Genial*

Fracture, *v.a.*, Break, rip, crack.
n., Break, breach, crack, breaking, rupture, cleft, fissure, rift, flaw, opening, rent.

Fragile, Brittle, feeble, weak, infirm, delicate, frail. *Strong*

Fragility, Brittleness, feebleness.† *Strength*

Fragment, Fraction, part, portion, piece, scrap, bit, remnant, morsel. *Whole*

Fragmentary, Broken, fractional, scattered, disconnected, disjointed. *Bodily*

Fragrance, Redolence, aroma, perfume, odour, scent, smell, balminess, balm. *Fetor*

Fragrant, Redolent, aromatic.† *Fetid*

Frail, Fragile, weak, delicate, slight, feeble, infirm. *Strong*

Frailty, Fragility, weakness, infirmity, defect, fault, feebleness, imperfection, failing, foible, faultiness. *Strength*

Frame, *v.a.*, Make, form, construct, build, fashion, fabricate, devise, invent, compose, forge, concoct. *Deform*
n., Structure, fabric, form, constitution, shape, skeleton, system, shell, carcass.
Condition, temper, state, mood, humour, feeling.

Franchise, Right, privilege, vote, exemption, immunity.

Frank, Honest, open, sincere, candid, straightforward, artless, ingenuous, unreserved. *Close*

Frantic, Raging, raving, furious, mad, wild, frenzied, distracted. *Calm*

Fraternity, Brotherhood, association, set, clan, league, company, society, circle.

Fraternize, Associate, league, coalesce, concur, unite, congregate, harmonize, co-operate, sympathize. *Abjure*

Fraud, Trick, deceit, deception, hoax, artifice, wile, imposture, stratagem. *Honesty*

Fraudulent, Tricky, trickish, deceitful, wily, dishonest, treacherous, crafty, false, knavish. *Honest*

Fraught, Full, filled, loaded, charged, laden, stored, pregnant, abounding, big, burdened. *Devoid*

Fray, *v.a.*, Chafe, wear, fret, rub, shred, ravel.
n., Conflict, battle, fight, combat, contest, war, affray. *Peace*

Freak, Fancy, vagary, whim, crotchet, whimsy, humour, quirk, caprice.
Monstrosity, abnormality, abortion.

Freakish, Fanciful, whimsical, odd, humoursome, capricious, erratic. *Consistent*
Monstrous, abnormal. *Normal*

Free, v.a., Liberate, release, discharge, emancipate, manumit, loose, disenthrall, enfranchise. *Bind*
Rid, relieve, disengage, extricate, unbind, clear, unchain, disencumber. *Encumber*
Privilege, exempt, immunize.
a., Independent, liberated, emancipated, released, delivered, loose. *Slave*
Unrestricted, unrestrained, unimpeded, unhampered, unobstructed, clear, open, exempt, immune, unbridled, unfettered, unshackled, privileged, allowed, permitted, open, devoid, empty. *Clogged*
Familiar, affable, informal, easy, lax, loose, unlicensed, frank, ingenuous, candid, sincere, affable, bold, careless. *Formal*
Liberal, bounteous, lavish, extravagant, generous, bountiful, prodigal, profuse, ready, prompt, willing, eager. *Close*
Gratuitous, willing, gratis, available, spontaneous. *Unwilling*
Freebooter, Brigand, robber, pirate, bandit, buccaneer, footpad.
Freedom, Liberty, independence, emancipation, immunity. *Slavery*
Looseness, familiarity, laxness, affability, informality. *Formality*
Range, scope, play, room, margin, swing.
Freeze, Chill, numb, congeal, solidify. *Melt*
Freight, v.a., Lade, charge, load, burden, burthen.
n., Cargo, load, lading, burden, shipment.
Frenzy, Fanaticism, fury, madness, raving, rage, lunacy, insanity, wildness, delirium, fire, aberration, derangement, excitement. *Calm*
Frequent, a., Common, everyday, usual, familiar, customary, habitual. *Unusual*
Recurrent, repeated, numerous, many, incessant, constant, persistent, continual. *Rare*
v.a., Haunt, resort, visit, attend.
Frequently, Often, repeatedly, regularly, commonly. *Seldom*
Fresh, New, novel, recent, renewed, revived. *Old*
Young, hearty, vigorous, lively, keen, unimpaired, undecayed, unwearied, unexhausted, strong, unfaded, unwithered, flourishing, blooming, rosy, ruddy, florid, fair, healthy, well, hardy. *Stale*
Stiff, brisk, strong, refreshing, bracing, keen, invigorating, pure, clean, sweet. *Close*
Unsalted, uncured, unsmoked, undried. *Salt*
Raw, unskilled, untrained, inexperienced. *Skilled*

Freshen, Refresh, invigorate, reinvigorate, revive.
Fret, v.n., Fume, worry, chafe, rage.
v.a., Fray, chafe, wear, rub, abrade, corrode.
Annoy, vex, worry, harass, tease, irritate, provoke, ruffle, weary. *Pacify*
Fretful, Irritable, petulant, peevish, snappy, snarling, waspish, splenetic, captious, touchy, testy, fractious, cross. *Genial*
Friable, Crumbling, powdery, pulverable. *Tough*
Friction, Attrition, abrasion, rubbing, grating, contact.
Dissension, disagreement, wrangling. *Agreement*
Friend, Companion, associate, ally, intimate, chum, confidant, familiar, adherent, supporter, comrade. *Foe*
Friendly, Amiable, amicable, benevolent, kindly, kind, brotherly, neighbourly, fraternal, cordial, affectionate, peaceable, favourable, propitious, advantageous. *Hostile*
Friendship, Amity, amicability, friendliness, kindliness, kindness, regard, benevolence, love, affection, attachment, fondness, intimacy. *Hostility*
Fright, Affright, fear, dismay, consternation, alarm, panic, terror, dread. *Composure*
Frighten, Affright, dismay, alarm, terrify, scare, intimidate, stampede. *Reassure*
Frightful, Fearful, dreadful, terrible, alarming, awful, dire, direful, dread, ghastly, fearsome, gruesome, hideous, terrific, horrible, horrid, monstrous. *Pleasing*
Frigid, Cold, cool, formal, stiff, exact, precise, prim, forbidding, rigid, chilling, icy. *Warm*
Frigidity, Coldness, coolness.† *Warmth*
Frill, Edge, edging, border, ruffle.
Affectation, mannerism.
Frisk, Wanton, sport, play, leap, jump, skip, frolic, dance, romp, gambol. *Mope*
Frisky, Wanton, sportive, playful, frolicsome, lively, coltish, gay. *Sedate*
Fritter, Waste, idle, dissipate, dribble. *Economize*
Frivolity, Frivolousness, folly, levity, lightness, flippancy, puerility, facetiousness. *Seriousness*
Frivolous, Foolish, light, flippant, idle, facetious, puerile, silly, petty, trivial. *Serious*
Frolic, v.n., Wanton, sport, frisk, gambol, dance, romp, play. *Mope*
n., Gambol, escape, lark, prank, fun, play.

Frolicsome, Sportive, frisky, wanton, gay, lively, playful, coltish.   *Sedate*

Front, *v.a.,* Face, confront, encounter, oppose.   *Flinch*
n., Face, anterior, obverse, frontage.   *Rear*
Head, breast, forepart, van.   *Back*
Impudence, assurance, effrontery.
a., Forward, anterior, foremost, frontal, headmost, fore.

Frontier, Boundary, marches, confine, limits, border.

Frosty, Cold, chill, chilly, frigid, freezing, wintry, icy, stinging.   *Warm*

Froth, *n.,* Foam, spume.
Emptiness, nonsense, triviality, balderdash.

Froward, Refractory, cross, captious, disobedient, wayward, perverse, contrary, untoward, ungovernable, peevish, contumacious, unyielding.   *Amenable*

Frown, Scowl, glower.   *Beam*

Frowsy, Rough, disorderly, tangled, unkempt, disordered.   *Neat*
Rank, musty, stale, rancid, offensive, fetid, noisome.

Fructify, Produce, bear, teem, multiply, abound.   *Wither*

Frugal, Sparing, economical, provident, careful, thrifty, temperate, saving, parsimonious.   *Extravagant*

Frugality, Economy, providence, care, thrift, carefulness, parsimony.   *Extravagance*

Fruit, Product, produce, crop, harvest, issue, result, outcome, profit, advantage, consequence, offspring, outgrowth.   *Cause*

Fruitful, Productive, fertile, fecund, prolific, abounding, abundant, plenteous, plentiful, rich, teeming.   *Barren*

Fruition, Fulfilment, perfection, conclusion, enjoyment, possession, gratification.   *Loss*

Fruitless, Barren, infecund, unproductive, unfertile, unfruitful, sterile, futile, vain, useless, bootless, abortive, ineffectual, unsuccessful, unavailing, idle.   *Productive*

Frustrate, Thwart, balk, confound, foil, defeat, baffle, upset, overthrow, discount, check, disappoint, circumvent.   *Encourage*

Frustration, Thwarting, balking, defeat.†

Fuddle, Muddle, inebriate, intoxicate, stupefy, confuse.

Fuddled, Muddled, inebriated, intoxicated, drunk, stupefied, confused, tipsy.   *Sober*

Fuel, Firing, combustibles, wood, coal, gas, oil.

Fugacious, Fugitive, transitory, transient, brief, passing, ephemeral, fleeting, short, evanescent.   *Permanent*

Fugitive, *a.,* Fugacious, transitory.†
Escaping, fleeing, flying.
n., Deserter, runaway, escaper, refugee, vagabond, wanderer.

Fulcrum, Support, prop.

Fulfil, Complete, accomplish, effect, do, effectuate, consummate, realize, execute, obey, answer, satisfy, perform, discharge, observe, meet, fill.   *Ignore*

Fulfilment, Completion, accomplishment.†

Fulgent, Shining, dazzling, resplendent, bright, radiant, brilliant.   *Dull*

Fuliginous, Smoky, sooty, dusky, dark.   *Clear*

Full, *a.,* Replete, filled, glutted, sated, satiated, saturated, abounding, complete, entire.   *Empty*
Large, broad, comprehensive, extensive, capacious, ample, loose, flowing, voluminous.   *Small*
Copious, plentiful, plenteous, abundant.
Strong, distinct, clear, deep, loud.
Exhaustive, detailed, circumstantial.
adv., Fully, entirely, completely, perfectly, quite, exactly, precisely, directly.   *Partly*

Fully, Full, entirely.†

Fulminate, Explode, burst, detonate.
Roar, thunder, vociferate, denounce, anathematize, curse.   *Laud*

Fulmination, Denunciation, malediction, threat, curse, ban.   *Eulogy*
Explosion, detonation.

Fulness, Completion, perfection, completeness, entireness.
Clearness, clarity, strength, distinctness, loudness, resonance.
Repletion, copiousness, abundance, profusion, plenty, plenitude, affluence.   *Emptiness*

Fulsome, Sickening, nauseous, disgusting, offensive, loathsome, repulsive, excessive, extravagant.   *Scanty*

Fulvous, Fulvid, yellow, tawny.

Fumble, Stumble, bungle, grope, feel.

Fume, *v.n.,* Reek, smoke.
Rage, fret, storm, rave, chafe, bluster.
n., Reek, smoke, vapour, steam, exhalation.
Rage, storm, passion, agitation, fret.   *Calm*

Fumigate, Smoke, disinfect.   *Infect*

Fun, Sport, entertainment, gaiety, merriment, jollity, joy, pleasantry.   *Sobriety*

Function, *v.n.*, Work, operate, answer, act.

n., Operation, exercise, execution, performance.

Duty, business, occupation, office, employment, province, part, ceremony.

Fund, Stock, store, supply, capital, investment, endowment, accumulation, reserve. *Outlay*

Fundamental, Primary, basic, essential, principal, indispensable, radical, important, constitutional, organic, cardinal, elementary, underlying. *Minor*

Funeral, Burial, interment, inhumation, sepulture, obsequies.

Funereal, Sad, mournful, woeful, sombre, dark, gloomy, lugubrious, dismal. *Joyous*

Fungous, Sudden, upstart, mushroom, transient, transitory, ephemeral.

Funicle, Fibre, filament, cord, ligature, stalk.

Funk, Fear, panic, terror, fright, timidity.

Funny, Droll, amusing, comic, comical, diverting, entertaining, laughable, ludicrous, humorous, farcical, ridiculous. *Sad*

Odd, strange, queer, curious.

Furbish, Polish, brighten, rub, burnish. *Tarnish*

Furcate-d, Branching, divaricating, furcular, forked, branched.

Furious, Wild, raging, fierce, frantic, mad, frenzied, infuriated, violent, tempestuous, impetuous, vehement, stormy, tumultuous. *Calm*

Furl, Wrap, fold, roll, stow. *Unroll*

Furnish, Equip, supply, provide, contribute, afford, bestow, give, produce, yield.

Furniture, Effects, fittings, decorations, appliances, apparatus, equipment.

Furore, Enthusiasm, craze, keenness, rage, excitement, fury. *Apathy*

Furrow, Groove, trench, channel, rut, cutting, hollow, fluting, seam, cut, wrinkle. *Ridge*

Further, *v.a.*, Advance, promote, help, forward, encourage, aid, strengthen. *Hinder*

a., Farther. *Nearer*

Additional, more.

adv., Furthermore, besides, moreover, also.

Farther.

Furtherance, Advancement, promotion, help, aid.

Furthermore, Further, besides, moreover, also.

Furthest, Farthest, remotest. *Nearest*

Furtive, Secret, sly, clandestine, hidden, dark, stealthy, stolen, surreptitious. *Open*

Fury, Frenzy, rage, fierceness, turbulence, wildness, madness, violence, tempestuousness, impetuosity, vehemence. *Calm*

Hag, vixen, shrew, termagant.

Fuse, Melt, smelt, liquefy, consolidate, commingle, intermix, amalgamate, blend, match, coolness, intermingle. *Diffuse*

Fusion, Melting, smelting, liquefaction.†

Fuss, *v.n.*, Bustle, fret, worry, fidget, fume.

n., Bustle, worry, fidget, flurry, stir, ado, excitement, tumult, perturbation, agitation. *Peace*

Fussy, Bustling, fidgety. *Serene*

Fust, Mould, mildew, mustiness.

Fustian, Bombast, rant.

Nonsense, balderdash, trash, inanity, stuff. *Wisdom*

Fusty, Mouldy, musty, mildewy, rank, ill-smelling. *Fresh*

Futile, Useless, fruitless, bootless, weak, ineffective, ineffectual, unavailing, vain, idle, profitless. *Cogent*

Futility, Uselessness, fruitlessness, vanity, worthlessness. *Cogency*

Future, Forthcoming, coming, subsequent, prospective, hereafter. *Past*

G

Gabble, *v.n.*, Prate, prattle, chatter, palaver, gossip, babble, jabber.

n., Prate, prattle,† jargon.

Gag, Muzzle, muffle, stifle, silence, choke, throttle, hush.

Gage, *v.a.*, Engage, pledge, pawn, impawn. **Redeem**

n., Pledge, pawn, security.

Gauntlet, glove, challenge, defiance.

Gaiety, Mirth, joy, hilarity, glee, joviality, jollity, joyousness, cheerfulness, buoyancy, merriment, liveliness, animation, vivacity. **Sorrow**

Gain, *v.a.*, Acquire, get, win, secure, procure, obtain, earn. **Lose**

Benefit, profit.

Reach, attain, arrive at.

n., Advantage, profit, earnings, winnings, emolument, benefit, lucre. **Loss**

Gainful, Advantageous, paying, profitable, remunerative, beneficial, lucrative, productive. **Unprofitable**

Gainsay, Deny, controvert, contradict, dispute, oppose. **Affirm**

Gait, Walk, carriage, bearing, step, stride, pace.

Galaxy, Bevy, assembly, assemblage, collection, throng, bunch, crowd, group.

Gale, Hurricane, tempest, squall, storm, wind. **Calm**

Gall, *v.a.*, Vex, annoy, irritate, harass, plague, tease, chafe, fret, incense, provoke, exasperate, torment, sting. **Appease**

n., Rancour, wormwood, bitterness, spite, malignity, malice, maliciousness. **Charity**

Gallant, *n.*, Paramour, lover, suitor, wooer, aspirant.

Beau, spark, blade.

a., Polite, courteous, chivalrous, noble, honourable, knightly, magnanimous. **Churlish**

Brave, valorous, valiant, courageous, fearless, doughty, dauntless, undaunted, heroic, intrepid, bold, daring. **Cowardly**

Gallantry, Politeness, courtesy.† **Churlishness**

Bravery, valour.† **Cowardice**

Gallery, Passage, corridor.

Balcony, circle, veranda, platform, loft.

Gallop, Hurry, speed, fly, dash, rush. **Trot**

Galvanize, Electrify, excite, stimulate.

Gambol, *v.n.*, Play, frolic, frisk, dance, jump, leap, caper, romp.

Gambol, *n.*, Frolic, frisk, dance, romp, caper, prank.

Game, *n.*, Pastime, recreation, frolic, sport, amusement, diversion, contest. **Work**

Quarry, prey.

a., Courageous, gallant, intrepid, dauntless, undaunted, fearless, bold, brave, heroic, valorous, valiant, unflinching, resolute. **Timid**

Disabled, lame, useless.

Gammon, *v.a.*, Cheat, hoax, deceive, beguile, hoodwink, circumvent, bamboozle, delude, outwit, overreach, inveigle, *cozen, chouse.* **Guide**

n., Hoax, deception.†

Gamut, Compass, range, scale.

Gang, Crew, collection, crowd, party, troop, company, coterie, horde, band, set.

Gangway, Path, aisle, passage.

Gaol, Prison, jail, dungeon.

Gap, Hole, breach, break, cleft, rift, cranny, interstice, chink, opening, crack, crevice.

Gape, Yawn, stare, gaze.

Garb, Dress, array, clothes, robes, attire, raiment, vesture, habit, habiliment, garments, costume, apparel. **Tatters**

Garbage, Rubbish, trash, stuff, refuse, offal.

Garble, Misquote, misrepresent, pervert, colour, corrupt, falsify, mutilate. **Quote**

Gargantuan, Enormous, huge, big, large, tremendous, immense, prodigious, elephantine, mammoth. **Minute**

Garish, Gaudy, tawdry, flaunting, flashy, showy, glaring, dazzling. **Quiet**

Garland, Wreath, coronal, coronet, crown, chaplet, festoon.

Garments, Clothes, dress, array, attire, robes, garb, raiment, habit, habiliment, vesture, apparel, costume.

Garner, Store, collect, gather, hoard, husband, reserve, deposit, save, accumulate. **Waste**

Garnish, Deck, bedeck, adorn, embellish, ornament, beautify, decorate, grace. **Strip**

Garniture, Adornments, embellishments, ornaments, decorations.

Garret, Loft, attic. **Basement**

Garrulity, Verbosity, loquacity, loquaciousness, chatter, babble, talkativeness. **Taciturnity**

Garrulous, Verbose, loquacious.† **Taciturn**

Gas, Vapour, fume, damp.

Gasconade, Vaunt, swagger, bluster, brag, boast.

Gash, Cut, incision, slash, score, slit, wound.

Gasp, Pant, blow, puff, choke. ***Breathe***

Gather, *v.n.*, Assemble, muster, congregate, collect, meet, parade. ***Disperse***
Collect, fester, thicken, suppurate.
v.a., Assemble, muster, congregate, collect, convoke.
Pick, pluck, glean, reap, bunch, stack.
Gain, acquire, get, win.
Deduce, infer, conclude.
Fold, plait, pucker.
Collect, amass, hoard, garner, accumulate. ***Dissipate***

Gathering, Meeting, assembly, assemblage, muster, congregation, concourse, collection, company. ***Dispersal***
Tumour, ulcer, sore, boil, fester, abscess, pustule.
Collecting, collection, accumulation, acquisition, procuring. ***Dissipation***

Gaudy, Garish, tawdry, flaunting, flashy, showy, glaring. ***Quiet***

Gauge, *v.a.*, Measure, estimate, appraise, probe, fathom. ***Guess***
n., Measure, standard, estimate.

Gaunt, Thin, lanky, lank, lean, hungry, attenuated, emaciated, slender, slim, meagre. ***Sleek***

Gawk, Boor, clown, lout, bumpkin, simpleton, booby.

Gawky, Boorish, awkward, ungainly, loutish, clumsy, boobyish. ***Graceful***

Gay, Merry, joyous, bright, jovial, jolly, lively, animated, gleeful, cheerful, happy, gladsome, hilarious, vivacious, blithe, blithesome, sprightly. ***Sad***
Bright, brilliant, smart, flashy, flaunting, gaudy, showy. ***Sombre***

Gaze, Look, stare, regard, contemplate, view. ***Glance***

Gazette, Journal, newspaper, paper.

Gear, Array, dress, equipment, accoutrements, accessories, appurtenances, appointments, harness, armour, furniture, trappings, tackle, paraphernalia, appliances.
Machinery, mechanism, apparatus, appliances, cogs.

Gelatinous, Gummy, viscous, lentous, glutinous.

Gelid, Cold, icy, frigid. ***Warm***

Gem, Jewel, stone, treasure.

Genealogy, Descent, pedigree, derivation, history.

General, *n.*, Chief, leader, head, generalissimo, captain.

General, Total, whole.
a., Catholic, universal. ***Local***
Vague, loose, inaccurate, inexact, indefinite, ill-defined, lax. ***Particular***
Usual, ordinary, common. ***Rare***

Generate, Engender, beget, create, make, form, produce, procreate, propagate, cause, breed. ***Stifle***

Generation, Creation, procreation, production, propagation, formation.
Family, breed, race, offspring, children, progeny.
Day, age, epoch, period, time, era. ***Eternity***

Generic, Common, collective, general. ***Particular***

Generosity, Liberality, charity, bounty, bountifulness, bounteousness, munificence, magnanimity, nobleness, disinterestedness. ***Meanness***

Generous, Liberal, charitable, bountiful,† honourable. ***Mean***

Genial, Hearty, cordial, pleasant, jovial, jolly, cheering, encouraging, enlivening, warm, inspiring. ***Cold***

Genius, Master, adept, proficient. ***Imbecile***
Gift, talent, power, aptitude, turn, bent, faculty, power, skill, cleverness, intellect, brains, creativeness. ***Inanity***
Spirit, djinn.

Genteel, Polite, civil, courteous, refined, polished, gentlemanly, elegant, well-bred, aristocratic, fashionable, stylish. ***Boorish***

Gentility, Politeness, civility, courteousness,† urbanity. ***Boorishness***

Gentle, Tender, mild, kind, considerate, compassionate, tame, docile, bland, soft, meek, merciful, clement, pacific, quiet, lenient, indulgent, humane. ***Rough***
Gradual, slight, easy, light, moderate, mild, soft, bland.
Genteel, courteous, polite, civil, refined, polished, gentlemanly, elegant, aristocratic, well-bred. ***Boorish***

Gentlemanly, Genteel, courteous, honourable, polite,† cultivated, urbane.

Genuine, True, veritable, pure, real, sound, authentic, unadulterated, unalloyed, uncorrupt, honest, right, proper, unaffected, frank, sincere. ***Spurious***

Genus, Order, class, species, kind, sort, universal, relative.

Geoponic, Agricultural, husbandry, tillage.

Germ, Seed, embryo, ovule, ovum, nucleus. ***Fruit***
Origin, cause, source, beginning.

Germane, Appropriate, relevant, fitting, pertinent, suitable, apposite. ***Irrelevant***

Germane, Related, cognate, allied, akin, kindred, homogeneous. *Alien*

Germinate, Vegetate, sprout, shoot, bud, push, grow, generate. *Decay*

Gesticulate, Gesture, signal, motion, beckon.

Gesticulation, Gesture, gesturing, action, signalling, beckoning, motioning.

Gesture, *v.n.*, Gesticulate.

n., Gesticulation, gesturing, action, sign, signal, motion.

Get, *v.a. & n.*, Gain, obtain, win, secure, procure, earn, acquire, receive, realize, achieve. *Forfeit*

v.a., Bring, fetch, procure, carry.

Persuade, influence, dispose, induce.

Learn, memorize, master, finish.

Engender, generate, produce, create, procreate, propagate, breed.

v.n., Become, go.

Arrive, reach, win.

Gewgaw, Trinket, trifle, gaud, bauble, toy.

Ghastly, Frightful, shocking, terrible, horrible, fearful, death-like, pale, dismal, cadaverous, wan, grim, hideous, grizzly, pallid, spectral. *Comely*

Ghost, Spirit, sprite, spectre, apparition, soul, phantom, spook.

Ghostly, Weird, spectral, shadowy.

Spiritual.

Giant, *a.*, Gigantic, enormous, elephantine, huge, tremendous, large, immense, big. *Dwarfish*

n., Monster, colossus. *Dwarf*

Gibber, Gabble, prate, prattle, babble, jabber.

Gibberish, Drivel, nonsense, prattle, prate, gabble, jargon, babble. *Sense*

Gibbosity, Protuberance, swelling, convexity. *Concavity*

Gibbous, Protuberant, swelling, convex, rounded, hunched, gibbose. *Concave*

Gibe, Jeer, jest, sneer, scoff, ridicule, taunt, deride. *Compliment*

Giddy, Whirling, dizzy, vertiginous.

Inconstant, unsteady, thoughtless, careless, flighty, irresolute, unstable, fickle, changeable, mutable, vacillating, heedless, headlong, wild, reckless. *Thoughtful*

Gift, Present, benefaction, donation, grant, boon, bounty, endowment, bequest, gratuity, allowance, legacy, subscription, contribution. *Forfeit*

Faculty, talent, aptitude, endowment, capacity, ability, power, turn, bent.

Gifted, Talented, apt, able, skilful, powerful, inventive, intelligent, sagacious. *Stupid*

Gigantic, Huge, immense, tremendous, large, enormous, giant, vast, colossal, prodigious, elephantine. *Minute*

Giggle, Snigger, laugh, cackle, grin, titter.

Gild, Adorn, illuminate, embellish, brighten.

Gin, Snare, trap, spring, noose, net, toil.

Gingerly, Cautiously, daintily, warily, carefully, circumspectly, tenderly. *Boldly*

Gird, Girdle, engird, encircle, surround, enclose, encompass, begird, environ, hem. *Open*

Invest, equip, furnish, clothe. *Strip*

Girdle, Gird, engird, encircle.†

Girl, Maiden, maid, lass, lassie, wench, virgin, damsel. *Boy*

Girth, Circumference, breadth, girdle, cinch.

Gist, Substance, pith, essence, marrow, core, kernel.

Give, *v.n.*, Yield, retreat, retire, recede.

v.a., Grant, bestow, accord, afford, spare, supply, furnish, present, confer, impart, donate, proffer, contribute. *Withhold*

Pronounce, utter, emit, render.

Produce, yield, occasion, cause.

Supply, devote, surrender, addict.

Giver, Donor, donator, disposer, bestower, granter. *Recipient*

Glabrous, Bald, polished, hairless, shiny, smooth, glassy. *Shaggy*

Glacial, Frozen, icy.

Glaciate, Freeze, congeal.

Glad, Delighted, pleased, joyous, happy, gratified, elated, cheerful, joyful, merry. *Sorry*

Pleasing, joyful, cheering, gratifying, pleasant, bright, animating, delightful. *Dismal*

Gladden, Delight, please, gratify, elate, cheer, animate, rejoice, exhilarate. *Grieve*

Gladness, Delight, pleasure, gratification, cheer, cheerfulness, animation, joy, joyousness, joyfulness. *Sorrow*

Gladsome, Pleasing, joyful, cheering, pleasant, bright, animating, delightful. *Dismal*

Glamour, Glow, witchery, bewitchment, enchantment, hallucination, fascination.

Glance, Gaze, look, glimpse.

Shine, flash, flit, dart, ricochet.

Glare, *v.n.*, Sparkle, glisten, gleam, shine, beam, glitter, dazzle, flare.

Glower, frown.

n., Flare, glitter, gleam, dazzle, sparkling. *Dulness*

Glaring, Sparkling, glistening, gleaming, dazzling, glittering.

Glaring, Open, manifest, notorious, conspicuous, barefaced. *Secret*

Glaze, *v.a.*, Burnish, furbish, polish, gloss, calender.

n., Varnish, polish, finish, enamel, coat, lustre.

Gleam, *v.n.*, Shine, beam, radiate, glisten, glitter, glimmer, sparkle, flash.

n., Glimmering, glimmer, beam, ray. Brightness, radiance, lustre, splendour. *Dulness*

Glean, Gather, collect, cull, pick, get, harvest. *Scatter*

Glebe, Sod, clod, turf, ground, earth, soil, field, land.

Glee, Gaiety, liveliness, hilarity, mirth, merriment, jocundity, jollity, joviality, exhilaration. *Sorrow*

Gleeful, Gay, lively, hilarious.† *Sorrowful*

Glen, Valley, vale, dell, dingle, dale.

Glib, Smooth, easy, fluent, ready, voluble, facile, talkative, flippant. *Hesitating*

Glide, Slide, slip, sail, float, skate, skim, roll, run, flow.

Glimmer, *v.n.*, Shine, glare, flare, glitter, glisten, gleam.

n., Beam, gleam, ray, glimmering.

Glimpse, Glance, view, look. *Scrutiny*

Glisten, Glitter, glare, gleam, glimmer, shine, flare, flicker, sparkle.

Glitter, *v.n.*, Glisten, glister, glare, gleam.†

n., Lustre, brightness, beam, brilliance, shine, splendour, glister, sparkle. *Dulness*

Gloaming, Dusk, twilight, nightfall, gloom.

Gloat, Revel, crow, cackle, feast, rejoice, exult, triumph.

Globate, Round, spherical, globose, globular.

Globe, Orb, sphere, ball, earth.

Globule, Drop, bead, spherule, particle.

Gloom, Dark, darkness, gloaming, dusk, shadow, obscurity, dimness. *Light* Melancholy, depression, dejection, despondency, sadness. *Gaiety*

Gloomy, Dark, dusky, shadowy, obscure, dim. *Light* Depressing, sad, dismal, cheerless, dark, saddening, lowering, dispiriting, disheartening, melancholy. *Cheering* Depressed, sad, dismal, cheerless, glum, dispirited, disheartened, melancholy, despondent, dejected, crestfallen, chapfallen, pessimistic, downcast. *Cheerful*

Glorify, Magnify, ennoble, exalt, extol, honour, aggrandize, adorn, elevate. *Defame*

Glorious, Noble, exalted, honourable, illustrious, famous, famed, renowned, celebrated, eminent, distinguished, lofty, high, splendid. *Base* Brilliant, bright, splendid, resplendent, radiant. *Dull*

Glory, *n.*, Gloriousness, nobleness, exaltation, honour,† grandeur. *Baseness* Brilliance, brightness, splendour, effulgence, radiance, pride. *Dulness* Parade, dignity, magnificence, pomp, state, show.

v.n., Boast, triumph, exult.

Gloss, Polish, varnish, brighten. Colour, varnish, palliate, disguise, extenuate.

Glossary, Vocabulary, dictionary, index.

Glossy, Smooth, sheeny, shining, bright. *Rough*

Glow, *v.n.*, Shine, gleam, glisten.

n., Brightness, gleam, incandescence, luminosity, blaze, brilliance. Warmth, eagerness, ardour, enthusiasm, fervour, vehemence. *Apathy*

Glower, Glare, frown, stare, scowl.

Glum, Gloomy, despondent, dispirited, dejected, disheartened, sad, crestfallen, chapfallen, melancholy, downcast. *Elated* Glowering, morose, splenetic, frowning, sullen, moody, crusty, crabbed. *Pleased*

Glut, *v.a.*, Surfeit, satiate, cloy, sate, fill, cram, stuff. *Disgorge*

n., Superfluity, superabundance, surplus, repletion. *Scarcity*

Glutinous, Viscid, viscous, clammy, gluey, sticky, adhesive, gummy.

Glutton, Gourmand, gormandizer, gobbler.

Gluttony, Gormandizement, voracity, greed. *Temperance*

Gnarl, *v.n.*, Snarl, growl, grumble, murmur.

n., Knot, protruberance, contortion, snag.

Gnaw, Bite, corrode, erode, consume, champ, nibble, eat.

Go, *v.n.*, Travel, proceed, walk, pass, depart, move, wend, fare, hie, disappear, journey. *Come* Extend, stretch, reach, range, run, lead, elapse. Concur, tend, avail, contribute. Eventuate, fare.

interj., Hence, avaunt, away, begone, aroynt.

Goad, Sting, prick, point, plague, worry, harass, annoy, irritate, spur, provoke, rouse, incite, stimulate, instigate, impel, urge. *Deter*

Goal, Object, objective, end, aim, ambition, design, destination, mark, limit, home, bound. *Course*

Gobble, Swallow, bolt, gorge, gulp. *Disgorge*

Gobbler, Glutton, gourmand, gormandizer.

Goblin, Spirit, sprite, apparition, spectre, hobgoblin, gnome, elf, ghost.

God, Deity, Godhead, Divinity, Creator, Father, Lord, Almighty, Jehovah. *Devil* Idol, image.

Godless, Ungodly, wicked, profane, irreligious, atheistic, depraved, immoral, sinful. *Righteous*

Godly, Righteous, good, pious, religious, holy, saintly, devout. *Wicked*

Goggle, Stare, squint, look.

Golden, Splendid, resplendent, excellent, precious, brilliant, bright, aureate. *Worthless*
Favourable, opportune, auspicious, propitious.
Happy, glorious, delightful, blest.

Good, *n.,* Goodness, righteousness, virtue, morality, excellence. *Evil*
Benefit, profit, gain, advantage, interest, utility, welfare, prosperity, weal. *Harm*
a., Righteous, moral, excellent, virtuous, pious, upright, religious, true, serious. *Bad*
Benevolent, kind, merciful, gracious, kindly, friendly, obliging, humane, genial, cheerful, cheering, sociable, companionable, agreeable, pleasant. *Niggardly*
Beneficial, profitable, advantageous, useful, serviceable. *Harmful*
Skilful, clever, adroit, dexterous, practised, competent, able, expert, ready. *Useless*
Proper, fit, convenient, appropriate, opportune, right. *Wrong*

Goodly, Comely, seemly, beautiful, pleasing, well-favoured, pleasant, agreeable, happy, fair. *Unpleasant*
Large, considerable. *Inconsiderable*

Goodness, Good, righteousness, morality, excellence, virtue, honesty, probity, rectitude, uprightness. *Evil*
Benevolence, kindness, mercy, grace, kindliness, friendliness, humaneness, humanity.

Goods, Chattels, effects, property, belongings, movables, furniture, commodities, wares, stock, merchandise.

Goodwill, Custom, favour, patronage, kindness, benevolence, zeal, ardour, earnestness. *Enmity*

Gore, *v.a.,* Pierce, stab.
n., Blood.
Gusset.

Gorge, *v.a.,* Swallow, gulp, eat, devour bolt, stuff, cram, fill, cloy, satiate, surfeit. *Starve*
n., Pass, defile, ravine, gulch.

Gorgeous, Magnificent, superb, rich, resplendent, brilliant, splendid, costly, showy, dazzling, glittering, fine, shining. *Dingy*

Gorgon, Hobgoblin, goblin, spectre, spirit, sprite, ogre.

Gormandize, Gorge, eat, stuff, gobble.

Gormandizer, Gourmand, glutton, gobbler.

Gory, Bloody, ensanguined.

Gospel, News, tidings, message.
Doctrine, teaching, creed.

Gossip, *v.n.,* Prate, prattle, chat, gabble, tattle, babble.
n., Prate, prattle, chatter, tattle, talk, babble.
Prater, prattler, chatterer, tattler, babbler.

Gourmand, Gormandizer, glutton, gobbler.

Govern, Rule, sway, conduct, control, guide, manage, direct, regulate, supervise, command, steer, restrain, curb, bridle. *Misrule*

Governable, Obedient, tractable, disciplined, manageable, controllable. *Wild*

Government, Rule, sway, conduct, control, autonomy, discipline, dominion, guidance, management, direction, regulation, supervision, command. *Misrule*
Administration, executive, cabinet.

Governor, Ruler, controller, manager, director, supervisor, commander, overseer, superintendent.
Executive, tutor, instructor, guardian, master.
Regulator.

Grab, Clutch, seize, snatch, grip. *Drop*

Grace, *v.a.,* Honour, dignity, adorn, deck, bedeck, embellish, decorate, ornament. *Defile*
n., Polish, refinement, elegance, gracefulness, comeliness, beauty, ease, symmetry. *Awkwardness*
Favour, love, mercy, kindness, benignity, pardon.
Devotion, piety, devoutness, love, religion, holiness. *Impiety*
Prayer, petition, thanks, blessing.

Graceful, Elegant, comely, beautiful, becoming, seemly, easy, natural, flowing, rounded. *Awkward*
Happy, tactful, felicitous.

Graceless, Shameless, abandoned, profligate, hardened, lost, wicked, depraved, obdurate, degenerate, vicious, reprobate, worthless, corrupt, dissolute. *Virtuous*

Gracious, Friendly, affable, courteous, civil, polite, elegant, kind, kindly, benign, benevolent, merciful, loving, easy, gentle, mild, condescending, benignant. *Churlish*

Grade, Degree, rank, step, stage, brand, intensity.

Gradient, incline, slope, ascent, descent.

Gradient, Grade, incline, slope, ascent, descent.

Gradual, Progressive, continuous, regular, slow. *Sudden*

Graduate, Regulate, adjust, adapt, proportion, divide.

Grain, Corn, cereals.
Seed, kernel.
Part, particle, atom, piece, bit, portion.

Graft, Sprout, slip, shoot, scion.
Fibre, texture, humour, temper.

Grand, Splendid, resplendent, fine, gorgeous, magnificent, superb, glorious, noble, stately, exalted, illustrious, august. majestic, princely, lordly, lofty, sublime, imposing. *Inferior*
Chief, principal, leading, main, superior. *Minor*

Grandeur, Splendour, magnificence, glory, nobility, stateliness, majesty, lordliness, loftiness, vastness, elevation, greatness, pomp. *Paltriness*

Grandiloquence, Fustian, bombast, verbosity, turgidity, pomposity. *Simplicity*

Grant, *v.a.*, Give,† vouchsafe, confer, bestow, yield, concede, cede, allow, admit, allot. *Withhold*
n., Gift,† concession, present, bounty, benefaction, boon, donation, largess.

Graphic, Striking, vivid, picturesque, pictorial, illustrative, descriptive, telling. *Dull*

Grapple, Grip, clasp, gripe, grasp, seize, clutch, hold. *Loose*

Grasp, *v.a.*, Grip, clasp, gripe.†
n., Grip, clasp, hold, possession, reach, power, scope, compass.

Grasping, Greedy, avaricious, rapacious, covetous, miserly. *Generous*

Grate, *v.a.*, Rub, abrade, scrape, rasp, comminute, scratch.
v.n., Rasp, jar, grind, creak, irritate, offend.
n., Bars, screen, grating, basket.

Grateful, Thankful, pleased, obliged, beholden, indebted. *Thankless*
Welcome, pleasant, agreeable, acceptable, delicious, delightful, gratifying, charming, satisfying, satisfactory. *Unpleasant*

Grateful, Soothing, alleviating, comforting, invigorating, refreshing.

Gratification, Satisfaction, pleasure, enjoyment, delight, indulgence. *Pain*

Gratify, Satisfy, please, delight, charm, humour, grant, fulfil, gladden. *Displease*

Gratifying, Pleasing, pleasant, welcome, agreeable, acceptable, delicious, delightful, charming, grateful. *Unpleasant*

Grating, Disagreeable, displeasing, irritating, harsh, offensive, jarring. *Pleasant*

Gratitude, Thankfulness, pleasure, obligation. *Thanklessness*

Gratuitous, Free, voluntary, spontaneous, uncompensated. *Obligatory*
Groundless, unwarranted, baseless, unfounded, wanton.

Gratuity, Bonus, bounty, gift, present, benefaction, donation, dole, grant, largess, charity.

Grave, *v.a.*, Engrave, carve, imprint.
a., Serious, staid, sober, solemn, sad, thoughtful, quiet, sedate. *Frivolous*
Serious, heavy, important, momentous, cogent, weighty. *Trivial*
n., Tomb, sepulchre, pit, mausoleum.

Graveyard, Churchyard, cemetery, necropolis.

Gravitate, Incline, descend, tend.

Gravity, Seriousness, sobriety, sadness, solemnity, thoughtfulness, quietness, sedateness. *Frivolity*
Seriousness, heaviness, importance, momentousness, moment, weight. *Triviality*
Weight, heaviness.

Graze, Scrape, touch, shave, skim, rub, scratch, glance, brush.
Feed, browse.

Greasy, Oily, fatty, unctuous, sebaceous.
Smooth, slippery.

Great, Huge, vast, wide, tremendous, large, enormous, big, immense, colossal, bulky, gigantic. *Small*
Excessive, much, decided, high, pronounced, numerous, countless. *Little*
Eminent, grand, exalted, lofty, famous, noble, high, illustrious, celebrated, distinguished, noted, famed, renowned. *Obscure*
Chivalrous, noble, exalted, generous, august, grand, elevated, majestic, dignified, sublime, magnanimous. *Ignoble*
Chief, main, principal, leading, grand, important, superior, weighty. *Minor*

Greatness, Vastness, immensity, largeness, bulk, size, enormity, magnitude. *Smallness*

Greatness, Eminence, grandeur, exaltation, fame.†   *Obscurity*
Chivalry, nobility, generosity.†

Greediness, Greed, gluttony, voracity, eagerness, covetousness, desire, longing, avidity, selfishness, rapacity, avarice.
    Unselfishness

Greedy, Gluttonous, voracious, eager,† grasping.   *Unselfish*

Green, *a.*, Fresh, undecayed, flourishing, recent, new, verdant.   *Decayed*
a., Raw, inexperienced, inexpert, unskilled, unskilful, immature, ignorant, young, crude, unseasoned, novice.
    Expert
n., Lawn, verdure, common, greensward.

Greet, Accost, hail, salute, address, welcome.

Greeting, Salutation, salute, welcome, hail.   *Farewell*

Grief, Regret, tribulation, trouble, woe, affliction, sorrow, distress, heartbreak, heartache, anguish, sadness, agony, misery.   *Joy*
Disaster, failure, mishap.

Grievance, Injury, hardship, wrong, complaint, oppression, burden, trial, grief, distress.   *Boon*

Grieve, *v.a.*, Afflict, hurt, pain, distress, agonize, sadden.   *Soothe*
v.n., Lament, sorrow, mourn, complain.
    Rejoice

Grievous, Sad, hard, intolerable, lamentable, deplorable, painful, afflicting, distressing, hurtful, dreadful, gross, iniquitous, flagrant, intense, outrageous, heinous, atrocious, heavy.   *Light*

Grim, Ferocious, fierce, dire, terrific, dreadful, hideous, horrible, horrid, grisly, terrible, awful, appalling, cruel, savage.
    Benign

Grime, *v.a.*, Begrime, smear, smudge, taint, sully, soil, dirty, defile, befoul.
    Cleanse
n., Dirt, foulness, filth, smut.

Grimy, Dirty, foul, filthy, unclean, begrimed, smutty, sooty.   *Clean*

Grind, Pulverize, triturate, bruise, crush, crunch, grate, sharpen, whet.
Afflict, overwork, plague, torment, oppress, persecute, trouble.

Grip, *v.a.*, Seize, grasp, clutch, hold.
    Lose
n., Gripe, clash, clutch, hold.

Gripe, *v.a.*, Seize, grasp, clutch, hold, squeeze, pinch, press.   *Lose*
n., Grip, clasp, clutch, hold.
Pinching, affliction, distress, griping.
    Ease

Grisly, Grim, ferocious, fierce, dire,

terrific, dreadful, awful, hideous, horrible, horrid, appalling, cruel, savage.   *Benign*

Grit, Gravel, sand, dirt, bran.
Courage, decision, nerve, firmness.

Groan, Moan, complain, grumble.
Creak.

Groom, Servant, valet, waiter.

Groove, Channel, way, cutting, canal, furrow, rut, cut, score.   *Ridge*

Grope, Feel, search, pick, stumble.

Gross, Great, large, big, massive, bulky, dense, thick.   *Small*
Plain, apparent, manifest, palpable, glaring, flagrant, outrageous.
Impure, indelicate, coarse, indecent, rough, low, common, vulgar, sensual, dull, stupid.   *Refined*
Whole, entire, total, aggregate, bulk, amount.   *Net*

Grossness, Greatness, largeness, bigness.†
Impurity, indelicacy, coarseness.†

Grotesque, Wild, fantastic, fanciful, odd, bizarre, strange, whimsical, absurd, ludicrous, ridiculous.   *Graceful*

Ground, Earth, clod, soil, sod, turf, field.
    Firmament
Land, territory, region, domain, country, estate.
Basis, base, reason, motive, cause, support, foundation, inducement, excuse, opinion, consideration.

Groundless, Gratuitous, false, baseless, unfounded, fanciful, unauthorized.
    Substantial

Grounds, Estate, land, fields, yard, premises, gardens.
Dregs, sediment, lees, deposits, grouts, precipitate.
Reasons, motives, supports, arguments, considerations.

Groundwork, Source, base, basis, origin, support, foundation, background, bottom.   *Summit*

Group, *v.a.*, Array, arrange, order, set, place, dispose.   *Disarrange*
n., Clump, cluster, bunch, collection, assemblage.

Grove, Wood, thicket, copse, spinney.

Grovel, Crawl, cringe, sneak, fawn. *Soar*

Grovelling, Crawling, cringing, sneaking, fawning, base, low, servile, mean, slavish, vile, abject.   *Lofty*

Grow, *v.n.*, Increase, expand, enlarge, advance, extend, swell, develop, improve.   *Decline*
Sprout, shoot, develop, germinate, vegetate.
Wax, become.
v.a., Cultivate, produce, raise.

Growl, Snarl, grumble, murmur, complain, repine. *Purr*

Growth, Increase, **advance,** expansion, enlargement, extension, development, progress, improvement, growing. *Decline*

Vegetation, produce, product, cultivation.

Sprouting, shooting, germinating.†

Maturity, adulthood.

Grudge, *v.a.,* Begrudge, envy, covet.

n., Malice, envy, hatred, enmity, dislike, malevolence, malignity, spite. *Charity*

Gruesome, Grim, grisly, terrible, dreadful, awful, horrible, frightful, repulsive. *Attractive*

Gruff, Surly, churlish, rough, blunt, ungracious, harsh, rude, impolite, uncivil, uncourteous, grumpy. *Affable*

Grumble, Murmur, complain, growl, snarl, repine, roar, rumble.

Grumbling, Murmuring, complaint, repining.†

Grumpy, Surly, irritable, sour, sullen, churlish, short, snappish, snarling. *Affable*

Guarantee, *v.a.,* Insure, assure, warrant.

n., Surety, assurance, warrant, pledge, security, earnest.

Guard, *v.a.,* Defend, protect, watch, shelter, shield, safeguard. *Neglect*

n., Defence, protection, security, shield, ward, safeguard, bulwark, rampart. custody.

Sentry, sentinel, watch, watchman, escort, guardian, warden, keeper, patrol, conductor, conduct, convoy, defender.

Watchfulness, preparation, caution, heed, circumspection, care, attention.

Guarded, Careful, cautious, circumspect, watchful. *Rash*

Guardian, Keeper, protector, defender, preserver, warden, custodian.

Guerdon, Reward, prize, remuneration, recompense. *Penalty*

Guess, *v.a.* & *n.,* Conjecture, surmise, judge, think, fancy, imagine, believe, suspect, suppose. *Prove*

Solve, fathom, penetrate.

n., Conjecture, surmise, supposition.

Guidance, Lead, direction, government, control. *Misdirection*

Guide, *v.a.,* Lead, direct, control, govern, pilot, manage, conduct, regulate, steer, superintend. *Mislead*

Guide, *n.,* Leader, director, pilot, controller.†

Key, directory, thread, index, clue, landmark, signpost, itinerary.

Guild, Association, fellowship, fraternity, set, band, company, society, union, corporation.

Guile, Deceit, artfulness, cunning, wiles, duplicity, artifice, craft, deception, fraud, trickery. *Honesty*

Guileful, Deceitful, artful, cunning.† *Honest*

Guileless, Honest, artless, ingenuous, open, sincere. *Crafty*

Guilt, Sin, wickedness, iniquity, wrong, criminality, culpability, guiltiness. *Innocence*

Guiltless, Sinless, innocent, pure, blameless, unspotted, spotless, unsullied. *Wicked*

Guilty, Sinful, wicked, wrong, criminal, culpable. *Innocent*

Guise, Garb, semblance, aspect, appearance, shape, figure, costume, dress, form, fashion, manner, mode.

Behaviour, air, mien, demeanour.

Habit, custom, practice, manner, pretence, disguise.

Gulf, Chasm, abyss, opening.

Gull, Cheat, deceive, dupe, trick, beguile, circumvent, *cozen, chouse.* *Guide*

Gullible, Confiding, trustful, unsuspecting, credulous. *Mistrustful*

Gumption, Common sense, ability, skill, capacity, power, cleverness, shrewdness, sagacity.

Gurgle, Purl, ripple, murmur.

Gush, Flow, stream, spout, outpour, burst. *Drip*

Gushing, Flowing, rushing.

Sentimental, demonstrative. *Restrained*

Gust, Burst, outburst, blast, fit, squall. *Calm*

Gusto, Relish, zest, zeal, eagerness, avidity, enjoyment, pleasure, liking. *Apathy*

Gutter, Channel, conduit, groove.

Guttural, Hoarse, gruff, thick, deep, throaty.

Guy, Scarecrow, fright, effigy.

Guzzle, *v.a.,* Drink, swill, quaff.

v.n., Drink, gorge, tipple, carouse.

Gyration, Revolution, spinning, turning, rotation, whirling.

Gyves, Chains, fetters, bonds, shackles.

H

Habiliment, Clothes, dress, garments, habit, array, apparel, vesture, vestments, robes, uniform, costume, raiment, garb, attire. *Undress*

Habit, *n.*, Habiliment, clothes, dress, garments.†

Practice, manner, way, usage, wont, custom.

v.a., Clothe, dress, array, robe, attire, garb, accoutre. *Strip*

Habitation, Dwelling, abode, domicile, home, dwelling, quarters, lodging.

Habitual, Customary, wonted, usual, ordinary, familiar, regular, common, accustomed, confirmed, inveterate. *Rare*

Habituate, Use, train, inure, harden, accustom, familiarize.

Hack, *v.a.*, Cut, chop, hackle, hew.

a., Hired, hackney, mercenary, hireling.

Hackneyed, Threadbare, trite, worn, stale, commonplace, common. *Original*

Haft, Handle, stock, hilt.

Hag, Beldam, vixen, virago, fury.

Haggard, Wild, gaunt, wasted, worn, weary, wrinkled, attenuated, spare, meagre, lean. *Chubby*

Haggle, Bargain, chaffer, higgle, tease, worry, harass, annoy, bait. *Yield*

Hail, Greet, salute, welcome, address, accost, call, signal, speak. *Pass*

Halcyon, Tranquil, still, quiet, calm, undisturbed, unruffled, serene, placid, peaceful. *Stormy*

Hale, Hearty, healthy, robust, strong, sound, well, hardy. *Weak*

Half, Moiety, bisection. *Whole*

Hall, Vestibule, auditorium, lobby, passage, corridor, chamber.

Hallow, Sanctify, dedicate, consecrate, devote. *Desecrate*

Hallowed, Holy, sanctified, sacred, blessed. *Profane*

Hallucination, Delusion, dream, illusion, blunder, error, mistake, fallacy, aberration, delirium, phantasm. *Reality*

Halt, *v.n.*, Stop, stay, stand, hold, rest. *March*

Hesitate, stammer, stumble, dubitate, falter, limp, hobble.

a., Lame, crippled, limping, disabled. *Sound*

n., Stop, stand.

Limp, gait.

Halve, Bisect, divide.

Hammer, Beat, forge, cudgel.

Hamper, Hinder, impede, encumber, clog, entangle, restrain, shackle, fetter, embarrass, restrict, confine, bind, curb. *Help*

Hand, *v.a.*, Present, give, pass, transmit, deliver, conduct, lead, guide.

n., Palm, fist. *Foot*

Labourer, artisan, employee, operative, craftsman, worker.

Participation, part, share, agency, intervention.

Handicraft, Trade, occupation, craft, art, work, handiwork.

Handicraftsman, Hand, labourer, craftsman, artificer, artisan.

Handiwork, Work, labour, workmanship, manufacture, handicraft.

Handle, *v.a.*, Manipulate, manage, use, wield, direct, deal, treat, discuss. *Bungle*

Feel, touch.

n., Stock, haft, hilt.

Hands, Clutches, power, grip.

Handsome, Fair, beautiful, fine, comely, stately, graceful, becoming. *Ugly*

Liberal, magnanimous, generous, noble, ample, plentiful, large, sufficient. *Niggardly*

Handy, Clever, skilful, expert, dexterous, useful, ready, adroit, skilled, proficient. *Clumsy*

Close, near, convenient. *Remote*

Hang, *v.n.*, Dangle, depend, rest, cling, swing, impend, stick, loiter, lean, rely. *Stand*

Float, hover, play.

Droop, drop, bend, incline, decline.

v.a., Suspend, attach.

Execute, truss.

Drape, adorn.

Hanker, Desire, long, covet, crave, yearn, hunger. *Loathe*

Hankering, Desire, longing, craving, yearning, hunger, want. *Antipathy*

Hap, Luck, chance, fortuity, accident, fortune. *Design*

Haphazard, Chance, aimless, random, disorderly. *Orderly*

Hapless, Unlucky, luckless, ill-fated, unfortunate, miserable, unhappy, wretched. *Lucky*

Haply, Perhaps, probably, possibly, perchance, peradventure, maybe, mayhap.

Happen, Occur, come, chance, befall, betide.

Happiness, Bliss, delight, joy, blessedness, pleasure, cheerfulness, joyfulness.

merriment, gaiety, brightness, felicity, enjoyment. **Sorrow**

Happy, Blissful, delighted, joyous.†
Sorrowful

Lucky, fortunate, felicitous, prosperous, successful. **Hapless**

Expert, able, apt, ready, skilful, adroit.

Opportune, pertinent, befitting, seasonable, favourable, bright, auspicious.
Dull

Harangue, n., Oration, address, speech, tirade, declamation.

v.a., Address.

v.n., Speak, declaim. **Mumble**

Harass, Annoy, distress, trouble, plague, vex, worry, torment, harry, molest, weary, tire, fatigue, exhaust, disturb, chafe, tease, irritate. **Relieve**

Harbinger, Precursor, herald, announcer, forerunner. **Follower**

Harbour, v.a., Protect, shelter, lodge, indulge, secrete, cherish, entertain, foster.
Expel

n., Haven, port, shelter, refuge, retreat, asylum, cover, sanctuary, home, anchorage, destination. **Afloat**

Hard, a., Solid, dense, rigid, firm, stubborn, resistant, adamantine, compact, unyielding. **Soft**

Stony, obdurate, callous, unfeeling, unkind, hard-hearted, insensible, oppressive, cruel, harsh, exacting. **Tender**

Difficult, arduous, intricate, complex, perplexing, puzzling, wearying, laborious.
Easy

Painful, unpleasant, distressing, grievous, disagreeable, calamitous. **Agreeable**

Rough, acid, sour, harsh.

adv., Energetically, laboriously, earnestly, diligently, painfully, severely, forcibly, violently, vehemently.

Near, close.

Harden, Indurate, nerve, steel, brace, strengthen, confirm, consolidate, fortify, compact. **Soften**

Inure, discipline, train, habituate, accustom.

Hardened, Inured, confirmed, impenitent, depraved, obdurate, reprobate, incorrigible. **Softened**

Hard-headed, Sagacious, wise, astute, keen, shrewd, clever, intelligent. **Simple**

Hard-hearted, Stony, hard, obdurate, callous, unfeeling, unkind, insensible, oppressive, cruel, harsh, exacting, fell, merciless, ruthless, ferocious, relentless, savage. **Tender**

Hardihood, Courage, pluck, bravery, manhood, firmness, strength, fortitude,

intrepidity, resolution, determination, audacity, brass, effrontery, assurance.
Timidity

Hardly, Scarcely, barely, narrowly, just.
Easily

Severely, harshly, roughly, rigorously, cruelly, unkindly. **Mildly**

Hardness, Solidity, density, firmness, compactness. **Softness**

Trouble, difficulty, perplexity, hardship, tribulation, suffering, trial, severity, cruelty, rigour. **Sympathy**

Hardship, Trouble, tribulation, trial, suffering, persecution, affliction, misfortune, hardness, grievance.
Recreation

Hardy, Courageous, plucky, brave, manly, intrepid, firm, strong, determined, bold, audacious, resolute, heroic, valiant, daring. **Timid**

Strong, healthy, hale, hearty, firm, stout, lusty, sturdy, tough, rugged, sound, robust. **Weak**

Hark, Hearken, hear, listen, attend.

Harlequin, Jester, clown, fool, buffoon.

Harlot, Whore, strumpet, courtezan, prostitute, trull.

Harm, v.a., Hurt, damage, injure, abuse, maltreat, molest, desecrate, scathe.
Benefit

n., Hurt, damage, injury, detriment, mischief, ill, misfortune, prejudice, disadvantage, evil, wickedness, wrong, criminality. **Good**

Harmful, Hurtful, injurious, deleterious, detrimental, pernicious, baneful, baleful, disadvantageous, noxious, mischievous.
Beneficial

Harmless, Inoffensive, inoffending, innocuous, safe, unhurtful, innocent, innoxious. **Pernicious**

Harmonious, Harmonic, concordant, accordant, congruent, congruous, agreeing, consistent, agreeable, friendly, amicable, cordial, neighbourly, fraternal. Musical, dulcet, melodious, tuneful, smooth, euphonious, mellifluous. **Discordant**

Harmonize, Accord, comport, correspond, agree, tally, cohere. **Differ**

Harmony, Accord, concord, congruity, consonance, accordance, concordance, agreement, unison, order, fitness, smoothness. **Discord**

Peace, friendship, amity, understanding, feeling. **Enmity**

Harness, Gear, tackle, accoutrements, equipment.

Harp, Repeat, reiterate, dwell, iterate.

Harping, Reiteration, repetition, iteration, dwelling.

Harrow, Tear, wound, lacerate, torment, harass, torture. *Relieve*

Harry, Plunder, raid, pillage, rob, ravage. Harass, plague, vex, annoy, fret, torment, torture, molest, tease, trouble, worry, harrow, chafe, disturb. *Appease*

Harsh, Jarring, discordant, grating, rough, raucous, strident, metallic. *Musical*

Churlish, sour, tart, acrid, biting, hard, severe, stern, corrosive, sharp, caustic, bitter, rude, uncivil, blunt, gruff, acrimonious, morose, crabbed, austere, unfeeling, unkind. *Gentle*

Harshness, Discordance, roughness. Churlishness, sourness, tartness.† *Kindliness*

Harvest, Crop, result, fruits, produce, yield, consequence, effect, product, issue, outcome. *Seed*

Hash, Chop, mangle, mince.

Haste, Hurry, speed, celerity, quickness, promptitude, despatch, expedition, precipitance, alacrity, velocity, rapidity, hustle. *Delay*

Hasten, *v.n.*, Hurry, speed, haste. *Dawdle*

v.a., Hurry, speed, accelerate, expedite, quicken, despatch, urge, press. *Retard*

Hasty, Quick, fast, speedy, rapid, brisk, swift, hurried, superficial, cursory, slight. *Deliberate*

Reckless, rash, headlong, precipitate, impetuous, indiscreet, thoughtless. *Thoughtful*

Excitable, peevish, petulant, testy, irritable, touchy, fretful, passionate, fiery, abrupt, hot, choleric, irascible, waspish. *Reflective*

Hatch, Incubate, breed, quicken.

Prepare, devise, scheme, concoct, plot, contrive, plan, brew, project. *Frustrate*

Inlay, engrave.

Hate, *v.a.*, Detest, loathe, abominate, abhor, dislike. *Love*

n., Detestation, enmity, hatred, antipathy, abhorrence, dislike, abomination, animosity.

Hateful, Detestable, loathsome, abominable, abhorrent, execrable, shocking, horrible, horrid, vile, foul, offensive, nauseous, repulsive, obnoxious, odious, repugnant, revolting, malignant, malicious, spiteful. *Delightful*

Hatred, Hate, detestation, enmity, antipathy, abhorrence, dislike, abomination, animosity, odium, disfavour, estrangement, alienation. *Love*

Haughtiness, Arrogance, pride, contemptuousness, superciliousness, loftiness, contempt, disdain, hauteur. *Meekness*

Haughty, Arrogant, proud, contemptuous.† *Meek*

Haul, Pull, draw, tow, tug, lug, drag, trail. *Push*

Haunt, *v.a.*, Inhabit, frequent. *Forsake*

Follow, dog, importune, obsess. *Avoid*

n., Retreat, resort, den.

Hauteur, Arrogance, pride, haughtiness, contemptuousness, superciliousness, loftiness, contempt, disdain. *Meekness*

Have, Own, hold, possess, keep, cherish, exercise, enjoy, experience. *Need*

Get, gain, acquire, obtain, receive, accept, take. *Lose*

Feel, entertain.

Haven, Harbour, port, home, shelter, retreat, refuge, asylum.

Havoc, Destruction, damage, harm, injury, desolation, devastation, ravage, waste, carnage, ruin, wreck. *Benefit*

Hawk, Sell, retail, cry, peddle.

Hazard, *v.a.*, Peril, imperil, risk, adventure, jeopard, venture, endanger. *Secure*

n., Chance, risk, peril, danger, jeopardy, accident. *Certainty*

Hazardous, Risky, perilous, dangerous, unsafe, uncertain, insecure. *Safe*

Haze, Mist, fog, cloud, pall, fume, obscurity, miasma.

Hazy, Misty, foggy, cloudy, obscure, murky, filmy. *Clear*

Confused, vague, indistinct, uncertain.

Head, *n.*, Top, acme, summit, zenith, apex, height. *Foot*

Mind, brain, intellect, thought, understanding.

Section, category, division, class, department.

Individual, person.

Origin, source, beginning, commencement.

Leader, master, director, manager, chieftain, chief, captain, commander, superintendent, principal, ruler. *Subordinate*

v.a., Lead, govern, rule, direct, command, guide, control.

Intercept, turn, halt.

v.n., Aim, tend, steer.

a., Leading, chief, principal, main, first. *Least*

Adverse, contrary. *Back*

Headland, Cape, promontory, foreland, bluff, cliff, escarpment.

Headlong, *a.*, Sheer, precipitous, steep. *Gradual*

Hasty, rash, precipitate, inconsiderate,

reckless, dangerous, perilous, impulsive, ruinous, thoughtless, foolhardy. *Cautious*
adv., Hastily, recklessly, rashly.† *Cautiously*

Headstrong, Wilful, self-willed, obstinate, stubborn, unruly, froward, intractable, heady, violent, wayward, ungovernable, dogged. *Amenable*

Heady, Headstrong, wilful, self-willed, obstinate.†
Impetuous, violent, rash, precipitate, rushing, headlong, hasty, impulsive, inconsiderate, thoughtless. *Cautious*

Heal, Restore, repair, cure, remedy, amend, compose, settle, harmonize, assuage, soothe. *Wound*

Healing, Restorative, restoring, remedial, assuaging, gentle, mild, comforting, soothing, curative, lenitive. *Wounding*

Health, Soundness, robustness, strength, tone, sanity. *Illness*

Healthy, Sound, robust, strong, hale, hearty, well, lusty, vigorous. *Ill*
Salubrious, wholesome, salutary, bracing, healthful, hygienic, invigorating. *Noxious*

Heap, v.a., Pile, gather, collect, accumulate, store, amass. *Scatter*
n., Pile, collection, accumulation, store, mass, lot, mound, abundance.

Hear, v.n., Listen, attend, hearken, learn.
v.a., Listen to, attend to, hearken to, heed, regard. *Ignore*
Try, examine, judge, interview.

Hearing, Audience.
Trial, examination, interview.

Hearken, Listen, attend, hear, heed, regard.

Hearsay, Report, rumour, talk, gossip.

Heart, Core, centre, kernel, interior, essence, meaning, nucleus. *Exterior*
Courage, hardihood, resolution, firmness, spirit, fortitude, boldness. *Timidity*
Feeling, love, affection, conscience, passion, purpose, intent, will, mind, inclination, disposition.

Heartache, Distress, sorrow, anguish, grief, woe, bitterness, affliction, dole. *Joy*

Hearten, Enhearten, encourage, embolden, cheer, rouse, assure, reassure, stimulate, animate, inspirit, rally, cheer, comfort, console, incite. *Depress*

Heartfelt, Sincere, hearty, deep, cordial, profound. *Feigned*

Hearth, Fireplace.
Fireside, home.

Heartless, Harsh, cruel, unmerciful, merciless, savage, pitiless, brutal, hard, unfeeling. *Tender*

Hearty, Sincere, honest, warm, cordial, heartfelt, profound, deep, unfeigned, genuine, true, earnest. *Feigned*
Active, earnest, energetic, warm, zealous, vigorous.
Strong, hale, robust, vigorous, sound, healthy, well, energetic, animated, abundant, heavy, full. *Delicate*
Rich, nourishing, nutritious.

Heat, v.a., Warm, stir, excite, rouse, stimulate. *Cool*
n., Warmth, excitement, ardour, zeal, flush, fever, passion, violence, vehemence, rage, frenzy, fierceness. *Coolness*

Heath, Moor, common, plain, heather.

Heathen, Pagan, gentile, idolater. *Christian*

Heave, v.a., Throw, cast, toss, fling, hurl, lift, hoist, raise, elevate, send. *Drop*
v.n., Pant, dilate, swell, expand, rise, struggle, strive.

Heaven, Paradise, Elysium, happiness, bliss. *Hell*

Heavenly, Angelic, divine, holy, celestial, cherubic, seraphic, beautiful, saintly, glorious, blissful, blessed, rapturous, delightful, ravishing, enrapturing, transporting. *Abominable*

Heaviness, Weight, gravity, ponderousness. *Lightness*
Despondency, gloom, sadness, depression, dejection, melancholy. *Buoyancy*
Languor, inertia, sluggishness, dulness, stupidity. *Activity*
Severity, grievousness, oppressiveness. *Triviality*

Heavy, Weighty, ponderous, hefty, massive. *Light*
Despondent, gloomy, sad,† downcast, downhearted, sorrowful, crestfallen, chapfallen. *Gay*
Languid, inert, sluggish, sleepy, inanimate, dull, stupid, dilatory, indolent, torpid, inactive. *Active*
Severe, grievous, oppressive, afflictive, burdensome, cumbersome, serious, hard, onerous, difficult, laborious, wearisome, tedious. *Trivial*
Stormy, rough, tempestuous, turbulent, strong, boisterous, roaring, deep, loud. *Calm*
Burdened, loaded, encumbered, weighted.
Dense, gloomy, dark, cloudy, overcast, oppressive. *Fresh*

Hebetate, Blunt, obtuse, dull, torpid. *Sharp*

Hectic, Feverish, fevered, heated, hot, flushed. *Cool*

Hector, v.n., Swagger, bully, boast, bluster, vaunt. *Cower*

Hector, *v.a.*, Bully, browbeat, harass, menace, threaten, domineer, vex, tease, annoy, harry, worry, irritate, provoke, fret.

n., Bully, swaggerer, boaster, blusterer.

Hedge, *v.a.*, Enclose, surround, crib, cabin, confine, environ, hinder, impede, obstruct. *Open*

Fortify, protect, guard.

n., Fence, barrier, limit, hedgerow.

v.n., Dodge, evade, hide, skulk, disappear.

Heed, *v.a.*, Mind, attend, notice, regard, observe, mark, obey. *Ignore*

n., Mindfulness, attention, notice,† care, watchfulness, regard, caution. *Disregard*

Heedful, Watchful, careful, cautious, observant, circumspect, wary, attentive, regardful, mindful, considerate. *Careless*

Heedless, Careless, unwatchful, inattentive, unmindful, inconsiderate, regardless, reckless, rash, thoughtless, negligent, unobservant, neglectful. *Careful*

Heel, *n.*, Bottom, foot, remnant, crust.

v.n., Lean, incline, follow.

Hegemonic, Chief, ruling, supreme, predominating, controlling, leading, predominant, prevailing. *Subordinate*

Hegemony, Rule, supremacy, predominance, control, leadership, headship.

Height, Altitude, tallness, elevation, eminence, dignity, grandeur, perfection, exaltation. *Depth*

Top, summit, acme, zenith, apex, head, climax, pinnacle. *Base*

Mountain, hill, eminence.

Heighten, Increase, augment, enhance, intensify, aggravate, improve. *Temper*

Raise, dignify, exalt, elevate, magnify, honour, aggrandize, ennoble. *Lower*

Heinous, Nefarious, infamous, scandalous, crying, outrageous, atrocious, odious, wicked, monstrous, villainous, enormous, flagrant, flagitious, serious. *Laudable*

Heir, Inheritor, offspring, child.

Hell, Hades, Gehenna, Avernus, Tophet, Inferno, torment, misery. *Heaven*

Hellish, Infernal, demoniac, demoniacal, fiendish, damnable, accursed, devilish, diabolical, monstrous, nefarious. *Angelic*

Helm, Helmet, casque, morion.

Rudder, wheel, tiller, control.

Command, rule, direction, control, reins.

Helmet, Helm, casque, morion.

Helot, Slave, bondslave, serf, bondsman. *Freeman*

Help, *v.a.*, Assist, aid, abet, encourage, back, second, further, support, serve, prevent. *Hinder*

Relieve, aid, succour, sustain, save, alleviate, improve, heal, remedy, restore, ameliorate, cure. *Aggravate*

Prevent, hinder, stop, resist, repress, forbear, withstand, control, avoid. *Incur*

n., Assistant, aider, abettor.† *Opponent*

Relief, assistance, support, remedy, aid, succour.† *Aggravation*

Helper, Assistant, aider, abettor, backer, second, supporter, ally, co-operator, coadjutor, partner, colleague, auxiliary, helpmate. *Opponent*

Helpful, Advantageous, useful, profitable, beneficial. *Useless*

Benevolent, kind.

Helpless, Weak, impotent, powerless, infirm, feeble, defenceless, unprotected, abandoned. *Strong*

Helpmate, Helper, aider, colleague, associate, partner, ally, companion. *Opponent*

Hem, Environ, enclose, crib, cabin, confine, hedge, border, edge, skirt, beset, surround, gird.

Sew.

Hence, Henceforward, henceforth, away. Therefore.

Henchman, Crony, supporter, follower, retainer, servant, attendant.

Herald, *v.a.*, Announce, proclaim, publish, tell.

n., Harbinger, messenger, crier, precursor, forerunner.

Herbage, Grass, vegetation, pasture, herbs, plants.

Herculean, Sturdy, powerful, vigorous, mighty, strong, muscular, brawny, sinewy, athletic, stalwart, robust, strapping, great, gigantic, huge, colossal. *Puny*

Laborious, heavy, hard, arduous, difficult, toilsome. *Light*

Herd, *n.*, Multitude, crowd, collection, populace, rabble.

Drove.

v.a., Tend, gather, lead, drive.

Hereditary, Inherited, lineal, ancestral, transmitted. *Acquired*

Heresy, Error, unorthodoxy, schism, heterodoxy. *Orthodoxy*

Heretical, Erring, unorthodox, schismatic, schismatical, heterodox. *Orthodox*

Heritage, Inheritance, bequest, legacy, patrimony, portion. *Merit*

Hermetic-al, Mystic, symbolical, emblematic, occult, mysterious, secret. *Open*

Hermit, Solitary, anchorite, anchoret, ascetic, recluse.

Heroic, Valiant, daring, brave, intrepid,

bold, dauntless, undaunted, gallant, courageous, fearless, noble. *Cowardly*
Epic.

Heroism, Valour, daring, bravery,† fortitude. *Cowardliness*

Hesitate, Demur, falter, pause, halt, waver, vacillate, delay, dubitate, doubt, scruple, stammer. *Decide*

Hesitation, Hesitancy, halting, indecision, wavering, vacillation, dubitation, doubt, uncertainty, reluctance.
Decision

Heterodox, Heretical, erring, unorthodox, schismatic, schismatical, recusant, uncanonical, apocryphal. *Orthodox*

Heterodoxy, Heresy, error, unorthodoxy, schism. *Orthodoxy*

Heterogeneity, Dissimilarity, dissimilitude, difference, contrast, unlikeness, opposition, contrariety. *Similarity*

Heterogeneous, Dissimilar, different, contrasted, unlike, opposed, contrary, diverse, mixed, indiscriminate. *Similar*

Hew, Chop, hack, cut, fell.
Fashion, smooth, form.

Hiatus, Gap, rift, opening, cleft, hole, crevice, break, chasm, interval.

Hidden, Obscure, dark, secret, concealed, latent, covered, masked, veiled, suppressed, blind, private, cloaked, covert, covered, secreted, occult, close, mystic, mysterious, cabalistic, clandestine, recondite, abstruse, hermetic. *Open*

Hide, *v.a.*, Conceal, cloak, cover, screen, secrete, mask, ensconce, disguise, dissemble, suppress, bury, shelter, veil, hoard. *Reveal*
n., Skin, pelt, coat.

Hideous, Ghastly, horrible, horrid, frightful, terrible, monstrous, unshapely, appalling, shocking, revolting, dreadful, grisly. *Beautiful*

Hie, Hasten, haste, speed, fly, go.
Dawdle

Hieratic-al, Priestly, sacerdotal, sacred, consecrated.

Higgle, Haggle, negotiate, bargain, chaffer, peddle, hawk.

Higgledy-piggledy, Disorderly, confused, helter-skelter, pell-mell, topsy-turvy, haphazard. *Orderly*

High, Exalted, elevated, noble, lofty, dignified, superior, eminent, distinguished. *Base*
Tall, extreme, great, strong. *Low*
Proud, arrogant, overbearing, supercilious, haughty, lordly, domineering, boastful, bragging, despotic, tyrannical, oppressive. *Lowly*
Shrill, sharp, acute.

High, Strong, violent, tumultuous, turbulent, boisterous, heavy. *Light*

Highwayman, Footpad, robber, brigand, bandit, freebooter, marauder, outlaw.

Hilarious, Jolly, joyful, gay, merry, jovial, mirthful, jocund, cheerful, exhilarated, noisy, boisterous.
Despondent

Hilarity, Jollity, joy, joyfulness, gaiety,† glee. *Despondency*

Hill, Mount, mountain, eminence, elevation, hillock, rise, ascent, knoll, mound.
Dale

Hind, *a.*, Back, rear, posterior, hindmost.
Front
n., Churl, boor, peasant, clown, lout, clodhopper, bumpkin, rustic.

Hinder, Impede, check, thwart, obstruct, prevent, stop, retard, oppose, encumber, embarrass, delay, bar, restrain, dog, interrupt, *let*. *Help*

Hindrance, Impediment, check, obstruction,† restraint.

Hinge, Turn, depend, hang, rotate, move, circulate.

Hint, *v.a.*, Insinuate, suggest, intimate, imply, mention.
n., Insinuation, suggestion, intimation, allusion, trace.

Hire, *v.a.*, Rent, engage, commission, secure, employ, charter, lease, bribe. *Let*
n., Pay, remuneration, reward, salary, wages, stipend, allowance, rent, compensation.

Hireling, Mercenary, venal.

Hirsute, Shaggy, hispid, bristly, hairy, rough, coarse, rude, rustic, uncouth.
Smooth

Hispid, Hirsute, shaggy.† *Bald*

Hiss, *v.n.*, Whistle, sibilate, shrill, whirr, whiz.
v.n., Deride, scout, ridicule, scorn. *Cheer*
n., Sizzle, fizzle, hissing, sibilation.

Historic-al, Authentic, genuine, true, real. *Legendary*
Famous, celebrated, noteworthy, memorable.

History, Chronicle, annals, record, account, story, memoir, biography, recital, narrative, narration, relation. *Legend*

Histrionic, Theatrical, dramatic, acting, Thespian.

Hit, *v.a.*, Strike, beat, knock, hurt.
Attain, gain, win, secure, reach, suit, fit
v.n., Collide, clash, strike. *Miss*
n., Stroke, collision, clash, blow, impact.
Succeed, carry, gain.
Chance, luck, hazard, fortune, venture, stroke.

Hitch, *v.a.*, Tie, fasten, join, attach, connect, unite. ***Sever***
v.n., Catch, jam, stick, hang. ***Flow***
n., Catch, check, obstacle, hindrance, impediment, jerk.
Knot, noose.

Hoard, Garner, store, husband, save, secrete, amass, accumulate. ***Dissipate***

Hoarse, Rough, grating, guttural, husky, raucous, low, harsh. ***Mellow***

Hoary, Grey, silvery, frosty, white. ***Dark***
Venerable, old, ancient.

Hoax, *v.a.*, Cheat, deceive, gull, gammon, fool, befool, dupe, trick, bamboozle, hoodwink. ***Enlighten***
n., Cheat, deception, trick, fraud, imposition, imposture.

Hobble, Halt, limp, falter, hop. ***Run***
n., Halt, shackle, fetter, clog.
Strait, difficulty, embarrassment.

Hobby, Pastime, pursuit, amusement, recreation, speciality, whim, avocation, fad, pursuit, object. ***Nuisance***

Hobgoblin, Goblin, apparition, spirit, sprite, bogey, spectre, spook.

Hog, Pig, swine, grunter, porker, glutton, beast.

Hoggish, Swinish, sordid, mean, grasping, selfish, greedy, brutish, filthy. ***Noble***

Hoist, Raise, heave, lift, elevate. ***Lower***

Hold, *v.n.*, Last, endure, persist, stand, remain, abide, continue. ***Perish***
Stick, cleave, cohere, adhere, cling. ***Disintegrate***
Believe, think, agree, stand, prove. ***Disagree***
v.a., Grip, grasp, gripe, clutch, keep, retain, occupy, seize, clasp, possess, hold. ***Drop***
Stop, check, arrest, detain, restrain, imprison, confine, bind, unite, connect, fasten lock, withhold. ***Release***
Maintain, declare, believe, regard, think, consider, deem, esteem, count, account, reckon, support, sustain, manage, prosecute, judge.
Admit, contain, receive, accommodate, stow, carry. ***Vacate***
Convene, assemble, conduct. ***Dissemble***
Celebrate, solemnize.
n., Grip, grasp, gripe, clutch, anchor, bite, embrace, control, purchase, possession.
Claim, footing, vantage, prop, stay, support.
Stronghold, fortress, castle, keep, fort, fortification, defence.

Hole, Opening, cleft, rift, aperture, breach, break, gap, crevice, perforation, cavity, concavity, hollow, pit, gulf.

Hole, Cave, cavern, hovel, den, retreat, lair, cover, burrow, chamber.

Holiday, Festival, fête, celebration, anniversary, vacation, playtime.

Holiness, Saintliness, sanctity, godliness, devotion, devoutness, piety, goodness, purity, divineness, religiousness, sacredness. ***Profanity***

Hollow, *a.*, Empty, vacant, void, concave, cavernous. ***Solid***
False, artificial, insincere, sham, faithless, deceitful, treacherous, hypocritical, opportunist. ***Sincere***
Deep, rumbling, muffled, low, reverberating.
n., Depression, basin, bowl, cavity, pit, hole, cavern, cave, dent, dimple, groove, channel, cup, pocket, canal, sag.

Holy, Saintly, godly, devout, pious, good, pure, divine, religious, sacred, righteous, spiritual. ***Profane***

Homage, Devotion, loyalty, allegiance, fealty, fidelity, duty, obedience, honour, respect, deference, worship, adoration, reverence. ***Defiance***

Home, *n.*, House,† household, abode, dwelling, residence, domicile.
Seat, habitat, quarters, destination, goal, asylum.
a., Internal, interior, domestic, family. ***Foreign***

Homely, Homelike, simple, domestic, plain, unpretentious, inelegant, coarse, uncomely. ***Grand***

Homicide, Murder, manslaughter.

Homily, Sermon, address, discourse.

Homogeneous, Similar, uniform, congruous, accordant. ***Heterogeneous***

Hone, Sharpen, whet, strop. ***Blunt***

Honest, Fair, just, honourable, open, straightforward, upright, sincere, trusty, trustworthy, virtuous, conscientious, faithful, true, reliable, genuine, ingenuous. ***Deceitful***

Honesty, Fairness, justice, honour,† probity, integrity. ***Deceit***

Honour, *v.a.*, Exalt, magnify, glorify, dignify, elevate. ***Debase***
Reverence, respect, revere, worship, venerate, adore. ***Slight***
n., Exaltation, glory, dignity, elevation, distinction, eminence, fame, renown, repute, reputation, esteem, nobility. ***Abasement***
Reverence, respect, worship, veneration, adoration, civility, homage, deference. ***Slight***
Fairness, justice, uprightness, sincerity, virtue, conscience, probity, integrity, honesty. ***Deceit***

Honourable, Exalted, dignified, elevated, distinguished,† illustrious, great. *Low*
Fair, just, upright.†
Right, respected, proper, reputable, estimable, esteemed.

Honorary, Gratuitous, unpaid, unremunerative. *Professional*

Honours, Decorations, titles, dignities, privileges, glories, adornments.

Hood, Cowl, cover, cloak, shelter, protection.

Hoodwink, Dupe, deceive, hoax, fool, befool, gull, trick, cheat, delude, overreach, circumvent, *cozen*, *chouse*. *Enlighten*

Hook, *v.a.*, Snare, ensnare, catch, trap, entrap. *Release*
Curve, bend, incline. *Straighten*
n., Snare, trap.
Hasp, clasp, catch, fastener.
Cutter, sickle, reaper.

Hooked, Curved, curvated, bent, crooked. *Straight*

Hoop, Band, ring, circlet.

Hoot, decry, denounce, hiss, yell, shout, boo, execrate, sibilate. *Cheer*

Hop, Leap, jump, dance, caper, skip, spring, bound.
Limp, hobble, halt.

Hope, *n.*, Faith, trust, confidence, reliance, longing, expectancy. *Despair*
v.n., Trust.
Anticipate, await.

Hopeful, Confident, longing, eager, ardent, expectant, optimistic, sanguine, anticipatory. *Despairing*
Auspicious, encouraging, propitious, promising. *Discouraging*

Hopeless, Despairing, downcast, despondent, disconsolate, forlorn, desperate, crushed. *Confident*
Irreparable, irremediable, helpless, incurable. *Promising*
Impossible, lost, forlorn, impracticable.

Horde, Crowd, multitude, throng, gang, crew, clan, group, company, pack, collection, troop, host.

Horizontal, Level, flat, plane. *Perpendicular*

Horrible, Horrid, terrible, alarming, dreadful, awful, fearful, appalling, terrific, dire, formidable, horrifying, hideous, ghastly, hateful, detestable, abominable, revolting. *Pleasant*

Horrid, Horrible, terrible, alarming.†

Horrify, Terrify, alarm, frighten, appal, shock. *Reassure*

Horror, Terror, alarm, fear, dread, awe, panic, dismay, fright. *Assurance*

Horse, Stallion, steldeed, ging, mare, filly, colt, pony, sheltie, palfrey, nag, cob, charger.
Cavalry, horsemen.
Frame, support, stand, back.

Horseman, Rider, cavalryman, cavalier, equestrian, dragoon.

Hortative, Exhorting, inciting, persuasive, homiletic. *Deterring*

Hospitable, Neighbourly, sociable, kind, friendly, charitable, attentive, bountiful, generous, liberal. *Niggardly*

Hospitality, Hospitableness, neighbourliness, sociability.† *Unfriendliness*

Host, Throng, multitude, crowd, assemblage, army, number, horde, legion, force, array. *Handful*
Entertainer, innkeeper, landlord.

Hostage, Surety, sponsor, bail. *Dictator*

Hostile, Adverse, unfriendly, inimical, contrary, opposite, opposed. *Friendly*

Hostilities, War, warfare, operations. *Peace*

Hostility, Unfriendliness, opposition, hatred, repugnance, variance, animosity, enmity. *Friendliness*

Hot, Heated, burning, warm, fiery, oppressive, scalding, roasting, flaming, boiling, parched. *Cold*
Passionate, hasty, violent, vehement, ardent, impetuous, eager, irascible, fervent, fervid, enthusiastic, animated. *Apathetic*
Pungent, sharp, acrid, peppery, piquant.

Hotel, Inn, public-house, tavern, hostel, hostelry, pension.

Hound, Hunt, chase, pursue, harry, harass, prosecute, persecute, incite, spur, drive, urge. *Liberate*

House, *n.*, Home, residence, domicile, dwelling, abode, place, habitation, mansion, cottage.
Race, family, tribe, kindred, lineage, household.
Firm, concern, business, establishment, partnership, company.
v.a., Protect, shelter, domicile.

Household, *n.*, Family, house, home.
a., Domestic, family, home.

Hovel, Hut, hole, cabin, shed, den, cot, retreat. *Palace*

Hover, Vacillate, flutter, wave, hang.

However, But, still, yet, notwithstanding, nevertheless, though.

Howl, Cry, roar, yell, weep, lament, wail, yowl, alarm. *Quiet*

Hubbub, Noise, uproar, tumult, confusion, din, disorder, riot, disturbance, outcry, clamour, alarum. *Quiet*

Huddle, Heap, pile, mix, jumble, derange, confuse, crowd. *Sort*

Hue, Tint, tinge, colour, shade, tone, complexion.

Hueless, Colourless, livid, pàllid, white, achromatic, untinged, uncoloured, pale, dull.   *Coloured*

Huff, Rage, passion, fury, anger, temper, tiff, quarrel.

Huffish } Enraged, passionate, furious,
Huffy } angry, petulant, pettish, irritable.   *Appeased*

Hug, Squeeze, embrace, clasp, cling, hold. Cherish, retain.

Huge, Enormous, tremendous, vast, large, great, immense, colossal, elephantine, gigantic, bulky.   *Minute*

Hull, Husk, shell, peel, rind, shuck.

Hullabaloo, Uproar, din, racket, clamour, outcry, hubbub, confession, disturbance.   *Quiet*

Human, Anthropological, cosmical, ethnical, rational.   *Inhuman*

Humane, Tender, compassionate, merciful, kind, benevolent, benign, benignant, charitable, clement, sympathetic. *Cruel*

Humanity, Manhood, man.   *Beast*
Tenderness, compassion, mercy.†   *Cruelty*

Humanize, Civilize, educate, enlighten, refine, polish, cultivate, soften, improve, ameliorate.   *Brutalize*

Humble, *v.a.*, Degrade, subdue, lower, crush, shame, mortify, humiliate, abash.   *Exalt*

a., Meek, lowly, low, unpretending, unassuming, modest, unobtrusive. *High*

Humbug, Fraud, trick, dodge, cheat, hoax, imposture, hypocrisy, quackery, charlatanry.
Impostor, cheat, quack, charlatan.

Humdrum, Tiresome, wearisome, dreary, monotonous, dull, uninteresting, prosaic, prosy, dry.   *Interesting*

Humid, Damp, moist, wet, vaporous, dank.   *Dry*

Humiliate, Humble, degrade, subdue, lower, crush, shame, mortify, abash.   *Exalt*

Humiliation, Humbling, degradation, lowering, shame, mortification, abashment, crushing.   *Exaltation*

Humility, Humbleness, meekness, lowliness, modesty, submissiveness.   *Haughtiness*

Hummock, Knoll, hillock, ridge, pile, knob, hump.   *Gully*

Humorous, Funny, amusing, comic, comical, droll, witty, facetious, laughable, ludicrous.   *Serious*

Humour, *v.a.*, Favour, gratify, indulge, pamper.

Humour, *n.,* Disposition, mood, temper, feeling, whim, fancy, caprice.   *Will*
Moisture, fluid, vapour.
Fun, amusement, wit, facetiousness, jocularity, pleasantry.   *Seriousness*

Humoursome, Capricious, wayward, perverse, petulant, testy, whimsical.

Hunch, Protuberance, lump, hump, knob. Push, punch, nudge, shove.
Premonition, intuition.

Hunger, Desire, hanker, long, crave, covet.

Hungry, Desirous, longing, craving, ravenous, famishing.   *Satisfied*

Hunk, Hunch, lump, slice, portion, piece, chunk.

Hunt, *v.n.*, Search, look, seek.
v.a., Hound, follow, chase, pursue, stalk, trail, drive, seek.
n., Hunting, sport, chase, pursuit.

Hurl, Sling, throw, cast, fling, pitch, precipitate.

Hurricane, Gale, storm, cyclone, tempest, typhoon, tornado.   *Calm*

Hurried, Cursory, slight, quick, hasty, superficial.   *Thorough*

Hurry, *v.a.*, Hasten, despatch, accelerate, quicken, speed, urge, precipitate, expedite, drive.   *Retard*
v.n., Hasten, haste, move, scurry.   *Dawdle*
n., Haste, despatch, quickness, speed, precipitation, precipitancy, expedition, celerity, flurry, bustle, hustle, perturbation, promptitude, confusion, agitation.   *Leisure*

Hurt, *v.a.*, Harm, injure, pain, damage, wound, afflict, bruise, grieve, offend, impair, mar, spoil.   *Benefit*
n., Harm, injury, pain,† detriment, damage, mischief, disadvantage.   *Heal*

Hurtful, Harmful, injurious, detrimental, deleterious, pernicious, baneful, baleful, noxious, mischievous, disadvantageous, damaging.   *Beneficial*

Husband, Store, hoard, save, economize.   *Waste*

Husbandry, Agriculture, tillage, farming, frugality, thrift.

Hush, *v.a.*, Silence, quiet, still, calm, repress, appease, console, assuage, allay.
interj., Silence, quiet, whist.
n., Quiet, stillness, silence.

Husk, Coating, covering, bark, rind, hull.   *Kernel*

Husky, Guttural, hoarse, grating, harsh, raucous.   *Melodious*

Hustle, Jostle, crowd, push, bustle, rush, elbow, hasten, hurry, speed.   *Dally*

Hut, Hovel, shed, cabin, den, cot. *Castle*

Hutch, Box, bin, chest, coffer, coop, shed, hut.

Hyaline, Transparent, translucid, glassy, crystalline. *Opaque*

Hybrid, Mongrel, impure, mixed, mule, cross-breed. *Thoroughbred*

Hydra, Hobgoblin, goblin, gorgon, spirit, spectre, bogey, ogre.

Hyemal, Hiemal, wintry, cold, frosty, chilly, chilling, biting, freezing. *Warm*

Hymeneal, Conjugal, nuptial, bridal, matrimonial, connubial.

Hypnotic, Mesmeric, soporific, somniferous, opiate.

Hypochondria, Depression, dejection, melancholy, spleen. *Elation*

Hypochondriac-al, Depressed, dejected, melancholy, splenetic, despondent, dispirited. *Elated*

Hypocrisy, Deceit, cant, pretence, humbug, pharisaism, sanctimoniousness, dissimulation. *Sincerity*

Hypocrite, Deceiver, pretender, pharisee, dissembler, impostor, feigner, humbug, cheat. *Saint*

Hypocritical, False, dissembling, canting, hollow, pharisaical, sanctimonious, deceitful. *Sincere*

Hypostasis, Principle, elements, substance, subsistence, person.

Hypothesis, Theory, conjecture, supposition. *Proof*

Hypothetical, Theoretical, conjectural, conditional, suppositional. *Proved*

I

Ice, Congeal, chill, freeze. *Heat*

Icy, Cold, chilly, freezing, frigid, frosty, gelid, arctic. *Warm*

Idea, Belief, doctrine, sentiment, opinion, supposition. *Reality*
Notion, conception, image, fancy, conceit, imagination, fiction, fantasy, impression, thought. *Object*

Ideal, Fanciful, fancied, fantastic, illusory, perfect, consummate. *Real*
Mental, intellectual, conceptional.

Identical, Same, self-same, equivalent, tantamount. *Different*

Identify, Integrate, unite, incorporate. *Confound*
Recognize. *Differentiate*

Identity, Personality, individuality, unity, sameness. *Difference*

Ideology, Sensualism, sensationalism, empiricism.

Idiocy, Imbecility, insanity, aberration, foolishness, fatuity. *Sanity*

Idiosyncrasy, Singularity, peculiarity, eccentricity, temperament, speciality. *Generality*

Idiot, Imbecile, fool, dolt, natural, simpleton, booby. *Sage*

Idiotic, Imbecile, foolish, doltish, fatuous, irrational, inane, witless, senseless. *Sagacious*

Idle, Indolent, inert, lazy, inactive, unemployed, unoccupied, sluggish, slothful, leisure. *Busy*
Fruitless, vain, abortive, useless, unused, vacant, bootless, futile, ineffectual, unprofitable, trivial, trifling, unimportant, frivolous, foolish. *Useful*

Idler, Trifler, sluggard, drone, dawdler, lounger.

Idol, Hero, god, image, illusion, sham, pretender, favourite, pet, darling, beloved.

Idolize, Adore, deify, venerate, worship, reverence, love. *Execrate*

If, Suppose, provided, admitting, allowing, though, whether, granting.

Ignite, Kindle, inflame, light, burn, fire. *Extinguish*

Ignoble, Low, base, mean, unworthy, contemptible, worthless, dishonourable, disgraceful, shameful, infamous, ignominious. *Honourable*

Ignominious, Disgraceful, contemptible, disreputable, worthless, unworthy, dishonourable, shameful, infamous, ignoble, despicable, base, scandalous. *Distinctive*

Ignominy, Disgrace, contempt, disrepute,† discredit, obloquy, odium, abasement, opprobrium. *Credit*

Ignoramus, Dunce, dullard, dolt, simpleton, fool, donkey, ass. *Genius*

Ignorance, Blindness, darkness, illiteracy, nescience. *Knowledge*

Ignorant, Blind, dark, illiterate, untaught, unread, uneducated, unlearned, unenlightened, uninformed, uninstructed, unlettered, unaware, unwitting, unconversant. *Wise*

Ignore, Disregard, overlook, neglect, skip, pass. *Notice*

Ill, *a.,* Unfortunate, bad, unlucky, unfavourable, evil, hard.
Wrong, bad, evil, wicked, vile, naughty, unjust, unrighteous, iniquitous. *Good*
Indisposed, unwell, sick, diseased, disordered, ailing. *Well*
Peevish, hateful, surly, ugly, cross, malicious, unkind, malevolent, crabbed.
adv., Badly.
n., Misfortune, harm, affliction, visitation, evil, pain, hurt, suffering, misery, calamity.
Wickedness, evil, wrong, depravity. *Good*

Ill-bred, Rude, discourteous, uncivil, impolite, unpolished. *Civil*

Illegal, Illicit, unlawful, forbidden, prohibited, unauthorized, illegitimate, contraband, unlicensed. *Lawful*

Illegible, Undecipherable, indecipherable, unreadable.

Illegitimate, Illicit, improper, unlawful, unauthorized, *Lawful*
Spurious, bastard.

Ill-fated, Unfortunate, luckless, unlucky, ill-starred. *Fortunate*

Ill-favoured, Plain, ugly, offensive, unpleasant. *Beautiful*

Illiberal, Miserly, mean, narrow, stingy, ungenerous, parsimonious, selfish, penurious, close, niggardly. *Generous*

Illicit, Illegal, unlawful, illegitimate, forbidden, unauthorized, unlicensed, improper, wrong, criminal. *Lawful*

Illimitable, Vast, infinite, unbounded, boundless. *Finite*

Illiterate, Ignorant, unlearned, untaught, unread, uneducated, unlettered, uninstructed. *Learned*

Ill-mannered, Discourteous, impolite, rude, uncivil, uncouth. *Polite*

Ill-natured, Unkind, malevolent, cross, peevish, unfriendly, sullen, perverse, petulant, sour, morose, churlish, unamiable, sulky, crusty, acrimonious, crabbed, bitter.   *Kind*

Illness, Malady, complaint, ailing, ailment, disease, distemper, disorder, sickness, indisposition.   *Health*

Illogical, Faulty, inconsistent, unsound, fallacious, inconclusive, absurd, incorrect, unreasonable, invalid.   *Sound*

Illtreat, Misuse, injure, abuse, mishandle, maltreat.

Illuminate, Illume, illumine, light, irradiate, enlighten.   *Darken*

Illusion, Delusion, dream, deception, mockery, snare, phantasm, hallucination, vision, error, chimera, fantasy.   *Reality*

Illusive ⎱ Fugitive, deceptive, deceitful,
Illusory ⎰ imaginary, unreal.   *Solid*

Illustrate, Exemplify, explain, interpret, elucidate, demonstrate, shew, adorn.   *Obscure*

Illustrative, Explanatory, elucidative.

Illustrious, Famous, renowned, glorious, splendid, great, celebrated, deathless, brilliant, bright, eminent, distinguished, conspicuous.   *Infamous*

Ill-will, Hate, hatred, enmity, envy, spite, grudge, venom, hostility, animosity, dislike, malice, rancour.   *Goodwill*

Image, Likeness, picture, representation, effigy, figure, resemblance, copy. Statue, idol. Conception, idea, reflection.

Imaginary, Unreal, fanciful, fancied, illusive, illusory, shadowy, unsubstantial, ideal, visionary, chimerical, assumed, supposed, conceivable.   *Real*

Imagination, Fancy, conception, invention, illusion, notion, fantasy, perception, image, idea, scheme, device.   *Reality*

Imaginative, Fanciful, visionary, inventive, creative, plastic, dreamy.   *Prosaic*

Imagine, Fancy, conceive, invent, dream, picture, pretend, devise, contrive, project, create.   *Represent* Think, suppose, believe, assume, deem, guess, apprehend.   *Prove*

Imbecile, *n.*, Idiot, fool, dotard.   *Sage* *a.*, Idiotic, foolish, doting, fatuous, feeble, weak, drivelling, decrepit, infirm.   *Clever*

Imbecility, Idiocy, foolishness, fatuity,† childishness, debility.   *Cleverness*

Imbibe, Acquire, absorb, drink, swallow, receive, assimilate, gather, gain.   *Discard*

Imbrue, Damp, wet, soak, drench, moisten, steep.   *Dry*

Imbue, Impregnate, infect, dye, stain, tint, colour, tincture, tinge, bathe, infuse, steep, pervade, permeate, inoculate.   *Purge*

Imitate, Copy, repeat, follow, mimic, impersonate, emulate, echo, forge, duplicate, personate, ape, burlesque, parody, mock.   *Alter*

Imitation, *n.*, Copying, copy, mimicry, burlesque, travesty, parody, likeness, resemblance.   *Alteration* *a.*, Counterfeit, false, spurious, artificial.   *Genuine*

Immaculate, Perfect, pure, stainless, spotless, unspotted, untarnished, undefiled, unstained, unsoiled, untainted, unsullied, unpolluted, unblemished, clean.   *Untidy*

Immanent, Innate, inherent, congenital, intrinsic, ingrained, inborn, indwelling, internal, subjective.   *Transitive*

Immaterial, Trivial, unimportant, unessential, minor, insignificant, trifling.   *Important* Incorporeal, spiritual, ethereal, mental, bodiless.   *Physical*

Immature, Imperfect, crude, unprepared, unready, unripe, raw, unfinished, green, undeveloped, hasty, premature, untimely.   *Ripe*

Immaturity, Imperfection, crudeness, crudity.†   *Ripeness*

Immeasurable, Illimitable, vast, boundless, infinite, limitless, unbounded, immense, unfathomable.   *Finite*

Immediate, Near, close, proximate, next, contiguous.   *Distant* Instant, instantaneous, direct, present, prompt.   *Future*

Immediately, Nearly, closely, proximately.   *Distantly* Instantly, directly, forthwith, straightway, now.   *Later*

Immemorial, Ancient, primitive, olden, remote, archaic, hoary.   *Modern*

Immense, Huge, enormous, vast, large, great, titanic, monstrous, colossal, gigantic, tremendous, stupendous, prodigious, infinite, boundless, unbounded, limitless, illimitable, unlimited, immeasurable.   *Small*

Immerse, Duck, submerge, plunge, douse, dip, bathe, souse, sink, inundate, involve. Baptize.

Immesh, Ensnare, entangle.   *Disentangle*

Immethodical, Irregular, erratic, unmethodical, unsystematic, slovenly, disorderly, desultory.   *Orderly*

Imminent, Threatening, impending, coming, hovering, perilous, alarming. *Past*

Immission, Injection, insertion, introduction. *Ejection*

Immobile, Still, immovable, inflexible, steady, steadfast, fixed, stable, motionless, stationary, static, impassive, stolid, stiff, rigid. *Flexible*

Immoderate, Extreme, excessive, exorbitant, extravagant, inordinate, unreasonable, intemperate. *Reasonable*

Immodest, Bold, shameless, brazen, forward, impudent, indecorous, indecent, gross, coarse, rude, obscene, impure, unchaste. *Bashful*

Immoral, Depraved, wicked, bad, wrong, loose, corrupt, unrighteous, dissolute, profligate, unprincipled, vicious, sinful, licentious, abandoned, indecent.
Virtuous

Immorality, Depravity, wickedness, badness.† *Virtue*

Immortal, Deathless, eternal, everlasting, undying, indestructible, incorruptible, imperishable, unfading, perpetual, endless, uneasing, ceaseless, lasting, permanent, abiding. *Perishable*

Immortality, Deathlessness, indestructibility, incorruptibility, incorruption, perpetuity. *Death*

Immovable, Steadfast, steady, unshaken, firm, fixed, secure, unalterable, unchangeable, stable, stationary. *Unsteady*

Immunity, Exemption, freedom, liberty, privilege, right, charter, franchise, exoneration, release. *Liability*

Immure, Incarcerate, imprison, confine, entomb. *Release*

Immutable, Constant, invariable, fixed, permanent, unalterable, stable, unchangeable, inflexible. *Changeable*

Imp, Scamp, demon, sprite, brat.
Cherub

Impact, Contact, shock, stroke, collision, impulse, impression, touch. *Avoidance*

Impair, Injure, damage, spoil, mar, blemish, ruin, deface, enfeeble, enervate, weaken, deteriorate, vitiate, harm, lessen, reduce, diminish. *Improve*

Impalpable, Indistinct, shadowy, imperceptible. *Clear*

Impart, Bestow, confer, give, grant, vouchsafe, share, divulge, disclose, tell, communicate, reveal. *Withhold*

Impartial, Just, disinterested, unbiassed, equitable, unprejudiced, neutral, fair.
Prejudiced

Impassable, Impenetrable, impervious, pathless, impermeable. *Penetrable*

Impassible, Insusceptible, insensible, indifferent, impassive, unfeeling.
Susceptible

Impassioned, Passionate, fervent, fervid, eager, ardent, impetuous, excited, animated, zealous, warm, vehement, eloquent. *Cool*

Impassive, Impassible, insusceptible, insensible, calm, passionless, indifferent, unfeeling. *Susceptible*

Impatient, Hasty, eager, impetuous, ardent, vehement, precipitate, violent, restless, unquiet, fretful, irritable, testy, uneasy. *Quiet*

Impeach, Indict, accuse, arraign, criminate, denounce, censure, discredit, asperse, impair, lessen. *Vindicate*

Impeccable, Innocent, faultless, sinless, pure, unstained, stainless, immaculate.
Guilty

Impede, Obstruct, hinder, prevent, restrain, stop, thwart, check, clog, delay, retard, block, encumber, interrupt, let.
Accelerate

Impediment, Obstruction, hindrance, prevention,† obstacle, difficulty, bar, encumbrance. *Acceleration*

Impel, Urge, press, drive, move, push, send, persuade, instigate, actuate, constrain, compel, induce, stimulate, incite, influence. *Deter*

Impend, Threaten, come, hover, approach. *Pass*

Impenetrable, Impassable, impervious, pathless, dense, proof, unfathomable, reticent, impermeable. *Passable*

Impenitent, Unrepentant, incorrigible, hardened, obdurate, uncontrite, seared.
Repentant

Imperative, Urgent, obligatory, binding, peremptory, dictatorial, authoritative, commanding, important, necessary.
Optional

Imperceptible, Invisible, minute, small, fine, undiscernible, impalpable, inaudible, gradual. *Visible*

Imperfect, Faulty, defective, lacking, wanting, poor, crude, deficient, incomplete. *Entire*

Imperial, Majestic, regal, royal, kingly, sovereign, supreme, magnificent, grand, superb. *Paltry*

Imperil, Peril, endanger, hazard, risk, jeopardize.

Imperious, Despotic, arrogant, domineering, authoritative, exacting, tyrannical, lordly, haughty, overbearing, urgent, compelling, imperative. *Mild*

Imperishable, Eternal, immortal, deathless, unending, undying, everlasting, endless, incorruptible, indestructible, un-fading. **Corruptible**

Impersonate, Personate, imitate, mock mimic, copy, ape, act, enact, parody.
Expose

Impertinence, Rudeness, sauciness, sauce, impudence, insolence, front, effrontery, pertness, assurance, face, boldness, forwardness, incivility.
Politeness
Irrelevance, irrelevancy. **Relevance**

Impertinent, Rude, saucy, impudent,† meddling, officious. **Polite**
Irrelevant, inapplicable, inapposite.
Relevant

Imperturbable, Composed, collected, serene, calm, cool, urbane, unruffled, even, tranquil, placid, impassive, un-disturbed, sedate, unmoved. **Excited**

Impervious, Impassable, impenetrable, impermeable. **Penetrable**

Impetuous, Hasty, precipitate, violent, sudden, passionate, impassioned, vehe-ment, eager, furious, hot, fierce, head-long, thoughtless. **Deliberate**

Impetus, Force, energy, momentum.

Impiety, Wickedness, sin, iniquity, un-godliness, profanity, irreverence.

Impinge, Strike, clash, hit, dash, im-fringe, encroach. **Avoid**

Impious, Profane, irreverent, irreligious, blasphemous, wicked, bad, unrighteous, unholy, sinful, iniquitous, ungodly.
Righteous

Implacable, Immovable, stern, unyield-ing, unbending, relentless, unrelenting, inexorable, pitiless, merciless, vindictive, harsh. **Lenient**

Implant, Plant, ingraft, sow, instil, infuse, infix. **Eradicate**

Implement, Appliance, tool, utensil, instrument.

Implicate, Involve, entangle, associate, connect, enfold, criminate. **Extricate**

Implicit, Tacit, implied, inferred, in-dicated, understood. **Expressed**
Firm, unwavering, unshaken, unhesi-tating, steadfast, constant, undoubting, unreserved. **Hesitating**

Implore, Beg, pray, beseech, entreat, supplicate, crave, adjure, petition, ask, solicit. **Demand**

Imply, Mean, hint, suggest, indicate, import, connote, insinuate, signify, pre-suppose. **Declare**

Impolite, Uncivil, rude, insolent, im-pertinent, impudent, unmannerly, un-gentlemanly, uncourteous, discourteous.
Civil

Impolitic, Unwise, indiscreet, inexpedi-ent, imprudent. **Wise**

Import, v.a., Imply, purport, betoken, signify, mean, denote.
Introduce, bring. **Export**
n., Purport, intention, meaning, significa-tion, sense, gist, drift, spirit, tenor, bearing. **Statement**
Moment, weight, importance, signifi-cance, consequence. **Triviality**

Importance, Import, moment, weight, significance, concern, pomposity, conse-quence.

Important, Momentous, weighty, signifi-cant, notable, valuable, considerable, urgent, influential, prominent, esteemed, consequential, serious, grave. **Trivial**

Importunate, Pressing, pertinacious, urgent, entreative, solicitous. **Diffident**

Importune, Press, urge, entreat, solicit, pester, crave. **Sacrifice**

Impose, Lay, inflict, place, put, set.
Remove
Charge, force, tax, enjoin, prescribe, dictate, appoint.

Imposing, Impressive, majestic, grand, fine, noble, stately, regal, striking, dignified, august, commanding, effective.
Insignificant

Imposition, Burden, charge, oppression, restraint, tax.
Imposture, trick, fraud, deception.

Impossible, Unfeasible, unthinkable, unattainable, unachievable, impracti-cable, absurd, inconceivable. **Likely**

Impost, Tax, levy, toll, rate, duty, excise, tribute, custom. **Revenue**

Impostor, Cheat, pretender, dissembler, rogue, deceiver, charlatan, mountebank, trickster, humbug, hypocrite. **Guide**

Imposture, Cheat, pretence, dissembling, deception, trick, fraud, wile, hoax, ruse, artifice. **Honesty**

Impotent, Incapable, feeble, disable, weak, helpless, powerless, incapacitated, infirm, inefficient, incompetent.
Powerful
Sterile, barren. **Potent**

Impound, Imprison, confine, cage. **Free**

Impoverish, Ruin, beggar, exhaust, drain, deplete. **Enrich**

Impracticable, Impossible, unthinkable, unattainable, unachievable. **Possible**

Imprecate, Curse, execrate, maledict, anathematize. **Bless**

Impregnable, Invincible, strong, un-assailable, invulnerable, secure. **Weak**

Impregnate, Saturate, fill, soak, dye, tinge, permeate.
Fructify, fertilize.

Impress, Imprint, stamp, fix, print. *Efface*

Impression, Imprinting, edition, stamping, printing, stamp, mark, impress, brand.
Notion, idea, recollection, remembrance, effect, influence, feeling, sensation.

Impressive, Imposing, striking, stirring, moving, affecting, powerful, touching. *Ridiculous*

Imprint, Print, impress, mark, stamp.

Imprison, Immure, incarcerate, confine, jail, commit. *Release*

Imprisonment, Durance, duress, incarceration, confinement, restraint, constraint. *Liberty*

Improbable, Unlikely, doubtful, uncertain, problematic. *Certain*

Improbity, Fraud, dishonesty, falseness, faithlessness, unfairness. *Honesty*

Impromptu, Extempore, extemporary, unrehearsed, improvised, unpremeditated, off-hand, unprepared. *Prepared*

Improper, Incorrect, false, inaccurate, wrong, inexact, erroneous. *Correct*
Indecent, unbecoming, unseemly, unfit, unsuitable, indecorous, indelicate. *Fit*

Improve, *v.n.*, Gain, mend, better, increase, rise. *Deteriorate*
v.a., Mend, better, amend, ameliorate, correct, rectify, use, cultivate. *Spoil*

Improvement, Amelioration, bettering, mending, amending, amendment, progress, advance, betterment. *Deterioration*

Improvident, Thriftless, wasteful, extravagant, prodigal, unthrifty, careless, heedless, unready, spendthrift, imprudent. *Thrifty*

Improvise, Invent, extemporize, impromptu.

Imprudent, Unwise, careless, heedless, rash, hasty, injudicious, indiscreet. *Wise*

Impudence, Sauciness, sauce, presumption, face, front, effrontery, boldness, audacity, insolence, shamelessness, rudeness, assurance. *Civility*

Impudent, Saucy, presumptuous, bold.† *Civil*

Impugn, Oppose, gainsay, contradict, deny, resist, attack, assail. *Support*

Impulse, Impetus, pull, push, thrust, momentum.
Influence, motive, inclination, instinct, proclivity, appetite, passion, incitement, feeling.

Impulsive, Hasty, quick, precipitate, impetuous, careless, rash, hot, heedless, passionate. *Deliberate*

Impure, Unclean, dirty, foul, smirched, sullied, stained, tarnished, defiled, filthy, polluted, adulterated, mixed. *Clean*
Immoral, unclean, unchaste, loose, gross, licentious, coarse, indecent. *Chaste*

Imputation, Accustom, charge, blame, reproach.

Impute, Charge, attribute, ascribe, refer, imply, insinuate. *Retract*

In, During, within, present, into.

Inability, Incompetence, incompetency, incapacity, impotence, incapability, disability. *Competence*

Inaccurate, Inexact, incorrect, faulty, wrong, false, improper, erroneous, mistaken. *Correct*

Inactive, Inert, indolent, inoperative, lazy, slothful, dilatory, idle, torpid, supine, sluggish, slack. *Diligent*

Inadequate, Imperfect, unsatisfactory, insufficient, lacking, faulty, defective, incomplete, disproportionate, unequal. *Sufficient*

Inadvertence, Oversight, blunder, error, slip, carelessness, inattention, negligence, heedlessness. *Attention*

Inadvertently, Accidentally, unintentionally, carelessly, negligently, thoughtlessly, heedlessly. *Purposely*

Inane, Fatuous, stupid, foolish, puerile, vain, worthless, trifling, frivolous, vapid, silly, senseless, empty, void. *Sensible*

Inanimate, Dead, lifeless, extinct, breathless, inert, dull, soulless. *Living*
Mineral, inorganic.

Inapplicable, Irrelevant, unsuitable, inapt, impertinent, unfit, inappropriate, inapposite. *Relevant*

Inapposite, Inapplicable, irrelevant, unsuitable.†

Inappreciable, Slight, little, minute, imperceptible, infinitesimal, small, trifling. *Considerable*

Inappropriate, Inapposite, unsuitable, unsuited, unadapted, inapt, unbecoming, unfit. *Proper*

Inapt, Inappropriate, inapposite, unsuitable.†
Dull, slow, clumsy, awkward, stupid, unapt. *Clever*

Inattention, Inadvertence, carelessness, negligence, neglect, heedlessness, disregard, thoughtlessness. *Care*

Inaudible, Low, still, mute, silent, noiseless, faint, muffled, indistinct. *Loud*

Inaugurate, Commence, begin, start, initiate, originate, induct, introduce, install, institute, invest. *Terminate*

Inauguration, Commencement, beginning, start.† *Termination*

Inauspicious, Unpromising, untoward,

ill-omened, unfortunate, ominous, bad, black, unlucky, unfavourable, unpropitious. *Favourable*

Inborn, Inbred, innate, congenital, inherent, immanent, ingrained, natural. *Acquired*

Incalculable, Great, immense, enormous, countless, unknown, inestimable, numberless, innumerable. *Minute*

Incantation, Magic, witchcraft, witchery, charm, conjuration, spell, invocation. *Exorcism*

Incapable, Incompetent, unqualified, weak, unable, unfitted, disqualified. *Qualified*

Incapacitate, Disqualify, weaken, unfit, disenable, cripple, disable. *Fit*

Incarcerate, Immure, confine, imprison, commit, jail. *Release*

Incase, Inclose, enclose, encase, enshrine, batten, board. *Expose*

Incautious, Imprudent, unwise, injudicious, impolitic, indiscreet, rash, headlong, precipitate, unwary, heedless, negligent, thoughtless, careless, reckless. *Careful*

Incendiary, Inflammatory, factious, dissentious, seditious, firebrand.

Incense, *v.a.*, Rouse, enrage, provoke, exasperate, excite, madden, enkindle, anger, irritate, inflame, gall. *Pacify*
n., Fragrance, perfume.
Applause, adulation, admiration.

Incentive, Inducement, encouragement, instigation, impulse, goad, cause, motive, stimulus, incitement, spur. *Deterrent*

Inception, Inauguration, beginning, start, commencement. *End*

Incessant, Unceasing, ceaseless, continual, unremitting, eternal, constant, everlasting, perpetual, uninterrupted. *Intermittent*

Inchoate, Initial, commencing, beginning, incipient, starting. *Finish*

Incident, Occurrence, event, happening, affair, episode, circumstance.

Incidental, Minor, concurrent, casual, concomitant, accidental, subordinate, occasional, adventitious. *Important*

Incipient, Inchoate, commencing, starting, beginning, rudimentary. *Ending*

Incision, Cut, gash, penetration.

Incisive, Sharp, cutting, biting, satirical, sarcastic, acute, trenchant, severe. *Mild*

Incite, Animate, rouse, stir, encourage, stimulate, foment, impel, spur, arouse, excite, goad, provoke, prompt. *Dissuade*

Incitement, Incentive, stimulus, motive, encouragement, impulse, spur, goad. *Deterrent*

Incivility, Impoliteness, rudeness, discourtesy, discourteousness, unmannerliness, disrespect. *Politeness*

Inclement, Severe, rough, rigorous, cruel, boisterous, stormy, harsh, tyrannical, unmerciful, vigorous. *Mild*

Inclination, Predisposition, disposition, bias, turn, twist, predilection, bent, propensity, aptitude, leaning, proclivity, tendency, liking, partiality. *Aversion*
Leaning, slope, slant, trending, verging. *Ascending*
Desire, taste, wish, fondness. *Distaste*
Nod, bow, obeisance.

Incline, *v.a.*, Predispose, dispose, bias, turn, bend.
v.n., Slope, tend, trend, bend, lean, slant, point.

Inclose, Enclose, encase, incase, pen, include, surround, encircle, envelop, wrap.

Include, Contain, embrace, comprehend, embody, comprise, hold. *Exclude*

Incognito, Disguised, unknown, concealed.

Incoherent, Disunited, unconnected, inconsistent, rambling, discursive, loose, confused, wild, detached, irrational, unintelligible. *Intelligible*

Income, Gains, proceeds, pay, revenue, profits, emolument, receipts, return. *Expenditure*

Incommensurate, Unequal, disproportionate, insufficient, inadequate. *Equal*

Incommode, Inconvenience, disturb, vex, trouble, annoy, molest. *Assist*

Incommodious, Awkward, inconvenient, unwieldy, cumbrous, cumbersome, unhandy. *Convenient*

Incomparable, Unique, inimitable, peerless, unequalled, unmatched, transcendent, surpassing, unrivalled. *Ordinary*

Incompatible, Irreconcilable, unsuitable, incongruous, unadapted, inconsistent, contradictory. *Consistent*

Incompetent, Incapable, unfit, unfitted, disqualified, powerless, unable, insufficient, inadequate. *Capable*

Incomplete, Imperfect, faulty, lacking, wanting, partial, unexecuted, deficient, defective, unfinished. *Perfect*

Incomprehensible, Unfathomable, mysterious, enigmatical, unimaginable, inconceivable, unintelligible, unthinkable. *Plain*

Inconceivable, Incomprehensible, unfathomable, mysterious.† *Comprehensible*
Unimaginable, vast, huge, enormous.

Inconclusive, Uncertain, indecisive, unconvincing.   *Decisive*

Incongruous, Incompatible, irreconcilable, inconsistent, contradictory, unfit, discrepant, unsuitable, grotesque, absurd.   *Consistent*

Inconsequent, Illogical, disconnected, desultory, loose, irrelevant, fragmentary.

Inconsiderable, Insignificant, small, unimportant, trivial, immaterial, minor, slight, petty, trifling.   *Important*

Inconsiderate, Unkind, thoughtless, unthoughtful, uncharitable.   *Thoughtful* Rash, precipitate, hasty, impetuous, thoughtless, heedless, careless, indiscreet, imprudent, headlong.   *Cautious*

Inconsistent, Incongruous, incompatible, irreconcilable, contradictory, discrepant.   *Congruous* Variable, inconstant, changeable, vacillating, wavering, unsteady, unstable, erratic.   *Constant*

Inconsolable, Forlorn, sad, disconsolate, hopeless, comfortless.   *Reconciled*

Inconstant, Variable, changeable, vacillating, wavering, unsteady, unstable, erratic, inconsistent, mutable, mercurial, volatile, unsettled, capricious, fickle, uncertain, fluctuating.   *Steady*

Incontestable, Certain, sure, indisputable, indubitable, unquestionable, incontrovertible, unassailable, undeniable.   *Doubtful*

Incontinent, Impure, unchaste, vicious, lewd, licentious, unrestrained, lascivious, lustful, debauched.   *Pure*

Incontrovertible, Incontestable, certain, sure, indisputable, indubitable, unquestionable, unassailable, undeniable.   *Doubtful*

Inconvenience, Trouble, annoyance, difficulty, vexation, awkwardness, disturbance, disadvantage.   *Ease* Incommodiousness, awkwardness, unwieldiness, cumbersomeness.   *Commodiousness*

Inconvenient, Troublesome, troublous, annoying.†   *Easy* Incommodious, awkward, unwieldy, cumbersome, unhandy.   *Commodious*

Incorporate, Consolidate, blend, mix, unite, combine, merge, embody.   *Sever*

Incorporeal, Disembodied, bodiless, immaterial, spiritual, supernatural.   *Material*

Incorrect, Wrong, erroneous, inexact, inaccurate, untrue, false, faulty, unsound, improper, unbecoming.   *True*

Incorrigible, Incurable, irreclaimable, hopeless, hardened, irremediable, remediless, irrecoverable, irretrievable, irreparable, reprobate, recreant, lost, obdurate.   *Remediable*

Incorruptible, Immortal, deathless, lasting, permanent, imperishable, everlasting, undying, indestructible, abiding.   *Perishable* Honest.

Increase, *v.a.,* Enlarge, extend, augment, intensify, greaten, enhance, aggravate.   *Decrease* *v.n.,* Grow, multiply, extend, accrue, advance, mount.   *Diminish* *n.,* Enlargement, extension, augmentation, expansion, growth, increment, addition. Gain, product, profit. Issue, offspring, progeny, descendants.

Incredible, Absurd, unbelievable, non sensical.

Incredulity, Unbelief, disbelief, mistrust, distrust, doubt, scepticism.   *Belief*

Increment, Increase, enlargement, extension, augmentation, expansion, growth, addition.   *Decrease*

Incriminate, Criminate, accuse, charge, impeach, involve, prejudice, inculpate, blame.   *Clear*

Incubus, Load, burden, encumbrance, drag, dog, hindrance.

Inculcate, Infuse, ingraft, instil, implant, impress.

Inculpable, Innocent, blameless, faultless, guiltless, sinless, unblameable, irreproachable.   *Guilty*

Inculpate, Blame, reproach, censure, accuse, criminate, incriminate, charge, impeach.   *Acquit*

Incumbent, *a.,* Resting, reclining, leaning. Binding, obligatory, devolvent.   *Optional* *n.,* Holder, occupant.

Incur, Acquire, gain, run, contract, meet.   *Elude*

Incurable, Irremediable, remediless, hopeless, irreparable, cureless, irrecoverable.   *Remediable*

Incursion, Raid, sally, encroachment, invasion, foray, inroad, descent.   *Retreat*

Incurvate, *v.a.,* Curve, bend, bow, crook.   *Straighten* *a.,* Curved, bent, bowed, hooked, angular, crooked.   *Straight*

Indebted, Owing, beholden, obliged.

Indecent, Improper, indelicate, unseemly, indecorous, obscene, coarse, foul, dirty, impure, gross, unchaste, filthy, offensive, lewd, outrageous.   *Pure*

Indecipherable, Undecipherable, illegible, unintelligible, unreadable, inexplicable. *Legible*

Indecision, Weakness, vacillation, fickleness, wavering, irresolution, hesitation, changeableness. *Resolution*

Indecisive, Inconclusive, uncertain, unconvincing, unsettled, wavering, hesitating, undecided, dubious, irresolute. *Conclusive*

Indecorous, Improper, indecent, unbecoming, rude, unseemly, impolite. *Seemly*

Indeed, Really, truly, certainly, verily, absolutely, actually, strictly, veritably, positively.

Indefatigable, Persistent, assiduous, unwearied, tireless, persevering, sedulous, unflagging, untiring, indomitable, unremitting. *Indolent*

Indefeasible, Immutable, unalterable, irreversible, irrevocable. *Mutable*

Indefensible, Inexcusable, untenable, unwarrantable, unjustifiable, unsound, wrong, faulty. *Justifiable*

Indefinite, Vague, undefined, indecisive, nondescript, general, obscure, confused, uncertain, indeterminate, undetermined, unfixed, unsettled, loose, indistinct, ambiguous, doubtful. *Certain*

Indelible, Indefeasible, ingrained, indestructible, ineffaceable, fast, fixed, permanent. *Transient*

Indelicate, Indecent, coarse, indecorous, unseemly, broad, unbecoming, improper, rude, lewd, unchaste, immodest, gross, obscene, low, vulgar, filthy. *Refined*

Indemnify, Requite, satisfy, compensate, reimburse, repay, remunerate, repair, secure, guarantee, pay. *Fine*

Indentation, Dent, notch, jab, bruise, depression, hollow.

Independence, Liberty, autonomy, freedom, separation, distinctness, competence, ease. *Subjection*

Independent, Autonomous, free, unrestrained, unfettered, self-governing, self-directing, unrestricted. *Subject*

Indescribable, Unutterable, wonderful, ineffable, inexpressible. *Ordinary*

Indestructible, Everlasting, incorruptible, imperishable, enduring, lasting, abiding, endless, permanent. *Perishable*

Indeterminate, Vague, indefinite,† undefined, obscure, confused, uncertain, undetermined, unfixed, unsettled. *Definite*

Index, Pointer, forefinger, hand, director, exponent.

Indicate, Denote, mark, show, evince, specify, declare, manifest, designate, betray, betoken, till, register, exhibit. *Conceal*

Suggest, intimate, hint, imply.

Indication, Mark, token, sign, suggestion, symbol, hint, symptom, proof, evidence, demonstration. *Surmise*

Indictment, Assignment, impeachment, charge, accusation, crimination, prosecution. *Acquittal*

Indifference, Apathy, coolness, unconcern, unconcernedness, coldness, inattention, carelessness, heedlessness, negligence. *Ardour*
Impartiality, neutrality, disinterestedness. *Bias*
Insignificance, triviality, unimportance. *Importance*

Indifferent, Apathetic, cool, unconcerned.† *Ardent*
Impartial, disinterested, neutral, unbiassed. *Biassed*
Mediocre, ordinary, passable, tolerable, middling. *Important*

Indigenous, Native, inherent, aboriginal, home-grown. *Exotic*

Indigent, Poor, needy, necessitous, insolvent, penniless, impecunious, reduced, straitened, destitute, distressed, pinched. *Rich*

Indignant, Irate, ireful, wroth, wrathful, angry, furious, annoyed, provoked, exasperated, incensed. *Gratified*

Indignity, Slight, insult, affront, outrage, reproach, obloquy, abuse, disrespect. *Respect*

Indirect, Roundabout, tortuous, oblique, circuitous, devious, collateral. *Straight*

Indiscernible, Invisible, imperceptible, slight, indistinguishable. *Visible*

Indiscreet, Unwise, imprudent, reckless, rash, incautious, headlong, precipitate, injudicious, inconsiderate, heedless, foolish. *Wise*

Indiscretion, Folly, rashness, mistake, blunder, imprudence. *Caution*

Indiscriminate, Mixed, assorted, confused, medley, promiscuous, miscellaneous, mingled. *Select*

Indispensable, Essential, vital, necessary, needed, needful, requisite. *Unnecessary*

Indisposed, Unwell, ill, sick, ailing. *Well*
Unwilling, loath, disinclined, averse, reluctant. *Eager*

Indisputable, Undeniable, unquestionable, incontrovertible, incontestable, certain, sure. *Doubtful*

Indissoluble, Indestructible, lasting,

imperishable, incorruptible, everlasting, permanent, abiding, enduring. ***Transient***
Inviolable, inseparable.

Indistinct, Dim, doubtful, hazy, obscure, faint, confused, blurred, vague, indefinite, ambiguous, undefined, uncertain, indistinguishable. ***Clear***

Indistinguishable, Indistinct, dim, doubtful.† ***Conspicuous***

Indite, Write, dictate, compose, prompt, pen, word.

Individual, *n.*, Person, being, character, personage, someone, somebody, body, head.

a., Independent, separate, particular, unique, special, marked, peculiar, single, singular, personal, proper. ***General***

Indivisible, Indissoluble, inseparable, ultimate. ***Separable***
Decided, definite, positive.

Indocile, Perverse, stubborn, intractable, ungovernable, froward, untamable, obstinate, unteachable, refractory, unruly, unmanageable, headstrong. ***Amenable***

Indoctrinate, Instruct, teach, imbue, initiate. ***Mislead***

Indolent, Idle, inert, inactive, slothful, lazy, sluggish. ***Diligent***

Indomitable, Invincible, unconquerable, unyielding, irrepressible. ***Feeble***

Indorse, Countersign, superscribe, support, approve, ratify, sanction, confirm. ***Cancel***

Indubitable, Indisputable, unquestionable, incontestable, undeniable, certain, sure, incontrovertible. ***Doubtful***

Induce, Persuade, urge, encourage, impel, incite, influence, spur, move, actuate, prompt. ***Deter***
Effect, cause, produce, lead, motivate.

Inducement, Incentive, encouragement, spur, impulse, incitement, influence, reason, motive, stimulus, cause, consideration. ***Deterrent***

Induct, Install, introduce, inaugurate, initiate. ***Expel***

Indue, Assume, endow, supply, clothe, invest. ***Divert***

Indulge, Pamper, humour, satisfy, gratify, allow, suffer, permit. ***Discipline***

Indulgent, Gentle, lenient, moderate, lax, kind, forbearing, clement, tender, tolerant, compliant, yielding, soft. ***Harsh***

Indurate, Harden, strengthen, inure, sear, consolidate. ***Melt***

Industrious, Assiduous, sedulous, busy, laborious, active, diligent, persevering. ***Lazy***

Industry, Assiduity, assiduousness, toil, labour, sedulousness, activity, diligence, perseverance, work, efforts, persistence. ***Idleness***

Inebriation, Inebriety, insobriety, intemperance, drunkenness, intoxication. ***Sobriety***

Ineffable, Indescribable, unutterable, unspeakable, inexpressible, wonderful. ***Commonplace***

Ineffaceable, Indelible, indestructible, ingrained.

Ineffectual, Useless, unavailing, bootless, fruitless, abortive, weak, inefficient, inefficacious, ineffective, powerless, impotent, feeble, futile. ***Efficacious***

Inefficacious, Ineffectual, useless, unavailing.† ***Effectual***

Inefficient, Incapable, weak, feeble, ineffectual. ***Efficient***

Inelegant, Unrefined, coarse, unpolished, uncourtly, rude, uncouth, plain, homely, ungraceful, ungainly, stiff, awkward, clumsy, crude. ***Polished***

Ineligible, Unqualified, disqualified, undesirable, inexpedient, objectionable. ***Qualified***

Inept, Foolish, inane, stupid, senseless, nonsensical, pointless, silly. ***Sane***
Unapt, inapposite, unsuitable, unbecoming, improper, inappropriate, unfit. ***Apt***
Worthless, futile, useless, null, void. ***Useful***

Inequality, Diversity, unevenness, disparity, roughness, irregularity, difference. ***Similarity***

Inequitable, Unfair, unjust. ***Just***

Inert, Indolent, slack, lazy, slothful, sluggish, inactive, torpid, dull, heavy, idle. ***Brisk***

Inertia, Indolence, slackness, laziness.† ***Activity***

Inestimable, Valuable, precious, invaluable, priceless. ***Worthless***

Inevitable, Unavoidable, necessary, sure, certain. ***Uncertain***

Inexact, Inaccurate, incorrect, faulty, crude, careless, loose. ***True***

Inexactitude, Falsehood, lie. ***Truth***

Inexcusable, Unjustifiable, indefensible, unwarrantable, inadmissible, unpardonable. ***Justifiable***

Inexhaustible, Unfailing, perennial, boundless, unlimited, indefatigable, exhaustless. ***Limited***

Inexorable, Inflexible, unbending, unyielding, harsh, unrelenting, relentless, cruel, merciless, implacable, immovable, firm. ***Indulgent***

Inexpedient, Imprudent, injudicious,

indiscreet, disadvantageous, unwise, unadvisable. *Profitable*

Inexperienced, Fresh, new, raw, unversed, unschooled, untrained, unpractised, unskilled, inconversant, ignorant, unfamiliar. *Expert*

Inexpiable, Unpardonable, irremissible, inexorable, unatonable. *Pardonable*

Inexplicable, Incomprehensible, enigmatical, mysterious, unaccountable, strange. *Obvious*

Inexpressible, Indescribable, unutterable, ineffable, wonderful, unspeakable, infinite, surpassing, boundless.
Commonplace

Inextricable, Involved, entangled, perplexed, intricate. *Simple*

Infallible, Sure, certain, dependable, reliable, unfailing, unerring. *Uncertain*

Infamous, Nefarious, shameful, disgraceful, disreputable, dishonourable, base, low, wicked, outrageous, vile, heinous, dark, scandalous, detestable, odious, bad, atrocious, ignominious.
Glorious

Infamy, Shame, disgrace, disrepute,† obloquy, opprobrium, discredit. *Honour*

Infant, Baby, babe, child, youngster, suckling, nursling. *Adult* Minor.

Infantile, Babyish, childish, puerile, weak, puny, infantine. *Mature*

Infatuation, Stupefaction, folly, madness, foolishness, fatuity. *Wisdom*

Infeasible, Impracticable, impossible, unfeasible. *Practicable*

Infect, Corrupt, contaminate, defile, taint, vitiate, pollute, befoul, poison. *Purify*

Infection, Corruption, contamination, contagion, taint, pollution, defilement, poison, virus, germ. *Antidote*

Infectious, Corrupting, contaminating, contagious,† catching, sympathetic.

Infecund, Sterile, unfruitful, unproductive, barren, infertile, unprolific.
Fruitful

Infelicitous, Unfortunate, inauspicious, calamitous, wretched, unhappy, miserable. *Happy* Unfitting, unapt, inappropriate.

Infer, Gather, conclude, deduce, argue, reason, draw, derive, glean, guess, presume, surmise.

Inference, Conclusion, deduction, argument, corollary, consequence, surmise.

Inferior, Lower, subordinate, minor, junior, secondary, mediocre, poor, indifferent, lesser, bad, mean, deficient, imperfect. *Superior*

Infernal, Demoniacal, devilish, diabolical, damnable, satanic, fiendish, accursed, abominable. *Angelic*

Infertile, Infecund, sterile, unfruitful, unproductive, barren, unprolific, poor.
Fruitful

Infest, Overrun, throng, beset. *Withdraw* Pester, harass, plague, annoy, disturb, torment, vex, worry, tease, molest, trouble. *Gratify*

Infidelity, Disloyalty, faithlessness, unfaithfulness, perfidy, unbelief, scepticism, treachery, adultery. *Loyalty*

Infinite, Limitless, illimitable, unbounded, boundless, stupendous, great, vast, immense, enormous, wide, unlimited, interminable, immeasurable, absolute, eternal. *Limited*

Infinitesimal, Minute, inconspicuous, small, inappreciable, microscopic. *Vast*

Infirm, Feeble, frail, weak, decrepit, debilitated, faltering, irresolute, wavering, vacillating, unstable, unsound, insecure. *Strong*

Infirmity, Feebleness, frailty, frailness, weakness, debility, failing, defect.
Strength

Infix, Implant, ingraft, fix, plant, set, place, fasten, infuse, instil. *Eradicate*

Inflame, Kindle, fan, rouse, incense, infuriate, excite, madden, stimulate, fire, animate, arouse, enrage, provoke, nettle, exasperate, irritate. *Pacify*

Inflammable, Combustible, ignitible, excitable.

Inflammation, Heat, burning, conflagration, violence, rage, anger, excitement.

Inflate, Expand, swell, distend, blow, bloat, increase, enlarge. *Compress*

Inflated, Swollen, distended, bloated, enlarged, magnified, turgid, pompous, bombastic, grandiloquent, magniloquent, declamatory, tumid. *Simple*

Inflect, Curve, incurvate, bend, bow, decline, conjugate. *Straighten*

Inflection, Curve, curvity, curvature, bend, bending, flexure, crook. Variation, accidence, comparison, declension, conjugation, modulation.

Inflexible, Stubborn, resolute, obstinate, firm, pertinacious, hard, obdurate, unyielding, steadfast, inexorable, immovable, rigid, stiff, persevering, dogged, intractable, refractory. *Ductile*

Inflict, Impose, bring, lay, judge, punish, put. *Spare*

Inflorescent, Blooming, flowering, blossoming.

Influence, *v.a.*, Persuade, urge, move, impel, incite, instigate, lead, direct, control, modify, sway.

Influence, *n.*, Control, sway, power, spell, authority, effect, reputation, credit, magnetism.

Influential, Forcible, powerful, persuading, potent, guiding, controlling. *Weak*

Inform, Enlighten, instruct, apprize, notify, tell, acquaint, advise. *Mystify*

Informal, Unconventional, free, easy, unceremonious, simple, familiar, natural, irregular. *Ceremonious*

Informant, Informer, accuser, complainant, adviser, advertiser.

Information, Knowledge, intelligence, advice, notice, facts, warning, word, message, instruction.
Denunciation, accusation, complaint, charge.

Infraction, Violation, breach, breaking, infringement. *Observance*

Infrequent, Rare, unusual, uncommon. *Plentiful*

Infringe, Violate, break, transgress, disobey, trespass, intrude. *Observe*

Infringement, Violation, breach, breaking, infraction, transgression. *Observance*

Infuriated, Furious, angry, wrathful, wroth, enraged, annoyed, wild, mad, incensed, raging, provoked. *Calm*

Infuse, Ingraft, inculcate, instil, introduce, inspire, plant, implant, steep, soak. *Eradicate*

Infusion, Inculcation, instillation, introduction.† *Eradication*

Ingenious, Ready, clever, gifted, prompt, smart, bright, adroit, shrewd, talented, inventive, adept, able. *Awkward*

Ingenuity, Ingeniousness, readiness, skill, cleverness,† aptness, aptitude, capability, acuteness. *Awkwardness*

Ingenuous, Artless, simple, honest, open, frank, naïve, straightforward, sincere, truthful. *Cunning*

Ingenuousness, Artlessness, simplicity, honesty.†

Inglorious, Infamous, ignominious, disgraceful, shameful, scandalous, humiliating, despicable, base, mean, low, vile. *Splendid*
Unknown, unhonoured, unrenowned, obscure, humble, lowly, unnoted, unmarked. *Renowned*

Ingraft, Fix, infix, plant, implant, inculcate, infuse, instil, graft. *Eradicate*

Ingrain, Impregnate, imbue.

Ingredient, Constituent, component, part, particle, element.

Ingress, Entrance, entry, entre. *Exit*

Inhabit, *v.n.*, Dwell, abide, live, sojourn, reside.

Inhabit, *v.a.*, Occupy, tenant, people.

Inhabitant, Dweller, resident, occupant, occupier, tenant, citizen, denizen, native, inmate. *Visitor*

Inharmonious, Unmusical, clashing, jarring, grating, discordant, unharmonious, inharmonic. *Musical*

Inherent, Natural, native, innate, immanent, inborn, inbred, congenital, ingrained. *Extraneous*

Inheritance, Heritage, legacy, bequest, patrimony.

Inhibit, Forbid, restrain, prohibit, bar, debar, interdict, ban, stop, check, obstruct, repress, prevent, hinder. *Encourage*

Inhibition, Restraint, prohibition, bar,† embargo. *Encouragement*

Inhospitable, Unkind, unfriendly, cool, illiberal, mean, prejudiced, intolerant, narrow, ungenerous. *Friendly*
Barren, wild.

Inhuman, Fell, ruthless, cruel, heartless, savage, barbarous, pitiless, unfeeling, harsh, merciless, severe, remorseless, ferocious, brutal, hardhearted. *Merciful*

Inhume, Inter, bury, entomb, sepulchre. *Exhume*

Inimical, Antagonistic, hostile, contrary, adverse, harmful, repugnant, unfriendly, unfavourable, opposed. *Friendly*

Inimitable, Unique, peerless, incomparable, matchless, unmatched, unequalled, unrivalled, unexampled, unparalleled, transcendent. *Ordinary*

Iniquity, Sin, crime, wickedness, vice, sinfulness, wrong, misdeed, offence, unrighteousness. *Virtue*

Initial, First, early, beginning, starting, commencing, primal, primary, introductory, opening, original. *Final*

Initiate, Begin, start, commence, introduce, inaugurate, open. *Close*
Teach, instruct, induct, prime, ground.

Injudicious, Imprudent, unwise, rash, hasty, unwise, foolish, precipitate, indiscreet, incautious. *Wise*

Injunction, Order, behest, command, enjoinder, mandate, precept, bidding.

Injure, Abuse, hurt, harm, damage, maltreat, mar, spoil, disfigure, impair. *Benefit*

Injurious, Hurtful, harmful, damaging, noxious, iniquitous, detrimental, deleterious, pernicious, evil, destructive, disadvantageous, baleful, baneful, mischievous. *Beneficial*

Injury, Wrong, damage, hurt, harm, injustice, evil, ill, detriment, mischief, loss, prejudice. *Reparation*

Injustice, Unfairness, grievance, wrong. *Justice*

Inkling, Intimation, suggestion, hint, whisper, innuendo.

Inland, Internal, interior, home, civil, domestic. *Foreign*

Inlet, Ingress, opening, passage, entrance, gap, bay, bight, creek, arm, cove. *Outlet*

Inmate, Inhabitant, resident, dweller, occupant, guest, denizen. *Outsider*

Inmost, Innermost, secret, deepest. *Outermost*

Inn, Public-house, tavern, hotel, hostelry.

Innate, Inherent, inborn, inbred, ingrained, natural, congenital, native. *Extraneous*

Inner, Interior, inward, internal. *Outer*

Innermost, Inmost, secret, deepest, close. *Outermost*

Innocent, Guiltless, guileless, clear, sinless, upright, unspotted, spotless, unfallen, pure, unstained, clean, blameless, harmless, faultless, innocuous, innoxious, inoffensive. *Guilty*

Innocuous, Innocent, wholesome, harmless, inoffensive, innoxious. *Deleterious*

Innovation, Novelty, alteration, change. *Archaism*

Innoxious, Innocuous, innocent, harmless, inoffensive. *Deleterious*

Innuendo, Allusion, suggestion, insinuation, hint, inkling.

Inoculate, Infect, vaccinate.

Inoffensive, Innoxious, innocuous, innocent, harmless, unoffending. *Noxious*

Inoperative, Ineffectual, inefficient, inefficacious, inactive. *Potent*

Inopportune, Untimely, inconvenient, unseasonable. *Timely*

Inordinate, Excessive, exorbitant, extravagant, disproportionate, immoderate. *Moderate*

Inorganic, Inanimate, unorganized, mineral. *Organic*

Inquietude, Disquiet, disquietude, uneasiness, anxiety, restlessness. *Easiness*

Inquire, Ask, question, investigate, interrogate.

Inquiry, Question, query, investigation, interrogation, examination, scrutiny, exploration, research, study, search. *Guess*

Inquisitive, Prying, curious, inquiring, meddlesome. *Indifferent*

Inroad, Incursion, invasion, foray, raid, irruption, encroachment. *Retreat*

Insalubrious, Unhealthy, unwholesome, noxious. *Healthy*

Insane, Mad, demented, crazy, crazed, deranged, lunatic, delirious, distracted. *Sensible*

Insanity, Madness, dementia, craziness,† aberration, lunacy, mania.

Insatiable, Rapacious, voracious, greedy, ravenous, omnivorous, unappeasable, insatiate. *Moderate*

Inscribe, Write, print, imprint, engrave, letter, label, cut, carve, impress. *Erase* Dedicate, address.

Inscrutable, Mysterious, incomprehensible, unfathomable, undiscoverable, impenetrable, hidden, inexplicable. *Obvious*

Insecure, Uncertain, unsure, unsafe, risky, perilous, dangerous, hazardous, exposed, unprotected. *Safe* Unstable, weak, shaking, infirm, tottering. *Steady*

Insensate, Insensible, indifferent, blind, unperceiving, inanimate, dull, stupid, torpid, apathetic, unconscious, unsusceptible. *Sensitive*

Insensible, Insensate, indifferent, blind.†

Inseparable, Indissoluble, indivisible.

Insert, Inject, interpolate, introduce, infix. *Extract*

Inside, *a.,* Internal, interior, inner. *Exterior* *prep.,* Within, internally. *Without*

Insidious, Crafty, artful, cunning, deceptive, sly, wily, subtle, tricky, secret, treacherous, designing, guileful. *Straightforward*

Insight, Penetration, perception, understanding, discernment.

Insignificant, Trivial, minor, petty, small, unimportant, trifling, immaterial, paltry. *Important*

Insincere, Hollow, perfidious, false, untrue, dishonest, faithless, deceitful, dissembling, empty, disingenuous, hypocritical. *Honest*

Insinuate, Intimate, hint, suggest. Ingratiate, worm, introduce, insert, infuse, instil, inculcate. *Retract*

Insinuation, Intimation, hint, suggestion, allusion, innuendo. Ingratiating, introduction, insertion, infusion, instillation, inculcation.

Insipid, Vapid, flat, tasteless, flavourless, savourless, stale, uninteresting, dull, tedious, heavy, tame, prosy, spiritless, characterless, prosaic. *Engaging*

Insist, Demand, maintain, stand, contend, urge. *Waive*

Insobriety, Drunkenness, intoxication, inebriety, ebriety, intemperance. *Sobriety*

Insolence, Rudeness, sauciness, contumacy, impertinence, pertness, malapertness, impudence, contumely, frowardness, arrogance.   *Deference*

Insolent, Rude, insulting, contumacious,† domineering, overbearing, disrespectful, contemptuous, saucy, pert.   *Deferential*

Insolvent, Bankrupt, penniless, ruined, failed, broken, beggared.   *Rich*

Inspect, Investigate, scrutinize, examine, overhaul, search, supervise, oversee, superintend.

Inspection, Investigation, scrutiny, examination, search, supervision, oversight, superintendence.

Inspector, Censor, critic, visitor,†

Inspiration, Exaltation, elevation, enthusiasm, frenzy.   *Depression*
Inhalation.

Inspire, Inspirit, enliven, cheer, encourage, animate, inflame, imbue, elevate, exalt, cheer.   *Depress*
Inhale.
Instil, infuse.

Inspirit, Inspire, enliven, cheer,† hearten, enhearten, invigorate.

Install, Induct, introduce, inaugurate, institute, invest, place, establish.   *Eject*

Installation, Induction, introduction.†   *Ejection*

Instalment, Portion, part, earnest.   *Whole*

Instance, *v.a.,* Specify, mention, quote, cite.
n., Case, example, illustration, exemplification.
Entreaty, request, solicitation, persuasion, prompting, incitement, instigation, urgency, impulse.

Instant, *a.,* Urgent, pressing, earnest, importunate.
Present, current.
Instantaneous, prompt, quick, immediate.   *Slow*
n., Second, moment, minute, twinkling, trice, flash.

Instantaneous, Instant, immediate, quick, prompt, sudden, abrupt.

Instantly ⎫ Forthwith, immedi-
Instantaneously ⎬ ately, now.
Instanter ⎭   *Presently*

Instauration, Renovation, rehabitation, restoration, reconstruction, reparation, renewal, reconstitution, reinstatement, re-establishment.

Instead, In lieu, rather.

Instigate, Persuade, incite, encourage, urge, move, impel, influence, prompt, rouse, spur, provoke, goad, actuate, stimulate.   *Deter*

Instigation, Persuasion, incitement, encouragement, impulse, influence, prompting, instance, solicitation.

Instil, Ingraft, implant, plant, fix, inculcate, insinuate, infuse, introduce, impress.   *Eradicate*

Instinct, Intuition, tendency, prompting, impulse, proclivity, inclination.   *Reason*

Instinctive, Impulsive, intuitive, spontaneous, natural, unreflecting.   *Reasoning*

Institute, *v.a.,* Found, appoint, establish, commence, originate, initiate, begin, erect, settle, fix, enact, pass, establish.   *Subvert*
n., Institution, school, college, seminary, academy.
Dogma, doctrine, maxim, principle, precept.

Institution, Founding, appointment, establishing.†
Institute, school, college, seminary, academy.

Instruct, Educate, inform, teach, enlighten, lead, edify, indoctrinate, school.   *Deceive*
Command, bid, order, enjoin, direct, apprise.

Instruction, Education, information, teaching,† tuition.   *Deception*
Command, behest, order, direction, mandate.

Instructor, Master, tutor, pedagogue, teacher, preceptor.   *Pupil*

Instrument, Utensil, tool, implement, device, appliance, apparatus, contrivance, means, medium, agent.
Document, writing, deed, charter, indenture.

Instrumental, Helpful, helping, serviceable, useful, conducive, assisting, subservient, auxiliary, subsidiary, ancillary.

Instrumentality, Agency, means, intervention, medium, mediation.

Insubordinate, Recalcitrant, unruly, refractory, disobedient, ungovernable, undutiful, riotous, rebellious, mutinous, seditious, turbulent.   *Obedient*

Insubordination, Recalcitrance, unruliness, disobedience,† insurrection, indiscipline, laxity, revolt.   *Obedience*

Insufferable, Unbearable, intolerable, unendurable, unpermissible, unallowable, disgusting, outrageous, detestable.   *Tolerable*

Insufficient, Deficient, lacking, inadequate, scanty, unsuited, unfitted, incapable, incompetent.   *Plenty*

Insular, Narrow, limited, restricted, contracted, petty, isolated, remote.

Insulate, Isolate, detach, sever, disconnect, separate, disunite, part.

Insult, *v.a.*, Abuse, mock, affront, ridicule, offend. ***Respect***
n., Abuse, mockery, affront, ridicule, offence, contumely, indignity, outrage, insolence.

Insuperable, Insurmountable, unsurpassable, impassable.

Insurance, Guarantee, assurance, security, providence. ***Jeopardy***

Insure, *v.a.*, Assure, secure, guarantee, provide, warrant. ***Imperil***
v.n., Underwrite.

Insurgent, *n.*, Rebel, rioter, mutineer, revolter.
a., Rebellious, riotous, mutinous, revolting, disobedient, seditious, insubordinate. ***Obedient***

Insurmountable, Insuperable, unsurpassable, impassable.

Insurrection, Rebellion, riot, mutiny, revolt, sedition, insubordination, rising, uprising, anarchy, tumult. ***Subjection***

Insusceptible, Unfeeling, insensible, indifferent, unimpressible, impassable. ***Sensible***

Intact, Whole, inviolate, unbroken, entire, unhurt, complete, sound, integral, untouched, unharmed, uninjured, scatheless, unimpaired. ***Broken***

Intangible, Impalpable, vague, shadowy, indefinite, dim, imperceptible, phantom. ***Definite***

Integral, Whole, total, entire, complete. ***Partial***

Integrity, Honesty, uprightness, virtue, rectitude, probity, conscientiousness, honour, purity, goodness, principle. ***Duplicity***

Intellect, Brains, understanding, mind, sense, intelligence, reason.

Intellectual, Mental, thoughtful, imaginative, reasoning.

Intelligence, News, knowledge, advice, notification, notice, instruction, information, tidings.
Understanding, discernment, acumen, brightness, sharpness, apprehension, comprehension, quickness, penetration. ***Dulness***

Intelligent, Discerning, acute, bright, sharp, quick, astute, alert, shrewd, clever. ***Dull***
Instructed, enlightened.

Intelligible, Comprehensible, plain, clear, distinct. ***Inscrutable***

Intemperate, Excessive, immoderate, inordinate, extravagant, extreme, uncontrolled, intoxicated. ***Moderate***

Intend, Purpose, design, contemplate, mean.

Intense, Great, extreme, concentrated, acute, deep, grievous.
Powerful, vigorous, strong, forcible, active, ardent, earnest, vehement, energetic. ***Mild***
Close, strained, intent, severe, strict.

Intensify, Quicken, strengthen, deepen. ***Moderate***

Intensity, Violence, force, power, vigour, strength, activity, ardour, vehemence, energy, earnestness, greatness, extremity, concentration, tension, eagerness. ***Debility***

Intent, *a.*, Set, bent, eager, fixed, earnest, close, attentive. ***Indifferent***
n., Purpose, design, contemplation, aim, meaning, object, end, intention, import, plan, scope.

Intention, Intent, purpose, design.†

Intentional, Intended, premeditated, designed, arranged, contemplated, wilful, deliberate, voluntary, studied. ***Accidental***

Inter, Inhume, bury, entomb, sepulchre. ***Exhume***

Intercede, Plead, interpose, interfere, intervene, mediate, advocate, arbitrate. ***Accuse***

Intercept, Interrupt, stop, catch, arrest, halt, seize, obstruct. ***Despatch***

Intercession, Pleading, interposition, interference, mediation, advocacy, arbitration, intervention, prayer, entreaty. ***Accustom***

Interchange, Alternate, vary, exchange, barter, swap, reciprocate. ***Intercept***

Intercourse, Communion, converse, communication, connection, dealings.

Interdict, Prohibit, ban, forbid, bar, proscribe, inhibit, disallow. ***Allow***

Interest, *v.a.*, Attract, engage, enlist, absorb, hold, occupy. ***Bore***
Touch, affect, concern.
n., Profit, advantage, gain, benefit, weal, good, share, part, stake, portion, premium, discount, profit. ***Loss***
Attention, regard, concern, curiosity, sympathy. ***Indifference***

Interested, Intrigued, engaged, attracted, concerned, attentive, occupied. ***Indifferent***
Partial, prejudiced, biassed, selfish. ***Impartial***

Interesting, Intriguing, engaging, attractive, entertaining, pleasing. ***Boring***

Interfere, Interpose, intervene, meddle, intermeddle, clash, conflict, oppose.

Interim, Interval, meantime.

Interior, Inner, inward, inside, internal. *Outside*
Inland, up-country, remote.

Interject, Insert, interpose, comment, exclaim.

Interlace, Interweave, inweave, cross, twine, intwine, intertwine, reticulate. *Unravel*

Interlock, Join, connect, lock, interchain.

Interlocution, Conversation, conference, colloquy, dialogue.

Interlope, Interfere, meddle, intermeddle, intrude.

Interloper, Meddler, intruder. *Member*

Intermeddle, Interlope, interfere.†

Intermediate, Interposed, interjacent, intervening, middle, transitional.

Interminable, Endless, unending, perpetual, infinite, protracted, long, limitless, unlimited, illimitable, unbounded, boundless, ceaseless, eternal. *Brief*

Intermingle, Mix, intermix, commix, mingle, commingle, blend. *Separate*

Intermission, Pause, stop, stoppage, interval, gap, rest, suspense, suspension, respite, interruption, remission, break, hiatus. *Continuity*

Intermittent, Spasmodic, broken, discontinuous, periodic, recurrent. *Smooth*

Intermix, Intermingle, mingle, commingle, blend, mix, commix. *Separate*

Internal, Inner, interior, inward, inside, intestine. *Outside*
Domestic, civil, home. *Foreign*

Internecine, Deadly, exterminating, destructive, mortal, sanguinary. *Bloodless*

Interpolate, Introduce, insert, add, interpose. *Expunge*

Interpose, Intrude, meddle, interfere, intermeddle, interpolate, intercede, arbitrate, mediate. *Retract*

Interpret, Expound, elucidate, explain, translate, define, unravel, decode, unfold, construe, render, decipher. *Distort*

Interpretation, Exposition, elucidation, explanation,† version, construction. *Distortion*

Interrogate, Question, ask, examine, inquire, catechise.

Interrupt, Stop, disturb, disconnect, break, disunite, hinder, divide, sever, dissever, cut, separate, disjoin, discontinue, suspend, intermit. *Continue*

Interruption, Stoppage, disturbance, disconnection.† *Continuance*

Intersect, Divide, cut, cross, interrupt.

Intersperse, Scatter, mix, interlard. *Expunge*

Interstice, Gap, hole, crevice, cranny,

cleft, rift, opening, chink, fissure, crack, interval. *Seam*

Intertwine, Interweave, interlace, intertwist, cross, reticulate, inweave, intwine. *Unravel*

Interval, Gap, interstice, interspace, space. *Continuity*
Period, time, moment, term, interregnum, spell, pause, recess, interlude, interim, season.

Intervene, Interfere, interpose, intrude, intercede, mediate, happen, befall, occur.

Interview, Consultation, meeting, conference, parley.

Interweave, Inweave, interlace, intertwine, intwine, cross, reticulate. *Unravel*

Intestine, Interior, internal, civil, home, domestic. *External*

Intimate, *n.*, Friend, confidant, crony.
a., Friendly, familiar, close, dear, near, special, confidential, bosom. *Distant*
v.a., Hint, tell, announce, declare, impart, insinuate, communicate, suggest, indicate. *Conceal*

Intimation, Hint, insinuation, suggestion, allusion, innuendo.

Intimidate, Dismay, frighten, affright, cow, terrify, scarce, alarm, appal, daunt, deter. *Encourage*

Intolerable, Unbearable, insufferable, unendurable. *Endurable*

Intolerant, Narrow, narrow-minded, bigoted, dictatorial, overbearing, imperious, tyrannical. *Liberal*

Intonation, Modulation, tone, cadence, accentuation, melody, resonance.

Intoxicated, Drunken, drunk, inebriated, muddled, fuddled. *Sober*

Intoxication, Drunkenness, inebriety, insobriety, inebriation. *Sobriety*

Intractable, Refractory, stolid, stubborn, perverse, indocile, obstinate, ungovernable, unmanageable, unyielding, unruly, froward, obdurate, stiff, inflexible, contumacious, headstrong, wilful, dogged. *Docile*

Intrenchment, Trench, ditch, dyke, fortification, defence, barrier, shield, protection, shelter, moat.
Invasion, infringement, encroachment, trespass, inroad. *Deference*

Intrepid, Brave, fearless, dauntless, undaunted, heroic, courageous, bold, daring, valiant, valorous, undismayed, doughty, gallant. *Timid*

Intricate, Involved, difficult, complicated, mazy, obscure, perplexed, entangled, tortuous, labyrinthine, complex. *Simple*

Intrigue, Conspiracy, machination, plot, scheme, cabal, manœuvre, ruse, artifice, design, stratagem, wile.   *Openness*

Intriguing, Scheming, wily, artful, crafty, subtle, deceitful, dishonest, cunning, tricky, insidious, crooked, designing, sly.   *Honest*

Intrinsic, Natural, inherent, inborn, inbred, inward, internal, innate, native, ingrained, immanent.   *Acquired*
Genuine, real, true.

Introduce, Conduct, bring, present, lead, induct, import, insert, inject.
Begin, initiate, commence, inaugurate, institute, start.   *End*

Introduction, Presentation, induction.
Preface, foreword, prelude, preliminary.   *Finale*

Intrude, *v.a.*, Obtrude, foist, thrust, encroach, interfere.   *Remove*
v.n., Trespass, interfere, meddle, intermeddle, interpose, interlope, infringe, encroach.   *Retire*

Intruder, Trespasser, meddler, intermeddler, interloper, stranger.

Intrust, Commit, consign, confine, deliver, hand.

Intuition, Insight, instinct, perception, knowledge, presentiment, clairvoyance, divination, apprehension.

Intumescence, Protuberance, swelling, inturgescence, turgescence, tumefaction.   *Concavity*

Intwine, Interlace, intertwine, interweave, inweave, reticulate, cross.   *Unravel*

Inundate, Submerge, swamp, flood, deluge, overwhelm, overcome, overflow, drown.   *Drain*

Inure, Accustom, harden, train, discipline, toughen, habituate, familiarize, use, acclimatize.

Invade, Assault, attack, raid, enter, occupy, infringe, violate.   *Evacuate*

Invalid, Null, void, unsound, useless, untrue, forceless, weak.   *Valid*
Ill, weak, infirm, sickly, sick, frail, feeble.   *Strong*

Invalidate, Annul, nullify, overthrow, cancel, reverse, quash, repeal.

Invaluable, Precious, inestimable, priceless, valuable.   *Worthless*

Invariable, Constant, changeless, unchanging, unchangeable, firm, unalterable, immutable, unvarying, uniform, set.   *Changeable*

Invasion, Assault, aggression, attack, raid, foray, violation, encroachment.

Invective, Vituperation, raillery, abuse, reproach, censure, attack, contumely,

denunciation, assault, obloquy, sarcasm, diatribe, satire.   *Panegyric*

Inveigh, Rail, denounce, vituperate, abuse, reproach, censure, blame, condemn.   *Praise*

Inveigle, Beguile, trap, entrap, decoy, ensnare, entice, lure, tempt.   *Guide*

Invent, Create, contrive, fabricate, concoct, conceive, make, devise, originate, imagine.   *Imitate*

Invention, Creation, contrivance, fabrication.†

Inventory, Roll, list, record, catalogue, register, schedule, account, invoice.

Inverse, Opposite, converse, reversed, inverted.   *Direct*

Inversion, Reversing, reversal, upsetting, transposition.   *Stability*

Invert, Reverse, upset, overturn, capsize.

Invest, Clothe, accoutre, robe, dress, deck, bedeck, array, cover.   *Strip*
Indue, endow, confer.
Besiege, surround, enclose, beset.

Investigate, Explore, examine, study, consider, overhaul, sift, probe, scrutinize.   *Disregard*

Investigation, Exploration, examination,† research, inquisition, inquiry.   *Neglect*

Investiture, Ordination, installation, induction, habitation.

Investment, Investing, clothing, robing, dressing, decking.
Clothing, clothes, array, dress, robe, garment, garments, habit, habiliment.

Inveterate, Established, habitual, habituated, confirmed, hardened, ingrained, besetting, obstinate, chronic, deeprooted.   *Undeveloped*

Invidious, Envious, unfair, odious, hateful, offensive, malignant.   *Just*

Invigorate, Quicken, animate, enliven, energize, fortify, strengthen, encourage, brace.   *Enervate*

Invincible, Indomitable, unconquerable, irresistible, insuperable, unsurmountable, irrepressible.   *Weak*

Inviolate, Virgin, stainless, unstained, unpolluted, whole, intact, unbroken, unimpaired, uninjured, unhurt, sacred, guarded.   *Betrayed*

Invisible, Unseen, imperceptible, hidden, undiscernible, unapparent, concealed.   *Apparent*

Invitation, Summons, call, challenge, bidding, request, solicitation.

Invite, Ask, request, bid, call, summon, solicit, attract, entice, allure, tempt.   *Forbid*

Inviting, Alluring, attractive, pleasant,

pleasing, fascinating, engaging, winning, captivating, bewitching, prepossessing, promising. *Repulsive*

Invocation, Prayer, supplication, invoking, petition, entreaty.

Invoice, Inventory, list, roll, register, record, schedule, bill.

Invoke, Adjure, conjure, imprecate, summon, beseech, beg, request, supplicate, pray, implore, entreat, call. *Ignore*

Involuntary, Compulsory, forced, unwilling, reluctant. *Willing*
Instinctive, automatic, mechanical, spontaneous, blind, reflex, unintentional.

Involve, Implicate, entangle, complicate.
Extricate
Wrap, inwrap, cover, envelop, surround, embrace, include.
Join, blend, mix, intertwine, twine, interweave, conjoin, connect, intertwist, interlace, mingle, unite. *Separate*

Invulnerable, Safe, secure, irrefragable, invincible. *Unsafe*

Inward, Inner, internal, interior, inside.
Outward
Private, secret, hidden, spiritual, mental.

Inweave, Weave, interweave, intwine, intertwine, interlace, reticulate. *Unravel*

Inwrap, Wrap, envelop, cover, enrobe, enfold, engross.

Iota, Scrap, atom, jot, tittle, bit, whit, mite, trace, glimmer, shadow, particle.

Irascible, Petulant, touchy, testy, irritable, splenetic, hasty, peppery, hot, choleric, snappish, waspish, snarling.
Mild

Irate, Angry, angered, wroth, wrathful, annoyed, provoked, incensed, irritated, piqued. *Calm*

Ire, Anger, wrath, irritation, choler, rage, fury, passion, annoyance, exasperation, resentment, indignation.

Ireful, Angry, angered, wrathful, wroth, annoyed, provoked, incensed, furious, passionate, irritated.

Iridescent, Opalescent, nacreous, pearly, prismatic, rainbow-like. *Neutral*

Irksome, Tedious, weary, wearisome, wearying, tiresome, boring, uninteresting, dull, monotonous, annoying.
Pleasant

Ironical, Sarcastic, mocking, derisive, satirical. *Complimentary*

Irony, Satire, mockery, banter, sarcasm.

Irradiate, Brighten, illumine, illuminate, illume. *Darken*

Irrational, Unreasonable, absurd, preposterous, foolish, injudicious, illogical.
Sensible
Brute, brutish, unreasoning.

Irrational, Crazy, insane, idiotic, fantastic, demented, brainless. *Sane*

Irreclaimable, Incurable, remediless, irremediable, hopeless, irreparable, irretrievable, irrecoverable, lost. *Curable*
Incorrigible, abandoned, reprobate, lost, hardened, recreant, impenitent, shameless, unrepentant, profligate, graceless.
Repentant

Irreconcilable, Incongruous, incompatible, inconsistent. *Compatible*
Implacable, hard, inexorable, immovable, unappeasable. *Appeasable*

Irrecoverable, Lost, irretrievable, hopeless.

Irrefutable, Unanswerable, unassailable, undeniable, indisputable, irresistible, incontrovertible, incontestable, invincible.
Faulty

Irregular, Fitful, uncertain, variable, capricious, unpunctual, unsettled, fickle, spasmodic, changeable, desultory.
Certain
Unmethodical, disorderly, loose, wild, dissolute. *Methodical*
Unusual, uncommon, anomalous, aberrant, devious, erratic, abnormal, exceptional, eccentric, crooked. *Normal*

Irrelevant, Impertinent, inapplicable, inapt, foreign, unrelated, illogical, apposite, inappropriate. *Pertinent*

Irreligious, Impious, ungodly, wicked, unrighteous, heathen, profane. *Godly*

Irremediable, Remediless, incurable, hopeless, irreparable, immedicable.
Curable

Irreparable, Irremediable, remediless, incurable.†

Irrepressible, Insuppressible, uncontrollable, invincible. *Suppressible*

Irreproachable, Faultless, spotless, blameless, unblamable, pure, innocent, inculpable, irreprehensible, irreprovable, stainless. *Blamable*

Irresistible, Unanswerable, invincible, overwhelming, overpowering, incontestable, impregnable. *Weak*

Irresolute, Weak, vacillating, hesitating, hesitant, unsteady, unstable, faltering, undecided, undetermined, unsettled, wavering. *Firm*

Irrespective, Independent, regardless.

Irresponsible, Untrustworthy, unanswerable, unaccountable. *Trusty*

Irretrievable, Lost, irrecoverable.

Irreverent, Profane, blasphemous, impious. *Devout*

Irreversible, Unalterable, unchangeable, unchanging, changeless, immutable, invariable, irrevocable. *Changeable*

Irrevocable, Irreversible, unalterable, unchangeable.†

Irrigate, Water, moisten, wash, submerge, inundate, flood, wet. *Drain*

Irritable, Touchy, testy, short, hasty, fretful, petulant, splenetic, irascible, fiery, hot, peevish, snarling, snappish, captious, passionate, susceptible, excitable, responsive. *Benignant*

Irritate, Exasperate, annoy, anger, excite, vex, provoke, gall, nettle, tease, offend, enrage, incense, chafe, stimulate, inflame. *Appease*

Irruption, Invasion, incursion, raid, inroad. *Retreat*

Isolate, Detach, insulate, separate, dissociate, sever, segregate, disconnect. *Unite*

Isolated, Single, separate, detached, solitary. *Connected*

Isolation, Detachment, insularity, separation, dissociation, segregation, disconnection. *Connection*

Isolation, Solitude, solitariness, loneliness. *Community*

Issue, *v.n.*, Proceed, flow, emanate, spring, come, originate, rise, arise, ensue, depart, emerge.
End, eventuate, result, terminate, conclude.
v.a., Deliver, distribute, emit, discharge, utter, publish, circulate.
n., Children, posterity, descendants, offspring, progeny.
Number, edition, impression, copy.
Delivery, delivering. *Suppression*
Result, end, consequence, conclusion, termination, head, upshot, outcome, event, consummation, effect. *Cause*
Egress, flow, outlet, exit, vent, escape.

Item, Number, particular, article, detail, entry.

Iterate, Reiterate, repeat.

Itinerant, Strolling, wandering, travelling, roving, unsettled, journeying, roaming, nomadic, peripatetic. *Stationary*

Itinerary, Route, circuit, guide.

J

Jabber, Chatter, prate, prattle, gabble.

Jacket, Jerkin, coat, casing, covering.

Jade, *v.a.*, Exhaust, fatigue, tire, fag, weary, wear.   *Refresh*

n., Hack.

Hussy, wench.

Jagged, Uneven, indented, serrated, notched, ragged.   *Even*

Jail, Prison, lockup, penitentiary, gaol.

Jam, *v.a.*, Crowd, press, squeeze, pack, wedge.

n., Preserve, conserve.

Press, pressure, crowd, crowding, crush, pack.

Jangle, *v.n.*, Clash, bicker, disagree, wrangle, dispute, contend, quarrel, squabble.   *Accord*

n., Clash, clashing, bickering,† discord, jangling, babel, jargon.   *Harmony*

Jangled, Inharmonious, discordant.   *Harmonious*

Jar, *v.a.*, Jolt, shake, disturb, agitate, vibrate.

v.n., Clash, jangle, grate, wrangle, squabble, quarrel, bicker.   *Accord*

n., Jolt, shake, disturbance, agitation. Clash, clashing, jangle.†   *Harmony*

Jargon, Nonsense, gabble, gibberish, palaver, balderdash, slang.   *Eloquence*

Jarring, Inharmonious, harsh, grating, discordant.   *Harmonious*

Jaunt, Excursion, outing, trip, tour, expedition, ramble, stroll.

Jaunty, Garish, showy, fine, airy, flaunting, flighty, sprightly, gay.   *Sedate*

Jealous, Covetous, envious, suspicious, resentful, distrustful.   *Content*

Anxious, watchful, vigilant, solicitous, apprehensive.   *Indifferent*

Jeer, *v.a.*, Spurn, despise, mock, ridicule, contemn, scoff, deride, taunt.   *Flatter*

v.n., Scoff, sneer, gibe, taunt, mock.

n., Scoff, sneer.†

Jehovah, God, Lord, the Deity.   *Satan*

Jejune, Scant, bare, barren, weak, sterile, bald, dry, thin, poor, uninteresting, meagre, lean.   *Exuberant*

Jeopardize, Imperil, peril, endanger, risk, hazard.   *Protect*

Jeopardy, Peril, danger, risk, hazard, venture.   *Security*

Jerk, Pluck, pull, twitch, flip, hitch, jolt.

Jest, *v.n.*, Joke, jape.   *Mope*

n., Joke, sport, fun, prank, quirk, quip, raillery.   *Earnest*

Jester, Joker, buffoon, droll, humorist, fool, wag, harlequin, clown.

Jewellery, Jewels, gems, trinkets.

Jingle, Tinkle, tingle, rhyme.

Job, Work, situation, employment, affair, business.

Jockey, *n.*, Rider.

v.a., Cheat, deceive, circumvent, overreach, delude, hoodwink, outwit, gammon, beguile, gull, inveigle, hoax, dupe, *cozen, chouse.*   *Guide*

Jocose ⎫ Bright, witty, humorous, droll,
Jocular ⎬ amusing, gay, merry, facetious,
Jocund ⎭ waggish, funny, mirthful, jolly, sportive, joyful, joyous, blithe, pleasant, lively, frolicsome, playful, jovial.   *Melancholy*

Jog, Push, nudge, hustle, jostle, jolt.

Remind, notify, warn.

Trot, trudge.

Join, *v.a.*, Unite, connect, conjoin, combine, fasten, cement, link, couple, attach.   *Part*

Joint, *n.*, Union, juncture, junction, seam, connection, hinge, splice, mortice, knot.

a., Combined, united, concerted.

v.a., Fit, unite, join.

Joke, *v.n.*, Jest, jape.

n., Jest, sport, fun, quirk, quip.

Jollity, Mirth, merriment, fun, gaiety, jocularity, joviality, hilarity, frolic.   *Sadness*

Jolly, Mirthful, merry, funny, gay, jocular, jocose, jocund, jovial, hilarious, frolicsome, blithe, playful, genial, joyful, joyous, sportive, lively, cheerful, cheery, sprightly.   *Sad*

Plump, lusty, stout, portly.

Jolt, Shake, jar, jog, jerk, shock.

Jostle, Jolt, jog, thrust, crowd, push, hustle, shake.

Jot, Tittle, iota, mite, bit, scrap, whit, atom, ace.

Journal, Diary, record, register, log.

Newspaper, paper, sheet, periodical, magazine, gazette.

Journey, *v.n.*, Travel, rove, wander, roam, ramble.

n., Travel, wandering, ramble, trip, expedition, excursion, tour, passage, voyage, jaunt.

Jovial, Jolly, gay, airy, blithe, genial, convivial.   *Gloomy*

Joy, Happiness, pleasure, gladness, glee,

delight, bliss, transport, felicity, rapture, ecstasy, ravishment, exultation. **Sorrow**

Joyful ⎱ Happy, pleased, glad, delighted,
Joyous ⎰ jolly, blithe, blithesome, gay, airy, merry, mirthful, jocund, buoyant, elated, enravished. **Sad**
Jubilant, Triumphant, exultant, exulting, joyous, rejoicing, triumphing. **Mournful**
Judge, v.n., Conclude, determine, decide, gather, pronounce, decree, infer.
v.a., Try, arbitrate, adjudicate, umpire, condemn, sentence, doom, criticise.
Think, count, esteem, consider, imagine, hold, regard, believe, suppose, deem, account, reckon, appreciate, estimate.
n., Justice, umpire, referee, arbitrator, arbiter. **Criminal**
Critic, authority, expert, connoisseur. **Novice**
Judgment, Decree, award, verdict, sentence, doom, censure, decision.
Discrimination, discernment, insight, penetration, sagacity, intellect, sense, prudence, intelligence, understanding, wisdom, brains. **Pleading**
Judicious, Wise, discreet, sensible, sagacious, prudent, cautious, rational, sound, reasonable, sober, cool, considerate, politic. **Rash**
Juggle, Conjure, shuffle, swindle, cheat.
Juicy, Succulent, watery, moist. **Dry**
Jumble, v.a., Confuse, disorder, disarrange, mix, muddle. **Arrange**
n., Confusion, disorder, muddle, chaos. **Order**
Jump, v.n., Hop, skip, leap, caper, bound, spring, vault.
v.a., Clear, take, vault, leap, skip.
Junction, Union, joining, joint, connection, combination, coupling, seam, linking. **Separation**

Juncture, Conjuncture, joint, moment, period, exigency, crisis, pass, strait.
Junior, Younger. **Senior**
Junto, Confederacy, federacy, cabal, clique, coalition, gang, party, combination, faction, coterie, society, set.
Jurisdiction, Judicature, rule, government, administration, sway, dominion, control, sphere, reach, province. **Independence**
Just, a., Fair, equitable, right, reasonable, honest, straightforward, conscientious, honourable, righteous, virtuous, upright, good, blameless, impartial. **Dishonourable**
Exact, correct, accurate, true, regular, normal, proportioned, proper. **Inexact**
Due, fitting, suitable, fit, appropriate, merited, deserved. **Disproportionate**
adv., Precisely, exactly, almost.
Barely, hardly, simply, quiet, very.
Justice, Fairness, equity, equitableness, right, impartiality, justness, propriety, reasonableness. **Unfairness**
Judge, magistrate, stipendiary.
Justifiable, Right, defensible, proper, fit, correct, warrantable, vindicable. **Unwarrantable**
Justification, Defence, plea, vindication, apology, exoneration, exculpation. **Protest**
Justify, Defend, vindicate, excuse, exculpate, support, approve, maintain, exonerate, warrant. **Censure**
Jut, Protrude, project.
Juvenile, a., Immature, young, childish, infantile, puerile, adolescent, youthful, boyish, girlish. **Mature**
n., Youth, child, adolescent, boy, girl. **Adult**
Juxtaposition, Adjacency, contiguity, contact, proximity.

K

Keen, Acute, astute, sharp, sagacious, shrewd, quick, penetrating, cutting, piercing, discerning.   **Dull**
Ardent, eager, hot, vehement, zealous, fervid, earnest, fiery.   *Indifferent*
Poignant, bitter, acrid, acrimonious, sour, severe, caustic.

Keenness, Acuteness, astuteness, sharpness.†   *Dulness*
Ardour, eagerness, heat,† zest, avidity.   *Apathy*
Poignancy, bitterness, acrimony,† pungency, asperity.

Keep, *v.a.*, Hold, withhold, retain, store, restrain, guard, possess, sustain, support, preserve, protect, detain.   *Discard*
Commemorate, honour, solemnize, celebrate.   *Ignore*
Observe, fulfil, obey.   *Break*
Continue, maintain, preserve.
v.n., Last, remain, endure, persist, stay, lodge, dwell, abide, continue.   *Cease*
n., Castle, fort, stronghold, support.

Keeping, Custody, charge, hands, care, ward, guardianship.
Consistency, agreement, conformity, harmony, accord, congruity.   *Inharmonious*

Ken, View, sight, vision, knowledge, cognizance, horizon.   *Oversight*

Kernel, Core, centre, heart.   *Husk*

Key, Solution, explanation, guide, clue, elucidation, translation, note, tonic.
Lever, clamp, wedge.

Kick, *v.a.*, Resist, spurn, punt.   *Soothe*
v.n., Calcitrate, rebel.   *Submit*

Kidnap, Abduct, capture, seize, steal.

Kill, Assassinate, slaughter, slay, murder, butcher, destroy, despatch.

Kin, *n.*, Relationship, consanguinity, blood.
Relations, kindred, relatives, family, race, connections, kinsfolk, kinsmen.
a., Akin, kindred, allied, related, cognate.   *Strange*

Kind, *n.*, Family, set, race, genus, breed, class, caste, species.
Manner, style, sort, description, order, type, make, brand, character, nature.
a., Generous, benevolent, obliging, benign, benignant, beneficent, gracious, tender, lenient, clement, humane, indulgent, sympathetic, charitable, loving, affectionate, bland, mild, forbearing, amiable, good, friendly, complaisant, accommodating, bounteous, compassionate, philanthropic.   **Hard**

Kindle, Enkindle, light, inflame, ignite, fire.   *Extinguish*
Inflame, rouse, arouse, provoke, excite, enrage, exasperate, stimulate, whet, foment, incite.   *Quiet*

Kindliness, Generosity, benevolence, benignity, beneficence, graciousness, tenderness, lenience, clemency, humanity, indulgence, sympathy, charity, love, affection, blandness, mildness, amiability, goodness, friendliness, compassion, philanthropy, bounty, kindness.   *Hardness*

Kindness, Kindliness, generosity, benevolence.†

Kindred, *n.*, Relationship, kin, blood, consanguinity.
Relations, kin, relatives, family, race, connections, kinsfolk, kinsmen.
a., Related, akin, kin, allied, cognate, sympathetic, congenial.   *Strange*

King, Monarch, ruler, sovereign, liege.

Kingdom, Monarchy, rule, sovereignty, sway, dominion, power, supremacy.
Land, country, realm, dominion, domain, province, region, tract.

Kingly, Regal, royal, imperial, majestic, monarchical, grand, imposing, stately, august, noble.   *Poor*

Kink, Entanglement, twist, bend, knot, curl, loop, crimp, crick, wrinkle. *Straight*

Kinsfolk, Kin, kindred, relations, relatives, family, race, connections, kinsmen.   *Stranger*

Knack, Aptitude, aptness, dexterity, skill, skilfulness, ability, expertness, adroitness, address, quickness, readiness, faculty.   *Clumsiness*

Knarled, Gnarled, knotty, knotted, knobbly.   *Smooth*

Knave, Rascal, rogue, rapscallion, villain, scamp, cheat, trickster, swindler, sharper.   *Fool*

Knavery, Rascality, roguery, trickery, villainy,† fraud, dishonesty, criminality.

Knavish, Rascally, roguish, villainous, tricky, swindling, dishonest, criminal, fraudulent, unprincipled. *Gentlemanly*

Knell, Toll, ring, sound.

Knight, Chevalier, cavalier.
Gallant, lover, partisan, champion.

Knit, Join, unite, bind, connect, interlace.   *Sever*

Knob, Bunch, hunch, protuberance, boss, handle.

Knock, Rap, beat, hit, strike, slap, cuff, buffet.

Knoll, Hill, hillock, mound.

Knot, *v.a.,* Tie, entangle, complicate.
Untie
n., Tie, bond, connection, joint.

Bunch, tuft, collection, group, crowd, set, gang, company, cluster, crew, clique, pack.

Complication, difficulty, intricacy, perplexity, muddle, entanglement, tangle.
Simplicity

Knotty, Complicated, difficult, intricate, perplexing, muddled, hard, involved.
Simple

Knotted, gnarled, knarled.

Know, Understand, comprehend, apprehend, perceive, recognize, discern. Distinguish, discriminate.

Knowing, Clever, intelligent, accomplished, skilful, astute, shrewd, cunning, penetrating, sagacious, sharp, expressive.
Simple

Knowledge, Erudition, learning, lore, scholarship, education, instruction, enlightenment, information, attainments, acquirements. *Illiterateness*

Cognition, cognizance, familiarity, notice, information. *Ignorance*

Discernment, comprehension, apprehension, understanding, perception.
Misapprehension

L

Laborious, Sedulous, diligent, assiduous, industrious, indefatigable, painstaking, toiling.   **Indolent**
Hard, tiring, tiresome, burdensome, arduous, difficult, onerous, wearisome, irksome, fatiguing, toilsome.   **Easy**

Labour, *v.n.*, Work, toil, drudge, slave, strive.   **Rest**
n., Work, toil, drudgery, slavery, striving, pains, effort, exertion, industry.

Labyrinthian⎫ Involved, tricky, intric-
Labyrinthine⎰ ate, confused, confusing, mazy, winding, obscure, difficult, perplexing.   **Simple**

Lace, Tie, bind, interlace, twine, intertwine, weave, interweave.

Lacerate, Tear, rend, lancinate, laniate, rip, claw, mangle, sever, wound, harrow.   **Bind**

Lack, *v.a.*, Need, want.   **Have**
n., Need, want, shortage, deficiency, insufficiency, shortness, scarcity, dearth, deficit, default, scantiness.   **Supply**

Laconic, Epigrammatic, terse, brief, short, concise, pithy, curt, succinct, compact.   **Prolix**

Lacquey, Flunkey, servant, footman, valet, attendant.

Lad, Boy, youth, youngster, stripling.   **Lass**

Lade, Load, burden, freight, laden.

Lading, Load, burden, freight, cargo, consignment.

Lag, Dawdle, loiter, linger, hang, dally, saunter, idle, tarry.   **Hurry**

Laggard, Lagger, loiterer, loafer, idler, saunterer.

Lair, Den, burrow, form, couch.

Lambent, Gleaming, twinkling, flickering, licking.

Lame, Halt, maimed, crippled, weak, faltering, hesitating, impotent, ineffective, hobbling, limp, feeble.   **Strong**

Lament, *v.a.*, Deplore, regret, bewail, bemoan, mourn.   **Welcome**
v.n., Wail, complain, mourn, sorrow, grieve, cry, weep, moan, repine. **Rejoice**
n., Lamentation, wailing, complaint, mourning, sorrow, grief, moan, moaning, dirge, plaint, threne, threnody.

Lamentable, Contemptible, poor, feeble, despicable, pitiful, miserable.
           Praiseworthy
Grievous, deplorable, regrettable, unfortunate.   **Fortunate**
Wailing, sorrowful, mournful.   **Happy**

Lamentation, Lament, wailing, complaint, plaint, mourning, sorrow, grief, moan, moaning, dirge.   **Rejoicing**

Lampoon, Ridicule, parody, satirize, lash.

Lancinate, Lacerate, laniate, sever, tear, mangle, rend, rip, claw.   **Bind**

Land, *v.a. & n.*, Debark, disembark.
           Embark
n., Earth, sod, soil, ground.
Country, nation, realm, district, tract, weald, province, region.

Landscape, Prospect, scene, view.

Language, Speech, utterance, expression, talk, conversation, diction, style, tongue, voice, phraseology, dialect, vernacular, idiom, parlance, slang.

Languid, Feeble, weary, faint, drooping, languishing, weak, exhausted, flagging, pining, spiritless, heavy, listless, enervated.   **Vigorous**

Languish, Faint, droop, flag, pine, decline, wither, sink, fail, fade. **Flourish**

Langour, Feebleness, weariness, faintness, weakness, exhaustion, heaviness, listlessness, debility, lassitude. **Vigour**

Laniate, Lancinate, lacerate, sever, tear, mangle, rend, rip, claw.   **Bind**

Lank, Long, lean, slender, emaciated, attenuated, tall, gaunt, slim, meagre, thin.   **Plump**

Lap, Fold, turn, twist, cover, wrap, lick.

Lapse, *v.n.*, Slip, sink, fall, slide, glide, flow.
n., Flow, flowing, gliding, passing.
Slip, falling, fall, decline, declension, error, failing, fault, void.

Larceny, Theft, robbing, robbery, pilfering, purloining, stealing.

Large, Big, massive, wide, extensive, bulky, capacious, great, immense, huge, full, copious, abundant, ample, broad.
           Small

Largess, Bequest, gift, present, donation, grant, bounty, alms, dole, endowment.
Generosity, liberality, kindness.
           Meanness

Lascivious, Lecherous,† prurient, lustful, incontinent, unchaste, lewd, loose, concupiscent, wanton.   **Temperate**

Lash, *v.a.*, Castigate, chastise, beat, scourge, whip, flagellate, chasten, flog, satirize, censure, upbraid.   **Caress**
Tie, join, bind.
n., Scourge, whip, thong.
Stripe, stroke.

Lass, Girl, maid, maiden, damsel, miss wench. ***Lad***

Lassitude, Languor, feebleness, weariness, faintness, weakness, exhaustion, heaviness, listlessness, debility. ***Vigour***

Last, *a.*, Ultimate, final, latest, hindmost, utmost, extreme. ***First***

v.n., Abide, remain, endure, continue, persist. ***Perish***

Lasting, Abiding, enduring, continuing, durable, persisting, permanent.
Transient

Late, Delayed, slow, tardy, overdue, behind.

Recent. ***Early***

Past, deceased.

Advanced.

Lately, Recently, latterly, late.

Latent, Secret, invisible, unseen, hidden, unobserved, inapparent, veiled, occult, concealed, potential, abeyant, undeveloped. ***Conspicuous***

Lateral, Oblique, parallel, indirect, incidental, secondary. ***Direct***

Latitude, Laxity, freedom, indulgence, licence, liberty.

Scope, compass, range, extent.

Latter, Recent, modern, previous. ***Early***

Latterly, Recently, lately, previously.

Laud, Praise, honour, magnify, extol.
Decry

Laudable, Praiseworthy, honourable, worthy, commendable. ***Despicable***

Laudation, Praise, eulogy, commendation, panegyric, encomium, compliment.
Criticism

Laughable, Funny, farcical, amusing, humorous, droll, ridiculous, comical, comic, ludicrous, absurd, diverting, entertaining. ***Serious***

Laughter, Fun, merriment, glee. ***Gloom***

Derision, ridicule, contempt. ***Respect***

Launch, *v.a.*, Hurl, propel, throw, dart, cast.

Start, inaugurate, initiate, begin, commence. ***Repress***

v.n., Expatiate, enlarge, descant, dilate.

Lavish, *v.a.*, Squander, pour, waste, spend, dissipate. ***Save***

a., Wasteful, prodigal, spendthrift, profuse, thriftless, unsparing, bountiful, extravagant. ***Economical***

Law, Statute, rule, enactment, order, decree, ordinance, regulation, edict, command, canon. ***Misrule***

Principle, idea, sequence, formula, form.
Chaos

Jurisprudence, code.

Litigation, suit, process.

Lawful, Legitimate, legal, constitutional,

right, rightful, just, valid, proper, permissible, allowable. ***Illegal***

Lawless, Disorderly, wild, rebellious.
Peaceful

Lawyer, Barrister, solicitor, counsel, attorney, advocate.

Lax, Loose, unexacting, latitudinarian, slack. ***Strict***

Negligent, neglectful, remiss. ***Attentive***

Dissolute, licentious, unprincipled, loose.
Conscientious

Laxity, Laxness, looseness, latitude, slackness. ***Strictness***

Negligence, neglect, remissness.
Attention

Dissoluteness, licentiousness, looseness.
Conscientiousness

Lay, *v.a.*, Place, put, deposit, establish.
Remove

Calm, quiet, allay, appease, pacify, still, settle. ***Arouse***

Produce.

Bet, wager, risk, venture, hazard.

Exorcise.

Assess, impose.

Charge, impute, ascribe.

a., Laical, laic, inexpert, inexperienced, non-professional.

Layer, Seam, stratum, bed, course.

Lazy, Sluggish, slothful, indolent, slack, idle, supine, inert, torpid, dronish, inactive. ***Industrious***

Lea, Meadow, sward, mead.

Lead, *v.n.*, Tend, conduce, serve, contribute, help.

v.a., Head, precede, surpass, excel.

Persuade, urge, entice, induce, allure.
Follow

Guide, convoy, direct, conduct, escort.
Misguide

Spend, pass.

n., Initiative, priority, pre-eminence, precedence.

Leadership, direction, guidance, control.

Leader, Guide, director, conductor, chief, chieftain, captain, commander, head, superior, ruler, dictator. ***Subordinate***

Leading, Chief, foremost, first, capital, main, principal, ruling, governing.
Minor

League, *v.n.*, Combine, coalesce, unite, confederate. ***Divide***

n., Combination, coalition, union, confederation, confederacy, compact, cabal, alliance.

Leak, *v.n.*, Ooze, percolate.

n., Percolation, hole, opening, cleft, rift, gap, fissure, crevice, chink.

Lean, *v.n.*, Repose, recline, rest, rely, trust, depend, confide, incline.

Lean, Tend, bend.

a., Thin, lank, emaciated, meagre, bony, gaunt, barren, scanty, slender, skinny, shrivelled, poor. *Fat*

Leaning, Bias, propensity, bent, inclination, tendency, liking. *Avoidance*

Leap, *v.a.,* Jump, clear, vault.

v.n., Jump, hop, skip, spring, bound, gambol, frisk.

n., Jump, hop, skip,† caper.

Learn, *v.a.,* Acquire, gather, collect, imbibe, attain, hear. *Forget*

Learned, Scholarly, lettered, literate, literary, informed, erudite, skilled, versed. *Ignorant*

Learner, Novice, beginner, pupil, tyro, student. *Authority*

Learning, Scholarship, erudition, education, knowledge, information, lore, attainments, acquirements. *Ignorance*

Least, Smallest, lowest, minutest, last, meanest. *Greatest*

Leave, *v.a.,* Forsake, quit, relinquish, abandon, renounce, desert, vacate. *Hold*

Bequeath, consign, commit, refer, devise, demise.

v.n., Cease, stop, forbear, desist.

Depart, go, withdraw, retire, quit. *Arrive*

n., Departure, withdrawal, retirement, farewell, adieu, congé.

Permission, license, liberty, allowance.

Leavings, Refuse, dregs, remains, remnants, scraps, fragments, bits, pieces, relics, lees.

Lecherous, Lustful, lascivious, lewd, unchaste, carnal, libidinous, concupiscent, incontinent, wanton. *Temperate*

Lecture, *v.a.,* Reprove, chide, reprimand, rebuke, sermonize, scold. *Praise*

n., Harangue, discourse, speech, prelection.

Reproof, chiding, reprimand, rebuke, scolding, censure, lesson.

Lees, Dregs, refuse, sediment, precipitate.

Legacy, Gift, bequest, devise.

Legal, Legitimate, lawful, licit, proper, constitutional, allowable. *Illegitimate*

Legalize, Legitimize, legitimatize, warrant, sanction, permit, authorize.
Prohibit

Legate, Ambassador, plenipotentiary, envoy, delegate, deputy.

Legend, Myth, fiction, fable, motto, caption. *Fact*

Legendary, Mythical, fictitious, fabulous.
Historical

Legible, Clear, plain, readable, apparent, decipherable, manifest. *Obscure*

Legion, Host, multitude, throng, army, horde.

Legitimate, Legal, lawful, proper, constitutional, genuine, allowable, licit.
Illegal

Fair, warranted, warrantable, logical, correct, valid. *Invalid*

Leisure, Ease, convenience, freedom, quiet, vacation. *Toil*

Lend, Advance, loan, accommodate, furnish, grant, present, give, bestow, afford. *Borrow*

Length, Extent, duration, reach.
Breadth

Detail, fulness, amplification.

Lengthen, Stretch, extend, elongate, prolong, protract. *Shorten*

Lengthy, Long, extended, detailed, protracted, diffuse, prolix, verbose, tedious.
Short

Lenient, Mild, merciful, compassionate, easy, kind, moderate, clement, forbearing, tender, gentle. *Hard*

Lenitive, Mitigative, soothing, palliative, emollient, balmy, sedative, assuasive.
Irritant

Lentiginous, Scabby, scurvy, freckly.
Clean

Leprous, Defiled, defiling, corrupt, vile, foul, infectious, polluting. *Pure*

Less, Smaller, inferior, minor, lower, lesser. *More*

Lessen, *v.a.,* Reduce, diminish, decrease, abridge, abate, mitigate, lower, disgrace, humble, degrade. *Increase*

v.n., Diminish, decrease, abate, shrink, contract, dwindle.

Lesser, Lower, smaller, inferior, minor, less. *Greater*

Lesson, Task, work, exercise.

Lecture, precept, instruction.

Warning, reproof, homily, chiding, scolding, admonition, censure, rebuke.

Let, *v.a.,* Permit, allow, suffer. *Stop*

Hinder, obstruct, impede, prevent, stop.
Help

Lease, hire.

n., Hindrance, obstruction, impediment, bar, stoppage, obstacle.

Lethal, Fatal, deadly, mortal, poisonous, venomous. *Vital*

Lethargic, Dull, sleepy, heavy, torpid, stupid, stupefied, drowsy, comatose, apathetic. *Energetic*

Lethargy, Dulness, sleepiness, heaviness,† oblivion, trance, apathy. *Energy*

Letter, Note, epistle, communication, missive.

Lettered, Learned, read, versed, erudite, educated, literary, literate. *Ignorant*

Letters, Culture, education, learning, erudition, literature.

Levee, Reception, party, entertainment.

Level, *v. a.,* Demolish, raze, destroy. ***Erect***
Point, aim, direct.
Flatten, smooth, plane. ***Roughen***
a., Even, plain, flat, horizontal, flush.
n., Plane, floor, surface, platform, ground.

Levigate, Grind, pulverize, crush, triturate, comminute, bruise, polish.
Compound

Levity, Frivolity, lightness, inconstancy, giddiness, flippancy, flightiness. ***Gravity***

Levy, Gather, collect, exact, muster, raise, impose. ***Surrender***

Lewd, Coarse, wicked, low, loose, vile, despicable, lustful, lecherous, libidinous.
Virtuous

Lexicon, Dictionary, glossary, vocabulary.

Liabilities, Debts, obligations, responsibilities, duties. ***Assets***

Liable, Responsible, answerable, accountable, amenable.
Open, likely, subject, exposed. ***Unlikely***

Liaison, Union, bond, relation, connection, intrigue, amour.

Libel, *v.a.,* Slander, defame, traduce, calumniate, lampoon. ***Eulogize***
n., Slander, defamation,† detraction.
Eulogy

Liberal, Generous, charitable, kind, unselfish, bounteous, munificent, profuse, plentiful, free, handsome, princely.
Mean
Wide, broad, large, catholic, tolerant, enlarged, unbigoted. ***Bigoted***

Liberality, Generosity, charity, kindness.† ***Meanness***
Width, breadth, largeness.† ***Bigotry***

Liberate, Loose, free, emancipate, release, deliver, manumit, discharge, disenthral, ransom. ***Confine***

Libertine, *n.,* Debauchee, rake, profligate. ***Saint***
a., Debauched, rakish, profligate, loose, dissolute, depraved, licentious, corrupt.
Pure

Liberty, Freedom, emancipation, immunity, liberation, independence, privilege, leave, license, permission.
Servitude

Libidinous, Lecherous, lustful, lascivious, lewd, wanton, unchaste, concupiscent, loose, incontinent, carnal. ***Temperate***

License, *v.a.,* Allow, permit, indulge, brook, suffer. ***Prohibit***
n., Permission, leave, authority, right, privilege, warrant, charter, certificate, dispensation.
Anarchy, laxity, looseness, disorder.
Restraint

Licentious, Dissolute, riotous, profligate, lewd, lascivious, lecherous, unchaste, lawless, lax, loose, disorderly, immoral, sensual, wanton, unruly, voluptuous, debauched, rakish, libertine, lustful, libidinous. ***Restrained***

Lid, Top, cover, coverlet.

Lie, *n.,* Untruth, falsehood, fabrication, mendacity, invention. ***Truth***
v.n., Rest, recline, repose, remain, be.
Rise
Consist.

Lief, Soon, gladly, willingly, freely, readily. ***Loath***

Liege, Lord, master, sovereign, superior.
Servant

Lieu, Place, stead, room.

Life, Energy, vitality, vigour, animation, alertness, spirit, sprightliness, briskness, vivacity. ***Lethargy***
Duration, existence.
Biography, memoir.
Behaviour, conduct, condition, deportment.

Lifeless, Dead, inanimate, defunct, deceased, extinct. ***Alive***
Lethargic, dull, passive, inert, sluggish, slow, tame, torpid, spiritless. ***Vigorous***

Lift, Elevate, raise, upraise, uplift, exalt.
Lower
Aid, help, assistance.

Ligament, Band, bandage, bond, tie, ligature, strap, brace.

Ligature, Ligament, band, bandage.†

Light, *v.a.,* Kindle, fire, ignite.
Extinguish
Illuminate, illumine, illume, irradiate, lighten, brighten. ***Darken***
n., Radiance, illumination, luminosity, brightness, gleam, beam, blaze.
Darkness
Lamp, candle, lantern, torch, taper.
Instruction, information, knowledge, understanding, explanation, elucidation, comprehension, illumination.
Mystification
a., Buoyant, imponderous, portable, unweighty, loose, sandy. ***Heavy***
Clear, bright, whitish. ***Dark***
Easy, simple, small, trifling, negligible, slight, moderate, trivial, inconsiderable.
Hard
Fickle, volatile, frivolous, capricious, vain, unthoughtful, thoughtless, unsettled, unsteady, characterless. ***Serious***
Buoyant, airy, light-hearted, gay, merry, joyous, joyful, lightsome, flimsy, feathery.
Depressed
Unburdened, unencumbered. ***Laden***

Lighten, Ease, disencumber. ***Load***

Lighten, Illumine, illuminate, brighten, irradiate, illume, light. *Darken*
Illumine, enlighten, instruct, inform. *Mystify*

Lightsome, Light, buoyant, airy, light-hearted, gay, merry, joyous, joyful. *Depressed*

Like, *v.n.*, Prefer, choose, desire, wish, elect.
v.a., Enjoy, relish, approve, fancy, love, esteem, affect. *Detest*
n., Equal, match, counterpart, peer, liking, preference, partiality.
a., Similar, equal, corresponding, resembling, same, allied, alike, cognate, analogous, parallel. *Different*

Likely, Probable, credible, suitable, pleasing, agreeable. *Improbable*

Likeness, Similarity, equality, correspondence, resemblance, sameness, copy, semblance, similitude, facsimile, image, counterpart, form, representation. *Dissimilarity*

Likewise, Similarly, moreover, further, also, so, too, besides, furthermore. *Otherwise*

Liking, Partiality, love, fondness, regard, affection, preference, predilection, desire, wish, taste, relish. *Aversion*

Lilliputian, Pygmy, tiny, puny, diminutive, small, dwarfish, little, short. *Elephantine*

Limber, Lithe, supple, pliant, flexible, limp, relaxed. *Stiff*

Limit, *v.a.*, Restrict, crib, cabin, confine, bound, hedge, restrain, condition, circumscribe.
n., Border, bound, march, frontier, confine, boundary, edge, termination, limitation, precinct, obstruction, check.

Limitless, Unlimited, unbounded, infinite, vast, unending, endless. *Finite*

Limp, Hobble, halt, stumble.
Flaccid, relaxed, flexible, slack.

Limpid, Transparent, translucent, pellucid, clear, crystalline, crystal, bright. *Opaque*

Line, Thread, row, rank, cord, stripe, streak, mark, cable, stroke, marking, stretch, rope, string.
Family, tribe, house, race, lineage, ancestry, succession.
Method, course, conduct, occupation, employment, business, pursuit.

Lineage, Family, tribe, house, race, line, ancestry, succession, descent, extraction, progeny, birth.

Linear, Direct, straight, rectilinear. *Zigzag*

Linger, Lag, saunter, dawdle, dally, tarry, loiter, delay. *Hurry*

Link, *v.a.*, Connect, tie, join, conjoin, fasten, bind, unite. *Sever*
n., Connection, tie, joint, bond.
Part, portion, member, particle, division.

Lion-hearted, Courageous, bold, fearless, intrepid, brave, valiant, valorous, daring, dauntless. *Timid*

Lip, Edge, labium, border.

Liquefy, Dissolve, melt, fuse. *Solidify*

Liquid, *n.*, Liquor, fluid. *Solid*
a., Fluid, fluent, running, soft, flowing, melting.

Liquidate, Pay, adjust, settle, discharge.

List, *v.n.*, Like, choose, prefer, desire, wish, elect.
n., Register, inventory, catalogue, roll, schedule, invoice.

Listen, Hark, hearken, attend, incline, hear, eavesdrop. *Ignore*

Listless, Heedless, careless, apathetic, torpid, languid, inattentive, uninterested, indifferent. *Eager*

Literally, Strictly, closely, precisely, exactly, really, actually. *Freely*

Literary, Scholarly, erudite, lettered, learned, literate, instructed, studious. *Illiterate*

Literature, Letters, erudition, learning, scholarship, lore.

Lithe, Supple, pliant, elastic, pliable, flexile, flexible, limber. *Stiff*

Litigious, Quarrelsome, contentious, disputatious, wrangling. *Genial*

Litter, *v.a.*, Derange, disarrange, strew, disorder, scatter, upset, mislay, discompose. *Tidy*
n., Derangement, disarrangement, confusion, disorder, shreds, fragments, rubbish, bedding. *Tidiness*

Little, Small, tiny, diminutive, brief, pygmy, short, trivial, inconsiderable, slight. *Large*
Mean, narrow, paltry, selfish.

Live, *v.a.*, Lead, spend, pass.
v.n., Exist, subsist, fare, feed, survive, grow, endure, remain, continue. *Die*
Reside, lodge, dwell, abide.
Act, behave.
a., Alive, living, breathing, growing, quick, animate, vivid, flowing, active, earnest. *Dead*

Livelihood, Living, sustenance, subsistence, support, maintenance. *Privation*

Livelong, Durable, lasting, enduring.

Lively, Animated, active, energetic, brisk, alert, eager, agile, vigorous, smart, keen, quick, blithe, nimble, buoyant, joyous, joyful, airy, spirited, gay. *Listless*

Livery, Uniform, costume, dress.
Living, *n.*, Livelihood, sustenance, subsistence, support, maintenance. ***Privation***
a., Alive, live, breathing, growing, quick, existing, active, animate. ***Dead***
Lo, Behold, look, see, observe.
Load, *v.a.*, Lade, burden, freight, cumber, encumber, oppress. ***Lighten***
Charge, fill.
n., Lading, burden, freight, cargo, pack, encumbrance, oppression, incubus, drag, weight.
Loaf, Lounge, dawdle, dilly-dally, idle.
Loafer, Lounger, vagrant, idler, vagabond, drone. ***Worker***
Loan, Lend, advance. ***Borrow***
Loath, Unwilling, averse, disinclined, reluctant, indisposed. ***Eager***
Loathe, Hate, abominate, detest, abhor, dislike. ***Love***
Loathing, Hatred, abomination, detestation, abhorrence, dislike, antipathy, disgust, repugnance, aversion. ***Liking***
Loathsome, Hateful, abominable, detestable, abhorrent, disgusting, repugnant, revolting, sickening, offensive, repulsive, nauseous, nauseating, execrable, shocking, odious. ***Attractive***
Local, Topical, regional, limited, provincial. ***Metropolitan***
Locality, Place, district, position, location, situation, spot.
Locate, Fix, place, find, settle, establish, set. ***Remove***
Loch, Lake, creek, pond, mere, bay.
Lock, *v.a.*, Close, seal, fasten, clasp. ***Open***
n., Seal, fastening, bolt, padlock.
Hug, grapple, embrace.
Bunch, tuft, tress, ringlet.
Locomotion, Movement, transport, passage, motion, travel. ***Fixture***
Lodge, *v.n.*, Stay, live, sojourn, tarry, reside, dwell, inhabit, stop, remain, abide.
v.a., Quarter, keep, harbour, cover, accommodate.
Place, lay, set, put, plant, deposit.
n., House, cottage, hut, cot, cave, hovel, haunt, den.
Lodging, Residence, quarters, abode, dwelling, habitation, refuge, shelter, cover, harbour.
Lofty, High, exalted, elevated, stately, noble, towering, tall, imposing, dignified, majestic, eminent. ***Low***
Arrogant, proud, haughty, overbearing, superior. ***Lowly***
Logical, Reasonable, sound, dialectical, valid, consistent, coherent. ***Fallacious***
Logomachy, Argument, debate, strife,

contention, wrangling, dispute, disagreement, discord, controversy, bickering, altercation. ***Agreement***
Loiter, Saunter, linger, dawdle, tarry, dilly-dally, idle, delay, lag. ***Hurry***
Loll, Sprawl, lounge, recline, rest, lie, lean. ***Stir***
Lone, Isolated, alone, lonely, solitary, apart, single, companionless, unaccompanied. ***Befriended***
Secluded, solitary, remote, apart, retired, uninhabited, unfrequented, unoccupied, deserted, lonely. ***Frequented***
Lonely, Lone, isolated, alone.†
Secluded, solitary, remote.†
Desolate, forlorn, miserable, wretched, cheerless, dreary, lonesome, gloomy, dismal. ***Cheerful***
Lonesome, Lonely, secluded, solitary, remote, apart, deserted. ***Frequented***
Desolate, lonely, forlorn, miserable, wretched, cheerless, dreary, gloomy, dismal. ***Cheerful***
Long, *a.*, Extensive, extended, lengthy, tall. ***Short***
Prolonged, protracted, prolix, tedious, diffuse.
Dilatory, lingering, tardy, slow, slack. ***Quick***
v.n., Yearn, desire, wish, crave, aspire.
Longing, Yearning, desire,† eagerness. ***Aversion***
Look, *v.n.*, Watch, regard, behold, see, contemplate, observe, gaze, scan, view.
Seem, appear.
n., Gaze, glance, glimpse, regard, peep, peer.
Appearance, air, manner, aspect, mien, complexion.
Loom, Appear, bulk. ***Recede***
Threaten, lower, glimmer.
Loop, Circle, noose, ring, bight, bend, crook, turn.
Loophole, Aperture, opening.
Plea, excuse, pretext, pretence.
Loose, *v.a.*, Release, untie, unbind, undo, loosen, liberate, relax, unlock, unfasten, disconnect, detach. ***Bind***
a., Untied, unbound, undone, unfastened, relaxed, disconnected, detached, slack, unattached, movable, free. ***Tight***
Vague, indefinite, diffuse, rambling, unconnected, indistinct. ***Exact***
Lax, dissolute, debauched, licentious, impure, unchaste, immoral, wanton. ***Strict***
Loosen, Release, untie, unbind, undo, liberate, relax, unloose, slacken. ***Tighten***
Loot, *v.a.*, Pillage, rifle, spoil, rob, plunder, ransack.
n., Spoil, booty, plunder.

Lop, Amputate, prune, cut, curtail, truncate, obtruncate, shorten, dock, crop, sever, detach.

Loquacious, Talkative, voluble, garrulous, babbling. *Taciturn*

Lord, Peer, noble, nobleman. *Commoner* Master, prince, king, ruler, sovereign, monarch, suzerain, governor. *Servant* Jehovah, God.

Lordly, Lofty, exalted, noble, dignified, majestic, magnificent, grand. *Low* Haughty, imperious, arrogant, proud, overbearing, domineering. *Lowly*

Lordship, Dominion, power, authority, sovereignty, domination, jurisdiction, rule, sway, control, direction, government, command. *Subjection*

Lore, Learning, instruction, wisdom, knowledge, counsel, lesson, advice, teaching, admonition, scholarship, erudition, doctrine.

Lose, Miss, mislay, forfeit, drop, squander, waste, displace, deprive, fail. *Find*

Loss, Mislaying, forfeiture, dropping, squandering, waste, deprivation. *Gain* Defeat, reverse, overthrow, ruin, disadvantage, damage, destruction, injury, detriment. *Victory*

Lost, Missing, mislaid, astray, forfeited, dropped, squandered, wasted, misspent. *Found* Abandoned, vicious, wicked, bad, profligate, corrupt, graceless, depraved, hardened, reprobate, incorrigible, dissolute, obdurate, shameless, vile. *Righteous* Distracted, wrapt, deep, puzzled, confused, bewildered, perplexed, abstracted, dreamy, absorbed, preoccupied. *Attentive*

Lot, Fate, destiny, doom, chance, hazard, fortune, portion, part, parcel, division.

Loth, Averse, reluctant, unwilling, disinclined. *Ready*

Loud, Resonant, resounding, sonorous, noisy, sounding, clamorous, obstreperous, turbulent, boisterous, stentorian, vehement, deafening, tumultuous, stunning, audible. *Soft*

Loudness, Resonance, noise, clamour,† uproar. *Softness*

Lounge, Loll, loaf, rest, lie, recline, idle. *Stir*

Lounger, Loafer, trifler, idler, loiterer.

Lout, Boor, clown, booby, bumpkin, clod, yokel. *Fop*

Lovable, Likable, sweet, amiable, charming, captivating, winning. *Detestable*

Love, *v.a.,* Like, adore, esteem. *Hate*

Love, *n.,* Liking, affection, esteem, regard, attachment, devotion, passion, fondness, inclination, delight. *Aversion* Charity, kindness, benevolence, friendship, tenderness. *Malice*

Lovely, Beautiful, charming, graceful, sweet, pleasing, pleasant, delightful, delectable, enchanting. *Hideous*

Low, *v.n.,* Bellow, moo. *n.,* Bellowing, mooing. *a.,* Depressed, sunk, abated, declining, deep, stunted, shallow, subsided. *High* Base, mean, vile, derogatory, dishonourable, degraded, unworthy, abject, menial, slavish, grovelling, servile, disreputable, disgraceful, ungentlemanly. *Honourable* Cheap, moderate, reasonable. *Exorbitant* Subdued, reduced, feeble, exhausted, weak. *Strong* Subdued, soft, gentle, repressed. *Loud*

Lower, *v.a.,* Depress, reduce, diminish, sink, drop, decrease, lessen, degrade, humiliate, humble, debase. *Raise* *v.n.,* Diminish, decline, decrease, sink, fall, subside. *Rise* Frown, glower. *Smile*

Lowering, Dark, threatening, clouded, cloudy, lurid, overcast, murky. *Bright*

Lowly, Meek, low, humble, modest, unassuming, unpretentious. *Lofty*

Loyal, True, allegiant, faithful, obedient, leal, constant, submissive, devoted. *Perfidious*

Loyalty, Allegiance, faithfulness, fidelity, obedience, constancy, submission, devotion, fealty. *Perfidy*

Lubberly, Awkward, clumsy, boorish, bungling, clownish, maladroit. *Clever*

Lubricate, Oil, smooth, grease, glaze, ease.

Lubricous, Smooth, greasy, oily, slippery. *Stiff* Wavering, unstable, uncertain.

Lucent, Bright, brilliant, effulgent, lucid, luminous, glittering, shining, radiant, beaming, resplendent. *Dark*

Lucid, Lucent, bright, brilliant.† Pellucid, limpid, crystalline, clear, transparent, diaphanous, pure. *Opaque* Plain, clear, intelligible, sane, sober, sound, distinct, rational, perspicuous, apparent. *Confused*

Luck, Fortune, chance, hazard, casualty, accident, fate, hap, success. *Design*

Luckless, Unlucky, unfortunate, ill-fated, ill-starred, unhappy, unsuccessful, disastrous. *Fortunate*

Lucky, Fortunate, favourable, auspicious, happy, prosperous, successful. *Unfortunate*

Lucrative, Paying, profitable, gainful, advantageous, remunerative.
Unremunerative

Lucre, Wealth, profit, gain, emolument, riches. *Poverty*

Lucubration, Study, reading, work, cogitation, meditation. *Idleness*

Luculent, Plain, clear, lucid, intelligible, distinct, rational, perspicuous, apparent, evident, unmistakable. *Confused*

Ludicrous, Absurd, amusing, funny, comic, comical, droll, laughable, farcical, odd, ridiculous. *Tragic*

Lug, Heave, pull, haul, tug, drag.

Luggage, Baggage, belongings, effects, impedimenta.

Lugubrious, Sad, doleful, depressing, melancholy, gloomy, dismal, sorrowful, complaining, mournful. *Cheerful*

Lukewarm, Tepid, thermal.
Cool, indifferent, apathetic, listless, dull, unconcerned. *Eager*

Lull, *v.n.*, Diminish, abate, wane, decrease, cease, subside. *Increase*
v.a., Assuage, calm, tranquillize, appease, pacify, still, compose, hush.
Aggravate
n., Quiet, peace, calm, tranquillity, stillness, cessation, hush, calmness.
Storm

Lumber, Rubbish, refuse, trash.

Lumbering, Cumbrous, cumbersome, clumsy, trudging, ponderous, awkward, unwieldy. *Adroit*

Luminous, Bright, radiant, lucent, resplendent, shining, brilliant. *Dark*
Clear, enlightening, perpsicuous, plain, lucid, comprehensible, luculent.
Confused

Lumpish, Heavy, dull, gross, bulky, stupid, cloddish, clumsy. *Nimble*

Lunacy, Madness, insanity, aberration, derangement, dementia, craziness, mania.
Sanity

Lunatic, *a.*, Mad, insane, deranged, crazy.
Sane
n., Madman, maniac.

Lunge, Thrust, pass.

Lurch, Roll, sway, toss.

Lure, *v.a.*, Allure, tempt, entice, attract, decoy, deceive, inveigle, seduce. *Repulse*
n., Allurement, temptation.† *Repulsion*

Lurid, Glowing, murky, dark, lowering, dismal, gloomy. *Bright*

Lurk, Skulk, hide, lie, wait. *Emerge*

Luscious, Delicious, delightful, sweet, palatable, savoury, attractive, tempting, goodly. *Nauseous*

Lush, Succulent, moist, watery, fresh, juicy, luxuriant. *Dry*

Lust, *v.n.*, Desire, covet, yearn, long.
n., Desire, longing, appetite, lechery, carnality, cupidity, concupiscence, lasciviousness, wantonness, lewdness, libidinousness, lubricity. *Indifference*

Lustful, Lecherous, lascivious, loose, libidinous, lewd, concupiscent, licentious, carnal, lubricious. *Temperate*

Lustration, Purification, washing, cleansing, expurgation, expiation. *Defilement*

Lustre, Radiance, brilliance, brightness, resplendence, splendour, glory. *Dulness*

Lusty, Strong, robust, vigorous, stout, healthy, sturdy. *Weak*

Luxate, Dislocate, displace, disjoint.

Luxuriant, Profuse, abundant, superabundant, exuberant, plenteous, plentiful. *Scant*

Luxuriate, Bask, flourish, revel, indulge, delight, wanton.

Luxurious, Pampered, voluptuous, intemperate, sensual, pleasurable, self-indulgent, epicurean, effeminate. *Ascetic*

Luxury, Luxuriousness, voluptuousness, intemperance, sensuality, pleasure, self-indulgence, epicurism, effeminacy, wantonness, delight, enjoyment, dainty, delicacy, treat. *Hardship*

Lying, False, untrue, untruthful, mendacious. *Truthful*

M

Macerate, Waste, rot, attenuate, soak, steep, wither, soften.   ***Replenish***
Mortify, torture, plague, harry, harass.

Machiavellian, Crafty, deceitful, artful, diplomatic, cunning, designing, tricky, wily, sly, subtle, arch, astute, shrewd, clever, crooked.   ***Open***

Machinate, Plot, plan, design, contrive, devise, form, scheme.   ***Detect***

Machination, Plot, complot, design,† intrigue, conspiracy, trick, ruse, stratagem.   ***Detection***

Machine, Instrument, agent, tool, engine. System, machinery, organization.

Maculate, Corrupt, impure, soiled, sullied, dirty, speckled, spotted, blotched, blotted, stained, unclean, defiled.   ***Spotless***

Mad, Lunatic, insane, crazy, demented, delirious, aberrant, maniac, deranged, crazed, distracted, raving, wild.   ***Sane***
Provoked, furious, infuriated, angry, raging, enraged, exasperated, incensed, wrathful.   ***Calm***

Madden, Provoke, infuriate, anger, enrage, exasperate, incense, craze, inflame.   ***Pacify***

Madness, Lunacy, insanity, craziness, delirium, aberration, distraction, derangement, mania, raving, wildness.   ***Sanity***
Fury, anger, rage, frenzy.   ***Calmness***

Magazine, Paper, booklet, periodical, pamphlet.
Storehouse, depository, repository, warehouse, depôt, receptacle.

Magic, Witchcraft, witchery, sorcery, enchantment, fascination.

Magisterial, Despotic, arbitrary, hard, domineering, dogmatic, arrogant, imperious, haughty, proud, overbearing, lordly, dictatorial, consequential, authoritative, lofty, pompous.   ***Modest***

Magnanimity, Clemency, forbearance, generosity, disinterestedness, loftiness.   ***Meanness***

Magnanimous, Clement, forbearing, generous, disinterested, lofty, chivalrous, noble, unselfish, liberal, heroic, dauntless, brave, elevated, honourable.   ***Mean***

Magnate, Grandee, noble, nobleman.   ***Nobody***

Magnetic, Attractive, enchanting, drawing.   ***Repulsive***

Magnificent, Sublime, superb, grand, majestic, splendid, imposing, stately, gorgeous, fine, exquisite.   ***Poor***

Magnify, Augment, enlarge, increase, multiply, exaggerate, amplify. ***Diminish***
Praise, extol, laud, honour, glorify, exalt, bless, elevate, celebrate.   ***Decry***

Magniloquent, Bombastic, turgid, tumid, grandiloquent, boastful, declamatory, swelling, pompous, inflated.   ***Simple***

Magnitude, Volume, size, extent, bulk, dimensions, mass, width, bigness, greatness, importance, consequence.   ***Smallness***

Maid   } Girl, virgin, damsel, lass, lassie.
Maiden }   ***Lad***

Maidenly, Modest, demure, reserved, bashful, gentle.   ***Bold***

Maim, Disable, mutilate, cripple, injure, mar, harm, hurt.   ***Strengthen***

Main, *n.*, Majority, bulk, gross, body.   ***Minority***
Strength, might, power, effort, force.   ***Weakness***
Ocean, sea, continent.
Conduit, pipe, duct, channel.
a., Leading, first, foremost, chief, principal, capital, cardinal, important, vital, necessary, essential, indispensable, requisite.   ***Minor***
Mighty, enormous, vast, huge.
Entire, direct, mere, absolute, sheer, pure.   ***Partial***

Mainly, Firstly, chiefly, principally, largely, entirely, absolutely.   ***Partially***

Maintain, *v.n.*, Hold, declare, allege, affirm, asseverate, believe, aver, contend.
v.a., Keep, hold, preserve, sustain, support.   ***Abandon***
Justify, vindicate, defend.   ***Attack***
Declare, allege, assert, say.

Maintenance, Provisions, subsistence, sustenance, victuals, livelihood, food, fare.
Defence, preservation, holding, support.

Majestic, Imposing, stately, grand, noble, august, princely, regal, royal, imperial, dignified, magnificent, pompous, lofty.   ***Paltry***

Majesty, Stateliness, grandeur, nobility.†

Majority, Bulk, mass, preponderance, greater, more.   ***Minority***
Manhood, adulthood.

Make, *v.a.*, Form, fashion, mould, create, figure, construct, cut, shape, fabricate, cause, effect, produce.   ***Destroy***
Constitute, form, compose.
Perform, execute, do, practise.   ***Undo***
Reach, attain, secure, gain, get, raise.

Make, Compel, force, cause, constrain, occasion.

n., Manufacture, construction, build, shape, form, constitution.

Maker, God, Creator.

Manufacturer, builder, constructor. ***Destroyer***

Maladministration, Misgovernment, misrule, malversation, corruption. ***Rule***

Maladroit, Clumsy, awkward, inapt, bungling, inexpert, unhandy, unskilled, unskilful, inefficient. ***Dexterous***

Malady, Illness, disease, complaint, sickness, distemper, disorder, indisposition, ailment, ail. ***Health***

Malapert, Impudent, impertinent, rude, saucy, insolent, forward, flippant, quick, bold. ***Respectful***

Malcontent, Dissatisfied, insurgent, rebellious, discontented, uneasy. ***Satisfied***

Malediction, Curse, cursing, anathema, imprecation, denunciation, execration, ban. ***Blessing***

Malefactor, Criminal, sinner, culprit, convict, outlaw, felon. ***Benefactor***

Maleficent, Hurtful, harmful, injurious, baneful, baleful, deleterious, mischievous, pernicious. ***Beneficent***

Malevolent, Spiteful, malignant, resentful, malicious, rancorous, revengeful, ill-disposed, ill-natured, mischievous, bitter, envious, rancorous. ***Kind***

Malice, Spite, spitefulness, malignity, resentment, rancour, revenge, hate, maliciousness, bitterness, enmity, venom, malevolence. ***Charity***

Malicious, Spiteful, malignant.†

Malign, Defame, calumniate, blacken, slander, traduce, asperse, revile, abuse, vilify, disparage, decry. ***Praise***

Malignant, Malicious, spiteful, resentful, rancorous, revengeful, bitter, malevolent. ***Kind***

Maleficent, hurtful, harmful, injurious, baneful, baleful, deleterious, mischievous, pernicious. ***Beneficent***

Malignity, Malice, spite, spitefulness.† ***Charity***

Malignancy, destructiveness, deadliness, harmfulness.

Malpractice, Malversation, misconduct, dereliction, mispractice, misbehaviour, misdoing, evil, sin. ***Right***

Maltreat, Injure, hurt, harm, abuse, ill-treat, ill-use. ***Assist***

Malversation, Malpractice, corruption, misconduct, misdoing. ***Integrity***

Mammon, Riches, wealth, opulence, possessions, property. ***Poverty***

Mammoth, Huge, large, elephantine, immense, colossal, enormous, gigantic, big, gargantuan. ***Tiny***

Man, Person, being, soul, individual, somebody, personage, human, body.

Mankind, humanity. ***Beast***

Male, husband. ***Woman***

Servant, workman, hand, employee, attendant, servant, dependant. ***Master***

Manacle, *v.a.*, Shackle, bind, tie, fetter, restrain, confine, chain, handcuff. ***Free***

n., Shackle, bond, tie.†

Manage, *v.n.*, Contrive, succeed, manœuvre, direct, administer. ***Upset***

v.a., Direct, control, regulate, rule, administer, conduct, supervise, superintend, govern, operate, transact, order, guide, handle, wield, mould, manipulate. ***Misconduct***

Manageable, Docile, controllable, tractable, easy, governable, tamable, amenable. ***Refractory***

Management, Contrivance, skill, care, address. ***Bungling***

Direction, control, regulation, rule, administration, conduct, supervision, superintendence, government, guidance, charge, treatment, negotiation, dealing, transaction, operation, manipulation.

Manager, Director, controller, regulator,† overseer.

Mandate, Charge, commission, order, command, edict, precept, injunction, requirement. ***Request***

Mangle, Crush, hack, mutilate, tear, rend, lacerate, destroy, mar, spoil, press.

Manhood, Virility, maturity, adulthood. ***Childhood***

Manliness, hardihood, fortitude, courage, bravery, intrepidity, strength, firmness, boldness, valour. ***Timidity***

Mania, Insanity, lunacy, madness, delirium, frenzy, desire, craziness, aberration, derangement. ***Sanity***

Maniac-al, Insane, lunatic,† demented, raving. ***Sane***

Manifest, *v.a.*, Exhibit, evince, show, reveal, disclose, declare, evidence, prove, expose, discover. ***Hide***

a., Visible, plain, apparent, palpable, obvious, clear, indubitable, open, evident, glaring, unmistakable, patent, conspicuous, undeniable. ***Dubious***

Manifestation, Show, revelation, exhibition, disclosure, declaration, exposure, discovery, display, exposition. ***Concealment***

Manifesto, Declaration, proclamation, protest.

Manifold, Numerous, many, varied, various, multifarious, multitudinous, diverse. *Few*

Manipulate, Handle, work, manage, operate, use.

Mankind, Man, men, humanity.

Manly, Hardy, daring, brave, dauntless, bold, fearless, intrepid, courageous, firm, strong, heroic, stout, vigorous, noble, valorous. *Weak*

Manner, Kind, sort, make, style.

Behaviour, way, conduct, deportment, mien, air, bearing, carriage, appearance, aspect, look.

Habit, practice, custom, degree, extent. Method, mode, style, fashion, way, form.

Mannerly, Polite, refined, well-bred, well-behaved, courteous, affable, ceremonious, civil. *Rude*

Manners, Behaviour, bearing, carriage, deportment, demeanour, morals, habits, breeding, conduct. *Rudeness*

Manœuvre, *v.n.*, Plot, plan, scheme, contrive, manage, intrigue.

n., Plot, plan, scheme, contrivance, management, intrigue, artifice, tactics, stratagem, operations, campaign, ruse. *Check*

Movement, evolution.

Mansion, House, residence, seat, dwelling, abode, place. *Cottage*

Mantle, Cover, covering, hood, cloak.

Manufacture, *v.a.*, Make, produce, fabricate, construct, mould.

n., Make, production, fabrication, construction, moulding.

Manumission, Liberation, release, emancipation, deliverance, enfranchisement. *Enslavement*

Manumit, Liberate, release,† free. *Enslave*

Manure, Compost, dung, fertilizer, dressing.

Many, Manifold, numerous, abundant, sundry, divers. *Few*

Map, *v.a.*, Draw, delineate, chart. Plan.

n., Chart, plot, diagram, plan.

Mar, Spoil, damage, disfigure, injure, impair, harm, deform, hurt, deface, ruin, mutilate. *Improve*

Marauder, Robber, brigand, freebooter, pirate, bandit, outlaw, plunderer, rover, pillager. *Guard*

Marcescent, Decaying, declining, failing, fading, withering. *Flourishing*

March, Walk, go, step, advance, progress. *Halt*

Marches, Boundaries, limits, confines, borders, frontier, precincts.

Marcid, Lean, wasted, withered, meagre, thin, gaunt, feeble, drooping. *Robust*

Margin, Brink, border, limit, edge, bound, boundary, brim, verge, lip.

Reserve, surplus.

Marine, Sea, oceanic, maritime, nautical, naval. *Land*

Mariner, Seaman, seafarer, sailor, tar. *Landsman*

Marital, Connubial, matrimonial, conjugal. *Celibate*

Maritime, Marine, sea, oceanic, nautical, naval. *Land*

Mark, *v.a.*, Brand, label, indicate, distinguish, stamp, differentiate, characterize, stigmatize.

v.a. & n., Note, observe, regard, see, notice, remark. *Ignore*

n., Sign, label, token, badge, symbol, proof, stamp, impression, character, print, brand, indication.

Object, target, butt.

Footprint, track, trace.

Distinction, eminence, fame, renown, consequence, importance. *Obscurity*

Marked, Prominent, notable, remarkable, eminent, distinguished.

Market, Emporium, shop, mart.

Marriage, Wedlock, matrimony, union.

Wedding, spousals, espousals, nuptials.

Marrow, Essence, quintessence, pith, best, kernal, gist, substance, cream.

Marry, Unite, join, wed, espouse. *Divorce*

Marsh, Bog, morass, swamp, quagmire, fen, slough.

Marshal, Array, arrange, order, place, rank, lead, guide, dispose, range, set. *Upset*

Mart, Market, emporium, shop.

Martial, Warlike, military, brave. *Peaceful*

Marvel, *v.n.*, Wonder, gape.

n., Wonder, astonishment, surprise, amazement, admiration. *Unconcern*

Wonder, prodigy, miracle, phenomenon.

Marvellous, Wonderful, wondrous, astonishing, surprising, amazing, stupendous, incredible, miraculous, extraordinary, prodigious. *Ordinary*

Masculine, Male, virile, manly, manlike, mannish, hardy, robust, strong, powerful. *Feminine*

Mash, Crush, knead, mix, beat, bruise, compound, amalgamate.

Mask, *v.a.*, Cloak, disguise, screen, veil, cover, shroud. *Expose*

n., Cloak, masquerade, revel, disguise,† blind, pretence, pretext, trick, evasion, subterfuge.

Masquerade, Revel, mask, disguise, veil, cover.

Mass, Lump, bulk, body, heap. ***Fragment***
Size, bulk, dimension, magnitude, whole, aggregate, body, sum.

Massacre, *v.a.*, Slaughter, slay, kill, butcher, destroy, murder.
n., Slaughter, killing, butchery, destruction, murder, carnage.

Massive, Big, bulky, large, immense, weighty, solid, ponderous, colossal, vast, enormous. ***Slight***

Master, *v.a.*, Conquer, subjugate, overcome, overpower, defeat, beat, vanquish, subdue. ***Yield***
Learn, acquire.
n., Ruler, governor, overseer, director, manager, chief, head, leader, principal, lord, superintendent, commander, employer, proprietor, holder, owner, controller. ***Man***
Pedagogue, teacher, professor, tutor, preceptor, instructor, adept, proficient. ***Pupil***

Masterly, Skilful, skilled, adept, dexterous, adroit, excellent, finished, smart, clever, expert. ***Clumsy***

Mastery, Supremacy, conquest, victory, ascendancy, sway, rule, command, superiority, dominion. ***Subservience***
Skill, ability, cleverness, dexterity, proficiency, attainment, acquisition.

Masticate, Eat, chew, manducate. ***Gobble***

Mat, Interlace, weave, inweave, interweave, entangle, twist. ***Disentangle***

Match, *v.n.*, Suit, tally, correspond, harmonize, agree. ***Clash***
v.a., Suit, adapt, fit, proportion, equal, rival. ***Fail***
Mate, marry, join, couple, combine.
Oppose, pit.
n., Mate, equal, rival, companion. ***Inferior***
Marriage, union.
Contest, competition, trial.

Matchless, Peerless, consummate, unequalled, unmatched, unrivalled, incomparable, inimitable, exquisite, excellent, perfect, unparalleled, surpassing, unique. ***Ordinary***

Mate, *v.a.*, Match, wed, marry, pair.
n., Companion, comrade, friend, associate, assistant, subordinate, fellow, compeer.

Material, *n.*, Stuff, substance, matter.
a., Essential, vital, necessary, weighty, momentous, important, relevant. ***Unimportant***

Material, Physical, bodily, earthly, corporal. ***Spiritual***

Materially, Essentially, vitally, importantly.

Maternal, Motherly, motherlike.

Mathematical, Accurate, strict, precise, rigid.

Matrimony, Marriage, wedlock, union.

Matrix, Mould, matrice.

Matron, Dame, mother, dowager, woman, wife. ***Miss***

Matronly, Motherly, elderly, sedate, grave.

Matter, *v.n.*, Signify, import, weigh.
n., Stuff, substance, material, body. ***Mind***
Question, topic, subject.
Trouble, difficulty, distress.
Business, affair, event, thing, concern, import, consequence, moment.

Mature, *v.a. & n.*, Ripen, mellow.
a., Ripe, complete, full, developed, perfect, mellow. ***Embryonic***

Matutinal, Early, waking, dawning, morning. ***Late***

Maudlin, Drunk, drunken, intoxicated, fuddled, inebriated. ***Sober***
Stupid, weak, sentimental, silly, mawkish. ***Sensible***

Maul, Disfigure, deform, injure, beat, hurt, harm, abuse, wound.

Mawkish, Maudlin, stupid, weak, sentimental, silly. ***Sensible***
Stale, flat, insipid, sickly, tasteless, vapid. ***Pungent***

Maxim, Dictum, saying, proverb, precept, saw, axiom, adage, rule, aphorism. ***Paradox***

Maximum, Limit, greatest, climax, acme, apex, utmost. ***Minimum***

Maybe ⎱ Possibly, probably, perhaps,
Mayhap ⎰ peradventure, perchance.

Maze, Intricacy, labyrinth, perplexity, confusion, bewilderment.

Meadow, Mead, field, lea, sward.

Meagre, Thin, skinny, lean, gaunt, lank, spare, emaciated, poor. ***Fat***
Poor, scanty, small, mean, barren, unfertile, sterile, unproductive. ***Rich***

Mean, *v.a. & n.*, Signify, denote, express, purport, imply, indicate, import, hint, suggest.
Purpose, intend, design, contemplate.
n., Medium, average. ***Extreme***
Method, mode, way, agency, measure.
a., Medium, average, middle, moderate, intermediate.
Common, vulgar, low, ignoble, coarse, humble, ordinary. ***Aristocratic***
Base, despicable, low, petty, paltry

contemptible, poor, small, wretched, vile, dirty, shabby, scurvy, sneaking, servile, grovelling, abject, dishonourable, spiritless, sordid, beggarly, sorry. *Honourable* Selfish, niggardly, near, ungenerous, stingy, close, parsimonious, miserly, mercenary, illiberal. *Generous*

Meander, Wander, wind, turn, twist.

Meaning, Significance, signification, import, purport, sense, explanation, interpretation, drift, force.
Purpose, intent, design, aim, idea, object, end, intention.

Means, Medium, method, mode, instrument, agency, way, resource, measure, step, expedient. *End*
Resources, money, wealth, income, substance, revenue, property, estate. *Poverty*

Measure, *v.a.*, Appraise, mete, gauge, estimate, value.
n., Standard, gauge, rule, meter.
Degree, limit, extent, amount.
Share, allotment, portion.
Step.

Measured, Steady, regular, uniform, equal. *Erratic*
Definite, limited, restricted, finite. *Infinite*

Measureless, Immeasurable, infinite, unlimited, limitless, unrestricted, unbounded, boundless, vast, endless, interminable, immense, illimitable. *Finite*

Measurement, Content, quantity, extent, size, bulk.

Mechanic, Craftsman, engineer, artificer, operative, workman.

Mechanical, Automatic, effortless, spontaneous, habitual, unreflecting, soulless, blind, involuntary. *Animated*

Meddle, Intermeddle, interpose, intercede, intrude, interfere.

Meddlesome } Intermeddling, interposing,† officious, obtrusive.
Meddling } *Unobtrusive*

Medial, Average, mean, mediocre.

Mediate, Arbitrate, intercede, reconcile, interpose, intervene.

Mediation, Arbitration, intercession, reconciliation, interposition, intervention, adjustment. *Neutrality*

Medicament } Remedy, cure, physic,
Medicine } drug, antidote, corrective. *Aggravation*

Medicinal, Curative, healing, medical, sanatory. *Poisonous*

Mediocre, Inferior, medium, middling, average, mean, indifferent, commonplace, ordinary, moderate. *Excellent*

Meditate, *v.n.*, Ruminate, think, reflect, ponder, muse, cogitate, consider.
v.a., Plan, contemplate, study, scheme, purpose, contrive, concoct, intend, devise, design. *Execute*

Meditation, Rumination, thought, reflection, musing, cogitation, consideration, contemplation, pondering, study.

Medium, *n.*, Means, agency, instrumentality.
Average, mean. *Extreme*
a., Average, mean, middling, mediocre.

Medley, Litter, jumble, confusion, mixture, miscellany. *Arrangement*

Meed, Prize, reward, guerdon, recompense, award, present, gift, remuneration. *Penalty*

Meek, Modest, unassuming, humble, gentle, mild, pacific, lowly, yielding, submissive, soft. *Proud*

Meekness, Modesty, humbleness, humility.† *Pride*

Meet, *v.a.*, Encounter, find, confront, engage, get, gain, receive. *Miss*
Satisfy, fulfil, gratify, answer. *Evade*
Cross, intersect, transect, join.
v.n., Converge, assemble, muster, collect, unite, congregate, coalesce, join. *Disperse*
a., Right, proper, fit, appropriate, befitting, fitting, becoming, suitable, adapted, qualified, convenient. *Wrong*

Meeting, Encounter, interview. *Avoidance*
Confluence, conflux, junction, joining, union. *Parting*
Duel, collision.
Gathering, assembly, congregation, company, crowd, concourse, conference, convention.

Melancholy, *n.*, Despondency, sadness, gloominess, gloom, depression, hypochondria, dejection, sorrow, unhappiness. *Elation*
a., Despondent, sad, gloomy,† moody, doleful, dispirited, disconsolate, glum, lugubrious, dismal. *Elated*

Mêlée, Contest, fray, fight, brawl, scuffle, broil.

Meliorate, Ameliorate, mend, emend, amend, improve, better, raise, advance, promote. *Impair*

Melioration, Amelioration, amendment.†

Mellifluous, Silvery, mellow, euphonic, euphonious, smooth, flowing, sweet, soft, dulcet. *Discordant*

Mellow, *a.*, Mellifluous, silvery.†
Ripe, perfected, rich, delicate, mature. *Immature*
v.a., Ripen, perfect, enrich, tone, soften, mature.

Melodious, Harmonious, musical, tuneful, sweet, dulcet, silvery. *Harsh*

Melt, *v.a. & n.,* Dissolve, fuse, liquefy, soften, thaw. *Solidify*

Member, Part, portion, limb, component, constituent, element. Head, branch, clause. *Body*

Memento, Souvenir, memorial, remembrance.

Memoir, Life, biography, journal, record, register.

Memorable, Remarkable, signal, extraordinary, notable, striking, conspicuous, great, famous, prominent, distinguished, celebrated, illustrious, noteworthy. *Insignificant*

Memorandum, Note, minute, record, account, article.

Memorial, Memento, monument, remembrance, record, celebration, inscription, relic. *Effacement*

Memory, Remembrance, recollection, retention, reminiscence, retrospect. *Forgetfulness*
Fame, renown, reputation, repute. *Oblivion*

Menace, *v.a.,* Threaten, alarm, intimidate, frighten. *Reassure*
n., Threat, threatening.

Mend, *v.n.,* Amend, improve. *Deteriorate*
v.a., Improve, amend, emend, meliorate, ameliorate, better, patch, rectify, correct, repair, restore, refit, retouch. *Impair*

Mendacious, Lying, false, untruthful, prevaricating, deceitful. *Honest*

Mendacity, Lying, falsehood, untruthfulness,† duplicity, deception. *Honesty*

Mendicity, Mendicancy, beggary. *Labour*

Menial, *n.,* Slave, attendant, servant, domestic, flunkey, lackey, serf, footman, valet. *Master*
a., Low, dependent, servile, base, mean. *Lordly*

Mensuration, Survey, surveying, measuring, geometry.

Mental, Intellectual, psychological, psychical. *Physical*

Mention, Name, cite, declare, tell, say, state, divulge, communicate, report, impart, disclose. *Omit*

Mentor, Guide, monitor, adviser, instructor, master, counsellor.

Mephitic, Baleful, baneful, poisonous, fetid, noxious, foul, pestilential, malarious, unhealthy, noisome. *Salubrious*

Mercantile, Trading, commercial, marketable, wholesale, retail.

Mercenary, Selfish, grasping, avaricious, parsimonious, near, stingy, close, mean, niggardly, penurious, covetous, sordid. *Liberal*
Paid, hired, hireling, venal. *Voluntary*

Merchandise, Goods, wares, commodities.

Merchant, Importer, exporter, trader, dealer. *Pedlar*

Merciful, Pitiful, clement, lenient, forbearing, forgiving, mild, compassionate, tender, gracious, humane, kind, benignant. *Harsh*

Merciless, Pitiless, unforgiving, unkind, hard, harsh, cruel, savage, barbarous, relentless, unrelenting, unmerciful, uncompassionate, inexorable, unfeeling, severe, fell, callous, ruthless. *Compassionate*

Mercurial, Volatile, mobile, changeable, flexible, fickle, changing, inconstant. *Fixed*

Mercy, Pity, clemency, lenience, lenity, forgiveness, forbearance, mildness, compassion, tenderness, grace, graciousness, kindness, benevolence, pardon. *Harshness*

Mere, *a.,* Simple, unmixed, unadulterated, pure, absolute, sheer, entire, bare. *Mixed*
n., Lake, pool, pond.

Merely, Simply, solely, barely, only, purely, utterly, entirely.

Meretricious, Sham, showy, spurious, false, gaudy, flashy, tawdry. *Real*

Merge, Lose, drown, sink, immerse, bury, involve, submerge.

Meridian, Zenith, apex, height, summit, culmination, top, pinnacle, acme, climax. *Nadir*
Noon, midday, noontide.

Merit, *v.a.,* Deserve, earn, incur.
n., Desert, value, goodness, worth, worthiness, credit, excellence. *Fault*

Meritorious, Deserving, good, worthy, excellent, praiseworthy, commendable. *Despicable*

Merriment, Mirth, happiness, pleasure, joy, jollity, joviality, gaiety, laughter, jocularity, amusement, sport, hilarity, cheer, glee. *Sadness*

Merry, Mirthful, happy, pleasant,† gleeful, jocund, gladsome, wanton, frolicsome, blithe, bright. *Sad*

Mesh, Snare, entanglement, trap. *Escape*

Mess, Confusion, muddle, medley, mixture, disorder, disarray, plight, perplexity, jumble. *Order*
Company, set.
Dish.

Message, Intimation, missive, communication, despatch, telegram, word, notice, note. *Interception*

Messenger, Courier, express, herald, forerunner, harbinger, precursor, carrier, envoy, emissary.

Metamorphic, Variable, changeable, mutable, inconstant. *Constant*

Metaphor, Allegory, image, similitude. *Literal*

Metaphysical, Subjective, psychical, psychological, intellectual, mental, ideal, general, conceptive, abstract. *Material*

Mete, Measure, bound, limit, divide, deal, distribute, weigh, apportion. *Misdeal*

Method, Order, system, regularity, rule, purpose, arrangement, scheme, plan, classification. *Disorder*
Mode, way, means, process, manner, course, procedure.

Methodical, Orderly, regular, systematic, exact, formal. *Disorderly*

Metropolis, Capital, city.

Metropolitan, Primate,† archbishop.

Mettle, Material, stuff, element, constituent.
Disposition, character, temper.
Spirit, fire, courage, ardour, feeling, animation, vigour, nerve, pluck. *Cowardice*

Mezzo, Medium, middle, mean.

Miasmatic, Mephitic, malarious, baleful, baneful, poisonous, noxious, foul, fetid, polluted. *Salubrious*

Microscopic, Minute, tiny, infinitesimal, small. *Huge*

Middle, *n.,* Midst, centre. *Edge*
a., Mean, medium, intermediate, medial. *Extreme*

Middling, Fair, ordinary, mediocre, average, mean, moderate, medium, tolerable, passable.

Midst, Middle, centre, heart, thick. *Edge*

Mien, Bearing, deportment, carriage, look, aspect, air, appearance, manner, countenance, demeanour.

Might, Force, strength, power, main, ability, efficacy, efficiency, potency. *Weakness*

Mighty, Forceful, strong, powerful,† dynamic. *Weak*

Migratory, Roving, wandering, nomadic, unsettled. *Settled*

Mild, Gentle, meek, tender, pitiful, compassionate, kind, lenient, clement, soft, merciful, pacific, suave, bland, indulgent, moderate, genial, calm, soothing, placid, tempered, forbearing, forgiving. *Savage*

Mildew, Mouldiness, mould, mustiness, must, smut, blast, rust, blight.

Militant, Warring, fighting, contending, struggling, combating. *Pacific*

Military, Soldierly, warlike, martial. *Civil*

Militate, Contend, war, fight.

Mill, *v.a.,* Comminute, powder, pulverize, grind, triturate.
n., Factory, works.

Mimic, Imitative, mimetic, ape, mime, mock. *Real*

Minacious⎱ Threatening, menacing.
Minatory⎰

Mince, Comminute, chop, hash, cut.

Mind, *v.a.,* Regard, heed, notice, obey, mark, note, observe. *Neglect*
v.n., Object, dislike.
n., Spirit, soul, intellect, brain, sense, understanding, reason. *Body*
Desire, inclination, intention, disposition, leaning, tendency, wish, will. *Aversion*
Thought, belief, opinion, idea, judgment, sentiment, reflection.
Memory, recollection, remembrance.

Mindful, Regardful, heedful, thoughtful, attentive, recollective, careful, observant. *Oblivious*

Mine, *v.a.,* Undermine, ruin, weaken, sap, destroy. *Prop*
n., Colliery, pit, shaft.

Mingle, Commingle, intermingle, mix, commix, intermix, blend, unite, compound, amalgamate, join, associate, confound, confuse, combine. *Separate*

Miniature, Tiny, small, little, diminutive, wee. *Large*

Minimum, Least, lowest, smallest, minority. *Maximum*

Minion, Crony, dependant, favourite, pet, darling, follower, parasite. *Master*

Minister, *v.n.,* Administer, serve, attend, wait, subserve, officiate, help, succour, aid. *Exact*
n., Servant, agent, assistant.
Priest, parson, churchman, clergyman, divine, pastor, ecclesiastic. *Layman*
Official, administrator, ambassador.

Ministry, Ministration, aid, service, agency, help.
Administration, government, cabinet.

Minor, Less, lesser, inferior, subsidiary, unimportant, subordinate, inconsiderable, petty, junior, small, smaller. *Major*

Minstrel, Bard, musician, singer.

Mint, Coin, stamp.
Make, produce, create, fabricate, mould, fashion, invert, forge.

Minus, Wanting, less, lacking. *Plus*

Minute, *a.,* Small, tiny, little, diminutive, week, microscopic, fine, slender. *Huge*
Exact, detailed, specific, critical, searching, precise. *Superficial*
n., Memorandum, note, record, article, account.

Miracle, Wonder, marvel, prodigy.
Ordinary

Miraculous, Extraordinary, wonderful, amazing, incredible, unbelievable, supernatural. *Natural*

Mire, Mud, slime, clay, ooze.

Mirk, Fog, gloom, dark, darkness.

Mirror, Paragon, pattern, glass, model, example, exemplar, reflection.

Mirth, Merriment, happiness, gladness, glee, joy, joyousness, gaiety, laughter, hilarity, joviality, jollity, pleasure, frolic, sport, festivity. *Melancholy*

Mirthful, Merry, happy, glad,† vivacious, lively, playful, jocund, cheerful, cheery.
Sad

Misadventure, Calamity, misfortune, disaster, mishap, mischance, failure, reverse. *Success*

Misanthropy, Cynicism, selfishness, egotism. *Philanthropy*

Misapply, Pervert, misuse, abuse, misemploy. *Apply*

Misapprehend, Mistake, misunderstand, misconceive. *Understand*

Misbecoming, Unseemly, indecorous, unbecoming, unfit, improper. *Seemly*

Misbehaviour, Misconduct, rudeness, impoliteness. *Bearing*

Miscarriage, Abortion, failure, defeat, frustration, mishap, misadventure, mischance, misfortune, disaster, calamity.
Success

Miscellaneous, Mixed, heterogeneous, varied, various, promiscuous, mingled, diverse, many, diversified. *Classified*

Miscellany, Mixture, variety, diversity, collection, medley, pot-pourri, jumble.

Mischance, Misadventure, accident, fortuity, calamity, disaster, misfortune, mishap. *Fortune*

Mischief, Ill, harm, damage, evil, injury, trouble, hurt, disservice, detriment, misfortune, disadvantage, prejudice, deviltry. *Good*

Mischievous, Harmful, evil, injurious, troublesome, hurtful, detrimental, pernicious, bad, wicked, vicious, malicious, wanton, spiteful, naughty, annoying.
Beneficial

Misconceive, Mistake, misunderstand, misapprehend, misjudge. *Understand*

Misconduct, Misbehaviour, rudeness.

Misconstrue, Misunderstand, misinterpret, misrender, mistranslate, misconceive, misapprehend. *Interpret*

Miscreant, Rogue, villain, scamp, rascal, scoundrel, vagabond, knave. *Gentleman*

Misdeed, Sin, offence, crime, misdoing,

fault, transgression, wrong, delinquency, misdemeanour, trespass.

Misdemeanour, Sin, offence, crime,† misconduct.

Misdoer, Sinner, offender, criminal, transgressor, delinquent, trespasser, malefactor.

Misdoing, Sin, offence, crime, misdeed, fault, transgression, wrong, delinquency, misdemeanour, trespass. *Rectitude*

Misemploy, Misapply, misuse, abuse, pervert. *Use*

Miser, Niggard, churl, skinflint, screw, scrimp. *Spendthrift*

Miserable, Wretched, pitiable, poor, forlorn, unhappy, abject, distressed, hopeless, disconsolate, comfortless. *Happy*
Low, contemptible, mean, worthless, abject, despicable. *Respectable*

Miserly, Mean, near, close, parsimonious, avaricious, niggardly, penurious, stingy, covetous. *Generous*

Misery, Wretchedness, unhappiness, distress, sorrow, woe, affliction, desolation, torment, suffering, agony, anguish, torture, pain, grief, desolation, tribulation. *Joy*

Misfortune, Mischance, mishap, misadventure, calamity, disaster, failure, blow, affliction, trouble, adversity, hardship, trial, distress, visitation, reverse, harm, ill. *Success*

Misgiving, Doubt, hesitation, uncertainty, suspicion, questioning, mistrust, distrust. *Assurance*

Misguide, Misdirect, mislead, deceive, delude. *Direct*

Mishap, Accident, misfortune, misadventure, calamity, disaster. *Luck*

Misinterpret, Misconstrue, mistranslate, misrender, misconceive, misunderstand, misapprehend, misjudge. *Interpret*

Misjudge, Misconstrue, mistake, misunderstand, misapprehend, misconceive.
Understand

Mislay, Lose, misplace. *Find*

Mislead, Deceive, delude, misguide, misdirect. *Guide*

Mislike, Dislike, aversion, disapprobation. *Approve*

Mismanage, Misconduct, fumble, misrule, mishandle. *Rule*

Misprision, Mistake, misunderstanding, neglect, oversight, contempt.

Misprize, Underrate, undervalue, slight, underestimate, belittle. *Value*

Misrepresent, Falsify, misstate, pervert.

Misrule, Anarchy, misgovernment, maladministration, disorder, riot, confusion, mismanagement. *Government*

Miss, *v.n.*, Fail, miscarry, fall, err, trip. *Succeed*

v.a., Want, desiderate, need, require. *Have*

Lose, overlook. *Find*

n., Failure, miscarriage, mistake, error, trip, slip, fault, blunder, oversight, omission.

Maid, maiden, spinster, damsel, lass, girl.

Misshapen, Deformed, misformed, misproportioned, ungainly, unshapely, ugly. *Shapely*

Missing, Wanting, lacking, absent, lost. *Found*

Mission, Duty, commission, business, object, charge, trust, office, errand.

Legation, delegation, embassy, ministry, deputation, commission.

Missive, Letter, despatch, communication, message, epistle.

Misspend, Waste, dissipate, misuse, squander. *Utilize*

Misstatement, Perversion, falsification, untruth, misrepresentation. *Truth*

Mist, Haze, fog, cloud.

Obscurity, perplexity, bewilderment, confusion. *Lucidity*

Mistake, *v.a.*, Misapprehend, misunderstand, misconstrue, misinterpret, misconceive, misjudge. *Apprehend*

v.n., Err.

n., Mistaking, misunderstanding, misinterpretation, misapprehension, misconception.

Error, oversight, slip, fault, blunder.

Mistaken, Wrong, incorrect, erroneous. *Right*

Mistreat, Maltreat, illtreat, misuse, abuse, injure, wrong, hurt, harm, damage. *Remedy*

Mistress, Governess, instructress, dame.

Paramour, flame, concubine.

Dame, matron, madam. *Master*

Mistrust, *v.a.*, Doubt, distrust, suspect, fear, surmise, apprehend. *Trust*

n., Doubt, dubiety, distrust, suspicion, fear, misgiving. *Assurance*

Misty, Dim, clouded, dark, obscure. *Clear*

Misunderstand, Mistake, misapprehend, misinterpret, misconceive. *Apprehend*

Misunderstanding, Mistake, misapprehension,† error.

Difference, dissension, conflict, quarrel, disagreement, discord, difficulty. *Agreement*

Misuse, *v.a.*, Misemploy, abuse, pervert, desecrate, profane, misapply, squander, waste. *Utilize*

n., Misemployment, abuse,† prostitution.

Mitigate, Lessen, abate, decrease, allay, diminish, soften, alleviate, assuage, moderate. *Aggravate*

Appease, mollify, pacify, calm.

Mix, Commix, mingle, commingle, blend, unite, combine, compound, join, associate, amalgamate, confound, intermix. *Separate*

Mixture, Medley, admixture, intermixture, compound, miscellany, pot-pourri, confusion, jumble, association, union, blend.

Moan, Lament, bewail, mourn, grieve, sorrow, deplore, bemoan, repine. *Rejoice*

Mob, Rabble, crowd, throng, multitude, populace.

Mobile, Ductile, variable, inconstant, changeable, volatile, movable, sensitive, mercurial. *Steady*

Mock, *v.a.*, Ridicule, flout, insult, jeer, deride, chaff, taunt, defy, delude, illude, deceive. *Respect*

Ape, imitate, counterfeit.

n., Ridicule, insult, jeering, derision, gibe, sneer.

a., Sham, false, spurious, assumed, imitation, feigned, pretended, mimic, counterfeit. *Genuine*

Mockery, Jeering, derision, scorn, ridicule, imitation.

Mode, Style, fashion, custom, manner, way, method, degree, variety, quality.

Model, *v.a.*, Mould, make, fashion, design, form, plan, shape.

n., Example, standard, pattern, archetype, prototype, exemplar, gauge, type, original, mould, norm, paragon, design.

Copy, representation, image, fascimile, imitation.

Moderate, *v.a.*, Diminish, abate, decrease, lessen, alleviate, assuage, mollify, modify, mitigate, allay, soften, temper, attemper, control, repress, regulate, subdue, soothe, appease, pacify. *Aggravate*

a., Mild, steady, temperate, calm, sparing, frugal, reasonable, even, cool, deliberate, judicious, gentle. *Extreme*

Middling, mediocre, fair, indifferent. *Excellent*

Moderation, Mildness, steadiness, temperance,† sobriety, restraint, forbearance, composure. *Intemperance*

Modern, New, recent, late, fresh, novel, existent, up-to-date, present, current. *Ancient*

Modest, Meek, retiring, unassuming, unostentatious, unobtrusive, unpretentious. *Arrogant*

Chaste, virtuous, pure, decent, proper, becoming. *Wanton*

Modification, Alteration, change, variation, form, state, manner.

Modify, Moderate, lessen, qualify, alter, change, vary, shape, lower.

Modulate, Attune, tune, harmonize, adjust, adapt, proportion.

Moiety, Part, portion, half, share, fragment.   *Whole*

Moist, Damp, clammy, dank, wet, humid.   *Dry*

Moisture, Dampness, dankness, wetness, humidity.   *Dryness*

Mole, Pier, jetty, dike, breakwater, quay.

Molecule, Atom, monad, particle.   *Bulk*

Molest, Vex, harass, harry, worry, plague, pester, annoy, torment, trouble, disturb, inconvenience, incommode, discommode, tease, irritate, upset, oppress, hector, chafe.   *Soothe*

Mollify, Soothe, assuage, alleviate, mitigate, modify, moderate, abate, lessen, decrease, diminish, qualify, pacify, quiet, compose, calm, soften, tranquillize, still, allay.   *Aggravate*

Moment, Second, minute, instant, flash, trice, jiffy, twinkling.   *Age*
Importance, import, weight, consequence, consideration, significance, signification, value, gravity, force, element, factor, constituent.   *Triviality*

Momentous, Important, weighty, significant, serious, grave.   *Trivial*

Momentum, Impetus, moment.

Monad, Atom, molecule, particle.

Monarch, Ruler, king, sovereign, liege, emperor, despot, tyrant, autocrat.   *Subject*

Monarchic, Kingly, sovereign, despotic, autocratic, arbitrary, royal. *Democratic*

Monastic, Recluse, secluded, monkish, celibate, conventual.   *Secular*

Monetary, Financial, pecuniary, fiscal.

Money, Cash, currency, coin, wealth, riches, means.

Moneyed, Wealthy, opulent, affluent, rich, comfortable.   *Poor*

Monitor, Advisor, mentor, counsellor, warner, overseer, instructor.   *Deceiver*

Monomania, Delusion, illusion, hallucination.

Monopolize, Engross, appropriate, forestall.

Monopoly, Privilege, possession, appropriation, exclusiveness.   *Competition*

Monotonous, Regular, uniform, unvarying, unvaried, weary, tedious, boring, dull, uninteresting.   *Interesting*

Monotony, Regularity, uniformity, dulness, tedium, sameness.   *Relief*

Monster, Brute, beast, fiend, wretch, demon, ruffian, villain.   *Human*
Marvel, wonder, monstrosity, prodigy.   *Trifle*

Monstrous, Dreadful, awful, hideous, horrid, horrible, frightful, vile, shocking, terrible, hateful, heinous, intolerable.   *Comely*
Huge, prodigious, immense, enormous, vast, tremendous, colossal, abnormal, stupendous, marvellous, wonderful, preternatural, unnatural, portentous.   *Ordinary*

Monument, Memorial, cenotaph, remembrance, stone, tomb, testimonial, record.

Mood, Disposition, temper, vein, feeling, humour, state.   *Mind*

Moody, Sullen, irritable, morose, gloomy, glum, sulky, perverse, sour, fretful, peevish, crabbed, melancholy, capricious, sad, variable, petulant, captious.   *Gay*

Moonshine, Stuff, nonsense, rubbish, sentiment.   *Sense*

Moor, *v.a.*, Fasten, fix, tie, secure, berth.   *Loose*
n., Heath, common.
Blackamoor, negro.

Moot, *v.a.*, Argue, discuss, ventilate, agitate, debate, dispute.   *Stifle*
n., Disputable, debatable, doubtful, nice.   *Certain*

Mopish, Gloomy, downcast, downhearted, sad, despondent, dejected, depressed, melancholy, spiritless, crestfallen, listless, dull, glum, chapfallen.   *Elated*

Moral, Ethical, good, honest, honourable, virtuous, upright, just, unexceptionable, faultless, excellent.   *Vicious*
Ideal, intellectual, abstract, mental, spiritual.   *Real*

Morals, Habits, conduct, behaviour, manners.

Morass, Bog, fen, swamp, marsh, quagmire, slough, ditch.

Morbid, Unhealthy, unsound, diseased, vitiated, sickly, tainted, corrupted.   *Healthy*

Mordacious } Pungent, biting, bitter,
Mordant } caustic, cutting, sharp, severe, stinging, acrid, sarcastic, satirical.   *Soothing*

More, *a.*, Further, additional, added, other.   *Less*
adv., Further, besides, again.

Moreover, Further, furthermore, too, likewise, also, besides.

Morning, Morn, daybreak, dawn, sunrise, forenoon.   *Evening*

Morose, Sullen, sour, crabbed, surly,

moody, crusty, austere, churlish, gruff, splenetic, spleenish. **Genial**

Morsel, Bit, piece, part, slice, fragment, bite, mouthful, titbit. **Whole**

Mortal, n., Man, being, person. **God**
a., Human, feeble, ephemeral. **Divine**
Deadly, fatal, final, destructive.

Mortality, Death, destruction, fatality. **Eternal**

Mortally, Deadly, fatally, irrecoverably.

Mortification, Humiliation, shame, chagrin, disappointment, discontent, displeasure, dissatisfaction, annoyance, vexation. **Delight**

Mortify, v.a., Kill, subdue, conquer, deaden. **Indulge**
Humiliate, shame, humble, abash, abase, disappoint, displease, dissatisfy, annoy, vex, chagrin, worry, trouble, harass, plague. **Delight**
v.n., Fester, putrefy, corrupt, gangrene.

Mortuary, Morgue, necropolis, cemetery.

Most, a., Greatest. **Least**
adv., Mostly, chiefly, mainly, principally, first, utmost.

Mother, Parent, origin, spring, source, head, mater, mamma. **Father**

Motherly, Tender, maternal, kind, affectionate, loving, careful.

Motion, Movement, passage, action, impulse. **Rest**
Proposal, proposition, suggestion, act.

Motionless, Still, stationary, quiescent, immobile, fixed, unmoved. **Moving**

Motive, Incentive, spur, inducement, reason, impulse, cause, ground, consideration, stimulus, prompting, purpose, design. **Effort**

Motley, Mixed, mingled, variegated, diversified, heterogeneous, mottled, composite. **Uniform**

Mottled, Mixed, motley, composite, piebald, speckled, spotted, variegated.

Mould, v.a., Make, form, model, shape, create, fashion, cast. **Distort**
n., Form, shape, fashion, cast, character.
Matter, material, substance.
Blight, mildew, rust, smut, mouldiness, mustiness.
Pattern, matrix, matrice.
Loam, soil, earth.

Moulder, Decay, crumble, perish, disintegrate.

Mouldy, Mildewed, musty, rusty, fusty. **Fresh**

Mound, Hill, hillock, knoll, pile, rampart, bulwark, defence.

Mount, v.a., Climb, ascend, scale. **Descend**
v.n., Ascend, rise, arise, tower, soar.

Mountebank, Charlatan, impostor, pretender, quack.

Mourn, v.a., Lament, bewail, deplore, regret, moan, bemoan. **Enjoy**
v.n., Lament, wail, moan, grieve, sorrow, repine. **Rejoice**

Mournful, Depressing, woeful, sad, lamentable, deplorable, grievous, distressing.
Sorrowful, sad, depressed, unhappy, lugubrious, doleful, tearful, melancholy. **Cheerful**

Mourning, Grief, lamentation, sorrow.

Mouth, n., Opening, aperture, gap, crevice, orifice.
Inlet, entrance.
v.n., Rant, declaim, vociferate.

Movable, Portable, light. **Stationary**
Variable, inconstant, changeable. **Steadfast**

Movables, Furniture, goods, chattels, belongings, effects, property, baggage. **Fixtures**

Move, v.n., March, go, stir, proceed, budge, remove. **Stay**
v.a., Stir, propel, remove, drive, impel, shift, start. **Stop**
Urge, incite, agitate, rouse, excite, incense, stir, affect, touch, awaken, prompt, persuade, influence. **Deter**
Propose, offer, suggest, recommend.
v.n., March, proceed, go, walk, stir, budge, act, change.
n., Motion, movement.
Proceeding.

Movement, Motion, move, crusade, passage, drive.
Rhythm, part, tempo, progression.

Moving, Pathetic, touching, eloquent, affecting, impressive.

Much, a., Plenteous, abundant, considerable. **Little**
adv., Greatly.
Almost, largely, nearly, practically.

Mucilaginous, Gelatinous, glutinous, slimy, viscid, viscous, gummy. **Crystalline**

Mud, Mire, clay, dirt, muck.

Muddle, v.a., Confuse, disarrange, derange, disorder. **Arrange**
n., Confusion, disarrangement, disorder, disarray, chaos, mess. **Order**

Muddy, Clayey, miry, dirty, impure, turbid. **Pellucid**

Muffle, Envelop, wrap, stifle, shroud, cover, conceal, disguise, blindfold, enfold, dull. **Expose**

Muffled, Stifled, dulled, suppressed, wrapped, deadened. **Clear**

Muggy, Damp, clammy, dank, vaporous, wet, moist, humid, warm, close, oppressive. *Clear*

Mulct, *v.a.*, Fine, penalize, amerce. *Reward*

n., Fine, penalty, amercement, forfeit, forfeiture, damages, indemnity.

Mulish, Obstinate, stubborn, stolid, intractable, headstrong, cross-grained, self-willed. *Amenable*

Multifarious, Manifold, many, varied, various, diverse, diversified, multitudinous, different. *Few*

Multiply, *v.a.*, Increase, augment. *Divide*

v.n., Increase, spread, grow, extend. *Decrease*

Multitude, Crowd, throng, concourse, number, host, horde, swarm, army, legion. *Sprinkling*

Mum, Mute, dumb, speechless, voiceless, silent.

Mummery, Buffoonery, sport, masking, mockery, masquerade, foolery.

Mumpish, Moody, morose, spleenish, splenetic, surly, cross, crabbed, sour, sullen, sulky. *Gay*

Munch, Chew, crunch, bite, nibble, masticate.

Mundane, Worldly, earthly, terrestrial, temporal, secular. *Spiritual*

Municipal, Civil, civic.

Munificent, Generous, bountiful, bounteous, liberal, princely, lavish, beneficent. *Mean*

Muniment, Defence, bulwark, fortress, support, stronghold, protection, fort, citadel, fortification.

Munition, Ammunition, military store, provisions, guns, armoury.

Murder, *v.a.*, Kill, slay, assassinate, destroy, slaughter, massacre. *Protect*

n., Assassination, slaughter, homicide.

Murderer, Killer, assassin, slayer.

Murderous, Fell, cruel, savage, barbarous, bloodthirsty, bloody, sanguinary, ruthless. *Kind*

Murky, Dark, cloudy, clouded, dim, lowering, overcast, gloomy, lurid, obscure, dusky. *Clear*

Murmur, *v.n.*, Whisper, mutter, mumble. *Shout*

Complain, mutter, grumble, repine, croak. *Rejoice*

n., Whisper, mutter, mumble, undertone. Complaint, mutter,† plaint.

Muscular, Strong, robust, vigorous, brawny, sinewy, lusty, sturdy, powerful, energetic, athletic, stalwart. *Feeble*

Muse, Ruminate, reflect, consider, turn, meditate, ponder, think, cogitate, dream, brood, contemplate, deliberate. *Act*

Mushroom, Transient, transitory, brief, evanescent, ephemeral. *Permanent*

Music, Harmony, poetry, melody, tune, symphony.

Musical, Harmonious, melodious, tuneful, symphonious, concordant, dulcet, sweet. *Discordant*

Musing, *n.*, Reverie, meditation, rumination, reflection, cogitation, dreaming, brooding, thinking, contemplation, wonder, abstraction. *Action*

a., Meditative, reflecting, dreaming, brooding, thinking, absent-minded, wandering, preoccupied, wool-gathering. *Attentive*

Muster, *v.a.*, Convene, convoke, collect, gather, congregate, marshal, assemble, rally. *Disperse*

v.n., Meet, congregate, collect, gather, assemble, rally.

n., Meeting, congregation, assembly, collection, rally.

Musty, Mouldy, rank, fusty, frowsy, fetid, old, stale, foul. *Fresh*

Mutable, Variable, changeable, changeful, inconstant, mobile, fickle, irresolute, unsteady, alterable, vacillating, wavering, uncertain, unstable, unsettled, fluctuating. *Changeless*

Mutation, Variation, change, alteration, fluctuation. *Constancy*

Mute, Speechless, dumb, silent, quiet, still, voiceless, taciturn, mum. *Loud*

Mutilate, Injure, mar, disfigure, deform, maim, cripple, mangle, dismember. *Mend*

Mutinous, Unruly, insubordinate, turbulent, rebellious, insurrectionary, wild, riotous, insurgent, seditious, refractory, contumacious. *Obedient*

Mutiny, Rebellion, rising, riot, sedition, revolt, insurrection, uprising.

Mutter, Murmur, mumble, whisper. *Exclaim*

Mutual, Interchangeable, common, correlative, reciprocal.

Myopic, Short-sighted, near-sighted, purblind.

Myriad, Innumerable, countless, many, multitudinous, manifold. *Few*

Mysterious⎫ Hidden, dark, unknown,
Mystic　　⎬ occult, abstruse, obscure, veiled, incomprehensible, unaccountable,

dim, unexplained, enigmatical, recondite, inscrutable, unintelligible, secret. *Plain*

Mystery, Enigma, riddle, secret.

Mystify, Perplex, puzzle, confuse, bewilder, nonplus, embarrass, obfuscate.
Enlighten

Myth, Legend, story, fable, tale, tradition, fiction, allegory, parable, falsehood, lie, untruth. *History*

Mythical } Fictitious, fabled, fanci-
Mythological } ful, fabulous, legendary, allegorical, imaginary.

Nacreous, Iridescent, opalescent, pearly, pearlaceous.   *Dingy*

Nag, Harry, harass, worry, torment, plague, hector, pester, bother.   *Soothe*

Naïve, Ingenuous, artless, simple, frank, candid, natural, innocent, unsophisticated, unaffected, plain, open. *Cunning*

Naked, Nude, denuded, bare, undressed, unclothed, uncovered, undraped, exposed.   *Clothed*

Unvarnished, simple, mere, sheer, plain, unexaggerated, uncoloured, evident, manifest, stark, open.   *Coloured*

Name, *v.a.,* Call, dub, style, christen, denominate, phrase, term, entitle.

Designate, specify, mention, indicate, nominate.

n., Title, denomination, designation, appellation, cognomen, sobriquet, description, epithet.

Reputation, character, credit, distinction, note, fame, celebrity, eminence, repute.

Nap, Slumber, doze, drowse.   *Wake*

Narcotic, Anodyne, sedative, opiate, anaesthetic.   *Stimulant*

Narrate, Report, relate, tell, recite, detail, describe, chronicle, rehearse, recount.   *Suppress*

Narration ⎱ Report, relation, chronicle,
Narrative ⎰ tale†, account, history, story.

Narrow, Strait, straitened, limited, contracted, close, cramped, scanty, confined, circumscribed, slender, spare, thin, pinched, incapacious.   *Broad*

Bigoted, illiberal, biassed, warped, prejudiced, intolerant.   *Unbiassed*

Nascent, Beginning, commencing, early, initial, youthful, budding, rudimental, incipient, dawning, opening. *Mature*

Nasty, Dirty, smutty, defiled, indelicate, filthy, impure, unclean, indecent, lewd, foul, polluted, ribald, gross, loose. *Pure*

Unpleasant, nauseous, offensive, odious, loathsome, sickening, disagreeable, repulsive, nauseating, revolting, disgusting.   *Pleasant*

Nation, People, race, country, land, realm, commonwealth, state.

Native, *n.,* Aboriginal.   *Foreigner*

a., Mother, domestic, home, own, vernacular.   *Foreign*

Genuine, real, original, natural.

Intrinsic, inborn, inherent, indigenous, natural, congenital, inbred. *Ascititious*

Natural, Normal, regular, usual, inevitable, consistent, legitimate.   *Abnormal*

Native, intrinsic, inborn, inbred, indigenous, innate, congenital, inherent.   *Ascititious*

Simple, naïve, artless, ingenuous, frank, open, candid, sincere, unaffected, unsophisticated, genuine, real, easy, free.   *Artificial*

Naturalize, Adapt, habituate, domesticate, acclimatize, accustom.

Nature, Structure, essence, constitution, creation, character, disposition, quality.

World, universe, creation, vitality.

Character, disposition, humour, temper, soul, mood, mind, intellect, intelligence.

Naught, Nought, nothing. *Everything*

Naughty, Bad, mischievous, wicked, corrupt, vile, base, sinful, worthless, froward, perverse.   *Good*

Nausea, Disgust, sickness, aversion, loathing, dislike, repugnance, repulsion.   *Relish*

Nauseate, Disgust, sicken, revolt, repel.†

Nauseous, Disgusting, sickening, loathsome.†   *Pleasant*

Nautical ⎱ Marine, maritime.   *Land*
Naval ⎰

Navigate, Sail, course, cruise, steer, plan, direct, guide, pilot.

Navy, Ships, shipping, fleet, vessels.

Near, *v.a.,* Approach.

a., Close, adjacent, neighbouring, nigh, adjoining, proximate, contiguous, approaching, imminent, forthcoming, impending.   *Distant*

Dear, intimate, allied, close, related, familiar, attached.

Short, direct, straight, immediate, close.

Parsimonious, close, mean, miserly, niggardly, stingy.   *Generous*

adv., Nearly, almost, closely, well-nigh.

Nearly, Near, approximately, almost, closely, well-nigh.   *Distantly*

Neat, Smart, clean, spruce, trim, tidy, orderly.   *Untidy*

Clever, dexterous, adroit, expert, finished, exact.   *Clumsy*

Pure, undiluted, unadulterated, unmixed.

Nebulous, Nebular, misty, hazy, cloudy, obscure.   *Clear*

Necessary, Essential, requisite, compulsory, involuntary, indispensable, inevitable, unavoidable, needful, certain.   *Optional*

Necessitate, Compel, impel, enforce, force, constrain, oblige.

Necessitous, Poor, needy, indigent, destitute, penniless, distressed, reduced. *Rich*

Necessity, Essential, requisite, compulsion, requirement, indispensableness, indispensability, inevitableness, certainty, destiny, fate, fatality, compulsion, unavoidableness, needfulness, need, want, exigency, urgency. *Choice*

Necromancy, Magic, witchery, witchcraft, wizardry, enchantment, sorcery, divination.

Need, *v.a.*, Lack, want, require, demand. *Have*

n., Lack, want, necessity, extremity, indigence, poverty, privation, distress, strait, readiness, destitution. *Possession*

Needful, Necessary, essential, vital, indispensable, requisite. *Unnecessary*
Needy, poor, necessitous, indigent, destitute, penniless. *Rich*

Needy, Needful, poor.†

Needless, Unnecessary, superfluous, useless. *Helpful*

Nefarious, Wicked, iniquitous, bad, execrable, vile, atrocious, abominable, outrageous, scandalous, detestable, flagitious, heinous, dreadful, villainous, horrible. *Admirable*

Negation, Reversal, opposite, disclaimer, denial, disavowal. *Assertion*

Negative, Indirect, denying, disclaiming. *Positive*

Neglect, *v.a.*, Overlook, disregard, omit, miss, contemn, ignore, forget, slight, despise. *Observe*

n., Disregard, omission, remissness, heedlessness, carelessness, inattention, default, failure. *Attention*

Neglectful Regardless, remiss, thought-
Negligent less, careless, inattentive, heedless. *Attentive*

Negligée, Undress, dishabille.

Negligence, Neglect, disregard, omission, remissness, heedlessness, carelessness, inattention, indifference, thoughtlessness, slackness, default, shortcoming, defect, failure. *Attention*

Negotiate, Treat, bargain, effect, transact, pass, circulate, sell. *Stop*

Neighbourhood, District, propinquity, vicinity, locality, environs, nearness.

Neighbouring, Near, adjoining, adjacent, close, nigh, proximate, contiguous. *Distant*

Neighbourly, Sociable, social, kind, friendly, civil, obliging, attentive. *Unfriendly*

Neophyte, Novice, beginner, learner, tyro, convert, disciple, proselyte, pupil. *Master*

Neoteric, Modern, recent, novel, new. *Ancient*

Nerve, *v.a.*, Steel, brace, strengthen, fortify, energize, invigorate. *Weaken*
n., Strength, vigour, courage, might, power, force, manhood, resolution, hardihood, fortitude, pluck, firmness, endurance, will. *Weakness*

Nervous, Weak, weakly, timid, afraid, fearful, agitated, irritable, timorous, hesitant, self-conscious. *Bold*

Nestle, Harbour, lie, snuggle, cuddle, nuzzle, lodge, rest.

Nether, Lower, bottom.

Nettle, Vex, provoke, plague, annoy, tease, chafe, aggravate, irritate, incense, harass, ruffle, exasperate. *Soothe*

Network, Mesh, interlacement, netting.

Neutral, Impartial, indifferent, unbiassed, non-partisan, aloof, neuter. *Partisan*

Neutralize, Balance, counterbalance, counteract, offset, destroy, invalidate, cancel, counterpoise, compensate. *Intensify*

Nevertheless, Notwithstanding, none-the-less, however, yet.

New, Recent, novel, modern, unused, fresh, unaccustomed, commencing. *Old*

News, Intelligence, tidings, advice, information, word, report, account.

Next, Near, bordering, close, joining.

Nice, Precise, exact, critical, accurate, correct, close, strict, definite. *Vague*
Delicate, fine, minute, scrupulous, exacting, finical, fastidious, particular. *Loose*
Fine, exquisite, neat, tender, tidy, pleasant, pleasing, delicious, agreeable, delightful. *Nasty*

Niceness Precision, exactitude, exact-
Nicety ness, accuracy, correctness, truth. *Vagueness*
Delicacy, fineness, scrupulousness, fastidiousness, discrimination. *Looseness*

Niche, Nook, corner, recess.

Nick, Dent, score, notch, dint, incision, indentation, cut.

Niggardly, Mean, near, close, parsimonious, miserly, selfish, stingy, avaricious, covetous, penurious, mercenary, illiberal. *Generous*

Nigh, *a.*, Near, next, close, proximate, adjacent, adjoining, contiguous. *Distant*
adv., Nearly, almost, near.

Night, Darkness, obscurity, dusk, nightfall. *Day*

Nimble, Active, agile, quick, prompt,

ready, smart, alert, alive, lively, speedy, sprightly, brisk, swift. ***Clumsy***

Nip, *v.a.,* Squeeze, pinch, crush, clip, compress, gripe, grip, bite.

n., Squeeze, pinch, clip, bite.

Sip, drop, drain, dram.

Nipple, Dug, teat, pap, udder.

Nobility, Gentry, aristocracy, peerage, lords, noblesse. ***Commoners***

Greatness, rank, exaltation, loftiness, dignity, eminence, nobleness, grandeur, elevation, worthiness, distinction, superiority. ***Meanness***

Noble, *n.,* Gentleman, aristocrat, peer, lord, nobleman, grandee. ***Commoner***

a., Lordly, patrician, great, exalted, lofty, dignified, eminent, grand, elevated, worthy, distinguished, superior, honourable, stately, magnificent, choice, excellent. ***Mean***

Nobly, Magnificently, grandly, heroically, bravely, honourably, magnanimously, splendidly. ***Poorly***

Nobody, Nonentity, cipher. ***Somebody***

Nocturnal, Nightly. ***Diurnal***

Nod, Bow, beck.

Node, Nodosity, protuberance, lump, knob, knot, swelling. ***Smooth***

Noise, Hubbub, clamour, row, racket, sound, blare, outcry, pandemonium, stir, talk, tumult, din, uproar. ***Quiet***

Noiseless, Silent, still, quiet, inaudible. ***Loud***

Noisome, Deleterious, noxious, hurtful, harmful, foul, bad, injurious, pestilential, unwholesome, unhealthy, baneful, baleful, detrimental, mischievous, poisonous, fetid, destructive, offensive. ***Beneficial***

Noisy, Loud, boisterous, clamorous, riotous, uproarious, obstreperous, turbulent, tumultuous, brawling, vociferous, blatant. ***Quiet***

Nomadic, Roving, migratory, wandering, vagrant, pastoral. ***Urban***

Nominal, Titular, formal, ostensible, professed, pretended. ***Real***

Nominate, Name, appoint, propose, present, specify, choose, define, invest, designate. ***Deprive***

Nonchalant, Easy, cool, indifferent, careless, calm, unconcerned, apathetic. ***Concerned***

Nondescript, Odd, indescribable, abnormal, unclassifiable. ***Select***

Nonentity, Nobody, cipher. ***Somebody***

Nonesuch, Paragon, pattern, nonpareil, model, acme, ideal.

Nonpareil, Matchless, unmatched, unequalled, peerless, unparalleled, nonesuch. ***Ordinary***

Nonplus, Astonish, astound, bewilder, puzzle, disconcert, confound, dumbfound, perplex.

Nonsense, Trash, absurdity, foolishness, fooling, folly, jest, inanity, trifling, silliness, stupidity. ***Wisdom***

Nook, Corner, recess, niche.

Norm, Type, standard, pattern, model, rule.

Normal, Typical, standard, model, regular, usual, ordinary, natural, wonted, legitimate, recognized. ***Unusual***

North } Northerly, arctic, boreal.
Northern } ***Southern***

Nosegay, Posy, bouquet.

Notable, Signal, remarkable, memorable, conspicuous, plain, extraordinary, noted, notorious, prominent, noticeable, famous. ***Commonplace***

Notch, Dent, dint, indentation, nick, incision, cut, score.

Note, *v.a.,* Remark, mark, notice, observe, register, record, heed, regard, designate, denote. ***Ignore***

n., Record, remark, memorandum, minute, catalogue, report, comment, annotation.

Letter, epistle, communication, billet.

Bill, account, reckoning.

Mark, fame, renown, repute, celebrity, distinction, credit, eminence, respectability, consequence, importance. ***Obscurity***

Remark, notice, regard, attention, consideration, heed, observation. ***Neglect***

Noted, Famous, renowned, reputed, reputable, celebrated, distinguished, eminent, important, notable, notorious, remarkable, conspicuous, illustrious. ***Obscure***

Noteworthy, Remarkable, noticeable, unusual, memorable, extraordinary, conspicuous, rare. ***Ordinary***

Nothing, Naught, nought, zero, cipher, nonentity, non-existence. ***Something***

Notice, *v.a.,* Observe, see, remark, note,† perceive. ***Miss***

n., Observation, note, heed, regard, attention.

Warning, notification, advice, information, instruction, order, direction, intelligence, news, intimation, premonition, announcement, communication.

Attention, respect, civility, consideration.

Remarks, comments, review.

Noticeable, Noteworthy, remarkable, unusual, extraordinary, conspicuous, rare. ***Ordinary***

Notification, Notice, warning, advice,

information, intelligence, advertisement, news, instruction, intimation, premonition, announcement, communication. *Concealment*

Notify, Warn, advise, inform, advertise, instruct, acquaint, apprise, publish, announce, declare. *Suppress*

Notion, Idea, belief, conception, theory, opinion, judgment, impression, conviction, estimation, view, concept, sentiment.

Notoriety, Publicity, reputation, fame, name, celebrity. *Privacy*

Notorious, Known, conspicuous, famed, noted, remarkable. *Obscure* Admitted, open, undisputed, recognized, allowed, known. *Suspected*

Notwithstanding, Yet, nevertheless, however, despite.

Nought, Naught, nothing, cipher.

Nourish, Nurture, support, feed, nurse, tend, maintain. *Starve* Cherish, foster, encourage, succour, promote, foment. *Banish*

Nourishing, Nutritive, nutritious, building, healthful, strengthening, wholesome, invigorating. *Weakening*

Nourishment, Nutrition, nutriment, food, sustenance, aliment.

Novel, *a.*, New, fresh, original, modern. recent, uncommon, rare, unusual, strange, *Stale* *n.*, Tale, story, book, romance, narrative, fiction.

Novice, Beginner, learner, pupil, fledgling, probationer, neophyte, disciple, tyro. *Master*

Noxious, Harmful, hurtful, injurious, baneful, baleful, deleterious, detrimental, noisome, unwholesome, unhealthy, objectionable, pernicious, poisonous, foul, pestilential, deadly, mischievous, destructive, bad, offensive, fetid. *Beneficial*

Nucleus, Centre, core, kernel.

Nude, Bare, naked, unclothed, undressed, uncovered, exposed, denuded. *Clothed*

Nudge, Push, poke, jog.

Nugatory, Futile, useless, worthless, ineffective, ineffectual, inefficacious, vain, bootless, unavailing, trifling, frivolous, magnificent. *Successful*

Nuisance, Annoyance, bother, pest, bore, plague, trouble, infliction. *Pleasure*

Null, Void, nugatory, useless, worthless, invalid, expressionless, characterless, inefficacious, ineffectual. *Valid*

Nullify, Abrogate, revoke, rescind, repeal, annul, invalidate, abolish, cancel, extinguish. *Establish*

Numb, Dead, deadened, benumbed, insensible, dulled, paralyzed, torpid. *Quick*

Number, *v.a.*, Count, calculate, compute, account, numerate, include, contain, enumerate, add, reckon, tell. *n.*, Figure, digit, numeral. Multitude, many, host, throng, crowd. *Few* Sum, total, aggregate, collection.

Numberless, Countless, innumerable, immeasurable, infinite. *Scarce*

Numeral, Number, figure, digit.

Numerate, Enumerate, count, calculate, number, compute, reckon, tell.

Numerous, Many, manifold, frequent, abundant. *Scarce*

Nuncio, Legate, messenger, ambassador, envoy.

Nuptial, Conjugal, connubial, hymeneal, bridal, marriage.

Nurse, Nurture, rear, tend, nourish, suckle, feed. *Neglect* Cherish, harbour, succour, promote, encourage, foster, manage. *Banish*

Nurture, Nourish, nurse, feed, rear, tend. Train, instruct, educate, discipline, school.

Nutriment, Nourishment, food, sustenance, sustentation, subsistence, nutrition, aliment. *Detriment*

Nutritious, Wholesome, feeding, building, nourishing, invigorating, strengthening. *Poor*

Nymph, Dryad, maid, girl, damsel, maiden.

O

OBSERVE

Oath, Vow, pledge, statement, asseveration, promise, affirmation.
Curse, imprecation, malediction, blasphemy, expletive.

Obdurate, Hardened, hard, unrelenting, relentless, harsh, unyielding, firm, inexorable, immovable, unbending, stubborn, obstinate, callous, dogged, unshakable, inflexible, unfeeling, insensible. *Docile*

Obedient, Submissive, subservient, deferential, compliant, yielding, respectful, regardful, dutiful, observant. *Refractory*

Obeisance, Homage, respect, reverence, worship, salutation, bow. *Haughtiness*

Obesity, Fatness, corpulence, corpulency, rotundity, plumpness, fleshiness. *Thinness*

Obey, Comply, submit, heed, mind. *Resist*

Obfuscate, Obscure, darken, cloud, confuse, bewilder, muddle. *Clear*

Object, *v.n.,* Protest, disapprove, mind, demur.
n., Thing, article, reality, phenomenon.
End, aim, goal, target, mark, intention, intent, design, motive, purpose. *Conception*

Objection, Protest, scruple, difficulty, obstacle, barrier, doubt.

Objective, External, entrinsic, outward, real, concrete, actual, positive. *Subjective*

Objectless, Desultory, purposeless, aimless, vague, wandering, senseless.

Objurgate, Scold, chide, censure, rebuke, rebuff, reprove, reprehend. *Praise*

Oblation, Sacrifice, gift, present, offering. *Sacrilege*

Obligation, Necessity, duty, debt, liability, engagement, responsibility, agreement, contract, bond, covenant, stipulation, compulsion. *Freedom*

Obligatory, Necessary, binding, coercive, compulsory, essential. *Optional*

Oblige, Necessitate, compel, bind, coerce, force, constrain. *Release*
Favour, accommodate, benefit, gratify, serve, please, convenience. *Annoy*

Obliging, Accommodating, considerate, compliant, complaisant, affable, friendly, kind, civil, polite, courteous. *Perverse*

Oblique, Slanting, aslant, sidelong, sloping, inclined, crooked, lateral, angular. *Straight*

Obliterate, Cancel, delete, efface, erase, eradicate, expunge, destroy, blot, remove. *Restore*

Oblivious, Forgetful, heedless, regardless, mindless, neglectful, negligent, careless. *Mindful*

Obloquy, Blame, aspersion, reproach, censure, defamation, calumny, detraction, contumely, odium, traducing, slander, reviling, invective. *Praise*

Obnoxious, Objectionable, offensive, nasty, hateful, unpleasant, unpleasing, horrible, horrid, pernicious, disgusting. *Pleasant*

Obscene, Loose, coarse, lewd, rude, indecent, indelicate, impure, unclean, nasty, foul, dirty, broad, ribald, unchaste, immodest, smutty, filthy, pornographic, shameless, gross, digusting, offensive. *Decent*

Obscure, *v.a.,* Eclipse, hide, cover, cloud, conceal, obfuscate, blot, disguise, dim, darken, shade. *Luminate*
a., Dim, dark, dusky, cloudy, shadowy, gloomy, indistinct, lowering, lurid, murky, sombre, rayless. *Bright*
Unknown, inglorious, humble, mean, unnoticed, unhonoured, nameless, unrenowed, unnoted, undistinguished. *Famous*
Hidden, recondite, mystic, mysterious, remote, secluded, abstruse, vague, incomprehensible, unintelligible, difficult, involved, intricate, doubtful, uncertain, indistinct, indefinite. *Clear*

Obsequious, Servile, flattering, fawning, cringing, deferential, slavish, sycophantic, submissive, subservient. *Independent*

Observance, Performance, discharge, fulfilment, respect, service, attention, heed, regard. *Neglect*
Rite, ceremony, form, ritual, custom, practice, usage, fashion.

Observant, Attentive, watchful, heedful, regardful, mindful, obedient, submissive. *Heedless*

Observation, Remark, note, notice comment, annotation.
Observance, attention, notice, experience, knowledge, study, contemplation, consideration. *Inattention*

Observe, *v.n.,* Remark, comment, say, attend, notice.
v.a., Notice, see, perceive, remark, mark,

195

note, watch, behold, see, discover, detect, descry. *Miss*

Obey, regard, fulfil, keep, follow. *Disregard*

Utter, mention, say, express, remark.

Observer, Spectator, watcher, beholder, student, examiner, keeper, bystander, looker-on.

Obsolete, Archaic, antiquated, ancient, old, past, disused, effete. *Modern*

Obstacle, Barrier, hindrance, impediment, check, obstruction, difficulty, objection. *Help*

Obstinate, Firm, resolute, immovable, stubborn, headstrong, refractory, obdurate, inflexible, mulish, contumacious, dogged, pertinacious, persistent, unyielding, unruly, perverse, wilful, heady, stolid, unshakable. *Docile*

Obstreperous, Uproarious, boisterous, clamorous, loud, noisy, tumultuous, turbulent. *Quiet*

Obstruct, Hinder, bar, impede, check, choke, stop, block, close, blockade, barricade, encumber, embarrass, retard, clog, prevent, arrest, interrupt. *Promote*

Obstruction, Hindrance, bar, impediment,† obstacle, difficulty. *Clearance*

Obtain, Acquire, procure, get, win, attain, achieve, earn, gain, secure. *Lose*

Obtrude, Intrude, thrust, force, interfere. *Withdraw*

Obtrusive, Intruding, intrusive, officious, interfering, forward. *Retiring*

Obtuse, Dull, dense, heavy, thick, stupid, stolid, unintelligent, slow. *Sharp*

Obverse, Opposite, facing. *Reverse*

Obviate, Prevent, remove, preclude. *Necessitate*

Obvious, Clear, apparent, plain, evident, manifest, visible, patent, palpable, distinct, undoubted, undeniable, unmistakable. *Obscure*

Occasion, *v.a.*, Create, produce, cause, originate.

n., Cause, reason, motive, ground, necessity, want, need, inducement.

Occurrence, conjuncture, opportunity, juncture, convenience, opening, incident, happening, event.

Occasional, Irregular, casual, incidental, rare. *Frequent*

Occult, Mystic, mystical, mysterious, hidden, recondite, deep, obscure, latent, secret, unrevealed, undiscovered, unknown, undetected, abstruse, invisible, veiled. *Open*

Occupant, Owner, inhabiter, holder, proprietor, resident, tenant, occupier, possessor. *Intruder*

Occupation, Occupancy, holding, tenure, use, possession, enjoyment, encroachment. *Evacuation*

Work, employment, situation, trade, calling, vocation, avocation, profession, pursuit, business, craft.

Occupy, Possess, own, hold, keep, inhabit, use, employ.

Engage, fill, follow, employ, busy.

Occur, Happen, befall, betide, chance, come, arise, appear, eventuate, supervene.

Occurrence, Happening, event, incident, accident, affair, adventure, proceeding, transaction.

Ocean, Deep, sea, main.

Odd, Singular, single, unmatched, uneven, sole, remaining, unusual, queer, extraordinary, unique, peculiar, eccentric, uncommon, strange, fantastic, quaint, whimsical. *Ordinary*

Odds, Difference, inequality, disparity. Probability, likelihood.

Supremacy, advantage, superior. *Disadvantage*

Odious, Detestable, abominable, hateful, shocking, nasty, unpleasant, offensive, execrable, damnable, loathsome, obnoxious, repulsive, disgusting. *Pleasant*

Odium, Obloquy, reproach, blame, censure, opprobrium, unpopularity, dislike, hate, hatred, antipathy, detestation, jealousy. *Popularity*

Odour, Smell, scent, redolence, fragrance, perfume.

Off, *adv.*, Away, from, over, done. *On prep.*, Opposite, along, against, facing, distant.

Offal, Carrion, waste, garbage, rubbish, refuse, bits.

Offence, Wrong, affront, injury, hurt, harm, indignity, insult, injustice, crime, misdeed, outrage, misdemeanour, transgression, delinquency, fault, trespass, sin. *Right*

Anger, wrath, resentment, displeasure, pique, umbrage. *Forgiveness*

Attack, onset, assault, aggression. *Defence*

Offend, *v.a.*, Annoy, wrong, affront, injure, hurt, harm, insult, outrage, vex, irritate, provoke, gall, fret, nettle, displease, shock, molest, mortify, pain, chafe. *Please*

v.n., Sin, err, trespass, fall, transgress.

Offender, Sinner, transgressor, malefactor, felon, convict, criminal, delinquent, trespasser, culprit.

Offensive, Annoying, injurious, insulting, outrageous, irritating, galling, painful, displeasing, unpleasant, disagreeable, disgusting, loathsome, nasty, nauseous, nauseating, sickening, repulsive, distasteful, obnoxious, objectionable, shocking, revolting, execrable, detestable, hateful, insolent, rude, abusive, impertinent. *Pleasant*

Aggressive, attacking, assailant, bold, invading. *Defensive*

Offer, *v.a.,* Proffer, tender, present, propose, give, exhibit, propound, furnish. *Withdraw*

v.n., Endeavour, dare, essay, venture, propose, volunteer, occur.

n., Proffer, tender, proposition, proposal, advance, overture, bid, attempt, essay, endeavour.

Offering, Sacrifice, gift, oblation, present.

Office, Post, position, situation, berth, station, work, place, charge, business, duty, service, employment, trust, function, appointment. *Sinecure*

Official, Professional, authoritative, functional, administrative. *Private*

Officiate, Perform, serve, act, supervise.

Officious, Interfering, meddling, intermeddling, meddlesome, pushing, intrusive, obtrusive, forward, pragmatical. *Modest*

Offset, Counterbalance, equivalent, counterpoise.

Offspring, Child, children, issue, progeny, posterity, descendant, descendants. *Parent*

Often, Oft, oftentimes, repeatedly, frequently. *Occasionally*

Ogre, Monster, demon, devil, spirit, giant.

Oily, Greasy, lubricous, smooth, oleaginous, fat, unctuous. *Viscous*

Old, Ancient, antique, pristine, aged, mature, matured, obsolete, elderly, antiquated, primitive, original. *New*

Oleaginous, Oily, greasy, lubricous, smooth, fat, unctuous. *Dry*

Omen, Augury, presage, sign, portent, prognostic, foreboding, foretelling, premonition.

Ominous, Portentous, foreboding, premonitory, monitory, unpropitious, inauspicious, threatening. *Favourable*

Omission, Oversight, neglect, exclusion, failure, default. *Notice*

Omit, Miss, disregard, neglect, exclude, skip, drop. *Include*

Omnipotent, Almighty, infallible, all-powerful. *Weak*

Omniscient, All-knowing, all-wise, all-seeing. *Ignorant*

On, *adv.,* Onward, forward, ahead, uninterrupted, unceasing. *Back*

On, *prep.,* Upon. *Off*

One, *n.,* Unit. *None*

Person, individual, head, being. *Nobody*

a., Single, united, undivided, integrated.

Onerous, Heavy, toilsome, oppressive, hard, difficult, burdensome, responsible, weighty, operose. *Light*

One-sided, Unfair, unjust, prejudiced, biassed, partial. *Fair*

Only, *a.,* Solitary, sole, single, alone.

adv., Solely, singly, simply, barely, merely.

conj., But.

Onset ⎫ Assault, attack, storming,
Onslaught ⎭ storm, charge. *Retreat*

Onus, Burden, responsibility.

Onward-s, On, forward, ahead, advancing. *Backwards*

Ooze, Drop, drip, leak, percolate, exude. *Rush*

Mud, slime, mire.

Opalescent, Nacreous, iridescent, pearly.

Opaque, Untransparent, turbid, thick, obscure, clouded. *Transparent*

Open, *v.a. & n.,* Begin, commence, start. *Close*

v.a., Unclose, unlock, unfasten, untie, undo.

Spread, expand, part.

Show, disclose, reveal. *Cover*

a., Unclosed, apparent, plain, visible, clear, evident, uncovered, spread, expanded.

Undefended, unprotected.

Clear, accessible, free, unobstructed, unrestricted, unenclosed. *Closed*

Candid, frank, honest, sincere, hearty, unreserved, cordial, ingenuous, artless, guileless, undesigning, undissembling, fair, above-board. *Secretive*

Undetermined, unsettled, debatable. *Settled*

Opening, *n.,* Start, commencement, beginning, dawn, inauguration, initiation. *Close*

Hole, crevice, gap, breach, aperture, orifice, cleft, rift, rent, chasm, fissure, flaw.

Opportunity, vacancy, chance, occasion, turn. *Lapse*

a., Beginning, starting, commencing, introductory, inaugural, first. *Closing*

Openly, Publicly, frankly, candidly, plainly, clearly. *Secretly*

Operate, Work, function, act, manipulate. *Rest*

Operation, Proceeding, performance, procedure, proceed, movement, action, motion, manœuvre. *Inaction*

Operative, *n.,* Hand, employee, artisan, workman, labourer.

Operative, *a.*, Active, acting, working, efficacious, effectual, effective, efficient. *Inoperative*

Operose, Burdensome, tedious, toilsome, onerous, heavy, weighty, hard, difficult, irksome. *Light*

Opiate, Narcotic, sedative, anodyne. *Stimulant*

Opine, Surmise, believe, think, suppose, conjecture, reckon, judge, fancy. *Know*

Opinion, Belief, supposition, judgment, fancy, estimation, persuasion, idea, notion, sentiment, impression, theory, conception. *Knowledge*

Opinionated } Dictatorial, dogmatic,
Opinionative } conceited, cocksure. *Diffident*

Opponent, Foe, antagonist, enemy, rival, adversary, competitor, opposer. *Ally*

Opportune, Suitable, favourable, timely, fit, happy, convenient, felicitous, auspicious, propitious, appropriate, fortunate. *Untimely*

Opportunity, Opening, chance, time, occasion, turn. *Omission*

Oppose, Prevent, hinder, resist, withstand, obstruct, check, oppugn, combat, bar, counter, thwart, contravene. *Aid*

Opposite, Conflicting, opposing, opponent, opposed, adverse, contrary, irreconcilable, inconsistent, antagonistic, inimical. *Agreeing*
Facing, fronting. *Coincident*

Opposition, Obstruction, hindrance, obstacle, antagonism, resistance, hostility, counteraction. *Agreement*

Oppress, Burden, overburden, overwhelm, overpower, load, persecute, tyrannize, crush, grind, abuse, subdue, maltreat, wrong. *Assist*

Oppression, Persecution, wrong, maltreatment, abuse, injury, suffering, hardship, misery, injustice, cruelty, severity, tyranny. *Encouragement*

Oppressive, Persecuting, cruel, severe, savage, tyrannous, tyrannical, overwhelming, heavy, overpowering, grinding, inhuman. *Mild*
Close, sultry, uncomfortable, stifling. *Fresh*

Opprobrious, Shameful, despicable, despised, disgraceful, infamous, dishonourable, scandalous, hateful, disreputable, scurrilous, reproachful, abusive, insolent, offensive, insulting. *Honourable*

Oppugn, Oppose, resist, withstand, contradict, contravene, cross, thwart, attack, assail. *Aid*

Optimistic, Cheerful, hopeful, bright, sanguine. *Pessimistic*

Option, Choice, wish, preference, election, selection, discretion. *Obligation*

Optional, Discretional, voluntary, elective. *Compulsory*

Opulent, Rich, moneyed, wealthy, affluent. *Poor*

Oracular, Portentous, foreboding, prophetic, ominous.
Sage, grave, dogmatic, authoritative, positive, wise, venerable. *Diffident*

Oral, Vocal, verbal, spoken. *Written*

Oration, Speech, discourse, declamation, harangue, address, rhetoric.

Orb, Circle, ring, sphere, orbit, ball, globe, disc.

Orbit, Path, circuit, sphere, revolution. *Deviation*

Ordain, Order, enjoin, command, enact, appoint, decree, bid, prescribe, institute, establish, regulate. *Cancel*
Consecrate, elect, appoint, destine, call, constitute.

Ordeal, Test, trial, probation, experiment, assay, proof, scrutiny. *Plea*

Order, *v.a.*, Direct, instruct, command, decree, enact, enjoin, ordain, bid, require. *Forfeit*
Arrange, manage, regulate, control, conduct. *Confuse*
n., Direction, instruction, command, injunction, requirement, mandate, precept, law, rule, canon, decree, regulation, commission.
Discipline, quiet, law, peace, tranquillity.
Regularity, arrangement, symmetry, plan, method, disposition. *Confusion*
Community, society, fraternity, class, association, brotherhood, rank, degree, kind.
Family, class, tribe.
Sequence, succession.

Orderly, Regular, equable, quiet, peaceable, sober. *Riotous*
Systematic, methodical, tidy, neat, shipshape. *Disorderly*

Ordinance, Law, decree, statute, enactment, edict, regulation, rule, order, appointment, precept, command.
Ceremony, ritual, rite, sacrament, observance, institution.

Ordinarily, Usually, generally, commonly, habitually.

Ordinary, Usual, common, commonplace, everyday, accustomed, customary, habitual, regular, wonted, normal, settled. *Unusual*
Plain, commonplace, homely.
Average, medium, indifferent, inferior, commonplace.

Organic, Vital, fundamental, radical, constitutional.

Organization, Constitution, system, structure, construction.

Organize, Frame, make, establish, constitute, arrange, adjust, systematize, construct, dispose, make. *Disrupt*

Orgy, Revel, carousal, feast, debauch.

Orifice, Aperture, opening, hole, mouth, perforation, bung, vent, pore. *Stopper*

Origin, Beginning, commencement, rise, source, root, cause, occasion, fount, fountain, foundation, spring, derivation. *Result*

Original, Fresh, novel, new, creative, inventive. *Old* Primary, primitive, primordial, primeval, pristine, aboriginal, ancient, old. *Later*

Originate, *v.n.,* Begin, commence, rise, spring, arise, emanate, proceed, flow, start. *End* *v.a.,* Begin, commence, start, initiate, create, cause.

Originator, Creator, inventor, author, maker, former, father.

Ornament, *n.,* Adornment, decoration, embellishment. *Disfigurement* *v.a.,* Adorn, decorate, embellish, beautify, deck, bedeck, garnish, emblazon, grace. *Disfigure*

Ornate, Ornamented, decorated, embellished, beautiful, bedecked, garnished, florid, adorned, rich. *Plain*

Orotund, Rich, full, round, musical, clear, ringing, mellow. *Harsh*

Orthodox, Sound, conventional, correct, true. *Heterodox*

Orts, Scraps, refuse, fragments.

Oscillate, Sway, swing, veer, vacillate, hesitate, fluctuate, vary.

Oscitant, Sleepy, gaping, yawning, dull, drowsy, tired. *Alert*

Ostensible, Outward, avowed, professed, pretended, shown, assigned, manifest, exhibited, visible, apparent, declared. *Real*

Ostentation, Parade, exhibition, show, display, vaunting, flourish, pomp, semblance, pageantry, appearance. *Reserve*

Ostentatious, Showy, vaunting, pompous, vain, boastful, flaunting, gaudy, vulgar. *Quiet*

Ostracism, Exclusion, banishment, rejection, expulsion, excommunication, separation. *Admittance*

Otiose, Indolent, idle, lazy, unoccupied, unemployed. *Busy*

Oust, Evict, eject, expel, dispossess, deprive, dislodge. *Install*

Out, Without, away, abroad, off. *In* Extinguished. Uncovered, disclosed, open, public, revealed. *Closed* Audibly, loudly, aloud.

Outbreak, Outburst, ebullition, eruption, explosion. Rebellion, rising, uprising, riot, revolt, broil, fray, commotion, row, conflict, insurrection. *Order*

Outburst, Outbreak, ebullition, eruption, explosion.

Outcast, Castaway, wretch, reprobate, exile, expatriate, vagabond, pariah.

Outcome, Consequence, sequel, issue, result, upshot, event. *Cause*

Outcry, Hue, cry, clamour, yell, scream, screech, tumult, vociferation, denunciation. *Plaudit*

Outdo, Outvie, exceed, eclipse, surpass, outstrip, beat.

Outer, Outward, outside, exterior, external. *Inner*

Outing, Expedition, excursion, holiday, airing, trip.

Outlandish, Strange, queer, alien, foreign, barbarous, exotic. *Fashionable*

Outlaw, Brigand, freebooter, robber, marauder, highwayman, bandit, footpad.

Outlay, Expenditure, disbursement, expense. *Receipt*

Outlet, Exit, vent, opening, egress, loophole. *Inlet*

Outline, Draft, sketch, plan, skeleton, contour, drawing, delineation.

Outlook, Prospect, future, view, sight, horizon.

Outlying, Distant, removed, remote, far. *Inner*

Outrage, *n.,* Offence, affront, indignity, maltreatment, injury, insult, abuse. *v.a.,* Offend, affront, maltreat, injure, insult, abuse, shock.

Outrageous, Wanton, excessive, monstrous, atrocious, nefarious, unwarrantable, inexcusable, vile, heinous, abominable, enormous, villainous. *Reasonable*

Outright, Entirely, completely, utterly, wholly, altogether. *Partly*

Outrun, Outstrip, beat, pass, surpass.

Outset, Start, beginning, commencement, opening, preface, inauguration. *End*

Outshine, Eclipse, overshadow, outvie, outrival, surpass.

Outside, *n.,* Exterior, surface. *Interior* Utmost, limit. *a.,* External, superficial, outward, outer, exterior.

Outskirts, Environs, suburbs, border, purlieus, precincts, outpost. *Centre*

Outspoken, Candid, open, blunt, frank, free, unreserved. *Secretive*

Outspread, Open, unfolded, extended, outstretched, expanded. *Folded*

Outstanding, Owing, unsettled, unpaid, uncollected, ungathered, unappropriated, due. *Settled*
Supreme, great, noticeable. *Insignificant*

Outstretch, Extend, expand, unfold, open, outspread. *Contract*

Outstrip, Outrun, outgo, outdo, outvie, surpass, exceed, eclipse, beat.

Outvie, Eclipse, surpass, exceed, beat, outdo, outrival.

Outward, Outer, outside, external, exterior, superficial, ostensible, visible, apparent. *Inward*

Outweigh, Offset, overbalance. *Balance*

Outwit, Circumvent, cheat, overreach, swindle, dupe, defraud, *chouse, cozen.*

Ovation, Applause, triumph, plaudit.

Over, *adv.,* Above, across, athwart, transversely. *Under*
Besides, additional.
Very, excessively, extremely, too.
Completely, throughout, through, past, by.
prep., Above, across, athwart.
Through, throughout.
Covering, immersing.
a., Outer, covering, upper, superior.

Overawe, Intimidate, affright, frighten, browbeat, daunt, scare, cow. *Reassure*

Overbearing, Domineering, lordly, overpowering, arrogant, haughty, dictatorial, imperious, dogmatic, oppressive, masterly. *Retiring*

Overcast, Cloudy, murky, dark, obscure, lowering. *Clear*

Overcharge, Surcharge, overload, burden, crowd, overstrain, overladen. *Undercharge*

Overcome, Conquer, vanquish, overpower, beat, defeat, meet, surmount, crush, subdue, overwhelm, subjugate, confound, rout, overthrow, prevail.

Overestimate, Overrate, overvalue, overprize, exaggerate, magnify. *Belittle*

Overflow, *v.a.,* Overrun, overwhelm, overspread, inundate, flood, deluge, cover, swamp. *Subside*
n., Exuberance, profusion, excess, redundancy, superabundance, surplus, luxuriance, copiousness. *Deficiency*

Overhaul, Inspect, examine, check, supervise, overtake.

Overload, Overlade, overcharge, overburden, encumber, cumber.

Overlook, Connive, disregard, ignore, forget, forgive, pardon, condone, pass, excuse. *Punish*
Neglect, miss, slight, disregard. *Mark*
Inspect, check, examine, supervise, superintend.

Overpower, Overwhelm, overcome, vanquish, subdue, conquer, defeat, beat, rout, crush, subjugate, master, worst.

Overpowering, Overwhelming, powerful, irresistible, subduing.

Overrate, Overvalue, overestimate. *Underrate*

Overreach, Circumvent, outwit, cheat, dupe, deceive, swindle, trick, defraud, *cozen, chouse.*

Override, Quash, annul, reverse, supersede, pass, outweigh. *Confirm*

Overrule, Cancel, annul, revoke, repeal, reject, supersede, rescind, nullify, repudiate.
Control, sway, govern, dictate.

Overrun, Infested, alive, swarming, full, replete.
Devastate, ravage, harass, subdue, oppress, despoil.

Overseer, Superior, superintendent, foreman, inspector.

Overshadow, Cloud, cover, overcloud, overshade.

Oversight, Slip, mistake, fault, error, omission, blunder, lapse, inadvertency, negligence, neglect, heedlessness, inattention. *Attention*

Overt, Open, public, manifest, avowed, deliberate, apparent, plain, clear, patent, palpable, glaring, notorious. *Secret*

Overthrow, *v.a.,* Subvert, upset, ruin, destroy, overturn, level, demolish. *Restore*
Vanquish, overcome, overwhelm, overpower, defeat, conquer, beat, rout, worst, master, subdue, subjugate, crush.
n., Subversion, ruin, destruction, demolition, fall, prostration. *Restoration*
Defeat, rout, subjugation, discomfiture, dispersion. *Victory*

Overture, Offer, proposal, proposition, invitation, advance. *Rejection*
Opening, prologue, prelude, lead, initiation. *Finale*

Overweening, Opinionated, opinionative, conceited, vain, haughty, arrogant, proud, smug, supercilious, superior, consequential, pompous, important. *Meek*

Overwhelm, Inundate, flood, deluge, overflow, drown, submerge, cover. *Rescue*

Conquer, vanquish, overcome, overthrow, beat, rout, defeat, master, overpower. *Reinstate*

Overwrought, Excited, elaborated, overdone, inflamed, laboured, overworked. *Calm*

Owing, Due, outstanding, unsettled. *Paid*

Own, Possess, have, hold.

Admit, acknowledge, confess, allow, grant, concede, recognize. *Deny*

Owner, Holder, possessor, proprietor.

P

Pace, *v.n.,* Walk, move, step, wander, hasten, hurry. ***Halt***
n., Speed, rate.
Step, gait, walk, amble.

Pacific, Peaceable, peaceful, quiet, mild, gentle, calm, tranquil, concilatory, appeasing, smooth. ***Turbulent***

Pacify, Appease, calm, tranquillize, compose, smooth, quiet, conciliate, still, allay, assuage, lull, hush, moderate, modify, quell, mollify, soothe, soften, mitigate. ***Exasperate***

Pack, *v.a.,* Compact, compress, crowd, store, stow. ***Disarrange***
n., Herd, flock, band, company, set, bevy, collection, lot, crowd, assemblage, clan, assortment, squad, gang.
Bundle, parcel, package, packet, bale, luggage, load, burden.

Pact, Agreement, compact, covenant, bond, bargain, stipulation, treaty, league, contract, concordat, convention, alliance.

Pagan, Heathen, paynim, idolatrous, paganic. ***Christian***

Pageant, Display, exhibition, show, parade, ceremony, procession, spectacle. ***Illusion***

Pageantry, Display, exhibition,† pomp, splendour, magnificence, state.

Pain, *v.a.,* Grieve, trouble, aggrieve, torment, worry, vex, hurt, distress, torture, harass, agonize, rack, disquiet, afflict, annoy, fret, chafe, plague. ***Please***
v.n., Smart, hurt, sting, twinge, ache, agony, torment. ***Relief***
n., Grief, trouble, torment,† ache, suffering, discomfort, misery, unhappiness, woe, pang, anguish, sorrow, dolour, wretchedness, bitterness. ***Ease***

Painful, Agonizing, torturing, tormenting, grievous, troublesome, vexatious, distressing, racking, disquieting, afflicting, afflictive, annoying, discomforting, displeasing, unpleasant, difficult, excruciating. ***Pleasant***
Toilsome, severe, hard, difficult, sore, arduous, laborious. ***Easy***

Painstaking, Industrious, diligent, assiduous, sedulous, careful, laborious, persevering, plodding, strenuous, conscientious. ***Lazy***

Paint, Portray, sketch, delineate, represent, describe, depict, limn.
Colour, tint, tinge, beautify, ornament, embellish, adorn.

Pair, *n.,* Couple, brace, two, twain.

Pair, *v.n. & n.,* Suit, fit, marry, match, mate, couple. ***Separate***

Palatable, Tasty, tasteful, luscious, enjoyable, savoury, pleasant, delicious, agreeable, dainty, delicate. ***Nasty***

Palatial, Grand, magnificent, stately, noble, splendid, elegant. ***Mean***

Palaver, Nonsense, prate, trash, chatter, twaddle, gibberish, jargon, talk, balderdash, colloquy, conference, conversation.

Pale, *a.,* Sallow, colourless, dim, white, wan, pallid, etiolated, faint, ashy, whitish, light. ***Dark***
n., Confine, boundary, limit, district, enclosure.

Pall, *v.a.,* Impair, weaken, deject, depress, discourage, enervate, dishearten, dispirit. ***Inspirit***
Satiate, sate, surfeit, glut, cloy. ***Whet***
n., Shroud, cover, clothe, invest, drape.

Palliate, Excuse, cloak, extenuate, cover, hide, lessen, gloss, conceal, mitigate, diminish, relieve, alleviate, allay, soften, abate. ***Expose***

Palliative, Emollient, softener, lenitive.

Pallid, Pale, white, whitish, ashy, colourless, wan, sallow. ***Ruddy***

Palling, Sickening, disgusting, repulsive, nauseating, nasty, loathsome. ***Pleasant***

Pallor, Paleness, pallidity, pallidness, whiteness, sallowness. ***Ruddiness***

Palm, Laurels, crown, prize, trophy. ***Brand***

Palmy, Thriving, prosperous, happy, wealthy, flourishing, victorious, successful, joyous, glorious, fortunate. ***Depressed***

Palpable, Material, tangible, corporeal, gross. ***Spiritual***
Obvious, plain, manifest, indisputable, undeniable, apparent, perceptible, glaring, unmistakable, evident, patent. ***Doubtful***

Palpitate, Throb, pulsate, beat, flutter, quiver, pant, tremble. ***Stop***

Palter, Prevaricate, quibble, trifle, dodge, equivocate, shuffle, haggle. ***Decide***

Paltry, Mean, low, abject, base, poor, small, insignificant, petty, despicable, shabby, worthless, contemptible, pitiable, vile, little, unimportant, slight, trivial, wretched, beggarly. ***Noble***

Pamper, Indulge, spoil, glut, gratify, fondle, coddle, feed, humour. ***Discipline***

Pamphlet, Booklet, brochure.

Panacea, Cure, remedy, medicine.

Pandemonium, Chaos, confusion, uproar, disorder. *Quiet*

Panegyric, Eulogy, praise, commendation, encomium, adulation, laudation, tribute. *Tirade*

Panegyrize, Eulogize, praise, commend, laud, extol. *Decry*

Panel, Body, list, array, board.

Pang, Convulsion, throe, paroxysm, twinge.

Panic, Consternation, terror, fear, fright, affright, alarm, confusion. *Calmness*

Pant, Gasp, puff, blow, throb, palpitate, heave, flutter, throe.

Paps, Dug, udder, nipple, breast, teats.

Paper, Newspaper, periodical, journal, publication, sheet.
Essay, lecture, dissertation, article, composition.
Writing, document, draft, deed, certificate.

Par, Equal, level, balance, equality, equivalent.

Parable, Fable, illustration, similitude, apologue, story, allegory. *History*

Parabolic, Allegorical, figurative, fictitious.

Parade, *v.a.*, Show, display, flaunt, vaunt. *Hide*
n., Show, display, flaunting, exhibition, vaunting, ostentation, pomp. *Modesty*
Pageant, procession, show, ceremony, spectacle, review.

Paradise, Heaven, elysium, Eden, bliss. *Purgatory*

Paradox, Contradiction, enigma, mystery, absurdity. *Truism*

Paragon, Model, example, standard, pattern.

Paragraph, Section, clause, passage, sentence, item, notice.

Parallel, *n.*, Counterpart, resemblance, similitude, likeness, similarity. *Converse*
a., Correspondent, similar, like, resembling, equal, congruous, analogous, concurrent, allied. *Different*

Paralyze, Deaden, numb, benumb, unnerve, palsy. *Quicken*

Paramount, Pre-eminent principal, chief, superior, dominant, supreme, leading. *Minor*

Paramour, Mistress, lover, concubine.

Parapet, Wall, breastwork, battlement, railing.

Paraphernalia, Baggage, luggage, trappings, belongings, impedimenta, equipment, equipage.

Paraphrase, Exposition, explanation, translation, wording.

Parasite, Toady, flatterer, sycophant.

Parcel, *n.*, Packet, package, bundle, batch, budget, lot, group, collection, set, number.
Piece, part, portion, plot, tract, patch.
v.a., Allot, assign, apportion, distribute, divide, share, mete, deal.

Parched, Dry, thirsty, arid, scorched, burnt. *Soaked*

Pardon, *v.a.*, Forgive, remit, pass, overlook, excuse, condone, acquit, absolve, clear, release, discharge. *Punish*
n., Forgiveness, remission, acquital, release, discharge, absolution, mercy, grace. *Punishment*

Pare, Peel, shave, cut, skive, diminish, reduce, lessen.

Parentage, Pedigree, descent, line, race, family, stock, lineage, birth, extraction, origin, ancestry.

Pariah, Outcast, wretch.

Parley, *v.n.*, Confer, converse, meet, talk, discuss, treat, discourse.
n., Conference, conversation, meeting.†

Parody, *v.a.*, Imitate, burlesque, caricature, travesty.
n., Imitation, burlesque.†

Paroxysm, Fit, twinge, convulsion, attack, seizure, spasm.

Parry, Frustrate, avert, meet, beat, prevent, avoid, evade.

Parsimonious, Mean, near, close, miserly, stingy, selfish, niggardly, avaricious, frugal, illiberal, sparing, grasping, sordid, covetous. *Generous*

Parson, Clergyman, priest, minister, rector, incumbent, preacher, churchman, divine, pastor, ecclesiastic. *Layman*

Part, *v.a.*, Separate, divide, sever, dissever, disunite, disconnect, dissociate, dismember, disjoin, detach, break, subdivide. *Join*
Divide, distribute, parcel, allot, apportion, mete, deal, dole. *Collect*
v.n., Quit, lose, divide, waive, depart, break, share.
n., Fragment, piece, portion, parcel, segment, scrap, share, division, section, ingredient, element, component, constituent. *Whole*
Concern, participation, interest, faction.
Character, rôle, office, charge, duty, function, work.
Clause, passage, paragraph, section, item.

Partial, Limited, restricted, imperfect, incomplete, unfinished, local, peculiar. *Total*
Favouring, biassed, unjust, predisposed, prejudiced, influenced, unfair, fond, prepossessed, inequitable, interested. *Disinterested*

Participate, Share, partake, help, assist.

Particle, Grain, piece, fragment, bit, atom, portion, scrap, speck, molecule.

Particular, *a.,* Critical, careful, exacting, exact, minute, definite, detailed, precise, finical, fastidious, faddy, strict, scrupulous, accurate. *Loose*
Special, especial, specific, single, distinct, local, individual, detailed, peculiar, separate, notable, respective, distinctive. *General*
Private, intimate, personal, own, individual.
Singular, strange, odd, peculiar.
n., Detail, feature, characteristic, item, point.

Particularize, Detail, specify. *Generalize*

Parting, *n.,* Division, separation, divergence, disruption, severing, severance, rupture, breaking, departure, farewell. *Meeting*
a., Departing, dividing, separating, diverging, breaking, final, last, farewell.

Partisan, *n.,* Votary, follower, supporter, disciple, adherent, champion, enthusiast.
a., Biassed, partial, factionary, prejudiced, interested. *Neutral*

Partition, Screen, division, separation, barrier, compartment, enclosure, distribution, allotment.

Partner, Co-partner, co-operator, colleague, ally, associate, confederate, co-adjutor, collaborator, helper, auxiliary, aider, abetter, accomplice, companion, consort, spouse. *Rival*

Partnership, Co-partnership, association, collaboration, firm, concern, establishment, business, house, company, union, interest, participation.

Parts, District, region, locality, quarters.
Intelligence, intellect, brains, ability, faculties, powers, talents, gifts, genius, mind. *Stupidity*

Parturition, Childbirth, delivery, travail, labour.

Party, Company, set, ring, body, clique, faction, cabal, circle, alliance, combination, league.
Individual, body, person, one.
Troop, detachment, squad.
Cause, interest, side, division, litigant, plaintiff, defendant.

Pass, *v.a.,* Experience, spend, undergo, suffer.
Surpass, overpass, overstep, exceed, transcend.
Ignore, neglect, disregard, omit. *Notice*
Ratify, enact. *Reject*
v.n., Move, go, proceed, journey.

Pass, Lapse, elapse, fade, vanish, disappear, die, cease.
Answer, suit, do.
Happen, occur.
n., Passport, visa, permit, voucher, ticket.
Passage, way, defile, gorge, ravine, road, avenue.
Plight, state, condition, situation.
Trick, transfer, thrust, push, lunge, tilt.

Passable, Fair, middling, mediocre, ordinary, tolerable, admissible, allowable, acceptable, current, good. *Excellent*

Passage, Road, way, pass, avenue, path, route, course, channel, thoroughfare.
Journey, voyage, crossing, tour, transit, going, progress, evacuation.
Access, reception, entry.
Corridor, hall, doorway, gate, gallery.
Sentence, clause, text, paragraph.
Fare.
Encounter, skirmish, contest, exchange, conflict, brush, collision.

Passenger, Voyager, traveller, tourist, wayfarer, itinerant, fare.

Passing, *a.,* Brief, evanescent, transient, fleeting, momentary, short. *Permanent*
adv., Surpassingly, excessively, exceedingly, enormously, remarkably, wonderfully, very, extremely.
prep., Beyond, exceeding, over.

Passion, Vehemence, feeling, ardour, emotion, fervour, excitement, rapture, zeal, wrath, ire, anger, fury, resentment, rage, indignation, lust, desire, animation, eagerness, warmth, keenness. *Apathy*

Passionate, Vehement, feeling, ardent,† earnest, fiery, burning, enthusiastic, violent, impassioned, impetuous, hasty, hot, choleric. *Apathetic*

Passive, Submissive, quiet, patient, dumb, enduring, suffering, unquestioning, resigned, unresisting, quiescent, inert, still, inactive. *Vehement*

Passport, License, pass, safeguard, credentials.

Password, Countersign, watchword.

Past, *a.,* Gone, behind, spent, done, over, finished, ended, accomplished, obsolete, ancient, former, bygone. *Present*
prep., Beyond, after, exceeding, above, farther.
n., Yesterday, history, heretofore. *Tomorrow*

Pastime, Sport, recreation, hobby, amusement, pleasure, diversion, entertainment. *Work*

Pastor, Clergyman, priest, divine, rector, minister, parson, ecclesiastic, churchman, shepherd. *Layman*

Pasture, Herbage, herbs, grass, pasturage, meadows, grassland.

Pat, Dab, tap, hit, rap, caress.

Patch, *v.a.*, Cobble, mend, piece, botch.

n., Piece, plot, square, parcel.

Patent, *a.*, Palpable, plain, obvious, evident, clear, manifest, open, apparent, undisguised, unmistakable, indisputable, notorious, glaring, public, unconcealed, conspicuous. **Obscure**

n., Copyright, privilege, right.

Path, Way, road, pathway, footway, track, trail, passage, course, route, avenue, access.

Pathetic, Sad, moving, affecting, touching, emotional, tender, plaintive.
Farcical

Patience, Endurance, suffering, calmness, imperturbability, composure, submission, resignation, fortitude, perseverance, quietness, persistence, constancy, forbearance, mildness, lenience. **Passion**

Patient, *a.*, Enduring, suffering, calm,† passive, uncomplaining, unrepining, contented. **Passionate**

n., Invalid, sufferer, subject, case.

Patrician, Aristocratic, noble, high, lofty, senatorial. **Plebeian**

Patrimony, Heritage, inheritance, hereditament.

Patron, Supporter, friend, helper, advocate, guardian, defender, customer.
Enemy

Patronize, Support, befriend, help, aid, guard, favour, assist, countenance, defend. **Oppose**

Pattern, Model, paragon, exemplar, example, specimen, sample, figure, shape, design, style, type, norm, archetype.
Caricature

Paucity, Rarity, scantiness, fewness, deficiency, lack, shortage, exiguity, poverty. **Abundance**

Pauperism, Destitution, penury, need, poverty, indigence, want. **Affluence**

Pause, *v.n.*, Halt, wait, cease, delay, stop, tarry, hesitate, desist, stay, breathe, rest, forbear, demur, waver, deliberate.
Proceed

n., Halt, wait, cessation, suspension, rest, interval, stoppage, hesitation, break, gap, interruption, intermission.

Pave, Prepare, smooth, facilitate.
Impede

Pawn, Pledge, security, surety, gage, earnest, risk, hazard, stake, wager.
Redeem

Pay, *v.a.*, Remunerate, reward, satisfy, recompense, requite, settle, liquidate,

discharge, defray, meet, honour, discount, give, offer, render. **Owe**

n., Payment, salary, recompense, remuneration, reward, stipend, wages, compensation, emolument, hire.

Paying, Lucrative, remunerative, profitable, gainful. **Losing**

Payment, Pay, recompense, remuneration, salary, reward, wage, fee, compensation, liquidation, settlement.

Peace, Concord, harmony, quiet, rest, calm, tranquillity, silence, pacification, repose, amity, agreement. **War**

Peaceable⎤ Quiet, calm, tranquil, pacific,
Peaceful ⎦ mild, moderate, gentle, placid, serene, restful, unwarlike, still, inoffensive, friendly, amicable, kindly.
Warlike

Peak, Top, acme, zenith, height, pinnacle, summit, apex, crown, crest, point. **Base**

Peal, *v.n.*, Roar, sound, echo, re-echo, resound, thunder, boom.

n., Roar, sound, blare, boom, blast, burst, clang.

Pearly, Translucent, pellucid, pure, clear, nacreous, iridescent.

Peasant, Countryman, villager, rustic, swain, boor, hind. **Townsman**

Peccable, Weak, feeble, frail, sinful, sinning, erring, imperfect. **Perfect**

Peccant, Bad, objectionable, offensive, corrupt, corrupting, malignant, defective, unhealthy, morbid, vicious.
Wholesome

Evil, wicked, criminal, sinful, erring, wrong, incorrect, bad, defective, guilty.
Righteous

Peculate, Steal, purloin, pilfer, rob, appropriate, embezzle.

Peculiar, Special, especial, particular, specific, individual, characteristic, personal, private. **General**

Unusual, uncommon, rare, strange, singular, queer, exceptional, odd, extraordinary, striking. **Ordinary**

Peculiarity, Speciality, particularity, individuality, characteristic, distinctiveness, singularity, idiosyncrasy.
Generality

Pecuniary, Monetary, financial.

Pedagogue, Master, schoolmaster, usher, teacher, tutor, pedant, dominie. **Pupil**

Pedantic, Strict, precise, finical, exact, exacting, particular, pragmatical, priggish, conceited, pompous, stilted. **Loose**

Peddle, Hawk, vend, sell, retail.

Pedigree, Extraction, race, family, line, lineage, descent, ancestry, house, breed, genealogy, stock. **Hybrid**

Pedlar, Bagman, dealer, hawker, chapman, vendor.

Peel, *v.a.,* Flay, bark, strip, pare, decorticate. *Cover*
n., Skin, coat, rind, bark, hull, covering.

Peer, Compeer, fellow, equal, mate, match, companion, comrade.
Lord, noble, nobleman, aristocrat. *Commoner*

Peerless, Matchless, unmatched, unequalled, unrivalled, unsurpassed, superlative, paramount, unique. *Ordinary*

Peevish, Petulant, pettish, irritable, fretful, waspish, snappish, snarling, touchy, testy, churlish, querulous, cross, captious, crabbed, acrimonious, splenetic, spleeny, crusty, sour, bitter, silly, childish, trifling, thoughtless. *Genial*

Pelf, Mammon, riches, gain, possessions, lucre, wealth, money, plenty. *Poverty*

Pellucid, Lucid, transparent, clear, vitreous, translucent, crystalline, limpid, diaphanous, bright, nacreous. *Opaque*

Pelt, Bombard, assail, belabour, batter, hurl, throw, cast, beat, strike.

Pen, *v.a.,* Write, indite, compose, inscribe.
Crib, cabin, confine, coop, impound, incarcerate, imprison, enclose. *Release*
n., Coop, enclosure, pound, penfold, pinfold, sty, paddock, corral.

Penal, Punitive, retributive, corrective, disciplinary. *Honorary*

Penalty, Punishment, retribution, correction, fine, mulct, amercement, pain, forfeiture. *Reward*

Penance, Humiliation, penalty, punishment, mortification.

Penchant, Turn, bent, inclination, propensity, leaning, liking, fondness, taste, bias.

Pendant, Hanging, pendulous, suspended, dangling, depending, overhanging, jutting, projecting. *Erect*

Pending, During, awaiting.

Penetrable, Pervious, impressible, permeable, vulnerable, susceptible. *Impervious*

Penetrate, Pierce, pass, enter, perforate, bore, cut, invade, soak, percolate.
Understand, perceive, comprehend.

Penetrating, Piercing, sharp, subtle, acute, intelligent, wise, clever, discerning, shrewd, keen, sagacious, astute, discriminating. *Dull*

Penitence, Sorrow, contrition, remorse, compunction, repentance, sadness, regret. *Satisfaction*

Penitential, Sorrowful, contrite, sad, doleful, dirgeful, wailing, mournful, regretful, repentant. *Glad*

Penitentiary, Prison, jail, gaol.

Penniless, Poor, destitute, penurious, moneyless, indigent, necessitous, needy, impecunious, reduced, distressed, pinched, straitened. *Rich*

Pennon, Streamer, colours, ensign, standard, flag, banner, pennant.

Pension, Annuity, grant, allowance.

Pensive, Musing, thoughtful, serious, meditative, sober, ruminating, wondering, dreamy, reflective, sad, solemn, grave, melancholy, mournful. *Careless*

Penurious, Niggardly, miserly, mean, near, close, parsimonious, covetous, avaricious, illiberal, stingy, sordid, mercenary, selfish. *Generous*

Penury, Poverty, want, indigence, need, necessity, destitution, privation. *Affluence*

People, Community, race, tribe, clan, nation, family, country, state.
Populace, mob, rabble, masses, herd, crowd, persons, folks.

Peppery, Hot, choleric, irritable, petulant, peevish, touchy, testy, acrimonious, hasty, excitable, snappy, snarling, surly, irascible, waspish, churlish, passionate. *Genial*

Per, Through, by, for, via.

Peradventure, Haply, mayhap, perchance, perhaps, probably, possibly, maybe. *Certainly*

Perceivable, Distinguishable, discernible, visible, perceptible, appreciable, noticeable, cognizable, palpable, obvious. *Imperceptible*

Perceive, Distinguish, discern, notice, note, descry, observe, mark, behold, see, discover. *Overlook*
Understand, appreciate, know, recognize, feel.

Perceptible, Visible, discernible, obvious, apparent, appreciable, noticeable, perceivable, palpable. *Invisible*

Perception, Understanding, discernment, apprehension, comprehension, feeling, seeing, recognition. *Ignorance*

Perchance, Peradventure, haply, mayhap, perhaps, probably, possibly, maybe. *Certainly*

Percolate, Drain, drip, ooze, exude, transude, penetrate, strain, filter.

Percussion, Crash, shock, collision, encounter, meeting, clash, concussion. *Repercussion*

Perdition, Destruction, downfall, loss, demolition, ruin, overthrow, damnation, wreck, condemnation, hell. *Salvation*

Peregrination, Travel, wandering, roaming, tour, journey. *Residence*

Peremptory, Arbitrary, absolute, authoritative, dogmatic, imperious, express, determined, decisive, imperative, positive, categorical.   ***Mild***

Perennial, Permanent, enduring, perpetual, lasting, deathless, undying, unending, endless, incessant, unceasing, continual, ceaseless, constant, unintermittent, uninterrupted, immortal, imperishable, unfailing.   ***Occasional***

Perfect, *v.a.,* Consummate, finish, accomplish, end, achieve, complete, elaborate.   ***Spoil***
a., Consummate, finished, accomplished, complete, completed, entire, full, whole, immaculate, spotless, faultless, pure, blameless, unblemished, impeccable, exquisite, excellent, capital, splendid, sound, absolute.   ***Incomplete***

Perfection, Consummation, finish, completion, wholeness, excellence, quality, beauty, perfectness, spotlessness, faultlessness.   ***Fault***

Perfectly, Completely, totally, entirely, fully, altogether, thoroughly, exactly, accurately, precisely.   ***Incorrectly***

Perfidious, False, faithless, unfaithful, disloyal, untrue, treacherous, traitorous, dishonest, untrustworthy, venal, deceitful.   ***Faithful***

Perforate, Penetrate, puncture, pass, pierce, bore, riddle, prick, drill.

Perforce, Necessarily, forcibly, violently, absolutely.

Perform, Execute, do, transact, compass, achieve, effect, accomplish, consummate, complete, fulfil, discharge, observe, mete, execute, observe, meet, satisfy. ***Neglect*** Act, play, represent.

Performance, Execution, deed, transaction,† exploit, work, action, feat.
Acting, play, representation, exhibition, entertainment, production, show.

Perfume, Smell, redolence, fragrance, scent, odour, aroma, balminess.   ***Stench***

Perfunctory, Mechanical, careless, indifferent, uninterested, slovenly, routine, thoughtless, heedless, reckless, negligent, formal.   ***Zealous***

Perhaps, Probably, possibly, peradventure, perchance, haply, mayhap, maybe.   ***Certainly***

Peril, *v.a.,* Imperil, endanger, risk, hazard, jeopard.   ***Safeguard***
n., Danger, risk, hazard, jeopardy, uncertainty, insecurity.   ***Safety***

Perilous, Dangerous, risky, hazardous, uncertain, insecure, unsafe.   ***Safe***

Period, Age, time, term, span, stage, season, era, epoch, cycle, date. ***Infinity***

Period, Continuance, duration, limit, end, conclusion, determination.

Periodical, *a.,* Recurrent, regular, systematic, stated, occasional.   ***Irregular*** *n.,* Magazine, paper, review.

Peripatetic, Wandering, itinerant, roaming.

Periphery, Circumference, perimeter, outside, surface.

Periphrastic-al, Roundabout, indirect, verbose, wordy, circumlocutionary.   ***Direct***

Perish, Pass, fade, fail, fall, decay, wither, die, expire, decease, waste, shrivel.   ***Last***

Perishable, Evanescent, transient, fleeting, short, brief, frail, fragile, mortal, destructible, ephemeral, decaying.   ***Permanent***

Perjured, False, untrue, perfidious, forsworn, treacherous, traitorous.   ***True***

Perky, Forward, trim, cheeky, airy, jaunty.

Permanent, Lasting, perpetual, enduring, abiding, durable, constant, persistent, fixed, changeless, unchanging, unchangeable, invariable, imperishable, indestructible, continuing, stable, fixed, immutable.   ***Transient***

Permeable, Penetrable, pervious, percolable, pervasive.   ***Impenetrable***

Permissible, Allowed, allowable, permitted, lawful, legal, proper, right, admissible, sanctioned.   ***Prohibited***

Permission, Allowance, permit, sanction, authority, power, leave, consent, license, liberty, warrant, authorization, tolerance, sufferance.   ***Prohibition***

Permit, *v.a.,* Allow, let, sanction, authorize, license, warrant, suffer, brook, countenance, tolerate, endure, empower, grant, admit, consent.   ***Prohibit***
n., Permission, allowance, sanction, authority, power, leave, consent, license, liberty, warrant, passport.

Permutation, Change, exchange, interchange, transference.   ***Sequence***

Pernicious, Baleful, baneful, hurtful, harmful, injurious, obnoxious, noxious, detrimental, deleterious, poisonous, mischievous, fatal, deadly, ruinous, destructive, damaging, noisome, evil, bad.   ***Beneficial***

Perorate, Declaim, speechify, harangue.

Perpendicular, Upright, vertical, erect, straight, plumb.   ***Slanting***

Perpetrate, Commit, execute, perform, do.

Perpetual, Continual, unending, endless, unceasing, ceaseless, incessant, constant, everlasting, permanent, uninterrupted, eternal, perennial, enduring, continuous, unintermitted, unfailing, interminable. *Temporary*

Perpetuity, Permanence, eternity, continuity, everlastingness, persistence. *Evanescence*

Perplex, Puzzle, confuse, bewilder, nonplus, mystify, worry, bother, disturb, trouble. *Enlighten*
Entangle, confuse, involve, complicate, encumber, embarrass, cloud, plague, harass, annoy, vex. *Simplify*

Perplexity, Entanglement, confusion, involution, complication, intricacy, complexity, difficulty, bewilderment, bother, trouble, doubt, dilemma, concern, care, anxiety, predicament, embarrassment, muddle, mess, puzzle, quandary, plight, fog. *Order*

Persecute, Harass, hunt, annoy, vex, molest, worry, torment, torture, afflict, oppress, pester, tease. *Support*

Perseverance, Persistence, tenacity, steadfastness, steadiness, resolution, determination, constancy, indefatigableness. *Weakness*

Persevere, Persist, resolve, determine, continue, maintain. *Waver*

Persiflage, Raillery, banter, badinage, mockery, jeering, ridicule.

Persist, Persevere, resolve, determine. Last, abide, remain, continue, stand, endure, keep. *Perish*

Persistent, Persevering, tenacious, steadfast, steady, resolved, determined, constant, stubborn, dogged, obdurate, pertinacious, perverse, obstinate, immovable, unshakable, fixed. *Weak*

Person, Individual, party, body, somebody, someone, one, being, entity, character, agent.

Personal, Private, special, individual. *Common*
Material, physical, exterior, corporal, bodily.

Personate, Act, represent, impersonate, imitate, simulate. *Be*

Perspective, View, sight, vista, panorama, prospect, proportion.

Perspicacious, Keen, astute, acute, sharp, shrewd, penetrating, discerning, sagacious, clever, intelligent. *Dull*

Perspicacity, Perspicaciousness, keenness, astuteness,† acumen, insight, cleverness, brains. *Dulness*

Perspicuity, Lucidity, lucidness, plainness, clarity, clearness, intelligibility, transparency, explicitness, distinctness. *Obscurity*

Perspicuous, Lucid, plain,† obvious, apparent. *Obscure*

Perspiration, Sweat, sweating, exudation.

Persuade, Influence, move, impel, incite, urge, encourage, sway, prompt, induce, incline, entice, advise, counsel, allure, lead, actuate, dispose, convince. *Deter*

Persuasive, Inducing, alluring, convincing, enticing, logical, sound, cogent, valid, persuasory, suasive. *Deterrent*

Pert, Impudent, rude, insolent, bold, forward, saucy, flippant, impertinent, lively, brisk, smart, dapper, sprightly. *Bashful*

Pertain, Appertain, belong, concern.

Pertinacious, Tenacious, dogged, persistent, persevering, steadfast, steady, resolute, determined, constant, firm, obstinate, stubborn, wilful, immovable, unshakable. *Irresolute*

Pertinent, Relevant, appropriate, apt, apposite, fit, suitable, proper, seemly, applicable. *Inappropriate*
Concerning, belonging, pertaining, regarding.

Perturb, Disturb, upset, embarrass, confuse, nonplus, agitate, trouble, disquiet. *Compose*

Perturbed, Disturbed, upset,† discomposed, distressed, worried, excited, vexed. *Calm*

Peruse, Read, scrutinize, examine, inspect, consider, study, digest, observe, survey.

Pervade, Fill, permeate, penetrate, saturate, overspread, impregnate, animate.

Perverse, Wayward, untoward, froward, stubborn, headstrong, mulish, obstinate, self-willed, wilful, bad, contrary, unyielding, intractable, dogged. *Docile*
Cross, peevish, petulant, surly, spiteful, ill-tempered, vexatious, troublesome.

Perversion, Abasement, abuse, misuse, corruption, debasement, deterioration, vitiation, prostitution, impairment, distortion. *Use*

Pervert, Abase, abuse, misuse,† falsify, stretch.

Pervious, Passable, permeable, penetrable, accessible, traversable. *Impenetrable*

Pessimistic, Gloomy, sad, despondent, hopeless. *Optimistic*

Pest, Curse, plague, pestilence, nuisance, scourge, annoyance, bane, thorn. *Blessing*

Pester, Plague, torment, worry, harass, annoy, vex, disquiet, tease, trouble, disturb, nettle, provoke, bother, chafe, fret, irritate. *Soothe*

Pestiferous, Pernicious, noxious, obnoxious, pestilential, mischievous, malignant, malign, insalubrious, unwholesome, vile, virulent, morbific, infected, infectious, contagious, destructive, poisonous, foul, venomous. *Pure*

Pestilence, Plague, contagion, outbreak, scourge, pest, epidemic, disease. *Purity*

Pestilential, Pestiferous, pernicious, noxious, obnoxious, mischievous, malignant, malign, insalubrious, unwholesome, vile, virulent, morbific, infected, infectious, contagious, destructive, poisonous, foul, venomous. *Pure*

Pet, *n.,* Favourite, fondling, plaything, darling, idol.

v.a., Caress, fondle, indulge.

Petition, *v.a.,* Ask, entreat, pray, beg, beseech, crave, solicit, supplicate, request. *Demand*

n., Entreaty, prayer, solicitation, supplication, request, address, suit, appeal, instance. *Protest*

Petrify, Stupefy, appal, astonish, astound, amaze, nonplus, dumbfound, stagger, stun. *Reassure*

Pettish, Petulant, touchy, testy, hasty, peevish, querulous, waspish, snarling, snappish, snappy, fretful. *Genial*

Petty, Trivial, minor, insignificant, small, trifling, unimportant, little, mean, slight, frivolous, paltry, inconsiderable. *Large*

Petulant, Pettish, touchy, testy, hasty, peevish, irascible, querulous, waspish, snarling, snappish, snappy, fretful, irritable, choleric, crusty. *Genial*

Phantasm, Delusion, chimera, illusion, idea, notion, vision, dream, hallucination, unreality, phantasy, phantom, apparition, fancy. *Reality*

Phantom, Apparition, ghost, spectre, spirit, spook, vision, phantasm, illusion. *Substance*

Pharisaical, Hypocritical, sanctimonious, ceremonious, self-righteous, formal. *Genuine*

Pharmacist, Druggist, chemist, apothecary.

Phase, Period, stage, aspect, appearance, state, guise, condition.

Phenomenal, Marvellous, wonderful, miraculous, prodigious, remarkable. *Ordinary*

Phenomenon, Fact, manifestation, appearance.

Marvel, wonder, prodigy, miracle.

Philander, Flirt, coquet, dally. *Love*

Philanthropic, Humane, kind, liberal, generous, gracious, charitable, loving, open, benevolent, benignant. *Selfish*

Philistinism, Vulgarity, vulgarism, utilitarianism, vandalism.

Philosopher, Student, theorizer, theorist, metaphysician. *Ignoramus*

Philosophic, Stoical, calm, serene, reasonable, imperturbable, cool, composed, collected, sane, rational, sound, sedate, wise, tranquil. *Uneasy*

Phlegm } Dull, sluggish, apathetic,
Phlegmatic } cold, unfeeling, impassive, calm, cold-blooded, uninterested, indifferent, unsusceptible. *Enthusiastic*

Phosphorescent, Luminous, phosphoric, phosphorical.

Phrase, *v.a.,* Put, express, utter, name, call, style, denominate, describe, entitle.

n., Expression, utterance, idiom, diction, phraseology.

Phraseology, Language, diction, style, expression, phrase, manner, speech.

Phthisis, Consumption, decline, wasting, emaciation, atrophy.

Phylactery, Amulet, charm, guard, spell, talisman.

Physic, Medicine, drug, dose, purgative, purge, remedy, cure, medicament.

Physical, Material, natural, substantial, corporeal, bodily, national, tangible, visible, external. *Spiritual*

Physician, Doctor, surgeon, practitioner, consultant, healer, curer.

Physiognomy, Countenance, face, visage, look, aspect, appearance.

Physique, Build, constitution, structure, frame.

Piacular, Expiatory, penitential. *Offending*

Picaroon, Adventurer, freebooter, rogue, cheat, pirate, rascal, buccaneer, outlaw.

Pick, *v.n.,* Steal, pilfer, embezzle.

v.a., Cull, select, choose, single. *Reject*
Pierce, peck.
Gather, collect, acquire, cut, pull, detach, pluck, get, glean, extract, rob.

n., Pickaxe, spike, pike.
Choice, selection, best.

Picket, Guard, sentry, sentinel, watchman.
Stake, pale, tether.

Pickle, Plight, quandary, predicament.

Picnic, Party, treat, outing, excursion.

Pictorial, Illustrated, graphic, picturesque.

Picture, *v.a.,* Imagine, see, glimpse.

n., Image, painting, drawing, etching, sketch, delineation, portrait, resemblance, likeness, semblance, description, representation.

Picturesque, Artistic, beautiful, graphic, graceful, scenic. *Ugly*

Piebald, Motley, mottled, mongrel, pied, mixed, diversified, irregular, variegated, heterogeneous. *Uniform*

Piece, *v.a.*, Cement, unite, join, patch, connect, complete, increase, augment. *Separate*

n., Part, portion, bit, fragment, particle, morsel, scrap, slice, chunk, shred. *Whole*

Pied, Motley, mottled, piebald, mixed, diversified, irregular, spotted, variegated, heterogeneous. *Uniform*

Pierce, Penetrate, perforate, pass, enter, bore, drill, transfix, puncture, stab. *Blunt*

Touch, thrill, affect, move, excite, rouse.

Piercing, Penetrating, perforating, acute, keen, sharp, cutting. *Dull*

Piety, Reverence, devotion, holiness, grace, sanctity, godliness. *Impiety*

Piggish, Hoggish, swinish, dirty, greedy, low. *Polite*

Pike, Spike, spear, point, halberd.

Pile, *v.a.*, Heap, amass, store, gather, accumulate, collect, stack. *Dissipate*

n., Heap, mass, store.†
Structure, building, erection, edifice, fabric.
Fabric, nap, surface.

Pilfer, Steal, thieve, purloin, embezzle, peculate, filch, abstract. *Restore*

Pilgrim, Wanderer, traveller, palmer, wayfarer, crusader, devotee, sojourner, tramp. *Dweller*

Pilgrimage, Wandering, travelling, journey, tour, sojourn, crusade, expedition, excursion.

Pillage, *v.a.*, Ransack, plunder, rifle, spoil, despoil, strip, sack, devastate, loot. *Adorn*

n., Spoliation, plunder, depredation, devastation, waste, ravage, loot, ravine, destruction.

Pillar, Post, support, prop, pier, column, upholder.

Pilot, *v.a.*, Guide, direct, steer, govern, rule, control, conduct. *Misguide*

n., Guide, director, aviator.

Pimp, Bawd, procurer, pander.

Pimple, Pustule, boil, blotch, spot, eruption.

Pin, *v.a.*, Fix, fasten, secure, hold, bind, pen, enclose, confine. *Loosen*

n., Peg, bolt, dowel, skewer.

Pinch, *v.a.*, Squeeze, gripe, compress, nip, hurt.

n., Squeeze, gripe, nip, pang. *Ease*
Emergency, crisis, pressure, exigency, stress, difficulty, push.

Pine, Droop, drop, waste, fail, decline, flag, languish, wither, decay, fade. *Revive*

Long, hanker, yearn, desire. *Possess*

Pinguid, Greasy, fat, oily, unctuous, oleaginous, adipose. *Dry*

Pinion, *v.a.*, Bind, fetter, fasten, restrain, shackle, chain. *Release*

n., Wing, arm, pennon, feather, plume.

Pinnacle, Peak, apex, top, acme, height, summit, crown, culmination, zenith. *Base*

Pious, Devout, godly, righteous, good, religious, filial, saintly, holy. *Ungodly*

Pipe, Conduit, tube, reed.

Piquant, Cutting, pungent, sharp, biting, severe, strong, keen, caustic, stinging, pointed, tart. *Soothing*

Interesting, enjoyable, racy, lively, stimulating, sparkling. *Insipid*

Pique, *v.a.*, Wound, offend, annoy, irritate, vex, chafe, fret, upset, displease, provoke, affront, nettle, sting, incense. *Pacify*

n., Offence, annoyance, irritation, vexation, displeasure, resentment, spite. *Pleasure*

Pirate, Rover, buccaneer, freebooter, corsair, picaroon.

Pit, *v.a.*, Set, match, oppose.

n., Hole, hollow, cavity, excavation, well, crater, mine, gulf, abyss, chasm.

Pitch, *v.a.*, Hurl, toss, fling, throw, cast, propel, plunge, heave. *Retain*

v.a., Set, place, plant, fix, establish, locate, settle, station. *Strike*

v.n., Fall, plunge, drop, lurch, reel. *Rise*

n., Extent, height, degree, rate, measure, range, elevation, slope, inclination, modulation.

Toss, cast, throw, jerk, plunge.

Pitcher, Vessel, pot, jug, jar, urn, ewer.

Piteous, Pitiable, lamentable, distressing, sad, sorry, sorrowful, woeful, grievous, affecting, moving, deplorable, wretched. *Enviable*

Pitfall, Snare, catch, trap, ambush, temptation.

Pith, Substance, gist, marrow, kernel, essence, quintessence, soul. *Dressing*

Vigour, force, power, energy, strength, importance, moment, weight. *Weakness*

Pithy, Brief, condensed, concise, terse, short, laconic, pointed, compact, pregnant. *Verbose*

Vigorous, forceful.†

Pitiable, Piteous, lamentable, distressing, sad, sorry, sorrowful, woeful, grievous, affecting, moving, deplorable, wretched. *Enviable*

Pitiful, Compassionate, merciful, tender,

kind, humane, mild, sympathetic, lenient, pathetic, piteous, wretched, deplorable, miserable. ***Harsh***

Pitiless, Harsh, merciless, hard, strict, ruthless, cruel, unfeeling, unkind, unsympathetic, inexorable, unsparing, relentless, unrelenting, implacable, callous. ***Compassionate***

Pittance, Dole, allowance, alms, charity, gift, modicum, driblet, drop, trifle. ***Profusion***

Pity, Compassion, mercy, tenderness, commiseration, condolence, sympathy, kindness. ***Cruelty***

Pivot, Hinge, axle, axis, centre, joint.

Placable, Mild, forgiving, appeasable, reconcilable. ***Inexorable***

Placard, Bill, poster, broadside, notice, advertisement.

Placate, Pacify, soothe, appease, conciliate, reconcile. ***Incense***

Place, *v.a.,* Put, lay, set, settle, establish, assign, locate, deposit, commit, allocate, order, fix, seat. ***Remove***

n., Spot, situation, locality, site, position, area, square, region, quarter, district, whereabouts, scene, premises.

Town, city, village.

House, mansion, estate, seat, residence.

Stead, room, office, position, appointment, post, occupation, calling.

Passage, paragraph, part, portion, point.

Placid, Calm, quiet, serene, tranquil, even, unruffled, collected, equable, unmoved, undisturbed, unperturbed, composed, unexcited, imperturbable. ***Ruffled***

Plague, *v.a.,* Torment, torture, harass, worry, vex, annoy, pester, harry, tease, trouble, molest, hector, afflict, distress, fret, chafe, gall, bother, inconvenience, incommode. ***Soothe***

n., Torment, torture, vexation, annoyance, trouble, affliction, distress, bother, nuisance, thorn, curse, pest, scourge. ***Blessing***

Pestilence, disease, epidemic, contagion, pest.

Plain, *n.,* Plateau, table-land, level, lowland, prairie.

a., Simple, unadorned, frugal, homely. ***Elaborate***

Level, smooth, even, flat, uniform, plane. ***Uneven***

Obvious, clear, manifest, apparent, undeniable, indubitable, palpable, notorious, glaring, open, visible, unmistakable, certain, evident, distinct, patent. ***Obscure***

Blunt, direct, easy, downright, candid, unsophisticated, frank, open, sincere, artless, ingenuous, straightforward, undesigning, simple, natural, unaffected. ***Cunning***

Plaint, Lament, lamentation, cry, complaint, sorrow, wail, moan. ***Gladness***

Plaintiff, Prosecutor, summoner, accuser. ***Defendant***

Plaintive, Woeful, sorry, sorrowful, sad, mournful, doleful, wailing, melancholy. ***Joyous***

Plait, Interweave, weave, interlace, lace, fold, gather, braid, intertwine, twine, mat. ***Unravel***

Plan, *v.a.,* Contrive, concoct, design, devise, figure, represent, study, calculate, manoeuvre, conspire, invent, prepare, hatch, project, arrange, scheme, plot.

n., Contrivance, design, device, project, arrangement, scheme, plot, idea, proposition, proposal, method, system, process, custom.

Sketch, plot, draught, diagram, map, illustration, chart.

Plane, Level, smooth, even, flat, plain. ***Uneven***

Plant, *v.a.,* Implant, fix, settle, establish, place, set, introduce, insert, inculcate. ***Eradicate***

Sow, scatter, implant, bed.

n., Equipment, works, machinery, factory, establishment. Vegetable, herb, organism.

Plastic, Soft, pliable, pliant, flexible, malleable, ductile, yielding. ***Hard***

Platitude, Truism, commonplace, flatness, insipidity, generality, banality, nonsense, verbiage, jargon, palaver, chatter. ***Novelty***

Plaudits, Applause, approval, approbation, acclamation. ***Execration***

Plausible, Passable, specious, colourable, superficial, suave, bland, smooth, glib. ***Genuine***

Play, *v.a.,* Perform, do, execute, enact act, exhibit, compete, represent.

v.n., Perform, act, personate, do, behave.

Revel, disport, sport, gambol, toy, caper, trifle, frisk, romp, frolic, wanton. ***Work***

n., Performance, drama, piece, tragedy, melodrama, comedy, farce. ***Reality***

Revel, sport, game, gambols, frolic, pastime, prank, jest, gamble, gambling, amusement.

Action, movement, motion, scope, range, latitude, sweep, opportunity.

Playful, Frolicsome, light, cheerful, buoyant, sportive, vivacious, jolly, gay, amusing, mirthful, merry, sprightly, giddy. ***Sedate***

Plea, Excuse, pleading, vindication, claim,

argument, allegation, defence, apology, appeal, pretext, action, suit, justification, ground. *Accusation*
Entreaty, call, request, prayer, petition.

Plead, Argue, reason, dispute, defend, appeal, answer. *Reject*

Pleasant, Delightful, welcome, agreeable, grateful, gratifying, acceptable, desirable, pleasing, delectable, pleasurable, charming, cheerful, gay, merry, amusing.
Obnoxious

Pleasantry, Facetiousness, wit, humour, gaiety, jocularity. *Sourness*

Please, *v.n.,* Like, prefer, choose, wish.
v.a., Delight, gratify, content, satisfy, gladden, rejoice, charm, oblige. *Offend*

Pleasing, Delightful, pleasant, welcome, agreeable, grateful, gratifying, acceptable, desirable, delectable, pleasurable, charming. *Obnoxious*

Pleasure, Gratification, indulgence, enjoyment, delight, delectation, joy, gladness, satisfaction, happiness, comfort.
Pain
Will, desire, wish, purpose, intent, mind, choice, preference, favour, kindness.

Plebeian, Low, common, vulgar, coarse, mean, ignoble, base. *Patrician*

Pledge, *v.a.,* Engage, gage, promise, plight, warrant, pawn, toast.
n., Gage, pawn, security, deposit, guarantee, earnest, warrant, surety, hostage, health.

Plenary, Entire, absolute, full, complete.
Partial

Plenipotentiary, Envoy, minister, ambassador, legate, consul.

Plenitude, Plenty, abundance, superfluity, fulness, completeness, copiousness, repletion. *Emptiness*

Plenteous } Abundant, full, complete,
Plentiful } copious, sufficient, ample, replete. *Scanty*

Plenty, Abundance, fulness,† enough, adequate, plenitude, profusion, overflow, exuberance. *Scarcity*

Pleonastic, Superfluous, redundant, diffuse, verbose, wordy, tautological, prolix. *Concise*

Plethora, Superfluity, redundance, superabundance, surfeit, excess. *Scarcity*

Pliable } Flexile, flexible, soft, supple,
Pliant } facile, limber, ductile, lithe, tractable, yielding, manageable. *Stiff*

Plight, *v.a.,* Promise, gage, engage, pledge, warrant, pawn.
n., Predicament, scrape, difficulty, state, dilemma, position, condition.

Plod, Trudge, jog, persist, persevere, drudge, toil, moil, labour.

Plodding, Painstaking, laborious, persistent, diligent, patient, jogging, persevering, industrious, studious. *Fitful*

Plot, *v.a.,* Plan, devise, scheme, concoct, contrive, frame, hatch, compass, brew, project.
v.n., Plan, scheme, contrive, conspire, intrigue.
n., Plan, scheme, conspiracy, stratagem, project, outline, skeleton, diagram, sketch, purpose, machination, intrigue.
Fable, story, intrigue.
Patch, allotment, field, plan.

Pluck, *v.a.,* Pull, pick, gather, collect.
Plant
n., Courage, bravery, daring, mettle, nerve, valour, heroism, grit, resolution, spirit. *Cowardice*

Plumb, Vertical, upright, perpendicular.
Slanting

Plump, Stout, fleshy, fat, portly, corpulent, burly, bouncing, bonny, chubby, brawny, strapping. *Lean*

Plunder, *v.a.,* Rob, ravage, fleece, sack, spoil, despoil, rifle, waste, pillage, loot.
n., Booty, spoil, pillage, loot, sack.

Plunge, *v.n.,* Dip, dive, pitch, duck, sink.
Emerge
v.a., Dip, duck, sink, immerse, souse, submerge, douse, precipitate.

Ply, Practise, apply, employ, use, exercise.
Urge, importune, ask, solicit, beg, tout.

Poach, Trespass, pilfer, steal, filch, purloin.

Pocket, Pouch, receptacle, hollow, cavity.

Poetical, Rhythmic, metrical, rhyming, lyric, lyrical. *Prosaic*

Poetry, Poesy, verse, rhyme. *Prose*

Poignant, Piercing, pungent, sharp, bitter, biting, penetrating, severe, intense, keen, caustic, acrid, piquant. *Dull*
Caustic, pointed, bitter, sacrastic, severe, keen, irritating.

Point, *v.a.,* Direct, aim, focus, level, train. Sharpen.
Show, indicate, designate, punctuate.
n., End, tip, apex.
Stage, period, phase, moment, instant.
Verge, eve.
Object, end, purpose, design, aim, intent, gist.
Place, spot, station, site, stage.
Subject, matter, question, respect.
Headland, cape, naze, promontory, projection.

Pointed, Sharp, peaked. *Blunt*
Pregnant, forcible, sharp, epigrammatic, telling, poignant, keen, expressive, explicit, distinct, significant, personal.
Vague

Pointer, Director, finger, index, tip, hand.

Pointless, Vague, vapid, flat, aimless, feeble, dull, inexpressive, futile, stupid. *Significant*

Poise, *v.a.*, Balance, weigh.

n., Balance, equipoise, equilibrium, gravity, weight, carriage.

Poison, *v.a.*, Pollute, contaminate, infect, corrupt, envenom, vitiate, canker, taint. *Purify*

n., Taint, virus, venom, pest, bane.

Poisonous, Pestiferous, baneful, baleful, noxious, deleterious, insalubrious, venomous, morbific, corruptive, peccant, pestilential. *Wholesome*

Poke, Push, shove, thrust, inject, punch, prod, jog.

Polar, Northern, arctic, antarctic, boreal. *Tropical*

Pole, Stick, rod, pointer, staff, post, mast. Rod, perch.

Polemic, Controversial, debatable, doubtful, moot. *Certain*

Disputatious, captious, cavilling, contentious. *Peaceful*

Policy, Statesmanship, administration, wisdom, plan, rôle, action, tactics, strategy, sagacity. *Aimlessness*

Polish, *v.a.*, Furbish, brighten, clean, burnish, rub, smooth, refine, glaze, levigate. *Scratch*

n., Brightness, shine, brilliance, lustre, splendour. *Dulness*

Refinement, politeness, elegance, finish, grace, accomplishment. *Roughness*

Polished, Bright, shining, brilliant, lustrous, glossy, glazed, refined, burnished, furbished, clean. *Dull*

Refined, polite, elegant, graceful, accomplished, cultivated, genteel. *Rough*

Polite, Refined, polished, elegant, graceful, accomplished, cultivated, genteel, courteous, courtly, urbane, affable, complaisant, obliging, civil. *Rude*

Politic, Political, civil, civic, public.

Sagacious, shrewd, artful, wise, cunning, astute, prudent, discreet, wary, cautious, wily, skilful, sly, diplomatic, crafty, subtle. *Rash*

Political, Civil, civic, public.

Pollute, Corrupt, taint, befoul, poison, tarnish, defile, stain, soil, debase, abuse, desecrate, contaminate, infect, violate, ravish. *Purify*

Poltroon, Recreant, scoundrel, coward, skunk, dastard, craven, hound. *Hero*

Pommel, Cudgel, bruise, thrash, flog, beat, baste strike, thump, belabour, maul, trounce. *Stroke*

Pomp, Show, ostentation, display, pride, parade, exhibition, magnificence, ceremony, pageantry, splendour, flourish. *Simplicity*

Pompous, Ostentatious, proud, showy, magnificent, splendid, gorgeous, sumptuous, pretentious, inflated, assuming, turgid, important, swelling, flaunting. *Modest*

Ponder, *v.n.*, Consider, meditate, think, ruminate, study, examine, cogitate, reflect, muse, wonder, deliberate.

v.a., Consider, examine, weigh, contemplate, study, meditate.

Ponderous, Massive, weighty, heavy, bulky. *Light*

Pool, *n.*, Pond, lake, puddle, mere, tarn, loch.

v.a., Contribute, combine, merge. *Distribute*

Poor, Needy, necessitous, indigent, penniless, straitened, moneyless, impecunious, pinched, reduced, distressed, destitute. *Rich*

Barren, unfruitful, unproductive, unprolific, unfertile, sterile, fruitless. *Fertile*

Feeble, weak, meagre, unsatisfactory, bad, inferior, useless, worthless, unsound, pitiful, wretched, contemptible, despicable. *Brilliant*

Insufficient, scant, deficient, inadequate, meagre, small, thin, bald, unsatisfactory. *Satisfactory*

Luckless, unlucky, wretched, miserable, unfortunate. *Fortunate*

Pop, Burst, detonation, explosion, clap, report, bang.

Populace, People, herd, rabble, mob, masses.

Popular, Favourite, accepted, received, approved, familiar, admired, liked. *Detested*

Common, prevalent, prevailing, current, general, cheap. *Exclusive*

Populous, Thick, crowded, thronged, dense. *Deserted*

Porch, Vestibule, portico, entrance, gallery.

Pore, *v.n.*, Brood, study, read, examine, dwell.

n., Opening, hole, orifice, spiracle.

Porous, Foraminous, percolable, pervious, permeable, pory, penetrable. *Impermeable*

Port, Haven, harbour, anchorage, roadstead, refuge, shelter, retreat.

Deportment, air, carriage, mien, bearing, demeanour, behaviour, appearance, look, aspect.

Portable, Light, handy, manageable, movable, transportable, convenient. *Ponderous*

Portend, Forebode, betoken, presage, threaten, indicate, foretell, foreshow, foreshadow, foretoken, bode, augur, herald, prognosticate. *Avert*

Portent, Sign, token, omen, augury, prognostic, presage, premonition, wonder, phenomenon, marvel.

Portentous, Ominous, inauspicious, unpropitious, threatening, premonitory. *Encouraging*

Wonderful, marvellous, monstrous, tremendous, extraordinary, amazing.

Portion, *v.a.*, Distribute, divide, deal, part, parcel, allot.

n., Part, bit, piece, fragment, half, scrap, morsel. *Whole*

Lot, share, quota, part, division, assignment, allotment.

Portly, Imposing, grand, stately, dignified, majestic, large, stout, burly. *Undignified*

Portrait, Picture, likeness, representation, sketch, drawing.

Portray, Depict, draw, sketch, delineate, describe, limn, represent, paint. *Caricature*

Pose, *v.a.*, Confound, nonplus, bewilder, embarrass, perplex, puzzle, dumbfound, mystify, stagger, daze. *Enlighten*

v.n., Stand, pretend, feign, affect.

n., Posture, attitude, pretence.

Poser, Enigma, riddle, puzzle, mystery.

Position, Standing, station, place, situation, locality, spot, post, site.

Condition, state, circumstance, phase.

Situation, post, job, berth, office.

Attitude, posture, bearing.

Rank, standing, dignity, status.

Positive, Actual, real, true, substantial, veritable, absolute. *Negative*

Certain, sure, convinced, assured, confident. *Doubtful*

Express, expressed, precise, definite, defined, explicit, direct, categorical, decisive, unequivocal, unconditional, unmistakable, imperative, clear, indisputable, incontrovertible. *Conditional*

Possess, Have, own, hold, keep, command, seize, obtain, control, enjoy, occupy. *Lose*

Possession, Control, monopoly, property, ownership, tenancy, tenure. *Surrender*

Possessions, Property, wealth, assets, effects, estate.

Possible, Practicable, likely, conceivable, accessible, feasible, potential. *Impracticable*

Possibly, Perhaps, mayhap, maybe, peradventure, perchance, haply. *Certainly*

Post, *v.a.*, Put, place, stick, station, fix, establish, set. *Remove*

Record, enter, register.

n., Column, pillar, support, picket, pier. Mail.

Place, position, station, situation, berth, seat, office, job, employment.

Poster, Notice, bill, placard, broadside, advertisement.

Posterior, Later, succeeding, subsequent, after, following, ensuing. *Precedent*

Back, hind, hinder, after, rear. *Front*

Posterity, Futurity, descendants, progeny, children, offspring, issue, heirs, family. *Ancestry*

Postpone, Delay, defer, prorogue, adjourn, procrastinate, shelve, table. *Despatch*

Postscript, Appendix, supplement, addition. *Preface*

Postulate, *v.a.*, Presuppose, assume, beseech, entreat, solicit. *Prove*

n., Supposition, assumption, hypothesis, conjecture, axiom, speculation, theory.

Posture, Position, situation, state, condition, attitude, pose, disposition, phase.

Pot, Can, pan, bowl, saucepan, jug, jar, cup, mug, tankard, kettle, utensil.

Potent, Efficacious, powerful, mighty, strong, forcible, efficient, able, effective, puissant, influential, active, energetic, cogent. *Weak*

Potentate, Ruler, emperor, king, prince, monarch, sovereign, lord.

Potential, Possible, immanent, virtual, undeveloped, implicit. *Actual*

Pother, Tumult, shouting, commotion, turbulence, confusion, bustle, noise, rush, flutter, turmoil, hullabaloo, uproar. *Quiet*

Potion, Draught, cup, dose.

Pouch, Bag, wallet, sack, case.

Pound, Impound, imprison, coop, cage, confine, enclose. *Release*

Beat, bruise, strike, thump, pulverize, levigate, powder, crush, triturate. *Amalgamate*

Pour, *v.n.*, Stream, issue, flow, rush, gush, run.

v.a., Emit, throw, lavish.

Pouting, Sullen, cross, disagreeable, perverse, sulky. *Pleasant*

Poverty, Want, indigence, need, necessity, destitution, penury, privation, distress, pauperism, straits, impecuniosity. *Wealth*

Paucity, scarcity, lack, want, need,

insufficiency, deficiency, shortage, poorness, smallness, barrenness. **Plenty**

Powder, *v.a.*, Pound, crush, pulverize, levigate, comminute, triturate.
Compound
Sprinkle, dab, dust.
n., Dust, gunpowder, explosive.

Power, Potency, force, efficacy, efficiency, might, strength, ability, energy, cogency, faculty, talent, gift, capacity, competency, capability. **Weakness**
Influence, control, sovereignty, sway, dominion, domain, domination, command, rule, government, authority, warrant. **Subjection**

Powerful, Potent, forcible, efficacious,† effective, puissant, influential, active, sturdy, robust, vigorous. **Weak**

Practicable, Possible, feasible, likely, attainable, achievable, usable, operative, passable. **Impossible**

Practical, Actual, working, workable, effective, useful. **Theoretical**
Practised, experienced, qualified, versed, trained, skilled, proficient.
Inexperienced

Practice, Work, exercise, pursuit, training, conduct, performance, application, action. **Theory**
Habit, use, procedure, usage, wont, custom.

Practise, Perform, exercise, do, pursue, apply, prosecute, perpetrate.

Practised, Experienced, qualified, versed, trained, skilled, proficient, practical, accomplished, *au fait*. **Inexperienced**

Pragmatical, Fussy, meddling, meddlesome, officious, interfering, intermeddling, intrusive, obtrusive, impertinent.
Indifferent

Praise, *v.a.*, Extol, laud, magnify, commend, applaud, eulogize, panegyrize, approbate, compliment, flatter, approve, exalt. **Censure**
n., Extolling, laud, laudation,† encomium, merit, desert.

Praiseworthy, Laudable, commendable, fine, worthy, meritorious. **Reprehensible**

Prank, Antic, trick, mischief, game, frolic, gambol, caper.

Prate } *v.n.*, Babble, talk, chatter, tattle,
Prattle } palaver, gabble.
n., Babble, talk,† nonsense.

Pray, Implore, adjure, ask, beg, beseech, entreat, desire, request, importune, crave, petition.

Prayer, Imploration, adjuration, asking, supplication, entreaty, petition, request. Communion, devotion, adoration.

Preach, Teach, exhort, urge, press,

declare, tell, publish, deliver, blaze, spread, proclaim, pronounce, inculcate.

Preamble, Preface, foreword, introduction, prologue, prelude, proem. **Epilogue**

Precarious, Uncertain, unsettled, unstable, dubious, unreliable, shaky, risky, hazardous, perilous, insecure, doubtful, unsteady. **Safe**

Precaution, Provision, providence, forethought, anticipation, caution, safeguard, care, prudence, foresight. **Improvidence**

Precede, Head, lead, herald, usher, introduce. **Follow**

Precedence, Lead, superiority, priority, pre-eminence, supremacy, advantage.
Subordination

Precedent, *n.*, Example, instance, pattern, warrant, custom, usage, authority.
Prohibition
a., Earlier, preceding, prior, antecedent, anterior, previous. **Subsequent**

Precept, Instruction, ordinance, direction, rule, law, command, behest, maxim, injunction, edict, decree, mandate, fiat, canon, order, regulation, principle, doctrine, dictate. **Impulse**

Preceptor, Pedagogue, instructor, tutor, teacher, master, dominie. **Pupil**

Precincts, Limits, confines, area, borders, bounds, boundaries, enclosures, environs, neighbourhood, district, purlieus.

Precious, Dear, valued, valuable, cherished, costly, priceless, inestimable, invaluable, treasured, prized, beloved, esteemed. **Worthless**

Precipitate, *v.a.*, Expedite, despatch, speed, accelerate, hasten, advance, promote, hurry, further, forward, urge, move. **Retard**
a., Rash, hasty, hurried, fast, reckless, heedless, sudden, abrupt, violent, indiscreet, thoughtless. **Cautious**

Precipitous, Steep, perpendicular, sheer, sudden, abrupt, headlong. **Gradual**

Precise, Nice, exact, fine, logical, careful, scrupulous, express, severe, accurate, formal, correct, strict, finical, definite, explicit, distinct. **Vague**

Precision, Nicety, exactitude, exactness.†
Vagueness

Preclude, Obviate, debar, bar, stop, prevent, check, prohibit, remove, hinder, inhibit, restrain. **Encourage**

Precocious, Forward, premature, clever, advanced. **Backward**

Precognition, Foreknowledge, foresight.
Reflection

Preconcerted, Concocted, prepared, prearranged, premeditated, faked.
Spontaneous

Precursor, Predecessor, harbinger, fore-runner, cause, sign, messenger, pioneer, omen, courier, herald. *Follower*

Precursory, Prefatory, introductory, pre-paratory, prior, previous, preliminary, initiatory, antecedent. *Final*

Predaceous, Voracious, ravenous, rapa-cious, greedy.

Predatory, Ravaging, plundering, wild, pillaging, destructive, greedy. *Peaceful*

Predecessor, Precursor, forerunner, an-cestor, forefather, progenitor. *Successor*

Predestination, Fate, doom, necessity, foredoom, predetermination, preordina-tion, foreordination, foreordainment. *Freedom*

Predetermined, Destined, fated, decided, foregone, appointed.

Predicament, Plight, situation, dilemma, difficulty, position, state, condition, case, extremity, mess, fix, emergency.

Predicate, Aver, assert, asseverate, main-tain, argue, declare, say, state. *Deny*

Predict, Prophesy, presage, prognosti-cate, foretell, portend, forecast, signify, see, augur, foreshadow.

Prediction, Prophecy, presage,† divina-tion.

Predilection, Bent, bias, preference, predisposition, prepossession, leaning, inclination, liking, partiality, fondness, desire, weakness. *Aversion*

Predisposition, Predilection, bent, pre-ference.† *Aversion*
Bent, proclivity, aptitude, propensity, capability, proneness, leaning.

Predominant, Supreme, pre-eminent, superior, prevailing, prevalent, ascen-dant, dominant, ruling, overruling, con-trolling. *Minor*

Predominate, Dominate, rule, prevail, preponderate. *Subordinate*

Pre-eminent, Predominant, supreme, superior, consummate, prevailing, excel-ling, excellent, unmatched, unrivalled, unequalled, unsurpassed, surpassing, paramount, peerless, transcendant. *Inferior*

Preface, Prelude, introduction, foreword, prologue, preliminary, proem, preamble, exordium. *Epilogue*

Prefatory, Prelusive, prelusory, intro-ductory, proemial, precursory, precur-sive, preparatory, preliminary, ante-cedent, initiative. *Final*

Prefer, Elect, select, choose, fancy, adopt, pick, single. *Reject*
Advance, promote, elevate, dignify, raise. *Degrade*

Preferable, Better, worthier, desirable.

Preference, Election, selection, choice, liking, priority, advantage, precedence.

Preferment, Advancement, promotion, elevation, dignity, exaltation. *Degradation*
Benefice, living.

Pregnable, Defenceless, weak, exposed. *Fortified*

Pregnant, Prolific, teeming, bursting, full, replete, fertile, fruitful, productive, filled, fraught. *Void*

Prejudice, *v.a.*, Harm, impair, injure, damage, diminish, involve, implicate.
Bias, warp, turn, incline.
n., Bias, prejudgment, predisposition, partiality, unfairness, preconception. *Impartiality*
Harm, mischief, detriment, impairment, injury, damage, implication.

Prejudiced, Biassed, warped, bigoted, partial, unfair, hostile, influenced, partisan, narrow. *Impartial*

Prelate, Archbishop, pope, metropolitan, bishop, primate, cardinal, pontiff.

Preliminary, *n.*, Preface, introduction, beginning, start, initiation, prelude, opening. *Finish*
a., Prefatory, introductory,† proemial, preparatory, prior, precursory, precur-sive, antecedent, precedent. *Final*

Prelude, Preliminary, preface, intro-duction, beginning, start, initiation, opening, prologue, preamble, proem, exordium. *Finish*

Prelusive ⎫ Preliminary, prefatory.†
Prelusory ⎭ *Final*

Premature, Untimely, unseasonable, crude, early, unprepared, immatured, un-ripe, previous, hasty, precipitate. *Late*

Premeditate, Plot, plan, intend, mean, predesign, predetermine, precontrive, prearrange, deliberate, preconcert. *Extemporize*

Premise, *v.a. & n.*, Preface, begin, announce.
n., Ground, hypothesis, antecedent, argument, support, proposition. *Conclusion*

Premises, Grounds, buildings, lands, place, antecedent.

Premium, Bribe, meed, reward, prize, guerdon, recompense, remuneration, en-couragement, bounty, bonus, fee, pay-ment, appreciation. *Penalty*

Premonish, Warn, forewarn, caution, advise.

Premonition, Warning, caution, fore-warning, advice, omen, sign, portent, presage.

Preoccupied, Lost, wandering, aberrant, absent, dreaming, inattentive, heedless, abstracted, absorbed, engrossed, absent-minded, musing, rapt, unobservant. ***Attentive***

Preordain, Predetermine, prearrange, doom, foredoom, predestine, predestinate, foreordain.

Preparatory, Preliminary, antecedent, prefatory, previous, prior, introductory, precedent, percursory, precursive. ***Final***

Prepare, Arrange, order, fit, adjust, adapt, qualify, concoct, fabricate, plan, make, lay, provide. ***Destroy***

Preponderant, Predominant, prevailing, prevalent, overbalancing, outweighing, dominant, supreme, ascendant. ***Insignificant***

Preponderate, Predominate, prevail, outweigh. ***Fail***

Prepossessing, Charming, delightful, attractive, inviting, enticing, alluring, fascinating, engaging, captivating, winning, bewitching, taking. ***Repulsive***

Prepossession, Preoccupation, inattention, aberration. ***Attention***

Preposterous, Ridiculous, ludicrous, absurd, farcical, monstrous, perverted, excessive, exorbitant, unreasonable, irrational, extravagant, wrong, foolish. ***Reasonable***

Prerogative, Right, privilege, liberty, advantage, claim. ***Disqualification***

Presage, *v.a.,* Predict, foretell, forecast, augur, forebode, prophesy, soothsay, prognosticate, foreshow, portend, indicate.

n., Prediction, foreboding, prophecy, prognostication, indication, augury, portent, sign, omen, premonition, presentiment. ***Realization***

Prescience, Prevision, precognition, foresight, forecast, foreknowledge.

Prescribe, Order, bid, command, enjoin, direct, dictate, ordain, decree, appoint, impose, establish. ***Prohibit***

Prescription, Order, bidding,† mandate, rule, law, ordinance, usage, custom.

Formula, recipe, remedy, receipt.

Presence, Company, personality, nearness, residence, neighbourhood, vicinity. ***Absence***

Air, carriage, demeanour, mein, appearance.

Present, *v.a.,* Offer, proffer, give, hand, deliver, bestow, grant, confer. ***Withhold***

Introduce, nominate.

Aim, level, point.

n., Offering, gift, grant, largess, gratuity, boon, favour.

Present, Time, stage, period, now, to-day. ***Future***

a., Here, near, ready, available. ***Absent***

Existing, existent, current, immediate, actual.

Presentation, Offering, gift, delivery, bestowal, grant, conferring, donation, giving, endowment. ***Withdrawal***

Introduction, exhibition, show, display, semblance.

Presentiment, Prescience, foreboding, foretaste, anticipation, apprehension, forecast.

Presently, Anon, later, shortly, soon, directly, immediately, quickly, forthwith.

Preservation, Conservation, care, protection, maintenance, safety, security, support, curing, soundness, keeping. ***Damage***

Preserve, *v.a.,* Conserve, protect, maintain, secure, uphold, save, keep, defend, guard. ***Destroy***

Confection, jam, jelly, marmalade, conserve, sweetmeat.

Preserver, Protector, defender, keeper, saviour, guardian. ***Destroyer***

Preside, Officiate, direct, control, rule, govern. ***Assist***

President, Officer, principal, chairman, superintendent, head, chief.

Press, *v.a.,* Crush, squeeze, compress, crowd.

Iron, smooth, flatten.

Urge, move, compel, force, constrain, harass.

v.n., Crush, crowd, push, fight, scramble, throng, encroach.

n., Crush, crowd, throng, multitude.

Hurry, urgency, pressure.

Journalism.

Pressing, Important, importunate, vital, urgent, immediate. ***Trivial***

Pressure, Weight, crushing, squeezing, compression, press, force.

Influence, force, urgency, hurry, stress, compulsion. ***Relaxation***

Presume, Assume, surmise, suppose, guess, reckon, think, apprehend, conjecture, anticipate, believe. ***Know***

Venture.

Presumption, Assumption, surmise,† opinion, hypothesis. ***Knowledge***

Boldness, audacity, assurance, forwardness, effrontery, arrogance, brazenness. ***Modesty***

Presumptive, Probable, apparent, antecedent.

Presumptuous, Bold, audacious, forward, arrogant, rash, foolhardy, venturesome, insolent, rude. ***Modest***

Presuppose, Postulate, imply, presume, assume, surmise. *Prove*

Pretence, Pretext, excuse, show, affectation, cloak, mask, simulation, fabrication, colour, semblance, guise, appearance. *Truth*

Pretend, Simulate, fabricate, mask, feign, affect, counterfeit, sham, claim, allege. *Verify*

Pretentious, Presuming, vain, conceited, assuming, affected, unnatural, conspicuous. *Modest*

Preternatural, Strange, extraordinary, unusual, abnormal, irregular, inexplicable, mysterious, unnatural, anomalous. *Normal*

Pretext, Pretence, excuse, show, affectation, cloak, simulation, fabrication, colour, mask, semblance, guise, appearance, justification, plea. *Truth*

Pretty, Fair, neat, beautiful, pleasing, comely, handsome. *Ugly*

Prevail, Preponderate, dominate, predominate.
Succeed, overcome, win, triumph, rule, exist, be. *Fail*

Prevailing⎱ Preponderating, dominant,
Prevalent⎰ controlling, predominant. *Powerless*
Superior, influential, ruling, successful, efficacious, effectual. *Subordinate*

Prevaricate, Equivocate, quibble, shuffle, palter, dodge, deviate, shift, cavil. *Affirm*

Prevenient, Introductory, prefatory, preliminary, initiatory, antecedent. *Subsequent*

Prevent, Hinder, stop, obstruct, hamper, thwart, restrain, check, impede, interrupt, bar, nullify, intercept. *Help*

Prevention, Hindrance, stoppage.† *Help*

Previous, Prior, preceding, antecedent, former, earlier, anterior, foregoing. *Later*

Prey, *v.a.,* Plunder, rob, pillage, despoil, feed on, devour.
n., Plunder, pillage, spoil, loot, booty, prize, rapine. *Dues*
Victim, quarry, game.

Price, Expense, cost, charge, value, worth, amount, outlay, estimation, rate, quotation, figure, valuation.
Compensation, recompense, reward, return.

Priceless, Invaluable, inestimable, valuable. *Cheap*

Prick, *v.a.,* Perforate, bore, pierce, puncture, cut, wound.
Goad, drive, urge, impel, incite, move, prompt. *Deter*

Prick, *n.,* Perforation, puncture, bore, hole, cut, mark, wound.
Goad, point.

Pride, Arrogance, vanity, conceit, self-sufficiency, self-exaltation, self-opinionatedness, self-complacency, assumption, haughtiness, hauteur, boastfulness, lordliness, loftiness. *Modest*

Priest, Parson, clergyman, divine, pastor, minister, cleric, rector, churchman. *Layman*

Priggish, Affected, conceited, prim, pedantic. *Unaffected*

Prim, Precise, formal, cold, stiff, strict, unbending, priggish, starched, demure. *Genial*

Primary, First, chief, main, principal, leading, prime. *Subordinate*
Primal, primitive, primordial, primeval, original, aboriginal, earliest, first. *Later*
Elementary, early, preparatory, first. *Secondary*

Prime, *a.,* Primary, first, chief.† *Subordinate*
Primal, primitive, primordial.† *Later*
Excellent, choice, perfect, capital, consummate. *Inferior*
n., Zenith, perfection, height, bloom, flower, spring. *Decadence*

Primeval, Primary, primordial, original, aboriginal, early, pristine. *Later*

Primitive, Quaint, old, crude, original, prehistoric, archaic, simple, rough. *Modern*

Primordial, Primeval, primary, original, early, earliest, pristine. *Later*

Prince, Sovereign, monarch, ruler, lord, potentate, leader. *Beggar*

Princely, Kingly, lordly, royal, imperial, stately, pompous, august, regal, magnificent, splendid, grand. *Beggarly*
Munificent, lofty, noble, exalted, dignified, elevated. *Mean*

Principal, *a.,* Main, leading, chief, first, head, prime, foremost, primary, preeminent, essential. *Minor*
n., Leader, chief, head, ruler, master. *Subordinate*

Principle, Probity, virtue, worth, goodness, integrity, uprightness, honesty, rectitude, honour. *Dishonesty*
Law, dogma, opinion, tenet, axiom, maxim, theory, substance, postulate. *Application*

Print, *v.a.,* Imprint, impress, press, stamp, brand, publish, issue.
n., Impress, impression, stamp, mark.

Prior, Previous, antecedent, anterior, former, foregoing, superior, earlier, precedent, first, preceding. *Subsequent*

Prison, Gaol, captivity, confinement, jail, dungeon, lock-up, reformatory.

Pristine, Primary, primeval, primordial, original, aboriginal, earliest. *Later*

Privacy, Retreat, solitude, concealment, retirement, secrecy, seclusion. *Publicity*

Private, Retired, solitary, sequestered, secret, secluded, concealed, clandestine, hidden. *Public*

Personal, particular, peculiar, individual, unofficial, own, special, confidential, privy. *Public*

Privation, Distress, want, lack, need, destitution, poverty, necessity, absence. *Wealth*

Privilege, Right, prerogative, liberty, immunity, favour, license, franchise, charter, grant, claim. *Prohibition*

Privy, Private, secret, solitary, retired, personal, individual. *Public*

Prize, *v.a.,* Value, esteem, appreciate. *Belittle*

Appraise, rate, estimate.

n., Reward, recompense, need, guerdon, trophy, honour, medal, cup, laurels, palm, booty, loot, capture. *Penalty*

Probable, Likely, reasonable, credible, possible. *Unlikely*

Probably, Likely, perhaps, perchance, mayhap, maybe, possibly, peradventure. *Certainly*

Probationer, Beginner, tyro, novice, learner, pupil, apprentice. *Master*

Probe, Scrutinize, investigate, examine, sound, verify, search, test, sift, prove, explore. *Miss*

Probity, Principle, uprightness, virtue, goodness, righteousness, soundness, integrity, rectitude, honesty, conscientiousness, honour, fairness, trustiness, worth, veracity, sincerity. *Dishonesty*

Problem, Riddle, puzzle, question, dilemma, enigma. *Certainty*

Problematical, Questionable, puzzling, unsettled, enigmatical, dubious, doubtful, uncertain, disputable, debatable, moot. *Certain*

Procedure, Conduct, performance, deed, action, operation, process, course, proceeding, practice. *Deviation*

Proceed, Advance, move, continue, progress. *Recede*

Emanate, come, rise, arise, flow, spring, issue, originate, accrue, result. *Ebb*

Act, behave, promote.

Proceeding, Action, act, performance, conduct, procedure, deed, transaction, step, process, course. *Discontinuance*

Proceeds, Profit, gain, yield, result, takings, returns, receipts. *Expenses*

Process, Procedure, proceeding, conduct, operation, course, practice, performance, deed, step, action, method. *Inaction*

Procession, Cavalcade, file, march, train, parade, retinue, caravan. *Cortège*

Proclaim, Declare, announce, promulgate, blazon, publish, herald, circulate, enunciate, advertise, bruit, cry, trumpet. *Conceal*

Proclamation, Declaration, announcement,† decree, order, ordinance, edict, command.

Proclivity, Bent, bias, leaning, fondness, liking, inclination, disposition, tendency, aptitude, ability, propensity, predisposition, proneness. *Aversion*

Procrastinate, Delay, wait, lag, loiter, postpone, adjourn, neglect, omit, prolong. *Hurry*

Procreate, Produce, beget, propagate, generate, engender, breed, get.

Procure, Gain, effect, manage, contrive, obtain, cause, attract, induce, secure, acquire, get, provide, compass. *Lose*

Prodigal, Extravagant, wasteful, spendthrift, reckless, lavish, profuse, careless. *Economical*

Prodigious, Strange, amazing, wonderful, unusual, extraordinary, uncommon, marvellous, portentous, astounding, astonishing, startling, surprising, miraculous, wondrous, staggering. *Ordinary*

Huge, immense, tremendous, enormous, monstrous, gigantic, large, colossal. *Small*

Prodigy, Wonder, marvel, miracle, portent.

Produce, Create, make, cause, originate, occasion, generate, engender, manufacture. *Destroy*

Show, adduce, exhibit.

Yield, furnish, afford, bear. *Retain*

Product, Produce, fruit, yield, result, proceeds, effect, issue, consequence, outcome. *Cause*

Productive, Fruitful, prolific, fertile, full. *Barren*

Proem, Introduction, preface, exordium, foreword, prelude, prologue, preamble, prolegomena. *Epilogue*

Profane, *v.a.,* Desecrate, violate, abuse, pollute, debase. *Hallow*

a., Blasphemous, irreligious, ungodly, impious, wicked, godless, irreverent, sacrilegious. *Reverent*

Secular, unconsecrated, unsanctified, unholy, unhallowed, worldly, temporal. *Sacred*

Profanity, Blasphemy, irreverence, impiety, sacrilege, profaneness. *Reverence*

Profess, Avow, claim, own, acknowledge, proclaim, declare, confess, aver, allege, affirm, avouch, pretend, feign.
Repudiate

Profession, Avowal, claim, acknowledgment.† *Repudiation*
Calling, vocation, avocation, trade, occupation, employment.

Proffer, Offer, tender, propose, volunteer.
Detain

Proficient, Qualified, competent, able, skilful, skilled, trained, versed, practised, conversant, accomplished, finished, good, expert, capable, clever, *au fait.*
Incompetent

Profit, *v.n.,* Benefit, improve, advance, gain. *Lose*
n., Benefit, improvement, advancement, gain, return, fruit, earnings, advantage, emolument. *Loss*

Profitable, Beneficial, advantageous, gainful, lucrative, remunerative, desirable, productive, paying, useful.
Unremunerative

Profitless, Unprofitable, fruitless, worthless, useless, valueless, bootless, futile.
Advantageous

Profligate, *a.,* Corrupt, dissolute, depraved, shameless, loose, lax, immoral, graceless, abandoned, wicked, lost, reprobate. *Virtuous*
n., Reprobate, libertine, rake, debauchee, *roué.*

Profound, Deep, abysmal, fathomless, bottomless, heavy.
Sagacious, penetrating, mystic, mysterious, learned, skilled, lively, vivid, complete, thorough, subtle, occult, recondite.
Shallow

Profuse, Bountiful, prodigal, extravagant, wasteful, free, lavish, spendthrift, copious, exuberant, ample. *Scanty*

Profusion, Bounty, prodigality,† excess, plenty, abundance, exuberance. *Scarcity*

Progeny, Issue, children, descendants, offspring, race, breed, stock, lineage, young, scion, family, posterity. *Ancestry*

Prognostic } Presage, augury, sign,
Prognostication } foreboding, indication, prophecy, symptom, omen, token, portent. *Record*

Prognosticate, Presage, augur, betoken, indicate, prophesy, forebode, portend, foreshow, foretell, foreshadow, foretoken.

Programme, Catalogue, plan, notice, outline, syllabus. *Analysis*

Progress, *v.n.,* Proceed, advance, continue, move, gain, mend, grow.
Retrogress
n., Progression, advancement, growth,

improvement, development, advance, circuit. *Retrogression*

Prohibit, Inhibit, forbid, stop, interdict, prevent, bar, disallow, hinder, debar, ban, veto. *Permit*

Prohibitive, Prohibiting, restrictive, forbidding. *Permissive*

Project, *v.a.,* Propel, hurl, cast, throw, fling, shoot, eject. *Attract*
Devise, contrive, scheme, plan, plot.
v.n., Jut, extend, protrude.
n., Proposal, plan, idea, design, purpose, scheme, intention. *Venture*

Projection, Propulsion, emission, throwing, hurling.
Prominence, protuberance, extension, bulge. *Cavity*

Prolegomena, Prologue, introduction, preface, proem, preamble, prelude, foreword, exordium. *Epilogue*

Proletariat, People, masses, workers, poor. *Bourgeoisie*

Prolific, Productive, fertile, fecund, fruitful, teeming. *Sterile*

Prolix, Verbose, wordy, long, diffuse, tedious, lengthy, wearisome, protracted, rambling, discursive, prosaic, circumlocutionary. *Terse*

Prologue, Introduction, preface, proem,† prelude. *Epilogue*

Prolong, Protract, lengthen, extend, continue, sustain. *Curtail*

Prominent, Conspicuous, notable, noted, famous, influential, marked, principal, celebrated, distinctive, distinguished, eminent. *Minor*

Promiscuous, Mingled, mixed, disorderly, confused, miscellaneous, indiscriminate, unselected. *Select*

Promise, *v.n.,* Agree, stipulate, bargain, warrant, guarantee.
v.a., Pledge, assure, engage, covenant, vow, swear.
n., Pledge, word, assurance, engagement, agreement, bargain, warrant, guarantee.

Promising, Hopeful, encouraging, inspiring, auspicious, likely. *Cheerless*

Promontory, Headland, cape, jutland.

Promote, Dignify, raise, exalt, aggrandize, honour, elevate, prefer. *Degrade*
Further, advance, help, assist, aid, cultivate, encourage, forward. *Hinder*

Promotion, Preferment, elevation, advancement. *Hindrance*

Prompt, *v.a.,* Urge, encourage, prick, impel, incline, incite, stimulate. *Deter*
a., Quick, ready, smart, active, agile, alert, apt, responsive, early, timely, punctual, immediate, instant. *Slothful*

Promulgate, Proclaim, announce, blazon,

publish, advertise, broadcast, spread, disseminate, divulge, declare. *Suppress*

Prone, Inclined, apt, disposed, tending. Recumbent, prostrate, horizontal. Ready, prompt, eager. *Averse*

Proneness, Inclination, aptitude, disposition, predisposition, propensity, proclivity, leaning, bent, fondness, tendency, bias. *Aversion*

Pronounce, Utter, declare, speak, say, announce, deliver, affirm, propound, assert, enunciate. *Suppress*

Pronounced, Distinct, definite, clear, defined, evident, certain. *Doubtful*

Proof, Trial, test, examination, scrutiny, ordeal, essay. *Failure* Evidence, demonstration, substantiation.

Prop, *v.a.,* Support, uphold, sustain. *n.,* Support, strut, stay, brace, pillar, buttress, pin.

Propaganda, Advertisement, inculcation, indoctrination.

Propagate, Engender, generate, breed, get, beget, produce, procreate. *Destroy* Spread, broadcast, disseminate, promulgate, diffuse, publish, blaze. *Suppress*

Propel, Project, hurl, cast, throw, fling. Drive, urge, move, impel, push. *Retard*

Propensity, Proclivity, proneness, tendency, aptitude, aptness, inclination, disposition, predisposition, bias, leaning, bent. *Aversion*

Proper, Correct, right, accurate, exact, real, formal, just, actual. *Wrong* Personal, own, particular, special, individual, peculiar. *Common* Seemly, fit, fitting, befitting, decorous, respectable, meet, suitable, becoming, decent. *Indecent*

Property, Possessions, goods, wealth, estate, assets, effects, chattels, rights, copyright, interest. *Poverty* Attribute, characteristic, quality, virtue, peculiarity.

Prophecy, Prognostication, augury, prediction, foretelling, divination.

Prophesy, Prognosticate, augur.†

Prophetic, Oracular, predictive, predicting, foretelling, premonitory. *Historic*

Propinquity, Proximity, contiguity, nearness, adjacency, neighbourhood. *Distance* Relationship, affinity, consanguinity, connection, kindred.

Propitiate, *v.a.,* Pacify, reconcile. win, appease, conciliate. *Offend* *v.n.,* Atone, intercede, mediate.

Propitious, Happy, lucky, fortunate, opportune, felicitous, auspicious, favourable, promising, timely. *Untoward*

Favourable, kind, gracious, obliging, benign, benignant, benevolent, friendly. *Hostile*

Proportion, *v.a.,* Adapt, adjust, arrange, fit, order, graduate, regulate. *n.,* Adaptation, adjustment, arrangement, uniformity, relation, symmetry. *Disparity* Portion, part, lot, division, share, ratio, quota, extent.

Proportional ⎫ Symmetrical, equal, proportionable, corresponding. *Unequal*
Proportionate ⎭

Proposal, Proposition, offer, proffer, suggestion, terms, idea, design, scheme, plan, tender, overture. *Warning*

Propose, *v.n.,* Intend, purpose, plan, design, mean, suggest. *v.a.,* Move, suggest, recommend, offer, proffer, propound, put. *Withdraw*

Propound, Promulgate, advocate, exhibit, suggest, offer, propagate, declare, propose. *Suppress*

Proprietor, Owner, master, possessor.

Propriety, Seemliness, correctness, decorum, modesty, decency, fitness, suitableness, appropriateness. *Indecency*

Prorogue, Adjourn, defer, postpone, prolong. *Convene*

Prosaic, Prosy, prolix, dull, tedious, dry, wearisome, tiresome, uninteresting, flat, boring, commonplace, tame, sober, unimaginative, vapid, uninspiring. *Lively*

Proscribe, Doom, expel, ostracize, outlaw. banish, reject, interdict, exclude, prohibit, condemn, denounce, excommunicate. *Sanction*

Prosecute, Sue, summon, arraign, indict. Continue, conduct, pursue, follow. *Abandon*

Prosecution, Undertaking, arraignment, pursuit. *Acquittal*

Proselyte, Convert, neophyte, disciple. *Infidel*

Prospect, Landscape, view, scene, vista, scenery, field, survey, spectacle, vision, display. *Obscurity* Chance, likelihood, probability. *Improbability* Promise, expectation, foresight, calculation, outlook, trust, anticipation, hope.

Prospective, Future, coming, expected, approaching, impending.

Prospectus, Syllabus, outline, scheme, programme, announcement, plan.

Prosper, Thrive, flourish, grow, succeed. *Fail*

Prosperous, Thriving, flourishing, successful, lucky, fortunate, wealthy, rich. *Unsuccessful*

Prostitute, *v.a.,* Abuse, misuse, misapply, sell.

n., Whore, strumpet, courtezan, harlot, trull.

Prostrate, *v.a.,* Overcome, overthrow, overturn, depress, destroy, demolish, upset, reduce, ruin, exhaust. **Revive**

a., Overcome, overthrown, depressed,† prostrated, prone, flat. **Erect**

Prosy, Prosaic, dull, prolix, tedious, dry, wearisome, tiresome, uninteresting, flat, boring, commonplace, tame, sober, vapid, uninspiring. **Lively**

Protean, Variable, inconstant, changeable, **Constant**

Protect, Guard, defend, secure, shelter, shield, cover, preserve, ward, screen, harbour, save, foster, fortify. **Expose**

Protection, Guard, defence,† safeguard, refuge, ward, bulwark, aid, support. **Exposure**

Protective, Guarding, defensive, sheltering, shielding, warding. **Offensive**

Protest, *v.n.,* Maintain, declare, asseverate, assert, object, demur, remonstrate, avow, testify, attest, expostulate.

n., Declaration, asseveration, assertion.† **Sanction**

Prototype, Type, archetype, model, pattern, original, precedent, example, exemplar. **Copy**

Protract, Prolong, elongate, lengthen, continue, postpone, defer, delay, extend. **Curtail**

Protrude, *v.a.,* Bulge, extend, project, jut. **Recede**

v.n., Project, thrust, show, exhibit, push. **Withdraw**

Protuberance, Bulge, lump, hump, convexity, bump, knob, swelling, prominence, bunch, excrescence. **Cavity**

Proud, Arrogant, imperious, domineering, boastful, haughty, presumptuous, lordly, uppish, supercilious. **Humble**

Vain, conceited, egotistical, self-satisfied, smirk, assuming, elated. **Lowly**

Lofty, noble, stately, imposing, grand, majestic, dignified, magnificent, splendid. **Mean**

Prove, Establish, show, demonstrate, verify, confirm, substantiate, manifest, evince, sustain, justify. **Refute**

Try, assay, examine, test, check.

Proverb, Saw, saying, maxim, adage, precept, aphorism, dictum. **Essay**

Proverbial, Acknowledged, notorious, unquestioned, current. **Questionable**

Provide, *v.a.,* Furnish, supply, afford, yield, give, produce, contribute, offer. **Neglect**

Provide, Procure, arrange, prepare, gather, store. **Divert**

v.n., Prepare, arrange, cater, purvey.

Agree, bargain, stipulate, guarantee, contract, engage.

Provided, Supposing, if, granted.

Provident, Economical, careful, cautious, considerate, prudent, wise, discreet, farseeing, frugal. **Reckless**

Province, Colony, dependency, department, county, division, district, region, territory, tract. **Capital**

Office, duty, function, business, sphere, place, department, division, charge.

Provision, Preparation, stock, supply, hoard, store, reserve, equipment, anticipation, arrangement. **Destitution**

Condition, stipulation, proviso, clause, reservation. **Oversight**

Provisional, Conditional, temporary, provisory, makeshift, contingent. **Absolute**

Provisions, Provender, victuals, food, rations, eatables, viands, supplies, fare. **Starvation**

Provocation, Vexation, affront, indignity, offence, insult, incitement. **Conciliation**

Provocative, Inciting, stimulating, rousing, moving. **Pacific**

Provoke, Incite, stimulate, rouse, move, excite, anger, annoy, vex, irritate, incense, stir, animate, inflame, instigate, kindle, enrage, exasperate, aggravate, nettle, sting, offend, infuriate, chafe, gall. **Appease**

Promote, cause, produce, instigate, call, evoke, occasion.

Provoking, Annoying, vexatious, irritating, exasperating, aggravating, offensive, vexing, tormenting. **Soothing**

Prowess, Skill, ability, strength, bravery, valour, dexterity, cleverness, adroitness, might. **Clumsiness**

Prowl, Prey, stalk, roam, rove, wander, sneak, slink. **Chase**

Proximity, Vicinity, neighbourhood, region, nearness, adjacency, contiguity, propinquity. **Distance**

Proxy, Substitute, deputy, lieutenant, delegate, representative, attorney, agent. **Person**

Prudent, Judicious, wise, discreet, wary, circumspect, cautious, provident, careful, considerate, thoughtful, frugal, thrifty, sparing, saving, economical. **Rash**

Prudish, Strict, narrow, puritanical, delicate, modest, demure, reserved, prim, precise, squeamish. **Tolerant**

Prune, Trim, clip, lop, dock, cut, dress, amputate, shape.

Prurient, Lustful, lecherous, desirous, covetous, eager, longing, itching, craving. *Apathetic*

Pry, Peep, inquire, examine, peer, search, look, question, investigate. *Overlook*

Prying, Peeping, inquiring, peering, curious, questioning, inquisitive. *Disinterested*

Psychological, Mental. *Physiological* Crucial, critical, decisive, important.

Public, Open, common, general, national, published, known, popular. *Private*

Publication, Promulgation, divulgation, dissemination, announcement, disclosure, report, advertisement, declaration, notification, proclamation. *Suppression* Pamphlet, book, booklet, magazine, periodical, edition, issue, paper.

Publicity, Notoriety, attention, advertisement, propaganda, outlet, spotlight. *Obscurity*

Publish, Promulgate, divulge, disseminate, proclaim, broadcast, declare, utter, propagate, blaze, blazon, disclose, announce, advertise, issue, reveal, impart, noise. *Suppress*

Pucker, Crease, furrow, wrinkle, crinkle, corrugate, cockle, contract, pinch. *Straighten*

Puerile, Childish, silly, weak, feeble, foolish, petty, idle, trivial, trifling, futile, simple. *Effective*

Puff, *v.n.,* Blow, pant, gasp. *v.a.,* Blow, swell, inflate. Flatter, advertise, compliment, praise. *Disparage* *n.,* Whiff, gust, breath.

Pugnacious, Bellicose, quarrelsome, contentious, fighting, warlike, belligerent. *Peaceable*

Puissant, Potent, mighty, able, strong, forcible, powerful, efficacious. *Weak*

Pull, Drag, draw, tug, haul, tow. *Push* Pluck, gather, tear, pick, extract, detach, rend, wrest. *Plant*

Pulpy, Pulpous, soft, succulent, fleshy. *Hard*

Pulsation, Palpitation, throbbing, throb, beat, beating.

Pulverize, Grind, powder, crush, bruise, comminute, triturate, levigate, bruise.

Pummel, Hit, stroke, beat, punch, belabour, thrash, maul.

Pump, Interrogate, examine, catechize, question. *Instruct*

Pun, Quibble, conceit, witticism, joke, quip.

Punch, *v.a.,* Strike, hit, beat, rap, push, pummel. Bore, pierce, perforate, puncture.

Punch, *n.,* Stroke, hit, blow, push, thrust. Fool, clown, jester, antic, buffoon, harlequin.

Punctilious, Exact, precise, nice, strict, punctual, careful, particular, ceremonious, scrupulous, conscientious. *Loose*

Punctual, Timely, prompt, seasonable, exact, punctilious, precise, regular, early. *Tardy*

Puncture, Punch, bore, pierce, perforate, prick. *Plug*

Pungent, Sharp, severe, stinging, caustic, acrid, acrimonious, hot, smart, biting, bitter, cutting, keen, stimulating, trenchant, tart, poignant, piquant, burning, pricking, mordant, painful, pointed, peevish, acute, satirical, waspish, penetrating, devastating. *Unctuous*

Punish, Correct, chasten, chastise, castigate, flog, scourge, whip, beat, lash, discipline, penalize. *Reward*

Punitive, Punishing, punitory, penal, corrective, disciplinary.

Puny, Feeble, frail, weak, ineffective, tiny, petty, small, pygmy, undeveloped, undersized, dwarfish, insignificant, stunted. *Sturdy*

Pupil, Scholar, learner, novice, disciple, beginner, student, neophyte, tyro. *Master*

Puppet, Marionette, doll, image, tool, pawn, catspaw. *Personality*

Purblind, Short-sighted, near-sighted, stupid, dull, myopic. *Farsighted*

Purchase, *v.a.,* Buy, procure, obtain, get. *Sell* *n.,* Bargain, buying, possession, property. Hold, force, power, leverage, advantage.

Pure, Clear, absolute, unmixed, unadulterated, neat, mere, perfect, sheer, simple, real, genuine. *Mixed* Chaste, uncorrupted, undefiled, clean, unstained, unspotted, unsullied, untarnished, stainless, clear, spotless, fair, untainted, unpolluted, incorrupt, guileless, blameless, honest, virtuous. *Corrupt*

Purgative, Cleansing, detergent, detersive, evacuant, cathartic, purifying, clearing, abstergent, abstersive.

Purge, Cleanse, deterge,† defecate. *Befoul* Pardon, absolve, shrive.

Purify, Cleanse, clarify, clear, clean, defecate, wash, purge. *Defile*

Purism, Fastidiousness, precision, nicety, exactness, squeamishness. *Looseness*

Puritanical, Prim, rigid, strict, exacting, narrow, prudish, ascetic. *Dissolute*

Purity, Clearness, perfection, simplicity, fineness.   *Impurity*
Chastity, modesty, piety, simplicity, cleanness, stainlessness, spotlessness, guilelessness, innocence, integrity, virtue, honesty.   *Corruption*
Purlieus, Environs, limits, borders, precincts, suburbs, confines, neighbourhood, district, outskirts, vicinity.   *Heart*
Purloin, Steal, embezzle, appropriate, filch, thieve, rob, abstract.   *Restore*
Purport, *v.a.*, State, convey, show.
Profess, intend, mean, signify.
n., Drift, import, meaning, significance, signification, gist, design, tendency.
Purpose, *v.a. & n.*, Mean, intend, design, propose, resolve, meditate, plan.
n., Meaning, intention, intent, design, plan, aim, resolve, view, sense, consequence, object, project, end.   *Hazard*
Purposeful, Dogged, tenacious, keen, eager, ardent, determined, strong, unshakable.   *Weak*
Purposely, Deliberately, intentionally, wittingly, designedly, knowingly, advisedly.   *Accidentally*
Pursue, Follow, track, chase, prosecute, conduct, hunt, continue, practise, seek.
                                                Abandon
Pursuit, Chase, prosecution, pursuance, race, hunt, search.
Occupation, business, employment, calling, vocation.
Pursy, Fat, stodgy, thick, podgy, corpulent.   *Lithe*
Purulent, Corrupt, feculent, festering, foul.   *Pure*
Purvey, Sell, retail, provide, procure, cater, obtain, furnish.
Purview, Scope, reach, limit, extent, range, compass, sphere.

Push, *v.a.*, Press, shove, impel, urge, thrust, jostle, propel, force, crowd, drive.
                                                   Pull
v.n., Press, thrust, jostle, crowd.
n., Charge, thrust, attack, onset, assault, endeavour.   *Retreat*
Pusillanimous, Timid, timorous, mean, cowardly, dastardly, effeminate, recreant, spiritless, frightened, feeble, fainthearted.   *Brave*
Pustule, Sore, fester, ulcer, blain, blotch, gathering, blister, abscess, pimple.
Put, Lay, place, set, deposit, impose, levy, enjoin, deposit, locate, plant, cast, inflict.
                                                Remove
Utter, express, offer, propose, present, state.
Putative, Supposed, reckoned, reputed, reported, alleged, deemed.   *Real*
Putid, Corrupt, decayed, stinking, rotten, foul, offensive, putrid, vile, low, worthless.   *Fresh*
Putrefy, Corrupt, decay, rot, decompose.
                                               Preserve
Putrid, Corrupt, decayed, stinking, rotten, foul, offensive, putid, decomposed. *Fresh*
Puzzle, *v.a.*, Bewilder, amaze, confound, confuse, perplex, mystify, stagger, nonplus, embarrass, entangle, complicate, gravel, pose.   *Enlighten*
n., Conundrum, poser, riddle, mystery, enigma, problem.   *Solution*
Dilemma, question, embarrassment.†
Pygmy, *n.*, Dwarf, midget.   *Giant*
a., Pygmean, dwarf, dwarfed, dwarfish, lilliputian, small, tiny, little, diminutive, stunted.   *Huge*
Pyrotic, Burning, acid, caustic. *Alkaline*
Pyrrhonism, Doubt, scepticism, incredulity, unbelief.   *Faith*
Pyx, Tabernacle, pyxis, vessel, box.

Q

Quack, Mountebank, impostor, charlatan, pretender, humbug, empiric. *Dupe*

Quaff, Swallow, gulp, drink, imbibe. *Disgorge*

Quagmire, Swamp, bog, marsh, fen, morass, slough.

Quail, Shrink, blench, cower, falter, flinch, faint, tremble, quake, crouch, sink, droop, succumb. *Stand*

Quaint, Unique, curious, odd, unusual, uncommon, extraordinary, fantastic, strange, droll, fanciful, singular, whimsical, archaic, antiquated, antique. *Commonplace* Abstruse, recondite, ingenious, subtle, affected, elegant, nice. *Common*

Quake, *v.n.,* Shake, quiver, shiver, move, tremble, rock, vibrate, shudder. *Stand* *n.,* Shake, shock, trembling, rocking, vibration, shudder, earthquake.

Qualification, Suitability, capacity, fitness, accomplishment, ability, preparation, requirement. *Incapacity* Restriction, condition, limitation, mitigation, proviso, stipulation, exception, modification.

Qualify, Capacitate, fit, prepare, adapt, equip, entitle, empower. *Incapacitate* Restrict, limit, mitigate, modify, moderate, narrow, restrain, regulate, reduce, abate, assuage, diminish, soften, lessen, temper. *Extend*

Quality, Characteristic, property, feature, trait, condition, nature, peculiarity, attribute. Sort, kind, character, rank, position, description, brand, make, status, gentry, aristocracy, nobility. *Nondescript*

Qualm, Pang, throe, attack, sickness, agony, fit, queasiness. *Ease* Penitence, remorse, regret, sorrow, compunction, uneasiness, scruple.

Quandary, Dilemma, difficulty, predicament, plight, doubt, dubitation, bewilderment, embarrassment, perplexity, strait, puzzle, uncertainty. *Facility*

Quantity, Amount, extent, size, measure, bulk, volume, number, portion, aggregate, sum. *Deficiency*

Quarrel, *v.n.,* Squabble, dispute, brawl, contend, strive, fight, argue, wrangle, bicker, row, clash, jar, altercate, disagree, differ. *Agree* *n.,* Squabble, dispute,† hostility, feud, fray, affray, misunderstanding, tumult. *Harmony*

Quarrelsome, Petulant, cross, testy, peevish, pugnacious, choleric, hasty, contentious, irritable, irascible, disputatious. *Conciliatory*

Quarry, Pit. Prey, victim, game, object.

Quarter, Fourth. Place, part, spot, locality, district, region, territory, abode, billet, lodging. Mercy, forbearance, clemency, pity. *Revenge*

Quarters, Shelter, lodging, abode, residence, dwelling, station, post, habitation.

Quash, Suppress, overthrow, crush, quell, annihilate, repress, abolish, invalidate, abate, extinguish, override, nullify, annul, subdue.

Quaver, Quiver, quake, shake, tremble, vibrate.

Quay, Dock, wharf, pier, landing-stage.

Queasy, Squeamish, qualmish, delicate, particular, fastidious, difficult. *Easy*

Queer, Quaint, odd, strange, unusual, uncommon, unfamiliar, extraordinary, whimsical, fantastic, peculiar, curious, irregular, abnormal, unique, singular. *Ordinary*

Quell ⎫ Suppress, crush, overcome, ex-
Quench ⎭ tinguish, subdue, overpower, curb, stifle, restrain, smother, repress, quash, check, moderate, allay, mitigate, cool, calm, modify, mollify, pacify, soothe, quiet, still, compose, deaden, blunt, dull, alleviate. *Excite*

Querulous, Peevish, complaining, dissatisfied, petulant, irritable, mournful, fretful, whining, murmuring, discontented, cross, malcontent. *Contented*

Query, *v.a.,* Question, inquire, ask, dispute, doubt, challenge. *Accept* *n.,* Question, inquiry, interrogation, challenge, issue, problem.

Quest, Search, suit, pursuit, journey, expedition. Examination, desire, request, invitation, demand.

Question, *v.a.,* Examine, interrogate, catechize, ask. *Answer* Query, dispute, doubt, challenge. *Accept* *n.,* Examination, interrogation, query, inquiry, investigation. *Reply* Motion, proposition, subject, matter, topic, theme, mystery.

Questionable, Uncertain, problematical, doubtful, equivocal, debatable, disputable, dubitable, suspicious. *Sure*

Quibble, *v.n.*, Equivocate, prevaricate, shuffle, trifle, cavil. **Reason**
n., Equivocation, prevarication, cavil, subtlety, subterfuge, evasion, sophism, quirk, pretence. **Truth**

Quick, Alert, active, prompt, brisk, smart, agile, speedy, sprightly, lively, ready, nimble, swift, hasty, rapid, fast, expeditious, animated, fleet. **Slow**
Living, alive, live, animate. **Dead**
Clever, adroit, skilful, smart, sharp, keen, expert, dexterous, intelligent, sensitive, acute, shrewd, apt. **Dull**
Passionate, irritable, hot, petulant, excitable, hasty, restless, testy, touchy, irascible, waspish, sharp, snappy, precipitate, choleric. **Mild**

Quicken, Revive, refresh, vivify, resuscitate, cheer, energize, rouse, animate, stimulate, reinvigorate, excite. **Deaden**
Expedite, accelerate, hasten, despatch, hurry, urge, speed. **Delay**

Quickly, Fast, quick, rapidly, soon, posthaste, immediately, forthwith, swiftly, speedily, promptly. **Slowly**

Quiescent, Quiet, still, restful, peaceful, reposing, resting, motionless, tranquil, serene, undisturbed, unruffled, placid, unagitated, calm. **Disturbed**

Quiet, *v.a.*, Still, calm, stop, arrest, lull, compose, alleviate, allay, appease, pacify, soothe, tranquillize, assuage, soften, mitigate, mollify, dull, blunt. **Disturb**
n., Quietness, calm, rest, peace, repose, tranquillity, serenity, stillness, silence, calmness, quiescence, quietude, ease. **Disturbance**
a., Calm, restful, peaceful,† quiescent, motionless, undisturbed, unruffled, unagitated, placid, smooth, contented, gentle. **Disturbed**
Unfrequented, secluded, retired, solitary. **Busy**

Quintessence, Essence, pith, marrow, substance, body, embodiment.

Quip } Sally, retort, remark, taunt,
Quirk } quibble, conceit, jest, repartee, evasion.

Quit, Leave, abandon, withdraw, desert, retire, forsake, forswear, relinquish. **Enter**
Relieve, release, free, deliver, acquit, liberate, clear, absolve, exonerate, resign, renounce, stop. **Bind**
Conduct, bear, behave, acquit.

Quite, *adv.*, Entirely, completely, fully, wholly, perfectly, positively, exactly, precisely, totally. **Partially**

Quiver, *v.n.*, Quaver, quake, tremble, shake, shiver, shudder, vibrate.
n., Quake, trembling, shake, shock, shiver, shudder, vibration.

Quixotic, Wild, visionary, romantic, impracticable, fantastic, fanciful, imaginary, freakish, mad, high-flown. **Practical**

Quiz, *v.a.*, Ridicule, hoax, puzzle, question, examine.
n., Riddle, joke, jest, hoax, conundrum, puzzle, enigma.

Quondam, Past, former, late.

Quota, Contingent, portion, share, assignment, proportion, allotment, quantity, part.

Quotation, Extract, selection, excerpt, reference, price, estimate.

Quote, Cite, mention, name, adduce, illustrate, instance, repeat, estimate. **Contradict**

Quoth, Spoke, said, *saith*, remarked.

R

Rabble, Mob, crowd, herd, populace, horde, riff-raff.   *Aristocracy*

Rabid, Raging, rampant, frantic, wild, mad, furious, infuriated, maniacal, intolerant.   *Rational*

Race, *v.n.,* Run, course, compete, contest. *v.a.,* Beat, outstrip.
n., Pursuit, chase, competition, contest. Tribe, stock, kindred, lineage, ancestry, family, clan, house, line, people, nation.

Racial, Lineal, ancestral.

Rack, *v.a.,* Torture, excruciate, agonize, torment, harass.   *Soothe*
n., Torture, agony, torment, anguish, pain.

Racket, Din, uproar, noise, confusion, disturbance, clamour, tumult, turmoil, ado, hubbub.   *Quiet*

Racy, Piquant, interesting, bright, pungent, strong, rich, spirited, lively, stimulating.   *Dull*

Radiant, Lustrous, bright, brilliant, beaming, glittering, gleaming, shining, resplendent, glorious, effulgent, luminous, sparkling, ecstatic, happy.   *Dull*

Radiate, *v.n.,* Beam, glitter, gleam, shine, sparkle.
v.a., Emit, disseminate, diffuse, spread, branch.   *Contract*

Radical, *a.,* Fundamental, organic, ingrained, essential, innate, original, constitutional.   *Superficial*
Extreme, unsparing, entire, thorough, complete.   *Moderate*
n., Reformer, Liberal.   *Conservative*
Base, root.

Radio, Broadcasting, wireless telegraphy, wireless telephony.

Raffle, Sweepstake, draw, lottery.

Rage, *v.n.,* Fume, rave, fret, storm, chafe.
n., Raving, wrath, frenzy, anger, madness, fury, passion, mania, vehemence, ferocity, calidity, excitement, rabidity.   *Calmness*
Fashion, style, mode, vogue, craze.

Ragged, Torn, shaggy, rough, rugged, jagged, uneven, tattered, rent.   *Smart*

Raging, Raving, wrathful, wroth, angry, mad, furious, infuriated, vehement, ferocious, rabid, excited, incensed.   *Calm*

Raid, *v.a.,* Invade, assault, forage, pillage, plunder.
n., Invasion, incursion, foray, irruption, forcing, plunder, pillage, attack, inroad.   *Retreat*

Rail, Scold, sneer, scoff, gibe, upbraid, reproach, censure, abuse.

Railing, Scolding, sneering,† vituperation, contumely, aspersion, invective.   *Praise*
Barrier, fence, pallisade, bar, balustrade.

Raillery, Satire, irony, jest, gibe, banter, ridicule, pleasantry, chaff, joke.   *Invective*

Raiment, Garments, dress, clothes, costumes, habit, habiliment, clothing, attire, garb, vestments, vesture, apparel, array.

Raise, Lift, uplift, elevate, hoist, heave, erect, construct.   *Lower*
Exalt, elevate, aggrandize, advance, promote, increase, advance, augment.   *Degrade*
Rouse, excite, heighten, awaken, wake, arouse, stir.   *Lull*
Rear, cultivate, grow, propagate, breed.   *Destroy*
Levy, impose, collect, get, assemble.

Rake, *v.n.,* Grope, search, scrape.
v.a., Scour, enfilade, ransack, collect, gather.
n., Debauchee, libertine, roué.

Rally, *v.n.,* Recover, revive.
Assemble, meet, convene, collect.   *Disperse*
v.a., Restore, reunite, reassure, animate, concentrate, gather, encourage, inspirit.   *Demoralize*
Taunt, banter, twit, deride, ridicule, satirize, mock.   *Flatter*

Ram, Stop, cram, dam, strike, butt, crowd.

Ramble, *v.n.,* Wander, stroll, rove, journey, roam, stray, range, saunter, maunder, digress.   *Hasten*
n., Wandering, stroll,† excursion, trip, tour.

Ramification, Divergence, branching, forking, radiation, divarication.   *Continuity*

Ramp, Incline, slope, declivity.

Rampant, Erect, standing, upright, salient.   *Couchant*
Exuberant, wanton, excessive.
Vehement, violent, headstrong, impetuous, unbridled, uncontrolled, uncontrollable, ungovernable, unrestrained.   *Curbed*

Rampart, Bulwark, fortification, fort, defence, guard, security, fence, mole, wall, breastwork, mound, elevation, embankment.

Ramshackle, Tumbledown, rickety, shaky, crazy. *Sturdy*

Rancid, Foul, rank, fetid, sour, musty, offensive, bad, fusty, smelling tainted, impure. *Fresh*

Rancour, Malice, venom, spite, malevolence, malignity, animosity, animus, enmity, spleen, hatred, antipathy, vindictiveness, grudge, bitterness. *Kindliness*

Random, Casual, haphazard, chance, fortuitous, accidental, irregular, aimless, purposeless, stray, vague, wandering. *Deliberate*

Range, *v.a.,* Dispose, array, arrange, rank, class, align, classify, order.
v.n., Rove, wander, cruise, extend, straggle, roam, stroll, ramble, stray.
n., Line, rank, file, tier, row.
Reach, scope, sweep, extent, compass, amplitude.
Order, class, sort, kind, assortment.
Register, compass.

Rank, *n.,* Line, file, tier, row, range. *Disorder*
Degree, class, quality, order, grade, position, condition, dignity, division, group, levies.
v.n., Count, class, range.
a., Excessive, exuberant, fertile, productive, rampant, gross, flagrant, luxuriant, extravagant, rich. *Thin*
Foul, fetid, rancid, fusty, musty, offensive, smelling, disgusting, coarse, bad. *Fresh*

Rankle, Fester, burn, smoulder. *Heal*

Ransack, Rifle, ravage, pillage, plunder, rummage, explore, strip, sack, loot. *Reconnoitre*

Ransom, *v.a.,* Release, redeem, rescue, indemnify, liberate, deliver, free. *Prosecute*
n., Release, redemption, expiation.† *Prosecution*

Rant, *v.n.,* Declaim, rave, vociferate.
n., Declamation, raving, exaggeration, fustian, flummery, bombast. *Moderation*

Rap, *v.a.,* Strike, hit, beat, knock.
n., Stroke, hit, knock, pat, cuff, thwack, blow, thump, slap.

Rapacious, Greedy, grasping, avaricious, ravenous, voracious, predaceous, preying, plundering. *Frugal*

Rape, Ravishment, violation, defloration, defilement.

Rapid, Fast, quick, swift, speedy, fleet, hasty, expeditious, hurried, accelerated, flying, brisk, smart, lively, agile. *Slow*

Rapidity ⎫ Quickness, speed, swiftness,
Rapidness ⎭ velocity, celerity, agility, despatch. *Slowness*

Rapine, Pillage, robbery, spoliation, plunder, loot, depredation, wasting.

Rapt, Lost, absent, transported, absorbed, ecstatic, entranced, charmed, delighted, fascinated, inspired, inattentive. *Attentive*

Rapture, Ecstasy, delight, ravishment, joy, pleasure, bliss, transport, beatitude, happiness, exultation. *Sorrow*

Rapturous, Ecstatic, delightful, ravishing.† *Sorrowful*

Rare, Scarce, unusual, infrequent, few, exceptional, extraordinary, uncommon, sparse, singular, valuable, fine, precious, incomparable, inimitable, excellent, choice. *Common*

Rarely, Seldom, infrequently. *Often*

Rascal, Scoundrel, rogue, vagabond, villain, blackguard, reprobate, knave, scamp, caitiff, miscreant. *Gentleman*

Rascally, Villainous, wicked, bad, roguish, knavish, blackguardly, vile, base, dishonest. *Honest*

Rase, Obliterate, efface, erase, expunge, cancel.
Destroy, overthrow, level, ruin, demolish. *Erect*

Rash, Hasty, reckless, precipitate, headstrong, headlong, incautious, indiscreet, unwise, careless, unwary, audacious, foolhardy, venturesome, impulsive, temerous. *Cautious*

Rate, *v.a.,* Appraise, value, estimate, compute, reckon, class, tax, assess. *Underrate*
Censure, chide, rebuke, scold, blame, upbraid, reprimand, reprove. *Praise*
n., Charge, tax, assessment, duty, impost, price, cost.
Degree, proportion, ratio.
Speed, velocity.
Standard.

Rather, Sooner, preferably.
Moderately, slightly, tolerably, somewhat. *Extremely*

Ratify, Establish, confirm, substantiate, seal, corroborate, settle, approve, bind, sanction, endorse. *Repudiate*

Ratio, Degree, proportion, rate, quota, percentage, comparison.

Ration, Portion, share, allowance, quota.

Rational, Reasoning, judicious, intellectual, sane, sensible, discreet, wise, intelligent, sober, enlightened, sagacious, sound. *Insane*
Reasonable, fair, equitable, just, right, proper, moderate, normal, fit. *Absurd*

Raucous, Hoarse, harsh, grating, rough, husky. *Oily*

Ravage, *v.a.*, Spoil, despoil, devastate, waste, sack, ransack, ruin, pillage, strip, plunder, destroy, desolate. *Preserve*
n., Spoliation, despoilment,† rapine, havoc.

Rave, Rage, fume, storm, fret, drivel, rant, wander. *Reason*

Ravel, Untie, untwist, undo, disentangle, unravel, unroll, unweave, unwind, separate. *Entangle*
Entangle, involve, confuse, complicate, perplex. *Disentangle*

Ravenous, Voracious, hungry, omnivorous, rapacious, greedy, insatiable, gluttonous, devouring. *Satiated*

Ravine, Gulch, gully, cleft, gorge, cañon, pass, defile.

Raving, *a.*, Mad, furious, raging, frenzied, delirious, distracted, frantic. *Sane*
n., Madness, fury.† *Sanity*

Ravish, Outrage, violate, debauch, deflower, abuse, strip, abduct, seize.
Charm, transport, delight, please, captivate, enchant, entrance, enrapture. *Repel*

Ravishing, Charming, delightful, pleasant, pleasurable, captivating, enchanting, entrancing, rapturous. *Repulsive*

Raw, Uncooked, unseasoned, unprepared. *Cooked*
Tender, sensitive, painful, open, bare, exposed, galled. *Healed*
Fresh, unripe, green, new, inexperienced, untried, unskilled, immature, crude, unpractised. *Finished*
Bleak, piercing, cold, exposed, chilly, cutting.

Ray, Beam, gleam, shaft.
Vision, notice, perception, sight.

Raze, Demolish, gut, destroy, level, overthrow, subvert, prostrate, ruin, reduce. *Raise*
Erase, efface, obliterate, remove.

Reach, *v.a.*, Attain, obtain, get, arrive at, grasp. *Fail*
v.n., Extend, stretch.
n., Extent, extension, stretch, expanse, scope, penetration, distance, range, compass, grasp.

React, Rebound, recoil, reciprocate.

Read, *v.a.*, Peruse, decipher, interpret, understand, comprehend, deliver, explain.
v.n., Study, learn.
a., Literate, learned, informed, erudite, scholarly, clever. *Ignorant*

Readily, Promptly, willingly, cheerfully, easily, quickly. *Reluctantly*

Reading, Rendering, recital, version interpretation, perusal.

Ready, Prompt, sharp, quick, expert, adroit, expeditious, dexterous, facile, nimble, alert, speedy, skilful, unhesitating, smart. *Clumsy*
Handy, near, commodious, convenient. *Remote*
Prepared, fitting, free, willing, inclined, disposed. *Reluctant*

Real, True, actual, veritable, genuine, authentic, existent, positive, substantial, absolute, certain. *Imaginary*

Reality, Truth, actuality, verity,† fact. *Image*

Realize, Feel, understand, comprehend, conceive. *Misunderstand*
Substantiate, gain, earn, obtain, acquire, sell, produce. *Dissipate*

Really, Truly, actually, veritably, verily, positively, absolutely, certainly, unquestionably, undeniably, indubitably, indeed. *Questionably*

Realm, Kingdom, dominion, country, land, province, domain, department, region.

Reap, Gather, obtain, get, receive, gain, harvest, crop. *Lose*

Rear, *v.a.*, Raise, breed, train, instruct, educate, grow, foster, nurse. *Kill*
Erect, build, construct, raise. *Demolish*
Lift, raise, uplift, elevate, toss, hoist. *Lower*
n., Back, tail, end, posterior, stern, rump, wake, train, heel. *Van*

Reason, *v.n.*, Argue, dispute, debate, consider, think.
n., Understanding, rationality, intellect, mind, sense, judgment.
Ground, cause, explanation, motive, consideration. *Pretence*
Aim, object, purpose, end, design.
Sense, wisdom, reasonableness, sanity, conception. *Folly*

Reasonable, Rational, sane, sober, sound, sensible, intellectual, judicious, enlightened, sagacious, wise, intelligent. *Absurd*
Moderate, just, fair, right, equitable, fit, suitable, tolerable, proper. *Excessive*
Inexperience, cheap, low-priced.

Reassure, Comfort, strengthen, rally, enhearten, hearten, encourage, inspire, inspirit, embolden, cheer. *Discourage*

Rebate, Allowance, reduction, discount, deduction, decrease, diminution, lessening. *Surcharge*

Rebel, *v.n.*, Revolt, rise, mutiny, strike. *Support*
n., Revolter, insurgent, traitor, mutineer. *Supporter*

Rebellious, Insurrectionary, mutinous, disobedient, defiant, insurgent, intractable, refractory, insubordinate, seditious, contumacious. *Servile*

Rebound, *v.n.*, React, recoil, reverberate, ricochet.

n., Reaction, recoil, reverberation, resilience, repercussion.

Rebuff, *v.a.*, Snub, check, discourage, rebuke, repulse, repel, oppose, resist, reject.

n., Snub, check.† *Encouragement*

Rebuke, *v.a.*, Reprove, reprimand, reprehend, chide, censure, upbraid, admonish, scold, blame, lecture, chastise, reproach. *Applaud*

n., Reproof, reprimand,† remonstrance. *Applause*

Rebut, Confute, meet, disprove, repel, rebuff, retort, oppose, refute, answer. *Accept*

Recalcitrant, Refractory, opposing, stubborn, disobedient, perverse. *Amenable*

Recall, Revoke, repeal, retract, supersede, annul, nullify, rescind, overrule, countermand, cancel, recant, withdraw, deny, repudiate, abjure, abrogate. *Confirm*
Summon, revoke.

Remember, recollect, commemorate, mind, revive. *Forget*

Recant, Retract, recall, renounce, abjure, disown, withdraw, repudiate, revoke, deny, annul. *Maintain*

Recapitulate, Rehearse, repeat, recite, summarize, restate, review, reiterate.

Recede, Retreat, ebb, retire, withdraw, desist, retrograde. *Advance*

Receipt, Acceptance, admission, reception, quittance.

Formula, recipe, prescription.

Receive, Get, obtain, reap, acquire, derive, accept, take. *Give*
Admit, welcome, entertain, greet, meet.

Recent, Modern, late, new, novel, fresh, latter, foregoing, preceding, retiring. *Ancient*

Receptacle, Store, place, repository, depository, container, bin, vessel, case, box, reservoir.

Reception, Welcome, entertainment, admission, greeting, meeting. *Rejection*
Party, entertainment.
Receipt, acceptance, acquittance.

Recess, Alcove, retreat, nook, niche, cavity, corner. *Projection*
Holiday, vacation, respite, rest, interval, break.

Recipe, Receipt, prescription, formula.

Recipient, Beneficiary, receiver, pensioner, assignee.

Reciprocal, Alternate, interchangeable, interchanged, mutual. *One-sided*

Reciprocate, *v.a.*, Interchange, exchange, requite.

v.n., Alternate, vary, return.

Recital, Relation, account, story, tale, narration, narrative, history, description. Concert.

Recite, Relate, tell, narrate, describe, enumerate, recapitulate, rehearse, detail, repeat, recount.

Reckless, Rash, incautious, headlong, headstrong, wild, careless, irresponsible, heedless, regardless, indiscreet, injudicious, imprudent, foolhardy, temerarious, thoughtless, venturesome, unsteady, foolish. *Cautious*

Reckon, *v.n.*, Calculate, estimate, compute, consider, judge. *Miscalculate*

v.a., Calculate, compute, count, cast, enumerate, number.

Esteem, deem, regard, consider, value, guess, estimate, account.

Depend on, rely on.

Reckoning, Calculation, consideration, computation, estimate.

Account, bill, charge, score, register, settlement, arrangement.

Reclaim, Rescue, recover, restore, improve, amend, save, reform, regain, reinstate. *Vitiate*

Recline, Lean, lie, rest, repose. *Stand*

Recluse, Hermit, solitary, ascetic, eremite, anchoret, anchorite, monk.

Recognize, Identify, remember, verify, apprehend.

Own, allow, admit, grant, acknowledge, confess, concede. *Repudiate*

Recoil, Rebound, ricochet, kick, retreat, react, withdraw, shrink, retire, falter, quail, flinch. *Spring*

Recollect, Remember, recall, mind. *Forget*

Recommend, Commend, approve, praise, endorse, commit, sanction. *Disapprove*
Advise, suggest, counsel, prescribe. *Warn*

Recompense, *v.a.*, Compensate, requite, indemnify, reward, redress, repay, remunerate, reimburse, redeem, satisfy. *Injure*

n., Compensation, requital,† amends, retribution. *Injury*

Reconcilable, Placable, forgiving, mild, appeasable. *Harsh*
Congruous, consistent, compatible. *Antagonistic*

Reconcile, *v.a.*, Appease, pacify, unite, reunite, appease, propitiate, resign, content, conciliate, compose. *Alienate*

Reconcile, Harmonize, adjust, settle, adapt, regulate.

Recondite, Deep, hidden, dark, mysterious, occult, abstruse, remote, profound, obscure, secret, mystic, concealed. *Patent*

Reconnoitre, Survey, spy, inspect, examine, view, search, scan. *Miss*

Reconstruct, Rebuild, reform, re-establish.

Record, *v.a.,* Enter, note, register, chronicle. *Suppress*

n., Entry, note, register, chronicle, memorandum, minute, account, docket, file, proceedings.

Attestation, witness, testimony, history, career, achievement.

Recount, Relate, recite, narrate, specify, detail, rehearse, enumerate, tell, describe, repeat.

Recourse, Refuge, resort, reference, recurrence, betaking. *Avoidance*

Recover, *v.n.,* Rally, revive, recuperate. *Deteriorate*

v.a., Reclaim, regain, retrieve, repossess, recapture, repair, rescue, save. *Lose*

Recovery, Recuperation, convalescence, cure, revival, redemption. *Relapse*

Restoration, repossession, regaining, replacement, retrieval. *Loss*

Recreant, *n.,* Coward, renegade, apostate, dastard, craven, wretch, traitor.

a., Cowardly, apostate, treacherous, dastardly, false, perfidious, unfaithful, renegade, base, faithless, pusillanimous, craven. *Staunch*

Recreation, Relaxation, diversion, entertainment, sport, amusement, pastime, refreshment, exercise. *Work*

Recrimination, Retort, answer, counter-charge, counter-accusation. *Confession*

Recruit, *v.a.,* Revive, renew, restore, refresh, repair, replenish, reinvigorate.

n., Novice, beginner, supporter, helper, tyro. *Veteran*

Rectify, Adjust, amend, emend, mend, settle, straighten, regulate, improve, correct, right, reform, redress. *Derange*

Rectitude, Honesty, uprightness, integrity, probity, righteousness, right, virtue, straightforwardness, justice, fairness, goodness, correctness. *Depravity*

Rector, Parson, vicar, minister, clergyman.

Recumbent, Lying, prostrate, prone, reclining, leaning, horizontal, reposing. *Erect*

Recuperate, Recover, regain, recruit, mend. *Decline*

Recur, Return, ebb, reappear, revert, intermit.

Recurrent } Repeated, frequent, return-
Recurring } ing, renewed, periodical, intermittent, reiterated. *Solitary*

Redeem, Ransom, save, regain, retrieve, repurchase, recover, deliver, liberate, free, rescue, reclaim. *Surrender*

Discharge, fulfil, keep, satisfy, perform.

Redemption, Ransom, salvation.† *Betrayal*

Discharge, fulfilment.† }

Redolent, Odorous, sweet, fragrant, scented, perfumed, odoriferous, balmy, aromatic. *Stinking*

Redouble, Increase, multiply, augment, reiterate, intensify. *Reduce*

Redoubtable, Formidable, frightening, doughty, awful, terrible, valiant, dreadful. *Ludicrous*

Redound, Conduce, lead, tend, contribute, incline, issue, result, reflex, accrue. *Miss*

Redress, *v.a.,* Rectify, right, remedy, compensate, amend, repair, correct, order, adjust, indemnify. *Wrong*

n., Rectification, remedy, compensation,† redressal, relief, atonement.

Reduce, Lessen, curtail, diminish, contract, decrease, abate, abbreviate, decimate, thin, abridge, shorten, attenuate. *Increase*

Weaken, impair, lower, degrade, debase, depress. *Elevate*

Subjugate, subject, subdue, vanquish, overcome, overpower, overthrow, conquer, master. *Strengthen*

Ruin, impoverish. *Enrich*

Redundant, Superfluous, excessive, unnecessary, superabundant, overflowing, plentiful. *Scanty*

Diffuse, circumlocutionary, verbose, wordy, lengthy. *Terse*

Re-echo, Resound, repeat, reverberate.

Reek, Smell, steam, smoke, vapour, fume, exhalation, effluvium.

Reel, *v.n.,* Stagger, spin, whirl, sway, swing, totter, falter, vacillate.

n., Cylinder, bobbin.

Re-establish, Reinstate, replace, restore, renew, renovate.

Refer, *v.a.,* Commit, hand, leave, direct, point, consign.

Attribute, advert, assign, impute, ascribe.

v.n., Allude, relate, advert, quote, cite.

Relate, touch, concern, point, respect, belong, appeal, consult, apply. *Misapply*

Referee, Umpire, arbitrator, arbiter, judge.

Reference, Allusion, remark, hint, intimation, relegation.

Regard, respect, relation, concern, connection.

Referendum, Plebiscite, vote.

Refine, Clarify, purify, defecate, cleanse. *Pollute*

Polish, civilize, cultivate, improve. *Barbarize*

Refined, Pure, purified, clear, clarified. *Turbid*

Polished, civilized, polite, elegant, civil, cultivated, stylish, accomplished, finished, courtly. *Rude*

Reflect, *v.a.*, Image, mirror, imitate, reproduce.

v.n., Muse, think, ponder, consider, cogitate, ruminate, meditate, contemplate, deliberate, study. *Wander*

Reflection, Image, shadow, echo.

Musing, thinking, thought, consideration, cogitation, rumination, meditation, contemplation, deliberation.

Thought, opinion, idea, remark.

Reproach, aspersion, slur, censure, criticism. *Honour*

Reflex, Introspective, reflective, reactive.

Refluence | Ebb, return, redound, re-
Reflux   } gurgitation. *Flow*

Reform, *v.a.*, Mend, amend, emend, improve, ameliorate, correct, rectify, better, remodel, restore, reconstruct, reclaim, reconstitute. *Corrupt*

v.n., Mend, amend, improve. *Deteriorate*

n., Reformation, mending, amendment, improvement, correction, rectification, reconstitution, progress. *Corruption*

Refractory, Obstinate, intractable, perverse, unyielding, stubborn, unruly, recalcitrant, contumacious, stiff, mulish, headstrong, dogged, unruly, rebellious, disobedient, ungovernable, unmanageable, mutinous. *Docile*

Refrain, *v.n.*, Forbear, forego, abstain. *Indulge*

n., Chorus.

Refrangible, Fallacious, refutable, refragable, weak. *Undeniable*

Refresh, Freshen, cool, cheer, revive, recreate, invigorate, exhilarate, enliven, brace, reanimate. *Weary*

Refreshment, Relief, cheer, food, invigoration. *Fatigue*

Refrigerate, Cool, chill, freeze. *Warm*

Refuge, Retreat, shelter, safety, protection, harbour, asylum, sanctuary, home, security. *Exposure*

Refulgent, Radiant, brilliant, shining,

lustrous, bright, splendid, effulgent, resplendent. *Dull*

Refund, Reimburse, repay, return, restore. *Withhold*

Refuse, *v.n.*, Decline. *Agree*

v.a., Deny, withhold, reject, repudiate, renounce, veto, exclude. *Grant*

n., Rubbish, dross, waste, trash, dregs, lees. *Prime*

Refute, Disprove, deny, confute, answer, negative, overthrow. *Confirm*

Regain, Retrieve, recover, recapture, repossess. *Lose*

Regal, Royal, kingly, imperial, princely, magnificent, stately, grand. *Mean*

Regale, Entertain, feast, feed, refresh, gratify, delight. *Stint*

Regalia, Decorations, emblems, insignia.

Regard, *v.a.*, Notice, heed, observe, remark, watch, see, look, gaze, consider, behold, esteem, reverence, honour, obey, mind, respect, value. *Ignore*

Reckon, deem, consider, hold, account, suppose, believe, esteem, judge.

n., Notice, heed, observation,† concern. *Neglect*

Consideration, notice, attention, estimation, esteem, affection, attachment, respect, liking, love, fondness. *Detestation*

Repute, note, reputation, esteem, eminence.

Reference, respect, relation.

Regardful, Mindful, heedful, considerate, attentive, thoughtful, careful, observing, watchful. *Heedless*

Regarding, Concerning, touching, about, respecting. *Omitting*

Regardless, Heedless, careless, mindless, inconsiderate, indifferent, unmindful, unconcerned, negligent, neglectful, inattentive, unobservant, disregarding, despising. *Cautious*

Regenerate, *v.a.*, Renew, revive, revivify, renovate, convert, change.

a., Renewed, regenerated, converted, new. *Degenerate*

Régime, Dispensation, rule, administration, government, system.

Region, District, country, tract, clime, province, land, territory, scene, locality.

Vicinity, neighbourhood, place, spot, sphere, part.

Register, *v.a.*, Record, enter, list, note, chronicle, portray. *Erase*

n., Record, list, roll, annals, archive, chronicle, inventory, catalogue, schedule entry, minute.

Range, compass, area.

Regnant, Ruling, reigning, ascendant, predominant, supreme, controlling.

Regress, *v.n.,* Retrogress, ebb, return, decline. ***Progress***
n., Retrogression, ebb, return, declension, reflux, retirement, retrocession, regression.

Regret, *v.a.,* Deplore, bemoan, bewail, lament, repine, rue, repent. ***Approve***
n., Sorrow, remorse, repentance, penitence, grief, lamentation, contrition, compunction. ***Satisfaction***

Regular, Orderly, steady, systematic, uniform, invariable, unvarying, unchanging, constant, punctual, consistent, certain, symmetrical, methodical, established, fixed. ***Erratic***
Normal, ordinary, customary, formal, usual, typical, conventional, fixed, stated, rhythmic, correct, recurring. ***Abnormal***

Regulate, Rule, direct, govern, control, dispose, adjust, manage, guide, order, systematize, methodize, arrange.
Disarrange

Regulation, *n.,* Rule, direction,† law.
Misrule
a., Formal, usual, official.

Regurgitation, Reflux, refluence, return, ebb.

Rehabilitate, Reinstate, renovate, reestablish, restore, reconstruct. ***Deprive***

Rehearse, Recapitulate, repeat, recite, recount, depict, relate, narrate, detail. Practise, drill, train.

Reign, *v.n.,* Rule, govern, command, prevail, administer. ***Submit***
n., Rule, power, sway, government, control, sovereignty, royalty.

Reimburse, Compensate, repay, requite, refund, indemnify. ***Defraud***

Rein, Restrain, control, check, hold, curb.
Indulge

Reinforce, Strengthen, support, fortify, augment. ***Weaken***

Reinstate, Rehabilitate, restore, replace.
Remove

Reiterate, Repeat, renew. ***Retract***

Reject, Refuse, renounce, repel, repudiate, discard, eject, dismiss, disallow, spurn, jilt, decline, exclude, rebuff, disapprove.
Accept

Rejoice, *v.n.,* Exult, triumph, glory, revel, joy. ***Mourn***
v.a., Cheer, delight, gladden, gratify, please, enliven, exhilarate, enrapture.
Grieve

Rejoinder, Reply, retort, answer, respond.
Sarcasm

Rekindle, Fan, reignite, relight.
Extinguish

Relapse, *v.n.,* Backslide, retrogress, deteriorate, revert, regress, lapse. ***Improve***

Relapse, *n.,* Backsliding, retrogression.†
Improvement

Relate, Narrate, recite, recount, tell, describe, report, mention, detail, connect.
Falsify

Relating, Concerning, respecting, touching, about, pertaining, relative, anent.

Relation, Relative, kinsman, connection, kin, affinity. ***Alien***
Connection, affinity, kinship, bearing, analogy, reference, respect.
Narration, narrative, recital, story, report, mention, detail, account, description.

Relative, *n.,* Relation, kinsman, connection.
a., Comparative, approximate, special, positive, definite, relevant. ***Absolute***

Relax, *v.a.,* Loosen, abate, slacken, loose, remit, mitigate. ***Intensify***
Lessen, abate, mitigate, diminish.
Enervate, debilitate, weaken, enfeeble.
Brace
v.n., Unbend, soften. ***Stiffen***

Relaxation, Loosening, slackening.
Tightening
Pleasure, recreation, sport, diversion, pastime, amusement, ease, rest. ***Work***

Relay, Reinforcement, relief, supply.

Release, *v.a.,* Free, liberate, unloose, loose, discharge, disengage, emancipate, extricate, disentangle, quit, acquit, clear, rid, exempt. ***Bind***
n., Freedom, liberation, liberty.†
Bondage

Relegate, Banish, remove, deport, exile, consign, expatriate, transfer, transport.
Reinstate

Relent, Soften, relax, yield. ***Harden***

Relentless, Unrelenting, hard, unyielding, implacable, cruel, pitiless, unpitying, remorseless, unforgiving, inexorable, unmerciful, harsh, merciless. ***Merciful***

Relevant, Apt, pertinent, apposite, appropriate, applicable, suitable, proper, fit.
Pointless

Reliable, Trustworthy, dependable, safe, unfailing, certain, constant, trusty.
Shaky

Reliant, Confident, sure, trusting.
Diffident

Relics, Remains, ashes, remnants.
Keepsake, memento, token, souvenir, memorial.

Relieve, Palliate, soothe, mitigate, lessen, diminish, soften, alleviate, assuage, allay, lighten, ease, abate. ***Aggravate***
Help, free, comfort, sustain, support, succour, assist, aid, refresh. ***Oppress***

Religious, Pious, godly, righteous, holy, good, devotional, devout, pure. ***Godless***

Relinquish, Yield, renounce, surrender, concede, forsake, quit, abandon, forgo, forswear, resign, vacate, cede, waive, abdicate, desert, leave, repudiate. *Retain*

Relish, *v.a.,* Like, appreciate, enjoy, approve. *Loathe*

n., Liking, appreciation, enjoyment, approval, inclination, fondness, gusto, zest, partiality, weakness. *Loathing* Flavour, savour, seasoning, piquancy, quality, taste, appetizer. *Insipidity*

Relucent, Lucent, shining, radiant, bright, effulgent, luminous, gleaming, resplendent, glittering. *Dull* Eminent.

Reluctant, Loath, unwilling, disinclined, indisposed, backward, averse. *Eager*

Rely, Depend, lean, hope, reckon, count, rest, confide, trust. *Distrust*

Remain, Continue, persist, abide, last, stay, endure, survive. *Perish* Tarry, stop, rest, sojourn, stay, abide, wait, halt, dwell. *Move*

Remainder, Remnant, residue, surplus, balance, remains, excess, leavings, rest. *Loss*

Remains, Relics, ashes, remnants, fragments, scraps, leavings, dregs.

Remark, *v.n.,* Say, declare, state, observe, comment.

v.a., Notice, note, observe, regard, heed. *Miss* Say, declare, observe, express, utter, state, mention.

n., Saying, declaration,† comment, note.

Remarkable, Extraordinary, singular, unusual, uncommon, strange, noteworthy, noticeable, peculiar, striking, conspicuous, prominent, rare, notable, wonderful. *Ordinary*

Remedy, *v.a.,* Restore, cure, redress, help, heal, palliate, amend, correct, rectify, relieve, repair, improve. *Aggravate*

n., Restoration, cure,† specific. *Aggravation*

Remember, Recollect, recall, mind. *Forget*

Remembrance, Recollection, memory, reminiscence, thought, consideration, regard. Souvenir, token, memorial, memento, keepsake, reminder.

Reminiscence, Remembrance, retrospect, recollection, memory. *Announcement*

Remiss, Dilatory, negligent, careless, inattentive, slack, lax, tardy, slow, backward, hesitant, idle, slothful. *Diligent*

Remission, Forgiveness, pardon, absolution, discharge, acquittal, release, exoneration, indulgence. *Punishment* Diminution, relaxation, abatement, lessening, decrease, modification. *Increase*

Remnant, Remainder, remains, residue.

Remonstrate, Protest, object, expostulate, argue. *Acquiesce*

Remorse, Sorrow, contrition, penitence, regret, compunction, repentance. *Satisfaction*

Remorseful, Sorry, contrite.† *Satisfied*

Remorseless, Relentless, unrelenting, ruthless, hard, harsh, pitiless, unpitying, inexorable, cruel, implacable, unmerciful, merciless. *Merciful*

Remote, Distant, far, removed, sequestered, isolated, secluded. *Near* Unconnected, separated, unrelated, alien, foreign. *Direct* Small, faint, inconsiderable, slight. *Real*

Remove, Dislodge, displace, move, transport, transplant, extract, abstract, carry, withdraw, take. *Replace* Dismiss, banish, eject, oust, expel, discharge, depose. *Reinstate*

Remunerate, Pay, recompense, reward, requite, reimburse, indemnify, repay. *Defraud*

Remunerative, Paying, profitable, gainful, advantageous, lucrative. *Honorary*

Renaissance, Awakening, revival, rebirth.

Rend, Tear, cleave, split, sunder, sever, rupture, break, lacerate, divide, rip. *Mend*

Render, Give, present, assign, furnish, supply, deliver, yield, restore, return. *Retain* Translate, construe, interpret.

Rendering, Version, interpretation, construction, rendition.

Renegade, Traitor, apostate, recreant, vagabond, runagate, rebel, backslider, deserter, wretch. *Zealot*

Renew, Repeat, reiterate, iterate, recommence. Restore, renovate, revive, refresh, repair, rejuvenate, replenish. *Exhaust*

Renounce, Relinquish, forgo, surrender, abjure, yield, desert, abandon, forsake, forswear, cede, drop, abdicate. *Retain* Repudiate, reject, deny, disown, disclaim, disavow, recant. *Acknowledge*

Renovate, Repair, restore, renew, revive, refresh. *Deteriorate*

Renown, Fame, celebrity, note, eminence, repute, honour, distinction, glory. *Disrepute*

Rent, *v.a.,* Hire, lease, let.

Rent, *n.*, Crack, hole, crevice, cleft, fissure, opening, breach, gap, flaw, laceration, tear, rupture, schism. *Union*
Revenue, rental, income.

Repair, *v.a.*, Mend, renovate, patch, restore, redress. *Injure*
v.n., Resort, go, wend. *Impair*

Reparation, Amends, indemnity, atonement, redress, repair, compensation, recompense, restoration, satisfaction. *Injury*

Repartee, Retort, answer, reply, rejoinder.

Repast, Victuals, meal, food, feast.

Repay, Reimburse, requite, refund, recompense, reward, return, compensate. *Defraud*
Revenge, avenge, retaliate. *Forgive*

Repeal, *v.a.*, Annul, rescind, abolish, abrogate, revoke, recall, reverse, nullify. *Confirm*
n., Annulment, remission.†

Repeat, Reiterate, iterate, renew, recapitulate, duplicate, double, rehearse, recite, relate, quote, cite, narrate, echo, reproduce. *Suppress*

Repel, Repulse, nauseate, sicken, disgust, deter, revolt. *Attract*
Rebuff, check, refuse, reject, resist, parry, withstand, disperse, scatter. *Welcome*

Repent, *v.a.*, Rue, regret, deplore.
v.n., Grieve, sorrow, relent, regret, rue. *Rejoice*

Repentance, Penitence, sorrow, regret, grief, compunction, contrition, remorse. *Satisfaction*

Repercussion, Recoil, rebound, reverberation. *Impact*

Repetition, Repeating, iteration, reiteration, redundancy, verbosity, recurrence, renewal. *Originality*

Repine, Grumble, murmur, complain, mope, pine, fret. *Rejoice*

Replace, Reinstate, restore, rehabilitate, substitute, supersede, refund. *Remove*

Replenish, Refill, fill, stock, supply, enrich, provide, furnish. *Impoverish*

Replete, Full, filled, exuberant, abounding, charged, stocked, fraught. *Empty*

Replica, Facsimile, duplicate, copy, reproduction. *Original*

Reply, *v.n.*, Answer, rejoin, respond, echo. *Ignore*
n., Answer, rejoinder, response, repartee, retort, acknowledgment.

Report, *v.a.*, Mention, tell, advertise, promulgate, publish, announce, declare, relate, narrate, noise, broadcast, rumour, communicate, annunciate. *Suppress*
n., Statement, account, relation, story, announcement, tidings, communication, annunciation, detail, recital, declaration, rumour, statement, narration, narrative, news, description.
Fame, repute, account, character, reputation.
Noise, reverberation, sound, detonation, explosion, discharge, clap. *Silence*
Minute, statement, note, bulletin, record.

Repose, *v.n.*, Lie, recline, rest, sleep. *Rise*
v.a., Place, lodge, put, rest. *Transfer*
n., Rest, ease, peace, quiet, tranquillity, quietness, relaxation, respite, stillness, peacefulness. *Tumult*

Reprehend, Blame, censure, reprove, rebuke, reprimand, upbraid, chide, reproach, admonish. *Praise*

Reprehensible, Blamable, censurable,† culpable, blameworthy. *Commendable*

Represent, Personate, mimic, personify. Portray, depict, reproduce, delineate, limn, image, exhibit, show, describe, symbolize. *Distort*

Representative, *n.*, Agent, proxy, delegate, substitute, deputy, lieutenant, vicar.
a., Typical, symbolical, figurative. Delegated.

Repress, Suppress, restrain, curb, damp, control, subdue, quell, overcome, overpower, crush, quash, check, smother, stifle, appease, calm. *Rouse*

Reprieve, Pardon, acquit, relieve. *Convict*

Reprimand, Reprehend, blame, censure, reprove, rebuke, reproach, upbraid, chide, admonish. *Praise*
n., Reprehension, blame.†

Reprisal, Retribution, retaliation, revenge. *Reprieve*

Reproach, *v.a.*, Reprimand, reprehend, blame, censure, reprove, rebuke, chide, upbraid, admonish. *Praise*
Asperse, traduce, vilify, taunt, revile, defame, disparage, malign, abuse. *Approve*
n., Reprimand, reprehension,† disapprobation, scorn, contempt, insolence, abuse, invective, reviling, railing.
Obloquy, disgrace, discredit, dishonour, shame, odium, ignominy, insult, opprobrium, indignity. *Honour*

Reprobate, *v.a.*, Denounce, upbraid, condemn, reject, disown, disapprove, abandon, discard, censure, rebuke. *Approve*
n., Outcast, villain, castaway, profligate, miscreant, wretch. *Paragon*
a., Wicked, lost, corrupt, abandoned,

profligate, irredeemable, castaway, base, hardened, graceless, vile, shameless. ***Virtuous***

Reproduce, Propagate, procreate, produce, generate, multiply. ***Exterminate*** Imitate, copy, exhibit, represent.

Reprove, Blame, reprimand, reprehend, censure, rebuke, upbraid, chide, rate, admonish, condemn, correct. ***Praise***

Repudiate, Disavow, disown, deny, disclaim, abjure, renounce, discard. ***Acknowledge***

Repugnant, Distasteful, offensive, contrary, adverse, inimical, antagonistic, opposite, opposed, hostile. ***Natural***

Repulse, *v.a.*, Repel, deter, rebuff, check, reject. ***Encourage*** *n.*, Repulsion, failure, check, rebuff, disappointment.

Repulsive, Repellent, nauseating, sickening, loathsome, revolting, forbidding, unpleasant, hateful, disagreeable, odious, unattractive, ugly. ***Charming***

Reputation } Character, report, name,
Repute } fame, account, standing, honour, distinction, renown, regard. ***Disgrace***

Request, *v.a.*, Ask, desire, require, solicit, beg, beseech. ***Command*** *n.*, Asking, desire, suit, demand, call, petition, entreaty, invitation, claim.

Require, Need, want, desire, lack. Ask, desire, request, demand, exact.

Requisite, Necessary, needed, needful, essential, imperative, vital, indispensable. ***Superfluous***

Requite, Repay, pay, reward, return, reciprocate, recompense, reimburse, avenge. ***Defraud***

Rescind, Repeal, revoke, annul, nullify, quash, countermand, reverse, cancel, abrogate, recall. ***Confirm***

Rescue, *v.a.*, Save, preserve, deliver, recover, redeem, extricate, liberate, ransom, release, free. ***Endanger*** *n.*, Salvation, preservation.†

Research, Analysis, inquiry, scrutiny, investigation, study, examination. ***Ignorance***

Resemblance, Likeness, similarity, semblance, similitude, analogy, affinity. ***Dissimilarity***

Resent, Dislike, repel, resist, hate, detest. ***Submit***

Resentful, Malicious, intolerant, irritable, bitter, hurt, indignant, angry, wrathful, wroth, irascible, choleric. ***Submissive***

Resentment, Indignation, anger, wrath, rage, displeasure, irritation, ire, vexation. ***Submission***

Reserve, *v.a.*, Keep, retain, hold, withhold, except. *n.*, Shyness, constraint, coyness, modesty, taciturnity, backwardness, restraint, reticence, closeness, demureness. ***Frankness***

Reserved, Kept, retained, held, withheld. ***Free*** Shy, constrained, coy,† cautious, distant, unsociable. ***Frank***

Reservoir, Receptacle, cistern, tank, reserve.

Reside, Live, dwell, abide, sojourn, stay, lodge.

Residence, House, home, place, seat, mansion, dwelling, domicile, habitation, abode, lodging. ***Migration***

Residue, Residuum, remnant, remainder, rest, leavings, excess, surplus, overplus. ***Loss***

Resign, Relinquish, surrender, abandon, yield, forgo, withdraw, abdicate, forsake, leave, quit, renounce, return. ***Retain***

Resignation, Relinquishment, yielding, surrender.† ***Retention*** Fortitude, endurance, patience, acquiescence, submission. ***Rebellion***

Resilient, Bounding, rebounding, springing, elastic, recoiling, buoyant. ***Stiff***

Resist, Withstand, check, thwart, oppose, hinder, assail, stop, block, baffle, rebuff, repel, confront. ***Tolerate***

Resolute } Steadfast, steady, determined,
Resolved } settled, decided, firm, fixed, constant, persevering, bold, staunch, dogged, unshaken, unflinching, unyielding, relentless. ***Weak***

Resolve, *v.n.*, Determine, decide, intend, purpose. Melt, dissolve, liquefy. *v.a.*, Determine, decide, declare. ***Vacillate*** Melt, dissolve, liquefy, reduce, analyse, separate, unravel, decipher, disentangle. *n.*, Resolution, determination, decision, intention, purpose, will.

Resonant, Loud, resounding, sounding, sonorous, sharp, ringing, vibratory. ***Silent***

Resort, *v.n.*, Go, fly, repair, retreat, assemble, congregate. ***Avoid*** *n.*, Retreat, haunt, rendezvous, spa. Recourse, expedient.

Resound, Echo, re-echo, ring, respond, reverberate, vibrate. Celebrate, extol, sound, praise.

Resource, Ingenuity, enterprise, ability, device, expedient.

Resources, Material, supplies, means, wealth, riches, funds, money. ***Drain***

Respect, *v.a.*, Venerate, regard, reverence, honour, revere, prefer, prize, value, esteem. *Despise*
Notice, observe, heed, consider.
n., Veneration, regard,† homage, deference. *Contempt*
Regard, particular, relation, reference.

Respectable, Worthy, laudable, praiseworthy, honourable, good, sound, honest, estimable. *Mean*

Respectful, Courteous, polite, civil, deferential, decorous, dutiful, modest, unassuming. *Haughty*

Respite, Pause, rest, delay, break, interval, stop, recess, reprieve, postponement.

Resplendent, Splendid, glorious, bright, brilliant, glittering, gleaming, shining, effulgent, luminous, flashing, burnished, gorgeous, beaming. *Dull*

Respond, Answer, rejoin, reply.
Correspond, accord, tally, suit, meet, agree. *Differ*

Responsible, Answerable, liable, guilty, accountable, trustworthy. *Unreliable*

Responsive, Sympathetic, answering, echoing, obedient, correspondent, responding, sensitive. *Deaf*

Rest, *v.n.*, Relax, recline, repose, sleep, unbend, slumber, lie, lean, lounge. *Stir*
Cease, stop, desist, halt, pause. *Continue*
v.a., Leave, lay, lean, place, deposit. *Move*
n., Quiet, repose, sleep, peace, stillness, tranquillity, ease, quiescence, security. *Tumult*
Pause, break, respite, interval, intermission, halt, cessation. *Continuity*
Surplus, remainder, remnant, residuum, residue, balance, overplus, others.
Stay, brace, support, pillar, prop.

Restitution, Restoration, return, reparation, requital, repayment, recompense, remuneration, indemnity, indemnification, satisfaction, amends, compensation. *Injury*

Restive, Restless, uneasy, recalcitrant, rebellious, unquiet, impatient, obstinate, stubborn. *Docile*

Restless, Restive, uneasy, unquiet, disturbed, agitated, turbulent, disquieted. *Calm*
Irresolute, changeable, inconstant, vacillating, unsteady, unstable, uncertain, unsettled. *Determined*
Wandering, nomadic, roving, active, unsettled, fidgety. *Still*

Restoration, Return, replacement, re-establishment, reinstatement, renewal, revival. *Removal*

Restoration, Reconstruction, renovation. *Deterioration*
Reparation, amends, restitution, cure, indemnification, compensation, requital, recovery. *Injury*

Restore, Return, replace, re-establish, reinstate, renew, revive, heal, cure. *Remove*
Reconstruct, renovate, repair, renew.
Repay, compensate, indemnify, requite, refund. *Injure*

Restrain, Repress, restrict, suppress, curb, confine, hamper, hinder, check, coerce, constrain, circumscribe, withhold, prohibit, prevent. *Incite*

Restrict, Circumscribe, confine, restrain, limit, hamper, bound. *Amplify*

Result, *v.n.*, Eventuate, come, end, rise, follow, accrue, terminate, ensue. *Begin*
n., Outcome, issue, consequence, end, conclusion, sequel, product, verdict, decision, termination, effect. *Cause*

Resume, Renew, recommence, continue. *Desist*

Résumé, Abstract, précis, epitome, summary, breviary, condensation, synopsis, compendium. *Amplification*

Resurrection, Resuscitation, regeneration, rising, revivification, revival, reanimation. *Extinction*

Resuscitate, Resurrect, regenerate,† quicken, renew. *Extinguish*

Retain, Keep, reserve, hold, withhold, detain, maintain, engage, employ. *Relinquish*

Retainer, Servant, dependant, henchman, attendant, lackey.

Retaliate, Revenge, requite, repay, return, answer, avenge, retort. *Forgive*

Retard, Hinder, delay, impede, obstruct, clog, postpone, slacken, check. *Accelerate*

Retention, Holding, grasp, detention, reservation. *Surrender*

Reticent, Taciturn, reserved, quiet, silent, close, uncommunicative. *Garrulous*

Retinue, Suite, party, escort, followers, attendants, train, bodyguard, entourage.

Retire, Recede, withdraw, depart, retreat, retrocede, leave, shrink. *Advance*

Retired, Private, secluded, solitary, secret, abstracted. *Public*

Retiring, Shy, diffident, withdrawing, modest, reserved, demure. *Forward*

Retort, *v.n.*, Reply, answer, rejoin, respond.
n., Reply, answer, rejoinder, response, repartee. *Acceptance*

Retract, Disavow, recant, withdraw, disown, revoke, recall, abjure, cancel, renounce, unsay, repudiate. *Repeat*

Retreat, *v.n.*, Retire, withdraw, recede, depart, retrocede, leave. *Advance*
n., Retirement, withdrawal.†
Asylum, refuge, recess, shelter, haunt, resort, habitat.

Retrench, *v.a.*, Decrease, lessen, abridge, cut, curtail, reduce, contract, abbreviate, clip, confine, limit. *Increase*
v.n., Economize, encroach.

Retribution, Penalty, visitation, punishment, reward, requital, recompense, reckoning, judgment. *Pardon*

Retrieve, Recover, regain, rescue, restore, recall, re-establish. *Lose*

Retrocede, Recede, retrograde, retire, retreat. *Advance*

Retrograde, Backward, inverse, degenerate, declining. *Advancing*

Retrospect, Review, reminiscence, survey, recollection. *Speculation*

Return, *v.a.*, Restore, render, requite, repay, refund, recompense, remit.
v.n., Revert, recur, recoil, reappear. *Disappear*
Retaliate, retort, reply, respond, answer.
n., Restoration, restitution, repayment, reward, recompense, reimbursement, requital.
Profit, advantage, yield, interest, benefit. *Loss*

Reveal, Disclose, divulge, expose, open, show, display, betray, uncover, discover, unveil, publish, communicate, tell. *Hide*

Revel, *v.n.*, Feast, carouse, wanton, indulge, disport. *Fast*
n., Feast, carousal, festivity, spree.

Revelation, Discovery, exposure, detection. *Concealment*

Revelry, Feasting, debauch, festivity, carousal, riot, orgy. *Mourning*

Revenge, *v.a.*, Avenge, repay, requite, vindicate, retaliate. *Forgive*
n., Vengeance, requital, retaliation, retribution. *Forgiveness*

Revengeful, Spiteful, malevolent, hard, malicious, malignant, vindictive, harsh, cruel, implacable, merciless, resentful, uncompassionate, unforgiving, vengeful. *Merciful*

Revenue, Income, proceeds, wealth, receipts, returns, reward. *Expenditure*

Reverberate, Re-echo, echo, resound.

Reverence, *v.a.*, Revere, venerate, adore, honour, respect, worship. *Despise*
n., Veneration, honour,† deference, awe, homage. *Contempt*

Reverent, Respectful, humble, deferential, submissive, reverential. *Contemptuous*

Reverie, Dream, musing, wandering, trance, phantasy, vision. *Attention*

Reverse, *v.a.*, Invert, subvert, upset, derange, up-end, revert, overthrow, overturn. *Range*
Change, counterchange.
Revoke, repeal, rescind, annul, override, quash. *Confirm*
n., Opposite, contrary, back, tail. *Obverse*
Defeat, check, misfortune, failure, mishap, mischance, misadventure, frustration, hardship, trial, affliction. *Success*
a., Opposite, contrary, converse, back.

Revert, Return, recur, reverse, repel, accrue. *Ignore*

Review, *v.a.*, Survey, examine, inspect, analyse, criticize, discuss, edit. *Dismiss*
Revise, reconsider.
n., Survey, examination, inspection, parade.
Review, retrospect, re-survey.
Notice, criticism, critique, analysis, commentary, digest, synopsis.

Revile, Slander, asperse, vilify, traduce, malign, reproach, abuse, calumniate, defame, upbraid. *Extol*

Revise, Review, reconsider, re-survey, amend, edit, correct, overhaul, alter, re-examine.

Revive, *v.a.*, Revivify, animate, rouse, reanimate, quicken, invigorate, recover, reinvigorate, resuscitate, cheer, awake, reawake, refresh. *Kill*
v.n., Recover, awake, rise. *Droop*

Revivify, Revive, animate, reanimate. *Extinguish*

Revoke, Retract, withdraw, disavow, recall, repudiate, reverse, repeal, nullify, annul, cancel, abrogate, quash, rescind, recant, abolish. *Confirm*

Revolt, *v.n.*, Rebel, rise, mutiny, kick. *Submit*
v.a., Nauseate, disgust, sicken, repel, offend. *Attract*
n., Rebellion, rising, mutiny, uprising, insurrection, revolution. *Loyalty*

Revolting, Sickening, repulsive, disgusting, offensive, shocking, horrid, horrible, nauseous, nauseating, abominable, abhorrent, hideous. *Attractive*

Revolution, Rotation, whirling, turn, gyration, circuit.
Change, reconstitution, alteration. *Conservation*

Revolve, Rotate, whirl, turn, circle, wheel.

Revulsion, Shrinking, change, withdrawal, abstraction. *Sympathy*

Reward, *v.a.,* Requite, repay, return, remunerate, indemnify, compensate, recompense, honour, decorate. *Punish* *n.,* Requital, repayment, return,† pay, guerdon, prize, award, premium, bonus, gratuity. *Punishment* Punishment, retribution, requital, visitation. *Forgiveness*

Rhapsody, Medley, effusion, rapture, composition.

Rhetorical, Oratorical, flowery, ornate, declamatory. *Simple*

Rhythm, Metre, measure, beat, number, poetry. Lilt, swing, cadence, pulsation.

Ribald, Obscene, filthy, lewd, loose, low, coarse, rough, base, indecent, indelicate, mean, gross, vile, rude. *Pure*

Rich, Affluent, wealthy, opulent, comfortable, moneyed. *Poor* Productive, fruitful, prolific, fertile, copious, ample, abundant, plenteous, plentiful, luxuriant, abounding. *Barren* Valuable, costly, expensive, precious, splendid, sumptuous. *Cheap* Luscious, delicious, sweet, savoury, soft, mellow, delicate. *Tasteless* Bright, deep, vivid, gay. *Pale*

Riches, Affluence, wealth, opulence, money, treasure, possessions, plenty, fortune, means. *Poverty*

Rickety, Weak, shaky, shattered, tottering, infirm, unsteady, unstable, imperfect. *Firm*

Rid, *v.a.,* Clear, free, deliver, release, disencumber, relieve, despatch, sever, divorce. *a.,* Clear, free, freed.†

Riddle, Conundrum, puzzle, enigma, problem, mystery.

Ridge, Ledge, crest, summit, elevation, chine, spine. *Rift*

Ridicule, *v.a.,* Satirize, mock, deride, taunt, banter, burlesque, scout, rally, lampoon. *Respect* *n.,* Satire, mockery,† sarcasm, raillery.

Ridiculous, Absurd, ludicrous, laughable, risible, farcical, funny, comic, droll, amusing, trivial, trifling, contemptible, preposterous, eccentric, queer, fantastic. *Serious*

Rife, Prevalent, prevailing, general, common. *Rare*

Rifle, Ransack, pillage, rob, plunder, strip, despoil, seize, fleece.

Rift, Hole, crevice, cleft, gap, fissure, opening, split, breach, crack, chink. *Ridge*

Rig, Clothe, deck, array, accoutre, dress. *Strip*

Rigging, Gear, tackle, ropes.

Right, *n.,* Justice, truth, integrity, honesty, rectitude, correctness, equity, uprightness, lawfulness, fairness, propriety. *Wrong* Privilege, claim, title, authority, due, prerogative, power. *Usurpation* *a.,* Just, true, honest, upright, lawful, fair, equitable. Proper, seemly, fit, fitting, suitable, appropriate, becoming. *Improper* Correct, true, real, actual, genuine, accurate. *Incorrect* Straight, direct. *Indirect* *v.a.,* Rectify, adjust, settle, correct, vindicate.

Righteous, Holy, good, pious, religious, devout, pure, conscientious, virtuous, godly, upright, incorrupt, saintly, honest. *Wicked*

Rightful, Just, legal, legitimate, lawful, proper, real, true, genuine, suitable, fitting. *Spurious*

Rigid, Stiff, tough, unyielding, unbending, inflexible, unpliant, unswerving, firm, staunch, unwavering, strict, stern, rigorous, exact, harsh, austere. *Pliant*

Rigour, Stiffness, inflexibility, hardness, firmness, staunchness, strictness, sternness, harshness, austerity, rigidness, rigidity. *Mildness*

Rigorous, Stiff, austere, firm.† *Yielding*

Rile, Vex, irritate, anger. *Pacify*

Rim, Edge, margin, brim, border, brink, flange. *Base*

Rimple, Rumple, wrinkle, crease.

Ring, *v.n.,* Tingle, sound, resound. *n.,* Tingle, sound, resonance. Circle, hoop. Trust, combine, combination, league, set. Arena, list, course. *v.a.,* Girdle, circle, enclose, encircle.

Rinse, Lave, clean, wash, clear. *Dirty*

Riot, Uproar, commotion, tumult, broil, noise, turbulence, disturbance, brawl, confusion, disorder, lawlessness. *Order* Excess, feast, revelry, orgy. *Sobriety*

Rip, Tear, rend, lacerate, split. *Mend*

Ripe, Mature, ready, prepared, complete, fit, perfect, developed, full, mellow, consummate, seasoned, advanced, finished. *Raw*

Ripple, Babble, gurgle, ruffle, lap, wave.

Rise, *v.n.,* Mount, tower, ascend, soar, arise, grow, climb, increase, swell. *Fall* Emerge, appear, happen, occur, *Vanish* Rebel, revolt, mutiny, kick. *Submit*

Rise, *n.*, Ascent, rising, growth, advance, increase. *Sink*
Elevation, rising. *Descent*

Risible, Ridiculous, absurd, ludicrous, laughable, farcical, funny, comic, droll, amusing. *Serious*

Risk, *v.a.*, Chance, hazard, stake, imperil, peril, endanger, venture, speculate.
n., Chance, hazard, venture, exposure, peril, danger, jeopardy. *Safety*

Rite, Custom, ceremony, form, usage, practice, ordinance, observance. *Disuse*

Rival, *n.*, Antagonist, opponent, competitor. *Friend*
v.a., Emulate, oppose, vie, match, equal.
a., Emulating, opposing, antagonistic, competing.

Rive, Split, cleave, rend, tear.

Road, Street, lane, way, pathway, path, track, route, highroad, course, highway, thoroughfare.

Roam, Rove, range, wander, stray, stroll, ramble, saunter, prowl, jaunt, straggle, meander. *Hasten*

Roamer, Nomad, vagrant, wanderer, rover, stroller.

Roar, *v.n.*, Vociferate, bellow, shout, yell, brawl.
n., Vociferation, bellow, bellowing, yell, shout, roaring. *Quietness*

Rob, Strip, deprive, denude, plunder, pillage, pilfer, embezzle, despoil, fleece, rook, defraud. *Enrich*

Robber, Thief, pirate, freebooter, brigand, plunderer, despoiler, desperado, marauder. *Protector*

Robbery, Theft, piracy, freebooting, peculation, larceny, depredation, spoliation, despoliation.

Robe, *v.a.*, Clothe, array, dress, deck, rig, bedeck, invest, drape, cover. *Strip*
n., Gown, dress, vestment.

Robust, Strong, hale, hearty, brawny, stout, vigorous, sound, lusty, sturdy, muscular, sinewy, firm, powerful. *Delicate*

Rock, *v.a.*, Soothe, lull, calm, pacify, tranquillize, quiet, still.
v.n., Totter, reel, stagger, move.
n., Stone, boulder, crag, reef.

Rod, Cane, twig, birch, stick, cudgel, wand. Pole, perch.

Rogue, Knave, scamp, rascal, villain, vagabond, scoundrel, cheat, caitiff, vagrant. *Gentleman*

Roguish, Knavish, rascally, fraudulent, villainous, tricky, dishonest, wanton, mischievous. *Honest*

Roisterer, Braggart, bully, swaggerer, boaster, gascon.

Rôle, Part, character, position, function, impersonation, task.

Roll, *v.n.*, Revolve, rotate, whirl, turn, wheel, spin, reel, lurch, yaw.
Welter, wallow, tumble, undulate, swell, billow.
v.a., Revolve, whirl, turn, wheel, spin, trundle.
Wind, swathe, enfold, envelop, wrap.
n., Rocking, pitch, toss.
Record, register, scroll, document, annals, chronicle, archives, volume, history.
Inventory, schedule, list, catalogue, book.
Booming, resonance, reverberation.

Rollicking, Frolicsome, frisky, lively, gay, jolly, jovial, sportive. *Staid*

Romance, Tale, fable, story, novel, legend, exaggeration, fiction. *Fact*

Romantic, Imaginative, fabulous, wild, fantastic, fanciful, extravagant, quixotic. *Ordinary*

Romp, Frolic, sport, gambol, frisk, caper.

Roof, Cover, ceiling, canopy, shelter. *Floor*

Rook, Cheat, rob, defraud, swindle.

Room, Chamber, apartment.
Stead, place.
Scope, expanse, extent, space, sweep, range, latitude, field, compass, margin. *Restriction*

Roomy, Wide, capacious, spacious, large, broad, ample, extensive, commodious. *Narrow*

Root, *v.a.*, Fix, plant, implant, ground, set, establish. *Eradicate*
Uproot, destroy, exterminate, eradicate. *Plant*
n., Radix, radicle, foundation, base, bottom, motive, parent, origin, cause.

Rooted, Deep, established, confirmed, radical, fixed, inveterate. *Superficial*

Rope, Bind, fasten, tie, secure. *Loose*

Roseate, Blooming, rosy, blushing, ruddy, rubicund, flushed, red, hopeful. *Pale*

Rostrum, Platform, pulpit, stage, stand.

Rosy, Roseate, blooming, blushing, ruddy, rubicund, flushed, red. *Pale*

Rot, *v.n.*, Decay, putrefy, corrupt, taint, decompose, rust, disintegrate, moulder, spoil. *Keep*
n., Decay, putrefaction, putrescence,† mildew.

Rotate, *v.n.*, Whirl, revolve, wheel, turn, spin, twirl, alternate.

Rotation, Order, series, succession, turn, course, sequence, round.

Rotten, Decayed, decaying, putrefied, corrupt, tainted, rusted, decomposed, spoilt, defective, putrid, putrescent, fetid, rank, foul. *Pure*

Rotundity, Roundness, rotundness, convexity, sphericity, globosity. *Angularity*

Rough, Wild, boisterous, tempestuous, stormy, untamed, blustering, rugged, uncourteous, uncivil, hard, ungentle, unpolished, churlish, blunt.   *Gentle*
Uneven, bristly, rugged, knotty, craggy, jagged, ragged, shaggy.   *Smooth*
Unpolished, crude, harsh, rude, coarse, impolite, churlish, indelicate, unrefined, uncourteous.   *Refined*
Severe, hard, harsh, sharp, stern, cruel, violent, heartless, unfeeling.   *Kindly*

Round, *a.*, Rotund, convex, spherical, circular, cylindrical, globular.   *Angular*
adv., Around, circularly, circuitously.
prep., Around, about.
n., Period, cycle, revolution, sphere, succession.
Tour, circuit, perambulation, compass, routine.
v.a., Turn, curve.

Roundabout, Tortuous, long, indirect, devious, circuitous, circumlocutory.   *Direct*

Roundly, Boldly, straight, openly, plainly.

Rouse, *v.a.*, Arouse, wake, excite, incite, stimulate, agitate, awaken, disturb, animate, enkindle, provoke, startle.   *Soothe*
v.n., Wake, awake, rise, stir, move.

Rout, *v.a.*, Vanquish, overcome, overthrow, defeat, dispel, scatter, chase, beat, overpower, discomfort, conquer.
n., Defeat, overthrow, discomfiture, flight, ruin.   *Victory*

Route, Way, road, path, course, itinerary, passage, march.

Routine, Order, system, custom, course, tenor, wont, practice, round.

Rove, Roam, wander, range, stray, ramble, stroll.

Rover, Roamer, wanderer,† nomad.

Row, Rank, string, file, line, thread, order, series.
Commotion, riot, brawl, uproar, tumult, disturbance.

Royal, Regal, imperial, kingly, princely, majestic, noble, stately, magnificent, grand, august, superb, splendid.   *Common*

Rub, *v.a.*, Chafe, scrape, smear, grate, abrade, scour, wipe, polish, clean, graze.
v.n., Grate, chafe.   *Smooth*
n., Friction, abrasion, rubbing.
Pinch, difficulty, obstacle, perplexity, obstruction, dilemma, hardship, embarrassment, hindrance.

Rubbish, Litter, waste, refuse, trash, lumber, dross, scum, confusion, débris.

Rubicund, Red, ruddy, flushed, florid, reddish, rosy, blushing.   *Pale*

Ruddy, Rubicund, red.†   *Pale*

Rude, Impolite, uncivil, churlish, rough, uncourteous, impudent, insolent, saucy, impertinent, unmannerly, low, blunt, coarse.   *Polite*
Coarse, unrefined, rough, uncivilized, barbarous, untaught, unlearned, savage, unskilled, untrained, primitive, illiterate, ignorant, boorish, vulgar, uncouth, crude, unpolished, inelegant, raw, rugged, uneducated.   *Polished*

Rudiment, Element, germ, embryo, seed, beginning, nucleus, commencement.   *Issue*

Rudimental
Rudimentary } Elementary, embryonic, primary, commencing, first, initial.   *Advanced*

Rue, Lament, regret, deplore, repent, grieve.   *Rejoice*

Ruffian, Rascal, scoundrel, bully, monster. wretch, villain, miscreant.   *Gentleman*

Ruffle, Disorder, disturb, rumple, crease, wrinkle, derange, disarrange, confuse.   *Smooth*
Agitate, excite, disturb, discompose, molest, worry, harass, plague, torment, vex, annoy, disquiet, trouble. *Compose*

Rugged, Rough, uneven, bristly, knotty, craggy, cragged, jagged, ragged, shaggy, coarse.   *Smooth*
Harsh, austere, surly, crabbed, blunt, bluff, churlish, rude.   *Polished*

Ruin, *v.a.*, Defeat, destroy, demolish, devastate, shatter, desolate, crush, overwhelm, seduce, violate, overthrow, overturn, subvert, discomfit, wreck. *Rescue*
n., Defeat, destruction,† wreck, prostration, downfall, perdition, undoing, fall, collapse.   *Reparation*

Ruinous, Mischievous, harmful, injurious, baneful, baleful, noxious, pernicious, deleterious, wasteful, calamitous, destructive.   *Prosperous*

Rule, *v.a.*, Control, command, direct, govern, lead, manage, guide, conduct, order, regulate.
v.n., Command, direct, govern, lead, settle, decide, establish.
n., Control, command, direction, sway, government, management, jurisdiction, mastery, dominion, authority, lordship.
Law, order, command, regulation, precept, maxim, canon.   *Exception*
Habit, custom, method, system, routine.

Ruler, Manager, director, dictator, lord, governor, monarch, master.   *Subordinate*

Ruling, Reigning, ascendant, controlling, governing.

Prevalent, prevailing, common, usual, predominant. *Rare*

Ruminate, Meditate, cogitate, muse, ponder, think, reflect, consider, brood. *Relax*

Rummage, Ransack, search, examine, explore.

Rumour, *v.a.,* Tell, publish, bruit, circulate, report.

n., Tale, story, report, bruit, gossip, hearsay, scandal, tidings, news, report, talk. *Truth*

Rumple, Ruffle, wrinkle, crease, rimple, pucker, corrugate. *Smooth*

Run, *v.n.,* Race, hurry, hasten, haste, speed, fly, sprint, career, trip, hie, glide. *Saunter*

Flow, stream, melt, fuse, leak, ooze, proceed. *Stanch*

v.a., Push, force, drive, thrust, propel, turn.

Risk, chance, venture, hazard.

n., Race, running, course, excursion, journey, tour, trip. *Walk*

Demand, pressure.

Rupture, *v.a.,* Break, burst, disrupt, tear, lacerate, fracture, sever, dismember. *Heal*

n., Breaking, bursting,† dissolution, separation. *Healing*

Rupture, Quarrel, dispute, feud, antagonism, hostility, disagreement. *Reunion*

Rural, Rustic, sylvan, pastoral, arcadian, country, agrarian. *Urban*

Ruse, Wile, trick, artifice, device, deception, stratagem, deceit, deception, *chouse*, manoeuvre.

Rush, *v.n.,* Dash, fly, flow, speed, charge, press, career, run, sally. *Lag*

n., Dash, change, course, run, sally, sortie, stampede, plunge.

Rust, Dross, mildew, canker, corrosion, blight, mould, mustiness, fust, must. *Polish*

Rustic, *n.,* Peasant, countryman, Hodge, clown, clod, lout, yokel. *Savant*

a., Rural, sylvan, pastoral, agricultural, country. *Urban*

Coarse, rough, plain, homely, simple, primitive, artless. *Elegant*

Rustle ⎫ Whisper, whispering, sighing,
Rustling ⎭ murmur, quiver, susurration. *Blast*

Ruthless, Pitiless, unpitying, merciless, unmerciful, harsh, cruel, savage, hard, unrelenting, inexorable, inhuman, uncompassionate, unsparing, unappeasable, truculent, ferocious, barbarous, fell. *Compassionate*

Rutilant, Flashing, flaming, meteoric, scintillating, coruscant. *Glowing*

S

Sable, Dark, black, ebon, sombre, dusky. ***White***

Sacerdotal, Priestly, clerical, hierarchical. ***Lay***

Sack, *v.a.*, Plunder, pillage, spoil, ravage, waste, loot, devastate, despoil, destroy. ***Preserve***

n., Plundering, pillage, spoliation,† havoc, desolation. ***Preservation***

Bag, pouch.

Sacred, Holy, consecrated, dedicated, devoted, divine, hallowed, sanctified. ***Profane***

Sacrifice, *v.a.*, Offer, surrender, forgo, immolate.

n., Offering, surrender, immolation, loss, oblation, destruction. ***Gain***

Sacrilege, Desecration, violation, profanation, impiety, irreverence. ***Reverence***

Sad, Sorry, sorrowful, heavy, downcast, dull, disconsolate, unhappy, despairing, gloomy, mournful, melancholy, afflicted, depressed, cheerless, dismal, lugubrious. ***Happy***

Serious, depressing, grave, sorry, dire, grievous, disastrous, calamitous, bad, deplorable, afflictive, melancholy. ***Good***

Saddle, Burden, load, encumber, impose, clog, charge. ***Rid***

Safe, Secure, secured, protected, unhurt, untouched, unharmed, unscathed, sound, undamaged, guarded, whole. ***Exposed***

Sure, reliable, trustworthy, trusty, dependable, certain. ***Dangerous***

Safeguard, *v.a.*, Protect, guard, defend, shield. ***Imperil***

n., Protection, guard, shield, defence, security, escort, convoy.

Sag, Drop, settle, bend, droop. ***Raise***

Sagacious, Shrewd, knowing, wise, keen, clever, judicious, intelligent, discerning, acute, rational, sapient, discriminating, penetrating, perspicacious, able, apt, sensible. ***Stupid***

Sagacity, Shrewdness, knowledge,† stupidity.

Sage, Savant, philosopher. ***Fool***

Said, Uttered, related, declared, reported, aforesaid.

Sail, *v.n.*, Cruise, glide, float.

Leave, depart.

v.a., Navigate.

n. Cruise, trip, journey.

Saintly, Godly, spiritual, holy, devout, pure, pious, religious. ***Sinful***

Sake, Account, interest, score, regard, consideration, reason, respect.

Reason, purpose, end, cause.

Salacious, Lecherous, lewd, lascivious, loose, lustful, impure, unchaste, wanton, concupiscent, incontinent, prurient, libidinous. ***Temperate***

Salary, Wages, income, pay, stipend, remuneration.

Sale, Auction.

Market, demand, vendition.

Salient, Prominent, projecting, striking, conspicuous, remarkable, outstanding, noteworthy, important, noticeable. ***Minor***

Sallow, Yellow, yellowish, pale. ***Ruddy***

Sally, *v.n.*, Rush, start, issue. ***Retire***

n., Sortie, rush, invasion, raid, incursion, excursion, escapade.

Repartee, answer, retort, joke, quirk, quip, jest, witticism. ***Confession***

Salt, *n.*, Flavour, savour, relish, taste, pungency, seasoning.

a., Saline, salted, briny. ***Fresh***

Bitter, sharp, biting, pungent. ***Sweet***

Salubrious ⎱ Wholesome, healthy, pure,
Salutary ⎰ healthful, good, beneficial. ***Unhealthy***

Salute, *v.a.*, Greet, hail, welcome, kiss, accost. ***Ignore***

n., Salutation, greeting, welcome, kiss, address.

Salvation, Saving, deliverance, rescue, preservation, redemption. ***Destruction***

Salve, *v.a.*, Rescue, raise, save.

Heal, remedy, help, cure. ***Aggravate***

n., Antidote, remedy, corrective.

Salvo, Fusillade, broadside, discharge, volley.

Same, Identical, corresponding, similar, like, ditto. ***Different***

Sample, *v.a.*, Try, taste.

n., Model, pattern, specimen, example, illustration.

Sanative ⎱ Curative, curing, healing,
Sanatory ⎰ remedial. ***Noxious***

Sanctify, Hallow, consecrate, purify. ***Pollute***

Sanctimonious, Holy, righteous, smug, pharisaical, satisfied.

Sanction, *v.a.*, Allow, permit, warrant, authorize, ratify, endorse, countenance, approve, support. ***Prohibit***

n., Allowance, permission.† ***Prohibition***

Sanctity, Sacredness, inviolability.

Sanctity, Piety, godliness, holiness, goodness, righteousness, purity, saintliness. *Profanity*

Sanctuary, Church, temple, shrine.
Refuge, retreat, asylum, security, shelter. *Snare*

Sane, Sober, sound, sensible, normal, lucid, intelligent, rational. *Mad*

Sang-froid, Calmness, coolness, indifference, unconcern.

Sanguinary, Bloody, truculent, savage, murderous, bloodthirsty, cruel, fell. *Mild*

Sanguine, Hopeful, optimistic, confident, enthusiastic, ardent, lively, animated. *Pessimistic*

Sanitary, Healthy, hygienic, clean. *Unhealthy*

Sanity, Soundness, wisdom, rationality, sensibility, lucidity, reasonableness, saneness. *Madness*

Sap, *v.a.*, Undermine, weaken, mine. *Strengthen*
n., Juice.

Sapid, Tasty, savoury, tasteful, palatable, delicious. *Distasteful*

Sapient, Wise, sagacious, discerning, discriminating, intelligent, clever, sharp, knowing, keen, acute, shrewd, astute. *Stupid*

Sarcasm, Irony, gibe, taunt, jeer, sneer, ridicule, satire. *Compliment*

Sarcastic, Ironical, bitter, biting, sneering, sardonic, mordacious, cutting, sharp, satirical, taunting. *Complimentary*

Sardonic, Bitter, malignant, sour, cross, tart, derisive, malignant, crabbed, surly, cynical. *Pleasant*

Sash, Belt, band, scarf, girdle.

Satanic, Devilish, diabolical, fiendish, infernal, demoniac. *Angelic*

Sate, Satiate, surfeit, satisfy, fill, gorge, overfill, overfeed, cloy, glut. *Starve*

Satellite, Subordinate, follower, vassal, associate, dependant, attendant, retainer. *Leader*

Satiate, Sate, surfeit, satisfy, fill, gorge, overfill, overfeed, cloy, glut. *Starve*

Satire, Sarcasm, irony, ridicule, lampoon, burlesque, wit, diatribe, skit. *Eulogy*

Satirical, Sarcastic, ironical, taunting, biting, poignant, cutting, mordacious, severe, sharp. *Flattering*

Satirize, Lampoon, ridicule, censure, lash, attack, abuse. *Praise*

Satisfaction, Pleasure, gratification, contentment, content, complacency, ease, enjoyment, comfort. *Annoyance*
Amends, reparation, indemnification, requital, recompense, compensation, atonement, redress, reward, payment, settlement, discharge. *Injury*

Satisfactory, Adequate, sufficient, convincing, conclusive, pleasing, gratifying.

Satisfy, Please, gratify, content. *Annoy*
Indemnify, requite, recompense, compensate. *Injure*
Meet, settle, discharge, pay, answer, fulfil. *Defraud*
Assure, persuade, convince.

Saturate, Soak, steep, drench, imbue, impregnate. *Drain*

Saturnine, Heavy, sad, gloomy, sombre, dark, grave, leaden, dull, morose, sedate, phlegmatic. *Jovial*

Sauce, Condiment, relish, appetizer, seasoning.

Saucy, Pert, impudent, insolent, rude, impertinent, malapert, forward, bold, disrespectful, flippant, light. *Civil*

Saunter, Stroll, loiter, lag, dawdle, dally, tarry, lounge, linger, delay, wander. *Hasten*

Savage, *n.*, Barbarian, native, aboriginal.
a., Wild, uncivilized, barbarous, fierce, untamed, rude, untaught, uneducated, primitive, backward. *Civilized*
Ferocious, brutal, brutish, fierce, cruel, inhuman, brute, beastly, rapacious, fell, murderous, bloodthirsty, truculent, merciless, unmerciful, ruthless, pitiless, relentless, malevolent, sanguinary. *Mild*

Savant, Sage, philosopher, scholar. *Fool*

Save, *v.a.*, Redeem, rescue, preserve, free, deliver, liberate, keep. *Abandon*
Spare, obviate, prevent. *Cause*
Husband, keep, hoard, reserve. *Lavish*
prep., But, except, excepting, excluding, bar.

Saviour, Deliverer, redeemer, preserver, rescuer, protector, defender, guardian. *Destroyer*

Savoury, Palatable, delicious, sapid, tasty, luscious, nice, delightful, piquant, appetizing, relishing, attractive. *Insipid*

Saw, *n.*, Adage, dictum, saying, proverb, precept, axiom, maxim, aphorism.
v.a., Cut, divide.

Say, *v.a.*, Tell, declare, utter, speak, pronounce, assert, express, affirm, allege, argue. *Suppress*
Assume, presume, suppose.
v.n., Speak, declare, assert, affirm, tell.
n., Statement, declaration, speech, voice, assertion, vote, affirmation.

Saying, Saw, adage, precept, maxim, proverb, dictum, aphorism.

Scaffold, Stage, staging, platform, frame. Gallows.

Scallawag) Scamp, rascal, villain, rogue,
Scallywag) scapegrace, knave, scoundrel.
Gentleman
Scale, *v.a.,* Mount, climb, ascend.
Descend
n., Gradation, balance.
Flake, plate, layer, lamina.
Scamp, Scallawag, rascal, villain, rogue,
scapegrace, knave, scoundrel.
Gentleman
Scamper, Run, speed, hasten, hurry, hie,
fly, scud. *Saunter*
Scan, Examine, search, view, scrutinize,
investigate.
Scandal, Disrepute, offence, reproach,
opprobrium, disgrace, discredit, shame,
dishonour, infamy, ignominy. *Honour*
Scandalize, Horrify, stagger, shock,
offend, defame, backbite, disgrace, libel,
calumniate, slander. *Respect*
Scandalous, Disgraceful, discreditable,
shameful, dishonourable, ignominious,
infamous, inglorious, odious, atrocious,
disreputable, opprobrious. *Creditable*
Scanty, Meagre, small, short, insufficient,
narrow, limited, sparing, chary, skimpy,
niggardly. *Ample*
Scar, Wound, hurt, injury, disfigurement,
mark. *Obliteration*
Scarce, *a.,* Rare, few, infrequent, sparse,
uncommon, short, deficient. *Plentiful*
adv., Scarcely, barely, hardly.
Scarcity, Rarity, infrequency, shortage,
deficiency, insufficiency, lack, dearth,
want. *Abundance*
Scare, *v.a.,* Frighten, affright, terrify,
alarm, dismay, intimidate, appal, daunt.
Reassure
n., Fright, terror, panic, shock, alarm,
dismay.
Scarify, Cut, scratch, deface, disfigure,
scar.
Scathe, *v.a.,* Damage, harm, hurt, injure,
wound, destroy, waste, blast.
n., Damage, harm,† mischief.
Scatheless, Undamaged, unharmed, untouched, unscathed, unhurt, uninjured,
sound, whole, intact. *Damaged*
Scathing, Mordacious, biting, cutting,
withering. *Pleasant*
Scatter, *v.a.,* Disperse, spread, distribute,
strew, dissipate, broadcast, sprinkle.
Gather
Dispel, overthrow, frustrate.
v.n., Disperse, separate, straggle, disband.
Scene, Sight, view, display, spectacle,
pageant, exhibition, show, representation.
Scenery, Prospect, view, landscape,
country.

Scent, Smell, odour, redolence, perfume,
fragrance.
Trail, track.
Sceptical, Incredulous, doubting, doubtful, unbelieving, questioning, uncon-
vinced. *Credulous*
Scepticism, Incredulity, doubt,† agnos-
ticism. *Faith*
Schedule, List, catalogue, inventory, roll,
appendix, document, register, table,
record, chronicle.
Scheme, *v.n.,* Plan, plot, intrigue,
contrive.
v.a., Plan, plot, contrive, devise, frame,
imagine, project, design.
n., Plan, plot,† machination, wile, ruse,
stratagem. *Blunder*
Theory, plan, system, outline.
Schism, Disunion, separation, division,
discord, faction, split, breach, dissent,
disruption. *Unity*
Scholar, Schoolboy, schoolgirl, student,
pupil, learner. *Master*
Pedant, savant.
Scholarship, Erudition, learning, knowledge, attainments, accomplishments.
Ignorance
Scholium, Note, annotation, comment,
remark, observation.
School, *v.a.,* Educate, instruct, teach,
discipline, train.
n., Academy, seminary, institute.
Denomination, sect.
Scientific, Philosophical, logical, sound,
rational. *Faulty*
Scintilla, Spark, atom, trace, shadow,
speck, jot, iota, tittle, ace, grain, particle,
scrap.
Scintillate, Sparkle, gleam, coruscate,
glitter, twinkle.
Sciolism, Superficiality, shallowness,
smattering. *Erudition*
Scion, Offshoot, shoot, sprout, branch,
descendant, heir. *Stock*
Scoff, Laugh, sneer, mock, gibe, deride,
jeer, taunt, ridicule, flout, scout. *Respect*
Scold, Upbraid, rate, reprimand, chide,
reprove, condemn, censure, blame,
rebuke. *Praise*
Scoop, Dig, hollow, excavate, remove.
Scope, Opportunity, room, liberty, space,
freedom, amplitude, margin, range.
Purpose, aim, end, object, design, view.
Scorch, Burn, singe, blister, char, roast,
parch, sear.
Score, Cut, mark, furrow, scratch.
Record, register, charge, enter.
Scorn, *v.a.,* Spurn, disdain, despise, slight,
contemn, disregard, scout, ridicule, de-
ride. *Respect*

Scorn, v.n., Disdain.
n., Disdain, contempt, derision, scoffing, mockery.

Scornful, Disdainful, scoffing, mocking, contemptuous, insolent, defiant. *Respectful*

Scot, Impost, tax, fine, shot, mulct, levy, imposition, custom, contribution.

Scoundrel, Rascal, rogue, scamp, knave, scallawag, caitiff, villain, reprobate, wretch, vagabond, cheat. *Gentleman*

Scour, Cleanse, clean, purge, wash, rinse, scrub, scrape, polish, brighten, whiten. *Soil*

Scourge, v.a., Whip, lash, punish, chastise, chasten, beat, correct. *Indulge*
n., Whip, lash, strap, rod, thong.
Punishment, chastening, infliction, bane, visitation, curse, plague, affliction, pest. *Blessing*

Scourings, Leavings, dregs, lees, refuse, dross, offal, scum. *Pickings*

Scout, v.a., Scorn, despise, disdain, spurn, slight, contemn, deride, ridicule, disregard. *Respect*
n., Spy, watchman, observer.

Scowl, v.n., Frown, glower, lower. *Smile*
n., Frown.

Scraggy, Uneven, rugged, rough, bony, angular, lean, thin, jagged, broken. *Round*

Scramble, v.n., Struggle, strive, bustle, hurry, fight, contest. *Loiter*
Clamber, climb.
n., Struggle, striving.† *Method*

Scrap, Piece, portion, bit, particle, part, fragment, atom, morsel, crumb. *Mass*

Scrape, v.a., Grate, abrade, scratch, rub, rasp, confricate, erase, bark. *Polish*
Save, husband, accumulate, gather, hoard, collect. *Lavish*
n., Distress, embarrassment, fix, difficulty, predicament.

Scratch, v.a., Claw, wound, cut.
Erase, obliterate, expunge.
n., Wound, cut, incision, laceration.

Scream, v.n., Screech, cry, yell, shriek, squall.
n., Screech, cry, yell, shriek, outcry. *Whisper*

Screen, v.a., Shroud, cloak, cover, hide, shade, protect, shelter, defend, fence, mark, conceal, veil, secrete. *Expose*
n., Shroud, cloak,† veil, guard, curtain.
Sieve, sift, riddle.

Screw, Twist, squeeze, contort, distort, wrench, press, force, rack.

Scribble, Scrawl, scratch, write.

Scribe, Writer, clerk, penman, scrivener, notary, secretary, amanuensis.

Scrimmage, Scuffle, riot, commotion, confusion, brawl, skirmish, tussle. *Order*

Scrimp, Stint, pinch, straiten, shorten, contract, reduce. *Lavish*

Scrivener, Writer, notary, scribe.

Scroll, Roll, document, parchment, list, register, table, schedule.
Flourish, ornament.

Scrub, Clean, cleanse, scour, wash, rinse. *Soil*

Scrubby, Insignificant, small, pygmy, diminutive, little, dwarfish, dwarfed, stunted, puny. *Immense*

Scrunch, Munch, crush, crunch.

Scruple, v.n., Waver, hesitate, halt, doubt, question.
n., Qualm, doubt, compunction, misgiving, hesitation, question, perplexity, reluctance. *Assurance*

Scrupulous, Punctilious, conscientious, cautious, strict, fastidious, exact, precise, nice, careful, circumspect, attentive. *Careless*

Scrutinize, Examine, probe, search, sift, investigate, study, explore, inspect. *Ignore*

Scrutiny, Examination, search, study, investigation, exploration, inspection, gaze, look. *Neglect*

Scud, Run, scamper, flee, hurry, hasten, bustle, drive, hie, trip, fly, post, speed. *Saunter*

Scuffle, v.n., Fight, struggle, contend, brawl, contest.
n., Fight, struggle, brawl, contest, fray, encounter, squabble, quarrel, tussle, discord, altercation. *Peace*

Scum, Scourings, dross, refuse, froth, scoria.

Scurrilous, Ribald, abusive, gross, low, obscene, foul, indecent, offensive, rude, insulting, insolent, vituperative, contumelious, opprobrious. *Complimentary*

Scurry, Scud, run, hurry, hasten, fly, run, scamper, scuttle, bustle. *Saunter*

Scurvy, Low, base, mean, despicable, paltry, contemptible, vile, sorry, worthless, dishonourable, ungentlemanly, offensive, malicious, objectionable. *Honourable*

Scuttle, Scurry, scud, hurry, hasten, scamper, bustle, run, fly. *Saunter*

Sea, Surge, wave, billow, ocean, main, briny.

Seal, Fasten, close, secure, shut. *Open*
Ratify, confirm, sanction, establish. *Annul*

Seam, Joint, fissure, commissure, crevice.
Stratum, vein, layer.

Seaman, Sailor, tar, mariner, seafarer.

Seamy, Unpleasant, unattractive, nasty, repulsive, dark, sordid. *Pleasant*

Seance, Session, sitting.

Sear, Wither, dry, burn, scorch,† blast, cauterize.

Search, *v.n.*, Seek, inquire, look, hunt, quest.

v.a., Examine, scrutinize, investigate, inspect, probe, sift, study, explore. *Ignore*

n., Examination, scrutiny,† inquiry, pursuit, quest. *Neglect*

Searching, *a.*, Keen, penetrating, close, inquiring, trying, probing. *Distant*

n., Misgiving, hesitation, uncertainty, doubt, perplexity, diffidence. *Assurance*

Seared, Callous, obdurate, hard, lost, unrepentant, irreclaimable, incorrigible, graceless, hardened, shameless. *Sensitive*

Season, *n.*, Time, period, while, spell, interval, term, conjuncture.

v.a., Harden, inure, accustom, habituate, acclimatize, use.

Fit, prepare, qualify, moderate.

Seasonable, Opportune, timely, suitable, appropriate, fit, convenient. *Untimely*

Seasoning, Relish, sauce, flavouring, condiment.

Seat, Bench, chair, stool.

Place, site, situation.

Mansion, estate, residence, abode, house.

Sebaceous, Greasy, fatty, fat, oily, unctuous. *Dry*

Secede, Withdraw, segregate, retire. *Adhere*

Secluded, Retired, remote, solitary, private, screened, sequestered, isolated, withdrawn, shaded. *Public*

Second, *v.a.*, Support, aid, further, help, promote, assist, abet, back, forward. *Oppose*

n., Supporter, aider,† ally. *Opponent*

a., Secondary, inferior, minor. *First*

Secondary, Subordinate, minor, inferior, unimportant. *Primary*

Secret, Hidden, covert, concealed, hid, unseen, veiled, privy, mysterious, occult, unknown, obscure, private, secluded, retired, clandestine, stealthy, underhand, sly. *Open*

Secretary, Clerk, scribe, scrivener, writer.

Secrete, Hide, conceal, veil, obscure, disguise, cloak, screen, shroud. *Expose*

Sect, Faction, schism, school, party, denomination.

Sectarian, Party, denominational, exclusive, schismatical, bigoted, narrow, intolerant. *Broad*

Section, Portion, piece, fragment, part, division, slice, segment. *Whole*

Secular, Lay, temporal, worldly, profane. *Religious*

Secure, *v.a.*, Procure, get, obtain, acquire, achieve. *Lose*

Fasten, guard, protect, assure, ensure, guarantee. *Release*

a., Safe, insured, protected. *Precarious*

Confident, assured, certain, sure, easy, unanxious, fixed, settled, firm, stable, fast, immovable. *Anxious*

Sedate, Staid, serious, sober, calm, quiet, demure, thoughtful, grave, placid, still, tranquil, serene, cool. *Giddy*

Sedative, *n.*, Narcotic, anodyne, opiate. *Stimulant*

a., Calming, allaying, balmy, soothing, lenient, composing, tranquillizing, lenitive, assuasive, hypnotic. *Irritant*

Sedentary, Motionless, inactive, torpid.

Sediment, Precipitate, lees, grounds, dregs, residuum.

Sedition, Treason, insurrection, rebellion, mutiny, riot, tumult, rising, revolt, insubordination. *Obedience*

Seditious, Treasonable, insurrectionary,† insurgent, refractory, turbulent. *Loyal*

Seduce, Tempt, corrupt, ensnare, entice, allure, betray, deceive, debauch, ravage, attract, inveigle, decoy.

Sedulous, Assiduous, laborious, diligent, painstaking, careful, industrious, active, energetic, tireless, persevering, close, unremitting, busy. *Idle*

See, *v.n.*, Look, beware, note, mark, heed, observe, examine, inquire, perceive, watch. *Disregard*

v.a., View, notice, descry, observe, mark, behold, regard, perceive. *Ignore*

Comprehend, understand, know, feel, discern, perceive.

interj., Look, watch, mark, observe, note, behold, lo.

n., Diocese, bishopric.

Seed, Germ, embryo, original, spring, root. *Fruit*

Children, progeny, offspring, descendants. *Ancestors*

Seeing, *n.*, Vision, sight, perception.

con., Because, since, considering, as.

Seek, Search, follow, hunt, prosecute, court, solicit, try, ask, inquire, attempt, endeavour. *Shun*

Seem, Look, appear, pretend. *Belie*

Seeming, *n.*, Look, appearance, guise, colour, semblance, show, aspect.

a., Apparent, appearing, ostensible. *Actual*

Seemly, Becoming, proper, appropriate,

fit, fitting, befitting, congruous, decorous, decent, meet, convenient, suitable, right. *Unbecoming*

Seer, Soothsayer, prophet, foreteller, augur, predictor.

Seethe, Boil, soak, steep.

Segment, Section, portion, fragment, piece, part, division, limb. *Whole*

Segregate, Part, exclude, dissociate, separate, isolate. *Unite*

Seize, Catch, grasp, hold, clutch, snatch, gripe, grip, grapple, hook, capture, take, apprehend, arrest, confiscate, impound, sequestrate. *Release*

Seldom, Rarely, infrequently, occasionally. *Often*

Select, *v.a.*, Pick, cull, choose, prefer.
a., Picked, choice, chosen, selected, prime, excellent, fine, good, preferable. *Coarse*

Selfish, Mean, ungenerous, illiberal, greedy, egotistical, narrow. *Generous*

Sell, Vend, exchange, hawk, retail, barter, peddle, betray. *Buy*

Semblance, Appearance, likeness, show, similarity, resemblance, similitude, air, seeming, aspect, mien, bearing. *Dissimilitude*

Seminary, Academy, college, school, institute.

Sempiternal, Eternal, everlasting, perpetual, continuous, unending, endless, infinite, undying, immortal, constant. *Transient*

Send, Forward, despatch, depute, commission, delegate, authorize, transmit. *Detain*
Hurl, propel, throw, impel, eject, fling, toss, cast.

Senile, Aged, doting, old, tottering, weak, infirm. *Young*

Senior, Older, elder, higher, superior. *Junior*

Sensation, Feeling, perception, sense.
Surprise, excitement, thrill, impression, stir. *Apathy*

Sense, Feeling, sensation, perception.
Understanding, mind, apprehension, tact, intellect, reason, brains, discernment, discrimination. *Insensibility*
Wisdom, sagacity, soundness, meaning, significance, import, purport, sanity. *Folly*

Senseless, Insensible, inert, unfeeling, dull, apathetic, unconscious. *Sensitive*
Nonsensical, absurd, foolish, stupid, silly, unwise, unmeaning, objectless, unreasonable. *Sagacious*

Sensible, Conscious, cognizant, aware, sensitive, mindful, observant. *Unconscious*

Sensible, Sagacious, wise, intelligent, sound, sane, understanding, rational, judicious, discreet. *Stupid*

Sensitive, Susceptible, sentient, affected, impressible, responsive. *Thick*

Sensual, Carnal, animal, bodily, fleshly, voluptuous, lewd, dissolute, licentious. *Abstemious*

Sensuous, Material, symbolical, aesthetic. *Abstract*

Sentence, *v.a.*, Condemn, judge, doom.
n., Condemnation, judgment, decision, doom, determination.
Phrase, clause.

Sententious, Laconic, brief, terse, pithy, short, condensed, pointed, axiomatic, compact, didactic. *Prosy*

Sentiment, Feeling, emotion, sensibility. *Reason*
Thought, idea, notion, opinion, saying, judgment, expression, maxim. *Preconception*

Sentimental, Emotional, romantic, tender. *Prosaic*

Sentinel⎫ Guard, guardian, watchman,
Sentry ⎭ warder, patrol, picket, keeper. *Decoy*

Separate, *v.a.*, Sever, dissever, divide, sort, disjoin, detach, eliminate, disunite, segregate, part, divorce, disconnect. *Join*
v.n., Divide, part, scatter, disintegrate. *Unite*
a., Severed, dissevered, divided,† alone, detached, dissociated, distinct, unconnected, independent, segregated, sequestered. *Joined*

Separation, Dissociation, disunion, disconnection, division, divorce, disjunction, segregation. *Union*

Sepulchral, Hollow, ghastly, grave, deep, lugubrious, funereal, gloomy, dismal, woeful, sombre, mournful, sad. *Cheerful*

Sequacious, Servile, slavish, obsequious, ductile, pliant. *Original*

Sequel, Conclusion, end, consequence, termination, issue, event, close, result, upshot, continuation. *Beginning*

Sequence, Order, continuity, arrangement, plan, progression, succession, series. *Disorder*

Sequestered, Quiet, retired, secluded, remote, separated, unfrequented, private, withdrawn. *Public*

Seraphic, Holy, heavenly, celestial, pure, sublime. *Diabolical*

Serene, Tranquil, calm, peaceful, placid, quiet, undisturbed, unruffled, sedate, unperturbed, composed, cool. *Agitated*
Unclouded, bright, fair, clear, calm. *Turbid*

Serf, Villein, slave, bondman, thrall, servant, labourer. *Master*

Series, Sequence, order, line, succession, concatenation, course.

Serious, Weighty, important, dangerous, momentous, grave, great. *Trivial*
Solemn, grave, thoughtful, earnest, sober, sedate, staid. *Jocose*

Sermon, Address, homily, exhortation, discourse.

Serpentine, Tortuous, winding, sinuous, anfractuous, anguine, meandering, spiral, twisted, crooked. *Straight*

Serrated, Indented, jagged, cut, toothed, notched. *Even*

Serried, Crowded, teeming, close, compact. *Empty*

Servant, Domestic, attendant, retainer, menial, servitor, maid, help. *Employer*

Serve, *v.n.*, Act, answer, do, perform, suit, attend, minister. *Command*
v.a., Observe, obey, attend, assist, aid, minister, benefit, advance, promote, succour, distribute, arrange. *Oppose*

Service, Labour, work, business, duty, employment.
Function, ceremony, rite.
Use, utility, benefit, advantage, avail, gain. *Uselessness*

Servile, Slavish, submissive, obsequious, sequacious, grovelling, abject, cringing, mean, base, sycophantic. *Independent*

Servitude, Serfdom, submission, service, subjection, enslavement, enthralment, bondage, slavery, obedience. *Mastery*

Set, *v.a.*, Place, put, seat, station, fix, locate, appoint, establish, settle, rest, lay, arrange, post, dispose, determine, plant. *Move*
Adorn, variegate, stud, ornament.
Adjust, regulate, rectify.
v.n., Sink, decline, subside. *Rise*
Congeal, harden, solidify, consolidate. *Melt*
n., Sect, band, clique, party, group, gang, collection, coterie, company, cluster.
a., Ordained, fixed, appointed, settled, established, ordered, determined, formal, prescribed, regular. *Casual*

Settle, *v.a.*, Arrange, regulate, determine, adjust, decide, fix, establish, confirm. *Derange*
Pay, discharge, meet, liquidate, finish, balance, *Awe*
People, colonize, plant, domicile, place, establish.
v.n., Reside, live, dwell, inhabit, abide. *Move*
Repose, rest.
Sink, decline, fall, subside. *Rise*

Settled, Fixed, steady, established, firm, stable, customary, decided, certain. *Uncertain*
Adjusted, regulated, arranged, orderly, quiet.

Settlement, Arrangement, regulation, adjustment, reconciliation.
Colony, colonization, post, installation, fixture, establishment.
Payment, discharge, liquidation.

Sever, Part, divide, cut, dissever, disjoin, disconnect, disrupt, disunite, detach, sunder, separate. *Join*

Several, Different, diverse, divers, own, various, separate, sundry, individual, independent, distinct, manifold, particular. *One*

Severe, Hard, sharp, bitter, biting, cruel, harsh, strict, relentless, unrelenting, austere, grave, stern, rigid, rigorous, inexorable, cutting, violent, afflictive, distressing. *Mild*
Plain, simple, restrained, chaste. *Gay*

Shabby, Poor, ragged, mean, old, worn, threadbare, faded. *New*
Paltry, despicable, low, mean, base, beggarly, contemptible, dishonourable. *Honourable*

Shackle, *v.a.*, Bind, manacle, tie, chain, fetter, obstruct, impede, encumber, restrict, trammel, hamper. *Free*
n., Bond, manacle,† handcuff, gyve.

Shade, *v.a.*, Screen, shadow, hide, cover, obscure, darken, shelter, cloud, eclipse, dim. *Expose*
n., Screen, shadow, darkness, umbrage, gloom, obscurity, dusk. *Glare*
Veil, blind, shutter, shelter, protection, cover.
Degree, touch, kind, sort.
Colour, hue, tint.

Shadow, Shade, screen, darkness, dark, umbrage, gloom, obscurity, dusk. *Glare*
Adumbration, image, reflection, shade, delineation, phantom, unsubstantiality. *Substance*

Shadowy, Shady, shaded, dark, gloomy, umbrageous, murky, dim, obscure. *Light*
Unsubstantial, imaginary, phantasmal, unreal, spectral, impalpable. *Real*

Shady, Shadowy, shaded, dark.† *Light*

Shaggy, Rugged, rough, uneven, craggy, cragged, coarse. *Smooth*

Shake, *v.a.*, Move, jar, jolt, convulse, agitate, loosen, weaken, impair. *Strengthen*
v.n., Quake, quiver, vibrate, tremble, move, shiver, shudder, totter. *Stand*
n., Shock, jar, convulsion, jolt, tremor, agitation.

Shaky, Trembling, unsound, tottering, weak, unstable. ***Firm***

Shallow, Superficial, slight, trivial, silly, trifling, empty, puerile, foolish, simple, ignorant, unintelligent. ***Deep***

Sham, *v.a. & n.,* Pretend, simulate, feign, counterfeit.

n., Pretence, feint, counterfeit, mockery, imposition, imposture, fraud, delusion, trick, humbug. ***Truth***

a., Pretended, feigned, counterfeit, mock, spurious, imitation, false. ***Real***

Shame, *v.a.,* Humiliate, humble, mortify, confuse, disconcert, embarrass, abash, confound, discompose.

n., Dishonour, disgrace, discredit, mortification, ignominy, humiliation, abashment, reproach, discredit, opprobrium, obloquy, infamy. ***Honour***

Shameful, Dishonourable, disgraceful,† base, disreputable, low, indecent, vile, nefarious, heinous, atrocious, scandalous, outrageous. ***Honourable***

Shameless, Brazen, bold, audacious, hardened, unabashed, unashamed, cool, impudent, insolent, abandoned, careless, reprobate, incorrigible, graceless. ***Penitent***

Shanty, Hovel, cabin, hut, shed, shack.

Shape, *v.a.,* Mould, form, create, make, model, fashion, figure, execute, adjust. ***Distort***

n., Mould, form, make, model, fashion, figure, image, apparition, cut, cast, build, appearance, aspect, guise.

Shapely, Comely, handsome, trim, neat, symmetrical. ***Ugly***

Share, *v.a.,* Portion, apportion, distribute, divide, participate, partake.

n., Portion, apportionment, part, ration, division, lot, quota, allotment, due. ***Whole***

Sharp, Fine, keen, pointed, thin, acute, cutting. ***Blunt***

Biting, bitter, caustic, sarcastic, acrid, pungent, acid, hot, stinging, severe, burning, piquant, keen, acrimonious, piercing, devastating, harsh, afflictive, distressing, mordacious, poignant, tart, trenchant. ***Gentle***

Clever, perspicacious, witty, smart, apt, acute, astute, shrewd, knowing, ready, sagacious, quick, discerning, intelligent, discriminating, ingenious, subtle, penetrating. ***Dull***

Intense, acute, violent, keen, piercing, afflictive, excruciating, poignant. ***Mild***

Sharper, Trickster, rogue, rascal, cheat, swindler, defrauder.

Shatter, Break, split, shiver, burst, crack, smash, disrupt, demolish, rend. ***Mend***

Shave, Pare, shear, clip, strip, slice, crop. Skim, graze, touch.

Shear, Shave, clip, cut, strip, fleece.

Sheathe, Cover, case, encase, hide. ***Draw***

Shed, *v.a.,* Drop, emit, cast, spill, effuse, diffuse, scatter. ***Retain***

n., Cabin, shanty, hovel, hut, cot, shack.

Sheen, Shine, brightness, resplendence, splendour, polish, lustre, brilliance, gloss, effulgence.

Sheepish, Bashful, timid, shamefaced, timorous, diffident, ashamed, abashed. ***Bold***

Sheer, Unadulterated, unmitigated, mere, clear, pure, unqualified, unmixed, simple, absolute, downright. ***Partial***

Precipitous, perpendicular.

Shell, Case, husk, shard, framework. Bomb, shrapnel, grenade.

Shelter, *v.a.,* Cover, hide, shroud, screen, protect, defend, shield. ***Expose***

n., Cover, covert, screen, protection, defence, shield, security, safety, retreat, haven, harbour, asylum, sanctuary, refuge.

Shelve, *v.a.,* Discard, dismiss. ***Pursue***

v.n., Incline, slope, slant.

Shibboleth, Watchword, test, criterion.

Shield, *v.a.,* Cover, screen, shelter, protect, defend, guard. ***Betray***

n., Cover, screen, shelter, protection, defence, bulwark, safeguard, buckler, guard, rampart.

Shift, *v.a. & n.,* Change, vary, move, alter, fluctuate, contrive, scheme, plan, manage. ***Fix***

n., Change, alteration, transference. Subterfuge, trick, wile, stratagem, ruse, contrivance, resource, resort, chicanery, artifice, expedient, device, evasion, fraud. ***Permanence***

Shifty, Deceitful, evasive, fraudulent, dishonest, tricky, artful. ***Honest***

Shillelagh, Cudgel, club.

Shimmer, *v.n.,* Glisten, glimmer, gleam, flash, shine.

n., Glistening, glimmer, gleam.

Shine, *v.n.,* Gleam, beam, glisten, flash, coruscate, sparkle, shimmer, radiate, glow, glitter. ***Wane***

n., Lustre, brilliance, sheen, brightness, resplendence, splendour, gloss, polish, effulgence.

Ship, Vessel, boat, steamer, craft.

Ship-shape, Neat, tidy, trim.

Shirk, Evade, avoid, neglect, malinger, escape. ***Perform***

Shiver, *v.n.*, Shudder, quiver, tremble, shake, quake, vibrate. ***Stiffen***
v.a., Shatter, break, disrupt. ***Mend***
n., Shuddering, trembling, shaking, shock, tremor, vibration.

Shoal, Swarm, horde, crowd, multitude, throng.
Shallow, bank, bar.

Shock, *v.a.*, Disgust, horrify, offend, outrage, sicken, shame. ***Please***
n., Blow, tremor, concussion, impact, collision, onset, shaking, force.

Shocking, Disgusting, horrible, sordid, outrageous, offensive, sickening, shameful, disgraceful, repulsive, hateful, vile, odious, detestable, loathsome, ghastly, execrable, foul, repugnant, revolting, obnoxious, abominable, dreadful, appalling. ***Pleasing***

Shoot, *v.a.*, Propel, discharge, fire, emit, dart, expel, hurl.
v.n., Fire.
Germinate, sprout, bud.
n., Sprout, bud, offshoot, scion, branch, twig.

Shore, Beach, coast, land, strand.
Support, brace, prop, stay. ***Undermine***

Short, Brief, contracted, terse, laconic, concise, compendious, condensed, pithy, sententious, limited, curtailed, succinct. ***Protracted***
Scanty, defective, deficient, insufficient, inadequate, lacking, imperfect, incomplete. ***Full***
Abrupt, blunt, brief, curt, laconic, sharp, unceremonious, pointed, uncivil, severe. ***Courteous***
Straight, quick, direct, near. ***Long***

Shorten, Cut, contract, curtail, abridge, abbreviate, reduce, diminish, lessen. ***Amplify***

Shortly, Briefly, succinctly, tersely, concisely. ***Diffusely***
Quickly, soon, directly. ***Later***

Shout, *v.n.*, Vociferate, cry, call, holloa, roar, cheer, clamour, exclaim, bellow. ***Whisper***
n., Vociferation, cry,† holloa.

Shove, Push, move, propel, jostle, press. ***Pull***

Show, *v.a.*, Display, exhibit, parade, present, reveal, indicate, blazon, flaunt, divulge, disclose, discover, unfold. ***Hide***
Demonstrate, evince, evidence, prove, manifest.
Explain, teach, inform, instruct, direct, demonstrate, expound, guide. ***Obscure***
n., Display, exhibition, presentation, spectacle, demonstration, parade, pomp, ceremony.

Show, Semblance, appearance, pretence, profession, illusion, pretext. ***Reality***

Showy, Flashy, gay, gaudy, garish, loud, gorgeous, ostentatious. ***Quiet***

Shred, Scrap, strip, tatter, bit, piece, atom, fragment, jot, particle. ***Whole***

Shrew, Vixen, virago, scold, fury, termagant, spitfire. ***Angel***

Shrewd, Sharp, clever, acute, keen, sagacious, knowing, wise, cunning, sly, astute, artful, intelligent, quick, awake, discriminating, discerning, penetrating. ***Dull***

Shriek, *v.n.*, Screech, yell, cry, scream, squeal.
n., Screech, yell.†

Shrill, Piercing, high, sharp, acute, piping. ***Deep***

Shrink, Contract, dwindle, decrease, wither, shrivel. ***Expand***
Recoil, retire, withdraw, blench, quail, wince, swerve. ***Dare***

Shrivel, *v.n.*, Shrink, contract.† ***Expand***
v.a., Parch, dry, burn.

Shroud, Veil, shelter, cover, conceal, hide, cloak, muffle, mask, screen. ***Expose***

Shrunk, Withered, shrivelled.† ***Swollen***

Shudder, *v.n.*, Shake, tremble, shiver, quiver, quake. ***Stiffen***
n., Shaking, trembling,† shuddering, tremor.

Shuffle, *v.a.*, Mix, intermix, confuse, derange, shift, jumble. ***Sort***
v.n., Quibble, cavil, equivocate, dodge, prevaricate, evade, dissemble, palter.
n., Quibble, cavil,† sophism, artifice, trick, fraud, ruse, stratagem, device, subterfuge, pretext, pretence. ***Frankness***

Shun, Avoid, elude, escape, evade, discard, eschew. ***Court***

Shut, *v.a.*, Close, lock, bar, fasten, secure, enclose, imprison, slam. ***Open***
a., Closed, locked.†

Shy, Timid, bashful, coy, diffident, chary, wary, cautious, retiring, reserved, shrinking, modest, timorous. ***Bold***

Sibilant, Hissing, buzzing, hooting.

Sibyl, Prophetess, hag, witch, sorceress.

Sick, Ill, unwell, disordered, diseased, distempered, indisposed, poorly, ailing, feeble, weak. ***Well***
Tired, disgusted, nauseated, weary.

Sicken, *v.a.*, Tire, disgust, nauseate, weary.
v.n., Languish, decay, ail, pine, droop, tire. ***Flourish***

Sickly, Delicate, unhealthy, morbid, languid, weak, feeble, infirm, diseased, faint, drooping. ***Flourishing***

Sickness, Disorder, disease, distemper,

indisposition, ailment, ail, complaint, illness, malady.   **Health**

Side, Edge, border, verge, flank, margin, face, half.   **Centre**

Interest, party, cause, behalf, sect, faction.   **Oppose**

Sift, Part, separate, examine, try, probe, scrutinize, discuss, fathom, analyze, sort.   **Confuse**

Sigh, Repine, mourn, complain, lament, grieve, long.

Sight, *v.a.,* See, glimpse, perceive, observe.   **Lose**

n., Vision, eye, seeing, perception, beholding.   **Invisibility**

View, visibility.

Spectacle, exhibition, show, prospect, scene.

Sightless, Blind, unseeing, eyeless.

Sign, *v.a.,* Beckon, indicate, signify, gesture.

Initial, autograph, endorse, subscribe.

n., Symbol, token, omen, password, countersign, indication, mark, proof, emblem, expression, note, manifestation. Signal, beckoning, beacon, indication, gesture.

Signal, *n.,* Sign, beckoning, indication, beacon.

a., Memorable, remarkable, noteworthy, notable, eminent, conspicuous, extraordinary.   **Ordinary**

Significant, Important, weighty, telling, momentous, suggestive, expressive, signifying.   **Trivial**

Signify, *v.a.,* Denote, show, tell, manifest, betoken, imply, declare, proclaim, utter, augur, portend, foreshadow, indicate, impart, announce, suggest.   **Conceal**

v.n., Matter.

Silent, Peaceful, calm, still, quiet, soft, restful, noiseless, hushed, undisturbed, quiescent.   **Noisy**

Taciturn, reticent, dumb, speechless, mute.

Silly, Simple, foolish, weak, shallow, witless, stupid, absurd, inept, senseless, nonsensical, unwise, imprudent, indiscreet.   **Wise**

Silt, Deposit, sediment, alluvium.

Silvery, White, bright, clear, sweet.

Similar, Like, alike, harmonious, congruous, resembling, correspondent, homogeneous, common, uniform.   **Different**

Simile, Metaphor, comparison, similitude.

Similitude, Likeness, similarity, congruity, resemblance, correspondence, uniformity, analogy.   **Difference**

Simile, metaphor, comparison.

Simmer, Boil, seethe, bubble, stew.   **Cool**

Simper, Smirk, smile, giggle.

Simple, Naïve, credulous, trusting, open, artless, unaffected, sincere, undesigning, ingenuous, frank, true, weak.   **Deep**

Plain, direct, bare, unadorned, single, unblended, uncompounded, natural, neat, clear, unstudied, elementary, unmistakable, intelligible.   **Complex**

Simply, Naïvely, artlessly, sincerely, frankly, openly, weakly, truly.   **Artfully**

Merely, only, absolutely, barely, solely.

Simulate, Sham, assume, pretend, affect, counterfeit, feign.   **Discard**

Simultaneous, Concomitant, concurrent, synchronous, coincident, contemporaneously.   **Separate**

Sin, *v.n.,* Trespass, transgress, fall, err, offend.

n., Trespass, transgression, error, offence, misdeed, wrong, iniquity, wickedness, crime, evil, delinquency, ungodliness, unrighteousness.   **Virtue**

Since, *adv.,* Ago.

conj., As, because, considering, seeing.

prep., After, subsequently.   **Before**

Sincere, Honest, artless, frank, open, genuine, plain, direct, candid, hearty, true, unfeigned, truthful, unaffected, pure.   **Feigned**

Sinewy, Strong, stalwart, muscular, firm, robust, brawny, powerful, vigorous, athletic, sturdy, healthy.   **Weak**

Sinful, Wicked, bad, depraved, wrong, unrighteous, iniquitous, criminal, immoral, mischievous, corrupt, unholy.   **Virtuous**

Singe, Scorch, burn, sear.

Single, *v.a.,* Choose, prefer, select, pick.

a., One, sole, only.   **Plural**

Solitary, alone, isolated, unique, particular, separate, individual.   **Numerous**

Unmarried, unwedded, celibate.   **Married**

Singular, Unique, peculiar, particular, single, individual, extraordinary, quaint, uncommon, unusual, rare, remarkable, notable, strange, unwonted, exceptional, unprecedented, eminent, unparalleled, unexampled, noteworthy, odd, eccentric, queer.   **Ordinary**

Sinister, Inauspicious, unlucky, malign, portentous, unfavourable, disastrous, baneful, injurious.   **Auspicious**

Evil, bad, wicked, wrong, foul, underhand, unfair, dishonest, fell, dishonourable, criminal.   **Honourable**

Sink, *v.a.,* Immerse, duck, submerge, drown, merge, engulf, dig, excavate.   **Raise**

v.n., Subside, fall, founder, descend,

drop, droop, decay, decline, decrease, flag, abate, waste, enter, penetrate. **Rise**

Sinless, Innocent, faultless, spotless, guileless, pure, undefiled, impeccable, untarnished, unsullied, unstained, guiltless, perfect, unblemished, virtuous, righteous. **Wicked**

Sinner, Criminal, transgressor, offender, delinquent. **Saint**

Sinuous, Serpentine, crooked, coiled, curved, winding, anfractuous, waving, tortuous, flexuous. **Straight**

Siren, Temptress, seducer.

Sit, Perch, rest, repose, settle, seat. **Stand**

Site, Location, locality, seat, place, spot, position, situation, ground, plot.

Situation, Site, position, locality, place, location, station, seat, spot, plot.

State, case, condition, predicament, pass, plight.

Place, position, post, berth, work, employment.

Size, Volume, extent, bulk, magnitude, greatness, largeness, bigness, breadth, dimensions, width.

Skeleton, Outline, draught, sketch, shell, framework, nucleus, cadre. **Body**

Sketch, v.a., Draw, delineate, portray, depict, limn, represent.

n., Outline, delineation, skeleton, plan, draught.

Skilful } Expert, versed, practised, adroit,
Skilled } clever, ingenious, intelligent, ready, competent, qualified, proficient, adept, apt, quick, accomplished, able, dexterous, conversant, trained, learned, experienced, cunning. **Clumsy**

Skill, Skilfulness, expertness, address, adroitness,† art, knack, facility. **Clumsiness**

Skim, Graze, touch, brush, skirt. **Penetrate**

Skin, v.a., Peel, pare, flay, excoriate.

n., Peel, hide, rind, covering, hull, pelt, epidermis. **Bone**

Skinny, Thin, lean, emaciated, poor, lank. **Fat**

Skip, Jump, dance, hop, leap, gambol, frisk, caper, spring, bound.

Omit, miss, pass, disregard, neglect.

Skirmish, Battle, conflict, fray, affair, collision, fight, contest, brush, engagement.

Skirt, v.a., Encircle, border, skim, edge. **Enter**

n., Hem, border, rim, edge, verge, margin. **Centre**

Petticoat, kilt, flap.

Skit, Burlesque, parody, satire, squib, pasquinade. **Eulogy**

Skittish, Nervous, shy, excitable, timid, fidgety. **Steady**

Wanton, fickle, capricious, coquettish. **Staid**

Skulk, Hide, lie, lurk, cower, sneak, slink. **Appear**

Sky, Heaven, heavens, firmament, stars, azure. **Earth**

Slab, Chunk, block, piece, square.

Slack, Loose, relaxed. **Tight**

Lazy, indolent, inactive, sluggish, idle, careless, remiss, negligent, dull, quiet, slow, dilatory, lax. **Busy**

Slacken, v.a., Loosen, moderate, relax, abate. **Tighten**

v.n., Tire, flag, languish, fail. **Freshen**

Slake, Quench, assuage, satisfy, allay, extinguish. **Create**

Slander, v.a., Abuse, asperse, traduce, malign, defame, disparage, vilify, libel, calumniate, decry. **Eulogize**

n., Abuse, aspersion,† scandal, obloquy, detraction. **Eulogy**

Slanderous, Abusive, libellous, defamatory, maligning, traducing, malicious, calumnious. **Eulogistic**

Slant, Slope, incline, shelve, tilt, list, lean. **Upright**

Slanting, Sloping, inclining,† oblique. **Perpendicular**

Slap, Smack, strike, pat, spank.

Slash, Cut, gash, slit.

Slatternly, Untidy, slovenly, sluttish, dirty, slipshod, negligent, careless. **Immaculate**

Slaughter, v.a., Slay, murder, butcher, massacre, kill, destroy, assassinate. **Protect**

n., Slaying, murder,† carnage, bloodshed, havoc.

Slave, n., Servant, bondman, thrall, serf, captive, drudge, vassal, menial. **Master**

v.n., Toil, work, drudge.

Slavery, Servitude, bondage, captivity, serfdom, vassalage, drudgery, enslavement, thraldom, enthralment. **Freedom**

Slavish, Servile, abject, fawning, mean, cringing, low, base, vile, obsequious, sycophantic, sneaking, grovelling, contemptible, despicable. **Independent**

Slay, Kill, murder, assassinate, destroy, massacre, slaughter, despatch. **Save**

Sleek, Smooth, soft, glossy, velvety, silken. **Rough**

Sleep, v.n., Doze, slumber, rest, repose, nap. **Wake**

n., Slumber, rest, repose, unconsciousness, siesta, drowse.

Sleepless, Wakeful, vigilant, disturbed, restless, agitated. **Restful**

Sleepy, Tired, drowsy, heavy, sluggish, lazy, dull, torpid, somnolent, slumberous. *Alert*

Sleight, Dexterity, smartness, cunning, skill, adroitness. *Clumsiness*

Slender, Thin, spare, slim, lean, slight, frail, flimsy, fine, narrow. *Corpulent* Slight, small, trivial, light, insufficient, scanty, meagre, inconsiderable, small, inadequate, superficial. *Deep*

Slice, *v.a.,* Cut, divide, sever, part, pare, split.

n., Piece, portion, morsel.

Slide, Slip, glide, skid.

Slight, *v.a.,* Despise, scorn, disregard, disparage, ignore, disdain, neglect, overlook, scamp. *Respect*

n., Scorn, disregard, disparagement, disdain, discourtesy, neglect, contempt, disrespect, inattention.

a., Trifling, trivial, little, small, slender, inconsiderable, unimportant, minor, slim, insignificant, cursory, petty, paltry, faint, scanty, weak, superficial. *Considerable*

Slim, Slight, slender, thin, spare, lean, narrow, lithe, lanky. *Plump*

Slime, Mire, mud, clay, ooze, sludge.

Slimy, Miry, muddy, oozy, clammy, damp, viscid, viscous, glutinous. *Dry*

Sling, Throw, fling, hurl, toss, cast. Suspend, hang.

Slink, Skulk, sneak, lurk, cower. *Show*

Slip, *v.n.,* Trip, fall, err, blunder, mistake. Slide, glide.

n., Trip, falling, spill, error, blunder, mistake, fault, indiscretion.

Twig, scion, cutting, shoot.

Slippery, Glassy, smooth, lubricated, unsafe, perilous, uncertain. *Firm* Perfidious, treacherous, faithless, shifty, evasive, untrustworthy, crafty, elusive, cunning. *Trustworthy*

Slipshod, Slatternly, slovenly, untidy, sluttish, careless. *Careful*

Slit, Tear, cut, split, rend, rip, slash, divide, sunder. *Mend*

Slope, *v.n.,* Incline, slant, shelve, list, lean, tilt.

n., Inclination, incline, ramp, gradient, pitch, cant, grade, slant, declivity, acclivity. *Level*

Sloping, Inclining, slanting,† oblique, declivious. *Straight*

Sloppy, Wet, muddy, splashy. *Dry* Emotional, sentimental, maudlin. *Manly* Loose, unsystematic, careless. *Thorough*

Sloth, Laziness, indolence, idleness, sluggishness, inertness, inaction, inactivity, torpor, supineness, dilatoriness, slowness. *Industry*

Slothful, Lazy, indolent, idle,† slack, dronish. *Industrious*

Slouching, Lubberly, uncouth, awkward, undisciplined, clumsy, ungainly, loutish. *Erect*

Slough, Morass, bog, deep, fen, marsh, swamp, quagmire.

Slovenly, Loose, disorderly, negligent, untidy, careless, unkempt, lazy. *Trim*

Slow, Tardy, late, behind, sluggish, slack, dilatory, deliberate, lingering, gradual, inactive, inert, dull. *Quick*

Sluggard, Lounger, drone, laggard, idler, slacker. *Worker*

Sluggish, Dronish, slothful, lazy, idle, slack, inert, inactive, indolent, drowsy, supine, torpid, dilatory. *Industrious*

Slumber, *v.n.,* Sleep, doze, rest, repose. *Wake*

n., Sleep, rest, repose, drowse, siesta, unconsciousness.

Slur, Stigma, stain, reproach, calumny, aspersion, disgrace, slight, brand, insinuation, innuendo. *Honour*

Sluttish, Slatternly, slovenly, untidy, careless, unclean, dirty, disorderly. *Trim*

Sly, Artful, cunning, clever, astute, crafty, knowing, shrewd, sharp, cautious, clandestine, stealthy, arch, wily, subtle, smart, underhanded. *Open*

Smack, *v.a.,* Slap, hit, beat, strike.

n., Flavour, tincture, taste, dash, tinge, savour, spice.

Crack, report, snap.

Small, Little, insignificant, tiny, minute, diminutive, miniature, slight, petty, trivial, paltry, inconsiderable, narrow, unimportant, microscopic. *Large*

Smart, *v.n.,* Rankle, suffer, pain.

n., Rankling, pain, suffering.

a., Stinging, forcible, pugnent, severe, poignant, painful, keen, sharp. *Dull* Trim, immaculate, neat, spruce, dressy, showy, elegant, fine, pretentious. *Shabby* Quick, prompt, brisk, sprightly, active, alert, witty, apt, ready, clever, nimble, agile. *Slow*

Smash, *v.a.,* Break, crack, disrupt, crush, shatter. *Mend*

n., Ruin, fall, destruction, disruption.

Smear, Besmear, plaster, daub, bedaub, coat, begrime, soil, pollute, sully, contaminate. *Scour*

Smell, *v.a.,* Scent.

n., Scent, aroma, odour, fragrance, perfume, stink, stench.

Sniff, inhale, breathe.

Smile, Smirk, grin, simper.

Smirk, Simper, smile.

Smite, Beat, hit, strike, buffet, knock.   *Caress*
Afflict, blast, visit, punish, chasten, destroy, slay, kill.

Smoke, *v.n.,* Exhale, fume, reek, steam.
n., Fume, fumigation, vapour, mist.
Triviality, emptiness, insubstantiality.   *Substance*

Smooth, *a.,* Plain, level, even, flat, soft, polished, sleek.   *Rough*
Oily, bland, easy, soft, suave, mild, glib, fluent.   *Blunt*
v.a., Level, flatten, ease.
Palliate, alleviate, alloy, mollify, calm, appease, assuage, pacify, mitigate.   *Ruffle*

Smother, Suffocate, strangle, suppress, repress, stifle, gag, choke, extinguish.   *Nurture*

Smoulder, Burn, simmer, smoke.   *Blaze*

Smudge, *v.a.,* Blur, besmear, stain, blot, soil.
n., Blur, smear.†

Smug, Comfortable, satisfied, content, self-satisfied, nice, easy.   *Uneasy*

Smut, Dirt, smudge, blot, stain, smear, blight, spot, soot.
Indecency, obscenity, ribaldry, coarseness, indelicacy, grossness, looseness, impurity.

Smutty, Dirty, smudgy,† foul.
Indecent, obscene.†   *Clean*

Snap, *v.a.,* Break, crack, snip.
n., Crack, smack.
Bite, nip, catch.
Catch, lock, clasp, fastening.

Snappish, Splenetic, waspish, touchy, acrimonious, testy, crabbed, acrid, tart, sour, irritable, irascible, pettish, surly, censorious, growling, snarling, peevish, perverse, captious, crusty, petulant, cross.   *Affable*

Snare, Trap, catch, device, noose, wile, net, toil, gin.   *Free*

Snarl, Growl, grumble, grouse, murmur.   *Purr*

Snarling, Snappish, splenetic, waspish, acrimonious, testy, touchy, crabbed, acrid, tart, sour, irritable, irascible, pettish, censorious, growling, peevish, perverse, surly, crusty, petulant, cross.   *Affable*

Snatch, *v.a.,* Clutch, grasp, gripe, grip, pluck, wrest, seize, pull, twitch.   *Release*
n., Clutch, grasp.†
Fragment, portion, bit, oddment.

Sneak, Lurk, slink, skulk, crouch, steal.

Sneer, *v.n.,* Jeer, scoff, laugh, gibe, mock.
n., Jeer, scoff, laugh, gibe, contempt, derision, taunt, scorn, disdain.   *Respect*

Sniff, Smell, inhale, breathe, scent.

Snigger, Laugh, giggle, titter.   *Snivel*

Snip, Cut, slit, clip, nip.   *Join*
Fragment, shred, piece, bit.

Snivel, Weep, whine, cry, whimper, blubber.   *Snigger*

Snowy, White, clean, spotless, unspotted, unsullied, unblemished, unstained, pure.   *Dirty*

Snub, *v.a.,* Reprimand, abash, mortify, shame, reprove, humiliate, disconcert, humble, slight.
Prune, cut, clip, dock, check.
n., Reprimand, reproof, slight, rebuke.   *Flattery*

Snug, Comfortable, cosy, trim, compact, neat, enclosed, sheltered.   *Bare*

So, Very, extremely.
Thus.
Therefore.
Likewise, similarly, provided.

Soak, Wet, moisten, drench, saturate, damp, absorb, steep, imbrue, macerate.   *Dry*

Soar, Mount, rise, fly, ascend, tower, aspire.   *Sink*

Sob, Weep, cry.

Sober, Temperate, steady, abstinent, abstemious.   *Drunk*
Calm, reasonable, rational, sane, sound, staid, composed, cool, solemn, serious, demure, sombre, sad, subdued, grave, sedate, steady, quiet, dispassionate.   *Extravagant*

Sobriety, Temperance, abstinence.†   *Intemperance*
Calmness, reasonableness.†   *Agitation*

Sociable, Genial, friendly, gregarious, social, companionable, communicative, affable, neighbourly.   *Close*

Social, Sociable, genial, friendly,† convivial, festive.   *Personal*
Civic, civil, politic.

Society, Union, association, company, fellowship, club, fraternity, partnership, community, brotherhood, corporation, body, sodality.   *Privacy*
Elite, public, community.

Sodality, Society, union, association.†

Sodden, Soaked, saturated, drenched, wet, steeped.   *Dry*

Soft, Yielding, impressible, pressible, pliable, plastic, malleable, flexible.   *Hard*
Tender, gentle, kind, mild, easy, lenient, bland, submissive, weak, compliant.   *Harsh*
Quiet, dulcet, smooth, delicate.   *Loud*

Soften, Melt, macerate, intenerate.   *Harden*
Palliate, alleviate, allay, lessen, assuage,

abate, blunt, temper, calm, mollify, modify, moderate, diminish, weaken, enervate, appease, pacify, quell, still, qualify. *Aggravate*

Soil, *v.a.,* Dirty, sully, taint, stain, daub, bedaub, defile, pollute, tarnish, bemire, foul, contaminate, besmirch, bespatter, begrime. *Clean*
n., Dirt, earth, ground, mould, loam.

Sojourn, Rest, abide, stay, dwell, tarry, remain, reside, stop, halt, quarter, lodge, live. *Travel*

Solace, Consolation, comfort, relief, cheer. *Affliction*

Sole, One, only, solitary, single, unique. *Numerous*

Solecism, Incongruity, absurdity, error, slip, fault, mistake, impropriety, blunder, *faux pas.*

Solemn, Serious, earnest, grave, sober, impressive, august, imposing, stately, staid, sedate. *Gay*
Sacred, venerable, ceremonial, religious, devotional, formal, ritual. *Profane*

Solemnize, Observe, keep, celebrate, commemorate, honour. *Desecrate*

Solicit, Ask, crave, beg, beseech, seek, pray, implore, importune, entreat, urge, petition, invite, canvass. *Demand*

Solicitous, Concerned, anxious, troubled, worried, disturbed, careful, uneasy, apprehensive. *Indifferent*

Solid, Hard, dense, compact, firm, congealed, substantial, strong, weighty, stout, stable, reliable, trustworthy, sound, safe. *Hollow*

Solidarity, Union, consolidation, community, fellowship. *Disintegration*

Solidify, Harden, congeal, petrify, consolidate. *Melt*

Solitary, Lonely, lone, isolated, alone, lonesome, desolate, companionless, cheerless, separate. *Accompanied*
Desert, deserted, unfrequented, private, remote, retired, secluded, lonely, isolated. *Frequented*
One, only, sole, single, individual. *Numerous*

Solitude, Loneliness, seclusion, isolation, remoteness, separation, privacy, retirement. *Society*

Solution, Dissolving, dissolution, melting, disintegration, separation, disruption, disunion, liquefaction. *Union*
Elucidation, explanation, disentanglement. *Complication*

Solve, Elucidate, disentangle, explain, clear, interpret, expound, unfold. *Complicate*

Solvent, Sound, healthy. *Insolvent*

Sombre, Dark, heavy, dull, doleful, cheerless, rayless, hopeless, melancholy, sad, dismal, lugubrious, gloomy, grave, funereal, sunless. *Bright*

Some, One, any, a, an.
About, more, less, near.
Several, part, portion.

Sometime, *a.,* Former, late.
adv., Formerly, once. *Never*

Somnolent, Drowsy, sleepy, dreamy, dozy. *Vigilant*

Song, Carol, lay, hymn, ballad, poem, canticle, anthem, psalm, sonnet, ode, ditty.

Sonorous, Resonant, resounding, loud, clear, audible, ringing, bold. *Soft*

Soon, Presently, quickly, shortly, early, promptly, betimes, anon. *Late*
Willingly, cheerfully, readily, gladly, lief.

Soothe, Compose, appease, pacify, calm, tranquillize, soften, assuage, allay, quiet, calm, still, palliate, temper, lull, mollify, moderate, mitigate, alleviate, ease, lessen, deaden, relieve, comfort, humour. *Irritate*

Soothsayer, Diviner, prophet, augur, seer, predicator, foreteller.

Sophism, Paralogism, fallacy, quibble. *Truth*

Sophisticate, Demoralize, spoil, corrupt, pervert, damage, vitiate, adulterate. *Reform*

Sophistry, Paralogism, paralogy, fallacy, quibble. *Truth*

Soporific, *n.,* Opiate, anodyne, narcotic, hypnotic, anaesthetic. *Stimulant*
a., Opiate, anodyne,† somniferous, slumberous, somnific, soporous, soporiferous, soporose.

Sorcery, Magic, witchcraft, wizardry, divination, necromancy, enchantment, spell, charm. *Exorcism*

Sordid, Mean, dirty, low, base, vile, ignoble, degraded, foul. *Honourable*
Greedy, niggardly, avaricious, mean, covetous, grasping, beggarly, illiberal, close, stingy, selfish, ungenerous, miserly. *Generous*

Sore, *n.,* Abscess, ulcer, boil, gathering, fester, pustule.
a., Tender, painful, afflictive, distressing, grievous, irritated, burdensome, heavy, ulcerous, raw. *Painless*
Hurt, vexed, pained, annoyed, grieved, galled, irritable, tender. *Pleasant*
adv., Sorely, severely, greatly, intensely, grievously, violently, profoundly, deeply, very, sadly. *Slightly*

Sorrow, *v.n.,* Mourn, grieve, moan, sigh, lament, repine, weep. *Rejoice*

Sorrow, *n.*, Mourning, grief,† sadness, affliction, woe, distress, trouble. *Joy*

Sorrowful, Mournful, grieved, sighing, sad, weeping, woeful, distressed, doleful, unhappy, depressed, afflicted, dejected, melancholy, lugubrious, dismal, sorry, disconsolate. *Joyous*

Sorry, Sad, grieved, hurt, pained, sorrowful, dejected, depressed, chagrined, mortified, regretful, compunctious, penitent. *Glad*

Miserable, pitiful, contemptible, poor, wretched, mean, worthless, shabby, vile, dismal, base, abject. *Splendid*

Sort, *v.a.*, Order, assort, arrange, array, classify, select, elect, choose, class, group. *Derange*

n., Kind, class, order, species, rank, group, nature, genus, race, family, description, denomination.

Way, manner.

Soul, Spirit, mind, reason, intellect, life, fire, vitality, ardour, fervour, feeling, sense. *Nonentity*

Essence, energy.

Soulless, Dead, unfeeling, spiritless, cold, lifeless, inanimate, sordid. *Fervent*

Sound, *v.a.*, Fathom, measure, test, try, gauge, search, probe, examine.

Pronounce, utter, proclaim, announce.

v.n., Resound.

n., Noise, report, tone, whisper, voice, resonance. *Silence*

Channel, passage, strait, narrows.

a., Whole, perfect, entire, undamaged, unimpaired, uninjured, unbroken, unhurt, intact, undecayed, good, strong, hale, hearty, healthy, vigorous, firm, hardy. *Impaired*

Correct, right, true, proper, sane, valid, rational, sensible, orthodox. *Fallacious*

Soundless, Noiseless, quiet, silent, dumb, mute. *Loud*

Bottomless, deep, abysmal, unfathomable. *Shallow*

Sour, *v.a.*, Embitter.

a., Tart, acid, bitter, acetous, sharp. *Sweet*

Acrimonious, acrid, surly, tart, caustic, severe, splenetic, rancid, waspish, cross, snarling, snappish, morose, crabbed, touchy, testy, pettish, petulant, rough, peevish. *Genial*

Source, Spring, cause, commencement, beginning, origin, rise, head, fountain, fount. *Issue*

Souse, Plunge, soak, dip, douse, pickle, drench, submerge, immerse, duck.

Souvenir, Keepsake, memento, reminder.

Sovereign, *n.*, Monarch, emperor, king, ruler, autocrat, prince, lord, potentate.

a., Supreme, head, chief, paramount, primary, principal, predominant. *Subordinate*

Efficacious, certain, effectual. *Useless*

Sow, Plant, scatter, spread, cast, broadcast, disseminate, disperse, propagate, strew. *Reap*

Space, Extension, extent, room, capacity, accommodation. *Limitation*

Interval, interspace, distance, pause. *Continuity*

Period, time, duration.

Spacious, Capacious, extensive, ample, large, wide, commodious, broad, roomy, vast. *Narrow*

Span, Extent, stretch, reach, width.

Period, spell, fathom.

Spar, *n.*, Pole, yard, beam, boom.

Box, fight, quarrel, dispute.

Spare, *v.a.*, Save, store, husband, withhold, reserve. *Squander*

Preserve, afford, save, give, allow, grant. *Spend*

a., Superfluous, additional, extra, supernumerary, surplus.

Scanty, frugal, lean, thin, poor, meagre. *Ample*

Sparing, Careful, chary, parsimonious, economical, frugal, saving. *Lavish*

Sparkle, Glitter, glisten, flash, shine, beam, scintillate, coruscate, radiate, bubble, effervesce, twinkle, gleam. *Smoulder*

Sparkling, Glittering, glistening,† brilliant. *Dull*

Sparse, Thin, scattered, scanty, meagre, infrequent. *Dense*

Spartan, Hardy, enduring, brave, bold, stoical, courageous, fearless, manly, valiant, heroic. *Effeminate*

Spasm, Throe, fit, twitch, paroxysm, seizure, cramp.

Spasmodic, Fitful, irregular, convulsive. *Regular*

Spatter, Sprinkle, splash, sputter.

Speak, *v.n.*, Talk, discourse, articulate, say, enunciate, converse, dispute.

v.a., Tell, say, articulate, enunciate, declare, utter, propound, deliver, express, pronounce, address, proclaim.

Special, Especial, specific, particular, peculiar, exceptional, uncommon, extraordinary, unusual, unique, marked, express, distinctive, distinct, definite. *General*

Specialist, Expert, connoisseur.

Specie, Money, cash, coin.

Species, Group, sort, class, collection, assemblage, kind, description, variety.

Specific, Special, especial, particular, peculiar, exceptional, uncommon, extraordinary, unusual, distinctive, distinct, definite, precise, limited. *General*

Specify, Name, particularize, indicate, individualize, detail, designate, mention, define. *Confound*

Specimen, Sample, example, pattern, copy, exemplar, type, mode, illustration, instance, model. *Freak*

Specious, Plausible, feasible, ostensible, obvious, manifest, colourable, illusory. *Absurd*

Speck, Spot, dot, stain, blot, atom, particle.

Spectacle, Sight, display, exhibition, pageant, scene, picture, parade, show, demonstration, review, vision, marvel, phenomenon, curiosity.

Spectator, Witness, observer, audience, bystander, beholder.

Spectre, Spook, ghost, hobgoblin, goblin, apparition, spirit, phantom, bogey. *Body*

Speculate, Wonder, ponder, contemplate, theorize, muse, meditate, ruminate, reflect, think, cogitate, consider, hazard. *Verify*

Speculation, Wonder, pondering, contemplation,† conjecture, view, theory, supposition. *Reality*

Speech, Address, oration, discourse, harangue, palaver.
Talk, words, language, utterance, tongue, dialect, idiom, parlance, conversation.

Speechless, Silent, dumb, inarticulate, mute. *Talkative*

Speed, *v.a.*, Hasten, hurry, accelerate, despatch, expedite, move, urge, quicken, press. *Delay*
Prosper, help, aid, assist, execute, further, advance. *Hinder*
n., Haste, hurry, celerity, acceleration,† swiftness, velocity, quickness, rapidity, rate, impetuosity. *Slowness*
Prosperity, success.

Speedy, Hasty, hurried, hurrying, quick, expeditious, prompt, impetuous, swift, rapid, fast. *Slow*
Early, soon, approaching, near. *Late*

Spell, Charm, fascination, witchcraft, incantation, magic.
Season, interval, period, term.

Spend, Disburse, exhaust, lavish, expend, squander, consume, dissipate, employ, use, bestow. *Save*

Spendthrift, Prodigal, wastrel, waster, spender, squanderer. *Miser*

Spent, Exhausted, weary, fatigued.

Sphere, Ball, globe, circle, orb. *Cube*
Field, scope, province, vocation, circle, department, beat.
Region, country, realm, rank, order, domain.

Spice, Flavour, savour, relish, seasoning, taste.
Smack, taste, tincture, dash, sprinkling.

Spicy, Aromatic, balmy, pungent, keen, racy, fragrant, piquant, pointed. *Insipid*

Spigot, Plug, faucet, stopper.

Spill, Upset, shed, effuse, empty. *Fill*

Spin, Whirl, twirl, turn, twist.
Lengthen, extend, protract, prolong.

Spinney, Thicket, wood, shrubbery, grove, coppice.

Spiracle, Vent, pore, aperture, orifice.

Spiral, Winding, twisting, turning. *Straight*

Spirit, Soul, life, breath, air, animation. *Body*
Essence, quintessence, substance, soul, character, nature, meaning, drift, sense, significance, intent.
Ghost, apparition, spectre, phantom, spook.
Temper, mood, feeling, disposition.
Vigour, enterprise, animation, courage, life, cheerfulness, energy, ardour, zeal, activity, enthusiasm, earnestness, fire, vivacity, liveliness, piquancy. *Listlessness*

Spirited, Vigorous, enterprising, alert, animated,† sprightly. *Listless*

Spiritless, Dull, listless, torpid, lifeless, heavy, dejected, discouraged, dispirited, depressed, cold, stupid, tame, insipid, apathetic, soulless. *Animated*

Spiritual, Sacred, religious, divine, holy, ethereal, incorporeal, immaterial, pure. *Fleshly*

Spite, *v.a.*, Annoy, mortify, thwart, vex, offend, displease, injure.
n., Malice, maliciousness, malevolence, vindictiveness, spleen, rancour, pique, malignity, hatred, gall. *Benevolence*

Spiteful, Malicious, malevolent, malign, rancorous, malignant. *Benevolent*

Spleen, Malice, spite, hatred, anger, wrath, irritability, malignity, rancour, malevolence, maliciousness, gall, pique, animosity, annoyance, irascibility. *Benevolence*
Hypochondria, despondency, dejection, melancholy, depression, megrims, dumps. *Cheerfulness*

Splendid, Brilliant, bright, resplendent, beaming, radiant, lustrous, effulgent, shining, glowing, refulgent. *Dull*
Magnificent, grand, superb, showy, fine,

pompous, gorgeous, stately, sumptuous, noble, signal, glorious, sublime, great, brilliant, excellent. *Poor*

Splendour, Brilliance, brightness.†
Dulness
Magnificence, grandeur,† parade, display.
Meanness

Splenetic, Sour, bitter, malevolent, testy, malicious, petulant, touchy, irascible, spiteful, melancholy, gloomy, irritable, peevish, pettish, snappish, snarling, waspish, fretful, cross, choleric, churlish, sullen, morose. *Genial*

Splice, Join, bind, connect, mortice.
Sever

Splinter, *v.a.,* Rend, split, shiver, tear, crack, cleave.
n., Piece, fragment.

Split, *v.a.,* Splinter, rend, tear, break, crack, cleave, burst, divide, cut, separate.
Unite
v.n., Break, burst, divide, separate, secede.
n., Rent, breach, gap, fissure, division, separation.
a., Divided, separated, disunited. *United*

Spoil, *v.a.,* Mar, vitiate, impair, injure, ruin, disfigure, corrupt, harm, damage, destroy. *Improve*
Plunder, pillage, waste, ravage, despoil, rob, fleece. *Endow*
v.n., Deteriorate, decay.
n., Plunder, booty, prize, gain, loot, pillage, spoliation, rapine.

Sponge, Expunge, obliterate, efface, clear, delete, clean, cleanse, purge.

Spongy, Spongeous, porous, compressible, elastic, absorbent.

Spontaneous, Instinctive, willing, impulsive, free, voluntary, gratuitous. *Coercive*

Sporadic, Dispersed, scattered, separate, infrequent. *Collective*

Sport, *v.n.,* Play, disport, gambol, frolic, wanton, romp, frisk.
n., Play, game, frolic, amusement, fun, gaiety, diversion, merriment, pleasure, entertainment, recreation, mirth, jollity, pastime. *Work*

Sportive, Playful, gamesome, hilarious, frolicsome,† vivacious, jocose, lively, sprightly. *Sedate*

Spot, *v.a.,* Speckle, stain, blot, soil, sully, tarnish. *Clean*
n., Speck, stain, blot, taint, mark, patch, speckle, fleck.
Place, site, locality, situation.

Spotless, Unspotted, clean, perfect, pure, stainless, undefiled, unsullied, untainted, untarnished, immaculate, perfect, unblemished, blameless. *Defiled*

Spouse, Consort, partner, companion, mate.

Spout, Gush, issue, spurt, squirt.

Sprain, Wrench, twist, turn, strain, rick.

Sprawl, Straggle, spread, lounge.

Spray, Sprig, shoot, bough, branch, twig.
Foam, froth, spume.

Spread, *v.a.,* Stretch, expand, extend, open, unfurl, unfold, dilate. *Fold*
Strew, scatter, sow, disseminate, blaze, distribute, broadcast, divulge, publish, propagate, promulgate, circulate.
Repress
n., Reach, scope, compass, range, stretch, expansion, extent.

Sprig, Spray, shoot, bough, branch, twig.

Sprightly, Blithe, gay, animated, lively, brisk, airy, buoyant, cheerful, joyous, jolly, jocose, vivacious, alert, vigorous, frolicsome, active, agile, blithesome.
Lifeless

Spring, *n.,* Well, fount, fountain, source, origin, cause. *Terminate*
Bound, hop, leap, jump, vault, skip.
v.n., Bound, hop, leap, jump, vault, skip.
Alight
Rise, arise, issue, emanate, commence, flow, come, start, proceed, originate, emerge. *Result*
Recoil, rebound, warp, bind.

Sprinkle, Scatter, strew, shower, bedew, besprinkle.

Sprite, Fay, elf, brownie, pixy, fairy, hobgoblin, imp, spirit.

Sprout, *v.n.,* Germinate, grow, shoot, spring, bud, vegetate, ramify. *Wither*
n., Sprig, spray, shoot, branch, twig.

Spruce, Smart, trim, tidy, neat, finical.
Slovenly

Spry, Brisk, nimble, active, supple, agile, lively, quick, alert, smart, dapper. *Stiff*

Spur, *v.a.,* Goad, prick, urge, incite, instigate, impel, rouse, arouse, animate, stimulate, drive, induce, encourage.
Deter
n., Goad, prick, stimulus, incitement,† incentive, provocation. *Deterrent*

Spurious, False, counterfeit, pretended, sham, fictitious, artificial, unauthentic, feigned. *Genuine*

Spurn, Scorn, scout, slight, disregard, disdain, despise, contemn, reject.
Respect

Spurt, Spout, gush, squirt, rush.

Spy, *v.a.,* Espy, see, discover, discern, observe, remark, notice, behold, detect.
Miss
n., Scout, detective, agent.

Squab, Squat, squabbish, fat, tubby, thick, short, stout, plump, dumpy. *Lank*

Squabble, *v.n.*, Quarrel, contend, brawl, argue, bicker, wrangle, dispute, altercate, row, struggle, fight. *Agree*

n., Quarrel, contention, brawl.† *Peace*

Squad, Band, company, gang, relay, crew.

Squalid, Foul, dirty, sordid, disgusting, unclean, filthy, nasty, repulsive. *Clean*

Squall, *v.n.*, Yell, cry, scream, shriek, bellow, bawl, squeal.

n., Yell, cry.†

Hurricane, gale, blast, gust, storm, tempest. *Calm*

Squander, Waste, dissipate, spend, expend, lavish, fritter, misuse. *Save*

Square, *n.*, Quadrate, quadrangle, parade.

v.a., Adapt, adjust, regulate, settle, accommodate, shape, balance.

v.n., Tally, agree, accord, harmonize, fit, suit.

a., Quadrilateral, perpendicular. *Round*

Fair, good, honest, just, true, upright. *Dishonest*

Even, adjusted, balanced, settled, exact, equal. *Uneven*

Squash, Squeeze, crush, mash, compress.

Squat, *v.n.*, Crouch, sit, cower. *Stand*

a., Squab, squabbish, fat, tubby, thick, short, stout, plump, dumpy. *Lank*

Squeal, *v.n.*, Squall, yell, cry, scream, shriek, bellow, bawl.

n., Squall, yell, cry.†

Squeamish, Particular, hypercritical, scrupulous, fastidious, finical, overnice, dainty. *Easy*

Squeeze, *v.a.*, Squash, crush, mash, nip, compress, constrict, force, pinch, press.

v.n., Crowd, press, jostle.

Squire, Escort, gallant, attendant. *Knave*

Squirm, Writhe, twist, wriggle, turn.

Squirt, Spout, spurt, gush, eject.

Stab, *v.a.*, Pierce, spear, wound, injure, gore, cut.

n., Wound, cut, thrust, injury.

Stable, Firm, constant, steady, durable, lasting, permanent, perpetual, secure, established, invariable, unchangeable, unchanging, immutable, steadfast, fast, unalterable, sure, fixed, unwavering, abiding. *Transient*

Staff, Rod, club, stick, cane, pole, prop, support, stay.

Employees, men, workmen, workers, personnel, force.

Stage, *v.a.*, Produce, present, perform.

n., Staging, platform, theatre, boards, playhouse.

Drama.

Point, step, degree, place, position.

Stagger, *v.a.*, Astound, astonish, shock, nonplus, surprise, dumbfound, amaze, pose, confound, bewilder. *Reassure*

v.n., Totter, reel, sway, vacillate, falter, waver, hesitate.

Stagnant, Still, quiet, motionless, inert, lifeless, tideless, quiescent, standing, sluggish, torpid, dull, inactive. *Flowing*

Staid, Sedate, serious, steady, grave, demure, sober, solemn, calm, composed. *Frivolous*

Stain, *v.a.*, Sully, taint, tarnish, blemish, soil, defile, discolour, spot, contaminate, befoul, blot. *Clean*

n., Taint, tarnish, blemish, spot, blot, imperfection, contamination, pollution.

Disgrace, shame, reproach, infamy. *Honour*

Stainless, Untainted, untarnished, pure, unsullied, spotless, unspotted, undefiled, unpolluted, unblemished, perfect, clean, blameless, faultless. *Defiled*

Stake, *v.a.*, Hazard, venture, jeopardize, risk, wager, imperil, peril.

n., Wager, bet, pledge, hazard, venture, adventure, risk, peril.

Pale, picket, stick, palisade.

Stale, Old, faded, vapid, musty, fusty, tasteless, flat, insipid, dry, hackneyed, effete, common, trite. *Fresh*

Stalk, *v.a.*, Hunt, follow, chase, pursue.

v.n., Parade, strut, march, walk, pace, stride. *Slink*

Stall, Recess, stable, compartment, stand, booth.

Stop, halt, check.

Stalwart, Sturdy, resolute, courageous, strong, redoubtable, stout, lusty, manly, athletic, indomitable, hardy, valiant, intrepid, bold, gallant, daring, formidable, powerful. *Weak*

Stamina, Strength, vitality, power, force, vigour. *Weakness*

Stammer, *v.n.*, Falter, stutter, hesitate.

n., Faltering, stutter, hesitation.

Stamp, *v.a.*, Brand, mark, print, imprint, impress, characterize.

n., Brand, mark, print, impression, impress.

Genus, kind, make, mould, cast, sort, description, character, type, cut.

Stampede, Rush, flight.

Stanchion, Prop, support, shore, stay.

Stand, *v.n.*, Rest, remain, continue, stop, abide, stay, endure, persist, halt, hold. *Move*

Rank, station, stop, halt, pause.

v.a., Abide, sustain, suffer, brook, allow, tolerate, endure, permit, bear. *Oppose*

n., Platform, booth, stall, place, station, post, rostrum.

Stand, Opposition, resistance.

Standard, *n.,* Colours, ensign, banner, flag.

Model, pattern, gauge, measure, criterion, test, type, rule, scale. ***Misfit***

a., Model, regulation, typical, uniform, regular. ***Irregular***

Standing, *n.,* Rank, status, position, reputation, degree, estimation, repute, status.

a., Set, settled, fixed, immovable, permanent, established. ***Temporary***

Staple, Chief, main, principal, leading, predominant. ***Minor***

Starchy, Stiff, formal, prim, rigid, exact, precise, punctilious. ***Free***

Stare, Look, gape, gaze.

Stark, *a.,* Rigid, stiff. ***Relaxed***

Absolute, sheer, downright, pure, simple, bare, gross, mere, unadulterated.

adv., Quite, wholly, absolutely, entirely, completely, fully. ***Partially***

Starry, Astral, lustrous, shining, bright, twinkling, brilliant, effulgent, sparkling. ***Dull***

Start, *v.a.,* Begin, institute, commence, initiate, evoke. ***End***

Rouse, disturb, scare, alarm, fright, startle.

v.n., Begin, commence, originate, arise, depart.

Wince, spring, flinch, shrink.

n., Beginning, commencement, outset, sally.

Movement, motion, fit, spasm.

Startle, Astonish, surprise, amaze, shock, astound, dumbfound, affright, frighten, alarm. ***Compose***

Startling, Astonishing, surprising,† unforeseen, unexpected, sudden, alarming. ***Stale***

Starve, *v.n.,* Perish, fail, famish, lack, want. ***Fatten***

v.a., Kill, deprive.

Starved, Famished, thin, lean, meagre, attenuated, emaciated, lank, gaunt. ***Fat***

State, *v.a.,* Assert, declare, asseverate, affirm, say, express, utter, specify, aver, maintain, avow, propound, narrate, recite. ***Deny***

n., Condition, position, case, situation, plight, pass, predicament, status, phase. Nation, country, commonwealth. ***Individual***

Pomp, majesty, display, grandeur, glory, parade, dignity, magnificence, splendour, rank, quality.

Stately, Pompous, majestic, grand,† imposing, lofty, imperial, regal, royal, princely, noble, august. ***Mean***

Statement, Assertion, declaration, saying, asseveration, expression, utterance, averment, avowal, narration, narrative, account, announcement, specification, recital.

Station, *v.a.,* Fix, post, locate, place, establish. ***Move***

n., Post, location, position, place, seat, situation, depot, terminal.

Position, standing, rank, status, degree, condition, character.

Stationary, Still, fixed, immovable, motionless, stable, quiescent. ***Mobile***

Stature, Height, size, tallness.

Status, Standing, rank, degree, station, condition, footing, position.

Statute, Decree, order, law, ordinance, regulation, enactment, act, edict. ***Precedent***

Staunch, Resolute, zealous, trusty, firm, steady, reliable, faithful, steadfast, loyal, strong, constant, unswerving, hearty, unwavering, stout, sound. ***Treacherous***

Stave, Ward, parry, forfend, fend, delay, burst. ***Provoke***

Stay, *v.a.,* Stop, hinder, halt, restrain, delay, arrest, detain, stall, obstruct, impede, check, curb, withhold, prevent. ***Hasten***

Uphold, sustain, support, prop.

v.n., Stop, halt, wait, linger, tarry, delay, rest, abide, sojourn, remain, repose. ***Move***

n., Stop, halt, wait.†

Prop, support, staff, buttress.

Steadfast, Firm, unwavering, resolute, unswerving, resolved, staunch, constant, fixed, grounded, fast, rooted, steady, pertinacious, persevering, unchangeable, stable. ***Vacillating***

Steady, Steadfast, firm, unwavering.†

Uniform, equable, regular, constant, undeviating, stable. ***Irregular***

Steal, Pilfer, purloin, take, embezzle, filch, thieve, peculate, smuggle.

Stealthy, Furtive, sly, clandestine, secret, underhanded, surreptitious, skulking, sneaking, private, dark, hidden, covert. ***Open***

Steam, *v.n.,* Evaporate, fume, smoke.

n., Vapour, fume, smoke, mist, reek.

Steamer, Steamship, steamboat, liner, ship, boat, vessel.

Steel, *v.a.,* Brace, nerve, prepare, fortify, strengthen, harden. ***Relax***

n., Iron, knife, blade, sword.

Vigour, sternness, hardness.

Steep, *v.a.,* Imbue, dip, soak, imbrue, permeate, pervade, macerate, drench, submerge, immerse. ***Exsiccate***

Steep, *a.*, Sheer, abrupt, precipitous, sudden.   *Gradual*

Steer, Pilot, guide, direct, control, rule, govern, conduct.

Stellar ⎤
Stelliferous ⎬ Astral, starry.
Stelliform ⎦

Stem, *v.a.*, Hold, stay, stop, check, resist, oppose, withstand, dam. •   *Liberate*
n., Body, stalk, trunk, branch, stock.   *Root*

Stench, Smell, odour, stink, effluvium, fetor.

Stentorian, Loud, powerful, thundering, bellowing, sonorous, deafening.   *Gentle*

Step, Pace, footfall, stride, gait, walk.
Stair, tread, rung.
Gradation, grade, remove, degree.
Proceeding, action, method, means, deed, thing, measure.

Sterile, Barren, infertile, infecund, unproductive, bare, unprolific, unfruitful, desert.   *Fertile*

Sterling, Sound, genuine, solid, true, pure, substantial, real.   *Specious*

Stern, Severe, strict, hard, inexorable, harsh, unbending, inflexible, austere, dour, rigid, grim, unrelenting, forbidding, unyielding.   *Lenient*

Stew, Cook, simmer, boil, seethe.
Confusion, scrape, mess, difficulty.

Stick, *v.a.*, Fix, attach, glue, paste, set.   *Remove*
Stab, thrust, transfix, pierce, penetrate.
v.n., Adhere, cling, cleave, stay, stop, remain, persist, scruple.   *Move*
n., Rod, cane, birch, club, staff, switch, stake, pole.

Sticky, Gummy, gluey, viscid, adhesive, glutinous, mucilaginous.   *Dry*

Stiff, Unbending, inflexible, rigid, firm, unpliant, unyielding.   *Pliant*
Tenacious, pertinacious, obstinate, stubborn, difficult, uncompromising.   *Easy*
Prim, constrained, starchy, stringent, strict, rigorous, severe, dogmatic, frigid, precise, ceremonious.   *Affable*
Crude, ungainly, cramped, inelegant, abrupt.   *Yielding*

Stifle, Choke, suffocate, smother, muffle, extinguish, quench, repress, suppress, subdue, deaden, muzzle, still. *Ventilate*

Stigmatize, Denounce, brand, reproach, defame, discredit, disgrace, dishonour, slur.   *Eulogize*

Still, *v.a.*, Quiet, calm, silence, placate, compose, lull, appease, pacify, subdue, tranquillize, smooth, check, suppress, hush, allay, alleviate, stop.   *Aggravate*

Still, *a.*, Quiet, calm, silent,† noiseless, mute, serene, inert, motionless, stationary.   *Agitated*
adv., Nevertheless, notwithstanding, yet, however.
Continually, ever, always, again.
n., Distillery, retort.

Stilly, Still, calm, quiet, peaceful, silent, tranquil, undisturbed, serene, placid.   *Stormy*

Stilted, Bombastic, pompous, turgid, grandiose, grandiloquent, pretentious, inflated.   *Simple*

Stimulate, Spur, goad, urge, prick, incite, inflame, kindle, animate, excite, rouse, wake, awaken, prompt, instigate, impel, inspirit, encourage, provoke.   *Deter*

Stimulus, Spur, incentive, incitement,† goad.   *Deterrent*

Sting, Wound, prick, afflict, hurt, pain.

Stingy, Mean, parsimonious, near, close, selfish, niggardly, illiberal, avaricious, miserly, covetous.   *Generous*

Stink, Stench, odour, fetor, effluvium, smell.

Stint, Limit, ration, pinch, begrudge, confine, restrain, bound.   *Lavish*

Stipend, Salary, remuneration, income, emolument, allowance, fee, honorarium, living, pay, wages, hire.   *Gratuity*

Stipulate, Contract, agree, engage, bargain, provide, condition.   *Deprecate*

Stipulation, Contract, agreement, condition, engagement, bargain, obligation.   *Refusal*

Stir, *v.a.*, Move, rouse, agitate, disturb, upset, excite, stimulate, goad, prick, urge, incite, instigate, spur, provoke, animate, awaken, prompt, impel.   *Still*
v.n., Move, go, appear, happen, budge.   *Stay*
n., Excitement, agitation, bustle, flurry, commotion, tumult, disorder, confusion, uproar, activity, hurry, bother, *pother*, fuss.   *Tranquillity*

Stirring, Moving, exciting, rousing, thrilling, animated, lively, active, brisk, diligent.   *Dull*

Stock, *v.a.*, Keep, store, reserve, hoard, save.
n., Store, reserve, hoard, supply, provision, accumulation.
Capital, property, principal, fund.
Body, trunk, stalk, stem.
Post, log, block, stake.
Handle, butt, haft.
Family, race, lineage, line, descent, house, ancestry, parentage, pedigree, breed.
a., Commonplace, usual, standard, stale, permanent, hackneyed.   *New*

Stoical, Philosophic, patient, cool, calm, indifferent, apathetic, phlegmatic, imperturbable, passionless, impassive. *Excitable*

Stolen, Pilfered, filched, purloined.

Stolid, Dull, foolish, stupid, heavy, phlegmatic, senseless, stubborn, slow, doltish, obtuse. *Quick*

Stomach, *n.*, Appetite, liking, relish, taste, leaning, desire, proclivity, inclination. *Dislike*
v.a., Swallow, tolerate, bear, abide, endure, brook, stand.

Stone, Boulder, rock, pebble, cobble. Jewel, gem.

Stony, Hard, flinty, fixed, rigid, cruel, inflexible, obdurate, adamantine, unfeeling, pitiless, inexorable. *Tender*

Stoop, Bend, cower, crouch, kneel, yield, condescend, descend, succumb, submit, surrender, bow. *Rise*

Stop, *v.a.*, Hinder, obstruct, impede, delay, stay, restrain, check, hold, repress, suppress, block, close, preclude, prevent, thwart. *Expedite*
Discontinue, end, terminate, cease, conclude, finish, arrest, suspend. *Continue*
v.n., Cease, end, terminate, conclude, finish, discontinue, halt, pause, stall, rest, tarry, desist.
n., Cessation, end, termination, break, interruption, intermission, conclusion, halt. *Continuity*
Impediment, bar, obstruction, obstacle.

Store, *v.a.*, Save, husband, treasure, garner, stock, reserve, hoard, accumulate. *Disperse*
n., Stock, supply, reserve, hoard, fund, accumulation, provision, treasure, abundance, deposit, garner.
Shop, market, emporium.

Storm, *v.n.*, Fume, rage, rant, scold, fret, bluster.
v.a., Assail, assault, attack. *Repel*
n., Tempest, hurricane, squall, tornado, gale. *Calm*
Turmoil, clamour, outbreak, attack, assault, onslaught.

Stormy, Tempestuous, blustering, wild, violent, furious, boisterous, rough, gusty, squally. *Still*

Story, Tale, narrative, narration, recital, account, rehearsal, relation, record, history, legend, anecdote.

Stout, Fat, corpulent, plump, round, rotund, obese, burly, large. *Thin*
Sturdy, strong, stalwart, lusty, vigorous, brawny, robust, hardy, staunch, valiant, bold. *Weak*

Straggle, Stray, rove, wander, roam, range, ramble, digress, err, deviate. *Abide*

Straight, Direct, undeviating, vertical, unswerving, near, short, perpendicular, retilinear, upright, right, erect. *Crooked*
Honest, fair, square, just, equitable, upright, straightforward, conscientious, honourable. *Dishonest*

Straightforward, Straight, honest, fair,† truthful, trustworthy, reliable, veracious, open, frank, sincere. *Deceitful*
Direct, plain, simple, straight.

Straightway, Forthwith, immediately, directly. *Soon*

Strain, *v.a.*, Wrench, sprain, stretch, tighten, force, exert, fatigue, tax, tire, press, squeeze, embrace, hug. *Relax*
Filter, filtrate, percolate, defecate, clarify, depurate, purify. *Thicken*
n., Wrench, sprain, tension, stress, exertion, fatigue. *Relaxation*
Manner, tendency, style.
Streak, element, smack.
Race, family, stock, pedigree, extraction.
Melody, tune, tone, song, lay, stove.

Strait, *n.*, Pass, predicament, difficulty, dilemma, plight, perplexity, exigency, distress.
a., Narrow, confined, limited, close, restricted, constrained, severe, rigorous, strict. *Broad*

Straitened, Difficult, reduced, limited, pinched. *Easy*

Strand, Shore, coast, beach.
Thread, fibre.

Stranded, Lost, ashore, wrecked, castaway, aground. *Rescued*

Strange, Uncommon, unusual, extraordinary, rare, unique, exceptional, surprising, odd, irregular, abnormal, singular, curious, anomalous, unnatural, unaccountable, inexplicable, peculiar, mysterious, wonderful, astonishing, new, marvellous, unfamiliar, exotic, alien, foreign, novel, queer. *Common*

Stranger, Alien, foreigner, visitor, outsider, newcomer. *Acquaintance*

Strangle, Throttle, suffocate, smother, choke, repress, suppress.

Stratagem, Ruse, artifice, scheme, wile, trick, manoeuvre, machination, device, plot, plan, contrivance, fetch. *Blunder*

Stray, *v.n.*, Err, wander, roam, rove, range, deviate, depart, ramble, swerve, digress. *Abide*
a., Strayed, erring, wandering,† sporadic, scattered.

Streak, Strip, stripe, line, band, vein, bar. Strain, element, smack.

Stream, *v.n.*, Flow, pour, issue, run, emanate. *Halt*
n., Brook, course, beck, burn, rivulet, run, current, tide, drift, gush, flow, rush, race.

Streamer, Pennon, flag, banner, ensign, standard.

Strength, Force, vigour, power, might, potency, nerve, puissance, sinew, energy, intensity, boldness, vehemence. *Weakness*
Validity, soundness, cogency, efficacy. *Hollowness*

Strengthen, Encourage, invigorate, steel, nerve, hearten, harden, energize, brace, fortify. *Weaken*
Increase, confirm, establish, support. *Shake*

Strenuous, Energetic, persistent, active, vigorous, earnest, zealous, ardent, keen, determined, resolute, eager. *Feeble*

Stress, *n.*, Urgency, strain, force, effort, tension, pull, weight, pressure, exigency, importance. *Triviality*
Accent, emphasis, weight.
v.a., Emphasize, accent.

Stretch, *v.a.*, Expand, extend, strain, elongate, tighten, spread, lengthen, display, unfold. *Shorten*
v.n., Expand, extend, reach, spread. *Contract*
n., Reach, extension, extent, range, compass, scope.

Strew, Spread, scatter, diffuse, sow, broadcast.

Stricken, Afflicted, smitten, wounded, struck, bruised.

Strict, Stern, austere, severe, rigorous, harsh, exacting, stringent. *Lenient*
Careful, particular, exact, precise, close, accurate, scrupulous. *Loose*

Stricture, Censure, blame, reprehension, animadversion, criticism. *Praise*

Stride, Step, gait, walk, stalk.

Strident, Harsh, grating, creaking, loud. *Soft*

Strife, Battle, conflict, contest, struggle, contention, disagreement, discord, brawl, quarrel, squabble, animosity, dispute. *Peace*

Strike, *v.a.*, Hit, touch, meet, beat, smite, knock, buffet, thump. *Caress*
v.n., Collide, touch, meet, clash, hit.
n., Revolt, lockout, mutiny.

Striking, Impressive, forcible, wonderful, moving, affecting, extraordinary. *Commonplace*

String, Cord, file, line, thread, twine, row, concatenation, series.

Stringent, Strict, stern, austere, severe, rigorous, harsh, exacting, binding. *Lenient*

Strip, *v.a.*, Peel, divest, deprive, denude, bare, skin, expose, rob, plunder, sack, loot, dismantle, fleece, shear, uncover. *Clothe*
v.n., Undress, disrobe, uncover. *Dress*
n., Piece, shred, slip, fragment, ribbon.

Stripe, Streak, line, band.
Lash, stroke, cut, blow.

Stripling, Youth, lad, boy.

Strive, Struggle, labour, toil, try, aim, endeavour, attempt, strain. *Yield*
Compete, contend, fight, struggle, vie.

Stroke, Blow, cut, hit, knock, thump, rap, cuff.
Caress, rub.
Attack, fit, shock, paralysis.

Stroll, *v.n.*, Ramble, roam, range, rove, wander, stray, straggle, walk.
n., Ramble, rambling, roving, excursion, walk, tour, trip. *Run*

Strong, Forceful, vigorous, powerful, mighty, potent, puissant, sinewy, hardy, energetic, intense, bold, vehement, firm, sturdy, robust, athletic, brawny, stout, stalwart, muscular, lusty, sound, healthy, hale, solid, zealous, tenacious, staunch, eager, ardent. *Weak*
Valid, sound, confirmed, binding, cogent, efficacious. *Hollow*
Hot, spicy, racy, piquant, biting, sharp, pungent. *Insipid*
Glaring, dazzling, intense, brilliant, vivid. *Feeble*

Stronghold, Fortification, fortress, fort, keep, castle, defence, bulwark, citadel, fastness, refuge.

Structure, Building, edifice, pile, fabric.
Make, composition, construction, form, constitution, erection, building, texture, formation. *Demolition*

Struggle, *v.n.*, Strive, fight, contend, try, wrestle, endeavour, labour, toil, writhe, flounder. *Yield*
n., Strife, fight, contention, contest, conflict, battle. *Peace*
Toil, effort, labour, exertion, pains, agony, distress, trouble, endeavour. *Ease*

Strumpet, Prostitute, whore, harlot, trull, courtezan.

Stubborn, Wilful, obstinate, perverse, unbending, unyielding, inflexible, stiff, unpliant, tough, hard, refractory, unruly, headstrong, contumacious, firm, mulish, positive, dogged, intractable, obdurate, unmanageable, ungovernable, indocile. *Docile*

Stubby, Short, stocky, truncated, thick, obtuse, blunt. **Long**

Studied, Wilful, deliberate, considered, premeditated. **Spontaneous**

Studious, Diligent, thoughtful, reflective, contemplative, meditative, attentive, careful, scholarly, lettered. **Thoughtless**

Study, *v.a.*, Learn, examine, read, scan, ponder, contemplate, search, watch, investigate, scrutinize. **Ignore**
v.n., Think, reflect, meditate, consider, ponder, muse, cogitate, work. **Dream**
n., Learning, thought, application, work, meditation, consideration, cogitation, contemplation, reflection, inquiry, research, diligence. **Idleness**

Stuff, *v.a.*, Crowd, pack, squeeze, cram, press, stow.
n., Material, cloth, fabric, substance, matter.

Stuffing, Padding, packing, wadding. Forcemeat, dressing.

Stuffy, Fusty, close, hot, musty. **Fresh**

Stumble, Fall, trip, err, stagger, lurch, blunder, chance, slip, happen.

Stump, Block, log, stub.

Stun, Stupefy, overpower, overcome, confound, overwhelm, dumbfound, amaze, bewilder, astonish. **Reassure**

Stunt, Performance, sensation, agitation, feat.

Stunted, Small, dwarfish, diminutive, little, tiny, undersized, pygmy, short. **Large**

Stupefy, Stun, benumb, dull, muddle, blunt, confuse, daze, petrify, bewilder, confound. **Revive**

Stupendous, Astounding, astonishing, amazing, marvellous, wonderful, vast, surprising, wondrous, tremendous, overwhelming, immense, prodigious. **Ordinary**

Stupid, Dull, senseless, witless, foolish, doltish, dazed, insensate, stolid, simple, sluggish, torpid, heavy, flat, lethargic, tiresome, idiotic, asinine. **Sagacious**

Stupor, Torpidity, torpor, stupefaction, dizziness, coma, lethargy, numbness, daze.

Sturdy, Stalwart, strong, stout, bold, hardy, powerful, brawny, athletic, firm, vigorous, muscular, robust, forcible, healthy. **Weak**

Stutter, Stammer, halt, falter, hesitate, stumble.

Stygian, Murky, gloomy, dark, black, sombre, sunless, rayless. **Celestial**

Style, *v.a.*, Call, name, dub, denominate, entitle, christen.
n., Manner, way, mode, form, method, kind, shape, character, vogue, fashion, pattern.
Phraseology, expression, diction, artistry.

Stylish, Fashionable, elegant, smart, modish, courtly, *à la mode*. **Dowdy**

Suavity, Gentleness, urbanity, agreeableness, sweetness, mildness, geniality, softness, pleasantness, affability, conciliatoriness, complaisance, politeness, courtesy, civility, decorum, amiability, evenness. **Harshness**

Subaltern, Subordinate, inferior.

Subdivision, Portion, piece, section, share, part.

Subdue, Subject, conquer, vanquish, overcome, overpower, overwhelm, foil, overbear, subjugate, beat, rout, defeat, discomfit, master, worst, crush, check, control, reduce, restrain, quell, tame, discipline. **Free**

Subject, *v.a.*, Subdue, conquer, vanquish.†
Expose, treat, submit, refer, surrender, undergo, abandon.
n., Subordinate, dependant. **Sovereign**
Thesis, theme, matter, text, topic.
a., Subordinate, dependent, obedient, subservient, inferior. **Superior**

Subjection, Subordination, dependence.† **Mastery**
Subjugation, subjecting, subduing, rout, conquering, conquest, defeat. **Independence**

Subjective, Internal, mental, intellectual, inward, imagined, illusory, fancied, introspective. **Objective**

Subjugate, Subject, subdue, conquer, rout, vanquish, overcome, overpower, overwhelm, master, beat, defeat, crush, overbear, discomfit, worst, check, quell, control, reduce, restrain, quash, tame. **Liberate**

Subjugation, Subjection, conquest, rout.†

Subjunctive, Annexed, added, joined, attached, subjoined. **Unattached**

Sublimate, Exalt, ennoble, dignify, refine, elevate, heighten, purify. **Degrade**

Sublime, Exalted, noble, dignified,† lofty, raised, stately, grand, majestic, eminent, glorious, superb, magnificent, fine. **Ridiculous**

Submerge } Drown, immerse, plunge,
Submerse } duck, dip, deluge, flood, overwhelm, sink, inundate, steep. **Raise**

Submissive, Docile, tractable, yielding, compliant, pliant, obedient, resigned, meek, passive, uncomplaining, humble, acquiescent, obsequious, subservient, amenable, patient. **Obstinate**

Submit, *v.n.*, Surrender, yield, succumb, capitulate, acquiesce. **Resist**

Submit, *v.a.*, Present, propose, suggest, refer.

Subordinate, *n.*, Dependant, subaltern, inferior, junior, underling. *Superior* *a.*, Dependent, inferior, junior, minor, secondary, subservient, ancillary.

Subscribe, Contribute, accede, consent, agree, assent.

Subsequent, Later, succeeding, following, after, ensuing, posterior. *Former*

Subservient, Instrumental, useful, helpful, serviceable, auxiliary, ancillary, subsidiary.
Obsequious, servile, slavish, cringing, inferior, subordinate. *Independent*

Subside, Sink, fall, settle, ebb, decrease, drop, diminish, wane, abate, lull, lessen, descend. *Rise*

Subsidence, Sinking, fall, settling,† refluence.

Subsidiary, Subservient, instrumental, useful, helpful, serviceable, auxiliary, ancillary, aiding, assistant, co-operating, corroborative. *Obstructive*

Subsidy, Aid, grant, dole, co-operation, help, support.

Subsist, Live, be, exist, continue, abide, manage, prevail, persist, endure. *Die*

Subsistence, Living, livelihood, existence, support, sustenance, provisions, maintenance, food, rations. *Death*

Substance, Material, matter, stuff, body, substantiality, reality, element, groundwork. *Shadow*
Gist, kernel, essence, meaning, import, drift, soul.
Wealth, means, property, income, estate, resources. *Poverty*

Substantial, Material, real, solid, actual, positive, existing, true, corporeal.
Imaginary
Firm, massive, valid, strong.

Substantiate, Prove, ratify, strengthen, confirm, corroborate, verify, establish.
Refute

Substantive, Name, noun.

Substitute, *v.a.*, Commute, exchange, replace, change, shift, duplicate, depute.
Fix
n., Agent, deputy, lieutenant, proxy, makeshift, equivalent.

Subterfuge, Artifice, stratagem, fetch, wile, trick, pretext, pretence, evasion, tergiversation, shuffle, quirk, dodge, excuse, shift. *Frankness*

Subtile } Cunning, clever, crafty, artful,
Subtle } ingenious, deep, shrewd, keen, smart, sly, astute, acute, arch, sharp, sophistical, designing, Jesuitical, Machiavellian. *Simple*

Subtract, Withdraw, deduct, remove, take. *Add*

Suburbs, Outskirts, environs, purlieus, confines, neighbourhood. *Centre*

Subversive, Revolutionary, destructive, upsetting. *Conservative*

Subvert, Destroy, upset, overthrow, overturn, demolish, ruin, raze, reverse, corrupt, injure, pervert. *Conserve*

Succeed, *v.n.*, Thrive, prosper, flourish, prevail. *Fail*
Ensue, follow, supervene, inherit.
Precede
v.a., Follow, replace.

Success, Prosperity, happiness, fortune, luck, victory, achievement, attainment, result, triumph. *Failure*

Successful, Prosperous, happy, lucky, fortunate, felicitous, auspicious, profitable, triumphant, victorious. *Unlucky*

Succession, Chain, series, concatenation, continuity, consecution, sequence, cycle, round, rotation. *Intermission*

Succinct, Brief, concise, compact, curt, condensed, compendious, close, short, terse, pithy, laconic, summary. *Prolix*

Succour, *v.a.*, Help, relieve, aid, support, tend, cherish, foster, nurse, assist, comfort, refresh. *Oppress*
n., Help, relief.†

Succulent, Juicy, moist, sappy, luscious, nutritive. *Dry*

Succumb, Surrender, yield, give, submit, capitulate, acquiesce, die. *Resist*

Such, So, similar, like.

Suckling, Babe, baby, infant, nursling, child. *Adult*

Sudatory, Sweating, perspiring.

Sudden, Abrupt, unanticipated, quick, unexpected, unforeseen, hurried, rapid, unpremeditated, fleet, brief, momentary.
Gradual

Sue, Summon, prosecute, solicit, petition, plead. *Defend*

Suffer, Bear, sustain, undergo, experience, feel, endure, tolerate, brook, allow, let, permit, admit. *Repel*

Suffering, *n.*, Pain, agony, misery, distress, passion, discomfort, torment.
Ease
a., Pained, agonized.†

Sufficient, Enough, adequate, ample, full, competent, capable, plentiful, plenteous.
Deficient

Suffix, Addition, ending, termination.
Prefix

Suffocate, Stifle, strangle, smother, choke, asphyxiate, extinguish.

Suffrage, Ballot, franchise, testimonial, vote, witness.

Suffuse, Cover, overspread, moisten, colour.

Suggest, Insinuate, indicate, intimate, hint, propose, advise, prompt, counsel, recommend. *Dictate*

Suggestion, Insinuation, allusion, plan, indication.† *Demand*

Suit, *v.a.*, Gratify, please, befit, fit, adapt, adjust, beseem, become, answer, match, accommodate. *Misfit*

v.n., Answer, tally, correspond, accord, comport, harmonize, agree. *Differ*

n., Address, solicitation, request, prayer, petition, entreaty.

Case, action, trial, cause.

Costume, habit, clothing.

Suitable, Convenient, appropriate, fit, proper, fitting, pertinent, becoming, apt, agreeable, relevant, apposite. *Inconvenient*

Suite, Set, collection, retinue, following, followers, escort, bodyguard, *cortège*, staff, train.

Suitor, Sweetheart, lover, admirer, wooer, gallant.

Petitioner, litigant, applicant.

Sulky, Morose, sullen, cross, splenetic, sour, surly, churlish, testy, moody, vexatious, perverse, glowering, lowering. *Genial*

Sullen, Sulky, morose, cross, splenetic.† *Cheerful*

Sully, Soil, taint, stain, defile, pollute, dirty, contaminate, tarnish, spot, spoil, disgrace, defame, slur. *Cleanse*

Sultry, Close, hot, warm, oppressive, humid, stuffy, stifling. *Cool*

Sum, Total, totality, aggregate, whole, entirety, amount. *Part*

Summarily, Briefly, concisely, shortly.

Summary, *n.*, Abstract, digest, epitome, breviary, synopsis, précis, compendium, conspectus, abridgment, syllabus, outline. *Amplification*

a., Curt, short, brief, terse, laconic, compendious, concise, succinct, pithy, condensed, rapid, quick. *Protracted*

Summit, Top, apex, zenith, acme, height, vertex, culmination, pinnacle, crown. *Base*

Summon, Call, bid, invoke, invite, cite, prosecute, charge, sue, arraign, subpoena. *Discharge*

Sumptuous, Rich, magnificent, superb, stately, costly, dear, expensive, grand, gorgeous, munificent, extravagant, splendid, luxurious. *Poor*

Sunder, Sever, dissever, disjoin, part, disunite, dispart, divide, dissociate, separate. *Join*

Sundry, Various, manifold, different, divers, several, many. *One*

Sunless, Dark, black, clouded, rayless, shaded, shady, beamless, unilluminated, dismal, gloomy, murky. *Bright*

Sunny, Bright, radiant, brilliant, clear, shining, warm, fine, unclouded. *Dark*

Joyful, happy, cheerful. *Gloomy*

Superable, Achievable, surmountable, conquerable, vincible, possible. *Invincible*

Superabundant, Superfluous, excessive, abundant, teeming, luxuriant, redundant, exuberant. *Scarce*

Superannuated, Old, aged, effete, passé, decrepit, antiquated, retired, pensioned. *Active*

Superb, Magnificent, gorgeous, stately, grand, sumptuous, splendid, august, noble, excellent, wonderful, majestic, exquisite, elegant. *Poor*

Supercilious, Proud, insolent, haughty, arrogant, domineering, overbearing, contemptuous, disdainful, scornful, lordly, overweening. *Respectful*

Supererogation, Needlessness, excess, redundancy, superabundance, surfeit, superfluity. *Deficiency*

Superficial, Light, shallow, slight, outer, external, showy, outward, exterior. *Profound*

Superfine, Choice, superior, excellent, prime.

Superfluous, Needless, superabundant, excessive, redundant, useless, exuberant, luxuriant, unnecessary. *Deficient*

Superhuman, Preternatural, miraculous, divine, supernatural, herculean. *Natural*

Superintend, Inspect, supervise, direct, manage, administer, control, conduct, oversee, overlook.

Superintendent, Inspector, supervisor, manager, overseer, director, controller, conductor, master, guardian, custodian, warder, warden. *Servant*

Superior, Better, higher, high, loftier, paramount, finer, supreme, matchless, unrivalled, superlative, excellent, good, preferable. *Inferior*

Principal, head, chief.

Superlative, Incomparable, excellent, supreme, transcendant, peerless. *Ordinary*

Supernumerary, Superfluous, surplus, unnecessary, odd, redundant.

Supersede, Displace, remove, overrule, suspend, replace, supplant, override. *Perpetuate*

Superstitious, Credulous, bigoted, simple, fanatical. *Sceptical*

Supervene, Happen, occur, succeed, accrue. *Pass*

Supervise, Superintend,† inspect, direct, manage, control, conduct. *Misdirect*

Supine, Lazy, torpid, languid, careless, sluggish, slothful, lethargic, otiose, idle, indolent, inert, slack, indifferent, dull, apathetic, sleepy, drowsy, inattentive, heedless, listless, thoughtless, negligent. *Energetic*
Recumbent, prostrate. *Upright*

Supplant, Supersede, displace, replace, remove, oust, overthrow, undermine. *Retain*

Supple, Yielding, pliable, pliant, flexible, flexile, elastic, bending, lithe. *Stiff*
Submissive, compliant, yielding, fawning, obsequious, sycophantic, grovelling, flattering, servile, slavish, adulatory, cringing. *Firm*

Supplement, *n.*, Addendum, addition, appendix, postscript, sequel, continuation.
v.a., Add, supply, fill. *Deduct*

Suppliant, *n.*, Supplicant, petitioner, suitor.
a., Supplicating, petitioning, begging, praying, imploring, craving, entreating, beseeching, asking, pleading. *Domineering*

Supplicate, Petition, beg, pray, implore, crave, entreat, beseech, ask, importune, solicit, plead. *Demand*

Supplication, Petition, prayer, entreaty, solicitation, request, invocation, pleading.

Supply, *v.a.*, Afford, provide, stock, equip, furnish, grant, give, contribute, bestow. *Consume*
n., Provision, stock, accumulation, store, hoard, reserve.

Support, *v.a.*, Forward, further, help, assist, patronize, back, aid, second, favour, advocate, abet, befriend, uphold, encourage, succour, promote, guard, protect, defend, prevent. *Oppose*
Prop, sustain, maintain, uphold, bear, brace, *Drop*
n., Furtherance, help, assistance.† *Opposition*
Sustenance, maintenance, stay, prop.

Suppose, *v.n.*, Imagine, think, conjecture, fancy, guess, opine, consider, conclude, ween, assume, surmise, suspect, believe. *Know*
v.a., Imagine, think, fancy,† judge, imply, presuppose, deem, apprehend, conceive. *Prove*

Supposition, Conjecture, imagination, guess, doubt, uncertainty, assumption, presumption, surmise, presupposition, hypothesis, postulate. *Proof*

Suppress, Repress, smother, restrain, quell, overpower, extinguish, subdue, crush, stifle, conceal, strangle, conquer, overthrow, check, quash. *Excite*

Supremacy, Lordship, mastery, power, sovereignty, pre-eminence, domination, predominance, dominion, ascendancy. *Subjection*

Supreme, Sovereign, pre-eminent, chief, predominant, leading, principal, main, first, foremost, greatest, highest, utmost, paramount. *Lowest*

Surcharge, Overcharge, overload, overburden. *Undercharge*

Sure, Certain, fixed, unerring, assured, secure, steady, permanent, abiding, lasting, enduring, strong, infallible, unfailing, stable, trustworthy, reliable, steady, safe. *Precarious*
Positive, certain, convinced, confident, assured, satisfied. *Doubtful*

Surety, Security, safety, support, pledge, guarantee, bond. *Option*

Surface, Outside, exterior, superfices. *Interior*
Covering, finish, appearance.

Surfeit, *v.a.*, State, satiate, glut, cloy, overfeed, gorge. *Starve*
n., Satiety, glut, excess, superabundance, plethora. *Deficiency*

Surge, *v.n.*, Roll, swell, move, heave, sweep, swirl, rush, rise, tower.
n., Billow, wave, rolling, swell, undulation. *Calm*

Surly, Sullen, sulky, sour, morose, cross, petulant, peevish, waspish, snarling, snappy, testy, touchy, perverse, rude, rough, uncivil, growling, gruff, crabbed, churlish, harsh, crusty, ungracious, fretful. *Affable*

Surmise, *v.a. & n.*, Suppose, imagine, fancy, guess, believe, conjecture, ween, opine, think, divine, assume, suspect, presume. *Know*
n., Supposition, imagination, guess.† *Proof*

Surmount, Overcome, surpass, conquer, meet, vanquish, subdue, climb, scale, clear. *Succumb*

Surpass, Eclipse, exceed, pass, outstrip, beat, excel, surmount, outdo, outvie, transcend. *Equal*

Surplus, *n.*, Remainder, residue, excess, balance, overplus. *Deficit*
a., Superfluous, unnecessary, needless.

Surprise, *v.a.*, Stagger, amaze, startle, astound, stun, astonish, dumbfound, bewilder, confuse. *Forewarn*
n., Shock, blow.

Surprise, Amazement, astonishment, confusion, bewilderment, wonder.

Surprising, Staggering, amazing, extraordinary, startling, astounding, wonderful, astonishing, marvellous, unexpected, remarkable.   ***Ordinary***

Surrender, *v.a.,* Resign, relinquish, cede, abandon, sacrifice, yield, give, waive, renounce, abdicate, forego.   ***Hold***
v.n., Submit, capitulate, yield.
n., Submission, capitulation, resignation, yielding, delivery, abandonment. ***Victory***

Surreptitious, Clandestine, underhand, stealthy, furtive, secret, hidden, sly.   ***Open***

Surrogate, Delegate, deputy, proxy, substitute, representative.

Surround, Environ, encircle, enclose, encompass, invest, hem, girdle, loop, beset.

Surveillance, Supervision, watch, care, superintendence, direction, inspection, charge, control, investigation, oversight.   ***Freedom***

Survey, *v.a.,* Scan, review, view, see, inspect, observe, reconnoitre, overlook, contemplate, scrutinize, examine. ***Ignore***
Estimate, plot, measure.
n., Review, inspection, scrutiny, sight, examination, retrospect, prospect.

Survive, Outlive, endure, subsist, abide, last.   ***Succumb***

Susceptible, Sensitive, impressionable, impressible, capable, inclined, predisposed.   ***Insensitive***

Suspect, Doubt, mistrust, distrust. ***Trust***
Conjecture, imagine, guess, surmise, think, consider, fancy, believe, suppose.   ***Know***

Suspend, Stop, delay, interrupt, discontinue, dismiss, debar, postpone, stay, hinder, arrest, intermit.   ***Continue***
Swing, hang, append.   ***Drop***

Suspense, Uncertainty, abeyance, doubt, hesitation, incertitude, indetermination, indecision, irresolution, waiting, wavering, vacillation, stoppage.   ***Decision***

Suspicious, Distrustful, unbelieving, suspecting, mistrustful.   ***Trustful***
Doubtful, questionable, strange.

Sustain, Support, uphold, maintain, help, bear, aid, assist, succour, relieve, comfort.   ***Weaken***
Suffer, bear, receive, endure, undergo, feel, experience.
Sanction, establish, confirm, approve, justify, ratify.   ***Suppress***

Sustenance, Support, subsistence, food, nourishment, nutrition, aliment, provision, nutriment.   ***Starvation***

Swagger, Brag, vaunt, boast, bluster, hector.   ***Crawl***

Swallow, Absorb, consume, eat, gulp, gorge, engross, imbibe, digest. ***Vomit***

Swamp, *v.a.,* Flood, inundate, drench, overwhelm, soak, saturate, sink, upset, capsize, wreck, embarrass.
n., Marsh, morass, quagmire, fen, bog, slough.

Sward, Lawn, grass, turf, sod.

Swarm, *v.n.,* Throng, crowd, teem, press, cluster, abound.
n., Throng, crowd, press, mass, shoal, multitude, concourse, flock, bevy, troop, herd, drove, host, army.   ***Sprinkling***

Swarthy, Dark, brown, swart, dusky, tawny.   ***Pale***

Swathe, Swaddle, wrap, bandage, bind, clothe.

Sway, *v.a.,* Wield, influence, govern, rule, direct, move, regulate, control, guide, prejudice.
v.n., Oscillate, swing, vacillate, totter, lean, incline, rock, roll.
n., Dominion, authority, influence, rule, direction, government, regulation, power, control, guidance, command, sovereignty.   ***Subordination***

Swear, Testify, vouch, avow, declare, assert, depose, affirm, vow, promise, state.   ***Deny***
Blaspheme, curse, profane.

Sweat, *v.n.,* Perspire, exude.
n., Perspiration, sweating, excretion, exudation, ooze, reek.

Sweep, *v.a.,* Brush, clear, clean, scour, rub.   ***Litter***
n., Bend, curve, curvature.
Compass, range, reach, scope.

Sweeping, Broad, comprehensive, wide, extensive, wholesale, exaggerated, unqualified.   ***Qualified***

Sweet, Luscious, sugary, saccharine, honeyed.   ***Bitter***
Gentle, mild, soft, tender, amiable, lovable, benign, benignant, attractive, serene.   ***Sour***
Fragrant, delicate, redolent, balmy, pure, fresh, clean, wholesome, sound. ***Putrid***
Dulcet, melodious, mellifluous, mellow, musical, harmonious, agreeable, silvery, delightful, soft, tuneful. ***Discordant***

Swell, *v.a.,* Enlarge, inflate, enhance, increase, extend, expand, dilate, amplify, augment.   ***Reduce***
v.n., Expand, increase, extend, distend, dilate, protuberate, puff, bulge.   ***Contract***

Swelling, *n.,* Bump, bulge, gathering, protuberance, rise, boil.

Swelling, Enlargement, inflation, expansion, increase, dilatation, augmentation, amplification, distension. *Reduction*

a., Stilted, pompous, inflated, turgid, bombastic, grandiloquent, declamatory, grandiose, pretentious, rhetorical. *Plain*

Swerve, Turn, depart, err, deviate, stray, wander, diverge, waver. *Continue*

Swift, Fast, rapid, speedy, quick, fleet, expeditious, accelerated, nimble, alert, prompt, sudden. *Slow*

Swimmingly, Easily, smoothly, successfully.

Swindle, *v.n.,* Trick, cheat, deceive, hoax, defraud, dupe, victimize, *cozen, chouse.* *n.,* Trick, imposition, deception, fraud, *chouse.* *Honesty*

Swindler, Trickster, cheat, impostor, rogue, villain, knave, scoundrel, sharper.

Swing, Vibrate, dangle, oscillate, sway, vacillate, hang, depend, incline, rock, revolve, brandish.

Swirl, Whirl, gyrate, eddy.

Switch, *v.a.,* Swing, snatch, whisk. Whip, lash, beat, birch, strike. *n.,* Twig, birch, rod, stick, cane. Bypass, shunt.

Swoop, *v.n.,* Descend, rush, stoop. *n.,* Descent, rush, stoop, scoop, seizure.

Sword, Rapier, steel, cutlass, sabre, blade, brand.

Sybarite, Sensualist, epicure, voluptuary. *Ascetic*

Sycophant, Flatterer, fawner, parasite, lickspittle, cringer, toady.

Sycophantic, Flattering, fawning, servile, parasitic, grovelling, obsequious, slavish, adulatory, cringing. *Independent*

Syllabus, Summary, abstract, compend, compendium, breviary, outline, digest, synopsis, epitome, précis, abridgment, skeleton.

Sylvan, Shady, woody.

Symbol, Token, sign, mark, emblem, representation, figure, type, exponent, badge.

Symmetry, Congruity, shapeliness, form, harmony, evenness, order, proportion, regularity, balance. *Disproportion*

Sympathetic, Kind, thoughtful, loving, tender, affectionate, compassionate, pitiful. *Harsh*

Sympathy, Kindness, thoughtfulness,† condolence, commiseration. *Harshness* Agreement, concord, congeniality, concert, harmony, affinity. *Antipathy*

Symphonic, Harmonious, musical, concordant. *Discordant*

Symposium, Festival, feast, banquet, revel.

Symptom, Sign, token, indication, note, mark.

Synchronous, Coincident, simultaneous, contemporaneous.

Syndicate, Trust, combine, combination, union, federation, amalgamation.

Synonymous, Equivalent, tantamount, similar.

Synopsis, Outline, skeleton, syllabus, breviary, abridgment, compend, digest, compendium, summary, abstract, précis, epitome. *Amplification*

Synthesis, Combination, composition, construction. *Analysis*

System, Method, order, plan, scheme, arrangement, rule, theory. *Chaos*

Systematic, Methodical, orderly, regular, intentional. *Casual*

T

TABETIC   **TASTE**

Tabetic, Emaciated, consumptive, wasting, phthisical.   ***Robust***

Table, Index, list, catalogue, syllabus, record, schedule.

Board, slab, counter, plate.

Tableau, Representation, picture, scene.

Taboo, Prohibited, banned, forbidden, barred.

Tacit, Implied, understood, implicit, unexpressed, silent, inferred.   ***Avowed***

Taciturn, Silent, reticent, reserved, mute, uncommunicative, close.   ***Loquacious***

Tack, Fasten, stitch, join, affix, attach, append.

Tackle, Gear, apparatus, equipment, effects, impedimenta, harness, weapon, implements.

Tact, Discrimination, sense, sensitiveness, adroitness, dexterity, judgment, skill, taste, perception, discretion, diplomacy, finesse.   ***Indiscretion***

Tactful, Discriminating, sensible, sensitive.†   ***Indiscreet***

Tactics, Manœuvring, policy, strategy, diplomacy.   ***Blunder***

Tail, End, rump, finish, conclusion, extremity.   ***Head***

Taint, *v.a.,* Sully, soil, stain, tarnish, begrime, tinge, infect, corrupt, defile, contaminate, befoul, pollute.   ***Purify***

n., Spot, stain, blot, infection, blemish, contamination, defilement, corruption, flaw, defect, fault.

Take, Grasp, clasp, seize, capture, gain, win.   ***Reject***

Hold, adopt, assume.

Accept, receive, get, obtain.

Lead, convey, transfer, carry, conduct.

Tale, Story, narrative, narration, fable, relation, rehearsal, account, romance.

Talent, Genius, capacity, ability, parts, faculty, endowment, aptitude, aptness, cleverness, gift, bent, turn.   ***Imbecility***

Talk, *v.a.,* Utter, speak, pronounce.

v.n., Speak, prate, deliberate, converse, reason, confer, discourse, parley.

n., Parley, conference, deliberation, conversation, discourse, dialogue, colloquy, chat, palaver.

Mention, rumour, report, gossip, scandal.

Talkative, Garrulous, communicative, chatty, chattering, loquacious, verbose.   ***Taciturn***

Tall, High, long, lofty, towering, elevated.   ***Short***

Tally, Agree, square, correspond, match, harmonize, mate, suit, square, accord, coincide, comport, fit.   ***Clash***

Tame, *v.a.,* Domesticate, break in, curb, subdue, subjugate, conquer, repress.

a., Domesticated, meek, subdued, tamed, broken, docile, spiritless, mild, gentle, crushed, submissive.   ***Wild***

Dull, flat, uninteresting, wearisome, tedious, boring, insipid, prosaic.   ***Interesting***

Tamper, Interfere, meddle, intermeddle, dapple.

Tang, Flavour, savour, taste, smack, quality.

Tangible, Material, substantial, real, palpable, plain, evident, obvious, tactile, corporeal, perceptible, solid, positive, concrete.   ***Abstract***

Tangle, *v.a.,* Twist, intertwist, interlace, interweave, intertwine, mat, involve, complicate, embarrass, perplex. ***Unravel***

n., Twist, muddle, jumble, intricacy, complication.

Tantalize, Tease, irritate, aggravate, torment, worry, annoy, provoke, cheat, frustrate, disappoint.   ***Satisfy***

Tantamount, Equivalent, equal.

Tantrum, Outburst, paroxysm, temper, fit.

Tap, Rap, knock, strike, pat, touch.

Tapering, Pointed, conical, narrowing, pyramidal.

Tardy, Slow, late, sluggish, dilatory, slack, loitering, reluctant, leisurely.   ***Prompt***

Target, Mark, objective, object, aim, butt.

Tariff, Tax, impost, charge, schedule, scale.

Tarnish, *v.a.,* Stain, spot, soil, sully, taint, begrime, tinge, infect, corrupt, contaminate, defile, befoul, pollute, dull, deface.   ***Cleanse***

n., Stain, spot, soil,† blemish, fault.

Tarry, Stay, remain, abide, linger, wait, sojourn, loiter, rest, halt, stop, delay.   ***Move***

Tart, Sharp, caustic, acid, bitter, sour, biting, pungent, harsh, virulent, keen, severe, acrimonious, touchy, snarling, testy, petulant.   ***Mild***

Task, Toil, drudgery, labour, work, business, exercise, employment, undertaking.   ***Leisure***

Taste, *v.n.,* Savour, smack.

v.a., Try, feel, experience, undergo.

271

Taste, *n.,* Savour, flavour, piquancy, relish. *Insipidity*
Perception, discrimination, discernment, judgment.
Culture, delicacy, polish, elegance.
Liking, desire, fondness, appetite, desire.

Tasteful, Elegant, smart, refined, quiet. *Ostentatious*

Tasteless, Insipid, vapid, flat, tame, dull, uninspiring, uninteresting. *Savoury*

Tattle, *v.n.,* Prattle, gossip, chatter, prate, babble.
n., Prattle, gossip,† twaddle.

Taunt, *v.a.,* Ridicule, deride, mock, chaff, scorn, flout, revile, upbraid. *Respect*
n., Ridicule, derision, mockery,† gibe, jeer.

Taut, Tense, tight, strained, stretched. *Slack*

Tautology, Iteration, reiteration, redundance, redundancy, repetition, verbosity. *Terseness*

Tawdry, Flashy, gaudy, meretricious, garish, showy. *Tasteful*

Tax, *v.a.,* Try, strain, burden, load, task.
n., Duty, tariff, impost, levy, tribute, toll, charge, custom, excise. *Bounty*

Teach, Educate, instruct, impart, tell, direct, inform, enlighten, show, counsel, admonish, warn, train, school, initiate, discipline, tutor, drill. *Mislead*

Teacher, Master, instructor, preceptor, pedagogue, tutor, adviser, preacher. *Pupil*

Tear, Sunder, sever, rend, split, part, rupture, lacerate, lancinate, laniate. *Mend*

Tearful, Weeping, mournful, maudlin. *Happy*

Tease, Tantalize, worry, aggravate, vex, irritate, provoke, annoy, molest, harass, torment, plague, chafe, disturb. *Pacify*

Techy, Peevish, irritable, touchy, testy, petulant, cross, sour, snarling, sullen, fretful. *Genial*

Tedious, Boring, wearisome, flat, slow, uninteresting, tiresome, fatiguing, irksome. *Interesting*

Teeming, Prolific, swarming, pregnant, multitudinous, overflowing, abundant, numerous. *Sparse*

Tell, Relate, narrate, rehearse, report, recount, describe, mention, communicate, divulge, inform, disclose, publish, reveal, utter, blab, recite, teach. *Repress*
Distinguish, discern, discover.
Count, enumerate, reckon, compute.

Telling, Powerful, potent, effective, pointed. *Weak*

Temerity, Rashness, audacity, boldness, recklessness, precipitancy, precipitation, foolhardiness. *Timidity*

Temper, *v.a.,* Mollify, modify, lessen, abate, qualify, allay, assuage, soften, deaden, blunt, dull, moderate, check, calm, restrain. *Aggravate*
n., Mood, humour, disposition, temperament, constitution, structure.
Anger, irritation, annoyance, passion, disposition, humour. *Calmness*

Temperament, Temper, mood, humour, disposition, habit.

Temperate, Abstemious, sober, sedate, moderate, restrained, cool, mild, calm. *Intemperate*

Tempest, Storm, hurricane, tornado, gale. *Calm*

Tempestuous, Stormy, squally, windy, boisterous, tumultuous, violent. *Calm*

Temporal, Earthly, worldly, mundane, secular, fleeting, transient, material, transitory. *Spiritual*

Temporary, Brief, fleeting, transient, transitory, short, limited, evanescent, ephemeral. *Permanent*

Tempt, Allure, decoy, entice, invite, seduce, inveigle, ensnare, persuade. *Deter*
Prove, try, test, essay, attempt.

Tempting, Attractive, seductive, alluring, enticing. *Repulsive*

Tenable, Sound, maintainable, rational, defensible, reasonable. *Fallacious*

Tenacious, Retentive, cohesive, firm, adhesive, stubborn, obstinate, zealous, dogged, determined, pertinacious. *Weak*

Tenant, Occupant, occupier, dweller, lessee, renter. *Owner*

Tend, *v.n.,* Lean, incline, trend, verge, conduce, contribute, mind. *Diverge*
v.a., Nurture, guard, watch, keep, serve, protect, nurse, accompany. *Desert*

Tendency, Leaning, inclination, trend, drift, bearing, propensity, proclivity, bent, bias, proneness, gravitation, turn, disposition, susceptibility. *Aversion*

Tender, *a.,* Kind, gentle, mild, pitiful, compassionate, lenient, merciful, affectionate, sympathetic. *Harsh*
Delicate, soft, fragile. *Hard*
Painful, sensitive, raw.
v.a., Proffer, offer, present, volunteer, propose, suggest. *Withhold*

Tenebrous, Dark, gloomy, obscure, cloudy, sombre, murky, dusky. *Light*

Tenement, Domicile, house, habitation, abode, dwelling, flat, apartment. *Mansion*

Tenet, Principle, dogma, doctrine, creed, belief, opinion, article. *Protest*

Tenor, Course, direction, drift, purport, intent, aim, meaning, sense. *Variance*

Tense, Strained, tight, taut, stretched, emotional, nervous, intent, exciting. *Slack*

Tension, Straining, stretching, strain, vigour, force, effort, stiffness, nervousness, excitement. *Relaxation*

Tentative, Experimental, speculative, empirical, probative, probatory. *Sure*

Tenuous, Small, slender, thin, minute. *Large*

Tenure, Holding, enjoyment, possession, occupancy, occupation, use.

Tepid, Lukewarm, moderate, mild. *Hot*

Tergiversate, Equivocate, shift, veer, vacillate.

Term, *v.a.*, Denominate, call, style, dub, name, designate, christen, entitle.

n., Denomination, name, designation, title, expression, phrase, word.

Space, season, spell, time, period.

Termagant, Shrew, scold, vixen, virago.

Terminate, End, cease, conclude, finish, stop, close, complete. *Begin*

Termination, End, ending, conclusion, finish, close, extent, limit, effect, issue, consequence, result, upshot. *Beginning*

Terminus, End, destination, boundary, limit, border.

Terrestrial, Earthly, worldly, mundane, sublunary. *Celestial*

Terrible, Awful, dreadful, frightful, fearful, terrifying, horrible, gruesome, shocking, dire, formidable, terrific, dread, severe. *Ordinary*

Terrific, Terrible, awful, dreadful.†

Terrify, Frighten, affright, fright, shock, horrify, appal, alarm, daunt, dismay, scare, startle. *Reassure*

Territory, Country, land, region, district, province, state, domain.

Terror, Fear, horror, alarm, dismay, awe, dread, consternation, fright, panic. *Reassurance*

Terse, Pithy, laconic, brief, compact, concise, succinct, curt, condensed, short, sharp. *Prolix*

Test, *v.a.*, Prove, assay, try, tempt.

n., Proof, trial, experiment, examination, ordeal, essay, attempt.

Criterion, standard, distinction.

Testify, Swear, state, depose, affirm, declare, certify, evidence, assert, attest, avow, vouch. *Deny*

Testimonial, Certificate, recommendation, credential, monument, voucher.

Testimony, Statement, evidence, deposition.†

Testy, Irritable, touchy, peevish, pettish, petulant, cross, sour, crabbed, irascible, acrimonious, captious, splenetic, waspish, snarling, snappy, techy, quick, surly. *Genial*

Tether, Tie, fasten, stake, chain. *Loose*

Text, Subject, theme, topic, clause, thesis, passage, words, treatise.

Texture, Composition, make, structure, fabric, constitution.

Thankful, Obliged, grateful, indebted, beholden, *Ungrateful*

Thankless, Unthankful, ungrateful. *Grateful*

Unprofitable, profitless, unacceptable, disagreeable, unpleasant. *Profitable*

Thaw, Melt, liquefy, dissolve, run, soften, fuse. *Freeze*

Theatre, Field, arena, scene, stage, seat, drama, playhouse.

Theatrical, Ostentatious, melodramatic, histrionic, Thespian, meretricious, scenic, showy, dramatic. *Simple*

Theft, Thieving, thievery, robbery, fraud, larceny, peculation, swindling, pilfering, purloining, stealing.

Theme, Subject, text, matter, thesis, topic, treatise, dissertation, composition.

Thence, Thenceforth, then, therefore. *Whence*

Theoretical, Hypothetical, presumptive, speculative, conjectural, postulatory. *Practical*

Theory, Hypothesis, presumption, conjecture, assumption, speculation, postulate. *Practice*

Thereafter, Subsequently, afterward, accordingly.

Therefore, Consequently, thence, hence, accordingly, so.

Thesaurus, Cyclopaedia, storehouse, lexicon, dictionary, glossary, treasury, repository.

Thesis, Subject, theme, dissertation, topic, essay, paper, proposition, treatise, composition.

Theurgy, Magic, witchcraft, sorcery.

Thews, Brawn, muscles, sinews, strength.

Thick, Condensed, dense, close, crowded, inspissate, inspissated, solid, fat. *Thin*

Misty, foggy, obscure, hazy, cloudy, dirty, muddy, turbid. *Distinct*

Inarticulate, confused, indistinct, hoarse, guttural. *Clear*

Abundant, numerous, multitudinous, frequent. *Sparse*

Familiar, friendly, intimate. *Distant*

Thicken, *v.n.*, Solidify, condense, harden, concrete. *Thin*

v.a., Condense, inspissate, coagulate, compact, confuse, obscure. *Clarify*

Thicket, Coppice, wood, shrubbery, copse, grove.   *Clearing*

Thief, Robber, burglar, peculator, cheat, embezzler, swindler, filcher, pilferer.

Thieve, Rob, peculate, embezzle, cheat, swindle, pilfer, filch, steal, purloin.

Thievery, Robbery, peculation,† theft, larceny.

Thin, Meagre, spare, attenuated, slender, fine, sparse, scanty, slight, gaunt, lean, lank, lanky, small, scraggy, skinny, slim, light, flimsy, delicate, emaciated, poor.   *Fat*

Thing, Something, object, article, body, being, entity, substance, matter.

Think, *v.a.,* Believe, conceive, consider, imagine, fancy, esteem, deem, regard, hold, suppose, judge, reckon.   *Misconceive*

v.n., Meditate, muse, cogitate, ponder, reflect, consider, speculate, ruminate, contemplate, reason, deliberate, understand.

Determine, imagine, fancy, conclude, believe, suppose, reckon, surmise.

Thinking, *n.,* Thought, meditation, cogitation, reflection, contemplation, speculation, rumination, musing, consideration.

a., Rational, reflecting, reasoning, sane.   *Unreflecting*

Thirst, *v.n.,* Crave, yearn, desire, long, hunger, hanker.

n., Craving, yearning,† appetite.

Thirsty, Dry, arid, parched, eager, craving, longing.   *Satisfied*

Thong, Lash, strap, whip, halter, reins.

Thorn, Prickle, spine.

Scourge, bane, infliction, bother, curse, nuisance, annoyance, plague, pest.

Thorny, Prickly, spinous, spiny, sharp, spiky, pointed, difficult, baneful, annoying, hard, vexatious, trying, harassing, troublesome.   *Smooth*

Thorough, Complete, unqualified, total, entire, perfect, downright, radical, unmitigated, absolute, consummate, painstaking, finished, laborious.   *Superficial*

Though, Although, notwithstanding, if, assuming, allowing, admitting, granting. However, nevertheless, yet, still.

Thought, Thinking, meditation, care, reflection, consideration, cogitation, concern, speculation, musing, rumination, contemplation, deliberation, attention, anxiety.   *Vacuity*

Idea, notion, view, fancy, conceit, belief, opinion, judgment, conception, design, intention, purpose.   *Misconception*

Thoughtful, Speculative, rapt, pensive,

reflecting, serious, quiet, contemplative, studious, reflective.   *Idle*

Considerate, mindful, regardful, careful, cautious, heedful, wary, circumspect, discreet, prudent, provident, attentive.   *Heedless*

Thoughtless, Inconsiderate, unmindful, heedless, careless, rash, indiscreet, remiss, imprudent, inattentive, regardless, unthinking, negligent, neglectful, mindless, improvident, trifling, reckless.   *Careful*

Thraldom, Serfdom, servitude, slavery, enslavement, vassalage, captivity, subjection, bondage, confinement.   *Freedom*

Thrash, Beat, whip, flog, drub, chastise, bruise, castigate, conquer, defeat.

Thrasonical, Bragging, vaunting, boasting, boastful, vainglorious.   *Modest*

Thread, Line, cord, string, filament, fibre. Course, continuity, drift, gist, import, tenor.   *Solution*

Threadbare, Worn, old, thin, trite, stale, commonplace, hackneyed.   *New*

Threat, Intimidation, menace, defiance, denunciation, portent.   *Encouragement*

Threaten, Intimidate, denounce, warn, menace, portend, forebode, augur.   *Reassure*

Threshold, Outset, start, entrance, opening, dawn, beginning.   *End*

Thrift, Economy, frugality, saving, care, thriftiness, growth.   *Extravagance*

Thriftless, Extravagant, improvident, unthrifty, prodigal, spendthrift, lavish, wasteful, profuse.   *Economical*

Thrifty, Economical, frugal, saving, careful, thriving, prosperous, provident, sparing.   *Extravagant*

Thrill, *v.a.,* Excite, agitate, affect, move, pierce, touch, rouse, electrify, stir.

n., Sensation, excitement, tremor, shock.

Thrilling, Exciting, stirring, gripping, moving, emotional, sensational.   *Tame*

Thrive, Prosper, flourish, succeed, grow, wax, improve, increase, luxuriate.   *Fail*

Thriving, Prosperous, flourishing, successful.   *Declining*

Throb, *v.n.,* Palpitate, beat, pulsate, vibrate, quiver.

n., Palpitation, beat,† throbbing.

Throe, Anguish, agony, paroxysm, pang.

Throng, *v.n.,* Press, come, go, crowd, flock, congregate.

v.a., Crowd, fill.

n., Crowd, horde, troop, multitude, mob, congregation, assemblage.

Throttle, Choke, suffocate, smother, strangle.

Through, During, throughout, within, among, consequently.

Throw, *v.a.,* Cast, fling, toss, hurl, propel, project, sling, pitch, whirl, overturn, fell, prostrate.   **Hold**

n., Cast, fling, toss.†

Thrust, *v.a.,* Drive, force, push, impel, urge, poke.   **Extract**

n., Drive, push, poke, pass, tilt, lunge, stab, attack, charge, assault.   **Withdraw**

Thud, Thump, blow, knock, shock.

Thump, *v.a.,* Beat, strike, hit, whack, knock, pommel, belabour.

n., Thud, blow, knock, shock.

Thunder, Roar, bellow, boom, detonate, sound, crash, roll, peal, rumble, resound, reverberate.

Thus, So, consequently.

Thwart, Frustrate, cross, balk, hinder, obstruct, oppose, contravene, defeat.   **Aid**

Ticket, Voucher, coupon, label, pass.

Tickle, Titillate, gratify, please, divert, delight, amuse.   **Irritate**

Ticklish, Difficult, delicate, nice, critical, risky, dangerous, precarious, unsteady, uncertain.   **Simple**

Tide, Current, course, flow, stream.   **Subsidence**

Tidings, News, information, word, report, intelligence, advice, announcement.   **Suppression**

Tidy, Orderly, spruce, neat, trim, shipshape.   **Slovenly**

Tie, *v.a.,* Bind, join, connect, unite, lock, fasten, link, fetter, manacle, knit.   **Loosen**

n., Bond, connection, link, knot.

Tier, Row, rank, line, series.

Tiff, Peevishness, anger, passion, rage. Quarrel, dispute, squabble, altercation.   **Harmony**

Tight, Firm, close, fast, compact, narrow.   **Open**

Stretched, taut, tense.   **Loose**

Till, Plough, tend, cultivate.   **Fallow**

Tillage, Cultivation, culture, agriculture, husbandry, farming.

Tiller, Helm, rudder, handle.

Tilt, *v.a.,* Slope, slant, incline, tip, cant.

n., Slope, slant, inclination, angle. Thrust, drive, lunge, pass. Canopy, covering, awning.

Timbre, Resonance, tone, quality.

Time, Period, season, duration, term, spell, age, era, epoch, day, generation, date, span, while.   **Eternity**

Timely, Opportune, seasonable, early, judicious, prompt, punctual, fortunate.   **Tardy**

Timid, Modest, shy, timorous, bashful, cowardly, afraid, fearful, pusillanimous, retiring, diffident.   **Bold**

Timorous, Timid, modest.†   **Audacious**

Tincture, Tinge, infusion, dash, smack, suggestion, suspicion, sprinkling, grain, hue, tint, taste, spice, flavour.

Tinge, *v.a.,* Colour, stain, tint, dye, affect.

n., Tincture, infusion, dash.†

Tinsel, *n.,* Glittering, glitter, tawdriness, trumpery, finery.   **Splendour**

a., Showy, gaudy, garish, glittering.

Tint, *v.a.,* Colour, tinge, stain, dye, affect.

n., Tinge, tincture, hue, colour, dye, complexion.   **Pallor**

Tiny, Small, minute, little, diminutive, wee, puny, microscopic, pygmy, lilliputian, dwarfish.   **Large**

Tip, *v.a.,* Tilt, incline, cant, overturn.

n., Point, head, end, extremity, peak, pinnacle, apex.   **Base**

Gift, donation, gratuity, perquisite, reward.

Tipsy, Drunk, drunken, intoxicated, inebriated.   **Sober**

Tirade, Diatribe, declamation, censure, invective, harangue, abuse.   **Eulogy**

Tire, Weary, exhaust, fatigue, jade, fag, harass.   **Refresh**

Tired, Weary, exhausted,† done.   **Refreshed**

Tiresome, Tedious, fatiguing, wearisome, exhausting, irksome, toilsome, annoying, troublesome, dull, difficult, laborious, hard, arduous.   **Pleasant**

Tissue, Web, fabric, structure, texture, membrane.

Concatenation, string, series, collection, conglomeration, combination, mass, set, accumulation.

Titanic, Gigantic, huge, vast, colossal, enormous, monstrous, herculean, large, mighty, immense.   **Small**

Titillate, Please, tickle.

Title, Name, appellation, designation, denomination, epithet, cognomen, inscription.   **Nondescript**

Claim, right, possession, privilege, due, prerogative, ownership.   **Disclaimer**

Titter, Giggle, laugh, chuckle, snigger.

Tittle, Particle, atom, whit, jot, iota, speck, grain, scrap, bit.

Together, Conjointly, simultaneously, concurrently, contemporaneously, concertedly, unitedly.   **Separately**

Toil, *v.n.,* Work, labour, travail, drudge, strive.   **Rest**

n., Work, labour, travail, drudgery, exertion, pains, fatigue, effort, task.

Toilet, Dress, costume, attire.

Toilsome, Hard, laborious, wearisome, tiresome, painful, difficult, fatiguing, tedious, onerous, heavy.   **Light**

Token, Sign, symbol, evidence, note, mark, keepsake, reminder, memento, memorial, demonstration, manifestation, illustration, exhibition, indication.
Misrepresentation

Tolerable, Sufferable, bearable, supportable, endurable, allowable, permissible.
Insufferable
Passable, fair, indifferent, middling, ordinary.

Tolerant, Indulgent, forbearing, liberal.
Bigoted

Tolerate, Suffer, bear, endure, support, allow, indulge, permit, abide, brook, admit. *Resist*

Toll, Duty, tax, charge, levy, impost, custom.

Tome, Volume, work, book.

Tomfoolery, Folly, nonsense, escapade, buffoonery, mummery.

Tone, Emphasis, accent, intonation, cadence, inflection, note, sound.
Colour, tint, shade, manner, tenor, style, cast, drift.
Mood, temper, spirit, strain.

Tonic, Stimulating, bracing, invigorating.

Too, Moreover, also, likewise, over, additionally.

Tool, Implement, machine, instrument, agent.

Toothsome, Savoury, luscious, palatable, agreeable, pleasant, nice, delicious.
Nasty

Top, Zenith, summit, head, apex, vertex, acme, meridian, height, pinnacle, crown, culmination, extreme. *Bottom*

Topic, Theme, subject, matter, question, text.

Topical, Particular, local, restricted, limited.

Topple, Totter, fall, tumble, collapse.

Torment, *v.a.*, Agonize, torture, harass, harry, plague, pain, tease, worry, vex, persecute, afflict, distress, importune, trouble, excruciate, rack, fret.
n., Agony, anguish, torture, pain, rack, persecution, affliction, distress, pang.
Ease

Tornado, Hurricane, storm, cyclone, whirlwind, tempest, typhoon, squall.
Calm

Torpid, Motionless, inactive, sluggish, dull, dormant, apathetic, numb, inert, indolent, lethargic, senseless, lifeless, inanimate. *Active*

Torpidity } Dulness, dormancy, apathy,
Torpidness } sluggishness, numbness, in-
Torpor } dolence, inertia, lethargy,
inactivity, insensibility. *Activity*

Torrefy, Parch, dry, roast, scorch, sear.

Torrent, Flood, current, downpour, stream. *Trickle*

Torrid, Parched, dry, dried, roasted, hot, fiery, scorched, arid, burning, scorching.
Arctic

Tortuous, Crooked, devious, sinuated, sinuous, winding, serpentine, curved, circuitous. *Straight*

Torture, *v.a.*, Torment, agonize, rack, pain, distress, excruciate, persecute.
Soothe
n., Torment, agony,† pang, anguish.

Tory, Conservative, Unionist. *Radical*

Toss, *v.a.*, Hurl, throw, fling, cast, pitch, propel, project.
v.n., Writhe, turn, roll. *Rest*
n., Hurl, throw, fling, cast, pitch.
Shake, movement, turn.

Total, *n.*, Totality, sum, whole, all, entirety, aggregate, mass, gross. *Part*
a., Entire, full, whole, complete, perfect, absolute, integral, undivided. *Partial*

Totter, Reel, flounder, falter, stagger, oscillate, rock. *Steady*

Touch, *v.a.*, Handle, hit, meet, strike, graze.
Concern, affect.
Affect, move, impress.
Reach.
n., Stroke, contact, feeling.
Suggestion, suspicion, hint, smack, taste, flavour, tincture, tinge, shade, sprinkling, little, dash, infusion.

Touching, *a.*, Moving, pathetic, affecting, tender, pitiable. *Ludicrous*
prep., Regarding, respecting, affecting, concerning, about, apropos, anent.

Touchstone, Standard, criterion, test, proof, assay.

Touchy, Testy, irritable, irascible, cross, peevish, splenetic, spleeny, sour, tart, snarling, snappish, waspish, petulant, fretful, choleric. *Genial*

Tough, Stiff, stubborn, resistant, fibrous, stringy, lentous, leathery, tenacious, adhesive, cohesive, inflexible, hard, rigid, durable. *Tender*

Tour, *v.n.*, Travel, journey.
n., Travel, journey, excursion, trip, course, circuit, round, expedition, outing, jaunt.

Tournament, Contest, joust, combat.

Tournure, Contour, figure, shape, curve, bend, turn.

Tousle, Ruffle, disarrange, derange, upset, touse, rumple, disturb. *Arrange*

Tow, Pull, draw, haul, tug, drag, heave.
Push

Towards, Nigh, near, nearly, almost, about.

Towards, Respecting, concerning, touching, regarding.

Tower, *v.n.,* Rise, soar, mount, transcend. *Sink*

n., Steeple, turret, spire.

Stronghold, castle, fortress, citadel, keep.

Town, Borough, city, metropolis, place. *Village*

Toy, *v.n.,* Play, wanton, trifle, sport.

n., Plaything, knick-knack, trifle, bauble. *Implement*

Trace, *v.a.,* Sketch, draw, delineate, limn.

Follow, pursue, track, investigate, trail, explore. *Miss*

n., Vestige, suggestion, hint, mark, trail, track, record, sign, indication, remains.

Track, *v.a.,* Trace, follow, pursue, trail. *Miss*

n., Vestige, trace, mark, trail, record, footmark, footprint, spoor.

Way, pathway, path, road, course.

Trackless, Unfrequented, pathless, wild, untrodden, desert. *Frequented*

Tract, Strip, plot, piece, part, portion, region, district.

Booklet, pamphlet, treatise, homily, sermon, dissertation, disquisition, discourse. *Tome*

Tractable, Amenable, docile, pliant, pliable, easy, adaptable, manageable, governable. *Refractory*

Traction, Pulling, drawing, dragging, heaving, towage, hauling.

Trade, Business, commerce, exchange, barter, traffic.

Calling, craft, office, profession, vocation, occupation, employment.

Traditional, Transmitted, unwritten, oral, customary. *Documentary*

Traduce, Calumniate, slander, libel, defame, vituperate, vilify, abuse, decry, depreciate, asperse, malign, disparage, revile, misrepresent. *Eulogize*

Traffic, Business, trade, commerce, exchange, barter, transport.

Tragedy, Disaster, catastrophe, calamity, adversity, affliction, drama. *Comedy*

Tragic, Disastrous, calamitous, shocking, sad, dreadful, terrible. *Comic*

Trail, *v.a.,* Haul, drag, pull, tug, heave, draw, tow, train. *Push*

n., Track, path, pathway, road, footpath. Footprint, trace, footstep.

Train, *v.a.,* Trail, haul, drag.†

Discipline, exercise, harden, educate, instruct, rear, school, drill. *Neglect*

n., Procession, retinue, followers, suite.

Line, chain, succession, series, course.

Trained, Skilled, versed, practised, fitted, proficient, expert, qualified, efficient. *Unskilled*

Trait, Characteristic, mark, feature, peculiarity, touch, stroke.

Traitor, Renegade, apostate, betrayer, rebel, mutineer, insurgent. *Loyalist*

Trammel, *v.a.,* Restrict, confine, clog, hamper, impede, shackle, cramp, fetter, cumber, curb, restrain. *Release*

n., Restriction, confinement, chain, net, impediment,† bond, fetter. *Freedom*

Tramontane, Barbarian, barbarous, alien, foreign, strange.

Tramp, *v.n.,* Walk, travel, march, trudge, hike. *Ride*

n., Walk, march, stroll, journey, tread.

Vagrant, vagabond, stroller.

Trample, Crush, tread, spurn, defy.

Trance, Rapture, ecstasy, exaltation, dream, coma.

Tranquil, Peaceful, still, quiet, calm, undisturbed, serene, untroubled, placid, unmoved, unruffled, composed, smooth, unagitated, easy. *Restless*

Tranquillize, Still, quiet, calm, smooth, pacify, soothe, compose, allay, alleviate, appease, quell, lull, hush. *Excite*

Transact, Do, execute, despatch, enact, conduct, manage, negotiate, perform. *Mismanage*

Transaction, Deed, doing, performance, execution, business, negotiation, action, proceeding, matter, affair. *Adjournment*

Transcend, Surpass, exceed, surmount, excel, eclipse, outrival, outvie, outstrip, outdo. *Fall*

Transcendent, Surpassing, exceeding,† pre-eminent, consummate, inimitable, unsurpassed, unparalleled, unmatched, unequalled, unrivalled, peerless. *Ordinary*

Metaphysical, metempirical, supersensible, transcendental.

Transcribe, Decode, copy, decipher.

Transcript, Duplicate, copy, imitation, engrossment.

Transfer, *v.a.,* Move, remove, transport, change, exchange, translate, transmit, transplant. *Fix*

n., Move, removal.†

Transfigure, Transform, dignify, metamorphose, idealize.

Transfix, Perforate, penetrate, pierce, impale, spear, stake.

Transform, Change, transmute, transfigure, metamorphose, translate, transmogrify, convert. *Perpetuate*

Transgress, v.n., Offend, sin, err, fall, trespass.

v.a., Break, disobey, violate, infringe, exceed, contravene. ***Observe***

Transgression, Offence, sin, error, misdeed, trespass, crime, fault, misdoing, wickedness, misdemeanour.

Breach, violation, infringement, infraction. ***Observance***

Transgressor, Sinner, culprit, offender, trespasser, delinquent, malefactor. ***Innocent***

Transient, Evanescent, ephemeral, brief, passing, fleeting, fugitive, short, hasty, transitory, temporary, momentary. ***Permanent***

Transit, Passage, going, conveying.

Transition, Passage, change, shifting, passing.

Transitory, Transient, evanescent, brief, ephemeral, passing, fleeting, fugitive, short, temporary, hasty, momentary. ***Permanent***

Translate, Render, interpret, do, construe, turn, decode, transform.

Remove, transfer, transport. ***Keep***

Translucent, Diaphanous, transparent, pellucid, crystalline. ***Opaque***

Transmission, Conveyance, communication, circulation, transference. ***Reception***

Transmit, Communicate, transfer, send, forward, remit, broadcast, carry, bear. ***Receive***

Transmutation, Transmuting, change, transfiguration, transformation, metamorphosis, conversion. ***Perpetuation***

Transparent, Pellucid, crystalline, clear, diaphanous, lucid, transpicuous, limpid, translucent, bright. ***Opaque***

Clear, patent, obvious, manifest, evident, explicit. ***Deep***

Transplant, Move, remove, transpose, transfer.

Transport, v.a., Convey, carry, bear, conduct, ship.

Entrance, enrapture, delight.

Expel, banish.

n., Carriage, conveyance.

Ecstasy, enravishment, rapture, joy, happiness, pleasure, felicity, delight. ***Agony***

Transpose, Change, interchange, shift, transfer, reverse. ***Fix***

Transude, Ooze, filter, exude, strain, percolate.

Transverse, Crosswise, oblique, thwart. ***Parallel***

Trap, v.a., Catch, snare, ensnare, net, springe.

Trap, n., Snare, pitfall, springe, gin, ambush, net, stratagem, artifice, wile, toil. ***Beacon***

Trappings, Paraphernalia, embellishments, haberdashery, adornments, gear, ornaments, accessories.

Trash, Rubbish, refuse, offal, dross. ***Treasure***

Nonsense, trumpery, balderdash.

Travail, v.n., Toil, labour, drudge.

n., Toil, labour, drudgery, heaviness, affliction. ***Rest***

Travel, v.n., Journey, tour, walk, rove, wander, ramble, roam, range, traverse. ***Settle***

n., Journey, tour, ramble, trip, excursion, expedition.

Traveller, Pilgrim, voyager, wayfarer, tourist, wanderer, roamer.

Representative, salesman.

Traverse, v.a., Cross, cover, survey.

Obstruct, thwart, cross, frustrate, oppose, contravene. ***Assist***

a., Cross, crossing, transverse.

Travesty, Caricature, parody, burlesque, imitation. ***Copy***

Treacherous, Perfidious, disloyal, faithless, deceitful, false, unfaithful, insidious, unreliable, treasonable, traitorous, untrustworthy, recreant. ***Faithful***

Treachery, Betrayal, perfidiousness,† perfidy. ***Faith***

Tread, v.a., Trample, crush, press.

v.n., Step, walk, go, march, tramp, pace.

n., Step, walk, gait.

Treason, Treachery, betrayal, disloyalty, insurrection, sedition, perfidy. ***Allegiance***

Treasure, v.a., Store, prize, hoard, value, garner, enshrine, idolize, accumulate, save. ***Disregard***

n., Store, valuables, gem, jewel, cash, money, bullion, funds, wealth. ***Trash***

Treasurer, Trustee, purser, banker, bursar.

Treat, v.a., Handle, use, manage, doctor, serve, attend. ***Maltreat***

Entertain, feast, regale.

v.n., Negotiate, deal, bargain.

n., Feast, entertainment, banquet.

Treatise, Discourse, dissertation, tract, disquisition, paper, pamphlet, essay, article, monograph. ***Memoranda***

Treatment, Use, management, dealing, handling, manipulation. ***Misuse***

Treaty, Agreement, pact, compact, contract, covenant, concordat, alliance, convention.

Tremble, Quaver, quiver, shake, shiver,

shudder, jar, vibrate, rock, quake, oscillate. **_Stiffen_**

Trembling, Quivering, shaking, shock, vibration, rocking, oscillation, tremor, trepidation. **_Steady_**

Tremendous, Terrible, terrific, horrible, awful, dreadful, overpowering, fearful, frightful, appalling, alarming, immense, monstrous. **_Ordinary_**

Tremor, Trembling, quivering, shaking, shock, vibration, oscillation, rocking, trepidation. **_Steadfast_**

Tremulous, Trembling, quivering.† **_Steady_**

Trench, Furrow, ditch, cut, channel, gutter, trough.

Trenchant, Severe, biting, bitter, cutting, sarcastic, keen, caustic, piquant, sharp, acute, pointed, straight, direct, incisive, unsparing. **_Mild_**

Trend, v.n., Tend, bear, incline, lean, turn, advance.

n., Tendency, bearing, inclination, leaning, direction, trending.

Trepan, Trap, entrap, ensnare, inveigle.

Trepidation, Fear, trembling, shaking, agitation, terror, emotion, excitement, disturbance, alarm, flurry, consternation, perturbation, fright, dismay. **_Courage_**

Trespass, v.n., Sin, offend, transgress, err. **_Respect_**
Encroach, infringe, intrude.

n., Sin, offence, transgression, error, crime, delinquency, misdoing, misdeed, fault.

Intrusion, invasion, injury, encroachment, infringement.

Trespasser, Intruder, invader, offender, delinquent, transgressor.

Trial, Test, testing, experiment, assay, ordeal, examination, proof.
Endeavour, essay, attempt.
Cause, case, suit, action, hearing.
Hardship, trouble, tribulation, vexation, suffering, grief, affliction, distress, pain. **_Relief_**

Tribe, Clan, race, family, class, order, division.

Tribulation, Trial, hardship, trouble, woe, unhappiness, sorrow, misery, grief, anguish, vexation, suffering, affliction, distress, pain. **_Joy_**

Tribunal, Court, bar, judicature, bench, assizes, sessions.

Tributary, Auxiliary, inferior, subject, subordinate. **_Main_**

Tribute, Impost, duty, tax, custom, toll, excise, offering, contribution.

Trice, Moment, second, instant, jiffy.

Trick, v.a., Dupe, gull, cheat, deceive, defraud, circumvent, overreach, _cozen_, chouse. **_Guide_**

n., Wile, stratagem, deception, fraud, artifice, ruse, chicanery, machination, contrivance, sleight, finesse, dodge, hoax, chouse, cunning, imposture, swindle, fetch. **_Artlessness_**
Practice, habit, mannerism, peculiarity.

Trickish, Wily, deceitful, artful, subtle, cunning, knavish, dishonest, clever, tricky. **_Artless_**

Trickle, Drip, drop, ooze, percolate, dribble, distil. **_Rush_**

Trifle, v.n., Toy, play, idle, wanton, dally. **_Tackle_**

n., Triviality, toy, bauble, gewgaw. **_Treasure_**
Trace, iota, particle, modicum.

Trifling, Trivial, small, inconsiderable, petty, minor, insignificant, slight, paltry, worthless, valueless, immaterial, unimportant. **_Important_**

Trill, Quaver, shake, warble.

Trim, a., Neat, spruce, compact, tidy, snug, smart. **_Deranged_**

v.a., Clip, prune, order, prepare, tidy, arrange, adjust, embellish, ornament, adorn, deck, bedeck, smarten, spruce, decorate, garnish. **_Derange_**

n., Condition, order, case, state.

Trinket, Jewel, ornament, bijou, bauble, toy.

Trip, v.n., Err, fail, fall, stumble, slip. **_Stand_**
Bound, dance, hop, skip, frisk.
v.a., Upset, overthrow, throw.
n., Fall, stumble, slip, error, failure, lapse, fault, blunder.
Tour, expedition, excursion, journey, outing.

Trite, Stale, hackneyed, common, worn, threadbare, thin, commonplace, obvious, unoriginal, familiar. **_Startling_**

Triturate, Pound, pulverize, grind, beat, powder, levigate, comminute, rub, bray, bruise. **_Compound_**

Triumph, v.n., Succeed, conquer, prevail, exult, win, rejoice, vaunt. **_Cower_**

n., Success, conquest, exultation, accomplishment, ovation, jubilee. **_Failure_**

Triumphant, Successful, conquering,† rejoicing, boastful, elated. **_Humiliated_**

Trivial, Trifling, small, inconsiderable, petty, minor, insignificant, worthless, slight, valueless, immaterial, paltry, unimportant. **_Important_**

Troglodyte, Outcast, castaway, wretch, pariah.

Trojan, Hero, warrior, champion.

Trollop, Slut, slattern.

Troop, *n.*, Company, party, detachment, contingent, band, throng, gang.
v.n., Flock, gather, crowd, throng, muster, collect.   *Disperse*

Trophy, Prize, palm, laurels, medal.

Troth, Faith, belief, allegiance, fidelity, honesty, sincerity, truth, veracity.

Trouble, *v.a.*, Disturb, worry, annoy, incommode, inconvenience, vex, distress, afflict, harass, grieve, tease, fret, pester, torment, plague, disquiet.   *Soothe*
n., Worry, annoyance, vexation,† trial, calamity, tribulation, adversity, care, suffering, embarrassment, irritation, uneasiness, torment, anxiety, perplexity.   *Joy*

Troublesome, Annoying, painful, hard, trying, tiresome, galling, distressing, difficult, irksome.   *Easy*

Troublous, Disturbed, agitated, restless, harassed, turbulent, tumultuous.   *Peaceful*

Trough, Furrow, trench, channel, groove, depression.

Truant, *a.*, Loitering, shirking, vagrant, vagabond, idling, loose.   *Sedulous*
n., Loiterer, shirker, vagrant, vagabond, idler, lounger.

Truce, Armistice, peace, rest, respite, intermission, lull, reprieve.   *War*

Truck, Exchange, barter, deal, hawk, trade, traffic.

Truckle, *v.n.*, Submit, cringe, knuckle, yield, stoop.   *Resist*

Truculent, Fierce, ferocious, relentless, savage, cruel, barbarous, bloodthirsty, brutish, ruthless, malevolent.   *Gentle*

Trudge, Tramp, march, jog, plod, go, shamble.

True, *a.*, Veritable, veracious, genuine, actual, truthful, real, authentic, correct, exact, accurate, faithful, legitimate, rightful.   *Inaccurate*
Loyal, faithful, trustworthy, staunch, honest, honourable.   *False*
adv., Granted, good, aye, yes, well.

Truism, Platitude, commonplace, proposition, axiom.   *Paradox*

Truly, Veritably, veraciously, truthfully, really, verily, assuredly, indeed, actually, faithfully.
Loyally, faithfully, honourably, constantly.
Candidly, sincerely, plainly, honestly, straight.   *Falsely*
Exactly, correctly, precisely.†

Trumpery, *n.*, Rubbish, nonsense, trash, tinsel.   *Treasure*
a., Worthless, shallow, showy, delusive, trifling.   *Valuable*

Trumpet, *v.a.*, Blaze, blazon, proclaim, promulgate, publish, advertise, announce.   *Suppress*
n., Bugle, clarion, horn.

Truncate, Cut, dock, lop, maim.

Truncheon, Club, cudgel, baton, staff, bollard.

Trundle, Roll, bowl, wheel, revolve, spin.

Trunk, Stalk, stem, stock, torso, bole, butt, body.
Chest, box, coffer.

Truss, *v.a.*, Tie, bind, fasten.   *Loose*
n., Packet, bundle, package, support, bandage, apparatus.

Trust, *v.a.*, Believe, credit, rely on, confide in, depend on.   *Doubt*
Commit, intrust, confide.
v.n., Hope, expect, believe.
n., Belief, credence, credit, reliance, confidence.
Hope, expectation, belief, assurance, faith, confidence.   *Despair*
Duty, commission, charge.

Trustee, Feduciary, depositary.

Trustworthy ⎱ Reliable, faithful, firm,
Trusty ⎰ honest, honourable, true, upright, staunch, strong, straightforward, straight.   *Fickle*

Truth, Verity, reality, fact, exactness, precision, correctness, nicety, accuracy, true.   *Falsehood*
Integrity, probity, faith, faithfulness, fidelity, fealty, honesty, straightness, honour, candour, straightforwardness, sincerity, frankness.   *Deceit*

Truthful, Faithful, honest, honourable, candid, sincere, straight, frank, artless, straightforward, ingenuous, true, open, guileless, trusty.   *False*
Veracious, true, reliable, accurate, exact, correct, trustworthy.   *Erroneous*

Try, *v.a.*, Test, examine, experiment with, *prove*, experience, attempt, essay.   *Abandon*
v.n., Endeavour, aim, attempt, strive.
n., Trial, endeavour, attempt, effort, experiment.

Trying, Hard, difficult, tiresome, severe, irksome, distressing, arduous, wearisome, irritating, annoying, provoking.   *Easy*

Tryst, Rendezvous, appointment, meeting, assignation.

Tuft, Bunch, collection, clump, cluster, knot, group.

Tug, Haul, heave, pull, draw, drag, tow.   *Push*

Tuition, Education, teaching, schooling, tutorship, training, instruction.

Tumble, Fall, topple, roll, toss, stumble, trip, sprawl.

Tumefy, Inflate, swell, enlarge, distend.

Tumid, Distended, inflated, enlarged, swollen, swelled, turgid, protuberant. *Smooth*
Pompous, rhetorical, turgent, inflated, grandiose, grandiloquent, declamatory, swelling, bombastic, fustian. *Subdued*

Tumour, Swelling, boil, carbuncle, tumefaction.

Tumult, Commotion, uproar, noise, ferment, turbulence, confusion, racket, disturbance, altercation, hubbub, stir, agitation, shouting, turmoil, disorder, riot, fuss, *pother*, flurry. *Peace*

Tumultuous, Uproarious, turbulent,† noisy, obstreperous, violent, irregular, boisterous, restless, disorderly, wild. *Quiet*

Tune, Harmony, melody, air, snatch, strain.

Tuneful, Harmonious, melodious, sweet, musical, dulcet. *Discordant*

Turbid, Muddy, cloudy, thick, feculent, foul, disordered, confused, unsettled, muddled. *Clear*

Turbulent, Tumultuous, noisy, riotous, uproarious, agitated, disturbed, wild, vociferous, disorderly, obstreperous, violent, restless, boisterous, irregular, insurgent, factious, blatant, blustering. *Quiet*

Turf, Earth, sod, sward, peat, grass.

Turgid, Swollen, enlarged, inflated, distended, tumid, swelled, protuberant, bloated. *Smooth*
Pompous, rhetorical, inflated, swelling, grandiose, grandiloquent, declamatory, fustian, bombastic, tumid. *Subdued*

Turmoil, Turbulence, tumult, confusion, commotion, uproar, noise, ferment, stir, disturbance, agitation, trouble, disorder, bustle, hubbub, racket, fuss, flurry, *pother*. *Peace*

Turn, *v.a.*, Revolve, spin, reverse. *Fix*
Round, mould, form, fashion, adapt, shape.
Inflect, deflect, cast, sway, twist, divert, bend. *Misshape*
Alter, transform, change, convert, suit, metamorphose, adapt, fit.
Apply, use, employ, direct, construe, render.
v.n., Revolve, spin, whirl, rotate, twirl.
Become, grow.
Ferment, curdle, acidify.
Hang, rest, hinge, depend.
Diverge, deviate, bend, incline.
n., Revolution, rotation, cycle, gyration.
Act, action, deed, office.

Turn, Shift, spell, bout, round, tunity, chance.
Talent, aptitude, faculty, inclination, genius, gift, bias. *Disinclination*
Change, alteration, vicissitude, variation, flexure, twist, deflection, deviation.
Shape, style, manner, form, cast, mould, fashion. *Malformation*
Exigence, purpose, requirement, need, occasion. *Oversight*
Stroll, ramble, circuit, run, round.

Turpitude, Vileness, baseness, villainy, depravity, wickedness, disgracefulness. *Nobility*

Turret, Tower, minaret, pinnacle, cupola.

Tussle, *v.n.*, Struggle, fight, wrestle, contend, scramble, scuffle.
n., Struggle, fight,† conflict.

Tussock, Clump, hillock, mound.
Tuft, lock, bunch.

Tutelage, Guardianship, charge, care, tutorship, protection. *Independence*

Tutor, *n.*, Master, teacher, instructor, pedagogue, coach, preceptor, professor. *Pupil*
v.a., Teach, instruct, educate, coach, train, drill, discipline.

Twaddle, Nonsense, gabble, jargon, prattle, prate, tattle, stuff, chatter. *Sense*

Tweak, *v.a.*, Pinch, twist, twitch, pull.
n., Pinch, twist.†

Twig, Stick, branch, shoot, spray, sprig. *Trunk*

Twin, Double, duplex, similar, like. *Singular*

Twine, *v.a.*, Entwine, wreathe, twist, wind, embrace. *Unravel*
v.n., Meander, bend, wind, turn, twist.
n., String, cord, thread.

Twinge, Pang, spasm, fit, convulsion, tweak, twitch.

Twinkle, Sparkle, shine, flash, scintillate, glimmer.
Wink, blink.

Twirl, Revolve, turn, twist, rotate, whirl, spin.

Twist, *v.a.*, Wind, twine, entwine, turn, screw, coil, wring, contort. *Unwind*
n., Contortion, winding, bending, bend, flexure.
Twine, cord, thread.

Twit, Taunt, ridicule, reproach, upbraid, rebuke, censure, blame. *Praise*

Twitch, Quiver, jerk, snatch, pluck.

Twofold, Double, duplicate, duplex, doubly. *Single*

Type, Kind, class, order, sort, stamp, species.

hetype, pattern, model, proto-
mple, exemplar.
mage, representation, emblem,
en, sign.

Typical, Representative, emblematic, symbolical, exemplary, indicative, illustrative, normal.   *Abnormal*

Typify, Represent, denote, figure, prefigure, indicate, exemplify, symbolize, embody.   *Realize*

Tyrannical, Imperious, inhuman, severe, haughty, despotic, absolute, autocratic, arbitrary, dictatorial, oppressive, cruel, domineering.   *Constitutional*

Tyranny, Autocracy, absolutism, despotism, dictatorship, oppression.
                Constitutionalism

Tyrant, Autocrat, oppressor, dictator, despot.   *Subordinate*

Tyro, Novice, neophyte, beginner, learner, student.   *Master*

U

Ugly, Ungainly, hideous, deformed, unsightly, ordinary, unlovely, shapeless, plain, uncomely, monstrous, horrid, horrible, frightful, ghastly, gruesome, loathsome. *Beautiful*

Ulcer, Sore, boil, gathering, pustule, fester.

Ulterior, Further, succeeding, beyond, remote, hidden. *Immediate* Indirect, unavowed.

Ultimate, Final, extreme, conclusive, last, eventual, farthest. *Preliminary*

Ultra, Excessive, extreme, radical, advanced. *Moderate*

Umbrage, Resentment, pique, offence, displeasure, grudge, jealousy. *Complacency* Shade, shadow. *Glare*

Umpire, Referee, arbiter, arbitrator, judge. *Disputant*

Unabashed, Undismayed, bold, assured, confident, undaunted, unshrinking. *Dismayed*

Unable, Powerless, incapable, impotent, incompetent, weak. *Capable*

Unacceptable, Unwelcome, disagreeable, unpopular, undesirable. *Welcome*

Unaccommodating, Ungracious, rude, churlish, disobliging, uncivil, unfriendly. *Obliging*

Unaccompanied, Solitary, unattended, alone.

Unaccustomed, New, fresh, unfamiliar, foreign, strange, unused. *Familiar*

Unacknowledged, Ignored, forgotten, slighted, unrequited.

Unadorned, Plain, unvarnished, simple, unembellished, unornamented, undecorated. *Ornate*

Unadulterated, Pure, whole, unmixed, genuine, undiluted, real, full. *Mixed*

Unaffected, Artless, simple, natural, naïve, plain, ingenuous, sincere, honest. *Artificial* Unchanged, untouched, unmoved, unaltered. *Changed*

Unaided, Helpless, unassisted, alone, single-handed. *Helped*

Unaltered, Unchanged, steady, firm, constant, the same.

Unanimity, Accord, harmony, concert, agreement, unity, unison, consensus, concord. *Dissent*

Unanimous, United, solid, full, agreeing, concordant. *Disagreeing*

Unanswerable, Conclusive, irresistible, strong, incontestable, incontrovertible, irrefutable. *Weak*

Unanticipated, Unexpected, unforeseen, sudden, abrupt. *Expected*

Unappalled, Undaunted, bold, fearless, intrepid, brave, undismayed, resolute, courageous, daring, unflinching. *Terrified*

Unappetizing, Tasteless, unsavoury, unattractive, insipid, vapid. *Delicious*

Unappreciative, Regardless, blind, deaf, heedless, undiscerning. *Heedful*

Unapprised, Ignorant, unaware, untold, uninformed, unacquainted. *Aware*

Unarmed, Defenceless, unprotected, unequipped, unguarded, naked, bare. *Prepared*

Unassailable, Impregnable, firm, sure, certain, safe. *Weak*

Unassuming, Modest, retiring, humble, unpretentious, unobtrusive, reserved. *Forward*

Unattached, Free, loose, at liberty, disjoined. *Bound*

Unattended, Solitary, unaccompanied, alone.

Unattainable, Inaccessible, insuperable, unobtainable. *Reachable*

Unattractive, Unprepossessing, repulsive, unappetizing, unalluring, uninviting, uninteresting, undesirable. *Alluring*

Unauthentic, Fictitious, false, spurious, pretended, feigned. *Genuine*

Unauthorized, Illegal, unlawful, unwarranted, unjustified, unlicensed. *Warranted*

Unavailing, Vain, fruitless, abortive, futile, useless, ineffectual, nugatory, bootless. *Successful*

Unavoidable, Unpreventable, certain, irresistible, necessary, inevitable. *Preventive*

Unaware, Ignorant, uninformed, unapprised, unacquainted. *Informed*

Unbearable, Insufferable, insupportable, intolerable, unendurable, afflictive, hard, heavy. *Moderate*

Unbecoming, Unseemly, unbefitting, indecorous, indecent, untimely, unsuitable, inappropriate. *Seemly*

Unbelief, Doubt, distrust, misgiving, disbelief, incredulity, scepticism, infidelity. *Faith*

Unbending, Stubborn, hard, inflexible, stiff, formal, unyielding, unpliable, rigid, unpliant, firm, resolute, mulish. *Pliant*

Fair, disinterested, neutral, impartial, unprejudiced, just. ***Prejudiced***

ose, undo, unfasten, unfetter, ain, release, liberate. ***Chain***

Unblemished, Undefiled, stainless, pure, spotless, unspotted, untainted, unstained, unsullied, unsoiled, clean, faultless, guileless, innocent, impeccable, untarnished, immaculate. ***Soiled***

Unblushing, Shameless, audacious, bold, impudent. ***Ashamed***

Unbounded, Boundless, unlimited, vast, interminable, illimitable, limitless, open, expansive, wide, uncontrolled, endless, immoderate, immeasurable, immense, enormous, huge. ***Scanty***

Unbridled, Wild, loose, lax, licentious, unrestrained, uncontrolled, ungovernable, wanton, violent, headstrong. ***Restrained***

Unbroken, Whole, safe, sound, fast, full, entire, complete, inviolate. ***Shattered***

Uncanny, Weird, strange, mysterious, unusual, ghostly, eerie.

Unceasing, Incessant, perpetual, endless, unending, ceaseless, unintermitting, uninterrupted, constant, steady, continual. ***Intermittent***

Unceremonious, Informal, plain, simple, familiar, · homely, rough, ready, bluff, offhand, brusque, curt, blunt. ***Formal***

Uncertain, Doubtful, dubious, indefinite, questionable, equivocal, ambiguous, unsettled. ***Definite*** Mutable, unreliable, changeable, shaky, precarious, variable, inconstant, fitful, capricious, irregular. ***Sure***

Unchallenged, Unquestioned, uncontradicted, undisputed.

Unchanging, Firm, steady, steadfast, immutable, fixed, constant, invariable, unalterable. ***Mutable***

Uncharitable, Illiberal, unkind, harsh, unchristian, censorious. ***Liberal***

Unchaste, Indecent, immoral, wanton, obscene, loose, dissolute. ***Pure***

Unchivalrous, Ungallant, discourteous, rude, ungracious, boorish, uncouth. ***Gallant***

Uncivil, Rude, rough, discourteous, illmannered, unmannerly, impolite, coarse, churlish, disobliging, disrespectful. ***Polite***

Unclean, Foul, dirty, impure, filthy, sullied. ***Pure***

Unclouded, Cloudless, unobscured, bright, clear, sunny, open. ***Lowering***

Uncoloured, Hueless, colourless, untinged. ***Tinged***

Uncoloured, Unvarnished, plain, simple, direct, real, genuine. ***Exaggerated***

Uncomfortable, Uneasy, unpleasant, disagreeable, displeasing, cheerless, dark, wretched, miserable, unhappy, troubled, dissatisfied. ***Easy*** Oppressive, close, heavy, dull, dismal.

Uncommon, Unusual, rare, singular, remarkable, extraordinary, exceptional, odd, queer, noteworthy, strange, scarce, choice. ***Ordinary***

Uncommunicative, Reserved, taciturn, reticent, quiet, unsociable. ***Loquacious***

Uncomplaining, Content, resigned, unrepining, patient, meek, satisfied.

Uncomplaisant, Disagreeable, churlish, uncivil, unmannerly. ***Pleasant***

Uncomplimentary, Rude, unflattering, straight, blunt, plain, candid, frank. ***Flattering***

Uncompromising, Decided, inflexible, unyielding, rigid, obstinate, firm, stiff. ***Vacillating***

Unconcerned, Cool, indifferent, easy, nonchalant, unmoved, careless, apathetic, disinterested. ***Anxious***

Unconditional, Absolute, full, complete, perfect, entire, positive, unqualified, total, categorical, unrestricted, unlimited, unreserved. ***Provisional***

Uncongenial, Abhorrent, unnatural, discordant, dissonant, disagreeable, alien, displeasing, antagonistic, unsympathetic. ***Sympathetic***

Unconnected, Disjointed, disconnected, illogical, unrelated, inconsequent. ***Related***

Unconquerable, Indomitable, invincible, victorious, insuperable, unmasterable, insurmountable. ***Weak***

Unconscionable, Unreasonable, absurd, preposterous, inordinate, monstrous, excessive. ***Reasonable***

Unconscious, Insensible, asleep, senseless. ***Awake*** Ignorant, unknowing, unaware. ***Aware***

Unconstitutional, Revolutionary, illegal, unlawful. ***Lawful***

Unconstrained, Natural, spontaneous, free, easy, artless. ***Stiff***

Uncontaminated, Pure, undefiled, clean, unsullied, untainted, unsoiled, unspotted, unpolluted. ***Defiled***

Uncontrollable, Headstrong, unruly, ungovernable, unmanageable, violent, intractable, independent, irrepressible. ***Servile***

Unconventional, Natural, free, easy, informal, odd, eccentric, peculiar, unusual, unceremonious. ***Stiff***

Unconvincing, Uncertain, indecisive, weak, inconclusive.   *Positive*

Uncouth, Clumsy, awkward, unrefined, strange, ungainly, unpolished, inelegant, boorish, lubberly, rustic, rough.   *Polished*

Uncover, Bare, strip, denude, discover, disclose, open, expose, reveal, show.   *Cloak*

Unction, Power, life, fervour, spirit, zest, ardour, verve, warmth, passion, feeling, animation, enthusiasm, force, emotion, energy.   *Vapidity*

Unctuous, Smooth, oily, fat, greasy, fulsome, flattering, fawning, adulatory, sycophantic, suave, bland.   *Blunt*

Uncultivated, Wild, untilled, sylvan, waste, fallow, rough.

Uncurbed, Unrestrained, loose, free, wild, uncontrolled, undisciplined, unbridled.   *Restrained*

Undaunted, Dauntless, resolute, brave, courageous, fearless, intrepid, bold, undismayed, unterrified, unappalled, gallant.   *Afraid*

Undeceive, Disabuse, disillusion, correct.   *Trick*

Undecided, Uncertain, undetermined, unsettled, doubtful, dubious, irresolute, wavering, hesitating, tentative, pending.   *Resolved*

Undefiled, Pure, uncontaminated, clean, unsullied, untainted, unsoiled, spotless, unpolluted, unspotted, untarnished, stainless.   *Contaminated*

Undemonstrative, Reserved, composed, staid, quiet, calm, sedate, placid, silent, unexcitable, even.   *Excitable*

Undeniable, Certain, evident, obvious, unquestionable, indubitable, incontestable, incontrovertible, indisputable.   *Doubtful*

Under, Beneath, below, underneath, lower, inferior, subject, subordinate.   *Above*

In.

Underestimate, Underrate, undervalue, disparage, belittle, minimize.   *Overrate*

Undergo, Experience, endure, sustain, bear, suffer.

Underhand, Clandestine, secret, sly, surreptitious, sinister, private, furtive, dishonest.   *Open*

Undermine, Sap, mine, ruin, weaken, impair.   *Strengthen*

Underneath, Under, beneath, below.   *Above*

Underrate, Underestimate, undervalue, disparage.   *Overestimate*

Understand, Comprehend, apprehend, perceive, know, grasp, realize, fathom, conceive, discern, gather, learn, interpret. Mean, imply.   *Misapprehend*

Understanding, *a.,* Intelligent, sensible, reasonable, knowing, thinking. *Foolish n.,* Knowledge, intelligence, judgment, sense, reason, thought, discernment, intellect, mind, brains, comprehension, perception.   *Ignorance* Agreement, unanimity, accord. *Rupture*

Undertake, *v.a.,* Attempt, try, essay, embark on. *v.n.,* Promise, bargain, agree, stipulate engage, guarantee.   *Omit*

Undertaking, Venture, project, adventure, effort, enterprise, task, affair, endeavour.   *Leisure*

Undervalue, Underrate, underestimate, disparage.   *Overrate*

Underwriter, Insurer, subscriber.

Undesigned, Unintended, accidental, unintentional, unpremeditated.   *Intentional*

Undesirable, Unpleasant, disagreeable, unwelcome, objectionable, inexpedient, distasteful, unacceptable, inconvenient, inadvisable.   *Welcome*

Undesirous, Loath, unwilling, reluctant.   *Eager*

Undetermined, Unsettled, irresolute, uncertain, doubtful, dubious, wavering, undecided, hesitating.   *Resolved*

Undeveloped, Immature, latent, rudimentary, primordial.   *Ripe*

Undeviating, Straight, direct, steadfast, steady, determined, regular, unswerving.   *Meandering*

Undignified, Unseemly, indecorous, uncouth, ungainly, unbecoming, ill-bred.   *Graceful*

Undiscerning, Unenlightened, stupid, dull, unintelligent.   *Clever*

Undisciplined, Raw, untrained, unruly, untaught, wild, callow.   *Trained*

Undiscoverable, Inscrutable, hidden, mysterious, occult, dark, obscure.   *Obvious*

Undisguised, Frank, open, plain, clear, sincere, honest, apparent.   *Veiled*

Undismayed, Fearless, bold, undaunted, dauntless, intrepid, resolute, gallant, courageous, unterrified, unappalled, unawed.   *Afraid*

Undisturbed, Composed, calm, cool, collected, impassive, unperturbed, mild, unruffled, serene, quiet, tranquil, gentle, peaceful, placid.   *Agitated*

Undivided, Complete, full, whole, entire, united.   *Partial*

Undo, Untie, open, unfasten, unravel, unfold, disengage, disentangle. *Tie*
Nullify, reverse, neutralize, counterbalance.
Ruin, destroy, crush.

Undoubted, Certain, evident, obvious, sure, plain, unquestionable, undeniable, indubitable, indisputable, unquestioned, undisputed. *Doubtful*

Undue, Excessive, extreme, immoderate, disproportionate, unwarranted, improper, inordinate. *Moderate*

Undulating, Rolling, uneven, waving, hilly. *Plain*

Unduly, Improperly, excessively. *Suitable*

Undutiful, Unfilial, disobedient, disloyal, refractory, rebellious. *Filial*

Undying, Immortal, deathless, lasting, permanent, endless, enduring, imperishable. *Transient*

Unearth, Disclose, reveal, discover, find, uncover, expose. *Bury*

Unearthly, Weird, supernatural, ghostly, uncanny, preternatural. *Common*

Uneasy, Disturbed, uncomfortable, stiff, restless, restive, impatient, awkward. *Content*

Uneducated, Ignorant, illiterate, rude, untaught, unenlightened. *Literate*

Unemployed, Idle, loafing, disengaged, unoccupied, out-of-work. *Industrious*

Unending, Endless, ceaseless, unceasing, incessant, perpetual, continual, eternal, interminable, everlasting, permanent, constant. *Brief*

Unequal, Inferior, insufficient, uneven, inadequate, incapable. *Uniform*

Unequalled, Peerless, paramount, unmatched, matchless, unrivalled, unique, unsurpassed, inimitable, transcendent, incomparable. *Inferior*

Unequivocal, Clear, plain, positive, sure, absolute, evident, certain, undoubted, unmistakable, explicit, unquestionable, indubitable, indisputable. *Ambiguous*

Unerring, Sure, straight, true, deadly, accurate, certain, exact. *Faulty*

Uneven, Rough, rugged, undulating, hilly, unequal, odd. *Level*

Uneventful, Eventless, quiet, ordinary, unexciting, dull, monotonous, commonplace. *Exciting*

Unexcelled, Unrivalled, unsurpassed. *Inferior*

Unexceptionable, Faultless, excellent, worthy, good, irreproachable, unobjectionable. *Faulty*

Unexpected, Unanticipated, unforeseen, sudden, abrupt. *Anticipated*

Unfailing, Constant, reliable, perpetual, certain, sure, inexhaustible. *Fickle*

Unfair, Dishonest, foul, unjust, false, dishonourable, interested, inequitable, wrongful, partial, biassed. *Just*

Unfaithful, Perfidious, false, faithless, deceitful, untrue, fickle, inconstant, treacherous, treasonable, recreant, disloyal, unreliable, untrustworthy. *Loyal*

Unfaltering, Bold, steady, steadfast, resolute, firm, determined, unhesitating. *Hesitating*

Unfamiliar, Unusual, uncommon, queer, odd, peculiar, strange, unaccustomed. *Common*

Unfashionable, Out-of-date, obsolete, antiquated, disused. *Modern*

Unfathomable, Deep, profound, soundless, immeasurable, abysmal, bottomless, mysterious, inscrutable. *Shallow*

Unfavourable, Inimical, adverse, bad, inauspicious, malign, discouraging, contrary, prejudicial, unpropitious. *Beneficial*

Unfeeling, Harsh, cruel, hard, unkind, callous, unsympathetic, insensible, numb, unconscious. *Sensitive*

Unfeigned, Genuine, real, true, sincere, honest, sterling, felt. *Assumed*

Unfetter, Loose, free, liberate, unbind, untie, release, unshackle, unchain. *Bind*

Unfinished, Imperfect, incomplete, unaccomplished, sketchy. *Perfect*

Unfit, Unsuitable, unqualified, incapable. *Suitable*

Unflagging, Indefatigable, tireless, constant, untiring, steady, unremitting. *Drooping*

Unfledged, Undeveloped, inexperienced, raw, untried. *Experienced*

Unflinching, Steady, bold, resolute, firm, hardy, unshrinking, brave. *Cowering*

Unfold, Open, unravel, display, unroll, expand, disentangle, disclose, reveal. *Shut*

Unforeseen, Unexpected, unanticipated, sudden, abrupt. *Expected*

Unforgiving, Relentless, unappeasable, hard, merciless, implacable. *Lenient*

Unfortunate, Unlucky, unhappy, illfated, calamitous, disastrous, luckless, ill-starred, deplorable, infelicitous, unsuccessful. *Lucky*

Unfounded, Baseless, groundless, idle, unnecessary.

Unfrequented, Sequestered, unoccupied, solitary, lonely, deserted, uninhabited, forsaken. *Busy*

Unfriendly, Antagonistic, unfavourable, opposed, hostile, adverse. *Neighbourly*

Unfruitful, Fruitless, barren, sterile, unproductive, infecund, unprolific, infertile. *Prolific*

Unfurl, Open, unfold, expand, display, unroll. *Wrap*

Ungainly, Awkward, uncouth, clumsy, stiff, inelegant, ungraceful, uncourtly, ugly. *Elegant*

Ungenerous, Mean, near, close, stingy, parsimonious, selfish, niggardly, illiberal. *Liberal*

Ungentlemanly, Rude, discourteous, unmannerly, uncivil, churlish, impolite, rough. *Polite*

Ungodly, Impious, bad, wicked, sinful, depraved, unrighteous, evil, godless, profane. *Righteous*

Ungovernable, Refractory, headstrong, rebellious, unruly, wild, uncontrollable, intractable, untamed, violent, unbridled. *Mild*

Ungracious, Discourteous, disobliging, unkind, rough, churlish, unfriendly. *Amiable*

Ungrateful, Thankless, unthankful. *Thankful*

Ungrudging, Willing, ready, voluntary, unsparing, cheerful, hearty, generous, free. *Niggardly*

Unguarded, Careless, thoughtless, naked, heedless, incautious, unprotected, undefended. *Protected*

Unhandy, Clumsy, awkward, maladroit, stiff, unskilled, unskilful, bungling. *Dexterous*

Unwieldy, awkward, inconvenient. *Convenient*

Unhappy, Miserable, sad, sorrowful, wretched, distressed, afflicted. *Gay*
Unlucky, unfortunate, calamitous, dire, disastrous, deplorable, grievous, sad. *Lucky*

Unharmed, Unhurt, immune, scatheless, uninjured, safe. *Hurt*

Unhealthy, Unsound, noxious, morbific, diseased, insalubrious, unwholesome, sickly. *Salubrious*

Unheeded, Ignored, disregarded, flouted, overlooked, neglected, unnoticed. *Marked*

Unhesitating, Instant, quick, prompt, ready, immediate, unfaltering. *Faltering*

Unhinge, Derange, upset, discompose, confuse, disorder, unsettle, unfix. *Order*

Unholy, Impious, profane, ungodly, evil, unrighteous, wicked, depraved, sinful, bad, irreverent, irreligious. *Devout*

Uniform, Regular, steady, undeviating, consistent, constant, unchanging, stable, changeless, equable, unvarying. *Irregular*

Unimaginative, Dull, prosaic, practical, unromantic, unpoetical. *Romantic*

Unimpaired, Undiminished, uninjured, unhurt. *Damaged*

Unimpassioned, Cool, placid, calm, serene, undisturbed, passionless, quiet, unexcited, impassive, dispassionate. *Excited*

Unimpeachable, Faultless, blameless, unexceptionable, irreproachable, satisfactory. *Faulty*

Unimportant, Minor, small, insignificant, trifling, trivial, little, inconsiderable, petty, slight. *Weighty*

Unimpressible, Immovable, apathetic, insensitive, cold, phlegmatic, impassive, dead. *Susceptible*

Uninhabited, Deserted, empty, solitary, sequestered, unfrequented, secluded, lonely. *Busy*

Unintelligent, Dull, doltish, simple, foolish, stolid, obtuse. *Clever*

Unintentional, Accidental, undesigned, unpremeditated, involuntary, fortuitous, inadvertent, casual. *Designed*

Uninteresting, Boring, tedious, dull, flat, stale, wearisome, prosaic. *Bright*

Uninterrupted, Continuous, continual, ceaseless, unceasing, incessant, constant, perpetual, unbroken, unintermitted. *Broken*

Uninviting, Repulsive, unattractive, unalluring, disagreeable, unpleasant. *Alluring*

Union, Conjunction, junction, joining, combination. *Parting*
League, coalition, confederation, confederacy, federacy, federation, alliance, combination, association.
Agreement, accord, concord, harmony, concert, unison, unity. *Discord*

Unique, Singular, single, peculiar, sole, rare, uncommon, choice, matchless, exceptional, unparalleled, unexampled. *Common*

Unison } Harmony, agreement, concord, **Unity** } accord. *Discord*

Unite, *v.a.*, Join, conjoin, connect, bind, combine, concert, amalgamate, attach. *Separate*
v.n., Join, combine, amalgamate, coalesce.

Universal, General, catholic, complete, comprehensive, wide, total, whole, entire, all-embracing. *Parochial*

Unjust, Unfair, biassed, inequitable, partial, interested, prejudiced. *Impartial*
Wicked, bad, wrong, heinous, nefarious, unrighteous, dishonourable. *Honourable*

Unjustified, Inexcusable, unwarranted, wrong, indefensible. *Proper*

Unkind, Cruel, hard, harsh, unfriendly, unsympathetic, unthinking. *Amiable*

Unknown, Obscure, nameless, hidden, dark, mysterious, undiscovered, unexplored, anonymous. *Known*

Unlace, Loose, unlatch, unfasten, open, untie, unloose, loosen. *Tie*

Unlawful, Illegal, unauthorized, illicit, prohibited, illegitimate, bastard. *Legitimate*

Unlike, Different, diverse, dissimilar. *Similar*

Unlikely, Improbable, unpromising. *Possible*

Unlimited, Infinite, limitless, boundless, unbounded, unrestricted, absolute, great, numerous. *Restricted*

Unload, Disburden, unlade, relieve, disencumber, empty, lighten. *Encumber*

Unlock, Open, unlatch, unbolt, unfasten. *Bolt*

Unloose, Unlace, loose, loosen, unlatch, unfasten, open, untie. *Tie*

Unlucky, Luckless, unfortunate, hapless, ill-fated, ill-starred, ill-omened, unhappy, unsuccessful, inauspicious. *Fortunate*

Unmanageable, Cumbersome, awkward, inconvenient, unwieldy, difficult, refractory, unruly, vicious. *Tractable*

Unmanly, Effeminate, weak, cowardly, dispirited, feeble, timid, dastardly. *Brave*

Unmannerly, Rude, impolite, boorish, discourteous, churlish, ungracious, uncivil. *Polite*

Unmatched, Incomparable, matchless, peerless, paramount, unequalled, unrivalled, consummate, perfect, unique, unparalleled. *Inferior*

Unmelodious, Discordant, harsh, grating, unmusical, inharmonious. *Musical*

Unmerciful, Ruthless, inhuman, cruel, unpitying, unsparing, merciless, harsh, inexorable, implacable, unrelenting, hard, pitiless. *Humane*

Unmerited, Unearned, undeserved. *Deserved*

Unmethodical, Unsystematic, slipshod, disorderly, irregular, careless, haphazard. *Systematic*

Unmindful, Mindless, regardless, forgetful, oblivious, careless, heedless, negligent. *Heedful*

Unmistakable, Plain, clear, evident, patent, obvious, palpable, manifest, certain, unquestionable, notorious, indubitable, positive, absolute. *Doubtful*

Unmitigated, Absolute, unqualified, perfect, thorough, complete, entire.

Unmoved, Impassive, cool, collected, calm, undisturbed, indifferent, placid, serene, quiet. *Excited*

Unshaken, unwavering, steadfast, firm, constant, unfaltering, resolute. *Shaken*

Unmusical, Unmelodious, discordant, harsh, grating, inharmonious. *Melodious*

Unnatural, Cruel, inhuman, unfeeling, heartless, stony, brutal. *Humane*

Monstrous, prodigious, anomalous, abnormal. *Usual*

Artificial, forced, affected, strained, stilted. *Real*

Unnecessary, Needless, unneeded, useless, superfluous, unessential. *Essential*

Unnoticed, Disregarded, ignored, unseen, unobserved, overlooked. *Recognized*

Unobservant, Inattentive, careless, dull, heedless. *Attentive*

Unobstructed, Clear, open, free, unhindered. *Impeded*

Unobtrusive, Retiring, unpretentious, unassuming, modest, reserved, quiet. *Pretentious*

Unoccupied, Empty, vacant, deserted, uninhabited, abandoned. *Tenanted*

Idle, unemployed, spare, leisure. *Working*

Unoffending, Harmless, innocent, inoffensive, unobjectionable. *Offensive*

Unorthodox, Heretical, unsound, untrue, incorrect, heterodox. *Correct*

Unpalatable, Unpleasant, disagreeable, repulsive, nauseous, bitter, disgusting, distasteful, unsavoury, offensive. *Sweet*

Unparalleled, Peerless, matchless, unmatched, incomparable, paramount, supreme, unrivalled, unexampled, unequalled, inimitable. *Inferior*

Unpardonable, Unjustifiable, unjustified, inexcusable, irremissible, wrong, unwarranted, indefensible. *Proper*

Unperturbed, Calm, quiet, cool, serene, collected, placid, undisturbed, unmoved, impassive, unexcited. *Excited*

Unpitying, Pitiless, cruel, harsh, hard, unmerciful, unrelenting, relentless, ruthless, merciless, uncompassionate, unsparing, implacable. *Merciful*

Unpleasant, Unpalatable, disagreeable, obnoxious, objectionable, offensive, displeasing, repulsive. *Delightful*

Unpliant, Inflexible, stiff, unpliable, firm, rigid, unyielding, unbending. *Flexible*

Unpolished, Rough, rude, coarse, unrefined, boorish. *Refined*

Unpolluted, Undefiled, unstained, pure, uncorrupted, untarnished, spotless, clean, unspotted. *Defiled*

Unpopular, Disliked, odious, obnoxious, detested. *Favourite*

Unpractical, Unqualified, inexperienced, unable, unskilled, untrained, ineffective, useless, unworkable. *Proficient*

Unpractised, Raw, unskilled, untrained, fresh, new, inexperienced, inexpert. *Expert*

Unprecedented, New, novel, fresh, unexampled, exceptional, unparalleled. *Frequent*

Unprejudiced, Fair, just, indifferent, unbiassed, impartial, disinterested. *Biassed*

Unpremeditated, Spontaneous, hasty, impromptu, unprepared, extempore. *Deliberate*

Unprepossessing, Ugly, repulsive, unattractive, uncomely. *Fascinating*

Unpretentious, Modest, retiring, quiet, unobtrusive, reserved. *Forward*

Unprincipled, Dishonest, immoral, bad, wicked, villainous, knavish, roguish, dishonourable. *Upright*

Unproductive, Barren, fruitless, sterile, unfruitful, unprolific, futile. *Fruitful* Unremunerative, unprofitable, unsuccessful. *Beneficial*

Unprofitable, Useless, worthless, futile, bootless, poor, fruitless, unfruitful, unproductive. *Useful*

Unpromising, Unfavourable, unlucky, unfortunate, inauspicious, unpropitious, dark, untoward. *Bright*

Unpropitious, Unpromising, unfavourable.†

Unprotected, Unguarded, defenceless, unsheltered, open, exposed. *Defended*

Unqualified, Thorough, complete, full, absolute, perfect, entire, decided. *Partial* Incompetent, unskilled, unpractised, untrained, unfit. *Skilled*

Unquestionable, Certain, obvious, plain, patent, evident, clear, apparent, irrefutable, undeniable, indubitable, incontestable, indisputable, incontrovertible. *Doubtful*

Unravel, Untwist, disentangle, explain, straighten, unfold, solve, decipher. *Twist*

Unreasonable, Excessive, immoderate, extravagant, extreme. *Moderate* Absurd, foolish, irrational, stupid, silly, mad, senseless. *Sensible*

Unrelenting, Relentless, harsh, severe, merciless, inexorable, implacable, pitiless, unpitying, hard, unmerciful, austere, ruthless, cruel, stern, uncompassionate, unsparing. *Merciful*

Unreliable, Untrustworthy, uncertain, independable, unstable, irresponsible, fickle. *Trustworthy*

Unremitting, Incessant, ceaseless, unceasing, diligent, persevering, continual, continuous, constant, perpetual. *Intermittent*

Unrepentant, Callous, hardened, seared, impenitent, obdurate, shameless, incorrigible. *Contrite*

Unreserved, Full, perfect, entire, open, unconditional. *Conditional*

Unrestrained, Unchecked, unrestricted, free, unhindered, unbridled, loose, wild. *Sober*

Unrestricted, Free, open, clear, unconfined, unlimited, unrestrained. *Confined*

Unrighteous, Bad, evil, sinful, depraved, wicked, ungodly, vicious, nefarious, heinous, iniquitous. *Godly*

Unripe, Undeveloped, immature, green, verdant, unready, crude. *Mature*

Unrivalled, Matchless, unmatched, unequalled, inimitable, peerless, unique, unparalleled, paramount, incomparable. *Inferior*

Unroll, Open, unfold, display, unfurl. *Fold*

Unruffled, Cool, calm, collected, placid, serene, undisturbed, unperturbed, quiet, peaceful, smooth, tranquil, composed, unmoved, impassive, imperturbable. *Agitated*

Unruly, Refractory, stubborn, rebellious, mutinous, turbulent, unmanageable, ungovernable, disobedient, headstrong, disorderly, obstinate, riotous, intractable. *Orderly*

Unsafe, Dangerous, hazardous, unsound, precarious, insecure, treacherous, risky, uncertain, perilous. *Secure*

Unsatisfactory, Poor, unsatisfying, unsuccessful, weak, feeble, mediocre. *Excellent*

Unsavoury, Vapid, insipid, tasteless, flat, unpalatable, unattractive, repulsive, rank, disgusting, unpleasing. *Appetizing*

Unscrupulous, Dishonest, unprincipled, dishonourable, unconscientious, shameless. *Particular*

Unseasonable, Untimely, inappropriate, inopportune, unfit, unsuitable. *Opportune*

Unseemly, Indecent, indecorous, unbefitting, unbecoming, improper, inappropriate. *Proper*

Unselfish, Charitable, liberal, generous, magnanimous. *Mean*

Unsettle, Upset, disorder, derange, confuse, disturb. *Smooth*

Unshackle, Emancipate, release, loose, manumit, free, liberate, unfetter. *Bind*

Unshaken, Firm, steady, steadfast, immovable, stout, resolute, determined, fixed, unmoved, convinced. *Wavering*

Unshrinking, Unhesitating, unflinching, fearless, firm, determined, resolute, unblenching, persistent. *Hesitating*

Unsightly, Ugly, repulsive, unpleasing, hideous, unpleasant, displeasing, disagreeable. *Beautiful*

Unskilful, Clumsy, awkward, maladroit, unhandy, inexpert, inapt, bungling. *Dexterous*

Unskilled, Inexpert, inexperienced.† *Expert*

Unsociable, Taciturn, sullen, reserved, quiet, solitary, uncommunicative, uncongenial. *Gregarious*

Unsoiled, Clean, spotless, unspotted, pure, unstained, untarnished, unsullied. *Dirty*

Unsophisticated, Innocent, guileless, honest, uncorrupted, pure, simple, artless, natural, ingenuous, undepraved, childlike, naïve. *Corrupted*

Unsound, Diseased, morbid, sickly, decayed, rotten, defective, impaired, imperfect, infirm, unhealthy, feeble, weak. *Perfect*
Fallacious, erroneous, unorthodox, false, invalid, heretical, faulty, untenable, illogical, wrong. *Right*

Unsparing, Profuse, lavish, untiring, ungrudging, liberal, unselfish, generous, bountiful. *Mean*
Hard, harsh, merciless, unmerciful, rigid, pitiless, unpitying, relentless, severe, unrelenting, ruthless, inexorable, cruel, unforgiving, stern. *Lenient*

Unspeakable, Unutterable, indescribable, inexpressible, ineffable.

Unspotted, Spotless, clean, pure, stainless, unstained, untainted, unsullied, unsoiled, untarnished, undefiled, uncorrupted, unpolluted. *Foul*

Unstable, Unsteady, inconstant, fickle, uncertain, insecure, precarious, erratic, wavering, vacillating, variable, changeable. *Firm*

Unstained, Unspotted, spotless, clean, pure, stainless, untainted, unsullied, unsoiled, untarnished. *Dirty*

Unsteady, Unstable, inconstant, unsafe, uncertain, tottering, wavering, variable, fickle, vacillating, changeable. *Firm*

Unstinted, Lavish, generous, full, ample, abundant, plentiful, bountiful, large. *Meagre*

Unstudied, Easy, natural, spontaneous, impromptu, unpremeditated. *Forced*

Unsubmissive, Refractory, stubborn, obstinate, contumacious, rebellious, disobedient, intractable, unruly, perverse, unmanageable, ungovernable, unyielding, independent. *Docile*

Unsubstantial, Airy, light, imaginary, unreal, illusory, shadowy, visionary, flimsy. *Solid*

Unsuccessful, Futile, ineffectual, vain, bootless, fruitless, unavailing, profitless, abortive. *Profitable*
Unlucky, unprosperous, unfortunate.

Unsuitable, Unfit, unfitting, improper, inappropriate, unbecoming. *Fitting*

Unsullied, Unspotted, spotless, clean, pure, stainless, unstained, unpolluted, unsoiled, untarnished, undefiled, uncorrupted. *Foul*

Unsurpassed, Paramount, supreme, pre-. eminent, unexcelled. *Inferior*

Unsusceptible, Phlegmatic, cold, dead, unimpressible, impassive, insensible, stoical. *Alive*

Unsuspecting, Trusting, credulous, confiding, unsuspicious. *Distrustful*

Unswerving, Straight, direct, undeviating. *Crooked*

Unsymmetrical, Irregular, shapeless, disproportionate. *Regular*

Unsympathetic, Unkind, harsh, hard, cruel, thoughtless, heartless, callous. *Kind*

Unsystematic, Unmethodical, slipshod, disorderly, irregular, careless, haphazard. *Methodical*

Untainted, Unsullied, unspotted, clean, spotless, pure, stainless, unstained, unsoiled, untarnished, undefiled, unpolluted, uncorrupted. *Foul*

Untarnished, Untainted, unsullied,† unblemished. *Dirty*

Untaught, Illiterate, ignorant, untrained, uneducated, unenlightened. *Educated*

Untenable, Unsound, fallacious, faulty, erroneous, weak, illogical. *Sound*

Unthankful, Thankless, ungrateful, unappreciative. *Grateful*

Unthinking } Careless, heedless, mind-
Unthoughtful } less, unmindful, hasty, regardless, inconsiderate, unreflecting. *Considerate*

Unthrifty, Prodigal, extravagant, lavish, wasteful, careless, profuse, thriftless, improvident. *Economical*

Untidy, Disorderly, careless, unkempt, slovenly. *Neat*

Untie, Undo, loosen, loose, unfasten, unloose, unlatch. *Knot*

Untimely, Inopportune, unseasonable, unsuitable, inappropriate. *Opportune*

Untiring, Tireless, indefatigable, endless, unwearying, unwearied, unremitting, ceaseless, unceasing, incessant. *Fitful*

Untold, Countless, innumerable, numberless, vast, immense, incalculable. *Minute*

Untouched, Whole, unscathed, unhurt, intact, unharmed, uninjured. *Damaged*

Unaffected, indifferent, apathetic, unmoved. *Moved*

Untrammelled, Free, unhampered, unfettered. *Bound*

Untroubled, Calm, composed, quiet, still, peaceful, tranquil, smooth, undisturbed, serene, placid. *Stormy*

Untrue, Incorrect, inaccurate, spurious, erroneous, false, fallacious, wrong. *Correct*

Perfidious, faithless, false, unfaithful, recreant, treacherous, traitorous, disloyal. *Faithful*

Untrustworthy, Unreliable, false, tricky, treacherous, disloyal, deceptive, deceitful, illusive. *Reliable*

Untruth, Falsehood, lie, deception, error, imposture, fabrication.

Untwist, Untwine, unravel, disentangle, ravel. *Twine*

Unusual, Rare, old, exceptional, strange, uncommon, extraordinary, remarkable, singular, queer, peculiar, curious, unwonted, unaccustomed. *Common*

Unutterable, Unspeakable, inexpressible, ineffable, indescribable.

Unvarnished, Plain, simple, unadorned, direct, unornamented, unembellished. *Ornate*

Unvarying, Invariable, constant, firm, unchanging, steady, reliable. *Changing*

Unveil, Reveal, unmask, expose, show, disclose. *Mask*

Unwarped, Unprejudiced, disinterested, unbiassed, indifferent, impartial. *Biassed*

Unwarlike, Peaceful, pacific. *Bloodthirsty*

Unwarrantable, Unjustifiable, unpardonable, inexcusable, indefensible, improper. *Justifiable*

Unwary, Incautious, careless, heedless, imprudent, rash, unwise, injudicious, hasty, indiscreet, unguarded. *Cautious*

Unwavering, Steady, steadfast, firm, constant, fixed, staunch, unhesitating, resolute, resolved, unvacillating, determined. *Hesitating*

Unwearied, Tireless, untiring, ceaseless, indefatigable, unremitting, incessant, unceasing, unflagging, persistent, persevering. *Fitful*

Unwelcome, Unpleasant, disagreeable, unpleasing, displeasing, unacceptable, distasteful. *Pleasing*

Unwell, Indisposed, ill, ailing, sick. *Healthy*

Unwieldy, Bulky, ponderous, unhandy, heavy, cumbersome, awkward, weighty, clumsy, inconvenient. *Handy*

Unwilling, Reluctant, averse, loath, indisposed, disinclined. *Eager*

Unwise, Injudicious, indiscreet, foolish, rash, hasty, precipitate, imprudent, mad. *Discreet*

Unwittingly, Unknowingly, unconsciously, unintentionally, inadvertently. *Purposely*

Unwonted, Rare, uncommon, peculiar, unusual, extraordinary, unaccustomed. *Usual*

Unworthy, Dishonourable, base, bad, discreditable, shameful, shabby, vile, despicable, worthless, contemptible, paltry. *Honourable*

Unwrap, Undo, unfold, unfurl, open. *Fold*

Unyielding, Firm, stiff, rigid, inflexible, hard, stubborn, pertinacious, steadfast, immovable, steady, staunch, resolute, determined, unbending, obstinate, intractable. *Weak*

Upbraid, Censure, rebuke, chide, blame, reprove, reproach, taunt, condemn. *Praise*

Upheave, Lift, raise, elevate.

Uphill, Hard, difficult, strenuous, toilsome, arduous. *Easy*

Uphold, Sustain, maintain, advocate, support, vindicate, defend, justify, aid. *Subvert*

Upright, Vertical, straight, erect, perpendicular. *Slanting*

Just, fair, honourable, honest, good, trustworthy, virtuous, conscientious. *Dishonest*

Uproar, Turmoil, tumult, disorder, riot, confusion, commotion, clamour, hubbub, disturbance. *Order*

Upset, Overthrow, overturn, subvert, invert, overbalance.

Confuse, derange, disorder, disconcert, perturb, discompose. *Calm*

Upshot, Consequence, conclusion, issue, end, result, event, effect, outcome. *Beginning*

Urbane, Courteous, elegant, refined, civil, suave, polished, polite, affable. *Rough*

Urge, Press, impel, propel, push, drive, force, prompt, incite, entreat, solicit, goad, encourage, spur, prick. *Deter*

Urgent, Pressing, important, imperative,

grave, serious, momentous, insistent, critical. **_Trivial_**

Usage, Custom, practice, habit, method, fashion.

Use, _v.a._, Employ, exercise, practise, apply. **_Neglect_**
Consume, waste, spend, exhaust. **_Save_**
_n._, Utility, usefulness, usage, custom, habit, benefit, service, advantage, avail, profit.
Employment, exercise, application.

Useful, Profitable, beneficial, valuable, serviceable, advantageous, helpful.
Unprofitable

Useless, Unprofitable, profitless, futile, disadvantageous, unavailing, fruitless, valueless, bootless, ineffectual, vain, worthless, abortive. **_Profitable_**

Usual, Ordinary, common, accustomed, general, normal, regular, customary, habitual, wonted, familiar. **_Exceptional_**

Usurp, Arrogate, appropriate, assume, seize. **_Inherit_**

Utensil, Implement, instrument, tool.

Utility, Use, usefulness, benefit, service, advantage, avail, profit. **_Futility_**

Utmost, Farthest, extreme, greatest, main, last, distant, remote. **_Nearest_**

Utter, _v.a._, Enunciate, express, declare, say, pronounce, promulgate, issue. **_Recall_**
_a._, Complete, total, unqualified, entire, absolute, perfect, thorough.

V

Vacant, Empty, unfilled, unoccupied, void, exhausted. *Occupied*
Mindless, thoughtless, dreaming, inane, expressionless, unthinking. *Alert*

Vacate, Evacuate, abandon, relinquish, quit, leave, surrender. *Hold*
Annul, rescind, repeal, abrogate, nullify, invalidate, quash, cancel, abolish. *Substantiate*

Vacation, Recess, holiday, intermission, recreation. *Term*

Vacillate, Fluctuate, sway, oscillate, waver, hesitate, dubitate. *Adhere*

Vacillating, Inconstant, fickle, uncertain, fluctuating, wavering, unsteady. *Firm*

Vacuous, Vacant, empty, void, unfilled, exhausted. *Full*
Unintelligent, expressionless, mindless, inane, vacant, dreaming. *Intelligent*

Vacuum, Void, emptiness, vacuity.

Vagabond, Wanderer, vagrant, tramp, lounger, nomad, loafer, scamp, rascal. *Worker*

Vagary, Freak, caprice, whim, fancy, humour, crotchet. *Purpose*

Vagrant, *n.*, Vagabond,† tramp, lounger, wanderer, nomad, loafer. *Resident*
a., Wandering, strolling, roving, roaming, itinerant, nomadic, peripatetic. *Settled*

Vague, Indistinct, uncertain, indefinite, obscure, doubtful, ambiguous, loose, lax, dim, undetermined. *Clear*

Vain, Conceited, opinionated, boasting, proud, vaunting, overweening, inflated, arrogant. *Modest*
Unsubstantial, empty, unreal, fruitless, void, shadowy, false, ineffectual, useless, worthless, bootless, futile, abortive, idle, unavailing. *Potent*

Vale, Valley, dell. *Hill*

Valediction, Farewell, goodbye, adieu. *Welcome*

Valiant, Brave, courageous, heroic, bold, intrepid, daring, dauntless, chivalrous, gallant, redoubtable, doughty, valorous, undaunted, fearless. *Cowardly*

Valid, Sound, defensible, cogent, logical, powerful, efficacious, conclusive, good. *Weak*

Valley, Dale, dell, glen, vale, dingle. *Hill*

Valour, Bravery, courage, heroism, boldness, intrepidity, daring, dauntlessness, gallantry, chivalry, fearlessness, spirit, prowess. *Cowardice*

Valuable, Precious, worthy, estimable, costly, expensive, rare. *Worthless*

Valuation, Estimate, value, assessment, worth, appreciation.

Value, *n.*, Worth, desirability, utility, price, usefulness, import.
v.a., Prize, appreciate, esteem, treasure. *Depreciate*
Rate, appraise, assess, compute, estimate.

Valueless, Worthless, useless, futile, vain. *Worthy*

Vandalism, Savagery, barbarism, ruin, destruction.

Vanish, Fade, disappear, depart, melt, dissolve. *Appear*

Vanity, Conceit, opinionatedness, pride, vaunting, arrogance, egotism. *Modesty*
Worthlessness, emptiness, triviality, unsubstantiality, hollowness, unreality, futility, falsity. *Reality*

Vanquish, Overcome, overthrow, beat, overpower, overbear, defeat, conquer, rout, destroy, subjugate, subdue, worst, discomfit, crush. *Yield*

Vapid, Insipid, flat, stale, savourless, dull, tasteless, flavourless, tame, feeble. *Pungent*

Vapour, Steam, moisture, smoke, mist, fog, fume, reek, exhalation.

Variable, Fickle, changeable, inconstant, unsteady, unstable, mutable, mobile, shifting, fitful, wavering, fluctuating, vacillating, versatile, mercurial. *Steady*

Variance, Disagreement, dispute, strife, dissension, difference, discord, change. *Agreement*

Variation, Deviation, diversity, change, alteration, mutation, departure, modification, difference, exception. *Fixity*

Variegated, Diverse, motley, mottled, pied, piebald. *Plain*

Variety, Difference, multiformity, multiplicity, diversity, medley, miscellany. *Uniformity*
Class, kind, sort, order, species, group, brand, type.

Various, Divers, multiform, manifold, many, multitudinous, sundry, several, numerous, different, variegated. *Identical*

Varnish, Embellish, adorn, decorate, glaze, gloss, lacquer, ornament, polish, garnish. *Deface*

Vary, *v.a.*, Change, alter, modify, transmute, alternate, variegate, transform.
v.n., Change, alter, alternate, deviate, depart, swerve.
Differ, disagree. *Agree*

Vassalage, Servitude, bondage, slavery, dependence, subjection. *Freedom*

Vast, Immense, huge, great, wide, spacious, enormous, colossal, expansive, extensive, measureless, boundless, unbounded. *Narrow*

Vaticination, Prophecy, prognostication, divination, augury, prediction. *Fulfilment*

Vault, *v.n.*, Leap, spring, jump, bound. *n.*, Cellar, cell, tomb, dungeon, crypt. Cupola, ceiling, dome, curvet, roof.

Vaunt, Boast, brag, crow, swagger, cry, flourish, parade, trumpet. *Disparage*

Veer, Change, turn, alter, shift. *Adhere*

Veering, Vacillating, turning, shifting, fickle, inconstant, changeable, variable, unstable, unsteady, mercurial. *Steady*

Vegetate, Sprout, grow, shoot, swell, germinate, spring. *Decay* Idle, bask, hibernate, sleep, luxuriate. *Work*

Vehement, Violent, passionate, fierce, fervent, fervid, hot, furious, impetuous, burning, ardent, mighty, powerful, strong, forcible. *Subdued*

Vehicle, Conveyance, carriage. Means, agency, instrument, medium.

Veil, *v.a.*, Cover, mask, cloak, conceal, hide, screen, disguise. *Expose* *n.*, Cover, curtain, mask, screen, shade, visor.

Vein, Streak, stripe, thread, seam, ledge, lode, course, current. Character, tendency, disposition, mood, humour.

Velocity, Speed, quickness, rate, swiftness, rapidity, acceleration. *Slowness*

Velvety, Smooth, soft, delicate. *Rough*

Venal, Sordid, mean, mercenary, corrupt, prostitute. *Pure*

Vendor, Hawker, seller, peddler. *Buyer*

Vendetta, Feud, enmity, hatred, grudge, vindictiveness.

Veneer, Coat, coating, cover, layer.

Venerate, Respect, revere, reverence, honour, esteem. *Despise*

Vengeance, Revenge, retribution, retaliation. *Forgiveness*

Venial, Pardonable, excusable, light, small. *Deadly*

Venom, Poison, sting, virus, malignity, virulence, rancour, malice, maliciousness, spleen, hate, hatred, malevolence, gall, spitefulness, spite, acerbity, bitterness.

Venomous, Poisonous, virulent, noxious, malignant,† envenomed. *Wholesome*

Vent, *v.a.*, Utter, emit, express. *Contain* *n.*, Opening, hole, outlet, spiracle, orifice, spout.

Ventilate, Air, oxygenate, purify, freshen. Discuss, examine, review, comment, scrutinize, publish.

Venture, *v.a.*, Risk, jeopardize, imperil, hazard, stake, chance. *v.n.*, Dare, undertake, adventure, presume. *n.*, Risk, jeopardy, peril, hazard, danger, chance, adventure, speculation, stake. *Certainty* Enterprise, project, work.

Venturesome, Bold, fearless, reckless, foolhardy, adventurous, intrepid, brave, daring, dauntless, audacious, courageous. *Timid*

Veracious, True, truthful, trustworthy, honest, reliable. *False*

Verbal, Spoken, oral, unwritten, literal, unrecorded. *Written*

Verbiage ⎱ Prolixity, wordiness, diffuse-
Verbosity ⎰ ness, redundancy. *Terseness*

Verdant, Green, fresh, fresh-coloured. *Withered*

Verdict, Decision, judgment, conclusion, finding, sentence, opinion.

Verge, *v.n.*, Approach, border, tend, lean, trend, incline, bear, approximate. *n.*, Brink, edge, border, skirt, brim, point. *Centre*

Verify, Authenticate, establish, confirm, substantiate, corroborate. *Falsify*

Verily, Really, truly, indeed, positively, certainly.

Verisimilitude, Probability, likelihood. *Improbability*

Veritable, Real, actual, genuine, true, positive, authentic. *Fictitious*

Verity, Truth, reality, actuality, fact. *Falsehood*

Vermicular, Wormlike, flexuous, sinuous, winding, waving.

Vernacular, Native, indigenous, vulgar, mother. *Foreign*

Versatile, Ready, plastic, mobile. *Stolid* Mercurial, volatile, fickle, inconstant, unsteady, adaptable, variable, changeable, capricious. *Constant*

Versed, Experienced, skilled, proficient, accomplished, practised, able, *au fait*, conversant, familiar, acquainted. *Ignorant*

Version, Rendering, account, translation, interpretation, reading.

Vertex, Apex, top, acme, point, zenith, culmination, summit, height, crown. *Base*

Vertical, Perpendicular, upright, erect. *Slanting*

Verticle, Joint, hinge, axis.

Vertigo, Giddiness, sickness, dizziness.

Verve, Vigour, energy, enthusiasm, force, rapture, ardour, animation, spirit, abandon. *Apathy*

Very, *adv.*, Extremely, exceptionally, excessively, absolutely, quite, highly, exceedingly, remarkably. *Slightly*
a., Real, true, genuine, actual, same.

Vest, Furnish, endue, endow, clothe. *Strip*

Vestal, Chaste, pure, spotless, virtuous. *Sensual*

Vested, Established, fixed, legalized.

Vestibule, Hall, lobby, ante-chamber, porch.

Vestige, Sign, track, trace, evidence, mark, indication. *Deletion*

Vestment ⎱ Robe, dress, garment, clothes,
Vesture ⎰ covering, raiment, apparel.

Veteran, Experienced, old, aged, expert, seasoned, proficient, practised. *Novice*

Veto, Prohibition, restriction, embargo, interdiction, ban. *License*

Vex, Trouble, annoy, provoke, plague, irritate, harass, torment, tease, worry, anger, agitate, offend, displease, chafe, fret, disquiet, disturb, afflict, bother, try, molest, hector, harry, persecute, perplex. *Soothe*

Vexatious, Troublesome, aggravating, annoying, provoking.† *Pleasing*

Vexed, Troubled, annoyed, provoked, plagued, irritated, harassed, worried, angry, agitated, offended, displeased, fretful, disquieted, disturbed, bothered, perplexed. *Appeased*
Contentious, contested, disputed.

Vibrate, Oscillate, vacillate, sway, swing, fluctuate, quiver, shiver.

Vicarious, Deputed, delegated, commissioned, substitutive, representative. *Personal*

Vice, Failing, fault, defect, flaw, evil, imperfection, blemish, corruption, sin, wickedness, iniquity, depravity. *Virtue*

Vicinity, Neighbourhood, proximity, nearness. *Distance*

Vicious, Depraved, bad, wicked, faulty, immoral, corrupt, imperfect, defective, demoralized, sinful, abandoned, lost. *Virtuous*
Spiteful, malignant, caustic, bitter, contrary, unruly. *Friendly*

Vicissitude, Change, mutation, alteration, alternation, fluctuation. *Stability*

Victimize, Swindle, cheat, dupe, gull, defraud, deceive, hoax, *cozen, chouse.*

Victorious, Conquering, triumphant, successful. *Defeated*

Victory, Conquest, triumph, success, achievement, mastery. *Defeat*

Victuals, Food, provisions, sustenance, viands, rations, eatables.

Vie, Strive, struggle, contend, compete, contest. *Yield*

View, *v.a.*, Watch, consider, survey, see, contemplate, behold, scan, explore, eye, inspect, examine, study. *Ignore*
n., Scene, vista, prospect, sight, outlook, perspective, panorama.
Survey, sight, vision, examination, inspection, observation.
Judgment, estimation, opinion, idea. *Delusion*
Object, end, intention, intent, meaning, purpose, design.
Judgment, belief, opinion, impression, idea, theory, sentiment. *Misconception*

Vigilant, Watchful, wakeful, observant, sleepless, careful, attentive, alert. *Heedless*

Vigour, Strength, energy, power, force, lustiness, liveliness, vitality, might, health, robustness, manliness, resolution. *Weakness*

Vigorous, Strong, energetic, powerful,† active, sturdy, lively, virile, lusty, hale, lively. *Weak*

Vile, Worthless, base, depraved, abject, shameful, bad, loathsome, despicable, contemptible, degraded, paltry, pitiful, wretched, miserable, abandoned, low, beggarly, grovelling, mean, sorry, cheap, ignoble, vicious, impure, valueless. *Honourable*

Vilify, Vituperate, slander, libel, defame, traduce, malign, calumniate, decry, slur, revile, asperse, abuse, disparage. *Praise*

Villain, Scoundrel, vagabond, miscreant, rascal, rogue, knave, cheat, scamp. *Hero*

Villainous, Vile, wicked, knavish, bad, dishonourable, mean, base, depraved, nefarious, atrocious, heinous. *Noble*

Vindicate, Justify, uphold, support, sustain, advocate, avenge, maintain, defend, establish, assert. *Destroy*

Vindictive, Implacable, relentless, unrelenting, revengeful, malicious, spiteful, malevolent, malignant, unforgiving, rancorous, vengeful, unmerciful, merciless. *Forbearing*

Violate, Infringe, transgress, disobey, break. *Keep*
Desecrate, abuse, pollute, defile, profane, outrage, ravish, debauch, deflour. *Respect*

Violent, Vehement, intense, passionate, furious, impetuous, boisterous, forceful, wild, fierce, tumultuous, turbulent, hot, raging, fiery, burning, ungovernable. *Cool*

Virago, Termagant, shrew, vixen, scold, fury.

Virgin, *n.*, Maiden, damsel, spinster, maid.

a., Fresh, new, maiden, pure, unspotted, unpolluted, undefiled, chaste, modest.

Virile, Manly, masculine, vigorous, forceful, robust. *Effeminate*

Virtual, Practical, potential, substantial, indirect, tantamount, essential, implied, implicit. *Actual*

Virtue, Uprightness, goodness, morality, chastity, innocence, purity, excellence, merit, efficacy, worth, rectitude, probity, integrity. *Vice*

Virtuoso, Master, expert, connoisseur.

Virtuous, Upright, good, moral,† honest, righteous, blameless, exemplary. *Bad*

Virulent, Poisonous, venomous, deadly, malignant, toxic, bitter, acrimonious, malevolent. *Mild*

Visage, Face, countenance, semblance, aspect, physiognomy.

Viscera, Intestines, entrails, bowels, inside.

Viscid } Sticky, semi-fluid, glutinous,
Viscous } cohesive, tenacious, gelatinous. *Limpid*

Visible, Discernible, conspicuous, plain, clear, noticeable, obvious, evident, perceptible, apparent, distinguishable, manifest, observable, patent. *Eclipsed*

Vision, Sight, seeing. *Blindness*
Apparition, spectre, phantom, ghost, chimera, dream, hallucination.

Visionary, *n.*, Zealot, fanatic, dreamer, enthusiast. *Cynic*
a., Romantic, imaginative, fanciful. *Prosaic*
Imaginary, unreal, illusory, fanciful, fantastic, unpractical, chimerical, wild, unsubstantial, shadowy. *Real*

Visit, *v.a.*, Frequent, haunt, survey, inspect, examine, affect.
v.n., Stop, call, tarry, stay.

Visitor, Caller, guest, company.

Vista, View, scene, prospect, retrospect.

Vital, Living, animate, alive. *Dead*
Important, essential, indispensable, necessary. *Immaterial*

Vitality, Life, animation, vigour, strength.

Vitalize, Animate, quicken, strengthen, vivify. *Kill*

Vitiate, Impair, corrupt, debase, pollute, contaminate, deprave, deteriorate, lower, spoil, injure, harm, adulterate. *Improve*

Vituperate, Revile, abuse, vilify, censure, upbraid, denounce, blame, reproach, rate, scold. *Praise*

Vituperation, Reviling, abuse,† railing, invective.

Vivacious, Lively, sprightly, animated, spirited, light, gay, cheerful, jocund, jocose, merry, sportive, frolicsome, jolly, active, pleasant. *Torpid*

Vivacity, Life, liveliness, sprightliness.† *Torpor*

Vivid, Bright, glaring, intense, brilliant. *Dull*
Clear, vigorous, strong, lucid. *Weak*
Striking, expressive, telling, graphic.

Vivify, Enliven, animate, vitalize, quicken. *Kill*

Vixen, Virago, termagant, shrew, scold, spitfire.

Vocabulary, Language, words, terms, glossary, dictionary, lexicon.

Vocation, Calling, trade, profession, business, avocation, employment, pursuit, occupation.

Vociferate, Shout, bawl, roar, clamour. *Whisper*

Vociferous, Noisy, obstreperous, loud, clamorous, blatant, uproarious. *Quiet*

Vogue, Fashion, custom, usage, favour, use, practice, mode. *Disrepute*

Voice, *v.a.*, Express, utter, say, declare.
n., Utterance, sound, tone, accent, language, articulation, expression, words. *Silence*
Wish, preference, opinion, say, option, vote.

Voiceless, Speechless, mute, dumb, silent. *Vociferous*

Void, Vacant,† empty. *Full*
Lacking, wanting, destitute, devoid, free, clear, bereft.
Null, invalid, ineffectual, nugatory. *Valid*

Volatile, Gay, lively, changeable, fickle, mercurial, unsteady, giddy, inconstant, flighty, frivolous, capricious. *Steady*

Volition, Will, determination, purpose, choice, preference, discretion, freewill. *Compulsion*

Volley, Salvo, shower, storm, emission, report, blast, explosion.

Voluble, Glib, fluent, loquacious, talkative. *Stammering*

Volume, Bulk, compass, mass, dimensions, contents, fulness.
Book, tome.

Voluminous, Bulky, ample, copious, big, full, great, large, diffuse. *Slight*

Voluntary, Free, optional, discretional, purposed, intentional, designed, willing, spontaneous, unconstrained, gratuitous. *Compulsory*

Volunteer, Proffer, offer, tender, tend, present, undertake. *Refuse*

Voluptuous, Sensual, licentious, carnal, luxurious, fleshly, epicurean. *Ascetic*

Vomit, Eject, spew, puke, belch, emit, disgorge. *Swallow*

Voracious, Greedy, ravenous, hungry, insatiate, rapacious, gluttonous. *Fastidious*

Vortex, Whirlpool, whirl, maelstrom, eddy.

Votary, Devotee, disciple, follower, zealot, enthusiast, adherent.

Vouch, Avouch, confirm, uphold, attest, warrant, declare, assert, asseverate, affirm, guarantee, support, back. *Repudiate*

Vouchsafe, Condescend, deign, stoop, descend.

Vouchsafe, Grant, allow, accord, give, concede, yield. *Refuse*

Vow, *v.a.*, Promise, pledge, dedicate, devote, consecrate. *Disavow*
n., Promise, pledge, oath, engagement.

Voyage, Trip, cruise, passage, sail.

Vulgar, Plebeian, coarse, low, unrefined, common, mean, base, gross, broad. *Genteel*
Ordinary, general, native, vernacular. *Foreign*

Vulgarity, Coarseness, lowness, baseness, meanness, rudeness, grossness. *Refinement*

Vulnerable, Assailable, sensitive, tender, susceptible, defenceless, accessible, weak. *Tough*

W

Waft, Convey, carry, bear, transport.

Wag, *v.a. & n.,* Shake, vibrate, oscillate.

n., Humorist, droll, jester, wit, joker.

Wage, *n.,* Pay, payment, emolument, salary, reward, remuneration, stipend, hire, compensation, earnings, allowance. *Gratuity*

v.a., Undertake, prosecute, conduct. *Abandon*

Wager, *v.a.,* Bet, pledge, hazard, lay, risk, stake.

n., Bet, pledge, stake.†

Waggish, Witty, jocular, mischievous, facetious, merry, sportive, humorous, sporting, droll, roguish. *Sedate*

Wail, *v.a., & n.,* Lament, moan, bemoan, bewail, deplore, cry, weep, grieve. *Rejoice*

n., Lament, lamentation, moan, weeping, cry, grief, wailing, plaint, complaint. *Joy*

Wait, *v.a.,* Await, expect, bide.

v.n., Tarry, halt, stay, stop, rest, linger, remain, abide, delay. *Press*

Attend, serve, minister, watch.

Waiter, Servant, servitor, attendant, steward.

Waive, Forego, remit, relinquish, resign, abandon, renounce, surrender, drop, yield. *Assert*

Wake, *v.n.,* Waken, awake, rise. *Slumber*

v.a., Waken, awake, rouse, reanimate, arouse, suscitate, animate, stimulate, revive, excite, provoke, kindle. *Allay*

n., Rear, trail, track, wash, path.

Wakeful, Awake, alert, vigilant, wary, watchful, observant. *Unwary*

Sleepless, restless, awake. *Asleep*

Waken, *v.n.,* Wake, awake, rise. *Slumber*

v.a., Wake, awake, rouse, arouse, kindle, resuscitate, reanimate, animate, revive, stimulate, excite, provoke. *Allay*

Walk, *v.n.,* Step, march, advance, move, go, progress, perambulate, stroll. *Run*

n., Stroll, perambulation, promenade, hike, tramp, saunter, ramble.

Way, path, avenue, pathway, footpath, alley.

Gait, step, carriage.

Field, sphere, course, career, province, beat.

Wallet, Bag, scrip, pouch, case, purse.

Wallow, Roll, welter, flounder, grovel.

Wan, Pale, colourless, bloodless, pallid, ashen, cadaverous, livid, lurid, haggard, worn. *Ruddy*

Wand, Rod, staff, stick, baton, mace.

Wander, Stroll, stray, straggle, roam, rove, range, ramble, deviate, depart, swerve, digress. *Settle*

Wandering, *a.,* Strolling, roaming, roving, migratory, ranging. *Settled*

n., Journey, travel, travelling, roaming, roving, ranging, rambling, straying, vagrant, itinerant.

Aberration, delirium, madness, raving, insanity. *Sanity*

Wane, *v.n.,* Diminish, decline, decrease, fade, fail, pale, ebb, sink, droop. *Wax*

n., Diminution, decline, declension.†

Want, *v.a.,* Need, require, lack, desire, covet, crave. *Possess*

v.n., Fail, lack, omit, neglect.

n., Need, necessity, requirement, desire, demand, longing, wish, craving. *Possession*

Lack, absence, scarcity, scarceness, deficiency, shortage, paucity, dearth, insufficiency, inadequacy. *Abundance*

Poverty, privation, indigence, penury, destitution, need. *Wealth*

Wanting, *a.,* Lacking, deficient, short, defective, backward. *Full*

prep., Without, less, minus, devoid.

Wanton, *v.n.,* Sport, gambol, frolic, caper, revel, play, flirt, disport. *Mope*

a., Sportive, frisky, playful, frolicsome, gay, coltish, irresponsible, capricious. *Sedate*

Luxuriant, unrestrained, exuberant, wild, abounding.

Lewd, licentious, unchaste, irregular, loose, dissolute, carnal, lecherous, lustful, lascivious, prurient, libidinous. *Chaste*

Motiveless, needless, groundless, wilful, careless, gratuitous. *Deliberate*

n., Flirt, baggage.

War, Hostility, enmity, strife, discord, contention, quarrel, fighting. Armageddon. *Peace*

Warble, Trill, sing, chant, carol.

Ward, *v.a.,* Protect, guard, defend, watch, shield, keep. *Betray*

Parry, fend, repel.

n., Custody, protection, defence, charge, confinement, garrison.

Minor, pupil.

District, quarter, division, apartment, room, precinct.

Warden, Keeper, guardian, protector, curator, custodian, gamekeeper, warder.

Wares, Commodities, goods, merchandise.

Warfare, War, hostilities, fighting, strife, belligerence.   *Peace*

Warily, Carefully, watchfully, heedfully, cautiously.   *Carelessly*

Warlike, Belligerent, martial, military, bellicose, hostile.   *Peaceful*

Warm, Hot, hottish, incalescent, thermal.   *Cold*
Ardent, enthusiastic, keen, zealous, fiery, animated, eager, hot, excited, hearty, fervid, fervent, earnest, vehement, intense, passionate.   *Apathetic*

Warmth, Heat, incalescence.   *Coldness*
Ardour, enthusiasm, keenness.†   *Apathy*

Warn, Caution, admonish, premonish, advise, forewarn, notify, inform.   *Induce*

Warning, Caution, admonition, advice, notification.

Warp, Twist, distort, pervert, bias, bend, contort.   *Straighten*

Warrant, *v.a.,* Vouch, avouch, secure, engage, guarantee, undertake, assure, certify, affirm, justify.   *Repudiate*
Justify, pardon, sanction, support, maintain, license, sustain, authorize.   *Invalidate*
n., Voucher, order, authority, permit, commission, writ, pass, summons.

Warrantable, Justifiable, pardonable, proper, defensible, right, allowable.   *Unjustifiable*

Wary, Guarded, careful, cautious, watchful, circumspect, suspicious, prudent, vigilant, heedful.   *Rash*

Wash, *v.n.,* Clean, cleanse, rinse, lave, absterge.   *Soil*
n., Washing, cleansing, lavation, ablution.

Washy, Weak, thin, insipid, watery, sloppy.

Waspish, Irritable, petulant, testy, sour, touchy, pettish, cross, peevish, splenetic, snarling, snappish, choleric, irascible, captious, fretful.   *Genial*

Waste, *v.a.,* Squander, consume, spend, expend, dissipate, fritter, lose, lavish.   *Husband*
v.n., Wither, decay, fail, decrease, wane, diminish, dwindle, shrivel, perish, pine.   *Flourish*
n., Desert, wilderness, wild.
Refuse, rubbish, débris, offal, dross.
Ruin, havoc, desolation, destruction, devastation, ravage.
Prodigality, dissipation, squandering, consumption, extravagance, expenditure, loss.   *Economy*
a., Desert, desolate, uninhabited, wild, uncultivated, dreary, bare, barren, untilled, abandoned, dismal.
Useless, superfluous, refuse, valueless.

Wasteful, Extravagant, prodigal, lavish, thriftless, unthrifty, improvident, profuse.   *Economical*

Watch, *v.a.,* Observe, note, notice, mark, guard, tend.   *Ignore*
v.n., Wait, wake.
n., Waiting, watching, watchfulness, vigil.
Sentry, sentinel, guard.
Timepiece, chronometer.

Watchful, Vigilant, wakeful, alert, wary, attentive, heedful, guarded, cautious, careful, circumspect.   *Heedful*

Watchword, catchword, countersign, password.

Water, Wet, moisten, damp, irrigate.   *Parch*

Wave, *v.a.,* Flourish, brandish, shake, beckon, signal.
v.n., Float, vibrate, stir, move, flutter, undulate, sway.
n., Undulation, ripple, ridge, breaker, billow.

Waver, Fluctuate, oscillate, sway, falter, hesitate, quiver, flicker, dubitate, vacillate.   *Decide*

Wavering, Fluctuating, oscillating, fickle, hesitating, faltering, vacillating, inconstant, unsteady, undecided, undetermined.   *Resolute*

Wax, Grow, increase, rise.   *Wane*

Waxy, Pliable, pliant, yielding, tender, soft, impressible.   *Firm*

Way, Route, course, road, progression, march, path, advance, passage, track.
Method, scheme, device, plan, course, manner, fashion, system, mode.
Habit, practice, usage, custom, style, behaviour, wont.

Wayward, Obstinate, perverse, wilful, capricious, headstrong, refractory, contrary, froward, stubborn, intractable, captious, ungovernable, unaccountable, unruly, freakish.   *Docile*

Weak, Fragile, feeble, delicate, infirm, frail, powerless, debilitated, unsound, unhealthy, sickly.   *Strong*
Inconclusive, ineffectual, unsubstantial, inefficient, poor, lame, unconvincing, illogical.   *Sound*
Foolish, pliable, pliant, soft, senseless, witless, imbecile, childish, stupid, erring, confiding, shallow, injudicious, indiscreet, imprudent.   *Wise*
Watery, diluted, insipid, thin.   *Potent*

Weaken, Enervate, debilitate, enfeeble, impair, unnerve, lower, reduce.   *Strengthen*

Weal, Ridge, stripe, streak.

Prosperity, profit, interest, happiness; welfare, comfort, good.

Wealth, Welfare, prosperity, happiness, comfort, content, profusion, abundance. *Scarcity*

Riches, affluence, possessions, opulence, property. *Poverty*

Wean, Alienate, ablactate, disengage, detach, withdraw. *Attract*

Wear, *v.a.*, Bear, carry, sport, display, don. *Doff*

Waste, consume, diminish, use, impair. *Augment*

v.n., Endure, last.

Wearied, Weary, fatigued, exhausted, tired, jaded, fagged, spent, worn. *Fresh*

Wearisome, Tiring, weary, fatiguing, trying, exhausting, tedious, irksome, monotonous, boring, dull, flat, slow, uninteresting. *Interesting*

Weary, *a.*, Wearisome, tiring, fatiguing.†
Fatigued, tired, exhausted, jaded, fagged, spent, worn. *Fresh*

v.a., Fatigue, tire.† *Refresh*

Weather, Stand, resist, bear, endure, last, survive. *Succumb*

Weave, Plait, intertwine, interlace, mat, intwine, unite. *Dissect*

Web, Structure, composition, texture, fabric, tissue.

Wed, Marry, espouse, couple, unite. *Divorce*

Wedding, Marriage, nuptials.

Ween, Suppose, imagine, think, guess, fancy, judge.

Weep, Lament, bewail, complain, sob, cry, moan, mourn. *Rejoice*

Weigh, *v.a.*, Balance, counterbalance, estimate, allot, ponder, examine, consider, regard, esteem.

v.n., Bear, press, gravitate, tell, count.

Weight, Pressure, load, heaviness, onus, burden, incubus. *Lightness*

Importance, consequence, significance, gravity, moment. *Triviality*

Weighty, Heavy, burdensome, onerous, ponderous. *Light*

Important, significant, momentous, considerable, grave. *Trivial*

Weird, Uncanny, supernatural, wild, preternatural, unearthly.

Welcome, *v.a.*, Greet, receive, salute, hail.

n., Greeting, reception, salutation.

a., Acceptable, pleasant, pleasing, agreeable, gratifying. *Distasteful*

Welfare, Wealth, prosperity, happiness, comfort, content, well-being. *Adversity*

Well, *n.*, Spring, fountain, fount, source, origin.

Well, *adv.*, Thoroughly, properly, rightly, justly, smartly, commendably, suitably, skilfully, adequately, accurately, correctly. *Badly*

a., Hale, hearty, healthy, sound. *Ill*
Satisfactory, beneficial, advantageous, useful, profitable, fortunate, favoured. *Bad*

Welter, Roll, wallow, flounder, tumble.

Wend, Betake, go, pass.

Western, West, occidental. *Oriental*
Westerly, west, westward. *Easterly*

Wet, *v.a.*, Damp, soak, moisten, water, dampen, sprinkle, drench. *Dry*

a., Damp, soaked, moist. watery, dank, drenched, humid.

Rainy, showery. *Fine*

Wharf, Dock, quay, pier.

What, Whatever, whatsoever, partly, how, which.

Wheedle, Cajole, coax, flatter, decoy, inveigle, humour, entice. *Coerce*

Wheedler, Fawner, coaxer, sycophant, toady, flatterer.

Wheel, *v.n.*, Turn, revolve, swing, diverge.

v.a., Turn, spin, whirl, rotate, twirl.

Whelk, Pimple, pustule, boil, fester, gathering.

When, While, whereas, then, whenever.

Whence, How, wherefrom, whither.

Whet, Sharpen, increase, stimulate, incite, heighten, rouse. *Deaden*

Whim, Fancy, crotchet, caprice, notion, humour, vagary, quirk, freak, whimsy.

Whimper, Whine, cry, moan. *Laugh*

Whimsical, Freakish, capricious, queer, fantastic, odd, humoursome, fanciful, singular, crotchety, quaint, strange, curious. *Staid*

Whimsy, Whim, fancy, crotchet, quirk, caprice, humour, vagary, freak.

Whine, Whimper, cry, moan, snivel. *Laugh*

Whip, Lash, flog, beat, castigate, thrash, chastise, flagellate, scourge.

Seize, snatch, jerk, whisk.

Whipping, Flogging, beating, castigation, chastisement, thrashing, flagellation.

Whirl, *v.a.*, Spin, rotate, twirl, wheel, turn.

v.n., Spin, rotate, twirl, revolve, turn, gyrate.

n., Rotation, twirl, revolution, gyration.

Whisk, Whip, seize, snatch, jerk, speed, hasten, rush.

Flap, beat.

Whisper, Murmur, intimate, hint, reveal, disclose. *Shout*

Whit, Particle, grain, jot, iota, scrap, bit, speck, scintilla, atom, tittle.

White, Light, pale, pallid, wan, snowy. ***Black***

Spotless, pure, innocent, unstained, unblemished, clean. ***Foul***

Whiten, Etiolate, blanch, bleach. ***Blacken***

Whittle, Cut, carve, slice, trim, reduce, prune.

Whole, *a.,* Entire, complete, perfect, all, total, intact, undivided, integral. ***Partial***

Sound, unimpaired, perfect, uninjured, well, restored. ***Sick***

n., Aggregate, sum, total, all, entirety, amount, gross, totality. ***Part***

Wholesome, Salubrious, salutary, beneficial, healthy, healthful, good, sound, helpful, nourishing, pure. ***Deleterious***

Wholly, Entirely, exclusively, utterly, completely, totally, fully, outright, perfectly, absolutely, altogether. ***Partially***

Whore, Harlot, courtezan, prostitute, strumpet, trull.

Wicked, Evil, sinful, bad, unrighteous, iniquitous, vicious, immoral, depraved, ungodly, godless, unprincipled, criminal, unjust, nefarious, heinous, atrocious, villainous, vile, worthless, abandoned, corrupt. ***Virtuous***

Wide, Broad, extensive, large, spacious. ***Narrow***

Rife, prevalent, widespread, remote, distant.

Wield, Control, sway, hold, use, exert, exercise, manage, handle, employ. ***Discard***

Handle, brandish, flourish, manipulate, ply.

Wild, Untamed, undomesticated, savage, barbarous, fierce, uncivilized, ferocious, ferine. ***Tame***

Uninhabited, desert, uncultivated. ***Cultivated***

Disorderly, irregular, turbulent, violent, unrestrained, boisterous, rough. ***Orderly***

Rash, reckless, heedless, careless, mad, unsound, foolish. ***Sane***

Chimerical, extravagant, imaginary, visionary.

Wile, Stratagem, ruse, artifice, trick, fetch, fraud, device, machination, dodge, contrivance, chicanery, manœuvre, deceit. ***Artlessness***

Wilful, Wanton, perverse, intentional, deliberate, obstinate, stubborn, wayward, contumacious, refractory, obdurate, headstrong, intractable, unruly. ***Docile***

Will, *v.a.,* & *n.,* Wish, desire, choose, want, decree, determine, leave, convey, bequeath.

Will, *n.,* Determination, resolution, decision, volition.

Pleasure, behest, decree, order, wish, command, direction, desire, request, demand.

Willing, Disposed, ready, eager, desirous, prepared, inclined. ***Loath***

Willingly, Readily, gladly, cheerfully, eagerly, voluntarily, spontaneously. ***Reluctantly***

Wily, Artful, clever, cunning, sly, arch, intriguing, insidious, tricky, scheming, crafty, underhand, deceitful, designing, subtle. ***Artless***

Win, Gain, earn, get, secure, procure, obtain, acquire, achieve, accomplish. ***Lose***

Persuade, sway, influence, induce, carry. ***Repel***

Wince, Flinch, startle, shrink, blench.

Wind, *v.a.,* Twist, coil, twine.

v.n., Turn, twist, meander, coil, bend, curve.

n., Air, breath, breeze, draught.

Winding, Serpentine, bending, turning, twisting, flexuous, curving, tortuous, meandering, sinuous. ***Straight***

Windy, Gusty, boisterous, blustering, squally, breezy, stormy. ***Still***

Verbose, wordy, diffuse, prolix, empty.

Winning, Captivating, engaging, alluring, attractive, seductive, charming, taking, bewitching, pleasing, enchanting, prepossessing, delightful, fascinating, winsome. ***Repulsive***

Winnow, Sift, sort, separate, part, divide, select.

Winsome, Winning, captivating, taking, engaging, alluring, attractive, seductive, charming, bewitching, pleasing, enchanting, delightful, prepossessing, fascinating. ***Repulsive***

Wintry, Cold, windy, cheerless, frosty, icy. ***Warm***

Wipe, Rub, clean, dry.

Wisdom, Sagacity, sense, judiciousness, enlightenment, discernment, knowledge, erudition, learning, light, judgment, prudence, reason, prescience, sapience, sageness, cleverness. ***Folly***

Wise, *a.,* Sagacious, sensible, judicious,† deep, sapient, intelligent, cautious. ***Foolish***

n., Way, manner, fashion, mode, method.

Wish, *v.a.,* & *n.,* Like, will, desire, choose, want, decree, determine.

n., Pleasure, behest, decree, will, order, command, direction, desire, intention, inclination, liking.

Wishful, Desirous, eager, anxious. *Indifferent*

Wistful, Pensive, reflective, musing, meditative, yearning, thoughtful. *Careless*

Wit, Intelligence, understanding, sense, mind, reason, penetration, discernment, intellect, insight. *Dulness*
Humour, fun, facetiousness. *Stupidity*
Humorist, wag.

Witchcraft ⎱ Magic, enchantment, spell,
Witchery ⎰ sorcery, necromancy, conjuration, charm.

With, Among, amidst, beside, through, accompanying.

Withdraw, *v.a.*, Retract, revoke, recall, abjure, disavow. *Repeat*
v.n., Retreat, retire, depart, decamp, flee. *Stand*

Wither, *v.n.*, Decay, fade, languish, pine, droop, shrivel, shrink, dry, waste. *Bloom*
v.a., Dry, shrivel, blast, blight. *Freshen*

Withering, Blasting, cutting, bitter, biting, devastating, ironic, sarcastic. *Mild*

Withhold, Retain, keep, reserve, hinder, suppress, restrain, check, detain. *Grant*

Withstand, Oppose, resist, confront, face, defy. *Support*

Witness, *v.a.*, Confirm, attest, prove, speak, corroborate.
See, notice, remark, observe, watch, mark, note. *Miss*
n., Evidence, confirmation, testimony, attestation, proof, corroboration.
Spectator.
Testifier, corroborator, deponent.

Witty, Humorous, funny, facetious, droll, jocular, amusing. *Dull*

Wizard, Magician, sorcerer, shaman, necromancer, charmer, conjurer, seer, enchanter, soothsayer.

Wizened, Shrivelled, dried, shrunken, aged, sharp, thin, pointed. *Fresh*

Woe, Grief, distress, affliction, sorrow, anguish, trouble, misery, calamity, pain, suffering, tribulation, agony, torment, torture, adversity, melancholy, depression, unhappiness, wretchedness. *Joy*

Woeful, Grievous, distressing, tragic, afflictive,† sad, deplorable. *Joyful*

Wonder, *v.n.*, Marvel.
Meditate, speculate, conjecture, ponder, question, muse.
n., Marvel, miracle, prodigy, curiosity, rarity.
Awe, bewilderment, admiration, surprise, amazement, astonishment, curiosity. *Indifference*

Wonderful, Marvellous, amazing, extraordinary, astonishing, astounding, surprising, staggering, startling, prodigious, miraculous, unprecedented, remarkable, awful, wondrous. *Commonplace*

Wondrous, Wonderful, marvellous.†

Wont, Custom, practice, rule, habit, use. *Exception*

Wonted, Customary, habitual, usual, ordinary, accustomed. *Unusual*

Wood, Forest, woodland, thicket, copse, grove. *Clearing*

Wooing, Courtship, suit, addresses.

Word, Expression, term. *Idea*
Command, signal, order, injunction, instruction.
News, tidings, information, report, intelligence, notification, advice.
Promise, assurance, pledge.

Wordy, Diffuse, verbose, lengthy, prolix, loquacious, garrulous, windy, tedious. *Terse*

Work, *v.a.*, Operate, exert, strain.
v.n., Function, act, operate. *Fail*
Toil, drudge, labour, slave. *Rest*
n., Toil, task, drudgery, labour, exertion. *Inertia*
Production, product, fruit, results, issue, performance, effect.
Business, trade, employment, occupation, function, office.
Book.

Worker ⎱ Operative, artisan, labourer,
Workman ⎰ craftsman, employee, hand. *Master*

World, Earth, universe, creation, globe.

Worldly, Temporal, earthly, mundane, secular, common, sordid. *Spiritual*

Worm, Wriggle, writhe, crawl, force, creep.

Worry, *v.n.*, Fret, fidget, chafe.
v.a., Vex, tease, annoy, bother, harass, plague, torment, pain, hector, disturb, molest, disquiet, trouble, persecute, harry, pester, irritate, importune. *Soothe*
n., Vexation, annoyance, bother,† care, anxiety, concern, fear, apprehension, uneasiness. *Delight*

Worship, *v.a.*, Adore, idolize, reverence, revere, venerate, esteem. *Contemn*
n., Adoration, reverence, veneration, homage. *Contempt*

Worst, Rout, defeat, beat, conquer, foil, overcome, overwhelm, overthrow, overpower, vanquish, discomfit, master, subjugate, subdue. *Yield*

Worth ⎱ Value, merit, excellence,
Worthiness ⎰ cost, estimation, virtue. *Demerit*

Worthless, Valueless, cheap, vile, useless, despicable, paltry, contemptible, base. *Excellent*

Worthy, Estimable, admirable, excellent, fine, meritorious, good, exemplary, noble, honest, deserving, upright, reputable, honourable. *Vile*

Wound, *v.a.,* Injure, hurt, harm, cut, damage, pierce, lacerate, bruise. *Heal*
n., Injury, hurt,† blow, detriment, grief, anguish.

Wrangle, *v.n.,* Brawl, squabble, quarrel, bicker, altercate, disagree, differ, spar, contend. *Accord*
n., Brawl, squabble, quarrel,† dispute, controversy.

Wrap, Wind, fold, muffle, swathe, cloak, enfold, envelop, cover. *Unfold*

Wrath, Anger, indignation, rage, fury, exasperation, ire, passion, resentment. *Pleasure*

Wrathful, Angry, indignant, furious, exasperated, ireful, passionate, annoyed, provoked, incensed, mad, raging, wroth, irritated, resentful. *Pleased*

Wreak, Exercise, execute, inflict, work, indulge.

Wreath, Festoon, garland, chaplet.

Wreck, *v.a.,* Ruin, destroy, disable, upset, break, shatter, blast, blight. *Build*
n., Ruin, blight, desolation, perdition, breakage, destruction, disablement. *Recovery*

Wrench, Strain, sprain, twist, pull, wring.

Wrest, Force, wrench, twist, pull, deflect, pervert, strain.

Wrestle, Fight, struggle, grapple, strive, contend.

Wretch, Villain, vagabond, miscreant, outcast, pariah, rogue, ruffian, rascal, knave.

Wretched, Miserable, pitiable, paltry, mean, despicable, sorry, poor, vile, contemptible, unhappy. *Fine*
Sorrowful, saddening, afflictive, afflicting, woeful, distressing, disastrous, deplorable, calamitous. *Joyful*

Wriggle, Worm, squirm, writhe.

Wring, Twist, squeeze, wrench, wrest, force, extort.

Wrinkle, *v.a.,* Crease, crumple, rumple, corrugate, pucker. *Smooth*
n., Crease, rumple, corrugation, pucker, furrow, rimple.

Writ, Summons, order, decree, precept.

Write, Pen, indite, scribe, scribble scrawl, inscribe. *Efface*

Writhe, Squirm, worm, turn, twist, roll, wriggle.

Wrong, *v.a.,* Abuse, injure, maltreat, oppress.
n., Injury, injustice, iniquity, unfairness, immorality, sin, offence, misdeed. *Right*
a., Iniquitous, inequitable, unjust, evil, unfair, immoral, wicked, improper, sinful. *Just*
Inaccurate, incorrect, false, mistaken, erroneous. *Correct*
adv., Falsely, improperly, erroneously, amiss, inaccurately. *Correctly*

Wroth, Angry, indignant, furious, ireful, wrathful, exasperated, passionate, mad, annoyed, provoked, incensed, raging, irritated, resentful. *Pleased*

Wrought, Effected, performed, done, worked.

Wry, Awry, askew, distorted, twisted crooked, contorted, deformed, deranged. *Straight*

X

Xanthic, Yellowish, fulvid, fulvous, tawny.

Xantippe, Scold, shrew, vixen, virago, termagant.

Xenodochium, Guest-room, guest-chamber.

Xenodochy, Hospitality, hospitableness, liberality, welcome. *Hostility*

Xiphoid, Ensiform, gladiate, sword-shaped.

Xylograph, Wood-cut, wood-engraving, wood-carving.

Xylophagous, Wood-feeding, wood-eating, wood-gnawing.

Xylotomous, Wood-cutting, wood-boring.

Y

Yap, Yelp, cry, bark.

Yard, Court, enclosure, close.

Yarn, Tale, story, anecdote, narrative.

Yea, Yes, aye, ay, verily. *Nay*

Yearly, Annual, anniversary.

Yearn, Long, hanker, desire, crave. *Loathe*

Yeast, Leaven, ferment, barm.

Yell, *v.n.*, Cry, shriek, bawl, screech, roar, scream, shout, bellow, vociferate.
n., Cry, shriek, screech.† *Whisper*

Yelp, Yap, cry, bark.

Yes, Yea, aye, ay, true, granted. *No*

Yet, *adv.*, Still, further, besides, now.
conj., However, nevertheless, notwithstanding, still.

Yield, *v.n.*, Surrender, capitulate, agree, submit, succumb, consent, acquiesce. *Struggle*
v.a., Produce, afford, furnish, supply, give, render, concede, bestow, accord, bear.
Surrender, relinquish resign, forego, abandon, abdicate, renounce. *Withhold*
n., Crop, produce, product, return.

Yielding, Flexible, flexile, facile, easy, submissive, docile, compliant, complying, pliant, pliable, affable, supple, weak, manageable, complaisant, accommodating. *Stubborn*

Yoke, *v.a.*, Couple, unite, link, interlink, join, conjoin, connect. *Liberate*
n., Link, tie, coupling, chain, ligament, ligature, bond, union.
Subjection, service, slavery, servitude, bondage. *Freedom*

Yokel, Rustic, boor, churl, clodhopper, bumpkin. *Townsman*

Young, Juvenile, youthful, childish, boyish, fresh, immature, recent. *Old*

Youngster, Child, boy, lad, youth, adolescent.

Youth, Lad, youngster, boy, child, stripling. *Man*
Adolescence, immaturity, minority, nonage, juvenility. *Age*

Youthful, Young, juvenile, childish, boyish, puerile, fresh, immature, early. *Aged*

Z

Zany, Half-wit, simpleton, clown, fool, jester, buffoon, mimic.

Zeal, Fervour, earnestness, passion, fire, ardour, enthusiasm, keenness, interest, eagerness, energy, heartiness, warmth, intensity. *Apathy*

Zealot, Partisan, fanatic, enthusiast, bigot, visionary.

Zealous, Fervid, fervent, earnest, keen, passionate, ardent, enthusiastic, hearty, energetic, fiery, warm, intense, eager. *Apathetic*

Zebrine, Zebra-like, striped.

Zenith, Height, acme, apex, vertex, top, summit, culmination, climax, pinnacle, crown. *Zero*

Zephyr, West-wind, gentle, mild, soft breeze. *Hurricane*

Zero, Nothing, nought, nullity, nil, nadir, cipher. *Zenith*

Zest, Piquancy, flavour, relish, savour, sharpness, taste. *Insipidity*
Relish, gusto, gust, avidity, appetite, keenness, eagerness. *Reluctance*

Zetetic, Seeker, searcher, inquirer.

Zigzag, Crooked, bending, tortuous, turning. *Straight*

Zoilean, Hypercritical, critical, finical, exacting. *Tractable*

Zone, Area, tract, region, circuit, climate, district, girdle, circumference.

Zymotic, Contagious, epidemic, endemic, infectious, bacterial, fermentative.